The **Rough Guide** to

Jamaica

written and researched by

Polly Thomas & Adam Vaitlingam

with additional contributions by
Polly Rodger Brown

ROUGH GUIDES

D0109885

NEW YORK • LONDON • DELHI
www.roughguides.com

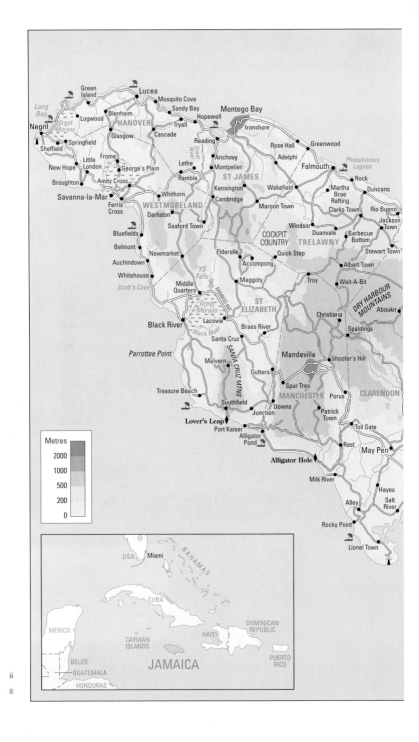

Introduction to

Jamaica

Rightly famous for its beaches and music, beautiful, brash Jamaica is much more besides. There's certainly plenty of white sand, turquoise sea and swaying palm trees, but there's also a huge amount to see away from the coast: spectacular mountains and rivers, tumbling waterfalls and cactus-strewn savannah plains. The towns and cities, meanwhile, affirm that the island is far more than just a tourist attraction, particularly Kingston – the dynamic,

sprawling metropolis which helped to inspire the music of Bob Marley and countless other home-grown reggae superstars.

Despite Jamaica's immense natural allure, it's not just the physical aspect that makes the country so absorbing and, to many visitors, so utterly addictive. Notwithstanding the invasion of tourists and American satellite TV, Jamaica retains an attitude – a personality – that's more resonant and distinctive than you'll find in any other Caribbean nation. It's a country with a swagger in its step – proud of its history, sporting success and musical genius – but also with a weight upon its shoulders. For Jamaica has not avoided the familiar problems of a developing country such as dramatic inequality of wealth, and social tensions that occasionally spill over into localized violence or worldwide headlines. The mixture is potent, and has produced a people as renowned for being sharp, sassy and straight-talking as they are laid-back and hip. People don't tend to beat around the bush here; Jamaicans get on with life, and their directness can

Fact file

• Ninety miles south of Cuba and six hundred miles south of Miami, Jamaica sits 18 degrees north of the equator. The largest English-speaking island in the Caribbean, Jamaica is 146 miles long, with widths varying between 22 and 51 miles. The island has 633 miles of coastline.

• Almost half of the island lies 327 feet above sea level; the highest point, Blue Mountain Peak, stands at 7402 feet.

• Jamaica boasts more than 120 rivers; the Plantain Garden River in St Thomas is the only one that flows to the west.

• Around 3800 varieties of flowering plants and ferns, some 720 of which are endemic, grow on the island.

• Jamaica's bee hummingbird is one of the world's smallest birds. The endemic Giant Swallowtail butterfly, with a wingspan of up to six inches, is the largest in the western hemisphere and the second-largest in the world.

• Sugarcane, bananas, plantains, mangoes, breadfruit, ackees, bamboo and coconut palms are not native to Jamaica, having been imported by the Tainos, Spanish, Africans and British.

• Jamaica's population is almost three million. Just over half of the island's residents live in urban areas, 22 percent in greater Kingston.

• Some 76 percent of Jamaicans are of African origin, 15 percent are of mixed African/European heritage, 3.5 percent are East Indian/African East Indian, 1.2 percent are Chinese/African Chinese and 0.8 are European.

sometimes make them appear rude or uncompromising. Particularly around the big resorts, this is taken to extremes at times, though the harassment of tourists that once bedevilled the resorts is a lot less noticeable these days.

But there's absolutely no reason to be put off. The Jamaican authorities have spent millions making sure the island treats its tourists right, and as a foreign visitor, your chances of encountering any trouble are minuscule. As the birthplace of the "**all-inclusive**" hotel, Jamaica has become well-suited for those who (like many people) want to head straight from plane to beach, never leaving their hotel compound. But to get any sense of the country at all, you'll need to do some exploring. It's

> Jamaica retains an attitude — a personality — that's more resonant and distinctive than you'll find in any other Caribbean nation

undoubtedly worth it, as this is a place packed with first-class attractions, oozing with character, and rich with a musical and cultural heritage; if you're a reggae fan, you're in heaven.

Where to go

Most of Jamaica's tourist business is concentrated in the "big three" **resorts** of Montego Bay, Negril and Ocho Rios, which between them pull hundreds of thousands of visitors every year. Probably the most evocative name in the Caribbean, **Montego Bay** is a busy commercial city with hotels lined up along its tourist strip, a stone's throw from a couple of Jamaica's most famous beaches. Though "MoBay" has lost some of its old lustre, the place retains an appealing vitality, with a busy street life and a great entertainment scene, most obvious during the annual **Reggae Sumfest** festival. West of here, its low-rise hotels slung along seven miles of fantastic white sand and two miles of dra-

Going off the beaten track

Though beaches and buzzing resort areas are Jamaica's most obvious draws, one of the island's greatest assets is its spectacular **interior**. With everything from mist-swathed mountains to steamy rainforest, lush wetland and cane-covered agricultural plains, the Jamaican countryside is a joy to explore, as much for its scenic delights as for its profusion of one-horse towns, where you can sink a few glasses of over-proof in the obligatory rum shop and get a flavour of life that couldn't be more different from life on the coast. And whether your goal is a swim in a waterfall or river, or a hike into the hills, the journey can be as much of a joy as the destination itself, especially if you stop off en route to sample pepper shrimp, roast yam and saltfish or jerk chicken from one of the country's innumerable roadside stalls.

matic cliffs, **Negril** is a different type of resort – younger, more laid-back, and with a long-standing reputation for unbridled hedonism that still carries a hint of the truth. East of MoBay, and the least individualistic of the big three, **Ocho Rios** embodies high-impact tourism – purpose-built in the 1960s to provide the ultimate package of sun, sand and sea. It's not an overly attractive place, and the beaches don't compare favourably with Negril and MoBay, but the tourist infrastructure is undeniably strong – the place is packed with shops, restaurants, bars and watersports – and you're right by some of Jamaica's leading attractions, including the famous **Dunn's River** waterfall, dramatic **Fern Gully** and the lovely **botanical gardens** at Shaw Park.

Away from these resorts, you'll have to look a bit harder to find your entertainment – Jamaica's quieter east and south coasts offer a less packaged product – but there are plenty of real gems worth hunting out, particularly if you're keen to escape the crowds. In the island's **east**, lush, rain-fed, sleepy **Port Antonio**, and its increasingly popular neighbour, **Long Bay**, provide gateways to some of Jamaica's greatest natural attractions, like the cascading **waterfalls** at Reach and Somerset, and outdoor activities such as **rafting** on the majestic Rio Grande and **hiking** through the dense rainforest of the John Crow Moun-

> If you're a reggae fan, you're in heaven

Jamaican music

Birthplace of **reggae** and of its most famous exponent, the inimitable Robert Nesta Marley, Jamaica's strongest cultural suit is its music – the lilting tones of ska and rocksteady, the militant posturing of roots reggae, the sweet soulfulness of lovers' rock, and the bass-heavy DJ-based sound of contemporary dancehall, these days heavily influenced by the US hip-hop scene that was kick-started by Jamaican DJs in the 1980s. Music is omnipresent in Jamaica, from the radios islandwide tuned to Irie FM or the speaker boxes that blare from buses, taxis and shop-fronts, but the best way to take in some tunes is to attend a sound-system dance, whether a high-profile Stone Love party packed with dancehall queens and bling-bling downtowners, or a simple country dance at a bamboo-fenced lawn in the middle of nowhere. If you prefer your reggae live, there's always a stageshow going on somewhere, from the vintage class-acts at the Heineken Startime series to international performers at Sumfest or Sashi or the best of the DJs at annual events such as Sting.

tains. The **south coast** offers different pleasures, from gentle beach action at the terminally easy-going **Treasure Beach** – the perfect base for exploring local delights like the YS waterfalls and the gorgeous lagoon and beach at Gut River – to boat safaris in search of local wildlife on the **Black River** or at **Alligator Hole**. Set in the upper reaches of the Santa Cruz Mountains, the south's inland towns, such as **Mandeville** and **Christiana**, offer respite from the heat of the coast.

Last, but in no way least, **Kingston** is the true heart of Jamaica, a thrilling place, pulsating with energy and spirit. This is not just the nation's political capital but the focus of its art, theatre and music scenes, with top-class hotels, restaurants and shopping, a clubbing scene that is second to none and legendary fried fish on offer at the fabulous **Hellshire beach**. A stunning backdrop to the city, the cool **Blue Mountains** are a captivating, gentle antidote, with plenty of marvellous hiking possibilities, while the nearby fishing village of **Port Royal**, once a great pirate city, and the former capital of **Spanish Town**, with its grand Georgian buildings, provide more historic diversions.

When to go

For many visitors, Jamaica's tropical **climate** is its leading attraction – hot and sunny all year. The weather is at its most appealing during the peak tourist season, which runs from mid-December to mid-April, when rainfall is lowest and the heat is tempered by cooling trade winds, known locally as the "Doctor Breeze". Nights can get chilly during this period, and you'll probably want to bring a sweater. Things get noticeably hotter during the summer and, particularly in September and October, the humidity can become oppressive. September is also the most threatening month of the annual hurricane season, which runs officially from June 1 to October 31, though it's worth bearing in mind that, on average, the big blows only hit about once a decade.

As you'd expect, prices and crowds are at their highest during peak season, when the main attractions and beaches can get pretty busy. Outside this period – from Easter to early December – everywhere is quieter and, though the main resorts throb with life pretty much year-round, quieter tourist areas like Port Antonio and Treasure Beach

Rastafari

Despite the fact that only a small portion of Jamaica's predominantly Christian population adheres to the faith, **Rastafari** is the island's most recognizable religion. Outwardly distinguished by the wearing of dreadlocks (usually tucked into a tam or wrapped in the turbans favoured by orthodox "Bobo" dreads), by the red, gold and green colours of the Rastafarian flag and by a penchant for ganja as an aid to free thinking and spiritual connection, Rastas believe in the divinity of the late Ethiopian king Haile Selassie, and champion black pride and self-determination as espoused by Jamaican son Marcus Garvey. However, not everyone with locks is a true Rasta. The resorts abound with so-called "rent-a-dreads", who sport locks to entice female tourists in search of a suitably exotic holiday romance, and happily consume the meat, processed foods, alcohol and tobacco regarded by true Rastas as polluting.

Roadside art

Whilst travelling round the island, keep an eye out for the variety of **artwork** and **signage** that adorns surfaces everywhere. Small business places are decorated inside and out with all manner of designs, from suitably big-bottomed ladies and muscular men dancing up a storm on a bar wall to psychedelic patterns in bright and vibrant colours on a shop-front or a beautifully illustrated biblical quote on a restaurant wall. Road signs are just as creative – "Walk, drive and ride good" and "Undertakers love overtakers" are roadside staples. Handwritten signs, using patois rather than standard English, are simply a joy: on a list of car-wash prices, vacuum becomes "vacanum" and a Hiace bus an "I-Ace", while an Ital restaurant becomes a "Rastawant".

can feel a little lifeless. The good news is that hotel prices everywhere fall by up to 25 percent, there are more bargains to be had in every field of activity, and a number of **festivals** – including the massive annual Reggae Sunfest in Montego Bay – inject some summertime zip.

Average daily temperatures and monthly rainfall

	Average daily temperature (°F max/min, then °C max/min)	Average monthly rainfall (inches, followed by mm)
Jan	86/67 30/19	0.9 23
Feb	86/67 30/19	0.6 15
March	86/68 30/20	0.9 23
April	87/70 31/21	1.2 30
May	87/72 31/22	4.0 100
June	89/74 32/23	3.4 86
July	90/73 32/23	3.4 86
Aug	90/73 32/23	3.5 89
Sept	89/73 32/23	3.8 96
Oct	88/73 31/23	7.0 178
Nov	87/71 31/22	3.0 76
Dec	87/69 31/21	1.4 36

These figures are for Kingston, but are virtually identical islandwide with the exception of Port Antonio and the Blue Mountains, where rainfall is considerably higher.

32

things not to miss

It's not possible to see everything that Jamaica has to offer in one trip – and we don't suggest you try. What follows is a selective and subjective taste of the country's highlights: outstanding natural features, marvellous beaches, festivals, clubs and delicious food and drink. They're arranged in five colour-coded categories to help you find the very best things to see, do and experience. All entries have a page reference to take you straight into the guide, where you can find out more.

01 Accompong Maroon Festival Page **281** • A celebration commemorating the 1739 treaty with the British, this is a unique showcase for Maroon culture at its proud best, finished off in true Jamaican style with a mammoth sound-system party.

02 **Treasure Beach Hook 'n' Line Fishing Tournament** Page **344** • A world away from high-octane deep-sea events, this hugely enjoyable, low-key festival sees local fishermen take to the water armed with the simplest of tools, while beachside parties and competitions keep up the carnival atmosphere back on shore.

| ACTIVITIES | CONSUME | EVENTS | NATURE | SIGHTS |

03 **Port Royal** Page **109** • This former pirate haunt and British military command centre bristles with atmosphere, from the cannon and quarterdecks of Fort Charles to the charms of its bars and renowned seafood restaurants, or the beachlife at nearby Lime Cay.

04

Swimming in the Blue Lagoon Page **169** • Shrouded by greenery, supposedly bottomless and frolicked in by Brooke Shields in the eponymous 1980s movie, this delicious mix of warm ocean waters and icy draughts from a mineral spring provides the ultimate refreshing dip.

05 Kingston from Skyline Drive Page 99 • High above the city in the foothills of the Blue Mountains, Skyline Drive is the perfect place to watch the sun go down and the lights twinkle on over the harbour.

06
Ackee and saltfish

Page 37 • Sample Jamaica's national dish, a delectable – and addictive – combination of salt cod and the little-known ackee fruit.

07
Beaches

Page 256 • From the north-coast strips of fine white sand to the wind-whipped breakers along the south coast, Jamaica's shore-line is immensely varied – but the gin-clear Caribbean is always warm.

08 **Jerked food** Page **38** • Seasoned to perfection and cooked slowly over pimento wood, jerked chicken, pork and even fish and lobster are the ultimate gourmet barbecue, best accompanied with a hunk of roast yam and an ice-cold Red Stripe.

09 **Hiking in the Blue Mountains** Page **137** • Cool, misty and fragrant with coffee and wild ginger flowers, the Blue Mountains are perfect hiking territory, the ultimate challenge being the highest point in Jamaica, Blue Mountain Peak.

10 Cockpit Country scenery Page **277** • The best way to appreciate the Cockpits' amazing eggbox landscape is from above – but the roads traversing the edges provide a tantalizing glimpse over this wild and wonderful area.

12 Bob Marley Birthday celebrations Page **47** • Jamaica's musical hero is remembered with lectures, seminars and – of course – by huge parties and concerts islandwide.

11 Conch soup Page **38** • The shells are a staple on craft stalls, and this thick, fortifying concoction – reputedly with aphrodisiac qualities – is equally ubiquitous at cookshops islandwide.

13 **Underwater Jamaica** Page **394** • From ancient forests of elk and staghorn coral to encrusted wrecks of sunken ganja planes, the waters around Jamaica teem with sealife.

14 **Cricket in Sabina Park** Page **53** • Cradled by the Blue Mountains, Sabina is the spiritual home of Jamaica's favourite game, and the best place to watch a Windies test is from the riotous home supporters' Mound stand.

15 **Devon House** Page **96** • Built in Uptown by Jamaica's first black millionaire, this graceful colonial house, with its surrounding gardens and restaurants, is the perfect place to escape the Kingston heat.

16

Cranbrook Flower Forest Page **219** • With fishing ponds, grassy greens for picnicking and a swimmable mineral pool as well as the gorgeous collection of tropical blooms, Cranbrook is perfect for a day's getaway.

17

Firefly Page **214** • Left just as it was when he died, and spectacularly perched above the St Mary coastline, Noël Coward's former home really does have a "room with a view".

18

Tropical fruit Page 39 •

If the weird and wonderful jackfruit proves too much of an acquired taste, there are always pineapples, guavas, otahetie apples and of course umpteen varieties of mango to quench the tropical fruit urge.

ACTIVITIES | CONSUME | EVENTS | NATURE | SIGHTS |

19

Drinks
Page **40** •

From a well-chilled jelly coconut to freshly made june plum juice or a killer rum cocktail, Jamaica's home-grown liquid refreshments are hard to resist.

20

YS Falls
Page **351** • In the midst of rolling pastures and surrounded by lush foliage, the falls here offer deep swimming pools and ropes to swing on for that Tarzan moment.

21 **Alligator Hole manatees** Page **347** • A boat trip through this protected stretch of river in search of the elusive "sea-cow" is a wonderfully gentle way to get close to nature.

22 **Asylum Club** Page **104** • The capital's hippest nightclub, Asylum is the place to catch up on whatever's hot on the dancehall scene.

23 **Sound-system jam** Page **49** • Stone Love put on some of the biggest sound system jams in Jamaica – and patrons dress to impress . . .

24 **Negril sunsets** Page **310** • Right at Jamaica's western tip, Negril is the best place for sunset-watching in Jamaica; head for the cliffs with cocktail in hand.

25 **Spanish Town** Page **118** • From the splendid cathedral to the orderly Georgian town square, with its intricate Rodney Memorial, imposing King's House and absorbing People's Museum, Spanish Town is drenched in history.

ACTIVITIES | CONSUME | EVENTS | NATURE | SIGHTS |

27

National Gallery Page

82 • This Kingston museum offers the country's premier collection of work by local and regional artists – look out especially for pieces by John Dunkley, Mallica "Kapo" Reynolds and Edna Manley.

28 **Waterfall climbing on Dunn's River** Page **196** • Tourist honeypot though it may be, the splashy climb up Jamaica's most famous waterfall is a sheer delight – if you can tear yourself away from the beach at the bottom.

29 **Royal Palm Reserve** Page **307** • Follow wooden boardwalks right into the heart of Jamaica's second-largest wetland, where a host of rare animals, birds and plants are dwarfed by splendid stands of graceful royal palms.

30 **Rio Grande Valley** Page **176** • Negotiate some of Jamaica's roughest roads all the way to the centre of the John Crow mountains, then splash around in the deep pools of the Rio Grande.

31 **Georgian Falmouth** Page **232** • This quiet country town boasts the best examples of Georgian Jamaican architecture in the country, all crumbling slowly in the salty sea air.

32 **Theatre and dance** Page **49** • From the Little Theatre Movement's spectacular annual pantomime and smaller-scale productions from eminent local directors to bawdier "roots" plays, Kingston's theatre scene is the best in Jamaica.

Contents

Using this Rough Guide

We've tried to make this Rough Guide a good read and easy to use. The book is divided into six main sections, and you should be able to find whatever you want in one of them.

Colour section

The front colour section offers a quick tour of Jamaica. The **introduction** aims to give you a feel for the place, with suggestions on where to go. We also tell you what the weather is like and include a basic country fact file. Next, our authors round up their favourite aspects of Jamaica in the **things not to miss** section – whether it's great food, amazing sights or a special hotel. Right after this comes a full **contents** list.

Basics

The Basics section covers all the **pre-departure** nitty-gritty to help you plan your trip. This is where to find out which airlines fly to your destination, what paperwork you'll need, what to do about money and insurance, about Internet access, food, security, public transport, car rental – in fact just about every piece of **general practical information** you might need.

Guide

This is the heart of the Rough Guide, divided into user-friendly chapters, each of which covers a specific region. Every chapter starts with a list of **highlights** and an **introduction** that helps you to decide where to go, depending on your time and budget. Likewise, introductions to the various towns and smaller regions within each chapter should help you plan your

itinerary. We start most town accounts with information on arrival and accommodation, followed by a tour of the sights, and finally reviews of places to eat and drink, and details of nightlife. Longer accounts also have a directory of practical listings. Each chapter concludes with **public transport** details for that region.

Contexts

Read Contexts to get a deeper understanding of what makes Jamaica tick. We include a brief history, articles about **religion** and **music**, and a detailed further reading section that reviews dozens of **books** relating to the country.

Language

The **language** section gives useful guidance for understanding Jamaican patois. Here you'll also find a glossary of words and terms peculiar to the country.

Index + small print

Apart from a **full index**, which includes maps as well as places, this section covers publishing information, credits and acknowledgements, and also has our contact details in case you want to send in updates and corrections to the book – or suggestions as to how we might improve it.

Map and chapter list

- Colour section
- Contents
- **B** Basics

- **1** Kingston and around
- **2** The Blue Mountains and the east
- **3** Ocho Rios and the north coast
- **4** Montego Bay and Cockpit Country
- **5** Negril and the west
- **6** The south

Contexts
Language

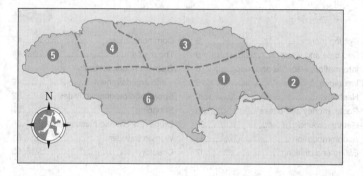

Contents

Colour section   i–xxiv

Basics   7–64

Guide   65–366

Contexts

Language

Index and small print

Map symbols

maps are listed in the full index using coloured text

══	Road	✈	Airport/airfield
━●━	Railway	ⓘ	Jamaica Tourist Board office
══	River/canal	⊠	Post office
----	County boundary	⌇	Golf course
━ ━ ●	Chapter division boundary	◉	Accommodation
◆	Site of interest	▣	Restaurant/bar/café
∴	Ruin	▬	Building
⌂	Cave	⊞	Church
𝄞	Waterfall	⊤	Cemetery
▲	Mountain peak	▦	Park
☀	Lighthouse	⋇	Marsh
ⵌ	Gardens	⬚ ⟲	Beach
⊞	Hospital		

Basics

Basics

Getting there

As one of the Caribbean's most visited islands as well as a regional transport hub, Jamaica is very well served with direct flights from North America, the UK and other parts of Europe. The majority of visitors purchase packages that include flight, accommodation and airport transfers, but there are plenty of good flight-only deals available for those who want to go it alone. Most airlines fly into Montego Bay, but many also land at Kingston as well – more convenient if you're heading for Port Antonio or the Blue Mountains.

Airfares always depend on the **season**, with the highest being around December to mid-January, when the weather is best; fares drop during the "shoulder" seasons – November and mid-January to April (excluding Easter) – and you'll get the best prices during the low season, May to November. If you're coming from Europe, however, the holiday months of July and particularly August are also busy travel periods when flight prices are hiked up and seats are at a premium.

You can often cut costs by going through a **specialist flight agent** – either a consolidator, who buys up blocks of tickets from the airlines and sells them at a discount, or a **discount agent**, who in addition to dealing with discounted flights may also offer special student and youth fares, and a range of other travel-related services such as travel insurance, rail passes, car rentals, tours and the like. Some agents specialize in **charter flights**, which may be cheaper than anything available on a scheduled flight, but again departure dates are fixed and withdrawal penalties are high. A further possibility is to see if you can arrange a **courier flight**, although you'll need a flexible schedule, and preferably be travelling alone with very little luggage. In return for shepherding a parcel through customs, you can expect to get a deeply discounted ticket. You'll probably also be restricted in the duration of your stay.

Booking flights online

Many airlines and discount travel websites offer you the opportunity to book your tickets **online**, cutting out the costs of agents and middlemen. Good deals can often be found through discount or auction sites, as well as through the airlines' own websites.

Online booking agents and general travel sites

Ⓦ travel.yahoo.com Incorporates a lot of Rough Guide material in its coverage of destination countries and cities around the world, with information about places to eat and sleep and etc.
Ⓦ www.cheapflights.com Bookings from the UK and Ireland only (for US, Ⓦ www.cheapflights.com; for Canada, Ⓦ www.cheapflights.ca; for Australia, Ⓦ www.cheapflights.com.au). Flight deals, travel agents, plus links to other travel sites.
Ⓦ www.cheaptickets.com Discount flight specialists (US only).
Ⓦ www.expedia.com Discount airfares, all-airline search engine and daily deals (US only; for the UK, Ⓦ www.expedia.co.uk; for Canada, Ⓦ www.expedia.ca).
Ⓦ www.flyaow.com Online air travel info and reservations site.
Ⓦ www.gaytravel.com Gay online travel agent, offering accommodation, cruises, tours and more.
Ⓦ www.geocities.com/thavery2000 Has an extensive list of airline toll-free numbers (from the US) and websites.
Ⓦ www.hotwire.com Bookings from the US only. Last-minute savings of up to forty percent on regular published fares. Travellers must be at least 18 and there are no refunds, transfers or changes allowed. Log-in required.
Ⓦ www.lastminute.com Offers good last-minute holiday package and flight-only deals (UK only; for Australia, Ⓦ www.lastminute.com.au).
Ⓦ www.priceline.com Name-your-own-price website that has deals at around forty percent off standard fares. You cannot specify flight times

(although you do specify dates) and the tickets are non-refundable, non-transferable and non-changeable (US only; for the UK, ⓦwww.priceline.co.uk).

ⓦ**www.skyauction.com** Bookings from the US only. Auctions tickets and travel packages using a "second bid" scheme. The best strategy is to bid the maximum you're willing to pay, since if you win you'll pay just enough to beat the runner-up regardless of your maximum bid.

ⓦ**www.smilinjack.com/airlines.htm** Lists an up-to-date compilation of airline website addresses.

ⓦ**www.teletext.com** Excellent deals on charter flights and package holidays from the UK.

ⓦ **www.travelocity.com** Destination guides, hot Web fares and best deals for car hire, accommodation and lodging as well as fares. Provides access to the travel agent system SABRE, the most comprehensive central reservations system in the US.

ⓦ**www.travelshop.com.au** Australian website offering discounted flights, packages, insurance, and online bookings.

Flights from the US and Canada

The popularity of the all-inclusive **package** holiday to Jamaica amongst North Americans means that many visitors to the island fly with a private charter company. However there are also plenty of daily **direct flights** from many parts of the US to Jamaica for those who wish to travel independently. Canada is not as well served and there are fewer direct flights.

Obviously from the US **flight duration** varies enormously. The flight from Miami to Montego Bay only takes 1hr 20min, making the city the main departure point for flights from the US to Jamaica; New York is also a popular departure point. Both cities have several daily flights to Jamaica year-round on a number of carriers. **Air Jamaica**, the island's national airline, has the most extensive timetable – it flies several times daily to Montego Bay and Kingston from Boston (6hr 30min), Chicago (3hr 50min), Los Angeles (5hr 45min), Miami and the New York area (JFK and Newark, 4hr). Its partnership with Delta airline means that flights from over sixty smaller US cities and towns are linked up to flights to Jamaica as conveniently as possible. Air Jamaica's high-and-low-season **fares** to Montego Bay average US$650/550 from

New York; US$520/419 from Miami; and US$820/700 from Los Angeles. Last-minute special deals with the airline are often very good value – eg US$272 from Miami or US$447 from Los Angeles. A number of other US airlines also fly to Jamaica: American Airlines flies direct from Los Angeles, Miami and New York; Continental from Newark; Northwest from Tampa, Detroit and Minneapolis; TWA from St Louis; and US Airways from Philadelphia and Pittsburgh.

Air Jamaica has daily direct flights from Toronto and Montreal in **Canada**, year-round. Air Canada has a direct daily flight to Montego Bay and Kingston from Toronto only (4hr) and low/high season **fares** average C$867/1035. Passengers from other parts of Canada have to either fly first to Toronto or to a regional hub in the US, and then take a connecting flight to Jamaica.

Airlines

Air Canada ☎1-888/247-2262, ⓦwww.aircanada.ca.
Air Jamaica US ☎1-800/523-5585, Canada ☎416/229-6024, ⓦwww.airjamaica.com.
American Airlines ☎1-800/433-7300, ⓦwww.aa.com.
Continental Airlines domestic ☎1-800/523-3273, international ☎1-800/231-0856, ⓦwww.continental.com.
Delta Air Lines domestic ☎1-800/221-1212, international ☎1-800/241-4141, ⓦwww.delta.com.
Northwest Airlines/KLM domestic ☎1-800/225-2525, international ☎1-800/447-4747, ⓦwww.nwa.com, ⓦww.klm.com.
TWA ☎1-800/892-4141, ⓦwww.twa.com
US Airways domestic ☎1-800/428-4322, international ☎1-800/622-1015, ⓦwww.usairways.com.

Courier flights

Air Courier Association ☎1-800/282-1202, ⓦwww.aircourier.org. Courier flight broker. Membership (3 months/$19, 1year/$29, 3year/$58, 5year/$87) also entitles you to twenty-percent discount on travel insurance and name-your-own-price non-courier flights.
International Association of Air Travel Couriers ☎308/632-3273, ⓦwww.courier.org. Courier flight broker with membership fee of $45/year or $80 for two years.

Discount travel companies

Airtech ☎ 212/219-7000, ⊛ www.airtech.com. Standby seat broker; also deals in consolidator fares and courier flights.

SkyLink US ☎ 1-800/AIR-ONLY or 212/573-8980, Canada ☎ 1-800/SKY-LINK, ⊛ www.skylinkus.com. Consolidator.

STA Travel US ☎ 1-800/781-4040, Canada 1-888/427-5639, ⊛ www.sta-travel.com. Worldwide specialists in independent travel; also student IDs, travel insurance, car rental, rail passes, etc.

TFI Tours ☎ 1-800/745-8000 or 212/736-1140, ⊛ www.lowestairprice.com. Consolidator.

Travac ☎ 1-800/TRAV-800, ⊛ www.thetravelsite.com. Consolidator and charter broker with offices in New York and Orlando.

Travel Avenue ☎ 1-800/333-3335, ⊛ www.travelavenue.com. Full-service travel agent that offers discounts in the form of rebates.

Travel Cuts Canada ☎ 1-800/667-2887, US ☎ 1-866/246-9762, ⊛ www.travelcuts.com. Canadian student-travel organization.

Worldtek Travel ☎ 1-800/243-1723, ⊛ www.worldtek.com. Discount travel agency for worldwide travel.

Tour operators

Air Jamaica Vacations ☎ 1-800/LOVEBIRD, ⊛ www.airjamaicavacations.com. All-inclusive trips to the island's premier tourist spots. Offers occasional good specials.

American Airlines Flyaway Vacations ☎ 1-800/321-2121, ⊛ www.aavacations.com. Organizes customized packages from budget to luxury, with a large range of hotels in Jamaica to choose from.

Caribbean Journey ☎ 1-888/343-2101, ⊛ www.caribbeanjourney.com. Low-key booking agent for tour operators to the Caribbean; also offers friendly personalized holiday-planning service at no extra charge.

Dragonfly Expeditions ☎ 1-888/9-WANDER, ⊛ www.dragonflyexpeditions.com/jamaica. A well-run and energetic company offering eco-tours through Jamaica, including snorkelling trips, bike rides, mountain trails, and other adventurous activities. Nine-day tours from Montego Bay include mountain biking, snorkelling, hiking and spelunking for US$1145 per person including lodging, food and transportation, but not flights. Check out the helpful website that explains its tour group philosophy.

Expo Garden Tours ⊛ www.infohub.com. Their

deluxe eight-day Jamaica package includes nights at the *Jamaica Inn* and *Strawberry Hill* hotels and visits to private and public gardens on the island including Cranbrook Flower Forest and Castleton Gardens. US$2438 per person.

Jamaica Reservation Service ☎ 1-800/JAMAICA, ⊛ www.jrstours.com. Booking service and customized tour company affliated with the Jamaica Tourist Board. Prices start at US$569 for three-night all-inclusive packages.

Spring Break Travel ☎ 1-800/678-6386, ⊛ www.springbreaktravel.com. Large tour company specializing exclusively in Spring Break holidays. Packages include airfare, hotel accommodation, transportation and drink coupons, and begin at US$719 per person. Accommodation options range from small hotels for students to crash in, to larger, private beachfront bungalows.

StudentCity.com ⊛ www.studentcity.com. Online Spring Break wholesaler – used by both travel agents and individuals. Lots of budget options and a range of package tours.

Sun Splash Tours ☎ 1-800/426-7710, ⊛ www.sunsplashtours.com. Specializes in budget/self-catering tours for college students and is one of the largest Spring Break tour organizers in the US (over 15,000 tours arranged per year). A week in Negril starts at US$470 per person and can get up as high as US$1369.

Tour Host International ☎ 1-866/SAY-HOST or 212/953-7910, ⊛ www.tourhost.com. Specialist tour operator with very helpful staff and an astonishing range of travel options, including adventure, natural history and eco- tours, coffee-tasting day-trips and architectural tours. Specializes in tours in Kingston.

TourScan Inc ☎ 1-800/962-2080 or 203/655-8091, ⊛ www.tourscan.com. This Caribbean specialist scans some 18,000 tours from two hundred brochures for the best-value deals (including hotels, flights and tours) on a variety of general and specialist packages, and publishes its findings in a catalogue. This is available for US$4, which is refundable if you use TourScan Inc to make your booking. They claim unique expertise, as every member of their staff has toured the Caribbean extensively. They're also one of the only tour operators offering sports tours in Jamaica – especially cricket.

Wings Birding Tours ☎ 1-888/293-6443, ⊛ www.wingsbirds.com. Specialists in birding holidays offer eight-day trips to Jamaica with visits to Rocklands Bird Sanctuary, Marshall's Pen in Manchester and Cockpit Country. US$1990 per person including food and accommodation, but not flights.

Flights from the UK and Ireland

The main carrier to Jamaica **from the UK** is Air Jamaica, which has nine direct flights per week from Heathrow to Montego Bay and Kingston (approx 10hr) and two from Manchester (9hr 45min). The only other airline that goes direct to the island is British Airways, which has three weekly flights from Gatwick to Kingston only (also 10hr). Average high-and-low season scheduled **fares** are £550/430 from Heathrow, £580/440 from Manchester.

It's also possible to fly to the US and then take an onward flight – this is most convenient via Miami. American Airlines, British Airways, Continental, Delta and Virgin all fly from London to Miami, with return fares as low as £199–£250 during the low season. From Miami, American Airlines and Air Jamaica fly direct to Montego Bay or Kingston, with return fares from around £150–£200, according to season.

You can also book a **charter flight** with companies such as Airtours (see opposite under "Tour operators"). These may be cheaper but tend to arrive and depart at anti-social hours and are usually valid for stays of one, two or three weeks only. Fares start from as little as £299 in low season, rising to £450-550 in high season. Your best bet for booking a charter is often ITV's Teletext (ⓦwww.teletext.com), though big-name high street travel agents can also turn up surprisingly low fares. The Charter Flight Centre (☎020/7854 8434, ⓦwww.charter-flights
.co.uk) is another useful resource.

There are no direct flights to Jamaica **from Ireland**, though there are decent connections via London, New York and Miami.

Airlines

Air Jamaica UK ☎020/8570 7999, ⓦwww.airjamaica.com.
American Airlines UK ☎0845/778 9789 or 020/8572 5555, Republic of Ireland ☎01/602 0550, ⓦwww.aa.com.
British Airways UK ☎0845/773 3377, Republic of Ireland ☎1800/626 747, ⓦwww.ba.com.
Continental Airlines UK ☎0800/776 464 or 01293/776 464, ⓦwww.continental.com/uk;

Republic of Ireland ☎1890/925 252, ⓦwww.continental.com/ie.
Delta UK ☎0800/414 767, Republic of Ireland ☎01/407 3165, ⓦwww.delta.com.
United Airlines UK ☎0845/8444 777, ⓦwww.unitedairlines.co.uk.
Virgin Atlantic Airways UK ☎01293/747 747, ⓦwww.virgin-atlantic.com.

Courier flights

International Association of Air Travel Couriers UK ☎0800/0746 481 or 01305/216 920, ⓦwww.aircourier.co.uk. Agent for lots of companies.

Discount flights and travel agents

Apex Travel Republic of Ireland ☎01/241 8000, ⓦwww.apextravel.ie. Specialists in flights to Australia, Africa, Far East, USA and Canada, and with good flight deals to the Caribbean also.
Aran Travel International Republic of Ireland ☎091/562 595, ⓦhomepages.iol.ie/~arantvl /aranmain.htm. Good-value flights to all parts of the world.
Bridge the World UK ☎0870/444 7474, ⓦwww.bridgetheworld.com. Specializing in round-the-world tickets, with good deals aimed at the backpacker market.
Flightbookers UK ☎0870/010 7000, ⓦwww.ebookers.com. Low fares on an extensive selection of scheduled flights.
Go Holidays Republic of Ireland ☎01/874 4126, ⓦwww.goholidays.ie. Package tour specialists.
Joe Walsh Tours Republic of Ireland ☎01/676 0991, ⓦwww.joewalshtours.ie. General budget fares agent.
Lee Travel Republic of Ireland ☎021/277 111, ⓦwww.leetravel.ie. Flights and holidays worldwide.
McCarthy's Travel Republic of Ireland ☎021/427 0127, ⓦwww.mccarthystravel.ie. General flight agent.
Newmont Travel ☎020/8920 1122, ⓦecommserver.newtravelsolutions.com/Index.html. Caribbean flight specialist that's been around for years and offers some excellent deals.
North South Travel UK ☎ & ℱ01245/608 291, ⓦwww.northsouthtravel.co.uk. Friendly, competitive travel agency, offering discounted fares worldwide. Profits are used to support projects in the developing world, especially the promotion of sustainable tourism.
Premier Travel Northern Ireland ☎028/7126 3333, ⓦwww.premiertravel.uk.com. Discount flight specialists.

Rosetta Travel Northern Ireland ☎ 028/9064
4996, ⓦ www.rosettatravel.com. Flight and holiday
agent.
Sackville Travel ☎ 020/7738 7077. Cheap
charter and scheduled fares.
STA Travel UK ☎ 0870/1600 599,
ⓦ www.statravel.co.uk. Worldwide specialists in
low-cost flights and tours for students and under-
26s, though other customers welcome.
Trailfinders UK ☎ 020/7628 7628,
ⓦ www.trailfinders.co.uk, Republic of Ireland
☎ 01/677 7888, ⓦ www.trailfinders.ie. One of the
best-informed and most efficient agents for
independent travellers; produce a very useful
quarterly magazine worth scrutinizing for round-the-
world routes.
Travel Cuts UK ☎ 020/7255 2082 or 7255 1944,
ⓦ www.travelcuts.co.uk. Canadian company
specializing in budget, student and youth travel and
round-the-world tickets.

Tour operators

Airtours UK ☎ 0870/238 7788,
ⓦ www.uk.mytravel.com. One of the largest
package operators into Jamaica, with a range of
holidays in all the tourist hotspots.
Caribtours UK ☎ 020/7751 0660,
ⓦ ww.caribtours.co.uk. Long-established company
offering tailor-made breaks – including trips
designed for families, spa-seekers, island-hoppers
and honeymooners – using scheduled flights to the
Caribbean.
Caribbean Centre UK ☎ 01444 455993,
ⓦ www.caribbeancentre.co.uk. Travel agent with
over forty years experience in the islands, offering a
wide range of hotel and resort options.
Complete Caribbean ☎ 01423/531 031,
ⓦ www.completecaribbean.co.uk. Tailor-made
holidays on most islands, including Jamaica, for
families, couples and adventure-seekers, with
accommodation in villas and hotels.
Expressions Holidays UK ☎ 020/7431 2131,
ⓦ www.expressionsholidays.co.uk. Luxury holidays
with accommodation in Jamaica's finest hotels;
seven nights from £1020 including return flights and
transfers.
Hayes & Jarvis UK ☎ 0870/898 9890,
ⓦ www.hayes-jarvis.com. Specialists in long-haul
holidays, particularly good on diving destinations.
Exotic weddings organized.
Kuoni Travel UK ☎ 01306/742 888,
ⓦ www.kuoni.co.uk. Flexible package holidays with
good family offers.
Sunbird Tours UK ☎ 01767/682 969,
ⓦ www.sunbirdtours.co.uk. Bird-watching holiday

specialists offering eight-day trips to Jamaica
covering Cockpit Country, Marshall's Pen Great
House and Portland, from £2020 all-inclusive.
Thomas Cook Holidays UK ☎ 0173/3417 100,
ⓦ www.thomascook.com. Package holidays, charter
and scheduled flights.
Trips Worldwide, UK ☎ 0117/311 4400,
ⓦ www.tripsworldwide.co.uk. High-end holidays in
luxury accommodation. Fifteen-day trips to Jamaica
include Negril, Blue Mountains, Treasure Beach and
Oracabessa, from £2850 per person.

Flights from Australia and New Zealand

There are **no direct flights** from Australia or
New Zealand to Jamaica; the best option for
travellers is to fly to the US, the UK or
Europe (Italy or the Netherlands) and pick up
an onward connection. The least expensive
and most straightforward **route** is via Los
Angeles or Miami, from where there are fre-
quent flights to Kingston or Montego Bay.
Both Air New Zealand and Quantas fly regu-
larly to Los Angeles; Air Jamaica and
American Airlines fly from Los Angeles to
Montego Bay and Kingston daily. Average
round-trip **fares** are A\$2500/NZ\$2940 and
A\$3000/NZ\$3530 from Sydney; add around
A\$500/NZ\$590 to fly from Darwin or Perth.

A viable alternative for Australasians with
lots of time to travel is a **round-the-world
ticket** (RTW). It's not an inexpensive option,
though. For example, a trip from Sydney to
the US, Venezuela, Trinidad, Jamaica,
England, Greece, Thailand and back home
again could set you back around
A\$6000/NZ\$7055.

Airlines

Air New Zealand Australia ☎ 13 24 76,
ⓦ www.airnz.com.au, New Zealand ☎ 0800/737
000, ⓦ www.airnz.co.nz.
American Airlines Australia ☎ 1300/130 757,
New Zealand ☎ 09/309 9159, ⓦ www.aa.com.
Cathay Pacific Australia ☎ 13 17 47,
ⓦ www.cathaypacific.com/au, New Zealand
☎ 09/379 0861 or 0508/800 454,
ⓦ www.cathaypacific.com/nz.
Continental Airlines Australia ☎ 1300/361 400,
New Zealand ☎ 09/308 3350,
ⓦ www.flycontinental.com.
Delta Air Lines Australia ☎ 02/9251 3211, New
Zealand ☎ 09/379 3370, ⓦ www.delta.com.

KLM/Northwest Airlines Australia ☏ 1300/303 747, ⓦ www.klm.com/au_en, New Zealand ☏ 09/309 1782, ⓦ www.klm.com/nz_en.
Qantas Australia ☏ 13 13 13, ⓦ www.qantas.com.au, New Zealand ☏ 0800/808 767, ⓦ www.qantas.co.nz.
United Airlines Australia ☏ 13 17 77, ⓦ www.unitedairlines.com.au, New Zealand ☏ 09/379 3800 or 0800/508 648, ⓦ www.unitedairlines.co.nz.

Travel agents

Flight Centre Australia ☏ 13 31 33 or 02/9235 3522, ⓦ www.flightcentre.com.au, New Zealand ☏ 0800/243 544 or 09/358 4310, ⓦ www.flightcentre.co.nz.
Holiday Shoppe New Zealand ☏ 0800/808 480, ⓦ www.holidayshoppe.co.nz.
New Zealand Destinations Unlimited New Zealand ☏ 09/414 1685 ⓦ www.holiday.co.nz.
Northern Gateway Australia ☏ 1800/174 800, ⓦ www.northerngateway.com.au.
STA Travel Australia ☏ 1300/733 035, ⓦ www.statravel.com.au, New Zealand ☏ 0508/782 872, ⓦ www.statravel.co.nz.
Student Uni Travel Australia ☏ 02/9232 8444, ⓦ www.sut.com.au, New Zealand ☏ 09/379 4224, ⓦ www.sut.co.nz.
Trailfinders Australia ☏ 02/9247 7666, ⓦ www.trailfinders.com.au.
Viator Australia ☏ 02/8219 5400, ⓦ www.viator.com. Bookings for hundreds of travel suppliers worldwide, including countries throughout Europe, North America, the Caribbean, Asia and the Pacific region.

Specialist agents

Adventure World Australia ☏ 02/8913 0755, ⓦ www.adventureworld.com.au, New Zealand ☏ 09/524 5118, ⓦ www.adventureworld.co.nz. Agents for a vast array of international adventure travel companies that operate trips to every continent.
Caribbean Destinations Australia ☏ 03/9614 7144 or 1800/354 104, ⓦ www.caribbeanislands .com.au. Specializes in festivals and hotel accommodation in Jamaica, Cuba, Antigua and the rest of the Caribbean.
Contours Australia ☏ 03/9670 6900 or 1300/135 391, ⓦ www.contours.com.au. Tours and independent travel, concentrating on island stays and flights throughout the Caribbean.
Creative Cruising ☏ 0800/803 599 ⓦ www.creative-cruising.co.nz. NZ-based cruise

holiday operator offering an array of fly/cruise packages that include hotel stays.
Harvey World Travel Australia, ☏ 08/9322 2914, ⓦ www.flightworld.com.au. Huge franchise operation, with 340 branches in Australia, that books Caribbean cruises and flights.
Silke's Travel Australia ☏ 1-800/807 860 or 02/8347 2000, ⓦ www.silkes.com.au. Gay and lesbian specialist travel agent.
travel.com.au and **travel.co.nz** Australia ☏ 1300/130 482 or 02/9249 5444, ⓦ www.travel.com.au, New Zealand ☏ 0800/468 332, ⓦ www.travel.co.nz. Comprehensive online travel company.
Wiltrans Australia ☏ 03/9696 9922. Luxury cruise and tour specialist, concentrating on Egypt, southeast Africa, the US, Patagonia and the Caribbean; Australian representative for Maupintour.

Cruises

The archetypal luxury vacation – a Caribbean cruise – is a relatively accessible reality in North America. A handful of corporate shipping companies peddle **all-inclusive cruises** of the Caribbean, and although prices on a luxury liner can scale the heights of silliness, a seven-day spin on a not-so-swanky ship should only set you back about US$700–900. All ships promise live entertainment and endless exotic drinks, and most now have swimming pools, gyms, tennis courts and Internet access. The downside of choosing a cruise is that as you only get to see the tourist ports – and only for a few hours at that – the glimpse you get of each island is both hurried and unrepresentative.

In Jamaica the biggest docking destination, by far, is **Ocho Rios.** The town now relies hugely on cruise-ship passengers for its tourist revenue and is very well set up with a wide roster of tours and local attractions. Other ports are Montego Bay and, much sleepier and only able to take the smallest ships, Port Antonio.

There are also several cruise operators in the **UK,** but because you'll have to fly stateside before getting on a boat, a cruise is not as good value an option from outside of the US.

A good place to start your research for a cruise trip is the **Internet**. Websites such as ⓦ www.cruise.com and ⓦ www.cruisereviews.com are helpful resources for deciding which cruise is best for you, taking into account price range, size of boat and length of trip. Travelocity.com also provides useful reviews of the major cruise companies. While some companies offer cruises only, there are still many others that negotiate rates with major airlines, allowing for fly/cruise options from most major airports in the US and the rest of the world.

Yachting between the US and the Caribbean is big business and a very pleasurable way of getting to the island. In February, there's a race from Miami to Montego Bay, called the Pineapple Cup, and a lot of yachters go over for the Montego Bay Easter Regatta. Marinas pepper the Jamaican coast; on arrival you have to go through customs and immigration, and pay a hefty tax. The US Coast Guard in Miami will steer you in the right direction (☏305/535-4470), or you can call US Sailing (☏1-800/US SAIL 1 or 401/683-0800) or, in Jamaica, the Montego Bay Yacht Club (☏979 8083). If you don't have your own boat and want to arrive in style, you can rent one for US$20,000 a week; contact ⓦwww.sailing-vacations.net.

Cruise lines

The fares quoted are for single person/double occupancy "inside" (no ocean views) cabins, outside of the high season (when prices can jump by US$300–500) and are exclusive of port charges, which add an extra US$200 or so.

From the US

Carnival Cruiselines ☏1-888/CARNIVAL, ⓦwww.carnival.com. A youthful cruise line with a big emphasis on fun, offering seven nights from Miami, Orlando or Fort Lauderdale from US$549.

Princess Cruises and Royal Caribbean ☏1-800/PRINCESS, ⓦwww.princesscruises.com. Seven-day luxury cruises (including spas and scuba diving) from Florida for upwards of US$599.

Radisson Seven Seas ☏1-877/505-5370, ⓦwww.rssc.com. Eleven-day circular cruises from Florida via the Caribbean and Central America, starting at US$4795.

From the UK and Ireland

Celebrity Cruiooo ☏0800/018 2525, ⓦwww.celebritycruises.com. Cruises with an emphasis on high-end pampering, including spas and art classes. Seven nights from Fort Lauderdale, Baltimore or San Juan from £429 (cruise only).

Fred Olsen Cruises ☏01473/742424, ⓦwww.fredolsencaribbean.co.uk. An extensive range of Caribbean cruises; fourteen nights from £1510, including a flight from London, Manchester or the East Midlands.

Royal Caribbean International ⓦwww.royalcaribbeaninternational.com. A rich variety of cruises throughout the Caribbean – seven nights from £429 – with additional flight options from throughout the UK and Ireland.

Cruise travel agents

Accent on Cruising ☏972/661-5151 or 1-800/317-3157, ⓦwww.accentoncruising.com. Agents for Celebrity, Princess, Radisson, Royal Caribbean and Silversea.

Adventure Travels ☏1-800/327-8967, ⓦwww.preferr.com. Agents for Carnival, Celebrity, Princess, Radisson, Royal Caribbean, Silversea and Windstar.

Cruise Discounters ☏1-800/268-0845, ⓦwww.cruisediscounters.com. Discount agent for most major cruise lines.

Red tape and visas

Entry requirements to Jamaica are fairly straightforward. Visitors from North America, the UK and Australasia do not need a visa and are allowed stays of up to six months without one. US and Canadian citizens don't need a passport either but do need proof of citizenship. This can take the form of a valid passport, a birth certificate supported by a driver's licence with photo, or a voter registration card supported by a driver's licence with photo.

On arrival, your passport will be stamped by an immigration officer who may ask you for proof of adequate funds, where you're staying during your holiday (if you don't know yet, pick any hotel in our listings, as you may be delayed if you can't name a place) and evidence of a return or onward flight. In most cases the stamp in your passport equates with the return date of your flight – you should always check, though, before you pass through immigration.

If you want to stay longer than six months, it's possible to apply for an **extension**, up to twelve further months. You'll need to contact the Ministry of National Security, located at the Mutual Life Building, North Tower, 2 Oxford Rd, Kingston 10 (℡876/906 4908 to 4933, ⊛www.mnsj.gov.jm) or, in Montego Bay, the Immigration Office at Overton Plaza, Union St (℡952 5381).

Jamaican embassies and consulates abroad

Canada Consulate-General of Jamaica, 214 King St West, Suite 402, Toronto, ON M5H 1K4 ℡416/598-3008, ℻416/598-4928
UK and Ireland Jamaica High Commission, 1-2 Prince Consort Rd, London SW7 2BQ ℡020/7823 9911, ⊛www.jhcuj.com.
US Embassy of Jamaica, 1520 New Hampshire Ave NW, Washington DC 20036 ℡202/452-0660, ℻202/452-0081, ⊛www.emjam-usa.com.

There are no Jamaican embassies or consulates in Australia or New Zealand.

Information, websites and maps

Before you leave home it's worth contacting the nearest branch of the Jamaica Tourist Board (JTB), which will send out plenty of glossy information on the country, including brochures on the main tourist attractions and forthcoming events and a good road map. Once in Jamaica, you can get the same information from JTB desks at the Kingston and Montego Bay airports and JTB offices in the main towns. The office in Kingston also has a small information library, with clued-up staff who can usually help with local queries. None of the JTB offices provides an accommodation-booking service.

Once you arrive in Jamaica, there are a number of **free publications** which you'll find distributed in tourist resorts – in hotels, bars and gift shops. These include *Destination Jamaica*, the "official visitor magazine of the Jamaica Hotel and Tourist Association", a thick glossy tome with useful contact numbers of tour companies and attractions; *Focus on Jamaica*, a small book published twice a year with a good inserted map; and *Jamaica International*, a twice-yearly newspaper printed in four European languages, with good articles and a focus on younger independent travellers.

Jamaica has no entertainments listings magazine, so to find out what's going on, you have to rely on the **radio** (particularly Irie FM), on **newspapers** (the *Daily Gleaner* and *Observer*, particularly on Fridays, for arts and music events and the *X-News* and *Hard Copy* for dancehall parties and stageshows), and – the usual way of announcing forth-coming events – **flyers and banners** posted up all around the towns. There are also a host of **websites** dedicated to entertainment listings; try ⓦwww.whaddat.com, ⓦwww.whatsonjamaica.com, ⓦwww.jamaicanlifestyle.com, ⓦwww.partyinc.com or ⓦwww.whata-gwan.com. We've given more specif-ic advice on finding out what's on in the indi-vidual chapters.

Lastly, there's a wealth of Jamaica-related sites on the Internet; we've listed some of the best and most useful sites below.

JTB Offices Abroad

There are no JTB offices in Australia, New Zealand or Ireland. The Jamaican Tourist Board websites are ⓦwww.visitjamaica.com and www.jamaicatravel.com.

United States

US Hotline ☎ 1-800/233-4JTB
Miami 1320 S Dixie Hwy, Suite 1101, Coral Gables, FL 33146 ☎ 305/665-0557, ⓕ 305/666-7239.

Canada

Canada Hotline ☎ 1-800/465-2624
Toronto 1 Eglinton Ave East, Suite 200, Toronto, Ontario M4P 3A1 ☎ 416/482-7850, ⓕ 416/482-1730.

United Kingdom

London 1-2 Prince Consort Rd, London SW7 2BZ ☎ 020/7224 0505, ⓕ 020/224 0551.

JTB Offices in Jamaica

Black River Hendriks Building, 2 High St, Black River ☎ 995 2074, ⓕ 965 2076.

Kingston 64 Knutsford Blvd, Kingston 5 ☎ 929 9200, ⓕ 929 9375.
Montego Bay Cornwall Beach, PO Box 67, Montego Bay ☎ 952 4425, ⓕ 952 3587.
Negril Coral Seas Plaza, Negril PO ☎ 957 4243, ⓕ 957 4489.
Ocho Rios Ocean Village Shopping Centre, PO Box 240, Jcho Rios ☎ 974 2582, ⓕ 974 2559.
Port Antonio City Centre Plaza, PO Box 151, Port Antonio ☎ 993 3051, ⓕ 993 2117.

Jamaica on the Internet

There's a vast amount of information about Jamaica available on the Internet, and hav-ing a browse before you leave is an excellent way to get a taster of the place. You can, of course, book flights and accommodation online, and it's possible to make a consider-able saving this way. For **music**-related sites see *Contexts*, p.418; for websites of **news-papers and radio stations**, see p.44–45. Websites also appear throughout the *Guide* wherever relevant.

Jamaica Tourist Board websites

Jamaica Travel ⓦ www.jamaicatravel.com
Official site of the JTB, with a regularly updated, searchable calendar of events, accommodation, resort and attraction listings and hoards of local information.
Visit Jamaica ⓦ www.visitjamaica.com Brand-new website from the JTB, which looks set to eclipse the old Jamaica Travel site (above); at the time of writing both were being regularly updated. Exhaustive and Flash-heavy, this one has all you'll ever need to know about Jamaica, with lots of practical information as well as loads of gorgeous pictures.

Other websites

Afflicted Yard ⓦ www.afflictedyard.com
The antidote to the slicker Jamaican sites, including a suitably volatile "Informer Corner" message board, beautifully cynical features, incisive discussion of current events, clips filmed in Jamaica and sound-system tapes from Kingston's best cassette vendors. Essential.
Discover Jamaica ⓦ www.discoverjamaica.com
Big site with lots of tourist info and links.
Jamaicas ⓦ www.jamaicans.com
All things Yard, from language,culture and music to cookery and tourist info, plus a busy message board.
Jamaica4u ⓦ www.jamaica4u.homestead.com
Comprehensive guide to Jamaica with entertainment

listings, practical information and history, cooking and patois tips. Good links, too.

Jamaican Information Service ⓦwww.jis .gov.jm Website of the ever-helpful Jamaica Information Service, unsurprisingly heavy on facts, figures and links to government agencies. You can email staff at the JIS with specific questions. Also has clips from JIS TV programmes.

Jamaica Irie ⓦwww.jamaica-irie.com Good range of links and tourist information on all the major resorts.

Members.Tripodⓦmembers.tripod.com/jamaica _wi/jamaica2.htm Comprehensive directory of links, organized into useful categories.

Reggae Boyzⓦwww.thereggaeboyz.com Site of the national football team, with lots of general info on the beautiful game, Yard-style, as well.

Top5Jamaicaⓦwww.top5jamaica.com Links to the most popular Jamaican sites on the Web, divided by category.

West Indies Cricket Board ⓦwww .windiescricket.com Homepage of the West Indies cricket board, with reports on regional and international matches, and lots of features.

Maps

For touring or driving around the island, the best map to get hold of is the **Shell Jamaica Road Map** (1:250,000), which is contoured and includes excellent street maps of Kingston, Montego Bay, Ocho Rios as well as Spanish Town, Mandeville and Port Antonio. It's sold at good book shops in Jamaica and in selected Shell petrol stations islandwide.

Of the other island maps, the JTB road map, *Discover Jamaica,* includes a 1:350,000 map of the entire island, a 1:34,000 map of Kingston and small maps of the other main towns. It's available from JTB offices abroad and, in Jamaica, from the offices in Kingston and Montego Bay – you may have to pay a small fee. Another two decent maps of the island are those from *Hildebrandt* (1:300,000) and *ITNB* (1:250,000), available at the map outlets below.

Map outlets

In the US and Canada

Adventurous Traveler.com US ☎1-800/282-3963, ⓦadventuroustraveler.com.
Book Passage 51 Tamal Vista Blvd, Corte Madera, CA 94925 ☎1-800/999-7909, ⓦwww.bookpassage.com.
Distant Lands 56 S Raymond Ave, Pasadena, CA 91105 ☎1-800/310-3220, ⓦwww.distantlands.com.
Elliot Bay Book Company 101 S Main St, Seattle, WA 98104 ☎1-800/962-5311, ⓦwww.elliotbaybook.com.
Globe Corner Bookstore 28 Church St, Cambridge, MA 02138 ☎1-800/358-6013, ⓦwww.globecorner.com.
Map Link 30 S La Patera Lane, Unit 5, Santa Barbara, CA 93117 ☎1-800/962-1394, ⓦwww.maplink.com.
Rand McNally US ☎1-800/333-0136, ⓦwww.randmcnally.com. Around thirty stores across the US; dial ext 2111 or check the website for the nearest location.
The Travel Bug Bookstore 2667 W Broadway, Vancouver V6K 2G2 ☎604/737-1122, ⓦwww.swifty.com/tbug.
World of Maps 1235 Wellington St, Ottawa, Ontario K1Y 3A3 ☎1-800/214-8524, ⓦwww.worldofmaps.com.

In the UK and Ireland

Blackwell's Map and Travel Shop 50 Broad St, Oxford OX1 3BQ ☎01865/793 550, ⓦmaps.blackwell.co.uk.
Easons Bookshop 40 O'Connell St, Dublin 1 ☎01/858 3881, ⓦwww.eason.ie.
Heffers Map and Travel 20 Trinity St, Cambridge CB2 1TJ ☎01865/333 536, ⓦwww.heffers.co.uk.
Hodges Figgis Bookshop 56–58 Dawson St, Dublin 2 ☎01/677 4754.
The Map Shop 30a Belvoir St, Leicester LE1 6QH ☎0116/247 1400, ⓦwww.mapshopleicester.co.uk.
National Map Centre 22–24 Caxton St, London SW1H 0QU ☎020/7222 2466, ⓦwww.mapsnmc.co.uk, ⓔinfo@mapsnmc.co.uk.
Newcastle Map Centre 55 Grey St, Newcastle-upon-Tyne, NE1 6EF ☎0191/261 5622.
Ordnance Survey Ireland Phoenix Park, Dublin 8 ☎01/802 5300, ⓦwww.osi.ie.
Ordnance Survey of Northern Ireland Colby House, Stranmillis Ct, Belfast BT9 5BJ ☎028/9025 5755, ⓦwww.osni.gov.uk.
Stanfords 12–14 Long Acre, London WC2E 9LP ☎020/7836 1321, ⓦwww.stanfords.co.uk, ⓔsales@stanfords.co.uk.
The Travel Bookshop 13–15 Blenheim Crescent, London W11 2EE ☎020/7229 5260, ⓦwww.thetravelbookshop.co.uk.

In Australia and New Zealand

Mapland 372 Little Bourke St, Melbourne, Victoria 3000 ℡03/9670 4383, ⓦwww.mapland.com.au. The Map Shop 6–10 Peel St, Adelaide, SA 5000 ℡08/8231 2033, ⓦwww.mapshop.net.au. MapWorld 173 Gloucester St, Christchurch

℡0800/627 967 or 03/374 5399, ⓦwww.mapworld.co.nz. Perth Map Centre 900 Hay St, Perth, WA 6000 ℡08/9322 5733, ⓦwww.perthmap.com.au. Specialty Maps 46 Albert St, Auckland 1001 ℡09/307 2217, ⓦwww.specialtymaps.co.nz.

Insurance

It's always sensible, and sometimes necessary, to take out an insurance policy before travelling to cover against theft, loss and illness or injury. Before paying for a new policy, however, it's worth checking whether you are already covered: some all-risks home insurance policies may cover your possessions while overseas, and many private medical schemes include cover while abroad. In Canada, provincial health plans usually provide partial cover for medical mishaps overseas, while holders of official student/teacher/youth cards in Canada and the US are entitled to meagre accident coverage and hospital in-patient benefits. Students will often find that their student health coverage extends during the vacations and for one term beyond the date of last enrollment.

After exhausting the possibilities above, you might want to contact a **specialist travel insurance company,** or consider the travel insurance deal we offer (see box below). A typical travel insurance policy usually provides cover for the loss of baggage, tickets and – up to a certain limit – cash or cheques, as well as cancellation or curtailment of your journey. Most of them exclude so-called dangerous sports unless an extra premium is paid: in Jamaica, this can mean scuba diving, white-water rafting, windsurfing and trekking, though probably not kayaking or jeep safaris. Many policies can be chopped and changed to exclude coverage you don't need – for example, sickness and accident benefits can often be excluded or included at will. If you do take medical

Rough Guides travel insurance

Rough Guides offers its own low-cost travel insurance, especially customized for our statistically low-risk readers by a leading British broker, provided by the American International Group (AIG) and registered with the British regulatory body, GISC (the General Insurance Standards Council). There are five main Rough Guides insurance plans: No Frills for the bare minimum for secure travel; Essential, which provides decent all-round cover; Premier for comprehensive cover with a wide range of benefits; Extended Stay for cover lasting two months to a year; and Annual Multi-trip, a cost-effective way of getting Premier cover if you travel more than once a year. Premier, Annual Multi-Trip and Extended Stay policies can be supplemented by a "Hazardous Pursuits Extension" if you plan to indulge in sports considered dangerous, such as scuba-diving or trekking. For a policy quote, call the Rough Guide Insurance Line: toll-free in the UK ℡0800/015 09 06 or ℡+44 1392 314 665 from elsewhere. Alternatively, get an online quote at ⓦwww.roughguides.com/insurance.

coverage, ascertain whether benefits will be paid as treatment proceeds or only after your return home, and whether there is a 24-hour medical emergency number. When securing baggage cover, make sure that the per-article limit – typically under US$730/£500 – will cover your most valuable possession. If you need to make a claim, you should keep receipts for medicines and medical treatment, and in the event of having anything stolen, you must obtain an official statement from the police.

 # Health

Health-wise, travelling in Jamaica is generally very safe. Food tends to be well and hygienically prepared and the filtered and heavily chlorinated tap water is safe to drink, so bugs and upsets are normally limited to the usual traveller's tummy. In rural homes not connected to mains pipes you may be offered rainwater – while this is generally safe it is up to you to decide whether to risk it.

Vaccinations and other precautions

Unless you have travelled to Asia, Africa, Central or South America, the Dominican Republic, Haiti or Trinidad and Tobago within six weeks of landing in Jamaica, **no vaccinations** are required to enter the island. However, you might want to have hepatitis A, typhoid and polio shots if you're planning to hike or swim in Jamaican rivers. Contact a travel clinic or doctor for up-to-the-minute advice on specific shots.

Jamaica is not malarial, but there are occasional outbreaks of **dengue fever**, carried by the *Aedes aegypti* mosquito, found throughout the island but particularly prevalent in Kingston. It's rarely fatal (only the infirm, very young or old are at serious risk), but at the first sign of symptoms – extreme aches and pains in the bones and joints, rashes around the torso, dizziness, headaches, fever and vomiting – you should take to your bed for a few days, and call a doctor if symptoms persist. There's no effective vaccination, so your best prevention is to avoid mosquitoes (see "Creepy crawlies" on p.22).

Have a **dental check-up** before you travel and bring **prescription medicines** with you. A pre-prepared **medical kit** (see box) is also

A traveller's first-aid kit

Here are some items you might want to carry with you – especially if you're planning on hiking (see "Sport and Outdoor Activities", p.52).

- Antiseptic spray or powder
- Insect repellent
- Plasters/Bandaids
- Lint and sealed bandages
- Emergency diarrhoea treatment
- Painkillers
- Multi-vitamin and mineral tablets
- Rehydration sachets
- Calamine lotion or aloe gel

- Hypodermic needles and sterilized skin wipes (more for the security of knowing you have them, than any fear that a local hospital would fail to observe basic sanitary precautions. A doctor's note is required if you want to carry hypodermic needles in your hand luggage – and is a good idea even if the needles are in your checked luggage.)

useful. The Yahoo! health website, ⓦhealth.yahoo.com, gives information about specific diseases and conditions, drugs and herbal remedies, as well as getting advice from health experts.

In the UK, you might also want to pick up the Department of Health's free publication *Health Advice for Travellers*, a comprehensive booklet available from post offices or by calling the Health Literature Line (☎0800/555 777). It includes immunization advice and is constantly updated on pages 460–464 of the BBC's CEEFAX; you can also consult it on the Internet at ⓦwww.open.gov.uk/. Another useful website, ⓦwww.24dr.com, outlines health risks in most countries.

Staying healthy in the heat

If you're unused to it, Jamaica's **humid climate** can bring on a host of minor medical complaints. Open wounds take longer to heal and easily become septic: clean wounds scrupulously as soon as they occur, and dress with iodine, dry antiseptic spray or powder – creams just keep a cut wet and slow down healing; for the same reasons, avoid dressing minor wounds. If you've no antiseptic to hand, white rum is an effective substitute. Among other bothersome ailments is **conjunctivitis** (pink eye), which thrives in heat and bright sunlight; wear sunglasses and bring your usual treatment if prone, or try the local remedy, aloe vera (see box, below). **Pityriasis** is a common, easily transmitted fungal infection that appears as circular crispy patches on white skin and as lighter patches of discoloration on black skin; it's easily treated with anti-fungal creams, sulphur-based lotions or anti-dandruff shampoos containing selenium. The same treatments apply for **athlete's foot** – to avoid it, wear open sandals as much as possible and flip-flops around pools and communal showers.

You'll need to be extra-scrupulous about personal hygiene, too, as blocked sweat ducts can cause uncomfortable and unsightly **prickly heat** rashes. To treat or avoid prickly heat, wear loose cotton clothes, take frequent cold showers without soap, dust with medicated talcum powder and don't use sunscreen or moisturizer on affected areas.

Given Jamaica's steamy heat, **dehydration** is easily achieved. It pays to dramatically increase your intake of water or coconut water (not fizzy drinks, alcohol, tea or coffee); it's wise to carry an insulated bottle of water wherever you go. Remember that if you feel thirsty, you're probably already

Aloe vera

Jamaicans are so convinced of the curative power of fast-growing **aloe vera** or "sinkle bible" (a corruption of the botanical name *Sempervivum*) that many dispense with titles altogether and simply call it the "healing plant". Noticeable for its thick, spiny-edged clusters of leaves growing close to the ground, aloe is the workhorse of Jamaican medicine. It's used to treat sunburn (for which it's particularly effective), heat rashes, cuts, bruises, burns and all insect bites; mixed with water to make an eye wash that soothes conjunctivitis; used to condition sun-damaged afro hair; prepared as a treatment for skin conditions like eczema and psoriasis; and drunk with garlic to cleanse the blood – a daring feat, as it's very bitter.

Rastafarians use aloe in place of the Biblical hyssop, but you're most likely to encounter it in the hands of hustlers who peddle bottles of "aloe massage" (aloe gel mixed with water) on north coast beaches. As aloe plants flourish throughout the island, you can usually find it for free, and it's much more effective (and hygienic) to use aloe straight from the plant rather than in a preparation. To extract the gel, slice the stem in two, cut off the serrated edges, lightly scrape the mauve jelly and wipe it on. Be careful not to get it on clothing – it leaves a stubborn purple stain. You'll also find pure aloe gel on the shelves of health-food stores at home.

dehydrated. **Heat exhaustion** is another potential (and more serious) problem. At the first sign of light-headedness, headache, or nausea, lie down in a cool place and drink as much as possible – packed with goodness, fresh coconut water is especially effective. If you become seriously dehydrated, a salt/sugar rehydration solution helps replenish lost minerals (see "Stomach problems", below). In case of serious **sunstroke** – signalled by vomiting and blurred vision – get to a doctor.

Stomach problems

While serious stomach disorders are rare among travellers in Jamaica, the climate and unfamiliar food might well result in a bout of **diarrhoea** – or "running belly", as the locals call it. Washing and peeling fruit and vegetables, being choosy about where you eat and always washing your hands before you do so lessen the risk. If you do come a cropper, rest and drink plenty of water, herb tea, fruit juice or clear soup; coconut water has excellent calmative properties and is packed with vitamins. Make up for lost minerals by drinking a glass of water mixed with a teaspoon of sugar and half a teaspoon of salt after every motion and once an hour. Eat plain foods like rice or bread and avoid fruit, fatty foods and dairy products. Conventional diarrhoea remedies alleviate symptoms but reduce the body's natural response to flush out the infection and should only be used if you cannot get to a toilet, such as before a long journey.

Creepy crawlies: bites and stings

Prevention really is better than cure when it comes to encounters with insects. Avoid being bitten by **mosquitoes** by wearing long sleeves and trousers, and by applying lots of DEET-rich repellent – especially in the early evening or after rain. Mosquito coils are sold everywhere and can be effective, if a bit smelly, and the widely available Skin So Soft has miraculous anti-mosquito properties, particularly if you're unwilling to spray on the chemicals. Another natural repellent, citronella, is also catching on in Jamaica, but even though sprays, oils (look for "Oil of No Mosquito" in the Starfish aromatherapy range) and scented candles are available from resort gift shops, you'll pay less if you bring it from home. Once you've been bitten (and you will be), anoint the bites with aloe or calamine – and **leave them alone.** Though hellishly tempting, scratching (or even a light investigative rub) will always lead to more irritation, and possibly infected sores and scarring.

Tiny and innocuous-looking, **sand flies** amass on beaches at dusk, inflicting a small, shiny bite with a lingering itch; Jamaicans use rubbing alcohol to soothe. Present wherever there is livestock, **ticks** and **grass lice** wait on grass stems to feast on passing feet; defy them by wearing trousers tucked into socks, as repellent can be ineffective. Ticks are present year-round, but their populations peak between October and January, although even then they're only a problem in rural areas. They can be safely plucked from the skin, though you should apply antiseptic or the locally available cream Rid and ensure that you have removed the head as well as the body – leave infested clothes out to air. A lighted cigarette efficiently dispatches the larger grass lice; locals dab with kerosene.

There are no **poisonous snakes** in Jamaica, and **black widow spiders** are shy enough to make an encounter unlikely, though you should see a doctor if you think you've been bitten. Watch out for the red and black "**forty legs**" **centipede**, which measures up to five inches and imparts a nasty scarring bite if touched, even when it's dead.

Hazards of the sea

Though they look vicious, **moray eels** and **barracudas** only attack if threatened, so keep away from them when snorkelling or diving. Other than the **nurse shark** occasionally seen around the reefs, and again only dangerous if cornered or harassed, sharks are rare along the heavily populated coast. **Spiny black urchins** are easily missed in a bed of sea grass – if you tread on one, remove the spines immediately, soak the skin in vinegar (or urine) and see a doctor; water heated as hot as you can stand is also useful for getting out the spines. Colourless **jellyfish** are quite common, particularly in harbours; the sting is painful but not serious and is easily treated by a doctor. Supreme care should be taken to avoid the trailing purple **Portuguese man o' war**, which is rare but toxic. Never touch **coral**; apart from the fact that contact usually kills the organism, it can cut and you'll come away with a painful, slow-to-heal rash. Fire coral is particularly nasty. If you do have a brush with the reefs, don't touch the affected area directly, but wash it with a diluted vinegar or ammonia solution; again, urine can be used if nothing else is available.

Sexual health

Jamaica has the third-highest incidence of AIDS in the Caribbean. Government figures claim that 25,000 people in Jamaica are HIV positive and 8000 of those have fully blown AIDS, though the figures are likely to be much higher. Given the high level of holiday liaisons and the local propensity for casual sex, figures seem set to rise and, even officially, have so far doubled every two years since the late 1980s. HIV is primarily a heterosexual problem in Jamaica, with tourist

Bush medicine

Many Jamaicans, particularly in rural areas, still make frequent use of "**bush medicine**" or "**balm**", a system of African herbal medicine introduced to Jamaica by slaves, fundamental to Maroon civilization for three hundred-odd years and still an important part of Myalist practice (see "Religion" in *Contexts*, p.403). Most Jamaicans have a rudimentary knowledge of plant medicine, using natural remedies for minor complaints as a matter of course, but "balmists", or herbalists, have a lifetime's experience, if no formal qualifications. One or two of these respected elders still prescribe from the traditional setting of a **balmyard**, distinguishable from other rural dwellings by coloured flags and hanging talismans. Consultations can be enlightening, but balmists tend to be secretive souls and you'll find a good one only through word of mouth.

Herbs can be taken as an infusion or decoction (usually as a tea), as a poultice, or in a hot "bush bath". Many households have a pot of cure-all **bush tea** permanently on the hob, made up of diverse ingredients like lemon, fevergrass, soursop, breadfruit leaves and pepper elder. Perhaps the most widely used single herb is **cerassee**, a climbing vine made into a very bitter tea – you can buy ready-made teabags if you develop a taste. It's said to cure practically everything, but is particularly good as a blood purifier and allegedly discourages mosquitoes. Inevitably, there are loads of plants geared around **male virility** – chainy root, jack-in-the-bush, medina, janta (or cow-hoof leaf), quassia – the list of "front end lifters" goes on and on, and many concoctions are now commercially bottled (see "Food and drink", p.40). **Ganja** is boiled into a tea for asthma and eye problems; **leaf of life** is said to conquer colds, hypertension and bronchial problems; **tuna cactus** is used to treat dandruff, nerves and chronic pain such as arthritis. Many of the medicinal herbs have rather fanciful names; among the best are **search mi heart** and **shame o' lady**, both used for colds and stomach problems, but the prize goes to **ram goat dash along**, good for arthritis and debility. Healing properties are also attributed to simple **fruits and vegetables.** Soursop is said to calm the nerves, and its leaves are used to help testy babies go off to sleep. Papaya (paw-paw) is reputed to relieve indigestion; guava leaves are good for diarrhoea; tamarind soothes itchy skin and chicken pox; and coconut water cleanses the bladder.

Though most balmists stick to medicine, some are associated with **obeah**, or witchcraft, prescribing what's said to be grave dirt mixed with substances such as "**Oil of Keep the Dead**" or "**Oil of Deliver Me**" to banish duppies, "**Oil of Come Back**" to win back a straying lover, or even "**Oil of Fall Back**", which dooms imbibers to fail in everything they attempt. These days, though, most Jamaicans regard such potions with a healthy degree of scepticism.

areas the worst affected; one in ten citizens in the Montego Bay area are HIV positive and one in five female prostitutes carries the virus. With an estimated 80,000 cases of other **STDs** (including syphilis) each year, Jamaica has a long way to go in sexual health education; as recently as the late 1990s, a radio advertising campaign saw fit to dispel the (widely believed) myth that STDs can be cured by having sex with a virgin. Things are slowly improving though – there are now widespread campaigns, with regular roadshows and educational programmes, to persuade Jamaicans to practise safe sex. The National Aids Committee (NAC, ☎967 1100/03/05/07, ⊛www.nacjamaica.com) offers advice and information on AIDS, HIV and STDs, as does Jamaica Aids Support (JAS, ☎978 2345, ⊛www.jamaicaaidssupport.com) or you can call JAS toll free on ☎1-888 991 4444.

Always use **condoms**. Bring them with you even if you don't plan on having sex. The main Jamaican brand, Rough Riders, and some US imports, including Durex, are available from pharmacies and street vendors – check the expiration date. In an attempt to sell safe sex to the ghetto massive, dancehall queen Carlene has lent her name to a range of condoms, Slam (the brand-name employs a local epithet for sex), complete with a suitably alluring picture of the lady herself on the packet. If you notice unusual symptoms, get treatment right away.

Women's health

It's an irritating inevitability that time in the tropics creates the perfect conditions for a bout of **thrush** – bring bifidum acidophilus capsules with you, and take them daily to balance yeasts. Canesten cream or pessaries are effective treatments, as is the more messy natural yoghurt, which is difficult to find in Jamaica. To avoid thrush, avoid using heavily perfumed products in this area and always wear cotton underwear. Dehydration and the stress of travel can encourage **cystitis**; to avoid it, drink copious amounts of water and be rigorous about personal hygiene. If you suffer regularly, bring sachets of acidifying remedies that contain potassium citrate.

You should bring more than enough **sanitary protection**, as your usual brand will be more expensive, and bear in mind that flushing towels and tampons down the toilet is usually a straight route to the sea.

Hospitals, doctors and pharmacies

There are tiny regional **hospitals** throughout Jamaica, but most are overcrowded, underfunded and poorly equipped; the general rule is the larger the town, the better the hospital. There are two good, sizeable public hospitals in Kingston, while Cornwall Regional in Montego Bay is the best equipped on the north coast. The easiest way to find a **doctor** in a hurry is to ask at your hotel; some have a resident nurse, and all will be able to recommend someone locally as every town has a doctor or medical clinic. Most of these are reliable, but you'll have to fork out for the treatment and claim on your insurance once back home, so make sure you get receipts.

Every town has at least one **pharmacy**, with those in resort towns well stocked with expensive brand-name products; they will only issue antibiotics with a doctor's prescription.

Hospitals, private doctors, clinics and pharmacies are found throughout the island and are listed in each chapter.

Medical resources for travellers

Websites

⊛www.fitfortravel.scot.nhs.uk UK NHS website carrying information about travel-related diseases and how to avoid them.
⊛www.health.yahoo.com Information on specific diseases and conditions, drugs and herbal remedies, as well as advice from health experts.
⊛www.istm.org The website of the International Society for Travel Medicine, with a full list of clinics specializing in international travel health.
⊛www.tmvc.com.au Contains a list of all Travellers Medical and Vaccination Centres throughout Australia, New Zealand and Southeast Asia, plus general information on travel health.
⊛www.tripprep.com Travel Health Online provides an online-only comprehensive database of necessary vaccinations for most countries, as well as destination and medical service provider information.

In the US and Canada

Canadian Society for International Health 1 Nicholas St, Suite 1105, Ottawa, ON K1N 7B7 ☎613/241-5785, ⓦwww.csih.org. Distributes a free pamphlet, "Health Information for Canadian Travellers", containing an extensive list of travel health centres in Canada.

Centers for Disease Control 1600 Clifton Rd NE, Atlanta, GA 30333 ☎1-800/311-3435 or 404/639-3534, ⓦwww.cdc.gov. Publishes outbreak warnings, suggested inoculations, precautions and other background information for travellers. Useful website plus International Travelers Hotline (☎1-877/FYI-TRIP).

International Association for Medical Assistance to Travellers (IAMAT) 417 Center St, Lewiston, NY 14092 ☎716/754-4883, ⓦwww.iamat.org, and 40 Regal Rd, Guelph, ON N1K 1B5 ☎519/836-0102. A non-profit organization supported by donations, it can provide a list of English-speaking doctors in Jamaica, climate charts and leaflets on various diseases and inoculations.

International SOS Assistance Eight Neshaminy Interplex; Suite 207, Trevose, PA USA 19053-6956 ☎1-800/523-8930, ⓦwww.intsos.com. Members receive pre-trip medical referral info, as well as overseas emergency services designed to complement travel insurance coverage.

MEDJET Assistance ☎1-800/9MEDJET, ⓦwww.medjetassistance.com. Annual membership program for travellers that, in the event of illness or injury, will fly members home or to the hospital of their choice in a medically equipped and staffed jet. US$175 for individuals, US$275 for families.

Travel Medicine ☎1-800/TRAVMED, ⓦwww.travmed.com. Sells first-aid kits, mosquito netting, water filters, reference books and other health-related travel products.

Travelers Medical Center 31 Washington Square West, New York, NY 10011 ☎212/982-1600. Consultation service on immunizations and treatment of diseases for people travelling to developing countries.

In the UK and Ireland

British Airways Travel Clinics 156 Regent St, London W1J 9HO ☎020/7439 9584, and 101 Cheapside, London EC2V 6DT ☎020/7606 2977; ⓦwww.britishairways.com/travel/healthclinintro. Vaccinations, tailored advice from an online database and a complete range of travel healthcare products.

Communicable Diseases Unit Brownlee Centre, Glasgow G12 0YN ☎0141/211 1062. Travel vaccinations including those for yellow fever.

Dun Laoghaire Medical Centre 5 Northumberland Ave, Dun Laoghaire, County Dublin ☎01/280 4996, ⓕ01/280 5603. Advice on medical matters abroad.

Hospital for Tropical Diseases Travel Clinic Mortimer Market Centre, 2nd floor, off Capper St, London WC1E 6AU ☎020/7388 9600, ⓦwww.masta.org. A consultation costs £15 which is waived if you have your injections here. A recorded Health Line (☎0906/133 7733; 50p per min) gives hints on hygiene and illness prevention as well as listing appropriate immunizations.

Liverpool School of Tropical Medicine Pembroke Place, Liverpool L3 5QA ☎0151/708 9393. Walk-in clinic; appointment required for yellow fever vaccination, but not for other jabs.

MASTA (Medical Advisory Service for Travellers Abroad) Forty regional clinics (call ☎0870/6062782 for the nearest). Also operates a pre-recorded 24-hour Travellers' Health Line (UK ☎0906/822 4100, 60p per min), giving written information tailored to your journey by return of post.

Nomad Pharmacy surgeries at 40 Bernard St, London, WC1N 1LE, and 3-4 Wellington Terrace, Turnpike Lane, London N8 0PX ☎020/7833 4114. They can give information tailored to your travel needs. Go in person for free advice, or phone the helpline (☎0906/863 3414, 60p per minute).

Trailfinders 194 Kensington High St, London W8 7RG ☎020/7938 3999. Immunization clinic; no appointments necessary.

Travel Health Centre Department of International Health and Tropical Medicine, Royal College of Surgeons in Ireland, Mercers Medical Centre, Stephen's St Lower, Dublin 2 ☎01/402 2337. Expert pre-trip advice and inoculations.

Travel Medicine Services PO Box 254, 16 College St, Belfast BT1 6BT ☎028/9031 5220. Offers medical advice before a trip and help afterwards if you contract a tropical disease.

Tropical Medical Bureau Grafton Buildings, 34 Grafton St, Dublin 2, ☎01/671 9200, ⓦtmb.exodus.ie.

In Australia and New Zealand

Travellers' Medical and Vaccination Centres 27–29 Gilbert Place, Adelaide, SA 5000 ☎08/8212 7522, ⓔadelaide@traveldoctor.com.au. 1/170 Queen St, Auckland ☎09/373 3531, ⓔauckland@traveldoctor.co.nz. 5/247 Adelaide St, Brisbane, Qld 4000 ☎07/3221 9066, ⓔbrisbane@traveldoctor.com.au. 5/8–10 Hobart Place, Canberra, ACT 2600 ☎02/6257 7156, ⓔcanberra@traveldoctor.com.au. Moorhouse Medical Centre, 9 Washington Way, Christchurch ☎03/379 4000, ⓔchristchurch@traveldoctor.co.nz. 270 Sandy Bay Rd, Sandy

Bay Tas, Hobart 7005 ☎ 03/6223 7577, ✉ hobart
@traveldoctor.com.au. 2/393 Little Bourke St,
Melbourne, Vic 3000 ☎ 03/9602 5788,
✉ melbourne@traveldoctor.com.au. Level 7,

Dymocks Bldg, 428 George St, Sydney, NSW 2000
☎ 02/9221 7133, ✉ sydney@traveldoctor.com.au.
Shop 15, Grand Arcade, 14–16 Willis St, Wellington
☎ 04/473 0991, ✉ wellington@traveldoctor.co.nz.

Costs, money and banks

In keeping with its reputation as a "luxury" destination, Jamaica is not a cheap country to visit. Some things, like car rental and international telephone calls, cost more than in Europe and a lot more than in the US; for the staples, like accommodation and food, there's usually something to suit every budget, though the pickings are slim at the bottom end of the lodging market. Don't be scared to negotiate on prices – particularly in taxis and at markets and roadside stalls, the first price quoted is often an opening gambit, and even hotels and guest houses are generally fair game for a bit of bargaining, especially during low season.

Currency

Jamaica's unit of currency is the **Jamaican dollar** (J$), divided into 100 cents. It comes in bills of J$1000, J$500, J$100 and J$50 and coins of J$20, J$10, J$5, J$1, J$.10, J$.05 and J$.01.

At the time of writing the **rate of exchange** was roughly J$60 to US$1 and J$90 to £1. Although the value of local currency has inexorably fallen in recent years, it was, at the time of writing, dropping dramatically on a weekly basis – a reflection of Jamaica's dire economic state. The **US dollar** has long served as an unofficial parallel currency, particularly at the north coast resorts, and prices for tourist services – hotels, restaurants, car rental and sightseeing tours – are usually quoted in US$ (note that US$1 is roughly equivalent to £0.60).

When paying a bill, though, check in advance that your change will be given in the same currency or, if in Jamaican dollars, at a decent exchange rate.

Costs

Accommodation is likely to be the major expense of your trip, although if you're prepared to put up with extremely basic options, you can find rooms in most of the main resort areas for around US$30 (£20) per night. For something more salubrious, expect to pay US$50 (£35), and a room with air conditioning and cable TV will cost US$60–80 (£40–55). Accommodation apart, if you travel around by bus or shared taxi and get your food from markets and the cheaper cafés and roadside stalls, you can just about survive on a daily budget of around US$25–30

Pricing policy

Because of the volatility of the Jamaican dollar and the widespread quotation of US dollars for major expenses such as hotels and car rental, we've largely given prices in US dollars throughout the Guide. Restaurants and bars vary, with some quoting US, others Jamaican; where we give prices, we do as they do. For minor items like bus fares, short taxi rides or roadside snacks, drivers and vendors will always quote Jamaican dollars, and we have followed their example. Bear in mind, though, that currency fluctuations mean that prices change frequently; hence some rates in Jamaican dollars listed in the guide may well be incorrect.

Insiders' Jamaica

In an attempt to get people out of the all-inclusives and into "explorer" mode – driving a rental car and staying at small hotels – the Jamaica Tourist Board unveiled the **Insiders' Jamaica** scheme in 1999. Insiders' members, who pay no fee to participate, are met at the airport and presented with a card for discounts at participating tours, attractions and restaurants, as well as an invitation to a Jamaican house party. The small hotels included in the scheme will also book you on at other participating properties. For more details, contact JTB offices on the island and worldwide, or check the website ⓦ www.insidersjamaica.com.

(£15–20) per day. Upgrading to one decent meal out, the occasional taxi and a bit of evening entertainment, expect to spend a more realistic US$35–50 (£22–35); after that, the sky's the limit.

Credit/debit cards and travellers' cheques

The easiest way to access funds in Jamaica is by using plastic. Banks in all major cities, most towns and some shopping malls and petrol stations have **ATM machines** that take any cards linked to Visa or MasterCard networks. The ATMs dispense local cash and, in large resorts, US dollars. (NB: There is no ATM in the Blue Mountains – your nearest options if you run out of cash are in Kingston or Buff Bay.) Major **credit cards** – American Express, Visa, MasterCard – are widely accepted in the larger tourist hotels, but don't necessarily expect the smaller hotels and restaurants to take them. You can also use your credit card to get **cash advances** at most banks, although this is an expensive option – you'll pay both a commission to the bank and hefty interest to your credit card company. **Debit cards** are more economical. The flat fee for using them is usually quite small – check with your card issuer before you go – and the exchange rate given when withdrawing cash is often the best you'll find.

Travellers' cheques, in US dollars or English pounds, are the safest method of carrying money in Jamaica. These are available for a small commission from most banks, and from branches of American Express and Thomas Cook; make sure you keep the purchase agreement and a record of cheque serial numbers safe and separate from the cheques themselves. Once in Jamaica, they can be cashed at banks and cambios (you'll need your passport or other photo ID to validate them) for a small charge.

A compromise between travellers' cheques and plastic is **Visa TravelMoney,** a disposable pre-paid debit card with a PIN that works in all ATMs that take Visa cards. You load up your account with funds before leaving home, and when they run out, you simply throw the card away. You can buy up to nine cards to access the same funds – useful for couples or families travelling together. It's a good idea to buy at least one extra as a backup in case of loss or theft. There is a 24-hour toll-free customer assistance number (☎ 0800/847 2399). The card is available in most countries from branches of **Thomas Cook** and **Citicorp.** For more information, check the Visa TravelMoney website at ⓦ usa.visa.com/personal/cards /visa_travel_money.html.

Banks and exchange

Banking hours in Jamaica are generally Monday to Thursday 9am to 2pm and Friday 9am to 3pm or 4pm. Other places to exchange money include **cambios**, which are found at some supermarkets across the country. Cambios usually offer a better exchange rate, particularly when the currency is fluctuating wildly. A firm favourite, with consistently good rates, are the islandwide branches of FX Trader, run by the Grace company and often conveniently situated within supermarkets and shopping malls; you can find out the location of the nearest office by calling toll-free on ☎ 1-888/398 7233. **Exchange bureaux** at the main airports offer rates slightly lower than the banks, and at **hotels**, the rate is invariably significantly lower – it's only worth changing money at hotels if you have no other choice.

Keep the official receipts when you change

money, as you'll need them to convert any Jamaican dollars back to dollars/sterling when you leave – you are not allowed to take Jamaican dollars out of the country. Whenever you exchange money, ask the cashier to give you some small bills – many shops, taxi/bus drivers and small restaurants won't be able to change a J$1000 note.

Wiring money

If you run out of money, you can arrange a **wire transfer** to Jamaica from your home bank account (or that of someone willing to lend you cash). Bear in mind, though, that having money wired from home is never convenient or cheap, and should be considered a last resort. Western Union has branches in banks as well as separate offices across the island; in Jamaica, call toll-free (☎1-888/991 2056) for locations of outlets islandwide. You can also wire cash from post offices and branches of Thomas Cook in the UK and the US via Moneygram, which is slightly cheaper than Western Union.

It's also possible to have money wired directly from a bank in your home country to a bank in Jamaica, although this is somewhat less reliable because it involves two separate institutions. If you go this route, your home bank will need the address of the branch bank where you want to pick up the money,

and the address and telex number of the Kingston head office, which will act as the clearing house; money wired this way normally takes two working days to arrive, and costs around £25/US$40 per transaction.

Money-wiring companies

American Express MoneyGram

Ⓦ www.moneygram.com.
Australia ☎1-800/230 100
Canada ☎1-800/933-3278
New Zealand ☎0800/262 263,
Republic of Ireland ☎1850/205 800
UK ☎0800/018 0104
US ☎1-800/955-7777

Thomas Cook

Ⓦ www.thomascook.com
US ☎1-800/287-7362
Canada ☎1-888/823-4732
UK ☎01733/318 922
Northern Ireland ☎028/9055 0030
Republic of Ireland ☎01/677 1721

Western Union

Ⓦ www.westernunion.com
Australia ☎1800/501 500
Canada and US ☎1-800/325-6000
New Zealand ☎0800/270 000
Republic of Ireland ☎1800/395 395
UK ☎0800/833 833

Getting around

A lot of people come to Jamaica, make straight for their hotel and spend the next fortnight lying on the beach. For those who want to see some of the island, and you'll have a far more rewarding stay if you do, there are a variety of ways to get around. Buses and minibuses run around the coasts, and to all towns and most rural communities in the interior. Renting a car offers maximum independence but will eat heavily into your budget; if you just want to make the odd excursion or short trip, it can work out cheaper to take a taxi, or even hire a private driver. For longer trips, internal flights are reasonably priced, and a good idea if you're short of time or considering a two-centre holiday – say, Negril and Port Antonio.

Buses and minibuses

According to the *Daily Gleaner* newspaper, Jamaica's public transport system is "a dreadful source of punishment and wasted time for those who are forced to use it". And though things are improving, there's no doubt that Jamaica's **buses** and **minibuses** – aside from the smarter "coasters" that ply the busier routes – can be a little disquieting if you're used to a more regulated system. Timetables are nonexistent, drivers can show little interest in the rules of the road, and passengers are often squeezed in with scant regard for their comfort.

On the other hand, public transport is a great way to meet people and get a window into a different side of the island. It's also absurdly cheap – about J$70 per fifty miles for a bus and J$100–140 per fifty miles for minibuses and coasters – and, if like most Jamaicans, you can't afford to fly, take taxis or rent a car, you'll be doing a lot of it. Throughout the book we've explained where to catch buses and, at the end of each chapter, detailed the main routes and journey times.

Each town has a bus terminal of sorts, often near the market. The destination is usually written somewhere on the front of buses, minibuses and coasters, squeezed between the vehicle's name: "Tings Coulda Worse", "Nuff Vibes", "God's Property", "Rude Boy Strength" and the like. The conductor will shout out the destination repeatedly before departure, scouting the area for potential passengers and cramming in as many as possible. Then the vehicle screeches off, jam-packed with humanity and often pounding with music. Buses and minibuses will stop anywhere en route to pick up or drop off passengers (except in major towns, where they are restricted to bus stops and terminals). If you want to get off somewhere before the terminus, tell the conductor and fellow passengers where you're going when you get on; yelling "one stop", or something similar, at the driver is the usual method of getting the bus to stop when you get there. To get on a bus, just stand by the side of the road and flag it down.

Always keep as close as possible to your luggage – it's probably unwise to stow your shiny new pack on the roof. Fares are paid to a conductor after boarding, and having the right change, or at least small bills, will make your life easier. Try also to travel during daylight, as arriving in an unfamiliar place at night will make things more difficult, especially if you have to find accommodation. In fact, the earlier in the day you travel the better – being stuck in a bursting Jamaican bus on a boiling afternoon is no picnic.

Cars

If you can afford it, **renting a car** is the best way of getting around and seeing Jamaica. Though some of the roads beggar belief – and knacker your suspension – it's a relatively easy country to drive in; distances are small, and a car can take you on some delightful back routes that you won't see if you're flying or travelling by bus. However, rental **prices** are high, starting at around US$70 per day in high season, including government tax (rates can go as low as US$40 at slow times). Third-party insurance is normally included in the rental rate; if you don't have a credit card that offers free collision damage waiver, you'll have to pay another US$12–25 per day to cover potential damage to the car. If you choose not to take out this cover, you're liable for every scratch on the car, whether caused by your own error or not.

There are **rental companies** all over the island, with the best selection in Kingston, Montego Bay and Ocho Rios, and we've listed them in the individual chapters. Renters range from reputable international chains to small but efficient local operators to dodgy one-man-and-his-dog outfits; though the latter may appear less expensive, you're often better off going with the known names, which will normally offer guaranteed roadside assistance and are less likely to palm you off with a shoddy vehicle. Most larger companies will also allow you to pick up and drop off in different major towns for no extra fee. To rent a car you'll need a current licence from your home country or an international driver's licence and, in theory, you'll need to have held the licence for at least a year. Most rental companies stipulate that drivers must be at least 21 years old (though some will rent only to drivers over 25). Before you set off, check the car fully to ensure that every dent, scratch or missing part is inventoried, and that the gas tank is full (bear in mind that you'll have to return the vehicle with the same amount of petrol). When returning the car undamaged, ensure that you collect and destroy any credit card deposit slip.

Car rental agencies overseas

In North America

Avis US ℡ 1-800/331-1084, Canada ℡ 1-800/272-5871, ⓦ www.avis.com.
Budget US ℡ 1-800/527-0700, ⓦ www.budgetrentacar.com.
Dollar US ℡ 1-800/800-4000, ⓦ www.dollar.com.
Hertz US ℡ 1-800/654-3001, Canada ℡ 1-800/263-0600, ⓦ www.hertz.com.
Thrifty ℡ 1-800/367-2277, ⓦ www.thrifty.com.

In Britain

Autobookers ℡ 020/8878 8333, ⓦ ww.autobookers.com.
Avis ℡ 0870/606 0100, ⓦ www.avis.co.uk.
Budget ℡ 0800/181 181, ⓦ www.budget.co.uk.
Europcar ℡ 0845/722 2525, ⓦ www.europcar.co.uk.
Hertz ℡ 0870/844 8844, ⓦ www.hertz.co.uk.
Thrifty ℡ 01494/751 600, ⓦ www.thrifty.co.uk.

In Ireland

Avis Northern Ireland ℡ 028/9024 0404, Republic of Ireland ℡ 01/605 7500, ⓦ www.avis.ie.
Budget Republic of Ireland ℡ 0903/277 11, ⓦ www.budget.ie.
Europcar Northern Ireland ℡ 028/9442 3444, Republic of Ireland ℡ 01/614 2888, ⓦ www.europcar.ie.
Hertz Republic of Ireland ℡ 01/676 7476, ⓦ www.hertz.ie.
Thrifty Republic of Ireland ℡ 1800/515 800, ⓦ www.thrifty.ie.

In Australia

Avis ℡ 13 63 33 or 02/9353 9000, ⓦ www.avis.com.au.
Budget ℡ 1300/362 848, ⓦ www.budget.com.au.
Hertz ℡ 13 30 39 or 03/9698 2555, ⓦ www.hertz.com.au.
Thrifty ℡ 1300/367 227, ⓦ www.thrifty.com.au.

In New Zealand

Avis ℡ 09/526 2847 or 0800/655 111,

ⓦ www.avis.co.nz.
Budget ℡ 09/976 2222, ⓦ www.budget.co.nz.
Hertz ℡ 0800/654 321, ⓦ www.hertz.co.nz.
Thrifty ℡ 09/309 0111, ⓦ www.thrifty.co.nz.

Rules of the road

Driving in Jamaica is on the **left**, and (unless otherwise specified) speed limits are set at 30mph in towns and minor roads and 50mph on highways. Wearing front seatbelts is now mandatory in Jamaica. The main A roads across the country are normally in pretty good condition, though once you come off them, you'll find the minor roads are often badly potholed. In parts of the country, including the Blue Mountains and Cockpit Country, roads are often little more than bare rock, and if you're planning to explore much in these areas, you should consider getting a **four-wheel-drive** (4WD) vehicle, though you'll pay a premium of around US$20 a day.

Jamaicans can be pretty cavalier behind the wheel, with many drivers (particularly those in charge of air-braked, diesel-spitting juggernauts) often dangerously macho and impatient. Always **drive defensively**; watch out for overtaking traffic coming towards you as overtaking a line of ten or more cars, even if it's impossible to see what's coming, is common practice. Be prepared to spend a lot of time stuck behind large lorries on smaller, winding roads, particularly the route between Ocho Rios and Kingston. At night, you'll also need to get used to being dazzled by other drivers' undipped headlights; to minimize the effects of the glare, keep your eyes on the left verge of the road and slow down. You should use your horn as freely as most Jamaicans do; a toot is just as likely to mean "thank you" as it is an indication of some kind of hazard such as "I'm planning to overtake as soon as we get to this blind corner". If someone does hoot to indicate that they're about to overtake, don't try to teach them a lesson by speeding up to prevent them from doing so, no matter how potentially dangerous you think they're being. Anywhere on the island, but particularly in Kingston, be extremely careful when driving in the rain; unsurprisingly, Jamaicans don't take kindly to being splashed, even if the water comes from a pothole that you didn't see. Daredevil stunts notwithstanding, you'll notice that on the whole Jamaican drivers are pretty courteous toward visitors, often offering loud vocal suggestions as to how best to handle situations and giving way to rental plates.

If you do have an **accident**, wait for the police before moving your car. Avoid making any admission of responsibility or, for that matter, accusations of blame – you don't want to get embroiled in a heated roadside argument.

Finally, the Jamaican police often set up **speed traps** and **roadblocks**; seen by the more cynical as a way for officers to augment their wage packets as the weekend approaches. Jamaican drivers have an informal system of flashing their lights to other drivers to indicate police presence ahead. If you're stopped, be friendly and polite. You'll normally be sent on your way fairly quickly, although drug searches are not uncommon – for more on this, see p.60.

Local drivers

If you don't drive – or don't want to – but still want to travel independently around the island, it might be worth hiring a **local driver** to ferry you about – generally for about US$70–100 a day (though you should be able to negotiate a little). They often make excellent tour guides, but, especially if you're a woman alone, you might find the prospect of setting off in a car with a stranger a bit daunting. Obviously, we only recommend reliable drivers, whose names and numbers appear at relevant points throughout the Guide.

Taxis

Although a rental car is useful for touring, if you're staying in one place for any length of time, you'll find that it often works out cheaper to get around by **taxi**.

What passes for a taxi in Jamaica varies from the gleaming white vans and imported cars of the **Jamaican Union of Travellers Association** (JUTA; ☏952 0813, 957 9197, 974 2292), the official – and expensive – carriers, to the Japanese estate cars that are the vehicle of choice for most taxi men. (The latter cars are called "deportees", they've been sent here in huge numbers as no one else wants them.) Officially licensed taxis carry red number plates with "PP" or "PPV" on them, but there are a number of rogue taxis, most of whom claim that their application for taxi status is being processed. The authorities advise against using the rogues but, obviously, it's up to you whether you trust them or not. Most towns have a reliable local taxi service that you can call (numbers are given throughout the Guide), but during the day, it's usually just as easy to head to the local taxi rank or flag them down in the street.

On the whole, taxi **fares** are pretty reasonable in Kingston and the less touristed areas, even for long journeys; on the north coast, prices are rather more hefty – around US$25 for ten miles, and you'll always pay a little more if you take a taxi licensed to a hotel. Bear in mind, though, that few of the cars have meters, so always establish a price before you get in (or over the phone if you're calling for a taxi). The first quoted price may well be just an opener, particularly if you hail a vehicle on the street; don't be afraid of negotiating. Once you've agreed on a price, a tip is unnecessary.

Shared taxis, or "route taxis", crammed with as many passengers as the driver/owner can fit in, operate on short, busy set routes around the main towns, picking up and dropping off people anywhere along the way in the same manner as

Hitching

Many Jamaicans **hitch** rides – and will expect you to offer a lift if you're driving through a rural area in a half-empty car. But very few tourists hitchhike, and it's not something we recommend. There's a common assumption that tourists have plenty of money so, at the least, you'll be looked on as a curiosity; at the worst, you're exposing yourself to danger. If you're short of cash, you're better off sticking to buses or shared taxis.

the buses and minibuses. Some shared taxis are marked by the PPV number plate, but many more are not, making them difficult to identify, except by the squash of passengers. Though they're normally perfectly safe, they are used more by Jamaicans than visitors, and it's not uncommon for a driver to assume that you wish to charter the whole taxi if you flag it down, in which case he will throw the other passengers out – make it clear that this is not what you want. Prices are much closer to bus fares than to taxi rates.

Motorbikes and cycling

Jamaica should be much better for **cycling** than it is. Places like the Blue Mountains, perfect for biking, are not well geared towards independent cyclists, though several tour companies offer an easy, and expensive, way of seeing them on a bike (see p.135). Throughout the island, rental outlets are thin on the ground – we've listed them where they're available. If you're interested in a bit of off-road **mountain biking**, contact Rusty's X-Cellent Adventures in Negril (℡957 0155, Ⓦwww.webstudios/rusty.com); excursions are detailed in that chapter, p.299.

Renting a **scooter** or **motorbike** is easier, and can be an exhilarating way of touring the island. Outlets abound in the main resorts, and at US$30–40 per day, prices are very reasonable, and though in theory you'll need to show a driving licence, these are rarely asked for. Under Jamaican law, all motorcycle riders must wear helmets – you'd be a fool not to in any case.

Zooming about on two wheels, though hugely enjoyable, is fraught with **danger** in Jamaica. One of the most common forms of injury to visitors is "road rash" courtesy of a motorbike incident, and you'll need to be a confident rider to tackle the major roads and Kingston streets. Cyclists should stick to minor roads, and everyone should be on the lookout for potholes, madcap drivers and daft goats and dogs.

Planes

If you're heading across country – say from Kingston to Montego Bay or Port Antonio – it's well worth considering one of the **internal flights** provided by Air Jamaica Express

(℡888/359 2475, Ⓦwww.airjamaica.com), which are quick, efficient and sensibly priced; numbers for Air Jamaica Express regional offices are given in the relevant chapters. There are domestic airports at Tinson Pen in Kingston (℡924 8850), Montego Bay (℡952 4300), Port Antonio (℡913 3692), Negril (℡957 4251), and Ocho Rios (℡726 1344). Sample one-way fares from Montego Bay are US$49.50 to Kingston, US$48.50 to Negril, US$45.50 to Ocho Rios and US$50 to Port Antonio.

Private **charters** are available from a number of operators, including International Air Link in Montego Bay (℡940 6660, Ⓦwww.intlairlink.com) and Timair in Montego Bay and Negril (℡952 2516 or 957 5374, Ⓦwww.timair.net). For **sightseeing tours,** you're better off with Island Hoppers, based in Ocho Rios (℡974 9756, ℻974 0002, Ⓔwwide@mail.infochan.com); a twenty-minute helicopter ride around Ochi costs US$60 per person, while longer charters vary in price – see p.192.

Air Jamaica Express flights

As Air Jamaica Express flight schedules are somewhat labyrinthine and subject to frequent changes, we've listed the minimum number of direct flights per day; call the airport you want to travel from to check current schedules before you plan your trip.

Kingston to: Montego Bay (6 daily; 35min); Negril (5 daily; 35min); Boscobel, Ocho Rios (2 daily; 15min); Port Antonio (2 daily; 15min).

Montego Bay to: Kingston (9 daily; 35min); Negril (6 daily; 15min); Boscobel, Ocho Rios (4 daily; 25min); Port Antonio (1 daily; 35min).

Negril to: Montego Bay (6 daily; 15min); Boscobel, Ocho Rios (1 daily; 35min); Port Antonio (1 daily; 45min).

Boscobel, Ocho Rios to: Montego Bay (4 daily; 25min); Port Antonio (2 daily; 15min).

Organized tours

There's plenty on offer if you're after an **organized tour**; hundreds of operators crowd the resorts, most schlepping off to well-known attractions like Rose Hall or Dunn's River Falls, or offering "highlight" tours of a specific area. At best, they're a hassle-free and comfortable means of getting around; at worst, they barely skim the

Caribbean island-hopping

People often like to do a bit of **island-hopping** while they're in the Caribbean. Many, certainly, can't resist the lure of **Cuba**, just seventy miles north. Both Cubana (℡978 3410, 🌐www.cubana.cu) and Air Jamaica (℡1-888/FLYAIRJ, 🌐www.airjamaica.com) fly to Havana from Kingston and Montego Bay for around US$170 return trip. Caribic Vacations (℡953 9878, 🌐www.caribicvacations.com) offer day-trips from Montego Bay (US$295) and longer package tours. Americans should note that the US government presently allows US citizens to visit Cuba but not to spend any money there.

Air Jamaica (see p.12) uses Montego Bay as a hub airport, with connections to Antigua, the Bahamas, Barbados, Bonaire, the Cayman Islands, Cuba, Dominica, the Dominican Republic, Grenada, Haiti, St Lucia, Trinidad, and the Turks and Caicos Islands. At present, round-trip flights to these islands start at around US$299 to St Lucia – though the airline already offers discounts for travellers visiting Jamaica on certain package holidays. It's also well worth bearing in mind that if you book a flight with Air Jamaica to another Caribbean destination, you can stop over in Jamaica for free.

More economical if you want to see a few islands is to buy a Caribbean **air pass** before you leave home. There are two currently available, one through **BWIA International Airways** and the other through Air Jamaica. Trinidadian BWIA (℡1-800/538-2942 in the US, 020/8577 1100 in the UK, 01/2859 222 in Ireland, 02/9285 6811 in Australia; 🌐www.bwee.com) sells thirty-day air passes to passengers whose international flights are booked with BWIA. The passes are valid for ten Caribbean destinations including Jamaica (the others are Barbados, Caracas, Grenada, Guyana, St Lucia, St Maarten, St Vincent, Trinidad and Tobago). The pass allows unlimited stops, though you can't visit one island more than once. The itinerary must be booked in advance and no backtracking is allowed.

Air Jamaica's Caribbean Hopper Program (℡1-800/523 5585 in the US, 020/8570 7999 in the UK, 1-888/FLYAIRJ in Jamaica; 🌐www.airjamaica.com) allows a passenger originating in the US to visit three or more islands within the airline's Caribbean and Central American network, which includes Bonaire, Barbados, Grand Cayman, Grenada, Havana, Jamaica, Nassau, Providenciale, and St Lucia. Tickets (US$399 for economy class and US$699 for first class) must be purchased along with the US-originating flight, and are valid year-round on Air Jamaica and Air Jamaica Express (economy only) for stays between three and thirty days. Backtracking is not allowed.

surface of the country and its culture from the shelter of an air-conditioned bus. There also tends to be little variation in tour content from one company to another. **Prices** are generally comparable, too, starting from around US$35 for a simple half-day excursion to US$100 for full day-trips, including meals. Tours of specific sights are listed in the relevant chapters throughout the Guide. Listed below are the largest operators, running trips throughout Jamaica, and several more **alternative-style** companies, whose tours tend to be more rewarding and, consequently, more expensive – booking in a group spreads the cost and always ensures cheaper rates. Almost every hotel in Jamaica will be able to book you with one of the conventional tour companies.

Conventional tour operators

Caribic Vacations ℡953 9878, 🌐www.caribicvacations.com.
Glamour Tours ℡979 8207.
Holiday Services ℡974 2948, 🌐www.holiday-services.com.
JUTA ℡952 0623 or 927 4532.
Tourwise ℡974 2323, 🌐www.ochoriosonline/tourwise.
Tropical Tours ℡953 9100, 🌐www.tropicaltours-ja.com.

Alternative tour operators

Barrett Adventures Rose Hall, Montego Bay ☎382 6384, ⓦwww.barrettadventures.com. Customized packages to waterfalls, plantations and beaches islandwide, from US$60 per person per day.

Chukka Cove Adventure Tours, Laughlands PO, St Ann ☎ & ⑤972 2506, ⓦwww.chukkacove.com. Excellent tour company doing great business. Its distinctively painted jeeps and reggae bus trundle along the north coast and into the interior to Marley's mausoleum and other local sights. Bus-based tours around the Ochi area include river tubing, horseback riding and Dunn's River Falls. Tours start at US$55 per person.

Cockpit Country Adventure Tours, Albert Town PO, Trelawny mobiles ☎610 0818, ⑤610 0819, ⓔstea@cwjamaica.com. Excellent, small-scale walks around Albert Town in the scenic fringes of Cockpit Country, from US$15–50 per person. The Quashie River Sinkhole trek is particularly rewarding.

Our Story Tours mobiles ☎699 4513 or 377 5693, ⓔourstorytours@hotmail.com. Thoughtful, offbeat and fascinating historical-based islandwide tours. Emphasis is on Kingston, Spanish Town and Port Royal, but offers some destinations farther afield in St Thomas, St Andrew, St Catherine and the rest of the island. It's the only company to offer trips to see the racing at Caymanas Park – unmissable. Rates range from US$50 for a half-day to US$100 for a full day.

Sun Venture 30 Balmoral Ave, Kingston 10 ☎960 6685, ⑤920 8348, ⓦwww.sunventuretours.com. Reliable, innovative and eco-friendly scheduled and custom-designed tours – the best on the island for offbeat excursions. Mainstays include Blue Mountain hikes, Cockpit Country hikes, south coast safaris, caving and city tours.

Treasure Tours Calabash Bay, Treasure Beach ☎965 0126, ⓦwww.treasurebeach.net. Small personal tour company with eight different day tours to south coast attractions, and a popular dayl-ong "non-tourist tour" (US$35 per person) that visits inland St Elizabeth and some of the local deserted and hidden beaches.

Community tourism

Community tourism is a relatively new concept in organized tours in Jamaica, the idea being to encourage closer connections between the tourist and the community through visits to private houses, farms, schools and craft centres. Countrystyle Ltd, based in Mandeville (☎962 3725 or 7758, ⓔcountrystyle@mail.infochan.com) is one of the main organizers, arranging accommodation and customized itineraries across the island; for more details, see p.355. A similar organization is the Southern Trelawny Environmental Association (STEA) in Albert Town, Cockpit Country (☎610 0818, stea@cwjamaica.com). The Jamaica Tourist Board also has a programme, Meet the People, which introduces holiday-makers to local Jamaicans with shared interests – religion, nature, art and culture – for no charge. You can register online (ⓦwww.jamaicatravel.com) or contact your local JTB branch.

Accommodation

Accommodation is likely to be your biggest single expense while travelling in Jamaica. Although the country has far more choice than you'll find on other Caribbean islands, it's rare to find anywhere to stay for less than US$20 per night in the large resorts, and you usually need to pay at least twice that for a place with reasonable security and comfort. At the other end of the scale, Jamaica has some of the world's finest luxury hotels, and there are also plenty of options in the middle. As you'd expect, you get what you pay for, although throughout the book we have emphasized places that we consider particularly good value.

The majority of visitors to Jamaica have their accommodation pre-arranged as part of a package deal, and though this can work out cheaper, you run the risk of being stuck in an unsuitable location. If you're not pre-booked, it's normally worth calling ahead to reserve a room for your first night or two to save hassle on arrival, and to satisfy immigration requirements (see p.16). After that, it's easy enough to call the next place you're heading to arrange a room, although if you've got your heart set on staying in a specific hotel or guesthouse, you should try to sort it out earlier.

A couple of times a year, the Jamaica Tourist Board posts a list of approved accommodation islandwide on its website (see p.17), with details of their latest rates. It's a reasonable guide to what's available, but there are plenty of perfectly acceptable hotels and guesthouses that aren't included because they don't meet the JTB's sometimes rather pedantic requirements. There also exist a couple of initiatives to help get visitors out of the all-inclusives and into Jamaica's many **small hotels.** The Port Antonio Guesthouse Association operates in Portland and represents some of the nicest accommodation options in the Port Antonio area (see p.160).

If you're in the mood, it is always worth **haggling** over the price of a room. Even in high season, a lot of hotels have surplus capacity and are sometimes desperate for custom – the boom in all-inclusives has hurt the independent sector badly. In low season, you have even more bargaining power, and it's not unknown for US$100 rooms to go for US$50. If you are going to negotiate, doing so over the phone will save you having to traipse around; if you do strike a deal, get the name of the person you're talking to in case the agreement has been forgotten by the time you arrive at the hotel.

Hotels and guesthouses

Jamaica has no youth hostels and the **cheapest** places to stay are usually small, family-run **guesthouses** with pretty basic facilities. At rock-bottom prices (US$20–35 a night), rooms make little concession to comfort; the ones that we recommend are normally clean and have some measure of security, though you can expect them to be cramped and box-like, with spartan furniture, shared bathrooms and a fan. Moving up in price, and into **hotel** territory, US$50–70 a night will normally secure a more tolerable place with a comfortable bed, hot water and, usually, a bar and maybe a place to eat; for a little more money you'll get a television and a phone and possibly air conditioning. Once you're paying US$75 per night, you can expect your hotel to have a swimming pool, a restaurant and air conditioning; for over US$100 you'll get a considerable degree of luxury. The top-price hotels are beyond most budgets but are often worth a visit – expect top-quality architectural design, lavish artwork in the rooms and lobby, impeccably dressed staff, and swimming pools carved in exotic shapes or with their own tumbling waterfalls.

All-inclusives

Jamaica was the birthplace of the **all-inclusive** hotel, where a single price covers your

Accommodation price codes

All accommodation listed in this guide has been graded according to the following **price categories:**

❶ under US$20
❷ US$21–35
❸ US$36–50

❹ US$51–70
❺ US$71–100
❻ US$101–150

❼ US$151–200
❽ US$200 and above

Rates are for the cheapest available **double** or **twin room** during the off-season – normally mid-April to mid-December. During the high season, rates are liable to rise by up to forty percent (though this is rare at the cheaper hotels), and proprietors may be less amenable to bargaining. Many of the all-inclusive hotels have a minimum-stay requirement – where this is the case, we have mentioned it in the text – and rates are quoted per person per night based on double occupancy. Although the law requires prices to be quoted in Jamaican dollars, most hotels give their rates in US dollars; payment can be made in either currency.

room and all meals, and often all drinks and watersports too. **Sandals** (☎1-800/SAN-DALS, ⓦwww.sandals.com) and **Superclubs** (☎1-800/GO-SUPER in the US, 020/8339 4150 in the UK; ⓦwww.super-clubs.com), are the best known of the all-inclusive chains, with around twenty hotels between them, but many other hotels are jumping on the bandwagon, offering all-inclusive deals side-by-side with room-only packages. Prices vary enormously, and it's possible to get bargain deals during low season.

The product offered by the all-inclusives is often excellent – sometimes verging on the madly luxurious – and, despite a blanket no-tips policy, staff are invariably as pleasant and accommodating as in other hotels. Also there is something undeniably seductive about the idea of unlimited access to a hotel's facilities without having to reach for your wallet every time. There is a downside, though. Jamaicans call these places "tourist prisons", and indeed many guests do feel rather trapped after a couple of days. The fact that everything is already prepaid discourages them from getting outside the hotel compound to sample the island's many great restaurants and bars, and the giddy thrill of trying twenty different types of cocktail in an evening quickly evaporates. Most all-inclusives offer **day or evening passes** for lunch, dinner or drinks and entertainment, so you might find it better to stay elsewhere and only visit once for a blow-out.

It's also worth bearing in mind that while all-inclusives remain the bedrock of Jamaican

tourism, with high occupancy rates even when the independent resorts are struggling, many establishments do very little for the local economy aside from the filter-down effect of employees wages. Much of the food the properties use is imported, and as the chains are often foreign-owned, Jamaica gets little direct benefit from their presence. For more on the ramifications of the all-inclusive trend, get hold of a copy of Polly Pattulo's *Last Resorts* (see *Contexts*, p.436).

Villas

Throughout Jamaica, there are hundreds of **villas** available for visitors to rent, normally by the week. Ranging from small beachside chalets to grand mansions, these are typically self-catering places, often with maid-service (occasionally with a cook and a security guard), and can make a reasonably priced alternative to hotels if you are travelling as a family or in a group. The Jamaica Association of Villas and Apartments (JAVA), PO Box 298, Ocho Rios (☎974 2508, ☎974 2967, ⓦwww.villasinjamaica.com) has comprehensive details of three hundred or so places to suit most budgets. Useful websites with details of villas in Jamaica include ⓦwww.caribbeanway.com and ⓦwww.villascaribe.com; for more unusual options, check out Carolyn's Cottages at ⓦwww.barrettadventures.com.

Camping

There are surprisingly few **camping** options around Jamaica, although you'll normally find one or two in each of the main tourist areas, and some of the cheaper hotels will let you set up a tent on their grounds for a small charge. Treasure Beach is fast becoming popular for camping, with several small properties offering sites. Expect to pay US$10–15 per person per night. **Camping** **rough** on the beaches is not recommended, as the risk of serious hassle and robbery is high. When camping at an official site, it's always wise to check on the security arrangements; fencing and an all-night guard are advisable unless you're in a quiet rural area or up in the Blue Mountains.

Eating and drinking

Jamaica's food reflects its motto – "Out of many, one people" – with distinctive contributions from each of the groups to have peopled the island. Though it's never made great strides outside West Indian communities overseas, Jamaican cuisine is undeniably excellent. From fiery jerk meat, probably the island's best-known culinary creation, to its inventive seafood and ubiquitous rice and peas, the national diet is surprisingly varied – though vegetarians may quickly tire of endless versions of sautéed cabbage and carrots with rice and peas. Snacking is good, too, with patties the staple fare, and there is a vast selection of fresh fruit and vegetables. Outside Kingston and the north coast resorts, international eating options are limited, although you will find pizza and Chinese restaurants in most towns alongside an ever-larger smattering of international fast-food chains such as McDonald's, Burger King, Wendy's (which has the gall to advertise itself as having the "best jerk chicken in Jamaica"), KFC and Pizza Hut.

Eating out

Cosmopolitan Kingston has the variety of eating options you'd expect in a capital city, and Negril, Montego Bay and Ocho Rios have a fairly wide range of places too, but elsewhere on the island, Jamaica's **restaurants** tend to be of two types: either the no-frills filling stations patronized mostly by locals and with a standard menu of West Indian staples, or tourist restaurants with more in the way of decor and a menu geared towards American and European palates. We've listed a cross-section of options throughout the Guide, but for quality of cooking (as well as cheaper prices), it's almost always best to go for Jamaican food; bear in mind, though, that such places often close early in the evenings – usually before 9pm.

In the cheapest of Jamaican places, expect to pay the equivalent of J$180–300 (around US$5–7) for a substantial plateful for breakfast, lunch or dinner. Going up a notch, moderately priced restaurants, which tend to price meals in US$, will charge more like US$10–15 for a main course, while at the upper end of the scale you'll be looking at US$20 plus for a similar dish.

Breakfast

The classic – and totally addictive – Jamaican breakfast is **ackee and saltfish**. The soft yellow flesh of the otherwise bland ackee fruit (see overleaf) is fried with onions, sweet and hot peppers, fresh tomatoes and boiled, flaked salted cod, producing a dish similar to scrambled eggs in looks and consistency but wildly superior in taste. You'll usually find it served with the leafy, spinach-like **callaloo**, boiled green bananas, a hunk of hard-dough bread (a dense, slightly sweet white loaf), fried or boiled dumplings, or **Johnny cake** – a sweet bread that varies widely in appearance from region to region. Other popular

Despite forming one half of Jamaica's national dish, **ackee** is a rather hazardous foodstuff. The fruits of the ackee tree must be picked only when their red pods have burst open to reveal the pale yellow arils inside. If forced open when unripe, ackees emit a toxic gas (hypoglycin) so poisonous that it's possible for people to die from what's known as "**Jamaica poisoning**".

morning options include delicious and filling cornmeal, plantain or peanut porridge, steamed fish or smoked mackerel "**rundown**" – flaked fish boiled with coconut milk, onions and seasoning. Inevitably, tourist demands have resulted in a wider availability of the continental breakfast (rolls, jam, juice and coffee), or American breakfast (bacon, pancakes and scrambled eggs), and most moderate and expensive hotels and restaurants will also have a good selection of local fruits.

Lunch and dinner

Most of Jamaica's cheaper restaurants and hotels offer **chicken** and **fish** as the mainstays of lunch and dinner. Chicken is typically fried in a seasoned batter, jerked or curried, while fish can be grilled, steamed with okra and pimento pods, brown-stewed in a tasty sauce or "**escovitched**" – served in a spicy sauce of onions, hot peppers and vinegar (tastier than it sounds). Red snapper and parrot are probably the most common varieties of fish, but you'll also be offered juicy steaks of kingfish, jackfish, tuna and dolphin fish (not the mammal). Other staples include stewed beef, curried goat, oxtail with butterbeans, and **pepperpot soup**, made from callaloo, okra and beef or pork. More adventurous palates might fancy "**mannish water**" (goat soup that includes the testicles, considered an aphrodisiac and traditionally served to a groom on his wedding night), **cowfoot** (a gelatinous and arguably delicious stew of bovine hooves) or **cow cod soup** (made from a bull's genitals and, unsurprisingly, touted as an aid to virility).

The tradition of "**jerking**" meat dates back to the seventeenth century, an invention of Maroon warriors keen to preserve the meat of wild pigs. It has since become the island's most idiosyncratic – and flavoursome – cooking style. Seasoned in a mixture of island-grown spices, including pimento, hot peppers, cinnamon and nutmeg, the meat – usually chicken or pork, but occasionally fish, lobster or sausage – is grilled slowly, often for hours, over a fire of pimento wood and under a cover of wooden slats or corrugated zinc sheets.

You'll find jerk on the menu at most tourist restaurants, though not so often in local places, and on the street in every town, where it's sold from smoking barbecues fashioned from oil drums (usually from Thursday to Sunday only) – head for the vendor with the longest line. With harddough bread and some roast breadfruit, yam or sweet potato (usually sold by the same vendors), jerk is the perfect picnic. If you're after the real McCoy, head for Boston Bay in Portland (see p.170) or Blueberry Hill in St Mary (see p.183), where you can get great meat from one of the original jerk centres, and a bottle of fiery marinade to take home.

Seafood is another Jamaican joy, with fresh **lobster** – occasionally curried but usually simply grilled with lemon or butter sauce – and **shrimp** on every upmarket restaurant menu. Freshwater **crayfish** (known locally as janga) are pulled from rivers across Jamaica, and you'll occasionally see groups of vendors offering bags of them, hotly peppered and ready to eat; a better alternative, however, is janga soup, a fortifying combination of whole janga and vegetables that's a popular aid to sexual potency. Though it's not the most visually appealing fruit of the sea, **conch** (the inhabitant of the huge pink shells sold in the resorts) is dense and delicious, cooked up into soup (yet another so-called source of virility) or curried in silver-foil parcels at roadside stalls and served with **bammy** (a substantial bread made from cassava flour which is soaked in milk or water and then fried or steamed). The more adventurous prefer to eat conch Cuban-style – raw, in a lime-and-garlic marinade. **Seapuss**, also occasionally on menus, is octopus.

Once known as the Jamaican coat of

In a bid to boost decimated fish stocks, the Jamaican government has enforced **closed seasons** on lobster and conch during their reproductive cycles – April 1 to June 30 and July 1 to October 31, respectively. It is **illegal** for restaurants to serve lobster or conch caught during these times, and while many will tell you that the stock is frozen and predates the deadline, this is obviously not always true, and you should avoid restaurants that don't comply with the law.

arms, **rice and peas** (rice cooked with coconut, spices and red kidney beans) is the accompaniment to most meals, though you'll sometimes get bammy, **festival** (a deliciously light sweet fried dumpling), sweet or regular **potatoes** (the latter known as Irish potatoes), yam, dasheen, Johnny cakes or fried or boiled **dumplings**.

Though the island produces a fabulous array of fresh produce, **vegetarians** are only really catered for at Rastafarian **Ital** restaurants, where meals are exclusively meat-free, and in theory, cooked without salt. Mainstays include ackee and vegetable stews served with rice and peas; tofu, gluten and soya are cooked up in various forms as alternative sources of protein. You should usually be able to get patties filled with pulses, soya chunks and ackee. The best places to eat Ital are in Kingston, though there are places in Ocho Rios, Montego Bay and Negril; many double up as health-food stores, stocking soya- or rice-based alternatives to dairy products.

Snacks

Along with jerked meat (see opposite), **patties** are Jamaica's best-known snack, a flaky pastry case usually filled with highly spiced minced beef, though occasionally with chicken, shrimp, ackee and saltfish or vegetables, and widely available in bakeries, cafés and snack bars. Many Jamaicans prefer **"bun and cheese"** – a sweet bun sold with a hunk of processed cheese that often passes for lunch – or **meatloaf** and **callaloo loaf**, both made with bread rather than pastry. Bakeries

also offer buttery folds of **coco bread** (eaten wrapped around a patty for the classic working-man's lunch), **bullas** (flat, heavy, ginger cakes, improved upon in the Portland area by the creation of lighter "holey bullas"), rock cakes, fruit cakes and **gizzadas** (small tarts filled with shredded coconut and spiced with nutmeg and ginger). If you're lucky, you'll find **duckanoo** (also known as "blue drawers"), an African dessert made from cornflour, sugar and nutmeg, wrapped in a banana leaf and steamed.

Jamaicans are enthusiastic **roadside** eaters, and you shouldn't miss out on breaking long journeys with a cup of fish tea (a tasty broth that's nicer than it sounds), conch or pepperpot soup, or a chunk of buttered roast yam with saltfish, which are all sold from steaming mobile cauldrons. Peanuts and cashews are also hawked at major road junctions, sold salted or "Ital"; if he's not holding a pile of them aloft, you'll recognize a "nuts man" by the high-pitched, steam-driven whine that emanates from the pushcart roasting equipment.

Fruits and vegetables

One of the delights of touring around Jamaica is stopping off at markets and roadside stalls to try the dozens of different **fruits** on sale. Bananas, oranges, pineapples and paw-paws (papaya) are the most common, but in season, there are plenty of others to choose from. **Mangos** come in all shapes and sizes (though the juicy, non-stringy Julie variety is a universal favourite), the suitably named **ugli fruit** looks like a disfigured grapefruit but is more tasty, while the origins and flavour of the Jamaican-bred **ortanique** are described by its hybrid name – orange, tangerine, unique. Something like a green-skinned lychee, with delicate flesh around a large pip, **guineps** (only available from July to October) are sold on the roadside all across the island; the brown, orange-sized **naseberries** (sapodilla) are sweeter and slightly gritty; **sweetsops**, or custard apples, look like pine cones and, as they ripen, the sections separate for eating. Other options include: **guavas**; **soursops** (a bigger, sharper and indescribably better version of the sweetsop); deep purple, milky-fleshed **star apples**; and the perfumed, rose-tinted flesh of **otaheite** (or "Ethiopian") **apples**, crimson-red and pear-shaped.

Ubiquitous **vegetables** include pumpkin and **dasheen**, like a yam but chewier. Of a variety of squashes, the watery **cho-cho** (also known as christophene) is the most common, and you'll also find **callaloo**, **pak-choy**, **okra**, **yams**, **cassava**, **breadfruit** and **plantains**, the latter ripened and served as a fried accompaniment to main meals.

Drinking

Jamaica's water is perfectly safe to drink, and locally bottled **spring water** is widely available, though not as cheap as you might expect – look out for the attractive red-gold-and-green labelling of the Cool Runnings brand. For a tastier non-alcoholic **drink** during the day, look no further than the roadside piles of coconuts in every town and village, often advertised with a sign saying "**ice-cold jelly**". The vendor will expertly open one up with a few strokes from a machete, and you drink straight from the nut (with a straw if you're lucky), after which the vendor will split the shell so you can eat the soft flesh, using a piece of the shell as your scoop. **Sky juice** – cones of shaved ice flavoured with sticky fruit syrup or fresh cane juice – is also popular, usually served in a plastic bag with a straw, though the hygiene element is sometimes questionable.

Elsewhere, you'll find the usual imported **sodas**, plus Jamaica's own D&G brands: Ting (a refreshing sparkling grapefruit drink), Malta (not surprisingly, a malt drink), and throat-tingling ginger beer. Most places also sell "**box drinks**" – additive-filled, over-sweetened peanut punch (curiously popular), egg-nog or orange juice. **Fresh fruit juices** – tamarind, June plum, guava, soursop, strawberry and cucumber – are always delicious if a bit over-sweet, while blended fruit juices are a meal in themselves; if you haven't got a sweet tooth, ask for yours to be made without syrup.

Jamaican **coffee** (see p.144) is usually excellent. The Blue Mountain brand, grown only in Jamaica's far eastern mountain slopes, is among the best and most expensive in the world, though the other local brews, such as High Mountain, Low Mountain or Mountain Blend, are also good. Made from balls of locally-grown cocoa spiced up with cinnamon and nutmeg and then boiled with water and condensed milk,

Stamina potions

Ever careful to safeguard his powerful libido, the average Jamaican man couldn't live without gallons of age-old potions concocted to ensure sexual stamina. With self-explanatory names such as **tan-pon-it-long**, these drinks are taken to thicken and enrich semen and supplement the diet, and are deemed necessary to see the Jamaican male through extended sessions of sexual olympics.

The most popular ingredient is **Irish moss**, a seaweed boiled and strained into a glutinous milky-white potion. Now available ready-processed in tins (as well as by the bag in its pure form from supermarkets and roadside vendors), Irish moss is the main component in many stamina drinks, including **magnum** (Irish moss and linseed), **strong back** (Irish moss, oats, peanuts, paw-paw, Dragon stout and a decoction of the strong back herb) and **pep-up** (Irish moss, Dragon stout, Red Label wine and liquified green corn). Most people have their own favourite blend with a suitably libidinous name to match.

Another popular tonic is **roots wine**, usually made by Rastafarian herbalists, who mix various quantities of roots and herbs such as arrowroot, chainy root, bridal wisp, strong back and occasionally ganja, boiling them with molasses or honey to make an evil-smelling brew. Most people have their own recipes, but as preparation is time-consuming, many prefer to visit their favourite "juice man", who sells old rum bottles full of the stuff in most markets. If you're female, don't be surprised if a potential purchase is refused on the grounds that such drinks are a "man's ting". These days, you can also buy commercially bottled roots wine from health-food stores: look out for the wonderfully-named "Put It In Wine" brand.

hot chocolate is a traditional but rather labour-intensive breakfast drink. **Tea**, in Jamaica, means any hot drink and includes regular tea, fish tea, herbal tea or even ganja tea; make sure you specify which one you want.

Alcohol and bars

Jamaica's national **beer** is the excellent Red Stripe, available in distinctive squat bottles (and occasionally in the inferior draught variety) islandwide, Red Stripe Light is a refreshing, lower-alcohol version. If you need an alternative, Heineken is widely available, as is locally brewed Guinness (stronger than British varieties), which competes with the sweeter Dragon as the island's stout of choice. Major hotels and restaurants as well as supermarkets sometimes stock a couple of other brands of beer; if you find it, try Carib, a light lager from Trinidad and Tobago.

Decent **wine** is a little more difficult to come by (though easier with each passing year), and if you order a glass in a restaurant, you pay a premium. A rum-shop staple, the local Red Label plonk is a pretty grim fortified tipple, while the sweetish Rosemont is not much better. However, you can buy imported wines, mostly Chilean, in most large supermarkets, and while the variety is never huge, prices are reasonable.

Rum is the liquor of choice, with a huge variety at a range of prices. Wray and Nephew make the classic white over-proof rum, the poor man's friend – cheap, potent, available everywhere and best knocked back with a mixer of Ting, though most hardened drinkers prefer water. Even more lethal is John Crow Batty; it's often over eighty percent proof and said to be as strong as the stomach acids that "John Crow" vultures need to digest their diet of rotting meat. There are plenty of better, less caustic, brands of white rum, the smoothest being C.J. Wray Dry, made principally for export but sold in larger supermarkets. If you're after taste rather than effect, you might prefer simple gold rums and the older, aged varieties, left to mature in (and taking their colour from) charred oak barrels; Appleton produce delicious twelve- and twenty-one-year old blends.

Rum-based **liqueurs** are the other local speciality; Sangster's make award-winning rum creams and liqueurs flavoured with orange, coffee, pimento and more. Finally, the coffee-flavoured Tia Maria is made on the island and widely available. **Alcopops** are becoming increasingly popular, with imported, vodka-based Smirnoff Ice competing for pole market position with X-Wray, a rum-based grapefruit drink.

Jamaica's **bars** – or rum shops – are generally rather macho enclaves, with groups of men sitting around drinking rum, playing dominoes and gazing at the scantily-clad ladies on the Red Stripe posters. They can present a good opportunity to meet local people, though single women won't always feel at home. Within the resorts, there are hordes of drinking holes, from sports bars to English-style pubs.

Communications

Communications have been revolutionized in Jamaica by two important factors: email and mobile phones. The rapid global spread of the **Internet and email** will benefit visitors to the island most. Locals have been more affected by the huge success in Jamaica of a **new mobile phone network**, Digicel, which has masts and hence range all over the island. It's now possible to keep in touch with home from almost anywhere in Jamaica efficiently and relatively cheaply.

Mail

Considering how small Jamaica is, it's amazing how long it can take for inland mail to get across the country. Don't expect a letter from Kingston to the north coast (or vice versa) to arrive in less than a week. International mail is also slow – reckon on around ten days to a fortnight for airmail to reach Europe or North America. Always use airmail, as surface mail takes forever. If you're really in a hurry to send something overseas, DHL or Fedex have offices in larger towns; check their websites for your nearest location. Within Jamaica, Tara Couriers (☎926 7982) will get packages from one side of the island to another within a day, as will Airpak Express (☎923 0371) and Air Jamaica Cargo (☎924 8750).

Most towns and villages have a **post office**, normally open Monday to Friday from 9am to 5pm; smaller postal agencies in rural areas keep shorter hours. Those in large towns have **poste restante** facilities – mail is held for about a month, and you'll need your passport or other identification to collect it – and a few have **fax machines.**

Stamps are sold at post offices and in many hotels. Rates are reasonable; for J$40 you can send a postcard to anywhere in the world.

Telephones

The national telecommunications network in Jamaica, run as a monopoly for many years by UK giant Cable & Wireless, has undergone a massive revolution recently, due to the arrival on the island of a hugely competitive mobile phone network, **Digicel**. Jamaicans are now said to have more

mobile phones per household than anywhere else in the world, and locals have all but abandoned the public phone system.

The success of Digicel doesn't really affect short-term visitors to the island, though the end of the Cable and Wireless monopoly means much more competitive rates for phone calls than previously. Finding a **public phone** is still not a problem in Jamaican towns (the rural areas are less well served); many hotel rooms have one and phone booths litter the island. If you're calling from your hotel, check the service charge first – most hotels impose a hefty mark-up, sometimes over a thousand percent, particularly on long-distance calls.

The easiest way to make international and local calls is to use WorldTalk **phonecards**, widely available – in denominations of J$100, J$$200, J$500 and J$1000 – from hotels, post offices, gift shops and supermarkets. These can be used either in public phone booths or from your hotel room. First of all, scratch off the silver strip on the back to reveal the security code, dial the access number, key in your code and you'll be told how much time you have on the card before you place your call. Remember to keep your security number very private – a common fraud is for someone to read it over your shoulder as you key it in, then transfer your credit to their card. Another good option for overseas calls and faxes are privately operated **call-direct centres,** where a call is placed on your behalf and you're directed to a phone. Most are open daily from mid-morning until around 11pm, in order to take account of time differences. Details of all these places are given throughout the Guide.

If you have a **mobile phone** bought in Europe, Australasia and Asia (but not the US), you'll be part of the GSM network and you can use your own mobile in Jamaica. The cheapest way to go about this is to buy a pay-as-you-go SIM card in Jamaica (the Digicel pay-as-you-go is called Flex, and cards are around US$10), and temporarily swap it for the existing one in your phone. You will then be connected to an islandwide network that allows you to make cheap local and international calls and send text messages. Both making and accepting calls can be very expensive if you use **roaming** with your home network; for advice, check out ⓦ www.telecomsadvice.org.uk/features/usin g_your_mobile_abroad.htm. It's also possible to rent a mobile phone from Max Touch Cell Phones in Jamaica (☎ 754 7833, ⓦ www.maxtouchjamaica.com) and some hotels.

If you have a US-bought cell phone, it won't work in Jamaica (unless it's a tri-band phone). You can either rent (see above) or buy one on the island, where they're relatively inexpensive.

All Jamaican telephone numbers (except some freephone ones) have **seven digits**. To dial locally (within the same parish), simply key in the number. To get a number in another parish, prefix the number with "1"; you also use the "1" prefix when dialling mobile (cellular) numbers; if you don't add the 1, you'll get a message saying the number is unobtainable. Finding numbers is easy – if there is no telephone directory in your hotel room or phone booth, call directory enquiries on t114.

Calling home from Jamaica

Note that the initial zero is omitted from the area code when dialing the UK, Ireland, Australia and New Zealand from abroad.
USA and Canada 00 + 1 + area code
Australia 00 + 61 + city code
New Zealand 00 + 64 + city code
UK 00 + 44 + city code
Republic of Ireland 00 + 353 + city code

Calling Jamaica from abroad

To call Jamaica from abroad, dial your international access code (see below) + 876 + seven-digit number.
UK ☎ 001
USA ☎ 011
Canada ☎ 011
Australia ☎ 0011
New Zealand ☎ 00

Email

Internet access is now widespread in Jamaica, though it hasn't yet reached the most rural parts of the island, there are frequent glitches and logging on is often infuriatingly slow. All the major resorts have a number of Internet cafés for sending and reading email; Internet access costs between US$2–5 per half hour. Parish libraries are also good places to use computers and, though busy, often have the cheapest rates in town.

The media

As in most countries, the best way to tap into the mood of Jamaica is to read its papers, tune in to its radio stations, or take a look at its television.

Newspapers

Of Jamaica's three daily **newspapers**, the broadsheet *Daily Gleaner*, founded in 1834, is the market leader, both in terms of circulation and quality journalism. Rarely afraid to voice an opinion, particularly during the 1970s when it regularly condemned the Manley administration, it eschews political partisanship these days and regularly harangues all parties. The paper's coverage of local news and sport is excellent, it enjoys the pick of the feature writers and has the best listings; overseas news is perfunctory but adequate. Its website (◉www.jamaica-gleaner.com) has weather forecasts, a business directory, chatrooms, personals, a webcam from the Gleaner building in Kingston, and an electronic version of the newspaper itself, with brilliant searchable archives.

The *Observer* (◉www.jamaicaobserver.com) was founded by Gordon "Butch" Stewart (owner of Sandals and Air Jamaica) in the early 1990s. Tabloid in form but broadsheet in content, it produces news and feature journalism that rivals the *Gleaner*, though it seems confused about its target readership. The *Star* (◉www.jamaica-star.com) is the island's tabloid, an afternoon publication from the *Gleaner* stable, full of salacious tittle-tattle; the truly enlightening "Dear Pastor" problem page is also worth a glance. Weekly *X News* (◉www.xnewsjamaica.com) plumbs even lower depths, but is excellent for entertainment listings and music news; the personal columns give an interesting insight into Jamaican relationships. Its newest competitor, bi-weekly *Hard Copy* (◉www.jamaicahardcopy.com) is, unlikely though it may seem, even more salacious. Regional titles include the *Western Mirror*, published in Montego Bay on Wednesdays and Saturdays and covering news and events on that side of the island, and the *North Coast Times*, based in Ocho Rios, with good tourist-oriented features and listings.

Sunday brings weekend issues of the *Gleaner* and *Observer*, similar to the dailies with a few advertisers' supplements, and the rather dull but weighty *Sunday Herald*.

International newspapers – the main US dailies and the UK's Sunday broadsheets – are sold in major pharmacies and the gift shops of the bigger hotels, usually a couple of days out of date.

A couple of glossy, full-colour **magazines**, published every other month, will appeal if you're interested in Jamaican music: *Jammyng* and *Reggae Times* print interviews with artists, features on the music scene and entertainment news; both cost J$100 and are usually available from bookshops and some gift shops.

Radio

Jamaica's **radio stations** are predictably awash with island sounds – including stageshow broadcasts, talent showcases and festival coverage – though music faces tough competition from the daytime talk shows and sports coverage. Radio is much more popular than television in Jamaica, and is an excellent way to appreciate the culture.

Irie FM (◉www.iriefm.net) is probably the most listened-to music station, with *Wake-Up Call* (6–10am), featuring the "Marley of the Morning" Wailers' tune daily, and Elise Kelly's *Easy Skanking* reggae (10am–2pm) giving way to harder-core dancehall as the day wears on. (For more on Irie, see p.199.) Also popular with die-hard music fans is **Zip FM,** a relatively new station with a slightly more eclectic mix of Jamaican musical styles. Irie has edged ahead of the more long-standing **RJR** (◉www.rjr94fm.com), where talk and sport dilute the music; Barbara Gloudon's *Hot Line* programme (Mon–Fri 10.30am–2.30pm) is one of RJR's better talk shows. For many Jamaicans, talk shows are essential listening, as evidenced by the animated groups you'll see gathered around radios during their broadcasts. Power 106 (®ww.go-jamaica.com /power) is perhaps the best bet for weekday talk shows; it offers *Independent Talk* (5.30–9am), hosted by notorious attorney Ronnie Thwaites, a former MP who had to resign his post in 2002 as a result of financial scandal. The anarchic Wilmott Perkins is the most entertaining presenter on Power 106 (10am–2.30pm), his ferocious attacks on authority figures attracting regular death threats and healthy ratings for his show, *Perkins Online*. Beverley Manley's *Breakfast Club* (Klas FM Mon–Fri 6–9am) is a good morning news brief. For something altogether different, radical dub poet Mutabaruka's *Cutting Edge*, (Irie FM, Wed 10pm–2.30am) lays down a Rastafarian viewpoint. Radio Mona, the University of the West Indies' own radio station, has a lively combination of music – jazz, Latin, Jamaican – with current affairs and cultural issues. Obviously, schedules change; if you can't find what you're after, ask around. Note that most of the radio station websites allow you to listen in live online.

Reception of the **BBC World Service** is patchy; early morning and late evening are the best times to find it. Consult the website ®www.bbc.co.uk/worldservice for further information. The websites for **Radio Canada** (®www.rcinet.ca), and **Voice of America** (®www.voa.gov) list their service frequencies around the globe.

Radio stations and frequencies

Hot 102 102FM
Irie FM 105.5/107.7FM
KLAS 89.7FM
Love 101.1FM
Power 106 106.5FM
Radio Mona 93.1FM
Roots 96.1FM (in Kingston area only)
RJR 90.5/91.1/92.9/94.5/103.3FM
Super Supreme 91.1/103.3/105.7FM
Zip FM 103 FM

Television

You'll find a **television** set in most hotel rooms, usually hooked up to the cable network with around thirty American-based channels as well as the two domestic channels, **TVJ** (®www.televisionjamaica.com) and **CVM** (®www.cvmtv.com), competent if rarely thrilling; look out, though, for the excellent music-based programme *Entertainment Report* on TVJ. Output is dominated by news, local sport and US reruns, though if you're a soap fan you'll want to catch the island's very own *Royal Palm Estates*. Those desperate for international sports coverage will find that most towns have one or two bars with big-screen TVs broadcasting major US sporting events – NFL and NBA games and occasionally baseball – though you won't find much from Europe. Try *Margaritaville* in Montego Bay and Negril, the *Jamrock Sports Bar* in Kingston, or the *Little Pub* in Ocho Rios.

Opening hours, festivals and entertainment

Jamaican offices are normally open for business between 8.30am and 4.30pm Monday to Friday, often closing for an hour at lunch, while shops are typically open from 8am to 5pm Monday to Saturday, although some close at noon on Saturdays. Sunday trading is rare, although you will find one or two pharmacies open in Kingston and at the major resorts, and we have listed these in the Guide. Museums normally close for one day a week, either Sunday or Monday, while most other places you'll want to visit – private beaches, waterfalls, gardens, churches and so on – are generally open daily.

Festivals and special events

Most of Jamaica's special events are timed to coincide with the winter tourist season; the main exceptions are: **Reggae Sumfest** (see p.50) in August, and **Spring Break** (see p.301) when young Americans take over the big resorts for a fortnight of raucous, beer-fuelled cavorting. Depending on the date of Easter, the month of February or March is **carnival** time – though not on the same scale as in Trinidad, Jamaica's Carnival is a growing event, with more and more parades each year. The smaller Negril Carnival is held in July. If you're in Jamaica in late July to early August, you're sure to come across **Emancipation Day** and **Independence Day** celebrations, which range from concerts to dance and theatre performances, family fun days, talks and parades; visit the websites of the JTB (see p.17) or Discover Jamaica (see p.17) for details of each year's programme.

The main **national holidays**, when virtually all shops and offices close, are:
New Year's Day (January 1)
Ash Wednesday
Good Friday
Easter Monday
Labour Day (May 23)
Emancipation Day (August 1)
Independence Day (first Mon in August)
National Heroes Day (third Mon in October)
Christmas Day (December 25)
Boxing Day (December 26).

We haven't given specific **dates** for most events listed below, as these change from year to year; all events (and each year's crop of new ones) appear in the JTB's annual "**Calendar of Events**" booklet, available from offices worldwide. Most of the bigger events are advertised nationally; local events are heralded on billboards.

Calendar of events

January

Accompong Maroon Festival Accompong, St Elizabeth ☏ 952 4546 (Kenneth Watson or Ava Simpson). All-day celebration of the 1739 Maroon peace treaty, held on January 6. Food and craft stalls, drumming, traditional dancing, speeches and a sound-system dance till dawn.

Air Jamaica Jazz and Blues Festival Wyndham Rose Hall, Montego Bay ☏ 1-800/LOVEBIRD (Air Jamaica) or contact JTB offices worldwide. This increasingly popular event has a fabulous setting and a big enough purse to attract some excellent international performers.

Annual National Exhibition National Gallery, Kingston ☏ 922 1561. Annual showpiece exhibition of new artists and established names.

Heineken Startime Various locations ☏ 960 2812 ⍟ www.startime.com.jm. Veteran artists perform at this consistently excellent reggae stageshow showcasing the cream of Jamaica's veteran performers. There's usually a show in January, but events take place throughout the year all over Jamaica; check with the JTB or call ahead to confirm dates.

LTM National Pantomine See "December" on p.48).

Rebel Salute Kaiser Sports Club, St Elizabeth ☏ 969 1111 (Patrick Barrett). Annual concert with cultural artists and DJs from Tony Rebel's Flames stable that attracts a large roots crowd. Sometimes held in February.

February

A Fi Wi Sinting Port Antonio. Daytime event highlighting Jamaica's African heritage, with dub poetry, drumming, fashion and traditional food and craft stalls.

Bob Marley Birthday Week Islandwide, with big parties at Marley's birthplace, Nine-Mile; the Bob Marley Museum in Kingston; James Bond Beach in Oracabessa; and Negril ☎ 070 2001 (Bob Marley Foundation), ⊛ www.bobmarley-foundation.com. Celebrations for the king of reggae are held on and around the anniversary of Marley's birthday on February 6. Ziggy Marley and the Melody Makers often perform alongside other artists, and you're guaranteed a party through the night.

Carnival Kingston, Ocho Rios and Montego Bay ☎ 923 9138 (Tony Cohen), 927 8662 (Andrea Gordon), or JTB offices on the island and worldwide; ⊛ www.jamaicacarnival.com or ⊛ www.bacchanaljamaica.com. Moveable party that takes place around the beginning of Lent (February or March). The main festivities begin in Kingston with "J'Ouvert", including costumed parades, live-music tents featuring Jamaican reggae and Trinidadian soca artists, and all-night fetes. The show then moves around the island, with a big party at Chukka Cove in St Ann towards the end.

LTM National Pantomine See "December" overleaf.

Negril Fat Tire and Music Festival Good Hope, Negril Hills ☎ 957 0155 (Nicole Kamens), ⊛ www.geocities.com/mountainbikejamaica. Week-long celebration of music and mountain biking, including scavenger hunts on bikes, cave parties and a street festival.

Misty Bliss Hollywell National Park, Blue Mountains ☎ 920 8279 (Jamaica Conservation Development Trust), ⊛ 64.45.40.146/index.html. Annual Sunday fair designed to showcase the mountain region and environmental matters, with market stalls selling herbs and spices grown in the area, nature tours, live mento and kumina music.

March

Jamaica Orchid Society Show Kingston ☎ 927 6713 (Claude Hamilton). Colourful flower show with over four thousand types of orchid sanctioned by the American Orchid Society.

Spring Break. In early March, American college students descend on the main resorts (particularly

Negril) for a two-week JTB-sponsored orgy of beer drinking and slapstick antics. Student ID obtains discounts on hotels and events.

Drax Hall Kite Festival Drax Hall, Ocho Rios ☎ 974 8258 (John Gosse). Affable family day attracting giant, flamboyant home-made kites as well as huge numbers of spectators. Stunt flying, pony rides, clowns and lots of fun.

April

Trelawny Yam Festival Albert Town, Trelawny ☎ 610 0818 (Hugh Dixon). This tiny town, with a stunning setting on the outskirts of Cockpit Country, plays host to an incongruously large open-air party. As well as the prize tubers, competition categories include cooking, best goat and best-dressed donkey, while sound systems and live entertainment take care of the music. A ten-kilometre race and a yam symposium complete the fun – unmissable.

May

Calabash International Literary Festival Treasure Beach, St Elizabeth ☎ 1-800/JAMAICA (Jamaica Reservations Service), ⊛ www.calabashfestival.org. Free festival highlighting the role of literature in unlocking creativity, with book and poetry readings and discussions.

June

Ocho Rios Jazz Festival Ocho Rios ☎ 927 3544 (Jazz Hotline), ⊛ www.ochoriosjazz.com. Jamaica's original jazz festival, attracting top performers from all over the world. Concerts take place in hotels and open spaces in Ocho Rios, with a few events in Montego Bay and Kingston.

Portland Jerk Festival Boston Bay ☎ 929 9200 (JTB). Live music, community dance groups and general festivities centred around the home of jerked meat in Jamaica.

July

Kumento Festival St Thomas ☎ 734 2449 (Devon Blake). All-day event highlighting traditional kumento drumming and its place in the island's cultural heritage.

National Dance Theatre Company's Season of Dance Little Theatre, Kingston ☎ 925 6129. This fabulous company performs modern dance throughout July and August.

National Festival Queen Competition Kingston ☎ 926 5726 (Jamaica Cultural Development Commission). As part of the JCDC's annual heritage celebrations, the fourteen giggling Parish Queens from the all around the island descend on Kingston to battle it out; the winner is judged on political, cultural and historical awareness, talent and deportment as much as on looks.

National Song Competition Finals Ranny Williams Entertainment Centre, Kingston ☎926 5726 (JCDC). National talent competition to find the island's best amateur musicians in the rather strange category of pop-reggae. The entrants get plenty of local media coverage, and the finals are great fun.

Negril Carnival Negril ☎957 3528 (Bernice Sinclair). A mixture of Trini-style carnival and traditional Jamaican festival, this celebration features costume parades, mento bands, soca fetes and concerts, traditional dance performances and sound-system jams in the streets.

August

Denbigh Agricultural Show Denbigh Showground, May Pen ☎922 0610. Creative displays of farm produce and livestock by farmers from across the country.

SASHI James Bond Beach, Oracabessa ☎929 9200. Huge R&B and reggae stage show.

September

Miss Jamaica World Coronation Kingston ☎927 7575 (Mr Haughton-James). Beauty pageants are still big business in Jamaica, and this is the crowning glory; it's sometimes held in September.

Jamaica Spice Food Festival Ocho Rios ☎929 9200 (JTB). Several days of food celebrations, with traditional recipes, cooking demonstrations and competitions.

October

Oktoberfest Jamaica German Society Headquarters, Kingston ☎926 4747 (Holger Waehling). Annual celebration of all things Teutonic, with stalls, German food, dancing, games, top Jamaican bands and the beer drinking contest.

Peter Tosh Birthday Celebration, Belmont, Westmoreland ☎957 7127 (Worrel King). Annual roots and culture tribute concert in memory of the reggae great, held on or around the anniversary of his October 19 birthday. Friendly, and one of the highlights of the stageshow year.

November

Jamerican Film and Music Festival Montego Bay ☎323 692 9537 (Island Girl Productions). Film makers and musicians from around the world gather to celebrate Jamaican contributions to the film business.

December

LTM National Pantomime Ward Theatre, Kingston ☎926 6129 or 968 0759. Unmissable annual theatrical institution, with ribald jokes, great costumes, political commentary and traditional Jamaican song and dance. The whole shebang moves to Kingston's Little Theatre in February, and occasionally tours around the island.

Reggae Kwanzaa Various venues islandwide. Kwanzaa, the African-American Christmastime cultural holiday (Dec 26–Jan 1), is celebrated in a large annual concert, held at venues across the island and featuring the best in cultural reggae.

South Coast Craft and Shrimp Festival, St Elizabeth ☎929 9200 (JTB). Sea and shellfish cuisine forms the centre of this local community festival. International food experts demonstrate recipes, from the simple to the exotic.

Sting Jamworld Entertainment Centre, Portmore, and other venues across the island. Annual New Year's Eve celebrations featuring current top DJs and singers. The atmosphere can get a bit hairy.

Entertainment

If you don't mind a musical policy of reggae, reggae and more reggae, then you'll find plenty on offer in the way of **live music** in Jamaica. Though touring American soul artists and the annual jazz festivals provide occasional alternatives, it's the home-grown scene that dominates. Jamaican **theatre** – particularly roots plays (see opposite) and the annual pantomime – is also hugely enjoyable, an idiosyncratic insight into the Jamaican way of life, and though the best productions are normally Kingston-based, many tour the island as well.

Stageshows

Most concerts – or **stageshows** as they're locally known – are well worth attending, as you'll see artists who seldom perform off the island sharing the bill with more familiar reggae luminaries like Beenie Man, Elephant Man, Sizzla, Freddie McGregor and John Holt. Most take place in open-air venues and are generally peaceful, with a friendly atmosphere and plenty of stalls selling drinks and food. Some of the DJ-based shows, however, attract a younger, predominantly male crowd and can get a bit fractious, so unless you're familiar with the scene, you might want to go with a Jamaican companion. Many are one-off affairs, but others – **Heineken Startime** – are established events that hire a fixed roster of artists and tour the island's venues; see the "Calendar of events" for further details.

Clubs

The party spirit is deeply imbedded in most Jamaicans, who like to dress up (turn up in a floppy T-shirt and shorts and you're guaranteed to feel underdressed) and let rip at the weekend. There's a lively **club scene** in Jamaica, at its most authentic in Kingston but also reasonably good along the north coast. Most clubs are sweaty and smoky in the extreme: the music is super-loud and dancers vie with each other as to who can wear the least and move the most. Away from some of the more sterile in-hotel establishments, many of which are all-inclusive, (meaning your entry fee covers drinks all night), clubbing is lots of fun and generally inexpensive; you'll rarely encounter a cover charge of more than US$6, and the frequent "ladies' nights" and weekday drinks promotions are well worth taking advantage of. Most towns also have a **go-go club** – generally full of men gawping at topless dancers, moving as rudely as only Jamaicans can.

For more on how to find out what's on in Jamaica, see p.17.

Sound-system parties

Altogether less formal, **sound-system parties** (known as "dances" or "jump-ups") take place all over the island at weekends (see *Contexts* p.415). Loyal followers travel for miles to hear their favourite selectors (usually well-known figures) spinning exclusive tracks and, on a good night, to see an established DJ take to the mike to improvise lyrics over the latest dancehall rhythms. Part club and part stageshow, most sound-system sessions are held in the open air at hurriedly fenced-in "**lawns**", and carry on until the early hours with the beer, rum and ganja consumption intensifying as the night rolls on. Most Jamaicans agree that the best dances are those held

in remote country areas; noise restrictions are seldom enforced and the atmosphere is usually a lot more friendly than at city sessions or at "clashes" between two well-known sound systems, where aggressive undercurrents often mar the fun. Tourists are infrequent but welcome visitors at dances. It's rare to be harassed – most Jamaicans are pleasantly surprised to see visitors taking an interest in this side of their culture – but as you're well off the beaten track and possibly in the company of drunken undesirables, you may want to tag along with a Jamaican escort.

Theatre and dance

Less energetic entertainment – though no less raucous – is available via a trip to the **theatre**, Jamaican-style. **Roots plays** are an institution, usually bestowed with titles – *Boops*, *Baby Faada* and so on – that reflect their bawdy vernacular content. With rich patois dialogue, plenty of easy-to-miss colloquial references and oceans of interaction from the audience, most performances are a riot, and you're sure to get the overall gist of a play even if you don't catch on to the more complex themes. Roots plays are staged at impromptu venues all around the island (listed in the relevant chapters throughout the Guide), but particularly in larger towns, and details of performances are advertised in local papers – don't miss the chance to get a uniquely unfettered view of the Jamaican psyche. Increasingly, local comedians such as Tony "Paleface" Hendricks are clubbing together with local performers to stage achingly funny **comedy reviews**; grab the opportunity if you're in Jamaica when they're in production.

If you're after more conventional drama, you're restricted to Kingston's Ward or Little theatres and the Fairfield Theatre in Montego Bay. If you're on the island between December and February, it would be a crime to miss out on the annual Little Theatre Movement **pantomime** (see "Calendar of events", p.48), a blend of folklore, song, dance and jokes that gets better every year. The Little Theatre is also the venue for performances by Jamaica's superb national dance company, NDTC, who combine African steps with European themes to great success, and often perform with the venerated NDTC singers. Among other companies to look out for is the innovative L'Cadco.

Cinema

If you tire of culture or partying, consider a trip to the **cinema**; most large towns have at least one, and away from the martial arts epics or cheesy B-movies that dominate

Reggae Sumfest

Every year, Jamaica's best-loved art form overwhelms Montego Bay as the massive **Reggae Sumfest festival** takes to the stage. The build-up to Sumfest is pretty frenetic: flights from the US and Europe become over-booked, beaches throng with fans from all over the globe, and the line-up – which usually reads like a reggae hall of fame – is worried over in rum bars and on radio talk shows. By the time the sound equipment and lights arrive from Miami, Montego Bay's hotel rooms are pretty much booked-out, the cost of living increases overnight and every available scrap of cardboard is appropriated by small-time entrepreneurs to be sold in the showgrounds as a "reggae bed" – an essential piece of equipment for tired legs, though only the foolhardy actually sleep on them.

A heady combination of ganja, rum, sea breezes and simply brilliant music, Jamaica's festival tradition began in 1978 when a small crowd of revellers enjoyed five trouble-free nights of roots reggae at Montego Bay's Jarrett Park. Jamaica's first Reggae Sunsplash set a positive tone; international attention was captured, and two years later a capacity crowd of Jamaicans and tourists alike rocked to a killer line-up featuring Bob Marley and a host of other headline acts. Promotion in the US and Europe drew huge crowds to the quintessential shows of the 1980s, which coincided with reggae's strongest phase and were characterized by the legendary, laid-back "good musical vibes" that still differentiate them from the cool reserve and farcical posturing of today's stageshows.

By the beginning of the 1990s, however, legal wrangles and a series of venue changes – including a couple of dismal years in Kingston that scared off tourists and journalists alike – left Sunsplash struggling to recapture its early success. In 1993, Reggae Sumfest muscled in, snapping up the coveted Montego Bay location (by then shifted to Catherine Hall Entertainment Centre) and outshining its rival in terms of line-up and fun factor; Sunsplash no longer takes place.

However, the festival scene is not what it used to be: where crowds once reached 30,000 nightly, even Sumfest is lucky to draw 20,000 today. As artist fees have risen, so ticket prices have become prohibitive for many Jamaicans, who increasingly prefer to attend sound-system jams rather than live shows. Some even argue that the changing focus of reggae – from the Bob Marley-style roots to today's immensely popular DJ-based dancehall – is just not appropriate to live performance anymore. Despite all this, Sumfest boasts an average of around a hundred acts spread over five themed nights, and you'll get no better overview of the Jamaican music scene.

Sumfest usually takes place during the last week of July or the first week of August, kicking off with a beach party on the Sunday, a sound clash at the *Pier One* club on Tuesday night, and the festival proper from Thursday to Saturday. Thursday is "Dancehall Night", with a DJ-based roster; Friday is "Conscious Night", when reggae stalwarts take to the stage; and Saturday is "International Night", when big-name R&B acts from overseas perform alongside the hottest names from Jamaica. Specialist Caribbean travel agents in the US, UK and Australia (see pp.11, 13 & 14) sometimes offer packages that include accommodation and entrance fees; you are issued a voucher to be redeemed for

matinee schedules, you'll usually find programming on a par with release times in America. Be prepared for a lot more audience participation than you're used to, particularly in the less upscale establishments, and you might be required to stand up for the national anthem at the start of a performance. The Jamaican film scene has been enlivened in the last few years with the release of homegrown classics such as *Dancehall Queen* and *Third World Cop* – for more on Jamaican movies, see *Contexts*, pp.427–430.

a ticket in Jamaica. Designated **ticket** outlets (including JTB offices) are found in all the resorts. Entry to the Sumfest beach party and sound clash cost around US$20 and US$10 respectively; Dancehall Night is US$25, and tickets for the shows on Friday and Saturday nights are US$40. Season tickets for all events cost US$110; VIP season tickets (which allow you backstage) cost US$140; you can also buy weekend passes, which cover Friday and Saturday nights (non-VIP US$75/VIP US$100). Bear in mind that all prices are likely to increase annually, and that you'll pay less if you purchase tickets in Jamaican dollars. For **Sumfest information**, call ☏ 953 2933 in Jamaica, or check the website, ⓦ www.reggaesumfest.com. Information on the festival is also available from JTB offices worldwide (see p.17).

Helpful hints for Jamaican stageshows

• Sumfest and most larger shows adhere to published timetables, and things are improving elsewhere, but nonetheless, Jamaican stageshows remain notorious for starting late; the gates may open at 10pm, but it's not uncommon for the first act to take to the stage at 1am. Ask local opinions (some promoters do have a good reputation for good timekeeping), but in general, it's not a great idea to leave your hotel too early; arriving at midnight will ensure an adequate view and enough stamina to last until the end.

• If it rains on the evening of an outdoor show, it's likely to be a washout – most Jamaicans won't leave home if it means getting wet.

• Wear clothing suitable for the night-time chill and the early morning sun – traditionally, stageshows continue well past daybreak. Despite having to stand in a field for ten hours, there are few pleasures more satisfying than watching the sun come up as the cream of the performers take to the stage.

• Jamaican entertainers can be uncompromisingly unreliable, and it's well worth checking that the artists you've come to see have actually turned up; bear in mind that even if the doorman confirms their presence, big names are unlikely to perform for a tiny crowd. Similarly, it's common for shows with mixed billings of veteran singers and dancehall DJs to rapidly empty once the latter have left the stage, leaving the vocal acts with no audience and an excuse to slope off early.

• Don't worry about eating before a show. Vast quantities of curry goat, mannish water and fried fish are available at almost every stageshow – mobile vendors sell cigarettes and confectionery as well.

• Don't be alarmed by the practice of throwing firecrackers or employing homemade flame throwers (achieved by way of a can of bug spray and a lighter) to demonstrate appreciation of an act; it's not aimed at hapless tourists, so move away if you don't like it. However, it may be wise to think about a taxi home if people start substituting real gunshots for the traditional finger salute – only really likely to occur in the roughest of DJ-based dancehall events.

Sport and outdoor activities

As you'll quickly discover, sport is a Jamaican obsession – hardly surprising in a country that has produced so many world-class athletes. In bars, buses and taxis, if the music isn't blaring then the chances are that they're tuned into the cricket, football or horse racing, while the newspapers are awash with sports reports and statistics from Jamaica and overseas. The island is also a great place to indulge your own sporting passion, with excellent watersports and top-class golfing in particular.

Spectator sports

Virtually every Jamaican has an opinion on **cricket**, the national game, and bringing it up in conversation is a sure-fire way to break the ice. If you get the chance to catch a match, you'll find the atmosphere very Jamaican – thumping reggae between overs and vendors hawking jerk chicken and Red Stripe. The Jamaican team is normally in action twice a year. In January, several matches of the Busta Cup – four-day games against the likes of Barbados, Guyana and Trinidad and Tobago – are held at Sabina Park in Kingston, Chedwin Park near Spanish Town and Alpart Sports Club in Nain, St Elizabeth. The more exciting one-day Red Stripe Limited Overs competition – against the same teams – is occasionally hosted in Jamaica in September/October at Sabina Park, Jarrett Park in Montego Bay, Chedwin Park, and Kaiser sports ground in Discovery Bay, St Ann. On a grander scale, from March to May the West Indies team plays a series of international test matches; one of the tests is always held at Sabina Park and is definitely worth catching if you can.

Since Jamaica's national team, the **Reggae Boyz**, qualified for the World Cup, **football** (soccer) has become another national obsession; it has become as popular with young people - if not more so - as cricket. Although international matches, held at the National Stadium in Kingston (popularly known as "The Office"), are relatively rare, the team's success has inevitably boosted local interest, with amateur leagues attracting large and passionate crowds at grounds across the island. Although there's no professional league in Jamaica (many of the best players play in the UK and US), the participation of the Reggae Boyz in the World Cup has proved them to be one of the best teams in the Caribbean.

Athletics is Jamaica's most internationally illustrious sporting field. Jamaicans have consistently won Olympic sprint medals from 1948, the year the island first entered the competition and Arthur Wint won his medal, through to the success of Deon Hemmings and Merlene Ottey in 1996. Most of the country's top athletes study and train abroad, and so major track meets on the island are unusual.

Finally, the influence of satellite television and the enormous salaries on offer have led to a growing interest in American sports, particularly **basketball**. You don't see that much of it being played around the country, but there is concern (as throughout the Caribbean) that this new enthusiasm is deterring youngsters from traditional sports, especially cricket, whose star players earn relatively little. Michael Jordan and rising star Vince Carter are idols for most young Jamaican males and, though few Jamaicans have yet made a big name for themselves in US sports, once they do, the rush to follow suit and abandon the cricket field is inevitable.

Participatory sports

Fabulous weather, excellent watersports, the widest variety of golf courses in the Caribbean and a host of hiking opportunities make Jamaica a dream destination for **active sports** enthusiasts.

The rules of cricket

The rules of cricket are so complex that the official rule book runs to some twenty pages. The basics, however, are by no means as Byzantine as the game's detractors make out.

There are two teams of eleven players. A team wins by scoring more runs than the other team and dismissing all the opposition – in other words, a team could score many runs more than the opposition, but still not win if the last enemy batsman doggedly stays "in" (hence ensuring a draw). The match is divided into innings, when one team bats and the other fields. The number of innings varies depending on the type of competition: one-day matches have one per team, test matches have two.

The aim of the fielding side is to limit the runs scored and get the batsmen "out". Two players from the batting side are on the pitch at any one time. The bowling side has a bowler, a wicket keeper and nine fielders. Two umpires, one standing behind the stumps at the bowler's end and one square on to the play, are responsible for adjudicating if a batsman is out. Each innings is divided into overs, consisting of six deliveries, after which the wicket keeper changes ends, the bowler is changed and the fielders move positions.

The batsmen score runs either by running up and down from wicket to wicket (one length equals one run), or by hitting the ball over the boundary rope, scoring four runs if it crosses the boundary having touched the ground, and six runs if it flies over. The main ways a batsman can be dismissed are: by being "clean bowled", where the bowler dislodges the bails of the wicket (the horizontal pieces of wood resting on top of the stumps); by being "run out", which is when one of the fielding side dislodges the bails with the ball while the batsman is running between the wickets; by being caught, which is when any of the fielding side catches the ball after the batsman has hit it and before it touches the ground; or "LBW" (leg before wicket), where the batsman blocks with his leg a delivery that would otherwise have hit his stumps.

These are the bare rudiments of a game whose beauty lies in the subtlety of its skills and tactics. The captain, for example, chooses which bowler to play and where to position his fielders to counter the strengths of the batsman, the condition of the pitch and a dozen other variables. Cricket also has a beauty in its esoteric language, used to describe such things as fielding positions ("silly mid-off", "cover point", etc) and the various types of bowling delivery ("googly", "yorker", etc).

Watersports

A calm Caribbean sea bursting with sumptuous coral reefs make **watersports** Jamaica's most obvious attraction.

Scuba diving and snorkelling is concentrated on the north coast, between Negril and Ocho Rios. The state of the reefs is variable – pollution and aggressive fishing techniques have affected many areas, and the whole stretch around Montego Bay is under enforced protection as a national marine park – but there are still some gorgeous sites very close to the shore. The fish are just as impressive, with multitudes of parrot fish, angel fish and trigger fish, as well as moray eels, turtles and the evil-looking barracuda. There are a handful of wreck dives – including several plane wrecks off the coast of Negril – and good trenches, overhangs and wall dives. There are fewer decent sites on the south coast, and visibility is usually worse, but Port Royal in Kingston is a divers' heaven, with hundreds of wrecks, excellent visibility and the possibility of turning up some real sunken treasure, tipped in – alongside most of Port Royal – during the earthquake of 1692.

See p.396 of *Contexts* for more on the ecological aspects of Jamaica's marine environment.

The main resorts are packed with operators offering dive trips and snorkelling excursions; the most reputable are listed throughout the Guide. For beginners, the most popular options are the one-day introductory **resort courses**, for US$70–100, which offer basic instruction and a short supervised shallow dive close to shore. The longer **PADI** (Professional Association of Diving Instructors) **open-water certification course** costs US$350–400 and takes a few days, with practical and theoretical tests, safety training and several dives. Once you're certified, you can dive without an instructor, though you'll still need to go with a licensed operator – expect to pay around US$70–80 for a two-tank dive, and remember to take your certification with you.

Parasailing, **jet-skiing**, **water-skiing**, **kayaking**, **glass-bottom boat rides** and **sailing** are also available at all of the major resorts. You can **surf** at Boston Bay and Long Bay in Portland (p.170 & 172–4) and Bull Bay just east of Kingston, though you're better off bringing your own board. **Deep-sea fishing** is best around Portland, particularly during October's Blue Marlin tournament. Fully equipped boats are available for rent in all the major resorts; at about US$400 per half-day, the pursuit of big fish doesn't come cheap, though.

Away from the coast, **river rafting** is the big aquatic attraction. It was first popularized in the 1950s by movie idol **Errol Flynn,** who saw that the bamboo rafts used to transport bananas along Portland's Rio Grande could be used for pleasure punting. The Rio Grande remains the most spectacular spot for an idle glide, but operators have also set up in Ocho Rios, Falmouth and Montego Bay (see pp.199, 235 and 274). Costs start at around $45 for a two-person raft.

River swimming is idyllic in Jamaica, particularly in the Rio Grande and the White River in Ocho Rios. Dunn's River in Ocho Rios offers the island's ultimate **waterfall climb**, but there are plenty more cascades, many untouristed. For more relaxing options, **mineral springs** and **natural spas** are Jamaica's hidden gems – locals flock to Bath in St Thomas (p.154), Rockfort in Kingston (p.109) and Milk River in Clarendon (p.348) for the restorative powers of the radioactive water. **River rising pools**, such as Roaring River in Westmoreland (p.321) or Cranbrook in St Ann (see p.219), are also a delight.

Golf

Jamaica boasts no fewer than thirteen **golf courses**, from the magnificent championship Tryall course near Montego Bay and the new, world-class course at the Ritz Carlton Hotel in Rose Hall, just east of Montego Bay, to less testing nine-hole links in Mandeville and Port Antonio. All are open to the public, except

Jamaica's golf courses

Kingston
Caymanas Golf Club ☏922 3386. 18 holes, 6844 yards, par 72.
Constant Spring Golf Club ☏924 1610. 18 holes, 6196 yards, par 70.

Mandeville
Manchester Club ☏962 2403. 9 holes (18 tees), 2863 yards, par 35.

Montego Bay
Half Moon Golf Club ☏953 3105. 18 holes, 6196 yards, par 70.
Ironshore Golf and Country Club ☏953 2800. 18 holes, 7119 yards, par 72.
Three Palms Ocean Course, Wyndham Rose Hall ☏953 2650. 18 holes, 6737 yards, par 71.
Tryall Golf and Beach Club ☏956 5681. 18 holes, 6920 yards, par 71.

White Witch at Ritz Carlton ☏953 2800. 18 holes, 6800 yards, par 71.

Negril
Negril Hills Golf Resort ☏957 4638. 18 holes, 6333 yards, par 72.

Ocho Rios
Sandals Golf and Country Club ☏975 0119. 18 holes, 6600 yards, par 71.

Port Antonio
San San Golf and Country Club ☏993 7645. 9 holes, 6124 yards, par 40.

Runaway Bay and Braco
Grand Lido Braco Golf Club ☏954 0010. 9 holes, 1357 yards, par 28.
Breezes Golf Resort ☏973 2561. 18 holes, 6870 yards, par 72.

during tournaments (Tryall sometimes closes to non-members in winter). **Greens fees** vary from US$16 to US$225 in winter, less in summer, and there are additional charges for caddies, club and cart rental.

Hiking

Though the heat doesn't encourage strenuous exercise, **hiking** is by far the best way to get a flavour of the Jamaican countryside. The best opportunities are in the dense wildernesses of the **Blue and John Crow mountains** and **Cockpit Country**, where trails originally blazed by Maroon warriors lead deep into the Jamaican interior, though there are enjoyable minor walks elsewhere; all are fully covered in the text.

It is strongly recommended that you use a **guide** for all but the shortest of hikes, as it's perilously easy to get lost (see p.34 for major operators). Always stick to paths and trails; veering off into uncharted foliage not only encourages disorientation, but can destroy plants and lead to soil erosion. Never throw rubbish when hiking; even cigarette butts should be pocketed – a carelessly discarded cigarette can easily start a massive bush fire.

Other activities

A labyrinth of caves networks Jamaica's limestone interior, and many have been opened up as attractions with lights and stairs, so you don't have to be an experienced spelunker to enjoy them. Best of the bunch are Nonsuch Cave in Portland (p.176), Roaring River in Westmoreland (p.321) and Runaway Caves in St Ann (p.224). Serious cavers should head for Cockpit Country, where the limestone is at its thickest and many of the caves are unexplored; Windsor (p.279) is the only easily accessible cavern. Contact Sun Venture Tours (see p.34) for caving trips. More information on caving in Jamaica is available on the Internet at Ⓦusers.skynet.be/sky33676/index.html.

Horseback trail riding is a lovely way of exploring the island, though some stables and their mounts are rather run-down; stick to those listed in the chapters or check with the JTB. The best stables are Hooves and Chukka Cove in St Ann, and the Half Moon Equestrian Centre in Ironshore, just outside Montego Bay (see p.217,218 and 270); the latter two also offer **polo**, **dressage** and **show-jumping** lessons.

Cycling is surprisingly under-promoted in Jamaica (see "Getting Around", p.32). An alternative to demure processions aboard colour-co-ordinated resort cycles is a guided **mountain-bike tour**, available in the Blue Mountains (see p.135); more serious mountain bikers should contact Rusty's X-cellent Adventures in Negril; Ⓣ957 0155, Ⓦwww.rxadventures@cwjamaica.com (see p.299).

Finally, many upmarket hotels offer **tennis courts**, and for those who can't survive without their workout, the top-notch resorts normally provide **gyms** and **aerobics classes**.

Clothes – warm, waterproof layers are best, especially in the wet and chilly Blue Mountains. Always wear long trousers or leggings to protect against scratchy ferns, brambles and grass ticks.

Shoes – unless you're planning to do a lot of walking, hiking boots aren't essential. A pair of stout shoes with good grip should suffice. Sneakers (training shoes) aren't advisable; they have less hold and don't allow feet to breathe. Clipping your toenails short will help you to avoid blistered toes, a particularly painful hazard of the descent from Blue Mountain Peak (see p.143).

Food and drink – concentrated high-energy foods such as chocolate, dried fruit or nuts keep you going, while a bag of cut sugarcane will maintain energy levels and quench thirst. Always bring water; isotonic sports drinks are available from larger supermarkets.

First-aid kit – see p.20 for a list of recommended medicaments.

Sundries – insect repellent, high-factor sunscreen, good sunglasses, a good flashlight with spare batteries, toilet paper and a rubbish bag.

Jamaica's sporting calendar

As cricket, golf and polo fixtures change each year, we haven't listed individual events. For an up-to-date rundown, get hold of a copy of the Jamaica Tourist Board's annual events calendar, available from offices worldwide. For more details on cricket in Jamaica, contact the Jamaica Cricket Association (℡967 0322). If you're interested in watching a polo match, contact Shane Chin at the Jamaica Polo Association (℡952 4370); fixtures are held throughout the year. Golf events are also held regularly at several of Jamaica's courses; contact the Jamaica Golf Association (℡925 2325, ⓦwww.jamaicagolfassociation.com) for details.

January

High Mountain 10km Road Race Williamsfield, Manchester ℡963 4211 (John Minott Jr). Strenuous annual mountain run undertaken by some of Jamaica's best athletes.

February

Pineapple Cup Yacht Race Montego Bay Yacht Club ℡979 8038 (Felix Hunter). Yacht race from Fort Lauderdale, USA, to Montego Bay, where the winner is crowned.

March

Bowden Invitational Marlin Tournament Bowden, St Thomas ℡922 7584 (Dwight Clacken). A major local fishing event centred around this quiet ex-sugarcane wharf.

Montego Bay Yacht Club Easter Regatta Montego Bay Yacht Club ℡979 8038. Annual boating fest that draws participants from the US as well as Jamaica, with a feast of maritime events.

May

Treasure Beach Off-Road Triathlon Treasure Beach, St Elizabeth ℡965 3000 (Jason Henzell at *Jake's* hotel), ⓦwww.breds.org. An arduous 400m swim, 18km mountain bike ride and a 4km run, with lots of parties alongside.

September

Montego Bay Yacht Club Blue Marlin Tournament, Montego Bay ℡979 8038 (yacht club). Forty years old in 2000, this event is still attracting top fishermen from the Caribbean and US.

October

Port Antonio Blue Marlin Tournament, Port Antonio Marina, Portland ℡927 0145 (Ron DuQuesnay). One of the oldest and most prestigious fishing competitions in the Caribbean, this still attracts anglers from all over the world.

Treasure Beach Hook 'n' Line Fishing Tournament Treasure Beach, St Elizabeth ℡965 3000 (Jason Henzell at *Jake's* hotel), ⓦwww.breds.org. If you want to go to a fishing tournament, pick this one – it's a million miles away from the big-boys-and-their-toys atmosphere of the marlin fishing events. Local fishermen are invited to catch what they can with only the simplest of equipment, and with sound systems and other events, it's a huge amount of fun.

World Championship of Dominoes Montego Bay ℡1-800/LOVEBIRD (Air Jamaica). Hugely popular dominoes tournament with two-player teams. All the locals noisily practice for weeks in advance.

December

Holland Bamboo Run, St Elizabeth ℡906 5455 (George Watson). Part of the St Elizabeth homecoming celebrations, this 5km run through pretty Bamboo Avenue finishes in Santa Cruz.

Reggae Marathon, Negril ℡929 9200 (JTB). Road race with reggae soundtrack blasting and all kinds of other festivities.

Shopping

The Jamaican souvenir industry is precisely that, with many of the carvings and knick-knacks mass-produced on a small scale with little variation from maker to maker. However, the most common products tend to be the best, and though your lignum vitae Lion of Judah may be a pitch pine copy of a thousand others, quality is generally good. Haggling is a natural part of the trade at craft markets and stalls, but not in hotel boutiques and the more expensive, air-conditioned shops.

Where to shop

Virtually every town in Jamaica has at least one **market**, most selling fruit, vegetables and other produce, and often a limited selection of crafts. The main tourist centres have dedicated craft markets, and these, along with the **craft stalls** (same products, higher prices) you'll see by the roadside everywhere, are the most enjoyable places to browse and buy. The range of T-shirts, wooden carvings, jewellery, straw goods, hats and assorted knick-knacks varies little from place to place, but the main **Craft Market** in Kingston (see p.83) is the cheapest.

Specialist **souvenir stores**, found islandwide, also have a good stock of crafts and indigenous art as well as rum and cigars, while local galleries often have paintings, sculptures and woodcarvings for sale. Both souvenir stores and galleries tend to be pricier than the markets and stalls, but the standard of merchandise is higher.

In-bond – or duty-free – shops are usually clustered together in glitzy plazas and malls, and their stock of perfume, spirits, designer clothes, brand-name watches, crystal, porcelain, diamonds and gold varies little. Savings range from twenty to forty percent; all goods must be paid for in foreign (basically that means US) currency, and major credit cards are usually accepted. You'll need your passport and proof of onward travel.

What to buy

There are many alternatives to "Rasta" tams with attached fake locks or Bart Marley (yes, Bart Simpson with dreadlocks and a spliff) T-shirts and bamboo shakers: a custom-designed pair of leather sandals, the ubiqui-

tous string vests, bandanas and red-gold-and-green tassels for car mirrors are all available in market areas of most towns.

Not surprisingly, **reggae music** is big business in Jamaica, and fans will have a field day rooting through the record racks. The best music stores are in downtown Kingston (see p.106), but there's an excellent CD shop in the Island Village complex in Ocho Rios, and there are adequate outlets in most other towns, though the latter are usually a little thin on older releases – don't expect to find a Studio One classic in downtown Ocho Rios, for example. Compilation tapes are available from roadside vendors throughout Jamaica; they also sell recordings of the most recent sound-system dances, like gold dust to dancehall fans back home.

Other good Jamaican gifts include the prettily packaged range of essential oils, soaps, candles and bodycare accessories from Blue Mountain Aromatics, made from natural local ingredients; Starfish Aromatherapy oils also make classy gifts. Both ranges are available from more upmarket gift shops.

Food and drink

For a taste of Jamaica back home, you can pick up fiery **jerk sauce** or viscous **guava jelly** at any supermarket – the main locally made brands, such as Walkers Wood and Busha Brown, are substantially cheaper when purchased in non-tourist shops. Jamaican **vanilla essence**, used in blended drinks, cakes and puddings; **cocoa tea** balls, used to make the local version of hot chocolate; fresh **nutmeg;** and the

Especially on the north coast, you'll see **coral** (particularly black coral) and "**tortoiseshell**", products (made from the endangered hawksbill turtle) on sale, but the trade in these protected species is **illegal.** Don't buy; you're liable to serious fines if you're caught with them. Though not illegal, conch shells, too, should be avoided, as demand has eclipsed supply and conch are slowly disappearing from Jamaican waters.

delectable **honey**, sold in old rum bottles at any market; will all bring your island memories flooding back.

Rum (see p.353) is an obligatory memento – gift shops sell cardboard "Jamaica Farewell" packages holding two or three bottles for easy transit, though these are usually cheaper in the airport departure lounge; savings can also be made if you buy from a wholesale liquor shop or supermarket. The Sangster's company produces excellent **liqueurs**, on sale everywhere, and the ubiquitous Tia Maria coffee liqueur is another must-have. Finally, a packet of **Blue Mountain coffee**, sold all over the island but most reasonably in situ, is

an essential souvenir; by far the best brand is Alex Twyman's Old Tavern, available in more upmarket outlets.

Groceries and provisions

Most sizeable towns have fairly large **supermarkets** selling most items you'll find in shops at home, but **food**, particularly imported goods, is not cheap. Fresh **fruit and vegetables** are best bought at the markets, though expect to bargain over price, and ask for your "brawta" (a little extra) when finalizing a purchase. Women market traders will give tips on preparation and will not usually rip you off, though prices may be a little higher for foreigners, black or white. Sadly, you'll find yourself paying more for produce grown in Jamaica, which is often better quality than the imported factory-farmed stuff grown on a huge scale in the US or Canada.

Smokers will find that the cheapest way to buy Jamaican brands (Craven A, Matterhorn, Rothmans) is by the carton at any wholesaler – you pay more at street stalls and small shops. Foreign brands are available at larger supermarkets, hotels and tourist gift shops.

Drugs, trouble and harassment

Jamaica has a terrible reputation for violent crime; foreign documentaries flash images of poverty and gangsterism around the world, and the impression that lingers is of drug-crazed, Uzi-toting political rivals battling it out in the bloodbath of Kingston. Such adverse publicity encourages international perceptions of a "dark" land in political and social turmoil. However, while the island's murder rate is undeniably high – the average is about a thousand per year – Jamaica's nightmare image is vastly exaggerated, a hangover from the late 1970s when the election violence that erupted during Michael Manley's turbulent administration (see *Contexts*, p.383) made headlines around the world.

The negative publicity has been difficult to shake off, and for a while in the early 1980s, potential visitors stayed away in droves. In response, the government initiated a mas-

sive clean-up of the island's north coast resorts. Today brigades of blue-uniformed tourist police patrol the boulevards, and the JTB are keen to stress that you are more

Police

The **emergency number** for the Jamaican **police** is ☏119. Individual police stations are detailed throughout the text.

likely to be mugged in New York than Montego Bay. You may even find that young men in the resorts are unwilling to be seen talking to, or walking with, tourists in case they're carted off by the tourist police for harassing visitors.

Most tourists still steer clear of the capital – even rural Jamaicans are wary of going into "Town", and you'll be warned against going at all of the resorts – but such trepidation is largely misplaced. You'll be surprised at how safe and friendly Kingston feels. Drug-related organized crime is a frightening reality, but it is a reality that affects poor Jamaicans rather than tourists. It's restricted to isolated ghetto areas – pockets of west Kingston that you're never going to go to; elsewhere, the vast majority of visitors experience no crime or violence during their stay. When the nation took to the streets in spring 1999 to protest against a forty-percent hike in gas prices, the troubles spread as far as Montego Bay and Negril – but not a single visitor was harmed, and most frolicked on the beach completely unaware of the demonstrations.

At the same time, robberies, assaults and other crimes against tourists do occur, and it's wise to apply the **precautions** you'd take in any foreign city. Don't flaunt your wealth with fat rolls of bank notes, avoid walking alone late at night, don't go mad smoking ganja in the street – in short, use your common sense and you'll prevent potential problems before they happen.

Hustling

Hustling – the hard-nosed, hard-sell pitches you'll be endlessly subjected to on the north coast – can be the chief irritation of time spent in Jamaica. In Montego Bay, Negril and, to a lesser extent Ocho Rios, the tourist trade has long been adversely affected by the stream of young hopefuls aggressively (or humorously) accosting foreigners in the street with offers of transport, ganja, aloe massages, hair braiding and crafts. It's wearisome, to be sure, but much of what is perceived as harassment is really nothing more than an attempt to make a living in an economically deprived country, and while an inevitable few see tourists as easy prey for exploitation, most street touts are genuine. Hustling is a game played in the true entrepreneurial Jamaican spirit; the sales pitch is finely honed and modified to match the perceived nature of the potential client, and the national aptitude for "lyrics" (artful banter designed to break down even the most hardened sensibility) can make encounters with street vendors an entertaining and educative experience rather than a trial.

Tourists are not the only victims of the entrepreneurial urge; city traffic lights are haunted by regulars selling everything from a window wash to brooms, flowers, doughnuts and newspapers, and the travelling peanut or cigarette vendors that pop up in the most unlikely places are often very convenient.

For a humorous insider's view of the hustler's art, consult *Hustling Jamaican Style – A Guide to Tourist Service* (see *Contexts*, p.437), which lists the most popular products and provides suggested responses to hustlers; p.254 of this book also has some suggestions.

Homophobia

Anyone familiar with Buju Banton's infamous hit Boom Bye Bye will know that Jamaica is overwhelmingly **homophobic**. Homosexuality is illegal in Jamaica, condemned as a sin by the church and the moral majority, and fuel for much hysterical press coverage. In 2002, Jamaican gay men successfully lobbied for asylum status in North America and the UK, claiming that they would be persecuted for their sexuality if forced to return to the island.

Attempting to argue with freely expressed prejudices is almost always a lesson in futility. But this doesn't mean that gay and lesbian travellers should avoid Jamaica – many hotels are managed by gay men, and a lot of the smarter ones won't turn a hair if you ask for a double room – but don't expect to be able to display affection in public without attracting catcalls, sniggers, downright aggression, and possibly physical violence. For more information contact J-Flag, the Jamaican gay and lesbian support group (℡978 1954, ⊛www.jflag.org).

Marijuana

Though tourism officials are loathe to acknowledge it, many people do come to Jamaica in search of what aficionados agree is some of the finest marijuana in the world, and certainly **ganja** is part-and-parcel of the culture here to a greater degree than in other Caribbean islands. Be warned that quite apart from being **illegal**, Jamaican ganja, or "herb", packs a mightier punch than anything you've probably experienced before, so don't plan on doing much if you decide to partake. Yellow-eyed Jamaicans who've been smoking since their teens can cope with a spliff before breakfast – fresh-off-the-plane visitors probably can't.

Most Jamaicans smoke their ganja **pure** in carrot-sized spliffs or a water pipe (chillum or cutchie), though some make a "blend" with ordinary cigarettes or whole tobacco leaf; this last, known as "fronta", is also used alongside dried sweetcorn husks or even paper bags as an alternative to rolling papers.

Bear in mind, though, that despite the stereotypical view of an island populated by ganja fiends, those Jamaicans who smoke are in a minority; most islanders are highly religious and neither take drugs, nor approve of those who do. And despite its links with the Rastafarian religion (see p.405) and frequent use as a medicinal draught, possession, use and export of any quantity of ganja is **against the law** and carries stiff penalties. Tourists are just as eligible for prosecution as Jamaicans; at any one time there are hundreds of foreigners serving sentences in Jamaican jails, in horrifyingly harsh conditions.

If you choose to smoke ganja, trust your instincts. You will be approached with offers;

buy only from someone you feel you can trust. Never accept a rolled-up spliff from someone you don't know – it may be what Jamaicans call a "seasoned spliff", laced with cocaine or crack. You should be equally wary of carrying ganja around the island; if you pass a car at the roadside flanked by a worried-looking white person and a swarm of cops, you can bet that the police are conducting one of their routine searches.

Finally, tempting as it may seem, do not attempt to smuggle ganja out of the country under any circumstances; however devious you think your method, customs officials have seen hollowed-out sculptures, training shoes or roasted breadfruits before. Even carrying rolling papers can prompt protracted questioning.

Other drugs

Though better known as a weed-smokers' paradise, **cocaine** and **crack** are also increasingly widespread in Jamaica, with addiction to both a major contributing factor in violent crime. Powder cocaine has long been the drug of choice for rich young Kingstonians, but the introduction of crack in the late 1980s ensnared a far wider following. Use is not restricted to the Kingston ghettos; Negril's reputation for drugs has attracted the inevitable quota of crack users, and cocaine has been a part of the scenery since wealthy tourists first brought it here in the 1970s. If you're fairly young, expect to be offered cocaine – and, less frequently, crack – in the tourist areas; if you're not interested, refuse calmly and firmly.

Cocaine trafficking between Jamaica and the UK in particular has become a huge problem in recent years, and in an effort to stem the flow, **scanning machines** have been installed at the airports. These can detect even the tiniest traces of the drug, and following a flurry of prosecutions, they seem to be acting as a fairly effective deterrent.

Women travellers

Violent sexual attacks against female tourists are very rare, and women travelling in Jamaica are likely to be more bothered by trivial catcalls than any serious threat – prepare yourself for a quite unusual degree of scrutiny. In the resorts particularly, unaccompanied women can expect to receive a barrage of attention from Jamaican men, from hopeful innuendo – "gal, me a cry for you"– to frankly pornographic propositions, and a walk down the street will have you sized up by a thousand eyes. All of this is somewhat wearing after the first couple of days, particularly if your idea of a good holiday doesn't include "climbing aboard the big bamboo".

As casual sex is part and parcel of Jamaican culture, and lots of women do come to the island in search of so-called "exotic" romance, it will inevitably be assumed that you are in Jamaica to find a man – or several. The news that you're not will often be greeted with incredulity, and the semi-professional gigolos (and full-blown male prostitutes) who work the resorts will do their best to get you to change your mind. Foreign black women are just as much of a target as white, though you might be treated to a "roots sister" approach. If you're not interested, saying "no" and meaning it, not wearing skimpy clothing off the beach and avoiding eye contact and idle chat with men you don't know are good lines of defence. As a last resort, you may want to assert that you already have a Jamaican boyfriend, though this can be seen to signify that you are playing the game and are a feasible challenge. Incidentally, the boyfriend-back-home excuse will only elicit, "But you're here for how long? Too long to go without".

In a social situation, Jamaican men are refreshingly direct, and while an open invitation to bed within the first five minutes of meeting can be disconcerting, you at least know where you stand; once the possibility of sex is out of the way you can move on to other agendas. Learn to listen to your instincts; the slightest hint of flirting means that you are probably about to be propositioned, so assume that even the most innocent reaction may be interpreted as a sign of acquiescence – agreeing to play a game of pool, for example, may well be read as a come-on.

If passion is on your agenda, don't have more than one partner in the same area; gossip spreads extremely quickly and Jamaican men do not take kindly to being "insulted" in this way (of course it's OK for them). Though most men will help if they see a woman being seriously bothered, don't expect Jamaican men (even friends) to extricate you from sticky situations of your own making, as this would encroach on another's machismo. Cope with your new status as a sex goddess with humility and humour; most of it probably has more to do with your foreign allure – or economic clout – than your personal charms, and a lot of the come-ons can be extremely amusing.

Jamaican women

As tourist centres are generally the preserve of male hustlers, it can be difficult to meet **Jamaican women**, and while many women are friendly and older ladies inclined to shower you with maternal protection, some display an understandable resentment towards the carefree, wealthy female visitors pursued by their men. Besides, most women are far too busy juggling childcare, cooking, cleaning and breadwinning to have time for idle chat.

From the dancehall queen to the market higgler, it's pretty obvious that strong women rule Jamaica. They make up 46 percent of the labour force, the highest per-capita ratio in the world. Many are employed at garment assembly factories or as domestic helpers

Women's organizations

Most Jamaican women's organizations are based in Kingston and are presided over by the **Association of Women's Organizations in Jamaica**, 2 Waterloo Rd, Kingston 10 (☎968 8260, ℱ968 0862), an umbrella group that aims to direct, unite and empower women as well as lobbying for change in the law and female opportunities. It can act as a conduit if you want to make contacts or want information on specific groups.

Woman Inc, 7 Denehurst Ave, Kingston 10 (☎929 9038), runs a counselling service and crisis centre for victims of incest, rape and domestic abuse; the number above is a national helpline.

Sistren Theatre Collective, 20 Kensington Crescent, Kingston 5 (☎968 0501), is an internationally recognized feminist theatre company, with a sideline in publishing. It regularly tours the island with consciousness-raising plays and produces a monthly magazine.

and earn an average weekly wage of J$1300 (US$25). On top of this, Jamaican women bear most of the brunt of childcare responsibilities. Single parentage is an institution in Jamaica – eight out of ten children are born out of marriage, with women usually having several children by several partners; the commonly used terms "**baby mother**" or "**baby father**" refer to parents who live apart. The impetus for women to have more than one baby father is more often economic than libidinous – if one man doesn't recognize his responsibilities, perhaps another will – and the family court in Kingston has dealt exclusively with paternity disputes for the past twenty years.

Despite the respect they earn as matriarchs and wage earners, Jamaican women have it tough in this sexist, macho and economically challenged country. They face an increasing threat of violence; the thousand or so rapes reported annually are estimated to be only a fraction of those that take place, and marital rape is not legally recognized. Incest and domestic violence are also on the increase, and there are virtually no sexual harassment laws. Legal abortions are so difficult to get that they might as well be barred; thousands of botched back-street attempts kill and maim women every year.

Directory

Airport Departure Tax For international flights, the departure tax is presently US$27, payable at the airport when you leave. There is no tax on domestic flights.

Children Pellucid seas, gently shelving beaches, no serious health risks and an indulgent attitude toward kids make Jamaica an ideal destination if you're travelling with babies, toddlers or children. Though many of the larger hotels (the *Sandals* chain in particular) operate under a couples-only policy, most welcome families. The Montego Bay *Holiday Inn* (☎953 2485), the *Franklyn D Resort* in Runaway Bay (☎973 4591), *FDR Pebbles* in Trelawny (☎954 0000), *Boscobel Beach* in Oracabessa (☎975 7331) and *Beaches* in Negril (☎957 9270) are all self-styled family resorts with extensive facilities, daily events and personal nannies. There are also plenty of other hotels with kids' clubs that offer vacationing parents an afternoon off.

Customs and immigration Entering Jamaica, customs allow a duty-free quota of 200 cigarettes, 25 cigars, a pound of tobacco, a quart (two pints) of any liquor except rum and a quart of wine. The import of weapons and farm products (including plants, fruit and meat) is heavily restricted and if you're crazy enough to try to smuggle drugs into the country you'll risk severe penalties. When you leave the island, crafts made in Jamaica attract no duty. Note that visitors are given an immigration card on arrival, which must be returned to the Jamaican customs on departure.

Disabled travellers Only the largest hotel chains, such as *Holiday Inn*, *Superclubs* and *Sandals*, have ramps or lifts on their properties; the JTB can provide a full list of hotels with suitable facilities. The Disabled Peoples' International at 9 Tunbridge Terrace, Kingston 19 (☎931 6155), acts as an umbrella agency for other groups on the island, lobbies on behalf of Jamaicans with disabilities, and is a useful source of further contacts and information. General holiday information for travellers with disabilities is available in the US from Travel Information Service, Moss Rehabilitation Hospital, 1200 West Tabor Rd, Philadelphia, PA 19141 (☎215/456 9600); in the UK from RADAR (Royal Association for Disability and Rehabilitation), 12 City Forum, 250 City Rd, London EC1V 8AF (☎020/7250 3222, minicom ☎020/7250 4119, ⓦwww.radar.org .uk); in Ireland from the Disability Action Group, 2 Annadale Ave, Belfast BT7 3JH (☎028/9049 1011); in Australia from ACROD, PO Box 60, Curtin ACT 2605, (☎02 6282 4333); and in New Zealand from the Disabled Persons Assembly, 4/173–175 Victoria St, Wellington (☎04/801 9100). A useful website is ⓦwww.access-able.com.

Electric current The island standard is 110 volts, with two-pin sockets, though a few of the older hotels still use 220 volts. Take adapters for essential items – some of the upmarket hotels and guesthouses have them, but you shouldn't rely on it.

GCT (General Consumption Tax) A government tax of fifteen per cent is levied on goods and services in most hotels, restaurants and stores, and is usually added to the bill (rather than included in the advertised price).

Getting married Jamaica is a hugely popular wedding destination. Only 24-hours' residence on the island is required before you can apply for a marriage licence. You'll need a valid passport or a certified copy of your birth certificate. If you're under 21 you'll also need written parental consent; if divorced, a certified copy of the decree absolute; and if widowed, a copy of your deceased partner's death certificate. Most people leave the bureaucracy to someone else and arrange the wedding through their hotel or tour operator – expect to have to provide the documents at least one month in advance. Alternatively, you can apply in person at the Ministry of National Security and Justice, Mutual Life Building, North Tower, 2 Oxford Rd, Kingston 10 (Mon–Thurs 9am–5pm, Fri

9am–4pm; ☎906 4908). A marriage licence costs US$40 and the paperwork as much as US$150.

Laundry Most hotels have a laundry service, but check prices before handing over a huge load as some charge as much as US$5 for a single shirt. Most large towns have at least one public laundry (listed in the relevant chapters), but in rural areas, your best option is to follow Jamaicans and have clothes washed by hand. Ask around for a trustworthy lady and bear in mind that your best garments may receive over-enthusiastic bleaching and scrubbing. A bag of clothes should cost US$6–10.

Measurements The country is slowly converting from the Imperial to the metric system – road signs, for instance, now give distances in kilometres – but the former still dominates and is used throughout this book. The archaic measurement of a chain – 22 yards – is still used, though if you're asking directions, "a few chains" can mean anything from 100 yards to a mile or more. Treat the directions "it's not far" and "just over there" with the same scepticism.

Photography Jamaica is made for pretty pictures. Take plenty of film and all the equipment you'll need – local costs for both are high, and you'll have difficulty finding good filters and lenses, even at the in-bond stores. Humidity is the photographer's main enemy – carry packets of silica gel in your camera bag, keep film cool and develop it quickly. Over-exposure can also be a problem: watch out for the glare from sea and sand, and try to take pictures early or late in the day when the sun is less bright. When photographing people (or their homes and property), always ask permission – some like it, others don't – and anticipate a request for a donation.

Time Jamaica is on Eastern Standard Time and does not adjust for Daylight Saving Time. Accordingly, it is on the same time as New York (one hour behind from spring to autumn) and five hours behind London (six hours from spring to autumn).

Tipping No tip is necessary at any restaurant that imposes an automatic service charge; ten to fifteen percent is the norm anywhere else. Tip taxi drivers at your discretion; route taxi drivers do not expect a tip.

Visa extensions If you want to extend your stay, you can either leave and re-enter the island or apply to the Ministry of National Security and Justice, Mutual Life Building, North Tower, 2 Oxford Road, Kingston 10 (Mon–Thurs 9am–5pm, Fri 9am–4pm; ☎906 4908), or the Immigration Office, Overton Plaza, Union St, Montego Bay (Mon–Fri 8am–1pm & 2–4pm; ☎952 5381).

Guide

Guide

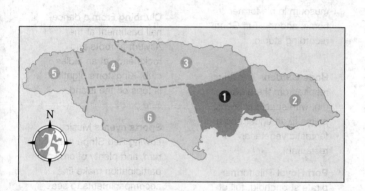

Kingston and around

CHAPTER 1

Highlights

* **National Gallery** A wealth of works from Jamaica's most important artists, from Edna Manley to Kapo. See p.82

* **Bob Marley** pilgrimage Tour the Trench Town Culture Yard, where Marley grew up; the museum in his former home; and the Tuff Gong recording studio. See p.85

* **Hope Gardens** A lovely respite from the urban din, with spacious lawns, palms to sit under and a fantastic vegetarian restaurant. See p.98

* **Port Royal** This former pirate stronghold, full of eighteenth-century military buildings, is an atmospheric place for a plate of fresh fish or a dance under the stars. See p.109

* **Hellshire** White sand, brightly-coloured fishing boats and a cool sea breeze provide the ideal backdrop for some of the best fried fish on the planet. See p.116

* **Clubbing** From a dance-hall bashment at the *Asylum* to roots and rocksteady at an oldies club, Kingston's nightlife is tops on the island. See p.102

* **Sports events** Music, flowing Red Stripe and rum, and plenty of crowd participation make fine accompaniments to seeing a football match at "The Office" or a few overs at Sabina Park. See p.107

△ Taino Cave art, Mountain River Cave

1

Kingston and around

Overwhelming and fascinating in equal measure, **Kingston** is quite unlike anywhere else in the Caribbean. Given its troubled reputation, it's hardly surprising that few tourists visit, and while the scare stories are absurdly exaggerated, Kingston is certainly not a place for the faint-hearted. In the 1950s, Ian Fleming called it a "tough city", and that still holds true today. Jamaica's capital is rough and ready, a little uncompromising, but always exciting and absorbing.

With just under 600,000 residents (22 percent of the island's total population), Kingston seethes with life, noise and activity, and if you venture downtown, you'll see the rough edges. Nonetheless, the capital offers a look at a side of Jamaica that couldn't be more different from the resorts. As well as being the seat of government and the island's administrative centre, Kingston is Jamaica's cultural heart, the city that spawned Bob Marley, Buju Banton, Beenie Man and countless other reggae stars. It's the only place on the island where you can fully appreciate the best of the country's art, theatre and dance.

If you do decide to visit – and it's well worth the effort for anyone with even a passing interest in Jamaican culture – you'll find that not only is it easy to steer clear of the troubled areas, but that there's little of the persistent **harassment** that bedevils parts of the north coast. In comparison to Ochi or Negril, the capital feels refreshingly real, with most Kingstonians far more interested in going about their business than wasting time on a tourist. That's not to say that city dwellers are unfriendly; in fact, it's far easier to strike up a decent conversation here than in more conventional tourist honeypots, where every interaction can seem like a precursor to a sales pitch. The pulsating, live-for-today vitality of the place injects a shot of adrenaline that often proves addictive, and its exuberant atmosphere is tempered by a cool elegance and a strong sense of national history. If you follow the herd and avoid the capital, you'll have missed one of Jamaica's undoubted highlights.

For many, the sights and sounds of the capital's non-stop street life are entertainment in themselves, but the city is packed with more substantial draws besides. A handful of interesting museums, galleries and churches can easily fill a couple of days of sightseeing; the island's best clubs, theatres and some great restaurants will take care of the evenings. Nearby, quite apart from the lovely Blue Mountains that overlook Kingston (and are covered in Chapter Two), plenty of other attractions surround the city. The area is littered with historic sites – Georgian monuments in **Spanish Town**, the forts of the English buccaneers in atmospheric **Port Royal**, and **Taino caves** from pre-Columbian times at **Mountain River**. For those who just can't cope without a beach, the white-sand **Hellshire beaches** and **Lime Cay** are the perfect places to get away from it all.

Kingston

Founded at the tail end of the seventeenth century, **KINGSTON** fast became the greatest city in the West Indies. The main impetus to growth was its fabulous location, built on an expansive **natural harbour** – the seventh largest in the world – which was to prove the cornerstone of Kingston's future trading success. Since those early days, the city streets have gradually found their way north and now reach as far as the foothills of the **Blue Mountains**, a truly glorious backdrop.

Kingston's main sights are divided between the area known as "downtown", which stretches north from the waterfront to the busy traffic junction of Cross Roads, and "uptown", spreading up into the ritzy suburbs of Jack's Hill and Cherry Gardens at the base of the mountains. **Downtown** is the city's industrial centre, its factories and all-important port providing most of the city's blue-collar employment; the law firms, stock exchange and the Bank of Jamaica are also prominent features. The peaceful, grassy waterfront provides a marked contrast to the busy streets of most of downtown, centred around **Parade Square**.

Uptown is different, and you may be surprised at how attractive and easygoing it feels, as suited businessmen and office workers go about their daily routines. Most of Kingston's hotels, restaurants, clubs and shopping centres are here, and it's where you'll spend most of your time. Some of the residential districts, such as **Mona** and **Beverly Hills**, are simply beautiful, while the central high-rises suggest a modern city anywhere in North America – although the coconut vendors and the odd stray goat tend to give the game away.

In terms of **highlights**, many visitors make straight for the **Bob Marley Museum**, former home of the island's greatest reggae star and musical ambassador. But there are also some grand old **colonial houses**, recently restored as museums, and an excellent **national art gallery**. There are plenty of good hotels and restaurants, and the city is the heartbeat of the country's music industry, with top-quality clubs and a busy live-music scene. The annual **Carnival** is well worth catching if you're on the island between February and April.

Some history

Though the Spanish first settled in Jamaica in 1510, replaced by British colonists in 1655, there was little development in present-day Kingston until 1692. The area held just a small pig-rearing village, glamorously known as Colonel Beeston's Hog Crawle, and a handful of fishing shacks. All of the action was across the harbour on the island of Port Royal, then Jamaica's second city (after Spanish Town) and home to most of the country's leading lights. In 1692, however, a violent **earthquake** devastated Port Royal; several thousand people died instantly and the rest went scurrying for a more hospitable place to live. The Hog Crawle was the obvious choice – on the mainland but beside the harbour – and the former citizens of Port Royal promptly snapped up two hundred acres of land there. The population was further expanded in 1703, when more Port Royalists fled to the other side of the harbour after a devastating **fire**.

Within a few months, the plans for the new town had been drawn up. Newborn Kingston was named in honour of William of Orange, king of

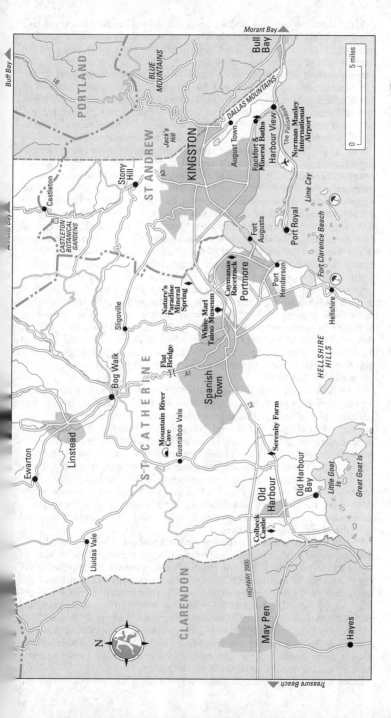

Morant Bay

Buff Bay

Bull Bay

PORTLAND

BLUE MOUNTAINS

B1

DALLAS MOUNTAINS

ST ANDREW

Jack's Hill

KINGSTON

August Town

Rockfort & Mineral Baths

Harbour View

Norman Manley International Airport

The Palisadoes

Castleton

Annotto Bay

CASTLETON BOTANICAL GARDENS

Stony Hill

A3

Lime Cay

Fort Augusta

Port Royal

Fort Clarence Beach

Sligoville

Nature's Paradise Mineral Spring

Caymanas Racetrack

Portmore

Port Henderson

Hellshire

HELLSHIRE HILLS

White Marl Taino Museum

Flat Bridge

A1

Spanish Town

Bog Walk

Mountain River Cave

Guanaboa Vale

A2

S T   C A T H E R I N E

Linstead

Ewarton

Serenity Farm

Lluidas Vale

Old Harbour

Old Harbour Bay

Little Goat Is

Great Goat Is

Colbeck Castle

CLARENDON

HIGHWAY 2000

May Pen

Hayes

N

Treasure Beach

0   5 miles

England from 1689 to 1702, and the town was laid out beside the water to take advantage of the existing **sea trade**. The road plan mostly followed a grid system (which remains largely intact today) with the big central square of the **Parade** left open in the heart of town.

By the early eighteenth century, Kingston had become a **major port** for the transhipment of English goods and African slaves to the Spanish colonies of South America. Merchants, traders and brokers made rapid fortunes and began to build themselves ostentatious homes, while fresh waves of **immigrants** piled into the booming city – some from Europe, some from other Caribbean islands, some from other parts of Jamaica, all in search of opportunity.

With its swelling population and rising wealth, the city soon began to challenge for the role of the **nation's capital**, though the authorities in Spanish Town – comfortably ensconced in their grand Georgian buildings – proved stubborn in handing over the title to their upstart neighbour. By 1872, when Kingston finally became Jamaica's capital city, many wealthy families were already moving beyond the original town boundaries to the more genteel areas that today comprise **uptown** Kingston. Meanwhile, the less affluent huddled downtown and in the **shanty towns** that began to spring up on the outskirts of old Kingston, particularly west of the city, their ranks swollen by a tide of former slaves hoping to find prosperity beyond the sugar estates.

Jamaica's turn-of-the-century boom, engineered by tourism and agriculture, largely bypassed Kingston's poor and helped to reinforce the divide between uptown and downtown. While the rich got richer and sequestered themselves in the new suburbs uptown, the **downtown** area continued to deteriorate, neglected by government and hit by a catastrophic earthquake in 1907 that destroyed almost all buildings south of the Parade. Those who could afford to do so continued to move out, leaving behind an increasingly destitute population that proved fertile recruitment ground for the **Rastafari** movement during the 1920s and 1930s.

There were major **riots** during the 1930s, with the city feeling the knock-on effects of an islandwide economic crisis sparked by the plunging price of key crops like bananas and sugar on world markets. The riots led to the development of local trade unions and political parties during the 1940s; these organizations spoke for the workers and the dispossessed, but improvements in working conditions and the physical infrastructure were slow in coming. Finally, in the 1960s, the city authorities began to show some interest in reversing the decay. Efforts were made to give the old downtown area a face-lift; redevelopment of the waterfront resulted in a much-needed expansion of the city's **port facility** (still a vital part of the city's commerce today) and a smartening-up of the harbour area with the introduction of shops, offices and even the island's major art gallery.

A mini-**tourist boom** was sparked by the new-look Kingston (and by the growing popularity of Jamaican music abroad), with cruise ships arriving to inject a fresh air of hope into the city. Sadly, the optimism proved short-lived. For the people of downtown Kingston, the redevelopment of downtown was only cosmetic. Crime – an inevitable feature in the crowded ghettos – was getting out of control, sponsored by politicians who distributed weapons and patronage to their supporters. At election time (particularly in 1976 and 1980), hundreds of people were killed in bloody campaigns, many of them innocent bystanders. Tourists ran for cover, heading for the new beach resorts on the island's north coast, and the city sank into a quagmire of unemployment, poverty and crime. (For more on Kingston's ghettos, see p.86.)

Today, Kingston remains a divided city. The wealthy have moved further and

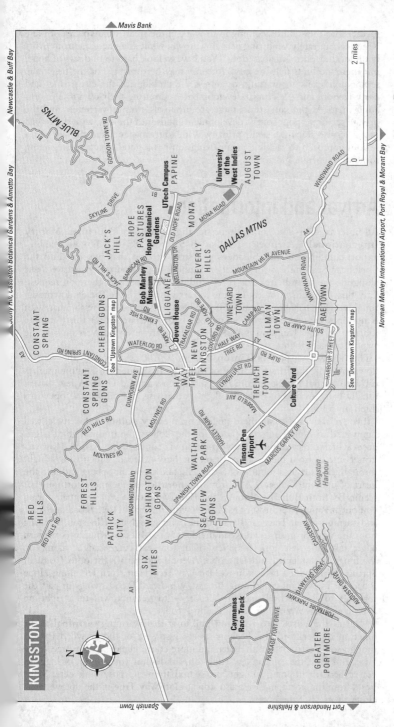

Mavis Bank

Newcastle & Buff Bay

Holly Hill, Castleton Botanical Gardens & Annotto Bay

BLUE MTNS

B1

GORDON TOWN RD

SKYLINE DRIVE

JACK'S HILL

JACK'S HILL RD

BARBICAN RD

CHERRY GDNS

CONSTANT
SPRING

CONSTANT
SPRING GDNS

CONSTANT SPRING RD

A3

RED HILLS RD

DUNROBIN AVE

MOLYNES RD

RED HILLS

RED HILLS RD

FOREST
HILLS

PATRICK
CITY

MOLYNES RD

WASHINGTON BLVD

CONSTANT
SPRING GDNS

SIX
MILES

A1

WASHINGTON
GDNS

WALTHAM
PARK

SEAVIEW
GDNS

SPANISH TOWN ROAD

HAGLEY PARK RD

Tinson Pen
Airport

MARCUS GARVEY DR

A1

HOPE
PASTURES

Hope Botanical
Gardens

UTech Campus

PAPINE

B1

University of the
West Indies

AUGUST
TOWN

MONA

MONA ROAD

OLD HOPE ROAD

WELLINGTON DR

Bob Marley
Museum

LIGUANEA

Devon House

E KING'S HSE RD

HOPE RD

NEW
KINGSTON

HALF
WAY
TREE

DEVON HSE

WATERLOO RD

TRAFALGAR RD

OLD HOPE RD

BEVERLY
HILLS

DALLAS MTNS

MOUNTAIN VIEW AVENUE

VINEYARD
TOWN

ALLMAN
TOWN

CAMP RD

A4

WINDWARD ROAD

RAE
TOWN

A4

WINDWARD ROAD

See "Uptown Kingston" map

HALF WAY
TREE RD

OXFORD RD

SLIPE RD

A3

TREE RD

LYNDHURST RD

TRENCH
TOWN

MAXFIELD AVE

A1

SOUTH CAMP RD

HARBOUR STREET

See "Downtown Kingston" map

Culture Yard

Norman Manley International Airport, Port Royal & Morant Bay

Kingston
Harbour

Caymanas
Race Track

PORT DRIVE

AUGUSTA DRIVE

DAWKINS DR

PORTMORE PARKWAY

CAUSEWAY

GREATER
PORTMORE

PASSAGE FORT DRIVE

Port Henderson & Hellshire

Spanish Town

KINGSTON

N

0   2 miles

further into the suburbs, coming in to work in the smart uptown area of New Kingston but rarely venturing near downtown, while the ghettos remain firmly under the control of area "dons". You have to look hard to find rays of hope, but there are hints that the city's fortunes may be turning. For the first time, senior politicians are starting to address the problem of the city's gangs and party factions and – a crucial development – admitting their own role in creating them. At the same time, there are proposals, from government and the private sector, to pour tourist development funds into the city, with the return of the cruise ships the main priority. With tourism-generated money and a serious approach to tackling crime, Kingston has a good chance of regaining some of its former glory.

Arrival and information

All international and some domestic **flights** land at **Norman Manley International Airport** (☎924 8452 or 8546, ⓦwww.manley-airport.com.jm) on the Palisadoes – a strip of land that juts out into the Caribbean Sea southeast of the city. A number of **car-rental** firms have desks alongside the arrivals area (see p.107); others will meet you there on request. City **bus** #98 runs from just outside the arrivals area to the Parade downtown roughly every half-hour (around J$40). However, unless you're familiar with Kingston, you're far better off opting for a **cab** – the fare for the thirty-minute journey to New Kingston is US$20–25; there are always drivers outside the airport to meet flights.

The domestic airport of **Tinson Pen** (☎923 0022) is just to the west of downtown on the fringe of some of the city's less salubrious communities. A cab into central Kingston from here should cost around US$8. A few drivers usually hang around to meet the flights; otherwise, call one of the operators listed on p.108.

If you're arriving by **car**, there are four main **entry points** to the city, all well signposted to New Kingston. (Look for the "follow the hummingbird" signposts, which direct you into New Kingston via South Camp Road.) Most visitors come in from the north coast on the busy A3 road, which runs straight through the northern suburbs of Stony Hill and Constant Spring and into the heart of uptown Kingston. Also from the north coast, the more tortuous but scenic B3 from Buff Bay through the Blue Mountains will eventually bring you out at Papine, northeast of town; following the main Hope Road due west, and turning left at Trafalgar Road, brings you into New Kingston. Coming from the west, Spanish Town Road divides at Six Miles on Kingston's western edge; take the left fork for New Kingston, carrying straight along on Washington Boulevard and Dunrobin Avenue and turn right onto Constant Spring Road, which takes you to Half Way Tree. Here, turn left along Hope Road for New Kingston. From the east, Windward Road swings in past the turn-off to Port Royal and the airport – to get uptown, turn right on Mountain View Avenue or South Camp Road.

Most of the **buses** into Kingston pull in at the swarming **terminal** at the junction of Beckford and Pechon streets, just west of the crowded Parade, though some terminate at the safer and more convenient Half Way Tree. Local buses run from there into New Kingston, although if you've a lot of luggage, you're best off hopping straight into a **taxi** from the busy rank here. Many buses from the north and west also stop at **Half Way Tree** in the uptown area, closer to most of the hotels.

Safety and harassment

The **pestering** of visitors, irritatingly widespread on the north coast, is relatively and refreshingly uncommon in Kingston. Nevertheless, as with any big city, there are plenty of scare stories and some places that you should steer clear of. There is serious poverty and political tribalism in large parts of residential downtown Kingston (see p.86) – these ghettos are not places for casual sightseeing and – with the exception of Trench Town Culture Yard (see p.86) – you shouldn't even think of straying in there without a good reason and the company of someone who knows the area well. The more central part of downtown, covered in this guide, has its dodgy areas; you'll usually be okay during the day, but once the business crowd has gone at around 5.30pm, it can be a bit risky. Unless you're seeing a show at the brightly lit Ward Theatre, there is little reason to head downtown after dark.

With an average of five hundred murders per year, the crime statistics for the city are undeniably ugly. But as the majority of violent crime is domestic or the result of drug-related gang disputes in the ghettos, visitors are unlikely to get mixed up in any trouble. Of course, criminal elements do venture out of these areas, and the well-to-do are increasingly protected behind high fences, barbed wire, security guards and dogs. During the day, though, the uptown area (and most of downtown) feels fine, particularly once you're familiar with the main roads. At night, you're best off getting a taxi if you're travelling any distance.

Information

The main office of the **Jamaica Tourist Board** (Mon–Fri 9am–4.30pm; ☎929 9200) is right in the heart of New Kingston at 64 Knutsford Boulevard. Staff dole out maps, brochures and lists of places to stay, and there's a useful little library. There's a smaller branch at Norman Manley Airport, normally open to meet flights (☎924 8024). The most useful **map** of the Kingston area is on the back of the JTB's Esso island map; there's also a smaller, more manageable version in the *Discover Jamaica* booklet; both have a handy separate plan of the city's downtown area.

There is no good **listings** section in any of the newspapers, but most of the theatres, cinemas and clubs advertise their activities on island radio stations Irie FM, Zip FM and Roots FM or in the national *Daily Gleaner* and *Observer* newspapers. The Friday editions of the papers carry the bulk of the ads, but there are daily listings, too. Look out, also, for posters slapped up around town heralding forthcoming stageshows and parties. Entertainment listings also appear online at ⓦwww.whatsonjamaica.com, ⓦwww.jamaicanlifestyle.com and ⓦwww.whaddat.com.

Getting around

Finding your way around Kingston is pretty straightforward. Downtown uses a grid system, while uptown is defined by a handful of major roads. You'll quickly get used to the main landmarks, and as a reliable fallback, the mountains to the northeast and the high-rises of New Kingston serve as good compass references. The heat and the distances between places mean you're not going to want to do a lot of **walking**, though the downtown sights, in particular, are easily navigable on foot. It's not advisable to walk the streets at night in any part of the city; most Kingstonians don't.

Taxis are the best way of getting around the city and are reasonably cheap; a ride from New Kingston to downtown costs around J$300. Bear in mind that cabs rarely carry meters and you'll need to fix a price before you get in. Although it's standard practice to call for a taxi (see p.108 for a list of companies), particularly at night, they can almost always be flagged down on the main streets (look out for red "PP" or "PPV" plates). There's also a bustling rank downtown at Parade and an unofficial one in New Kingston along Knutsford Boulevard. Since the establishment of the government-run Jamaica Urban Transit Company (JUTC) in 1998, Kingston's **buses** have become a viable option for visitors. Smart and clean new vehicles have replaced the motley crew of country-type buses operated by various private entities that formerly crawled through the streets, and their numbers are such that you'll rarely see the chronic overcrowding that was the bane of commuters' lives in previous years. Services cover all the main routes. All buses have numbers, but the dot-matrix boards at the front, showing destination and number, are often out of order. The best way to ensure you get to your destination is to ask – most bus users seem to have an exhaustive knowledge of schedules and services. For a full list of **routes**, visit Ⓦ www.mtw.gov.jm/index.html. **Fares** are absurdly cheap – no more than J$50 for any journey in and around the city; reckon on J$20 for short hops in the city centre. You can use cash to pay fares, but if you plan on using buses a lot, get hold of a pre-paid Smart Card; these cover multiple rides and are widely available at specialist outlets. Main bus terminals are at Parade and Half Way Tree; a new terminal is planned at the latter.

Though traffic jams are a real problem, particularly around the morning and evening rush hours, when traffic slows to a crawl along all the main roads, **renting a car** is the best way to explore Kingston. Signage on the roads has improved immeasurably in recent years, and if you plan on spending more than a couple of days in the capital, it'll work out cheaper to drive yourself than to keep forking out money for taxis. A car of your own also makes it a lot easier to check out Kingston's nightlife (it's not advisable to walk from venue to venue). Rental is usually cheaper in Kingston than at the resorts; for a list of reliable operators, see p.107.

Finally, **city tours** can be an excellent way to negotiate the main sights efficiently, and not all of the available roster are of the twenty-people-in-a-bus variety. For a list of operators, see p.108.

Accommodation

Most of Kingston's **hotels** are scattered around the small uptown district of **New Kingston**, a convenient base for sightseeing and close to many of the restaurants, theatres, cinemas and clubs (see map on p.81 for accommodation locations). There are some dirt-cheap hotels in and around **downtown**, but as these are only for the desperate and fearless, we don't recommend them. Few of the city's hotels cater specifically for the tourist trade, relying instead on a steady stream of Jamaican and international business visitors. As a result, prices are not as seasonal as in the resort areas, and there are few discounts available during the summer. Although it is normally wise to reserve in advance, finding a room in Kingston is rarely a problem.

If you don't fancy the hustle of the big city (and some of the hotels can get noisy at night), you might want to stay in Port Royal (see p.109) or Hellshire (see p.116). There are also a couple of small hotels and guesthouses in the foothills of the Blue Mountains just north of Kingston (see p.133). If you want to explore the city, though, it can be expensive and time-consuming getting back and forth from a hotel in one of the outlying areas. Unless you have a car, you're better off staying in town.

Alhambra Inn 1 Tucker Ave ☎978 9072–3, ⓔalhambra@cwjamaica.com. Pretty complex set back from the road near the National Stadium, with a pool, outdoor restaurant, lots of greenery and a fabulous collection of Jamaica ephemera, from rusting Appleton signs to gardening tools. The rooms offer parquet floors, king-size beds, telephone, a/c, cable TV and iron, and are superb value. Rates include breakfast. ⑤

Altamont Court 1 Altamont Terrace ☎929 4497-8, ⓦwww.altamontcourt.com. Easily the best midrange option in New Kingston, right in the heart of the action but tucked away from the noisy main drag, with a swimming pool, jacuzzi, restaurant and bar. The comfortable rooms have a/c, cable TV, phone and Internet jacks, and there are some lovely split-level suites, too. ⑤

Beverly Cliffs Hotel 200 Mountain View Ave ☎978 5288 or mobile 421 6817. Quiet, newly opened place opposite the National Stadium has one spacious, wood-floored room upstairs, and several smaller units downstairs with tiled floors; all have a/c and cable TV. There's a pool on site. ②

Central Court 47 Old Hope Rd ☎960 3982, ⓕ906 3402. Toward the Cross Roads end of Old Hope Road, this is an extremely basic option worth considering if you're on a tight budget. Rooms are tiny and in need of refurbishment, but each has a private bathroom, cable TV in a cage and either a/c or fan. Meals available. ①–②

Chelsea 5 Chelsea Ave ☎926 5803, ⓕ929 4746. Cheap and in the heart of New Kingston. The en-suite rooms have a/c, fan, cable TV and hot and cold water, and there's a restaurant and a bar with pool tables on site. Friendly service. ②–③

Christar Villas 99 Hope Rd ☎978 3933, ⓦwww.christarvillashotel.com. Appealing studios and suites in a great location near the Bob Marley Museum. All units have kitchen, a/c, phone and cable TV; the more luxurious ones feature private jacuzzi and exercise equipment. Also on the premises: a business centre, gym, pool, jacuzzi, sun deck, a/c restaurant and popular bar. ⑤

Courtleigh 85 Knutsford Blvd ☎929 9000, ⓦwww.courtleigh.com. Easily the most appealing of the New Kingston high-rise hotels, with a tasteful lobby decked out in Chinese style, a business centre, good restaurant, popular bar/nightclub, pool and gym. Each of the luxurious rooms has a

balcony and lots of welcome extras, from hair dryer to Internet jack. ⑥

Crieffe Court 10 Crieffe Rd ☎927 8033, ⓦwww.in-site.com/crieffe. No frills but good value at this functional place near the National Stadium. An eclectic collection of rooms with screened windows, a/c, ceiling fans, tiled floors and cable TV. There are studios with kitchenettes, and one- or two-bedroom apartments. ③–④

Four Seasons 18 Ruthven Rd ☎926 8805, ⓕ929 5964, ⓦwww.hotelfourseasonsja.com. Attractive, converted Edwardian home in New Kingston. Rooms in the original house are more atmospheric than those in the modern wing. ⑥

The Gardens 23 Liguanea Ave ☎927 5957, ⓔmlyn@cwjamaica.com, ⓦwww.forrespark.com. With centrality, seclusion and a homely, relaxing feel, this delightful complex of expansive two-bedroom townhouses is one of Kingston's best choices. Single rooms as well as two-bedroom apartments with living room and kitchen are available. The grounds offer gorgeous, flowered gardens and a pool. ④

Hilton Kingston 77 Knutsford Blvd ☎926 5430, ⓕ929 7439, ⓦwww.kingston.hilton.com. Landmark New Kingston hotel popular with visiting execs. All the *Hilton* trappings, from Olympic-size pool, tennis courts and health club to nightclub, business centre and three restaurants, including an excellent Japanese diner above the glitzy lobby. Rooms have all the mod cons, and there's a huge range of suites, too. ⑦–⑧

Holborn Manor 3 Holborn Rd ☎ & ⓕ929 3070. Friendly family-run guesthouse in New Kingston. The rather basic rooms are equipped with fans and cable TV. Jamaican breakfast is included in the rates. ④

Indies 5 Holborn Rd ☎926 2952, ⓔindieshotel@hotmail.com. Compact and clean little hotel next to *Holborn Manor*, set on two levels around a garden courtyard and small restaurant. The cheapest rooms are on the small side, with fan only, but there are more spacious a/c options, with cable TV, too. ②–④

Iris Inn 26 Tankerville Ave ☎978 2912, ⓕ978 2913. Off Mountain View Avenue (turn off onto Tucker Avenue, and it's straight ahead of you), near the National Stadium, this is an excellent choice if you're after a degree of independence. Spacious one- and two-bedroom apartments have fully-equipped kitchens, a/c bedrooms and pleasant, neutral decor. There's a small (and cheaper) studio, too. Excellent value. ④–⑥

Jamaica Pegasus 81 Knutsford Blvd ☎ 926 3690, ⓦ www.jamaicapegasus.com. Seventeen-storey business-oriented behemoth with a slightly 1970s air. The three hundred luxurious rooms and suites, in American-chic decor, all have a/c, phone, Internet jacks, hairdryer and a balcony. The hotel also offers a business centre, gym, two pools, floodlit tennis courts, jogging trail, four restaurants, two bars, a gaming room and acres of conference space. ⑥

Knutsford Court 16 Chelsea Ave ☎ 929 1000, ⓦ www.knutsfordcourt.com. Formerly the *Sutton Place* hotel, it's now under the efficient management of the *Courtleigh* team. Newly refurbished, it has lots of greenery outside and redecorated rooms with all mod cons. Business centre, coin-op laundry, pool and restaurant are on site. Rates include continental breakfast. ⑤

Mayfair 4 West King's House Close ☎ 926 1610, ⓦ www.in-site.com/mayfair. A sound choice in a quiet area, with a pool, restaurant and bar. Standard rooms have a/c, phone and a balcony (you pay more for a room with cable TV), and there are studios and suites with a dining/living room and kitchenette. ④–⑤

Medallion Hall 53 Hope Rd ☎ 927 5721, ⓕ 927 4081. Roomy 21-room property in a central location, popular for conferences and with execs whose budgets can't stretch to the more central business-oriented hotels. A range of units (some

sleep four) with a/c, cable TV and phone; ask for one of the breezier rooms upstairs. There's a good Jamaican restaurant, too. ④

Olympia Crown 53 Molynes Rd ☎ 937 2677, ⓕ 901 6688. Labyrinthine complex near Half Way Tree with restaurant, bar, gym, tennis courts and a large pool. Rooms are comfortable, if in need of refurbishment, with cable TV, phone and fan; you pay more for a/c. ③–④

Sandhurst 70 Sandhurst Crescent ☎ 927 8244, ⓕ 927 7239. Excellent value in a peaceful spot near King's House and behind the Bob Marley Museum. Rooms range from simple fan-only to units with a/c, cable TV and veranda. Other pluses are a nice pool and a terrace restaurant overlooking the mountains. ③

Shirley Retreat House 7 Maeven Ave ☎ 946 2679, ⓔ jeshirl@cwjamaica.com. Tucked down a quiet cul-de-sac off Hope Road, this is a pleasant getaway. The simple, spacious rooms have a/c, phone and cable TV. A restaurant is on site; rates include breakfast. ④

Sunset Inn 1A Altamont Crescent ☎ 926 2017, ⓔ sunsetinn@mindspring.com. Budget-conscious New Kingston guesthouse with a range of clean, pleasant rooms. All have fridge, a/c and cable TV; some have a kitchenette. ④

Terra Nova 17 Waterloo Rd ☎ 926 2211, ⓔ terranova@hotmail.com. Very smart little hide-away set in landscaped gardens, with a small pool. The elegant rooms are suitably upscale, with cable TV, hairdryers, bathrobes and Internet jacks. Rates include a buffet breakfast. ⑥

The City

Most people divide Kingston into two sectors – **downtown** and **uptown** – and we've adopted the same distinction. It'll take you a full day to check out the main sights downtown, and about the same amount of time to catch those uptown. Downtown, the **National Gallery**, by the waterfront, is the high-culture highlight, while the nearby **Craft Market** and Orange Street **record stores** have a throbbing, grittier atmosphere. The breezy waterfront is also the departure point for the **ferry** to Port Royal (see p.109). Ten minutes' walk north, the cacophonous **Parade** – one-time marching ground of the British army – is flanked by a couple of interesting **churches.** A little further from here, **Headquarters House** is a grand old colonial home stuffed with historical relics. In the midst of the notorious Trench Town community, the **Culture Yard** offers the opportunity to visit the former home of Bob Marley – though it's very much an attraction in the making, worth visiting more for the opportunity to soak up some inner-city atmosphere than for the place itself.

Uptown has the more popular attractions, including the must-see **Bob Marley Museum** and the striking **Devon House** – former home of the island's first black millionaire – with its clutch of gift shops, landscaped gardens

△ Fort Charles, Port Royal

and superb ice-cream outlet. Also uptown, at Half Way Tree, the seventeenth-century **St Andrews Parish Church** remains one of the key churches in Jamaica, second in historical importance only to the cathedral in Spanish Town (see p.121), while the **Hope Botanical Gardens** offer a quiet refuge from the noise of the city.

Downtown

Flattened by an earthquake in 1907, **downtown Kingston** has lost most of its grand eighteenth-century architecture. A handful of historic buildings can still be found along Rum Lane, Water Lane and King Street, however, and if you peer into the most unlikely yards you can occasionally find evidence of the intricate buildings that used to proliferate here.

Much of Kingston's economic strength still derives from its impressively huge natural **harbour**. It's one of the world's best, but grimly polluted these days, despite concerted government efforts to clean it up. Once buzzing with trading ships, the wind-whipped **waterfront** is a good spot to start a tour of the downtown area. It's close to the **National Gallery** and the **Craft Market**, and a short walk from the main **Parade**, above which you'll find **Headquarters House** and, just outside the old city boundaries to the north, **National Heroes Park**.

Nearby, and very much off the beaten track, are some of the country's most depressed ghetto areas – the stuff of many a reggae lyric – Trench Town, Jones Town, Tivoli Gardens, Rema, Hannah Town and Greenwich Farm. Explosive and creative, these areas are the birthplace of many of Jamaica's most successful musicians. It's now possible to visit Trench Town by way of the **Culture Yard**, a community initiative set up at Bob Marley's former home in an attempt to attract some much-needed tourist dollars to the area.

The waterfront

Despite the fuel silos, loading cranes and the container ships moored just offshore, the wind-whipped **waterfront** is a surprisingly pleasant place: people and pelicans fish off the concrete piers, couples and the odd vagrant sit on the harbour wall or walk the wide grassy boulevard between the road and the sea, and planes swoop overhead en route to Norman Manley Airport across the water. The chief beneficiary of the city council's 1960s' bid to beautify elements of downtown, the waterfront saw its historic buildings swept away and replaced by spanking new high-rises – the icons of the era.

Today, these modern monuments define the eastern end of the waterfront's main strip, Ocean Boulevard. They include the high-rise headquarters of the Bank of Jamaica on Nethersole Place, whose small **Coin and Note Museum** (Mon–Fri 9am–4pm; free; ⓦ www.boj.org.jm) is an exhibition on the country's currency that should fascinate the numismatic. The well-labelled and surprisingly interesting collection takes you through a history of money, from barley grains, cowrie shells and Taino beads to notes and coins, including the "anchors" and "Christan quatties" first issued by the British in Jamaica. Nearby at 14 Duke St, you can get a free tour of the enormous **Jamaica Conference Centre** (Mon–Fri 9am–4pm), built in 1981 to host meetings of the United Nations' International Seabed Authority. This in itself probably won't have you queuing at dawn, but the building's lofty design and abundant use of glass and local crafts make it feel unlike anywhere else in the city.

West of here, the large, pink, forlorn-looking building on Ocean Boulevard was, until the late 1980s, the **Oceana Hotel**, built as the government's flagship

DOWNTOWN KINGSTON

0   500 yds

for Kingston in an attempt to entice business travellers – and their expense accounts – downtown. The target guests ignored it entirely and continued to enjoy the smarter hotels and better nightlife of New Kingston, and the hotel flopped. The longstanding official claim that private investors are on the verge of reopening it seems more than a little optimistic. Nonetheless, the bristling satellite dishes on the adjacent apartment complex stand as testament to the few brave members of the middle classes who've decided that a harbour view outweighs potential security concerns. Further along the boulevard, at the bottom of King Street, is a reproduction of the sculpture **Negro Aroused** by the late Edna Manley, one of Jamaica's leading artists and wife and mother, respectively, of former prime ministers Norman Manley and Michael Manley. One of the icons of twentieth-century Jamaican art, the bronze sculpture captured the incipient labour movement and the spirit of unrest of the 1930s, and is dedicated to the workers of Jamaica (though you wouldn't know it, as the title plaque is long gone). Running parallel to the waterfront on the inland side of the boulevard, the rangy **Kingston Mall** should be a great place for a browse, but the empty, dusty store-fronts that predominate speak volumes about the unexploited potential of the area.

The National Gallery and the African-Caribbean Heritage Centre

The pleasantly air-conditioned **National Gallery**, at 12 Ocean Blvd on the corner of Orange Street (Tues–Thurs 10am–4.30pm, Fri 11am–4pm, Sat 10am–3pm; J$50), is one of the unexpected highlights of a visit to Kingston. The permanent collection here is superb, ranging from delicate woodcarvings to flamboyant religious paintings, while the several temporary exhibitions showcase the best of contemporary Jamaican art. Held from December to February in alternating years, and normally arranged in the first gallery you come to on entering the building, the Biennial and the Curators' Exhibition are the ones to look out for.

Guided tours of the gallery (J$800, call ☎922 1561–4 in advance to arrange, though it's usually possible to get a tour on the spot) are well worth taking. They provide essential background to, and interpretation of, the works on show.

At the core of the **permanent collection** are ten chronological galleries, housed on the first floor, representing the **Jamaican School**, 1922 to the present. The school's era is generally deemed to begin with Edna Manley's 1922 *Beadseller*, a dainty little bronze sculpture which married a contemporary artistic trend (Cubism) to a typical local image (the Kingston "higgler", or female street vendor) to create something distinctly Jamaican. Manley's sculpture and the absorbing paintings of John Dunkley (1891–1947) dominate the first galleries. Dunkley was a Kingston barber and the first and most important of Jamaica's self-taught artists. His dark, brooding and often eerie local scenes are a far cry from the jaunty colours of modern landscape painters – *Lonely Road* and *Banana Plantation* are particularly powerful. He and Manley paved the way for others to paint what they saw around them, and in the work of artists like Albert Huie and David Pottinger, you can detect the early stages of a movement giving value and artistic identity to Jamaica's own people and places. Particularly notable are Pottinger's *Nine Night*, with its mourners turned trance-like during the ritual nine nights of grieving after a death, and Huie's *Crop Time* and *Coconut Piece*, which illustrate sugar cane production and coconut processing in minute detail. Look out also for Gloria Escofferey's *The Old Woman*, which suggests the esteem in which elders are held in Jamaica.

The paintings of the prolific Carl Abrahams in the later galleries show a move towards abstraction that is capped by the idiosyncratically Jamaican surrealism of Colin Garland and the unsettling ghostly images of David Boxer, longtime curator of the gallery and a key figure in Jamaican modern art. Realism returns with Barrington Watson's *Conversation* and the tender and beautiful *Mother and Child*, a portrait of his partner and son, while Kay Brown's *Star Boy* sculpture perfectly captures the stance of Kingston's streetside newspaper vendors. Even more forcefully realistic is Dawn Scott's *A Cultural Object*, a spooky and powerful recreation of a Kingston ghetto, complete with Kisco cake wrappers, juice boxes, sound-system party posters and political graffiti. The work leads gallery visitors in ever-decreasing circles through graffiti-splattered corrugated tin alleys to a disturbing climax.

Look out, also, for the funky colours of Rastafarian Everald Brown (1917–2002) in spiritual works such as *Ethiopian Apple*. The religious theme is also seen in Karl Parboosingh's *Confrontation* and *Man with Abeng*, Gloria Escoffery's *Church Street*, and Ralph Campbell's black Christ and disciples in *Sea of Galilee*. An entire room houses the **Larry Wirth Collection** of African-style sculpture and paintings by Revivalist Shepherd Mallica "Kapo" Reynolds that depict themes from the Revivalist faith. As well as the hordes of beautiful wood sculptures, particularly striking are paintings *Watching Over Me* and *Peaceful Quietness*.

Downstairs, the **A.D. Scott Collection** displays a selection of Edna Manley's sculptures alongside some of the finest works of the island's biggest names. Highlights include Barrington Watson's *Banana Loaders*, beautifully capturing the toiling banana workers in Post-Impressionist style.

The rest of the permanent collection is rotated from time to time. It includes a modern photographic display; a pre-twentieth-century exhibit, with its series of landscapes by itinerant European painters; and an international collection featuring the work of such diverse artists as modern Cuban painters and the English Bloomsbury Group. You can ask to see works that are in storage if you've a special interest.

Just north of the gallery on Orange Street, the tiny **African–Caribbean Heritage Centre** (Mon–Thurs 9am–5.30pm, Fri 9am–3.30pm; free) is a library and small art gallery run by the Institute of Jamaica. It's also the home of the **Memory Bank,** an archive of oral histories collected in order to preserve Jamaica's folk traditions. Temporary cultural exhibitions are occasionally staged here, and the centre puts on regular events, from dance to lectures; call ☏ 922 4793 or visit ⓦ www.instituteofjamaica.org.jm/ACIJ for details.

Further north past the noisy Parade, Orange Street holds some of the city's best **record shops** (see p.106). They're essential stops if you're looking to pick up Jamaican vinyl past and present.

The Craft Market

The **Craft Market** (closed Sun), housed in an unprepossessing iron building at the western end of Ocean Boulevard, is all that's left of the formidable market that for centuries was held at the bottom of nearby King Street. Originally a Sunday market drawing thousands of slaves on their day off, it got shunted a few hundred yards west during the 1960s' redevelopment of the waterfront. Shopping here is generally a hassle-free experience, and you'll find loads of little stores selling T-shirts, carvings, jewellery and other souvenirs – some of the stock appears marvellously antiquated. Unlike most places, though, it's not a good place to bargain, as prices remain the lowest on the island.

The Parade and around

Opposite Edna Manley's *Negro Aroused* statue, King Street runs north to the **Parade**, a large square left open by the original city planners and used as a parade ground by British troops during the eighteenth century. It was also the site of public floggings and hangings – most famously the hanging of the slave hired to assassinate Venezuelan independence leader Simon Bolivar during his visit to the island in 1818. (The slave failed, but perished for trying.) Until recently, this was one of the busiest spots in town. Traffic still races around the central park, crowds mill around the taxi rank and the bus terminus, and music blares from radios and shop-front speakers, but the increasingly determined government initiative to remove the **vendors** who've traditionally hawked their wares in the street here has left Parade with a rather forlorn air. The authorities argue that the roadside displays of counterfeit designer wear, toys, shoes, tapes, and sundry miscellany obstruct the free passage of pedestrians. It's true that you can certainly move more easily around the area these days, but the absence of the vendors' entertaining sales pitches and tottering piles of goods means a less colorful scene – and a dilemma for those who've been made unemployed. Unwilling to decamp to newly constructed markets, which they say are unsafe – with only one entrance and exit, they'd become deathtraps in the event of an outburst of the gang warfare downtown is notorious for – the vendors feel they've been left high and dry. Demonstrations against the policy have been vociferous, and in early 2003, vendor Basil Brown was shot dead by the police after he allegedly drew a machete while being asked to move on from his regular pitch in front of Devon House. It was a tragic incident in what some see as a rather misguided deployment of police resources in this crime-raddled city.

In the middle of the Parade is **St William Grant Park**, originally Victoria Park but renamed in 1977 for the 1930s' leader of the infant Jamaican trade union movement. Cynically upstaged by the more charismatic Alexander Bustamante, Grant ended his life as a security guard for the Ministry of Social Security. Rather fierce statues of political rivals Norman Manley and Alexander Bustamante guard the park's north and south entrances, while Queen Victoria – the one-time "Supreme Lady of Jamaica" – stands to the east, looking a little lost among all the mayhem. There's an elaborate fountain in the centre of the park, prettily illuminated at night.

Just north of the park on North Parade, looking like an elaborately iced birthday cake, the elegant **Ward Theatre** occupies a site with a long theatrical tradition. It is reckoned that public performances have been staged here since at least the mid-eighteenth century and probably earlier. The Theatre Royal building, which originally stood on this spot, was destroyed in the 1907 earthquake. The present building, bestowed on the city by one-time Custos and rum baron Colonel Charles Ward, dates from 1911. It now hosts an annual **pantomime** every December and regular music and dance shows throughout the year; for more on these, see p.105. If you want to poke around, the building is normally open.

On South Parade, just below the park, the **Kingston Parish Church** was first built in 1699, although little of the present structure pre-dates the 1907 earthquake. Airy and spacious, the church is used for important state funerals and such, although the regular congregation has dwindled to almost nothing due to migration out of the downtown area. The south wall has a marvellously wordy elegy to midshipman Edward Baker, who died in 1796 in a sea battle off Santo Domingo, and there are plenty of marble monuments by John Bacon to such notables as British Admiral John Benbow, and John Wolmer, founder of Wolmer's School (see p.91). An eloquent testament to colonialism hangs on the west wall, where plaques honour soldiers of the West Indian regiment who died (mostly of fever) on unheard-of campaigns in West Africa in the 1890s.

Queen Street runs west and east of the park. To the west, **Jubilee Market** (Mon–Sat) spills over into **Coronation Market (same days)**, the island's biggest, busiest, and loudest – an experience even if you're not here to buy. Coronation has a distinctly chaotic feel: tattered tarpaulins flap over piles of everything from home-made graters fashioned from nail-punched tin cans to washing powder, underpants and, of course, artistically displayed produce amongst a backdrop of vegetable peelings and discarded corn husks. The dingy indoor section, its iron roof beams festooned with impressively abundant cobwebs, is laced by alleys patrolled by customers prodding, poking and bargaining. The sales banter of the vendors is always a joy; you'll need your wits about you to keep up with it. Backing onto the fringes of the volatile Tivoli Gardens area, Coronation is not a traditional tourist spot, and is best experienced in the company of someone who knows where he or she is going and can keep you out of the way of the wildly steered pushcarts that weave though the shoppers.

Tuff Gong and Culture Yard

If you're a Bob Marley devotee, you might want to jump in a taxi and head west of the markets via Temple Lane, along Port Royal Street and its western continuation Marcus Garvey Drive, a battered but wide thoroughfare lined with warehouses and factories. At 220 Marcus Garvey Dr you'll find the state-of-the-art **Tuff Gong Recording Studios** (daily, no set hours; ⊕923 9383, ⓦwww.bobmarley-foundation.com), established by Bob Marley and now staffed, in part, by members of his family, including Ziggy of Melody Makers' fame. A pressing plant and re-mastering facility, it's a commercial venture rather than a tourist site. But nonetheless, you can **tour** the facility (J$120; 45 min) to see the self-same mixing board used on Wailers' classics such as *Stir It Up*, *Concrete Jungle* and *No Woman, No Cry*. If the studios are in use, you may not get access to all areas – it's up to whoever's recording. While not wildly exciting, it's a nice stop for Marley disciples, with a gift shop for that essential CD or souvenir.

North of Marcus Garvey Drive spread the notorious ghetto communities of West Kingston: Tivoli Gardens, Denham Town, Jones Town and **Trench Town**. Eulogized in *Trench Town Rock* and lamented in *Concrete Jungle*, Trench Town was the first Kingston home of Bob Marley, who earned his nickname – the "Tuff Gong" – on the area's mean streets after his mother relocated to the capital when he was a small boy. She moved him into government-built tenement yards first on Second Street, and then on First Street. Trench Town is as infamous for its garrison politics and gang warfare (for more on which, see p.86) as it is for having spawned some of the biggest names in the reggae pantheon (Joe Higgs and Alton Ellis to name just two). It remains a harsh place to live, its inhabitants crammed into crumbling zinc-fenced yards along streets that are often impassable due to roadblocks set up by residents to deter drive-by shootings, but nonetheless is a vibrant, proud and creative community that holds an edgy allure for anyone with a serious interest in the roots of Jamaican culture.

Though Trench Town is still one of Jamaica's most impoverished areas, the picture isn't entirely bleak. In the last few years, enterprising members of this tight-knit community have clubbed together to find ways in which to regenerate their area. The first initiative was the establishment, in 1993, of the

Kingston's ghettos

Kingston's **ghetto communities** are the country's urban nightmare. Bob Marley sang fondly of growing up in the "government yards in Trench Town", but the reality is a huge underclass confined to crowded, makeshift tenement yards enclosed by rusting, graffiti-daubed zinc, their communities bearing suitably apocalyptic names, from Dunkirk and Jungle to Tel Aviv and Zimbabwe. Taking up huge swathes of downtown Kingston, both east and west (and some, such as Standpipe, located on the fringes of uptown Liguanea), Kingston's ghettos have seen some sporadic clean-up and regeneration campaigns, but it's an endless – and expensive – task.

In the city's early years, downtown Kingston was a popular residential zone – well laid out and central. In the twentieth century, though, an exodus of the wealthy to districts uptown led to downtown Kingston's decline, and a subsequent influx of the less well-off – men and women from rural Jamaica who headed for Kingston's bright lights but were unable to find either work or welfare. Crowded together, the very worst-off built their makeshift homes on the "**Dungle**" (dunghill) by Kingston harbour, where all the city's excrement was dumped before the introduction of a sewage system. There, they fought with each other, as well as with the dogs and vultures, for scraps of garbage from the dustcarts.

Criminal elements were quick to take advantage of the conditions, recruiting and arming gang members from the ranks of the poor, especially young men looking for the identity and protection offered by allegiance to a "posse". Robbery and drug sales brought in money and, with it, a measure of street credibility. The crime problem was exacerbated in the **1970s** as politicians provided guns and favours (including the construction of housing schemes, such as Edward Seaga's Tivili Gardens) for their supporters, asking them to intimidate – at the very least – opponents or drive them out of their "**garrisons**" or constituencies. The "PNP zone" or "JLP enter at your own risk" graffiti plastered over downtown walls stands testament to the strong political allegiances of the communities, many of which remain divided along political lines. During the worst of the violence in the 1980s, countless Jamaicans were murdered for wearing the "wrong" colour clothing (PNP is orange, JLP green) or simply ordering a "Labourite" Heineken beer or a "PNP" Red Stripe in a rival area.

While political violence still flares up at election times – 43 people died in the

---

Trench Town Reading Centre on First Street (mobile ☎301 8194, Ⓦwww.trenchtownreadingcentre.com), a library and resource centre with a mission to arm local people with information rather than weapons. By 1996, the aim had widened, and the **Trench Town Development Association** (TDA; ☎757 6739 or 922 8462) was formed to address the pressing issues of sanitation, security, housing, health and employment. On February 6, 2000 (the anniversary of Marley's birthday), in a ceremony presided over by Britain's Prince Charles, the TDA's Seventh Street offices were opened in conjunction with the inauguration of the **Culture Yard** (daily, no set hours; US$10), set in the tenement where Marley spent much of his youth. Marked by an "Iyabinghi" banner proclaiming the "oneness of the Trench Town community – United We Stand, Divided We Fall" – the Lower First Street centre is a museum in the making, with a few pieces of Marley memorabilia in the main office. After a look at resident artist Stoneman's found sculptures and rocks, whose markings are interpreted with much biblical significance, you progress to the yard's central open-air courtyard, where residents would formerly have cooked, washed clothes and socialized. The remains of Marley's powder-blue VW van lie rusting in a corner, and you can go into some of the tiny rooms that surround the courtyard, including the one in which Marley wrote *No Woman, No*

run-up to the 2002 poll – the people of the ghettos, like the rest of the population, have largely washed their hands of a system that seems to have done them no long-term favours despite the years of promises. Instead, many prefer to give their allegiance to high-profile "area leaders" or "**dons**"; the biggest names at present are east Kingston's Christopher Lloyd Coke, aka **Dudus**, son of (late) infamous original area don Jim Brown, and the diminutive Donald Phipps, or **Zekes**, brother of PNP MP Victor Cummings. These "enforcers", as they're sometimes referred to, earn the favour of their communities as much as by staging free "fun days" for local people and doling out school books and cash to the needy as through sheer fire power. Zekes is said to have initiated a kind of alternative justice system to police his downtown stronghold of Matthew's Lane, and both leaders regularly sponsor everything from community football teams to school-building programmes. Nonetheless, the ghettos remain violent places to live, with army-enforced night-time **curfews** in place for months on end, and so many drive-by shootings that residents routinely block roads with debris in an attempt to prevent the "shottas", or gunmen, from entering.

Since the establishment of the garrisons in the 1970s and 1980s, dons have been able to establish ever stronger and more extensive empires that are now profitable enough for their political allegiances to take a lower profile. It's estimated that some 100 metric tonnes of cocaine pass through Jamaica annually, generating US$3 million each year, and most Jamaicans believe that the dons, in addition to the high-ranking police and customs officers who smooth the drug's progress through the island, take a cut from the profits. In addition to this, both Zekes and Dudus run **protection rackets** in the capital, said to be worth some US$10 million annually. Given the amounts of money involved, it seems unlikely that the government will have much success in its recent efforts to curtail the dons' influence by way of regenerating the ghettos. For the time being, Zekes, Dudus and their compatriots appear to be here to stay.

Laurie Gunst's book *Born Fi Dead* (see *Contexts*, p.435) provides a gripping explanation of the development of Jamaican posse culture in Kingston and the US, while *Third World Cop* and Perry Henzell's *The Harder They Come* (see *Contexts*, p.427 & 430) provide a cinematic perspective on ghetto life.

Cry alongside Vincent "Tata" Ford. As there's not much to the museum itself, you'll probably want to pay another $5 to take a tour of the area, passing the reading centre and newly constructed school, and knocking on a few doors to get some authentic Trench Town history from area elders. A craft shop and restaurant are planned when funding allows (so far, the Yard has had assistance from the Franciscan Ministries and the tourist board's TPDCO, but no support from the Bob Marley Foundation). Donations of cash, equipment or expertise are gratefully accepted; call the Yard or the TDA, or write to PO Box 118, Kingston 5.

While your safety is pretty assured in and around the Culture Yard, Trench Town itself remains a volatile community, and getting to First Street presents something of a dilemma. It's not a good idea to drive a rental car into the area. Instead, call ahead to arrange transportation from Half Way Tree (around J$100) or take a taxi, though you may have a hard job persuading drivers to venture this far into the ghetto. It's also worth keeping an ear out for reports of trouble in the area; if things seem to be hotting up, you may want to reconsider visiting. Don't carry too much money with you – though if you take a tour of the area, you'll probably want enough to tip the guide and his or her entourage. It's also a good idea to start early, as you don't want to be touring here after dark. But you'll be fine if you come for the night-time concert that's staged here around the time of the Marley birthday celebrations.

Coke Chapel and around

Back in central downtown Kingston, east of the markets and in the northeast corner of the Parade, the large red-brick **Coke Chapel** is a Methodist church that dates from 1840. It was erected over the remains of a smaller eighteenth-century chapel built by Thomas Coke, an early missionary. Methodism, along with other nonconformist religions, played an important role in Jamaica, its missionaries actively fighting for improvements in the conditions of slaves and, eventually, against slavery itself. Because of this, the Methodist church found itself in conflict with the Jamaican authorities and, like others, the Coke Chapel was ordered to close for several years in the early nineteenth century. There's little to see in the rather spartan interior, but it's a quiet retreat from the sun and the crowds. The caretaker can usually be found nearby with a key – ask at the little shop in the compound.

Just south of Coke Chapel on Mark Lane, the bizarre octagonal **St Andrews Scots Kirk** was founded in the early nineteenth century by local merchants of Scottish ancestry. The St Andrews Cross can still be detected in the church's stained-glass window. If you want to have a look around, the resident caretaker has the key.

The Institute of Jamaica

Four blocks east of Coke Chapel, East Street runs south to the **Institute of Jamaica** (IOJ; Mon–Thurs 9am–5pm, Fri 9am–4pm; free; ⓦ www.instituteof-jamaica.org.jm). Here you'll find the **National Library** (ⓦ www.nlj.org.jm), home to the best collection of books and old newspapers in the country, and the eminently missable **National Museum** (entrance round the corner on Tower St; J$100) of Jamaica's natural history. Alongside the ranks of musty cabinets filled with dust-gathering stuffed birds, one of the more interesting displays explains the origins of the country's most important "economic plants" – sugarcane, bananas, coconuts and pineapples. Almost all imported from areas of Asia during the early years of Spanish and British colonialism, they are now widely grown for export. The museum has plenty of other interesting odds and ends – Taino *zemis*, African jewellery, old musical instruments – but, infuriatingly, these are only occasionally on display; most of the time they're mouldering away in the basement.

Lunchtime concerts, usually featuring reggae artists, are occasionally held at the IOJ on Thursdays at noon; call for details of what's on (☎ 922 0620).

Headquarters House and Gordon House

Two blocks west of East Street and just north of Parade, the fretworked Georgian edifice of **Headquarters House** on Duke Street (Mon–Fri 8.30am–4.30pm; free) affords a brief glimpse of Jamaican history. Built in 1755 by Thomas Hibbert, a wealthy local merchant, the house was part of a wager between four friends as to who could construct the most elegant building to impress a local woman. (Hibbert lost the bet, but the three other contenders are no longer in existence.) Jamaica's legislative assembly met here briefly in 1755 and moved in full time between 1872 and 1960. During the intervening years the house was commandeered by the armed forces to serve both as its military headquarters (hence the name) and as the residence of the local general in charge.

Today, Headquarters House is the home of the **Jamaica National Heritage Trust** (☎ 922 1287, ⓦ www.jnht.com). The trust offices are installed in the former bedrooms and on the now walled-in veranda, but it's usually possible to have someone take you around the rest of the house. The debating chamber, where the legislative assembly used to meet, is on the ground floor, filled with original furniture and a fine mahogany public gallery for visitors, and the walls hold large portraits of Jamaica's first political leaders and some of its National Heroes, including Sam Sharpe, Nanny and Paul Bogle (for more on these, see p.90). In the brick-built basement, the cool storage rooms contain more offbeat relics, including a bronze statue of Marcus Garvey. Dormer windows in the steamy attic afford good views over downtown Kingston, Port Royal and the Blue Mountains. From the lookout tower at the top of the building (no longer accessible due to the uncertain strength of the roof), Hibbert would watch his ships coming into the harbour, and later, the generals could keep an eye on any enemy boat movements. Behind the main house is an array of outbuildings, including servants' quarters and stables, which, at the time of writing, were undergoing a J$11.6 million restoration programme.

Next to Headquarters House is the rather less imposing **Gordon House**, a contemporary slab of concrete that's been home to the Jamaican parliament since 1960. It's named after national hero George William Gordon, a lay preacher who consistently advocated for the rights of the poor and proved a constant thorn in the side of the establishment. In 1865, the authorities arrested him for his nominal role in the Morant Bay Rebellion (for more on which, see p.152); he was arrested at Headquarters House and summarily executed, despite widespread protest from black Jamaicans. Today, the House of Representatives meets here most Tuesdays at 2pm (and at the same time on Wednesdays and Thursdays if there is sufficient business), while the Senate sits in the chamber on Fridays at 11am. At these times, surrounding streets are sometimes cordoned off. Entrance to the public gallery is free, and when the chamber is empty you can ask the marshal to show you around. The debates are normally pretty soporific for spectators, though you might want to catch political veterans like the Jamaican Labour Party's Edward Seaga in action.

The Jewish Synagogue

The striking white building on the opposite side of Duke Street above Gordon House is the **Jewish Synagogue**. It's kept locked, but you can normally find the caretaker on the premises during the week; you'll need to pay a small donation for him to open the place up. Jews were among the first Europeans to settle in Jamaica during the sixteenth century, fleeing the Inquisition in Spain. Even here, though, they were still obliged to practise their religion in secret, a fact remembered today by the sand scattered on the floor of the modern building, which symbolically muffles your footsteps as you wander around.

In 1882, the synagogues of the two Jewish congregations in Kingston, the Ashkenhazi and the Sephardic, were both destroyed by fire and an amalgamated synagogue was built on this site (although a handful of rebel members of each congregation refused to mix and went off to found their own synagogues). The present building dates from after the 1907 earthquake, with substantial repairs effected after Hurricane Gilbert in 1988. The exodus of Jamaica's Jews, both from downtown Kingston and from the island (part of the general flight of whites during the 1970s), means that the present congregation is tiny. But the building, with its mahogany staircase and gallery, is still worth a visit if you're passing.

East of Duke Street

A couple of blocks east of the synagogue, the **Gleaner Building** (closed to visitors) on the corner of North and East Streets holds the offices of the *Gleaner* and *Star* newspapers (ⓦwww.jamaica-gleaner.com). The *Gleaner* has reported on events in Jamaica since it was founded as *de Cordova's Advertiser* in 1834. Never afraid to voice its strident opinions, and particularly scathing during the first administration of Michael Manley, the paper remains the most influential and widely read of the country's dailies. Five minutes' walk further east along North Street will bring you to the Catholic Church's large-domed **Holy Trinity Cathedral**. A caretaker is supposed to guard the premises, but don't hold out too much hope of finding him there, or the cathedral open, except during services. During term-time, hundreds of schoolchildren mill around the area, spilling out of nearby high schools **Kingston College** and **St George's College**, the latter founded by the Jesuits in 1850.

Just around the corner from the cathedral is **Sabina Park**, home of the Kingston Cricket Club. The oldest sports club in the Commonwealth Caribbean, it's the venue for international test matches and many of the inter-island games. Even if you're not a cricket fan, attending a match here – particularly an international test – is an unmissable experience. Several ticket categories are available, from the bleachers, where you can immerse yourself in the colourful crowd commentary, to the all-inclusive Red Stripe Mound, home of the hard-core partyers, where the beer and rum flow and speakers blare out between overs. Call ⓣ967 0322 for tickets, and see *Basics*, p.53, for more on cricket.

National Heroes Park and around

A ten-minute walk north of the Gleaner Building, **National Heroes Park** is a large stretch of scrubby, sun-bleached grass enclosed by iron railings. If you're

Jamaica's National Heroes

Since independence, the Jamaican parliament has elevated seven of the island's greatest people to the status of **National Hero**, all of whom carry the title "The Right Excellent". As yet, none of the Heroes hail from the worlds of sport or music, but it is widely anticipated that Bob Marley will be next to join the pantheon. Michael Manley, who died in 1997, is another popular candidate. The present National Heroes are:

Paul Bogle (unknown–1865). Baptist preacher who led the 1865 Morant Bay Rebellion and was executed for his participation.

Alexander Bustamante (1884–1977). Labour leader, founder of the Jamaica Labour Party and first prime minister of the independent country from 1962 to 1967.

Marcus Garvey (1887–1940). Founder of the Universal Negro Improvement Association and widely viewed as the father of the black power movement.

George William Gordon (1820–65). "Free coloured" leader of Jamaica's nationalist movement after slavery, executed by the British for his part in the Morant Bay Rebellion.

Norman Manley (1893–1969). Lawyer, founder of the People's National Party and leader of Jamaica's movement for independence.

Nanny (birth and death years unknown). Legendary eighteenth-century female leader of the Windward Maroons in their battles with the English.

Sam Sharpe (1801–32). Baptist preacher executed after leading the 1831 slave rebellion in Jamaica's western parishes.

on foot it offers a chance to escape the traffic that hammers around it, but it's not a place for a promenade these days; its proximity to the volatile Vineyard Town community means that it's favoured more by grazing goats than casual strollers. The park held the city's racecourse for more than a century before it got shifted to the safer New Kingston, and from there to its present location west of the city at Caymanas Park. After independence, the government converted the southern portion of what was then the George IV Memorial Park into a monument to Jamaica's **National Heroes** (see box). Patrolled by gun-toting soldiers and guarded by two po-faced JDF sentries sweltering in full ceremonial uniform (there's a foot-stomping changing of the guard each hour), it feels a lot less hairy than it has in the past.

Norman Manley, Alexander Bustamante and Marcus Garvey are buried beneath the futuristic Shrine of Monuments – a series of stone, marble and bronze memorial busts and figures dedicated to each of the Heroes – at the south end of the park. Other local luminaries buried here include entertainer Ranny Williams, artist and Revivalist preacher Mallica "Kapo" Reynolds, and former prime ministers Donald Sangster and **Michael Manley**. The latter lies outside of the main area below a soaring monument that's "surging upwards toward a perfect state" and inscribed with quotations from the man himself, such as "Equality is nothing without freedom". Almost adjacent is the grave of reggae star **Dennis Brown**, who died on June 1, 1999, from respiratory failure associated with his long-term battle with cocaine addiction. The "Crown Prince of Reggae" was one of Jamaica's most prolific and best-loved artists, and his simple headstone reads "sadly missed". Adjacent to the main Heroes' plots is a bust of Antonio Maceo and a statue of Simon Bolivar, independence leaders in Cuba and Venezuela respectively, and inspirational to Jamaica's early nationalists. Bolivar was exiled to Jamaica for a year in 1814 following his unsuccessful revolt against Spanish rule in Venezuela. Whilst here, he survived an assassination attempt by the Spanish and penned his "Letter from Jamaica", in which he laid out the reasoning behind his struggle for South American liberation.

At the south end of the park, on the opposite pavement at the corner of New North Street, stalls sell boiled corn and land crab, and roast yam and saltfish. At the north end of the park, on Marescaux Road, are the colourful wooden buildings of **Wolmers High School** and **Mico College**. Wolmers, founded in 1729, has proved a formidable centre of academic achievement, counting prime ministers and governor generals among its alumni. Nearby Mico, the largest teacher-training school in the West Indies, owes its foundation in 1834 to the eleventh-hour refusal of Englishman Samuel Mico to marry one of the six nieces of his aunt, Lady Mico, back in 1670. The intended dowry was invested for a number of charitable purposes and eventually used to found teacher-training colleges in various parts of the Caribbean. Dedicated to "liberating minds from the bondage of ignorance", Mico was founded to fund education for newly emancipated Africans and was one of the only colleges in Jamaica that operated on non-racial grounds.

Inside the main Mico College building is a **museum** (Mon–Fri 9am–4.30pm; J$100; ☎929 5260) with a section on Mico's history as well as the excellent INAFCA (Indian, African and Caribbean Artefacts) collection, donated by old Miconian Dr Aston Taylor, which includes spears, shields, sculptures and masks. If you want a guided tour of the museum and the college – at no additional charge – you'll need to book a day in advance.

East of here on Camp Road are the headquarters of the island's army, the Jamaica Defence Force (JDF), and the notorious **Gun Court**. Established in 1972, during the early years of Michael Manley's first administration, to deal with the proliferating number of firearms offences, the place is still a harsh prison, protected by high-security fences and reams of barbed wire. The hugely busy **Cross Roads**, a quarter of a mile above Mico and the dividing line between uptown and downtown, marks the intersection where Kingston's principal roads – Half Way Tree Road, Slipe Road, Caledonia Avenue/South Camp Road, and Old Hope Road – meet. There's little to it other than a busy market and the **Carib Theatre**, the city's oldest cinema, which has been lavishly rebuilt after a catastrophic fire destroyed it in 1996.

Uptown

The phrase "uptown Kingston" is used as a catch-all for areas of the city north of Cross Roads, including the business and commercial centres of **Half Way Tree** and **New Kingston** as well as residential areas like **Hope Pastures Mona** and **Beverly Hills**. Up until the late eighteenth century, uptown was mostly rural, sprinkled with livestock farms (known as "pens") and sugar estates. Gradually, as Kingston's wealthy merchants acquired this land in a bid to escape from the noise and crowds downtown, the city began to spill out of its original waterfront site. The process has accelerated during the past half-century, and newer and more fashionable districts have been created further and further north of the old city, extending right across the old Liguanea Plain and into the foothills of the Blue Mountains.

The "heart" of uptown Kingston, running between Oxford and Trafalgar roads and known as **the "Strip"**, is Knutsford Boulevard, home to the city's largest hotels, a glut of restaurants and nightclubs, and the spanking new **Emancipation Park**, a breezy, manicured open space that commemorates the end of slavery. Away from the Strip, most visitors make a beeline for the **Bob Marley Museum** and the colonial-era **Devon House**, both just above New Kingston on the traffic-crazed Hope Road, uptown's central thoroughfare. Further east are the soothing **Hope Botanical Gardens** and Mona, home to the capacious **University of the West Indies** campus. To the north, the main arteries fan out into the Blue Mountains and the ritzy suburbs of Red Hills, Stony Hill and Jack's Hill.

New Kingston

The heart of uptown is the high-rise financial district of **New Kingston**, found in an eccentric triangle bounded by Trafalgar Road, Old Hope Road and Half Way Tree Road. In the early twentieth century this was an attractive grassy area, the location of the Liguanea Golf Club and later, briefly, the Knutsford Park racetrack. During the 1950s and 1960s, with the commercial areas of downtown getting increasingly choked and congested, the city planners decided to create a new self-contained business district here. The horse racing moved west to Caymanas Park, the Liguanea Club contracted, and bank, hotel and office buildings started to shoot up.

The chances are that you will **stay** and do much of your **eating** and **drinking** in or around this area; some of the interesting sights are within walking distance, the rest are a short bus or taxi ride away. There are few places of note in New Kingston itself, although the **Liguanea Club**, opposite the *Jamaica Pegasus* hotel on Knutsford Boulevard, still retains its old colonial buildings as well as lots of lovely tennis courts (available for hire). In theory the club is open to members only, but it's easily accessible if you're passing. The building served as the fictional Queens Club, where James Bond took cocktails on the veranda with Professor Dent in the classic movie *Dr No*. It's sometimes used for outdoor parties these days.

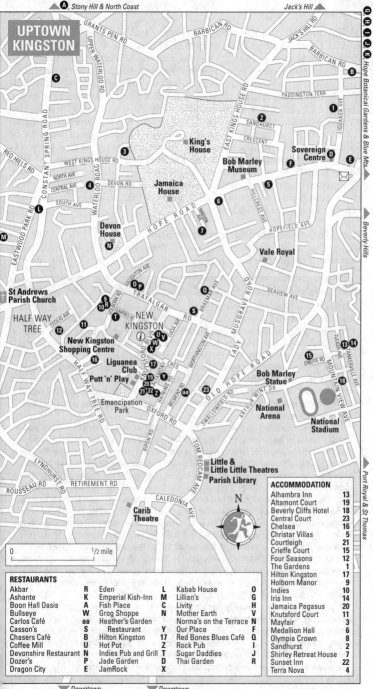

UPTOWN KINGSTON

Stony Hill & North Coast

Jack's Hill

G H I J K Hope Botanical Gardens & Blue Mts.

GRANTS PEN RD

BARBICAN RD

JACK'S HILL RD

BARBICAN RD

UPPER WATERLOO RD

PADDINGTON TERR

LIGUANEA AVE

SANDHURST CRESCENT

King's House

EAST KINGS HOUSE RD

Bob Marley Museum

Sovereign Centre

RED HILLS RD

CONSTANT SPRING ROAD

WEST KINGS HOUSE RD

NORTH AVE

CENTRAL AVE

SOUTH AVE

WATERLOO ROAD

DEVON RD

Jamaica House

HOPE ROAD

MARLEY AVE

HILLCREST AVE

HOPEFIELD AVE

Beverly Hills

EASTWOOD PARK RD

Devon House

Vale Royal

St Andrews Parish Church

HAUGHTON AVE

HALF WAY TREE

CECILIO AVE

TRAFALGAR RD

BRAEMAR AVE

SEAVIEW AVE

NEW KINGSTON

LUCAS AVE

MUSGRAVE ROAD

LADY

New Kingston Shopping Centre

HALF WAY TREE RD

KNUTSFORD BLVD

WORTHINGTON AVE

Liguanea Club

Putt 'n' Play

Emancipation Park

ALTAMONT CRES

BELMONT RD

HANING RD

OLD HOPE ROAD

Bob Marley Statue

CRIEFFE RD

TUCKER AVE

ANKERVILLE AVE

MOUNTAIN VIEW AVE

OXFORD RD

SWALLOWFIELD RD

ARTHUR WINT DR

National Arena

National Stadium

LYNDHURST RD

RETIREMENT RD

ROUSSEAU RD

RIPON RD

TOM REDCAM AVE

Little & Little Little Theatres

Parish Library

CALEDONIA AVE

Carib Theatre

N

0   ½ mile

Port Royal & St Thomas

Downtown   Downtown

ACCOMMODATION

Alhambra Inn	13
Altamont Court	19
Beverly Cliffs Hotel	18
Central Court	23
Chelsea	16
Christar Villas	5
Courtleigh	21
Crieffe Court	15
Four Seasons	12
The Gardens	1
Hilton Kingston	17
Holborn Manor	9
Indies	10
Iris Inn	14
Jamaica Pegasus	20
Knutsford Court	11
Mayfair	3
Medallion Hall	6
Olympia Crown	8
Sandhurst	2
Shirley Retreat House	7
Sunset Inn	22
Terra Nova	4

RESTAURANTS

Akbar	R	Eden	L	Kabab House	O
Ashante	K	Emperial Kish-Inn	M	Lillian's	C
Boon Hall Oasis	A	Fish Place	C	Livity	G
Bullseye	W	Grog Shoppe	N	Mother Earth	V
Carlos Café	aa	Heather's Garden		Norma's on the Terrace	F
Casson's	S	Restaurant	Y	Our Place	Q
Chasers Café	B	Hilton Kingston	17	Red Bones Blues Café	I
Coffee Mill	U	Hot Pot	Z	Rock Pub	J
Devonshire Restaurant	P	Indies Pub and Grill	T	Sugar Daddies	J
Dozer's	E	Jade Garden	D	Thai Garden	R
Dragon City	E	JamRock	X		

A little further down Knutsford, the concrete buildings give way to the open space of **Emancipation Park**, opened in 2002 as a memorial to the cessation of slavery in Jamaica in 1838. It's a manicured and well-maintained space, with more concrete than grass, piped jazz from speakers ensconced in fake boulders, a jogging track, a concert stage and a marvellous – though controversially nude – sculpture, **Redemption Song**, by local woman Laura-Facey Cooper. Though it's a nice spot to take a breather in the daytime, it comes into its own at night, when couples canoodle and families turn out to promenade and gaze at the central "sky cascade" fountain, its ever-changing jets of water lit by coloured lights to delightful effect. If you're here in the evening or at the weekend, you might want to head across the boundary road to **Putt 'n' Play** (Mon–Thurs 5–11pm, Fri 5pm–midnight, Sat & Sun 11am–midnight; US$6). It's a prettily landscaped 18-hole mini-golf course that attracts a healthy clique of Kingston teenagers after dark, and families at the weekends. There's usually a lively crowd at the bar and restaurant.

The National Stadium and around

Just east of New Kingston on Arthur Wint Drive, the 40,000 capacity **National Stadium**, known to sports fans as "The Office", hosts most of

Jamaica at the Olympics

Although, like other West Indian islands, Jamaica is world-famous for its cricket, it also has a tremendous record of achievement in other sports, particularly **athletics**. The country first entered the **Olympic Games** in 1948 when it was still a British colony. Arthur Wint and Herb McKinley took gold and silver in the 400 metres, and Wint picked up silver in the 800 metres. That record of achievement, remarkable for such a small country, has been kept up over the years, with sprinters like **Don Quarrie** and **Merlene Ottey** winning medals and acquiring a devoted following in the process. The success of Jamaican-born athletes who have run under the flag of other countries – Britain's Linford Christie is just one example – has only enhanced the country's reputation.

Two explanations are usually given for Jamaica's athletic excellence. First, success in athletics (as in most sports) offers a quick way out of the ghetto. A case in point is Merlene Ottey, born and raised in a poor rural village, who became *the* role model for many young Jamaican women. Although her usually exemplary conduct took an international knocking after she tested positive for the banned steroid nandrolone in July 1999, Ottey's reputation at home remained relatively unscathed. Most Jamaicans insisted that she'd been treated erroneously, and that the presence of nandrolone in her sample was down to a natural excess caused by her menstrual cycle combined with traces of the substance contained in a supplement she was taking. The fans' suspicions were confirmed when Ottey was cleared by the Jamaican Athletics Federation in November 1999. The International Association of Athletics Federations (IAAF) ban was lifted in June 2000, clearing the way for her to participate in the Sydney Olympics. (Ottey didn't clinch any medals, but Deon Hemmings brought home the silver for the women's 400-metre hurdles, as did Lorraine Graham in the 400-metre sprint.)

A second explanation for why Jamaicans excel in athletics is the vision of political leaders such as **Norman Manley** – who himself held a sprinting record in schoolboy athletics for over forty years. They made sure that young athletes were given top-class facilities, particularly the National Stadium, and the opportunity to compete for track scholarships to colleges in North America. This approach has been used by many Jamaican athletes as a springboard to international success.

Jamaica's premier sporting events. The stadium was built to coincide with Jamaica's independence celebrations in 1962; the first event here was the raising of the new nation's black, green and gold flag, followed soon after by the 1962 Commonwealth Games. The facilities for athletics and cycling are first-rate, but the centerpiece is the recently refurbished football pitch, surrounded by towering aisles of bleachers and overlooked by arc lights. The home of Jamaica's Reggae Boyz, the stadium comes alive when there's a game on. If the national team are playing, it's usually packed to capacity – Air Jamaica planes fly low overhead, and the shouts of "GOAAALLLL" can be heard across town. For information on tickets, call ☏929 4970. Just inside the railings by the car park is a statue of Jamaican athlete Herb McKinley coming off the starting blocks; at the 1952 Helsinki Olympics, McKinley became the first man in the world to run in the 200-, 400- and 800-metre races (see box opposite). A smaller stadium, for minor events, is adjacent.

The **National Arena** next door houses smaller-scale sporting events and other shows. There are plans to convert the grassy area opposite into a **Celebrity Park**, with statues of the island's leading names, but at present only a slightly mournful figure of Bob Marley, by local sculptor Alvin Marriot, stands by the road, while the back wall is decorated with murals of Jamaica's sporting heroes. The hills to the east of the complex house Jamaica's **Beverly Hills**, almost as affluent as the Los Angeles suburb it was named after. Once the first-choice neighbourhood for wealthy Kingstonians, it saw an exodus of the rich during Michael Manley's socialist 1970s administration. Manley's famous comment that there were five planes a day to Miami and that anyone who didn't like his policies should get on one, was taken to heart by those with the most to lose, and many of Beverly Hills' swankiest homes were swiftly deserted. Those brave enough to remain snapped up the properties, and it's often said that many of the newer homes were built by drug money. Nonetheless, the area still provides stunning **views** across the city and out to sea, which are best seen by taking a trip along Beverly Terrace/Montclair Drive from Old Hope Road.

Further south from the National Arena, on Tom Redcam Avenue, the squat, wooden **Little Theatre** was built in 1961 to house the Little Theatre Movement (LTM), which from its inception in 1942 pioneered organized theatre in Kingston. The theatre hosts the LTM's annual pantomime as well as seasons by the globally recognized National Dance Theatre Company and the Jamaican Folk Singers. The wooden memorial outside is to Greta Fowler, energetic founder of the LTM, while the small building next door is the site of the innovative **Little Little Theatre**, where the works of modern Jamaican playwrights are given an airing. For more on performances, see p.105. The unimposing **Parish Library** (Mon–Fri 9am–6pm, Sat 9am–5pm; free), half a block further down Tom Redcam Drive, has an expansive, if somewhat disorganized, West Indian collection, and visitors can borrow books on payment of a small deposit.

Half Way Tree

On the other side of New Kingston, a mile or so away, is the congested area known as **Half Way Tree**. Before it got swallowed up by the expanding city, Half Way Tree was a tiny village and the capital of the parish of St Andrew. Its central plaza – today a busy shopping area and one of Kingston's key road intersections – once provided a resting place for farmers travelling into the city's markets. The eponymous cotton tree under which they sheltered is long gone, and a clock tower (with a non-functioning timepiece) now stands in its place, a 1913 memorial to British King Edward VII. With back-to-back traffic sweltering under the sun, vendors hawking anything from doughnuts to sound-system tapes, and queues of hungry workers standing in line at the pretty-pink *Tastee Patties* outlet, Half Way Tree today is about as far away from a resting place as it's possible to imagine.

A handful of restored colonial buildings stand near the square, the most notable of which is the red-brick **St Andrews Parish Church** (always open; free). Though largely submerged by the modern buildings that have arisen around it, this is still a tranquil and gently alluring edifice. Built in 1666, it's one of the oldest religious sites on the island, though the present model is the fourth incarnation, renovated (with typical Victorian vigour) in 1879 after earlier ones were wrecked by hurricane and earthquake. Grand Latin memorials in the floor date back to 1692, the marble tablets on the walls commemorate English soldiers and Jamaican civil servants, and there are some delicate stained-glass windows. Outside, the massive **graveyard**, with its crumbling tombs, ancient and modern, is a fascinating spot to kill some time if you don't mind the company of large numbers of goats.

Striking north from Half Way Tree, **Constant Spring Road** boasts Kingston's largest conglomeration of shopping malls; it's also the route to the cool greens of the Constant Spring Golf Course (see p.107).

Devon House

Fifteen minutes' walk east from Half Way Tree, the immaculate **Devon House** at 26 Hope Rd (Mon–Sat 9.30am–5pm, tours run throughout the day and last half an hour; J$200, including guided tour) was built in 1881 by Jamaica's first black millionaire and is still the grandest house in the city.

Born in Kingston in 1820, building contractor George Stiebel made his fortune mining gold in Venezuela, returning home in 1873 to snap up 99 properties throughout Jamaica (ownership of a hundred was prohibited by law). Among these was Devon Pen, where he built the house that was his Kingston home until he died in 1896. Bought by the Jamaican government in 1967, the house has gradually been furnished with West Indian and European antiques as well as more modern Jamaican reproductions. It makes for a diverting hour's exploration, despite the enforced tour, which can be rushed and monosyllabic – don't be afraid to take your time. Some eccentric pieces – a folding bagatelle table, unique porcelain chandeliers and an 1821 Broadwood piano – offset the obligatory portraits and rather predictable furniture. There are a couple of obituaries of Stiebel on display in the games rooms; look out also for the print of French Admiral de Grasse surrendering to Admiral Rodney after the crucial naval battle of les Saintes in 1782, which confirmed British naval superiority in the Caribbean.

The landscaped grounds of Devon House make a fine place for a leisurely stroll, with plenty of breezy benches and shady spots to while away the midday heat. You've a good chance of running into one of the numerous wedding parties who come here for their photos. The former stables now house a handful of gift shops stocking a good range of rather expensive ephemera. But chief attractions are the shop selling heavenly home-made "**I Scream**" (soursop and Guinness flavours are sublime), and the *Brick Oven* bakery, which sells excellent gooey cakes and some of Kingston's best patties. You can also get a decent sitdown lunch at the *Grog Shoppe*, which is not as painfully quaint as its name would suggest, or even afternoon tea or a gourmet meal at the elegant *Norma's on the Terrace*; p.102.

Rumour has it that nearby Lady Musgrave Road, which circuitously bypasses Devon House, was built at the request of the wife of Anthony Musgrave,

Jamaica's governor from 1874 to 1883, so that she could get to King's House (see below) without having to pass such a fine house owned by a black Jamaican.

Jamaica House and King's House

Guardhouses further up Hope Road from Devon House mark the entrances to **Jamaica House** (closed to visitors), used as the prime minister's office, and **King's House** (Mon–Fri by appointment; free; ☎927 6424), official residence of the governor general. (The governor general, the Queen of England's representative in Jamaica, has the notional powers of a head of state, although like the Queen, he retains only vestigial political authority.) You can get a tour of a few of the latter's rooms, including the ballroom, with its portraits of Jamaica's governors through the centuries, and the banqueting room, which has full-length portraits of Britain's George III and Queen Charlotte. Bond fans might want to note that King's House served as Government House in the first 007 movie, *Dr No*. A little south of here on Montrose Road, **Vale Royal** is the official residence of the prime minister but is closed to visitors.

The Bob Marley Museum

For reggae fans, the **Bob Marley Museum** at 56 Hope Rd (Mon–Sat 9.30am–5pm, tours every 20min, last tour at 4pm; U$10; ☎927 9152, Ⓦ www.bobmarley-foundation.com) is the whole point of a visit to Kingston. Even if you're not a serious devotee, it's worth an hour of your time – though don't expect a Disney-type theme-park ambience. Hidden from the street by a red-, gold- and green-painted wall and marked by fluttering Rasta banners, this was Marley's Kingston home from 1975 until his death from cancer in 1981. It's still much as it looked when he lived here, a gentle monument to Jamaica's greatest musical legend. The hour-long **tour** starts as soon as you pass through the gates (no photography, filming or taping is allowed, but you can leave equipment in safekeeping here). The guide usually points out the mural *The Journey of Bob Marley Superstar*, which decorates the outside wall, and Rasta artist Jah Bobby's colourful statue of Marley with his preferred guitar and football. **Inside** the house, you'll see stage dresses of the I-Threes, Marley's backing singers, and his own favoured denim stage shirt as well as the Grammy Lifetime Achievement Award, posthumously presented in 2001. A back room has a rather bizarre hologram of the man himself.

Upstairs, there is a re-creation of Wail 'n' Soul – Marley's tiny, shack-like Trench Town record shop, where he once hung out with band members Peter Tosh and Bunny Wailer – and a room wallpapered with thousands of newspaper articles and a chart of all the cities he played worldwide. (Prominence is given to shows in Africa, particularly the independence celebrations in Zimbabwe in 1980.) Gold and platinum discs rewarding sales of the albums *Exodus* (1977), *Uprising* (1980) and *Legend* (1984) hang above the stairs, and familiar tracks are played as you explore the building. You can peek into Marley's bedroom and kitchen, the latter complete with the blender in which he made his natural juices, and the room where Marley was almost assassinated during the 1976 election campaign – the bullet holes still much in evidence. (After that he left Jamaica for a two-year exile in Britain.)

The tour ends behind the house in the air-conditioned movie theatre that once housed Marley's Tuff Gong recording studio. There's moving footage of the "One Love" concert held during the bloody election year of 1980, at which Marley brought together rival party leaders Michael Manley and Edward Seaga. Another film features interviews with the great man cut together with appropriate music videos – the return to Africa and *Exodus*, celebration of "herb" and *Easy Skanking*.

Afterwards, you can escape from the clutches of the guide to look at the excellent photo gallery. There are pictures of Marley in New York during his final tour, with the police after the assassination attempt, and playing a lot of football. In the yard opposite the cinema, a shop sells daughter Cedella's wonderful Catch a Fire clothing alongside hordes of Marley paraphernalia. CDs are sold in a shop to the right of the house's main entrance, and snacks and drinks are available from a café.

Hope Botanical Gardens and around

A quarter of a mile east of the Marley museum, just past the Sovereign shopping centre, Hope Road becomes Old Hope Road and heads east towards Papine and the Blue Mountains. On the way it passes the ample grounds of Jamaica College, one of the island's premier schools, which count both Norman and Michael Manley among its ex-pupils. In the early days of English settlement in Jamaica, Major Richard Hope, an officer with the invading British forces of Penn and Venables (see p.370), set up a thriving sugar estate here, with a stone aqueduct (parts of which can still be seen today) bringing water down from the Hope River. In 1881 the government acquired two hundred acres of land from the Hope Estate and laid out the **Hope Botanical Gardens** (daily 6am–7pm; free) in much the same form as you see them today.

Entered on your left as you head up Old Hope Road, the **gardens** took a heavy knock from Hurricane Gilbert in 1988, but remain a lovely escape from the clamour of the city and a popular venue for weekend strolls, picnics and get-togethers. There are huge lawns, bougainvillea walks, a disorienting privet-hedge maze in which to lose yourself and a dizzying variety of unusual trees, including a great collection of palms. After exploring, you can grab a bite at the wonderful *Ashante* vegetarian restaurant (see p.101) in the middle of the gardens; come on a Sunday afternoon and you'll hear live jazz as you eat. Adjacent to the gardens is a small and sadly underfunded **zoo** (Mon–Fri 10am–5pm, Sat & Sun 10am–6pm; J$20), with lions (one of which has managed to grow dreadlocks), crocodiles, monkeys, mongooses, tapirs, peccaries, snakes and tropical birds. A wooden tower overlooks the lot and provides a handsome view of the city. If you're driving from downtown or New Kingston, turn off the Old Hope Road about four hundred yards past the signposted main entrance to the garden and follow it around to the left to a small parking area.

Further along Old Hope Road, past the gardens, is the expansive campus of the **University of Technology** (UTech; Ⓦ www.utech.edu.jm). It's worth a quick visit for its **Sculpture Park** (no set hours; free), featuring works by Jamaican artists Kay Sullivan, Basil Watson, Christopher Gonzales and Laura Facey. The lovely *Lillian's* restaurant (see p.102) is adjacent to the park.

University of the West Indies

A few hundred yards west of Hope Gardens along Old Hope Road, and just before the Sovereign Centre mall, Mona Road swings southeast towards the extensive campus of the **University of the West Indies** (Ⓦ www.uwi-mona.edu.jm), usually just called UWI. It was first established here in 1948, as a College of the University of London, and achieved full university status in 1962. With sister campuses in Trinidad and Barbados, UWI accepts students from all over the Caribbean. Thanks to its grassy lawns and colonial relics, the campus is a good place for a soothing stroll. Look out for sections of the 1758 **Paine-Mona Aqueduct**, which once sluiced water from the Hope River in the Blue Mountain foothills to a sugar-processing works that was part of the old Mona, Hope and Papine estates. The university's Jamaican-Georgian **chapel**, located elsewhere on campus, has an interesting history. Built in 1799, the building was originally a warehouse on a Trelawney sugar estate, but was brought here and rebuilt brick by brick in 1955 at the suggestion of a former UWI chancellor. You can see the name of its former owner, one Edward Morant Gale, esquire, inscribed along the northern outer wall. If you're in Kingston around the February 6 anniversary of Bob Marley's birthday, try to attend the annual Marley lecture presented here by the university's Reggae Studies unit; past speakers have included Finance Minister Omar Davies discoursing on Peter Tosh, and there's usually a reggae performance afterwards. Otherwise, finish off your campus visit with a browse around the excellent bookshop.

Southeast past UWI, Mona Road inches into **August Town**, a somewhat impoverished valley-bound community with a volatile history. During the period of religious fervour that followed the 1860–61 Great Revival, one Alexander Bedward (see *Contexts*, p.400) founded his Native Baptist Church here. Bedward's self-made faith struck a chord with the disenchanted masses, and the pro-black religion attracted thousands of converts. Sadly, Bedward's tendency toward insanity was revealed when he failed to live up to his promised pledge to sprout wings and fly up to heaven on December 31, 1921. You're unlikely to see any Bedwardites in August Town these days; indeed, it's not a place accustomed to visitors at all. But reggae fans might want to check out Judgement Yard, the flag- and banner-adorned home of cultural reggae star **Sizzla**.

Skyline Drive and into the Blue Mountains

It is only a short drive from Kingston into the Blue Mountains. Even if you don't have time to make the trip, it's worth going up onto **Skyline Drive** for spectacular views across the city. To get there, follow either East King's House Road or Barbican Road to their northern end, where they join Jack's Hill Road for the climb onto Skyline Drive itself. The drive presents you with a series of great panoramas of Kingston and across the harbour to Port Royal – imagine watching the catastrophic earthquakes of 1692 or 1907 from up here – before bringing you out on the Gordon Town Road. From there you can turn right, to return to Kingston through Papine and onto Old Hope Road, or left to travel up into the mountains (see Chapter Two). Opposite the junction, woven bamboo walls and Rasta flags mark the **Black Lion Foundation**, a Rastafarian hangout better known by the nickname of its owner, the genial Daddy D. Perched on the side of the hill and affording a birds-eye view of Mona below, it's a good spot for a Guinness, an ital meal or a discourse on the merits of Rasta. Roots reggae blasts through the speakers each evening from Friday to Sunday.

Eating

After the sun goes down and the heat lifts, the Kingston area is hard to beat for **eating**. Particularly uptown – which is where you'll want to be in the evenings – you'll find a wider choice of **restaurants** than anywhere else in Jamaica and an excellent standard of food. Most places offer variations on traditional Jamaican fare, from tiny jerk bars to exquisite local seafood establishments, but there's also good Chinese, Indian, Italian and even Middle Eastern cuisine. Many places have tables outdoors to take advantage of the balmy night air, but there are plenty with air-conditioned dining rooms, something you'll appreciate in the heat of the day. Restaurants tend to be open daily (we've specified days of closing in the individual reviews), and keep serving until around 10.30pm (though many of the vegetarian places close at around 8pm). At the weekends, the big thing in Kingston is Sunday **brunch**. *Strawberry Hill* hotel in the Blue Mountains (see p.137) is a fabulous destination if you're looking to splurge and don't mind the short drive out, but if pockets aren't that deep, head for *Alhambra Inn* (see p.77) near the National Stadium, where brunch is J$650 (10am–1.30pm).

For food on the hop, **fast-food** chains abound. *McDonald's*, *Burger King*, *KFC*, *Taco Bell* and *Wendy's* (which, without a hint of irony, claims to produce the "best jerk in Jamaica") are dotted all around the city, concentrated uptown in the shopping malls along Constant Spring Road, and along Knutsford Boulevard and Hope Road in Liguanea. You'll get a better class of fast food, though, at the Jamaican-owned *Island Grill* on Constant Spring Road, particularly good for JA-style jerk chicken sandwiches and fish. For **patties**, *Tastee*'s most convenient branches are on Knutsford Boulevard and at Half Way Tree, or try the *Juicy Beef* outlet on Hope Road, just up from Sovereign Centre. *Juicy Beef* also does great breakfast; try the porridge. More substantial lunches of all kinds are available from the **food courts** at Sovereign Centre in Hope Road (where you can get a passable roti), Island Life Plaza on St Lucia Avenue, the huge Marketplace complex in the Constant Spring Arcade, or the two Manor Plazas on Constant Spring Road. If you don't feel like leaving your hotel, *Sumptin' Nice* (☎968 6423) will deliver Jamaican specials to your door, or you can call ☎925 JERK for jerk chicken, pork and fish.

Lastly, if you're after truly authentic **jerk chicken**, try any of the smoking oil-drum barbecues that set up on street corners. An excellent choice is the vendor just outside Northside Plaza in the Liguanea section of Hope Road, who sells from Thursday to Saturday.

Note that we've given a phone number only for those places where you might need to reserve a table.

Inexpensive

Coffee Mill 17 Barbados Ave. Just off Knutsford Boulevard, this air-conditioned café is a convenient option for a cup of excellent Blue Mountain espresso, cappuccino or latte and a sandwich or cake.

Dragon City Northside Plaza, Liguanea. Almost opposite the Liguanea Shopping Centre on Hope Road, this inconspicuous place serves up some of the tastiest Chinese food around, and it's reasonably priced to boot.

Emperial Kish-Inn 2 Hillview Ave, off Eastwood Park Rd ☎920 0541. Atmospheric ital eatery for bargain-priced breakfasts, lunches and dinners, such as stew with soya mince or tofu and vegetables. Natural juices and home-made cakes are available, as are lengthy discussions on Rastafari. Deliveries available in central Kingston.

Hot Pot 2 Altamont Terrace. Popular spot for typical Jamaican meals in the heart of New Kingston. Excellent breakfasts, including cornmeal and banana porridge and the unusual combination of baked beans and saltfish, and lunches of fish and bammy, curry goat, stewed beef and the usual Jamaican staples.

King Ital 4 Caledonia Crescent. Proper ital restaurant popular with Rastas, with tables on a covered patio. Breakfast (6–11am) could be ackee or saltfish fritters, calalloo or cornmeal/banana porridge. Choices for lunch or early dinner (till 6pm) include barbecue tofu, red peas or broad bean stew, fish and patties; also a great selection of natural juices and power punches.

Moby Dick Corner of Orange and Port Royal Streets. Simple, low-key downtown joint for Jamaican staples. Curry goat is particularly good.

Mother Earth 13 Oxford Terrace. Centrally located and businesslike vegetarian restaurant doing a cracking trade. The menu changes daily; expect good Jamaican staples for breakfast and imaginative lunches with lots of pulses, soya and tofu. Patties – chickpea, lentils, veg mince, ackee – are excellent, as are the natural juices and soya ice cream.

Rock Pub Gordon Town Rd. Small shack, peacefully situated on the far side of Hope River just past the turn-off to Skyline Drive; park by the sign, walk across the bridge, and it's on your left. A great place to get away from it all, it offers decent seafood and jerk chicken.

Sugar Daddies Gordon Town Rd, Papine. Simple, no-nonsense take-away serving tasty, inexpensive, no-frills Jamaican food. A good place to buy your lunch if you're heading into the mountains for a picnic.

Moderate

Ashante Hope Gardens. Right in the centre of the gardens, and with a waterfall running through the centre of the open-sided dining area, this wonderful vegetarian restaurant is an absolute must. The daily-changing lunch/early dinner menu always includes a delicious thick soup (split peas, red peas, pumpkin) and main dishes such as soya and veg balls served with rice, salad and ratatouille. Veg burgers with chutney, natural juices and soya ice cream also available. Unmissable.

Bullseye 57 Knutsford Blvd. Indoor, air-conditioned place with the feel of a chain restaurant, though convenient if you're staying in New Kingston. The speciality is steaks (meat is imported from the US and South America), served up with all the usual trimmings. Seafood is available too, as are a full range of gooey desserts.

Carlos Café 22 Belmont Rd. Friendly place off Oxford Road with appealing decor and excellent service. Decent and inexpensive, food ranges from salads and sandwiches to steaks, seafood and pasta. Monday is crab night, and "Fat Tuesday" offers two-for-one specials on drinks and meals.

Casson's 1d Braemar Ave. English pub with typical Brit meals including sausages and mash and Sunday lunch with all the trimmings, served up in a pleasant, air-conditioned dining room adjacent to the bar. Popular with high-commission workers.

Chasers Café 29 Barbican Rd. Busy and popular with an older crown, this indoor/outdoor restaurant is a pleasant place for Jamaican lunches (weekday specials), dinners, Sunday brunch or just a drink. Theme nights include Caribbean on Wednesday and "Seafood Splash" on Thursday.

Dozer's 38a Trafalgar Rd. Convenient for New Kingston, it's an open-air bar/restaurant set back from the road, offering a reliable if rather unimaginative menu of seafood and Jamaican standards to soak up the rum. Go for the Thursday "sidewalk grill" of conch, jerk fish, etc.

Eden Central Plaza, Constant Spring Rd. Air-conditioned restaurant at the back of this small shopping mall (head towards Eastwood Park Road).

Reliable, if uninspired, vegetarian food (tofu, gluten, veggie burgers, vegetable stew and patties) and natural juices are served until 8pm.

Fish Place 136 Constant Spring Rd. A bit of a ride from the centre of town, but worth it for the spicy conch soup alone, quite apart from excellent fish, scallops, crab and lobster.

Heather's Garden Restaurant 9 Haining Rd. Solid Middle Eastern and Jamaican food in a quiet location with an extensive, medium-priced menu and a daily seafood speciality.

Indies Pub and Grill 8 Holborn Rd, opposite *Indies Hotel*. Easy-going outdoor café-cum-bar with an eclectic, reasonably-priced menu featuring steaks, fish and chips, pizza and Lebanese dishes. Specials are cooked each night, and there's a good Sunday brunch (noon–2pm).

JamRock 69 Knutsford Blvd. A perfect and always busy combination of bar, hangout, restaurant and patisserie. Favourite among Jamaican-style dishes is the sumptuous "Jerk Nyamwich", and you can also get salads, burgers, tuna melts, pastrami sandwiches, excellent patties, pastries and espresso or cappuccino.

Livity 166 Old Hope Rd. Fabulous vegetarian restaurant in an open-air courtyard with shaded tables around the edges. The daily-changing menu offers soups (pumpkin, split peas, etc) and a couple of mains, including brown lentil, tofu and soya stews. There are also sumptuous salads; chickpea, veg or soya "yatties" (patties); lovely channa or hummus wraps; veggie burgers; natural juices/smoothies; and cakes and soya ice cream. Great service and a "thought for the day" with your bill. Open till 8pm weekdays, 9pm Fri & Sat.

Our Place 102 Hope Rd. Laid-back place offers excellent Jamaican cooking and attracts a regular crew of locals. All the staples, from conch soup to curry goat, and evening specials such as janga and seafood night on Fridays. The bar is nice for a quiet drink, and there's outdoor seating at the back.

Expensive

Akbar 11 Holborn Rd ☎ 926 3480. The best Indian food in town, in a tastefully decorated air-conditioned dining room. All the regular dishes, roti and plenty of vegetarian choices. The Monday to Friday lunchtime buffet (J$595) is well worth it if you're hungry – you eat as much as you like.

Boon Hall Oasis 4 River Rd, Stony Hill ☎ 942 3064. Quite a drive from town (turn right at Stony Hill square and follow the small green signs), this outdoor restaurant on the banks of the Wag Water River is wreathed with flowers and greenery. It's best for the good but pricey Sunday brunch.

Devonshire Restaurant Devon House; ☎929 7029. Classy, costly dishes – pasta, chicken Dijon, steak, roast suckling pig, flambéed shrimp – in a cool and elegant setting. Closed Sun.

Grog Shoppe Devon House ☎929 7029. Shady setting in the oasis of the Devon House grounds, serving standard Jamaican fare at lunchtime and dishes with a more European flavour (and price) in the evening. Theme nights include all-you-can-eat-crab and live jazz each Tuesday. Closed Sun.

Hilton Kingston 77 Knutsford Blvd ☎926 5430. Run by Japanese expats and boasting a lofty air-conditioned setting above the lobby, *Restaurant Japan* is the best option here, with excellent sushi, teriyaki and other Oriental delights. The *Terrace Café* buffet is good for breakfast, light lunches and afternoon tea, while the *Palm Court* offers a formal setting and international and local fare for lunch and dinner. Poolside theme nights with live entertainment are also worth checking out: an international buffet (Sat & Sun), carvery (Mon), Jamaican/Caribbean barbeque (Tues & Wed), Texan night (Thurs) and seafood (Fri).

Jade Garden Sovereign Centre ☎978 3476. Smart business-set restaurant with some of the best Chinese dishes in town, most of them J$500–800.

Kabab House 40 Trafalgar Road ☎968 0790. Up-market, open-air "Mediterranean" restaurant offering hummus, falafel, kibbe and tabbouleh starters, proper Arabic flatbreads and lots of meaty mains. Finish off your meal with a draw on a traditional hookah pipe filled with scented tobacco.

Lillian's University of Technology (UTech) campus, Old Hope Rd ☎970 2224. It's a training restaurant for students of the School of Hospitality and Tourism Management, though you'd never know it from the flawless service and excellent Caribbean food. Friday is International Night (Chinese, Italian, etc), and there's a good-value Sunday Jamaican brunch for J$695.

Norma's on the Terrace Devon House ☎968 5488. Kingston's most upscale eatery, situated on the terrace of the old Devon House stables and serving gourmet Jamaican food with an international twist. Menu highlights include peppered beef salad, smoked marlin and a chowder of crab, shrimp, conch and lobster, while afternoon teas feature delectable, light pastries. It's also good for a late-night cappuccino, latté or espresso accompanied by one of the superb desserts.

Red Bones Blues Café 21 Braemar Ave ☎978 6091, ⓦwww.redbonesbluescafe.com. Stylish, up-market restaurant-cum-music venue with a distinguished but laid-back atmosphere. Imaginative and delicious Jamaican/Mediterranean food, embellished with contemporary flavour, is served in the lovely open-air dining area.

Thai Garden 11 Holborn Rd ☎926 3480. Set in the shady backyard of *Akbar* restaurant and run by the same team, this is a pleasant spot for decent Thai food. The full range of starters – fish cakes, spring rolls – is offered, along with red and green curries and noodle dishes.

Drinking and nightlife

Kingston has legions of great places to head to for a **drink**, from sophisticated hangouts with live jazz and a long wine list to more local-style hangouts – and many of them also double up as restaurants. Hotel **bars** uptown also make decent venues for a swift beer or a more protracted soak – the *Hilton* poolside area has live entertainment nightly and karaoke on a Friday, while *Terra Nova* has a nice Friday night after-work jam by the poolside. Most regular bars put on some kind of **theme** each night, from karaoke or open mic sessions to poetry readings, pool tournaments or live music, and as these change regularly, the reviews below can give only a general idea of what's on; call ahead for specific details. It's also a good idea to check the entertainment sections of the *Gleaner* and *Observer* on a Friday, and keep an eye and an ear out for press and radio ads throughout the week; you can also visit ⓦwww.whatsonjamaica.com, ⓦwww.partyinc.com or ⓦwww.whata-gwan.com. When choosing a bar, bear in mind that you'll rarely want to walk between places at night, and taxis are the best way of getting around.

Kingston's active **club** scene ranges from jam-packed, air-conditioned indoor venues with big-name DJs, state-of-the-art equipment and the latest tunes to small, dark, oldies' clubs for the more mature dancers. At the time of writing, there were plans to reopen Portmore's *Cactus* club, formerly one of the capital's busiest venues. The owners were also planning a three-storey superclub in New Kingston; ask at the tourist board or check the newspapers for an update. Anticipate a cover of around J$300 – more if there's a live performance or a big-name sound system; the *Gleaner* advertises regular ladies' nights, when women get in free. As you'll find islandwide, nothing much happens before midnight except on Friday, when after-work jams pull an early evening crowd of bright young things. **Security** at most of the clubs is tight, and you'll often be searched on your way in. Despite the assiduous activities of the police enforcing the Noise Abatement Act and shutting down the music, you'll still find the odd **street party** happening around town, with a sound system stacked up and beer and jerk vendors ready at hand; one of the best is at Port Royal on a Friday and Saturday (see p.115). For some real Kingston ambience, check out the Sunday night open-air dances in downtown **Rae Town**. From around 11pm, crowds fill up the main Rae Street, centred around the genial *Capricorn Inn*. While good-natured (it's roots, lovers' rock and slow-dance soul and country rather than dancehall), Rae Town is in the heart of downtown Kingston, and it's best to go with someone who attends regularly.

Live music in the capital is less predictable, but often more interesting, than the anaesthetised reggae dished up for tourists on the north coast; some of the best shows to look out for are the regular Heineken Startime concerts, featuring the best of Jamaica's vintage artists; Startime also put on "back in times" parties at venues such as *Mas Camp Village* on Oxford Road. If you're in Kingston between January and April, you can take in Jamaica's **Carnival**. Adopted from the Trinidadian event, Carnival is on a smaller scale here and focused more on all-inclusive parties than a street parade (though it usually culminates with a parade through the capital's streets). Jamaica's top DJs, singers and bands are usually in action around the city, playing anywhere from the regular clubs to open-air parties at *Mas Camp Village* to the UWI and UTech campuses. Trinidadian and Bajan calypsonians and soca stars do the rounds, as do Jamaica's own Byron Lee and the Dragonaires; bandleader Lee was instrumental in bringing Carnival to Jamaica. For more on Carnival, contact the JTB (☎929 9200) or visit ⓦwww.jamaicacarnival.com or ⓦwww.bacchanaljamaica .com.

Otherwise, the busiest time, musically speaking, is during the summer, when the annual round of **Jamaica Cultural Development Commission** (ⓦwww.jcdc.org.jm) arts competitions swing into action. There are performances of traditional music and dance by both amateur and professional artists

---

Kingston's parties

Throughout the year (and particularly during the summer and Christmas periods), Kingston weekends see the more well-heeled of the capital's youth gather together for huge **outdoor parties** staged at venues such as the *Mas Camp Village*, *Liguanea Club*, *Cinema 2* or Caymanas Park. Most of them are **all-inclusive**; your entrance fee (anything from J$500 for a basic party to J$2000 for a high-profile event) covers drinks, and sometimes food, all night, as well as music from Jamaica's hottest **sound systems** – Renaissance, Adonai, Stone Love, Skyy Disco, Travellers – and live performances from singers and DJs. Each party draws a slightly different, though usually fairly peaceful, crowd of loyal revellers, but you'll need to enlist local help to decide which ones are likely to go with a bang. They're all advertised by way of flyers posted up around the capital; you can also visit the websites listed above.

all around town as well. Look out for amateur dramatics and music at the Ward Theatre, and the finals of the National Song Competition. The venue of the latter varies, but it's often held in either the Ranny Williams Entertainment *Centre* or the *Hilton*. In Kingston, Christmas means **panto season**, and the annual Little Theatre Movement (LTM) pantomime should not be missed.

Bars and clubs

Asylum 69 Knutsford Blvd; ☏ 929 4386. Kingston's busiest club, usually packed with patrons dressed to the nines checking out the latest dances under the dry ice and UV glare. Currently, Monday is the house and techno "rave" night; Tuesday is ladies' night, with dancehall on the decks and free entry and drinks for women; and Wednesday (probably the best time to make your first foray) is a little more sedate, with 1970s and 1980s reggae and R&B for an uptown crowd. Thursday is a hard-core, rude boy-filled dancehall night with Stone Love; Friday is a regular after-work jam, with dancehall and drinks promotions; Saturday sees a popular "dance party", with soul, hip hop and R&B in amongst the reggae; and Sunday features "Girls Gone Wild", with dance competitions and plenty of modelling from the female patrons.

Carlos Café 22 Belmont Rd. Small and very friendly place to sink a few drinks or shoot some pool, with various theme nights throughout the week: "Twisted Tuesdays" see lots of tequila and free pool (7–9pm); Thursday is Latin night; Fri & Sat are party nights; and there's a trance night on Sundays.

Casson's 1d Braemar Ave. Indoor, air-conditioned English-style pub with beer mats, beer bellies and UK food. There's a quiz night on Monday, and a dartboard out back.

Chasers Café, 29 Barbican Rd. Popular hangout with a decent beer selection. Monday offers karaoke; Tuesday is oldies night; there's an after-work jam on Fridays; and sports events are shown on TV throughout the week. See "Eating", p.101.

Club Juice 11 Knutsford Blvd. New indoor club at the quiet, Trafalgar Road end of the Strip, offering all-inclusive nights of debauchery to a youngish crowd as well as live music on Thursdays. Open Wed–Sat.

Dozer's 38a Trafalgar Road. This semi-open-air bar, popular amongst a mature crowd, is a good bet for a New Kingston drink. The various theme nights to pull in the punters are karaoke (Tues), soca night with two-for-one mixed drinks (Wed) and a Friday happy hour (5.30–8.30pm).

Drifter's Lounge Northside Plaza, Liguanea. Top-floor, open-air club and bar right at the back of this mini plaza, offering lovely views over the city's twinkling lights. Best for the Wednesday oldies night, popular amongst a mature crowd.

Epiphany II Knutsford Blvd. Indoor club next door to *Asylum*, attracting a mixed crowd. Friday, dancehall night, is the best bet. Open Wed–Sat.

Friends on the Deck 14 Trafalgar Rd. Spacious, easy-going and central open-air bar under a cavernous thatched roof, popular with a friendly, older set. Different snacks on offer each night, the DJ's oldies selection keeps things moving on the dance floor.

Grog Shoppe Devon House. In the grounds of Devon House, this is a good place to finish your day's sightseeing with a drink outside under the giant cotton tree. Especially nice on Friday, when a band (usually jazz) plays. See "Eating" p.102.

Half Time Sports Bar 69 Knutsford Blvd. Studenty upstairs pool hall with plenty of fair-quality tables, a few arcade games and TVs showing sports events or karate movies. Good for a quiet drink or a game of pool. Cover charge for men after 7pm.

Indies 8 Holborn Rd, opposite the *Indies* hotel. With a central location and a mellow atmosphere, it's popular with mature late-night revellers from Thursday to Saturday, when it stays open until 2am.

JamRock Sports Bar and Grill 69 Knutsford Blvd. Shiny, neon-clad US-style sports bar with an authentically Jamaican twist, popular for lunchtime and after-work drinks or a late-night espresso and pastry. Headline sports events are shown on the sprinkling of TV monitors.

Jonkanoo Lounge *Hilton Kingston*, 77 Knutsford Blvd ☏ 926 5430. Relatively smart and sedate, as you'd expect from a hotel-based venue. Rarely crowded, it attracts a mature and up-market clientele who come to dance or take in occasional live bands. Currently the Thursday Latin night is busiest, with dance classes from 6pm to 8pm, though Friday's ladies' night (women free till 10pm), the "Mature Mix" (1980s reggae and soul) on Saturday nights, and Sunday's 1970s, 1980s and 1990s music are all worth a visit.

Mingles *Courtleigh Hotel*, 85 Knutsford Blvd; ☏ 929 9000. Indoor and outdoor sections of this in-hotel nightclub provide pleasant settings for a drink during the week, with barbecue and jazz, R&B and reggae on Tuesday, karaoke on Thursday, after-work jam on Friday and Latin, with dance lessons, on Saturday, the busiest night (6–10pm).

Peppers 31 Upper Waterloo Rd. Late-opening and permanently popular outdoor bar that pulls in post-work drinkers and then younger clubbers who pack out the outdoor dance floor. There's a huge line of pool tables, and inexpensive Jamaican food is available.

Pool Bar *Hilton Kingston*, 77 Knutsford Blvd ☎926 5430. Adjacent to the *Hilton's* lavish pool, this is a pleasant spot for a cocktail, with a sense of being away from it all. A mento band play live on Monday, the Hummingbird Steel Orchestra accompany Tortilla night each Wednesday, there's karaoke on a Thursday, and Sunday evenings see a live jazz band.

Priscilla's 109 Constant Spring Rd. Pleasant and easy-going roof bar with views over the city. Sixties and Seventies Jamaican music on Friday and Saturday nights attracts the older media and professional set.

Red Bones Blues Café, 21 Braemar Ave ☎978 8262. Sophisticated place for a quiet drink amongst a mixed, uptown crowd. Look out for live music sessions, with everything from classical to blues and jazz, and a good wine list.

Vibes Sports Bar *Christar Villas*, 99 Hope Rd. Intimate little bar within a friendly villa complex overlooking Hope Road, with a pool table and TVs showing sports events. Good for a quiet drink.

Village Café Orchid Village Plaza, Barbican Rd. Currently Kingston's hottest bar, this open-air, split-level venue at the top of a small plaza stages a range of popular and ever-changing events, from open mic on Tuesdays to bikini modelling on Wednesdays. Cover (J$200–300) some nights.

Waterfalls 9 Mona Plaza, Liguanea ☎977 0652. New, indoor club that's best on a Friday, when there's a happy hour (6–9pm). Winston "Merritone" Black spins an excellent oldies selection (6–7pm), karaoke takes over from 9pm, and a soca party swings into action until the early hours.

Weekendz 80 Constant Spring Rd. Outdoor club/bar set off from the road in gardens and attracting a mixed-age, uptownish crowd who come to socialize and dance in the open air. Weekends are busiest, with a music policy ranging from dancehall and reggae to R&B, hip hop and house, and there are regular drinks promotions. Weeknights are quieter, with open mic on Tuesdays.

Theatre, dance and cinema

Next to nightlife, **theatre** is Kingston's strongest cultural suit. The performance scene is limited but buoyant, with a small core of first-rate writers, directors and actors – including Trevor Rhone, Oliver Samuels and David Heron – producing work of a high standard. Most of the plays are sprinkled with Jamaican patois, but you'll still get the gist. Comedies (particularly sexual romps and political satire) are popular, and the normally excellent annual **pantomime** – a musical with a message, totally different from the English variety – is a major event, running from December to April at both the **Ward Theatre** (☎922 0453; see p.84) and, later, the **Little Theatre** (☎926 6129; see p.95). Other theatres include the Barn, 5 Oxford Road (☎926 6469), and the New Green Gables Playhouse, 6 Cargill Ave (☎920 0858). For details of performances, check the *Gleaner* or *Observer* newspapers, particularly the Friday entertainment sections. Many of these venues also stage dance performances featuring the acclaimed National Dance Theatre Company or L'Acadco; check the press to see what's on. Kingston's **cinemas** invariably screen recent mainstream offerings from the States. Tickets are around J$250, and there's usually a snack interval in the middle of the show. Most of the cinemas are uptown, including the **Palace Cineplex** (☎978 3522) at the Sovereign Centre; the **Island Cinemax** (☎920 7964) at the Island Life Centre on St Lucia Avenue; and the **Odeon** (☎926 7671) at 11 Constant Spring Rd. Recently rebuilt and suitably plush, the **Carib Cinema** (☎926 6106) at Cross Roads is probably the most atmospheric choice. There's a **drive-in** cinema on the eastern outskirts of town at Harbour View (☎928 6066). The movie theatre at the Bob Marley Museum, 56 Hope Rd (☎978 2991) occasionally screens movies of a more alternative bent, including Jamaican-made classics such as *Life and Debt* and *Third World Cop*. For more on Jamaican film, see *Contexts* pp.427–430.

Shopping and galleries

A multitude of American-style malls means that **shopping** in Kingston is nothing if not convenient. The major players – the New Kingston Shopping Centre on Dominica Drive, the Sovereign Centre on Hope Road and the multitude of malls on Constant Spring Road – sell everything you can imagine buying. There are, however, more exciting places to look for fresh **food**: the heaving Jubilee Market downtown (see p.85) and the smaller markets at Cross Roads and, particularly, Papine (friendly and rich with super-fresh produce bused in from the Blue Mountains).

For **books**, the University Bookshop at the UWI in Mona is far and away the superior choice for both novels and books on Jamaica, though Sangster's (branches at Ward Plaza, 106 Old Hope Rd and 33 King St) and Bookland, 53 Knutsford Blvd, are reasonable and more central. Reader's, at Liguanea Plaza, 134 Old Hope Rd, has a decent second-hand collection. Downtown, Headstart Books, 54–56 Church St, concentrates on all things African and roots Jamaican, with an excellent collection of hard-to-find titles as well as Rasta-made crafts, greeting cards and posters. Similar books and merchandise are sold at Books About Us and Blakk Muzic, 2 Hillview Ave, owned by broadcaster and dub poet Mutabaruka.

As you'd expect, reggae fans are in shopping heaven in Kingston. Downtown's Orange Street is the place to go – you'll find loads of **record stores**, many of them attached to studios and pressing plants. For vinyl as well as CDs, GG's Records, on the corner of Orange Street and Parade, is particularly well stocked, and as vibrant and loud as its location. Prince Busta's, further down Orange Street, is known for its collection of rare oldies. Rockers International, 135 Orange St, carries an extensive stock of old rocksteady and reggae classics, and Techniques, at no. 99, has a good selection of old and new stock. Elsewhere, a good place to check is Rock and Groove Mix, 8 Northside Plaza in Liguanea. Just up the road there's an excellent selection of reggae CDs, old and new, above the *Livity* restaurant complex (see p.101). Mobile Music, at Lane Plaza in Liguanea, has helpful staff and a good selection of reggae and R&B; Derrick Harriot's One Stop in Twin Gates Plaza, Constant Spring Road, is good for old and new reggae.

For **souvenirs**, try the Craft Market downtown (see p.83). For more expensive choices, check out the gift shops at Devon House or Patoo, in the Upper Manor Park Centre, which have prints, books, spices, coffee and a host of other items. It's also worth browsing the malls on Constant Spring Road, which hold hordes of excellent, reasonably priced craft shops; Craft Cottage at 24c is particularly good.

Kingston also has a vibrant art scene, and there are excellent **galleries** across the city. The Frame Centre Gallery at 10 Tangerine Place is a fine place to start, with a good variety of local work on display and for sale. The Grosvenor Galleries at 1 Grosvenor Terrace and the Chelsea Galleries at 12 Chelsea Ave both host exhibitions by contemporary Jamaican artists. If you want to splash out, try the art shops at Devon House (Tues–Sat 9.30am–5pm) and the *Pegasus* and *Hilton* hotels. (The latter has a great collection of paintings by Portland artist Ken Abendana Spencer in its lobby.) Finally, the Art Centre (Mon–Fri 9am–5pm & Sat 10am–4pm), near Papine at 202 Old Hope Rd, sells local art, and there is a chaotic jumble of paintings and sculptures in the gallery opposite.

Listings

Airlines Air Canada, Norman Manley Airport ☎924 8211; Air Jamaica & Air Jamaica Express 72 Harbour St ☎922 4661, toll-free booking and info ☎1-888-359 2475; American Airlines, 26 Trafalgar Rd ☎920 8887, toll-free ☎1-800-744 0006; British Airways, 25 Dominica Drive ☎929 9020–5, Norman Manley Airport ☎924 8187; BWIA, 19 Dominica Drive toll-free ☎1-800-538 2942, Norman Manley Airport ☎924 8364; Cayman Airways, 23 Dominica Drive ☎926 1762; Cubana, 22 Trafalgar Rd ☎978 3406.

Airport information Norman Manley International Airport ☎924 8546, ⓦwww.manley-airport.com.jm; Tinson Pen (domestic flights) ☎923 0022.

Ambulances For a public ambulance, call ☎110 or St John's Ambulance on ☎926 7656; for a private ambulance, call ☎978 2327.

Banks The main banks have branches citywide; uptown branches with ATMs include: CIBC, 23 Knutsford Blvd, Manor Park Plaza; Citibank, 63 Knutsford Blvd; Bank of Nova Scotia, 125 Old Hope Rd, 2 Knutsford Blvd and 6 Oxford Rd; National Commercial Bank, 10 Oxford Rd, 30 Knutsford Blvd, 133 Hope Rd; RBTT Sovereign Centre, 106 Hope Rd, 17 Dominica Drive, 6 St Lucia Ave.

Car Rental Reliable firms include: Avis, Norman Manley Airport ☎924 8013; Bargain, Norman Manley Airport ☎924 8293, toll-free ☎1-888-991 2111; Budget, Norman Manley Airport ☎924 8762, 53 South Camp Rd ☎759 1793; Caribbean, 31 Old Hope Rd ☎926 6339; Econocars, 11 Lady Musgrave Rd ☎927 6761, ☎927 9989; Island, 17 Antigua Ave ☎926 8012, Norman Manley Airport ☎924 8075.

Doctors and dentists Your hotel should be able to make recommendations. Otherwise, for doctors call Dr Dianne Lewis-Tucker ☎928 7285 or Dr Trevor McCartney ☎927 7666. Reliable dentists include the Oxford Dental Centre, 22g Old Hope Rd ☎926 7311.

Embassies Almost all of the embassies and consulates are based in New Kingston. They include the British High Commission, 28 Trafalgar Rd ☎510 0700; the American Embassy, 2 Oxford Rd ☎929 4850; and the Canadian High Commission, 3 West Kings House Rd and 30 Knutsford Blvd ☎926 1500.

Golf Kingston has two excellent eighteen-hole golf courses, west of the city at Caymanas Park ☎922 3386 and north at Constant Spring (☎924 1610). Putt 'n' Play, 78 Knutsford Blvd ☎906 4814; offers nine holes of mini-golf.

Hospitals Kingston's best public hospital is the University Hospital at Mona (☎927 1620); other-

wise there's the Kingston Public Hospital downtown on North Street (☎922 0210), and the Bustamante Hospital for Children, Arthur Wint Drive (☎926 5721). There are a number of well-equipped private hospitals in New Kingston, including Medical Associates, 18 Tangerine Place ☎926 1400; Nuttall Memorial, 6 Caledonia Ave ☎926 2139; and Andrews Memorial, 27 Hope Rd ☎926 7401.

Internet One Stop Computers at the Island Life Mall on St Lucia Avenue in New Kingston, and Innovative Superstore in the Sovereign Centre on Hope Road in Liguanea offer Internet access in pleasant, air-conditioned surroundings for about J$150 per half-hour.

Laundry All of the hotels will wash laundry, often at a hefty price. Otherwise, Quick Wash at 1 Union Square in Cross Roads has coin-operated machines, and Joy Laundromat, 120 Barbican Rd, offer a drop-off/pick-up service; Fabricare, 144 Old Hope Rd in Liguanea also does dry-cleaning. VIP, 9 the Marketplace, Constant Spring Rd (☎754 3605), will collect from and deliver to hotels.

Newspapers Sunday newspapers from England, and many US publications, can be found at Bookland, 53 Knutsford Blvd; in larger pharmacies; and at the gift shops at the *Hilton* and *Pegasus* hotels in New Kingston. Supermarkets, pharmacies, gas stations and vendors at major road junctions sell daily papers.

Pharmacies There are pharmacies at most of the shopping malls. Late-opening options are Monarch, at the Sovereign Centre (Mon–Fri 8am–10pm, Sat 9am–10pm, Sun 9am–8pm), and York Pharmacy at the Half Way Tree junction (daily 8am–11pm).

Police The main station is at 79 Duke St ☎922 9321. Stations uptown include Matilda's Corner, Old Hope Rd ☎926 6517. In an emergency, call ☎119.

Post Offices The GPO is at 13 King St downtown, and there are post offices at 115 Hope Rd in Liguanea and at the airport. Stamps can also be bought at most hotels.

Sports International and major domestic soccer and cricket matches are played at the National Stadium (☎929 4970) and Sabina Park (☎967 0322), respectively. Horse racing and (occasionally) polo can be seen at Caymanas Park (☎922 3338). There's a fully equipped fitness centre at the *Crowne Plaza* hotel, 211A Constant Spring Rd (☎925 7676), where you can work out, take an aerobics class or sauna or play a game of squash; courts cost J$200 per hour.

Tours from Kingston

All of the places around Kingston can be explored on an **organized tour** from the city. You shouldn't need a tour to see Port Royal, which is easy to reach on the ferry and small, safe and relaxed enough to wander around alone. But a tour is not a bad option for Spanish Town, which is a bit awkward to get to and – as a major industrial city – can feel rather unwelcoming. However, you'll get a fuller perspective on all the sights by engaging the services of a tour company, many of which offer individualized, small-scale jaunts. **Our Story Tours** (mobiles ☎377 5693 or 699 4513, ℮ourstorytours @hotmail.com) is brilliant for historical perspectives, offering custom-designed tours of Kingston, Spanish Town and Port Royal as well as farther afield – Colbeck Castle, Mountain River Cave, Sligoville, and St Thomas. Costs start at US$50 per person plus transportation, but include any entry fees; trips to Caymanas Park for racing start at $50 per person, including lunch and access to the a/c lounge. Another good option is Kingston-based **Sun Venture** (30 Balmoral Ave, ☎960 6685, ℉920 8348, ⓦwww.sunventuretours.com), which offers an interesting, professional half-day city tour of the more conventional sights – the Bob Marley Museum, Devon House, etc – for US$35 per person for a group of four or more. Sun Venture is also your best choice if heading into the Blue Mountains. Former head of the Jamaica Cultural Development Commission Ainsley Henriques (mobile ☎759 7804, ℮ainsley @cwjamaica.com) offers an unusual tour of Kingston harbour aboard a fishing canoe. Music fans should look no further than Andrea Lewis (☎927 0859 or 970 3928, mobile 805 7364, ℮drialou@hotmail.com), who conducts brilliant tours of Kingston's recording studios as well as record-buying trips and nights on the town.

Taxis Reputable operators include JUTA (also for day tours and all-island transfers) ☎927 4534; Blue Diamond ☎926 2976; Checker (☎922 1777); Zenith ☎929 3559.
Telephones There are phone booths dotted around town; otherwise, there are several cheap international call centres on the Half Way Tree

roundabout, and many more scattered around town. However, it's easier and often cheaper to purchase a World Talk card (see p.42) and call from your hotel.
Travel Agents Great Vacations, 19 Knutsford Blvd ☎929 6290; ITS, 2 Belmont Rd ☎929 6331.

Around Kingston

There are some excellent options around Kingston if you want to escape from the city for a day or two. The one-time pirate haunt of **Port Royal** in particular is worth a half-day visit, with nearby **Lime Cay** providing a good spot for a swim afterwards. **Spanish Town**, the nation's capital from 1534 to 1872, offers the third limb of Jamaica's "Historic Triangle" (with Kingston and Port Royal). Again, half a day is more than ample to see the remains of the city's superb Georgian architecture and to tour the oldest Anglican cathedral in the "New World". Fragments of a more ancient culture remain in the old Taino haunt of **Mountain River Cave**, while the Blue Mountains (see Chapter Two) and **Castleton Botanical Gardens** offer hiking and undisturbed nature. For something even more relaxing, **Rockfort Mineral Baths** have reasonably priced spas. **Hellshire**'s lovely white-sand bays, just south of the city, are immensely popular at the weekend; you're best washing off the salt at the **Nature's Paradise mineral spring** behind Caymanas Polo Club.

East of Kingston

The main route east out of the city, newly widened Windward Road, follows the coastline out of Kingston, scything through an industrial zone of oil tanks and a cement works that towers over the ruined defensive bastion of Fort Rock, now the **Rockfort Mineral Baths**. If the scenery looks familiar, you may be recalling the classic scene in the **James Bond** movie *Dr No*, in which Bond leaves Norman Manley Airport in a nifty red Sunbeam Alpine. A mile or so further on, turning right at the roundabout takes you on to the **Palisadoes**, a narrow ten-mile spit of land that leads out past the international airport to the ancient city of **Port Royal**, from where it's a short hop to the tiny island of **Lime Cay**.

Rockfort Mineral Baths

Rockfort Mineral Baths (Mon & Wed–Sun 7am–5.30pm; J$100 to use the pool, J$700 for a two-person spa) offer one of the few public swimming pools in the Kingston area as well as some rather luxurious private spas seating two to twelve people. This was the site of the British Fort Rock, first strengthened against a threatened French invasion in 1694 and remanned in 1865 amid fears that the Morant Bay Rebellion further east might spread to Kingston. Today, the baths sit in a neat modern facility – an oasis in the surrounding dusty terrain – and offer visitors a chance to enjoy some laid-back pampering. Fed by a spring high in the hills that appeared following the 1907 earthquake, the mineral spas are all fitted with jacuzzis, and you're allowed to wallow in them for up to 45 minutes. Piped from a local spring, the mineral water is moderately radioactive; it's claimed that the radioactivity helps to infuse the therapeutic minerals into the body. Massage is available, and there's a canteen serving Jamaican food.

The hills above Rockfort rise up to the **Dallas Mountains**, named after Robert Dallas, a local eighteenth-century plantation owner whose grandson, George Miflin Dallas, became vice president of the United States in 1845 and founded the eponymous city in Texas.

Port Royal

PORT ROYAL (ⓦ www.portroyal-jamaica.com), a short drive or ferry ride from downtown Kingston, captures the spirit of early colonial adventure better than any other place in Jamaica. Originally a tiny island, this little fishing village is now joined to the mainland by the **Palisadoes**, a series of small cays that silted together over hundreds of years and, with a bit of human assistance, now form a roadway and a natural breakwater for Kingston's harbour. The cactus-strewn Palisadoes provided the setting for the opening scenes of the James Bond movie *Dr No* – it was here that the chauffeur of Bond's Sunbeam Alpine car tried unsuccessfully to poison him with a cyanide-laced cigarette.

For several decades in the late seventeenth century, Port Royal was a riotous town – the notorious haunt of cut throats and buccaneers, condemned by the church as "the wickedest city on earth". Only a few traces of those days remain – much of the old town is now a sunken city, submerged under fifty feet of water – but the Jamaican government and the private sector are slowly beginning to appreciate the potential allure of its romantic past. A major archeological museum is in the pipeline, and there is even talk of a cruise-ship port, though the prevailing "soon come" attitude combined with a lack of funding have ensured that none have yet been realized. For now, Port Royal retains a

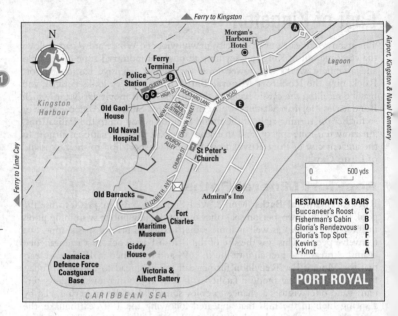

deliciously eerie, antiquated feel, a perfect place to catch a whiff of pirates and pieces of eight or to recall an egregiously proud city brought to its knees by natural disaster.

Some history

When Britain captured Jamaica from Spain in 1655, most of the country's population of two or three thousand lived in the capital city of Spanish Town, a few miles from what is now Kingston harbour. Two things were immediately obvious to British tacticians: first, that to prevent any other power from repeating the simple strategy with which they had conquered the island, strong **defences** were required all around the harbour. Second, with their navy tied up with wars in Europe, they needed to recruit local support to help defend the new colony.

Port Royal at this time was uninhabited, but, surrounded by deep water, it had been a perfect place for the Spanish to moor up their sailing ships for cleaning and caulking. Now the British turned it into a **battle station**, with five separate forts covering all of the angles from which enemy ships could approach, and a palisade at the north to defend against attackers coming over the cays. As added protection, they encouraged the buccaneers who had for decades been pillaging the area to sign up as "**privateers**" in the service of the king.

Port Royal boomed. Merchants took advantage of the city's great location to buy and sell slaves, export sugar, log wood and import bricks and supplies for the growing population. The privateers wreaked havoc on the ships of Spain, and the fabulous profits of trade and plunder brought others to service the town's needs; brothels, taverns and gambling houses proliferated, and by 1692 the population had swollen to six thousand. Rents were as high as in the most fashionable parts of London, and the world's finest wines and silks were readily available.

The huge **earthquake** that struck the city on June 7, 1692, dumped sixty percent of Port Royal into the sea, killing two thousand people in seconds; within a week, a thousand more had died. Of the remaining population, most fled for Kingston, while almost all of the rest died or deserted when a massive fire swept the island in 1703.

Despite the destruction, Port Royal continued to serve as the country's **naval headquarters**. All the great British admirals of the eighteenth and early nineteenth centuries were stationed here at some point in their careers, plotting the downfall of the French, whose presence in the area grew increasingly threatening up until the time of the Napoleonic Wars. However, the advent of steamships saw the British Navy close its Port Royal dockyard in 1905, and following the rapid expansion of Kingston during the last century, Port Royal has become increasingly marginalized. The settlement suffered further blows when hurricanes Charlie and Gilbert wreaked havoc in 1951 and 1988 respectively. Though Port Royal still retains its naval traditions as home to the JDF Naval wing and the Jamaican coastguard, it's a far less exotic – though nonetheless beguiling – place today. The small and tidy fishing village is proud of its very low crime rate and happy to serve up some of the tastiest fresh **fish** you'll find anywhere in Jamaica.

Getting there

Unless you are **driving** – in which case follow signs southeast from Kingston to the airport and keep going past the turn-off – the most pleasant and convenient way to get to Port Royal is on the little blue-and-white **ferry** that leaves from the pier at the bottom of Princess Street in downtown Kingston, near the National Gallery. Services depart Monday to Friday at 6am, 7am, 10am, 12.30pm, 5pm & 7pm; on Saturday at 6am, 8am, 10.30am, 12.30pm, 2pm & 6.30pm; and on Sunday at 10am, 12.30pm, 2pm, 4pm & 6.30pm. The ferry returns from Port Royal half an hour later. The one-way fare is J$20 during the week, J$30 at weekends and public holidays; journey time is about half an hour.

Bus #98 runs every half-hour between the Parade and Port Royal Square, while a **taxi** will set you back around US$25 in each direction.

The Town

Port Royal makes an impression before you even reach dry land; look back to sea as the ferry docks on the northwest shore and you'll get not only a great view of Kingston harbour, but a clear idea of the area's strategic military importance and a glimpse of its former limits. The **old city** once extended way out across the harbour, but since the 1692 earthquake, sixty percent of it has been submerged under fifty feet of water, its key sites marked by buoys.

Once on land, what remains of Port Royal is easily navigable on foot. Five minutes' walk from the ferry terminal, behind the old garrison wall, are the decaying red bricks of the **Old Naval Hospital**. Built by the Bowling Ironworks in Bradford, England, the two-storey iron prefab, shipped over and put up here in 1819, remains the oldest prefabricated structure in the New World. It somehow managed to survive hurricanes Charlie and Gilbert and was put into use in the aftermath of Hurricane Charlie as a refuge for displaced townspeople. Despite its ramshackle state, it now serves as offices of the National Heritage Trust. Although numerous artefacts have been recovered from the sea and stored in the building (you may be able to get staff to show you the collection of pewter and china), plans to reopen to the public remain on hold at the time of writing. Take a wander around if there's no one to show

Pirates and buccaneers

The early history of Port Royal is inextricably linked with adventurers. The first **buccaneers** were a ragged crew of outlaws and fugitives, European outcasts who banded together on the island of Tortuga, north of present-day Haiti. They lived by hunting wild pigs and cattle (first brought to the island by the early European explorers), which they smoked on a wooden frame known as a *boucan* (hence the name). As they grew more organized and more daring, they began to raid the treasure ships sailing between Spain and its New World colonies.

After Britain conquered Jamaica in 1655, the newly installed authorities embarked on an open-door policy, issuing a general invitation to these buccaneers to set themselves up in Port Royal and use it as their base for attacks on the Spanish enemy. In return for official status as **privateers**, they were obliged to deliver ten percent of their haul to the Crown. Privateering flourished, and Port Royal turned into a city marked by extreme wealth and a constant threat of violence.

The privateers' reversal of fortune came in 1671, when a peace treaty was signed between Britain and Spain. Despite the treaty, **Henry Morgan** – the most famous of the buccaneers – sailed from Bluefields Bay in Jamaica to plunder the wealthy Spanish colony of Panama. Although there is some evidence that the British authorities connived at this attack, Morgan and the Jamaican governor, Thomas Modyford, were recalled to the mother country to face official sanction. Modyford was sacked to appease the Spanish. Meanwhile Morgan, having insinuated his way into royal favour, was made lieutenant-governor in Modyford's stead, returning to Jamaica with a new brief – to stamp out piracy by persuading his former colleagues to adopt a life of peace.

Many of the buccaneers, now officially termed **"pirates"** to mark their loss of favour, refused to give up their exciting and profitable lifestyles and continued to plague ships throughout the Caribbean. In turn, they were ruthlessly hunted down by Morgan and his successors, and hangings at a spot called Gallows Point on Port Royal were frequent until as late as 1831. The most famous success for the authorities came in 1720 when "Calico Jack" Rackham and his sidekicks, female pirates Anne Bonney and Mary Read, were captured during a party on Negril beach (see p.307). Rackham was executed, his body squeezed into a tiny cage and left on Rackham's Cay, just east of Port Royal, as a warning to others. Conveniently, the women both declared themselves pregnant and were spared the gallows. Bonney disappeared without trace, but Read contracted yellow fever, died in prison and is buried in St Catherine.

you the place: A few rusting naval artefacts gather dust outside, but don't head upstairs without permission – only one of the staircases is strong enough to be climbed.

Ten minutes' walk away and on the main Church Street, **St Peter's Church** (irregular opening hours; when shut, ask around for local vendor Patsy, who usually has the key) was built in 1726 and, apart from the roof, has survived largely intact since. It's unremarkable apart from an intricately carved mahogany and cedar organ loft, which was made in 1743 by W.G. Dowles of Bristol, England; the organ was restored in the late 1990s by the same company, which still trades to this day. Marble tablets on the church walls emphasize the role of the navy in this area, and you should be able to get someone to show you a collection of silver plates, bowls and a jug said to have belonged to Henry Morgan. More interesting are the ancient tombs in the small and rambling graveyard, particularly that of the Frenchman **Lewis Galdy**. Swallowed by the earthquake in 1692, an eruption seconds later spat him out into the sea from where, amazingly, he scrambled to safety. No doubt a pillar of the church thereafter, Galdy lived until 1739. Next to Galdy's grave is a tomb for three small children who died in the earthquake and whose remains were found in the rubble of their collapsed house during underwater excavations in 1992.

A left turn out of the church leads down the main road to fascinating **Fort Charles** (daily 9am–5pm; J$100). It's approached through an expansive parade ground that was formerly Chocolata Hole – a part of the harbour and a sheltered spot for mooring ships before natural sea and land movements, combined with artificial filling during the eighteenth and nineteenth centuries, created the dry land of today. Originally known as Fort Cromwell (but renamed after King Charles II was restored to the British throne in 1660), this was the first of the five forts to be built here, though it never saw any action. The first structure was wooden, but following the Great Fire of London in 1666, British laws required that all such buildings in the colonies be made of brick. The present fort looks much as it did in 1692, except that then it was immediately bordered by the sea on three sides. The red-brick building to your left as you enter is the storage room, where the all-important gunpowder was kept dry. In the courtyard, the **Maritime Museum** gives a lucid history of Port Royal and displays items dredged up from the underwater city.

The raised platform on the other side of the small parade ground is known as **Nelson's Quarterdeck**; the great commander (incredibly still under 21) used to pace up and down here spoiling for a fight with the French. From the quarterdeck you can see how the land has built up around the fort – over a foot per year – as the sea has continued to deposit silt against the former island. The two structures that now stand between the fort and the water both date from the 1880s. The squat, rectangular **Giddy House** was an ammunition store, while the circular bunker beside it was the **Victoria and Albert Battery** – an emplacement for a nineteenth-century supergun that was fired only once, at a British soldier whose attempt to desert was swiftly curtailed. The 1907 earthquake dropped the gun turret several yards into the earth, while the storeroom somehow remained intact but tilted at a seventeen-degree angle. Try walking across it without slipping over.

There are two other points of minor interest in Port Royal. Heading back towards the main square, turn left after St Peter's Church, then right and third left onto Gaol Street. The distinctive block building on your right is the **Old Gaol House** (closed to visitors), built before the 1692 earthquake and once used as a women's prison. Slightly out of town on the road back to Kingston, the **Naval Cemetery** – its entrance marked by an anchor-shaped memorial to the crew of *HMS Goshawk*, who drowned when their vessel sank in Port Royal harbour – marks the final resting place of many of Port Royal's long-forgotten sailors. Buccaneer-turned-politician Henry Morgan (see box on previous page) was buried here too, but the earthquake tipped his body into the sea, along with a large part of the old graveyard. What remains today of the cemetery was laid out by the British in 1762, following successive outbreaks of yellow fever; Port Royalists still avoid what they perceive as a contaminated area to this day.

Finally, there are a couple of **beaches** around Port Royal, but both sea and sand are pretty dirty; if you want to **swim**, you're better off taking a boat out to Lime Cay (see p.114). Otherwise, the dive shop at *Morgan's Harbour Hotel* runs scuba certification courses as well as **diving** and **snorkelling** excursions to some of the best sites on the south coast, many of them centred around wrecked ships and frequented by the usual array of tropical fish and nurse sharks. At the time of writing, the dive shop was undergoing a management change; call to check prices. You can also arrange deep-sea **fishing** (4hr,

US$400; 8hr, US$650), and evening drop-line fishing (4hr, US$400) through the hotel. Alternatively, you could take a gentler **boat ride** into the mangrove swamps that parallel the Palisadoes road for a look at the local bird life, particularly impressive during the pelican breeding season from February to April. At all times, though, you'll also see frigate birds and egrets rooting in the trees.

Lime Cay and other islands

Just fifteen minutes from Port Royal, **Lime Cay** is a tiny uninhabited island with white sand, blue water and easy snorkelling. It was here that Ivanhoe ("Rhygin") Martin – the cop-killing gangster and folk-hero immortalized in the classic Jamaican movie *The Harder They Come* – met his demise in 1948. Boats run regularly from Port Royal; best option is to head to *Y Knot* (see opposite), whose boats are all well maintained and carry life jackets. The fare is J$300 return at weekends and holidays, or J$500 during the week; tell the boatman what time you want to be picked up. Alternatively, you can try at *Morgan's Harbour* hotel (see below), or ask one of the fishermen around the ferry pier to take you – their going rate is J$250 per person, round-trip. At weekends, when a good-natured crowd of Kingstonians descend on Lime Cay, food and drink stalls and sound systems are set up on the beach; at other times, take your own picnic. At the time of writing, Lime Cay had been leased to a private operator with a view to upgrading the facilities and charging a J$100 entry fee; protests from locals have been vociferous, however, and whether or not a fee will be imposed remains to be seen.

If you desperately want your own private island, ask to be dropped at **Maiden Cay**, a tiny, shadeless sandspit, or **Twin Cays**, shadier but with poorer swimming than at Lime Cay. En route to any of these, you'll pass the once heavily armed **Gun Cay**, still bearing evidence of its eighteenth-century fortification by the British, and the fast-disappearing **Rackham's Cay**, a visible victim of beach erosion.

Practicalities

The best place to **stay** in Port Royal is the elegant and atmospheric *Morgan's Harbour Hotel* (℡967 8030 or 8040, ⓦwww.morgansharbour.com; ⓺). It's convenient also for the airport, five minutes' drive away. The hotel is all dark wood and seafaring charm, with a pool and a salt-licked open-air bar. Room 105 here was the setting for the *Dr No* scene in which James Bond is woken by the attentions of a large spider. Bond also tumbles amongst crates of Red Stripe at the bar, transformed for the movie into "*Puss Fellers*" nightclub. Rates include a Lime Cay trip and, if you stay two or more nights, breakfast. Another option is *Admiral's Inn* (℡967 8669 or 856 5636, ⓕ967 8670, ⓔnautical@infochan.com; ⓶), by the Western Union office in the housing development behind Church Street, which has simple rooms with bathroom, a/c, cable TV, fridge and microwave. It's also worth asking around in the town square, as some local people will put up visitors in their homes.

Morgan's Harbour Hotel has a good restaurant, *Sir Henry's*, which affords marvellous views of the city and cooks up excellent seafood and international dishes. Several cheaper **eating** options near the ferry pier serve Port Royal's best fish and seafood, the stuff that Jamaicans will drive miles to get; all places offer steamed, fried or escovitch fish with bammy or rice, and the usual seafood combinations. The most popular is *Gloria's Rendezvous* at 5 Queen St, with tables right on the road and inside, where you can enjoy a tasty plate of fish and bammy and watch the pelicans and frigate birds fishing just offshore. Otherwise, there's *Buccaneer's Roost* next door, which has a lovely upstairs deck with a sea view and is also good for a drink, and, just down the road, *Fisherman's Cabin*, which is a lot less smart but has tables right by the water and on a short pier. In the housing scheme opposite the entrance to *Morgan's Harbour*, *Kevin's* also cooks up all things piscatorial, though in a less ambient atmosphere. You can also buy fried fish from stalls in the main square.

The *Angler's Club/MacFarlane's Bar*, at the corner of the square on Dockyard Lane, opens up for some hard **drinking**, and at weekends, speakers are stacked up in the square for an outdoor **party**, playing dancehall on Friday and oldies on Saturday. A friendly crowd piles down from Kingston, and it's a great opportunity to enjoy a very easy-going Jamaican street party. *Gloria's* is also the focus for a marvellous Sunday oldies party, and there's a small indoor club in the housing scheme, *Gloria's Top Spot*, which stages late-night dances at the weekends, around the back of town. These days, though, the more hip visitors head straight to *Y-Knot*, an excellent spot for a drink and a dance, set around a large wooden deck over the water adjacent to *Morgan's Harbour*. Most Kingstonians take their Lime Cay boats from here, and it's a busy scene at the weekends, with sand-dusted Cay visitors piling off the boats and heading straight to the bar, dancers staking out their portion of the deck, and swift business at the charcoal grill. The fish, lobster, chicken and shrimp are cooked to perfection here, and the conch soup is excellent.

West of Kingston

Southwest of Kingston, a **causeway** (closed to outgoing traffic from Mon–Fri 6.30–9am, and to incoming traffic Mon–Fri 4.30–7pm) connects the city to the bland but booming dormitory town of **PORTMORE**, currently in the parish of St Catherine but lobbying for municipal status of its own. Home to an estimated 120,000 people (and built to accommodate far fewer, as the recent strain on the sewage system illustrates), Portmore itself has nothing much of interest save its **racecourse** and a few shopping malls. But **Port Henderson**, a brief detour away, has a handful of colonial-era relics and fine views across Kingston harbour. Below Portmore, the road cuts across the eastern fringe of the **Hellshire Hills** – a vast and scrubby limestone expanse – and down to Hellshire's white-sand **beaches**. Further northwest, the former capital city of **Spanish Town**, a run-down shadow of its former self, still retains some graceful architecture, while the less accessible **Mountain River Cave**, **Colbeck Castle** and **Old Harbour** each offer a distinct glimpse into Jamaica's varied history.

Port Henderson

Established as a port in the 1770s, when it was the embarkation point for the ferry that provided a fast route to Spanish Town (then the capital city), **PORT HENDERSON** became a popular spa town and fashionable resort area during the Victorian era. It's now a small village with a few restored eighteenth- and nineteenth-century buildings, including the bar and restaurant at **Rodney's Arms**, named for the British admiral in charge of the local naval station during the late 1700s. Past here, towards the Jamaican Defence Force base, a trail leads up to **Rodney's Look-Out**, from where the admiral kept an eye peeled for French warships. The JDF keep-out signs aren't exactly welcoming, however, and you may prefer to take in the panorama by simply walking or driving up the hill past the restaurant.

To get to Port Henderson, take the left-hand exit as you cross the causeway from Kingston, then turn right onto Augusta Drive (also called Port Henderson Road) and left at the roundabout. En route, it's worth stopping off to look at the substantial old English fort at **Fort Augusta**, back at the causeway end of Augusta Drive. Built by the British on reclaimed land in 1740, it served as their main sea defence on Kingston's western side. Originally holding some eighty guns, the fort was struck by lightning in 1763, which ignited the three thousand barrels of gunpowder in the magazine and generated a big enough boom to kill three hundred people and break windows as far as seventeen miles away. It's now used as the island's only women's prison and is closed to visitors, though you can drive up as far as the gates. Many of the inmates here are "drug mules", who were caught attempting to smuggle cocaine out of the country by way of swallowing multiple packages of the drug.

Caymanas Racing

Once you've crossed the causeway, taking the right turn (Dawkins Drive) rather than the left onto Augusta Drive brings you into Portmore proper, an immense maze of identikit residential streets. You'll soon come to a roundabout adjacent to the Portmore Mall (home of the soon-to-be-reopened *Cactus* nightclub). Turn right at the PetCom gas station here onto Portmore Parkway, left at the sewage tank, and you'll see signs for **Caymanas Park** (℡ 988 2523). It's one of the best racetracks in the Caribbean, with a gorgeous backdrop of the Blue Mountains. Meets are held most Wednesdays and Saturdays (call ahead to check) and make a great day out, with much commentary and cursing from racegoers adding to the colourful scene. You can visit Caymanas on your own, but you'll undoubtedly have a better time if you go with Our Story Tours (see p.108), who charge US$48 for a day at the races, including lunch.

Practicalities

Buses and **minibuses** run to Port Henderson from Parade and to Portmore from Parade and Half Way Tree. There is nowhere to **stay** in Port Henderson itself, but Augusta Drive is lined with accommodation options, most of them short-time "motel no-tells" for couples seeking a discreet rendezvous. Despite being right on the sea, these aren't places with a holiday vibe, and there's little reason to stay here. However, *La Roose* (℡ 998 4654; ❸) has very reasonable air-conditioned rooms, while *Jewels* (℡ 988 6785; ❸), a little further on, has a nice pool beside its oceanfront restaurant. Both are on Augusta Drive, and while still considered "motel no-tells", they are slightly more respectable ones, where you might go to a show or for dinner. *Rodney's Arms*, justifiably the most popular local **eatery**, serves excellent seafood. The restaurant at *La Roose* is also good, dishing up fried chicken, fish and lobster, and there are plenty of fried-fish shacks along the causeway. In terms of **entertainment**, *La Roose* is a lively venue for dancehall shows and sound-system parties (go with a Jamaican friend), while *Jewels* is good for oldies sessions.

Hellshire and around

Covered in low, dense scrub and bushy cacti, the arid **Hellshire Hills** extend for around a hundred square miles west of Kingston. Around five hundred to a thousand years ago, this forbidding landscape was home to Taino Indians and, later, to runaway slaves. For now, though, virtually the only inhabitants are the migrant birds, a few conies and a handful of Jamaican **iguanas.** Thought extinct for half a century, the iguanas were rediscovered here in 1990 by a local man who had the foresight to take the specimen to the university for identification. Low rainfall and the unwelcoming limestone terrain have deterred people from settling out here, although the expansion of the suburb of Portmore threatens to encroach on the area's eastern half. It's not a bad place to **hike** if you're interested in seeing one of the island's genuine wilderness zones. Don't try it on your own – it's easy to get lost and there are some nasty sinkholes; Sun Venture Tours (see p.108) have excellent guides.

From Port Henderson, the signposted road to the Hellshire beaches runs under the flanks of the Hellshire Hills, passing a huge scar in the mountainside gouged out to provide marl for construction of Portmore's homes. Just before the quarry stands an abandoned high-rise building, formerly the *Forum Hotel*, built by the government in an unsuccessful attempt to entice tourists to the area. Past here, the road hits the coast again beside the **Great Salt Pond**. An old Taino fishing spot, the pond is a site of ecological significance that continues to be polluted by excesses from Portmore's woefully inadequate sewerage system. From there the road carries on to **Fort Clarence beach** (Mon–Fri 10am–5pm, Sat & Sun 8am–7pm; J$100), a pretty stretch of white sand and choppy waves (there's no outlying reef to protect the beach). Owned by the Urban Development Company (UDC), the beach has long been used as a venue for dancehall stageshows. At the time of writing, new management had just taken over, with a promise to refurbish the showers and changing rooms, upgrade the snack shop and add a go-kart track. They also plan to veto the stageshows, though it remains to be seen whether public demand will necessitate a rethink. Fort Clarence is usually very quiet, though lifeguards are on duty during opening hours.

If you're after atmosphere, though, it's far better to press on to **Hellshire beach** (no set hours; free), separated from Fort Clarence by a barrier reef that makes the Hellshire water a lot calmer. As the closest beach to the capital, Hellshire is buzzing at the weekends, with sound systems (particularly on a Sunday) and a party atmosphere. The powdery dunes are peppered with family groups that haven't been able to nab one of the wooden loungers set up under the shady eaves of the area's multiple **fish restaurants**, which compete to sell the freshest fish, lobster and festival. Most Jamaicans come here for the food as much as the sea and sand, and Hellshire fried fish, best eaten with festival and vinegary home-made pepper sauce, beats anything you'll find in town. The best cook shops are *Flo's* and *Seline's*, the latter with some wonderful wall art. You'll find that eating here can be expensive; expect to pay around J$1000 for four fish, four festivals and a couple of beers – a feast for two. Also present at the weekends are **watersports operators** offering jet skis and snorkelling equipment for rent, while horses (wearing fetching eye-gear to protect against flying sand grains) parade up and down giving children rides.

The only place to **stay** in the area is the friendly *Hellshire Beach Club* (☎989 8306; ❸), a cavernous white building with a pool and restaurant. The clean, tiled rooms have a/c, fan and TV; the ceiling mirrors are a hint as to why most people rent by the hour. Bus 1A from Parade and Half Way Tree in Kingston runs roughly every hour to the Hellshire beaches.

Nature's Paradise mineral spring

As there's no fresh water at Hellshire, a great way to sluice off the salt after a day on the beach is to head for the **Nature's Paradise mineral spring** (daily during daylight hours; J$40). From Hellshire, follow the signs to Spanish Town; when you meet the A1 Nelson Mandela Highway, go straight across into the road signposted for the Caymanas/Kingston Polo Club. Coming from central

Kingston, follow Washington Boulevard west out of town; just past the Ferry police station, turn right at the sign for the Caymanas/Kingston Polo Club. From the highway (and the Caymanas/Kingston Polo Club sign), a ten-minute drive through the lush surrounds of Caymanas estate brings you to the small community of Caymanas Bay. Here, to the right of the road, tall bamboo fences have been erected by the spring's Rasta caretakers, who open the gates so you can drive in and park within the compound. Seldom visited by tourists, and something of a Rasta hangout as well as a popular spot for baptisms, the spring is actually the point where the Fresh River rises from underground. You can see the water bubbling up from pipes once used to irrigate the cane fields. The river is clear, cool, refreshing and, at weekends, teeming with Jamaican swimmers who come to lark about and chill out to the music pumped from the small bar, where you can get snacks and drinks.

As the facilities are pretty basic (though there are toilets-cum-changing rooms), you're best off arriving in your swimming gear.

Spanish Town

Capital of Jamaica from 1534 to 1872, and still the island's second city, teeming, industrial **SPANISH TOWN**, twelve miles west of Kingston, today shows only vestigial traces of its former glory. Few tourists visit, and to be honest, it's not a place that you'll want to linger in for long. But the Georgian **square** – with possibly the finest collection of Georgian architecture in the Americas – and the great old **cathedral** – Jamaica's premier church and the oldest surviving Anglican cathedral outside England – repay the small effort involved in getting here from Kingston.

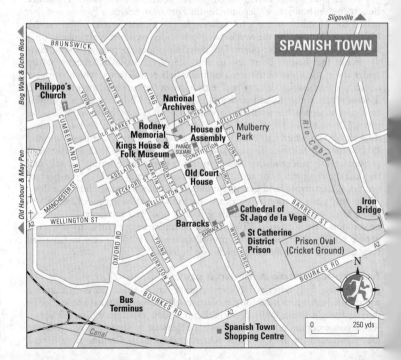

Some history

Spain's first attempt to create a city in Jamaica foundered when its chosen site at **New Seville** on the north coast proved well suited only to the spread of disease (see p.220). Its second choice at St Jago de la Vega (as Spanish Town was then known) proved more durable; there was fertile ground, no mosquito-ridden swamps and it was only a short march from two good south coast harbours (present-day Old Harbour and Kingston). The site also had great lookout points over the surrounding plains, although this proved of little help during English invasions in 1596 and 1643, when the city was comprehensively sacked. Sadly, there are almost no relics of the Spanish-era wooden and adobe buildings left today, although an extensive tunnel system – a hiding place for the Spaniards and their booty during English raids – is believed still to run under the centre of town.

Soon after the English captured Jamaica, the country experienced a boom in trade and, gradually, the newly created port city of Kingston began to flourish as the centre of population and commerce. Although huge sums were spent on Spanish Town's major public buildings in the late eighteenth century to boost the city's prestige, the authorities cut their losses and eventually moved the capital to Kingston in 1872, leaving Spanish Town to decay. Today, parts of the city are desolate, rumoured to be entirely controlled by political (or, some say, drug-running) gangs. More optimistically, though, there is some economic revitalization, with local industries – particularly in the busy free-trade zone – producing garments for export and cigarettes for the local market, and locals pushing hard for development funds and recognition of the area's potential as a "heritage tourism" site.

Arrival and orientation

Spanish Town lies to the west of the Rio Cobre, with Bourkes Road, the main highway from Kingston, running across its southern end, fifteen minutes' walk from the central square. If you're **driving** from Kingston, follow Washington Boulevard (from uptown) or Marcus Garvey Drive (from downtown) out of the city, a half-hour journey. **Bus** 21A runs regularly from New Kingston to the terminus on Bourkes Road, while a **taxi** from New Kingston costs about US$20. Once here, the main sights can easily be explored on foot, as the city is still laid out on its original neat grid system.

Parade Square

The starting point for any visit to Spanish Town should be the graceful **Parade Square**, centrepiece of the whole city. There is a charming little park at its middle, with a fountain and a few royal palms, while the buildings around are splendid showcase examples of Georgian architecture. On the north side, and boasting a new roof and a rather incongruous shade of orange paint on the walls, the **memorial to Admiral Rodney** was commissioned by the Jamaican House of Assembly. It commemorates Rodney's defeat of the French Navy at the battle of les Saintes, off Guadeloupe, in 1782 – a victory that ensured Jamaica's safety from invasion for centuries. The building houses a sculpture by English sculptor John Bacon. In accordance with the artistic convention of the time, Bacon put Rodney in classical dress, and the seaman is flanked by a couple of rare and intricate cannons, dated 1748, taken from the French flagship and still bearing the herald of the Sun King. In the 1870s the memorial was briefly moved to Kingston, but the aggrieved citizens of Spanish Town banded together and intimidated the authorities into returning it. Check out the stonework above Rodney, depicting his arms and motto

Jamaica's death row

The jail at Spanish Town, built right behind the cathedral, is home to Jamaica's notorious **death row**, the only place in the country that carries out capital punishment. In the recent past, hundreds of men have awaited their execution here in appalling conditions, some of them for as long as fourteen years. At present, twenty-plus men are on death row here; the last hanging, of Nathan Foster, took place in February 1988. In 1993 the cases of Earl Pratt and Ivan Morgan were brought before the Privy Council in London, which still sits as Jamaica's final court of appeal. Convicted of murder in 1979 and sentenced to hang, Pratt and Morgan had on three separate occasions heard the death warrant and been taken to the cells adjoining the gallows. Each time they received a last-minute reprieve. The Privy Council overturned the death sentence on the two men, finding that the length of time they had spent on death row was "cruel, inhumane and degrading". The verdict, which made future executions increasingly unlikely, didn't go down well with the vast majority of Jamaicans. In the face of soaring crime figures, they express widespread support for the penalty. The verdict has also increased pressure on the government to abandon the archaic reliance on the British House of Lords as the ultimate arbiter in Jamaica's legal matters, a hangover from colonial days.

In a bid to remove one of the international bodies to which death row inmates could lodge an appeal, and to speed up the legal process, Jamaica withdrew from the Optional Protocol to the International Covenant on Civil and Political Rights in January 1998. The 1999 hanging of nine men in Trinidad and Tobago further fuelled Jamaican debate on capital punishment, and as violent crime becomes ever more prevalent, popular opinion continues to urge the government to follow T&T's example. Following a campaign for the 2002 election that leant heavily on promises to expedite the death-penalty process, P.J. Patterson invited the opposition JLP to collaborate in drafting a constitutional amendment on hanging in December 2002; reform of the constitution requires a two-thirds parliamentary majority under Jamaican law. When passed (and it looks very likely that it will be), this amendment will reduce the level of legal protection afforded to death row prisoners, in breach of international law and standards. Condemned prisoners could be executed irrespective of the length of time spent on death row, while the prison's abysmal conditions would also become unlawful grounds for appeal. In June 2003, however, the amendment paled into significance with the ratification of a new Caribbean Court of Justice (see p.385), which will replace the British Privy Council as the island's final court of appeal and, effectively, clear the way for hangings. The fate of the men who remain on Spanish Town's death row seems increasingly inevitable. For more on Jamaica's death row and the issues surrounding capital punishment and human rights on the island, visit Amnesty International's website, ⓦwww.amnesty.org.

and a picture of the French ship sinking; the sides of the memorial show yet more ships being scuppered. A number of Spanish buildings, including a sixteenth-century tavern, were demolished to make way for the memorial and the adjoining buildings, which today include the **National Archives** (Mon–Thurs 9.30am–3.30pm, Fri 9am–3.30pm; free). Housed in a modern structure, the archives hold records dating back to the early days of English settlement. The courtyard outside the archives and memorial has been refurbished, with a few benches and understated landscaping. The former home of the archives, a cavernous Georgian structure adjoining the memorial, was undergoing refurbishment at the time of writing; a museum of Spanish Town is planned here in the near future. Directly opposite the memorial, on the other side of Parade Square, is the spanking new **courthouse**, built in Georgian style to replace the original nineteenth-century building, destroyed by fire in 1986.

On the west side of the square is the porticoed, red-brick facade of the **King's House**, built in 1762 and the official residence of the governor of Jamaica until the capital was moved to Kingston in 1872. It was here, in 1838, that one Lionel Smith stood on the front steps and read the proclamation declaring the full emancipation of Africans from slavery – an act that was only commemorated in 2001, when a plaque was unveiled here by Governor General Sir Howard Cooke. Following a catastrophic fire in 1925, the facade is all that remains of the King's House, but there's a great little **People's Museum** in the former stables at the back (Mon–Thurs 9.30am–4.30pm, Fri 9.30am–3.30pm; J$100). The main body of the museum has well-labelled displays on Jamaican architecture, agriculture, ways of life and crafts, with the emphasis firmly on upholding African traditions. Look out for the re-creation of a balm yard (see p.23) and a model of the square in its heyday.

The former **House of Assembly**, opposite the King's House, was built in the same year and to the same dimensions. The Assembly, comprised of representatives of the plantation owners and other bigwigs, met here until 1865, when, following the Morant Bay Rebellion (see p.152), Jamaica abandoned its constitution and became a Crown Colony with direct rule from Britain. Today the building is the seat of local government, reflecting Spanish Town's fall in the rankings. It is not officially open to the public, but you can normally sneak in to look at the grand mahogany staircase and the chamber upstairs.

The cathedral

From Parade Square, a five-minute walk south down White Church Street leads to the **Cathedral of St Jago de la Vega** (daily 9am–5pm; free), Jamaica's most important church and the oldest Anglican cathedral outside England. It stands on the foundations of the sixteenth-century Church of the Red Cross, and the black-and-white tiles in the aisle are thought to date from that Spanish building. Important monuments crowd the cathedral, many of them carved in England by leading sculptors of the time such as John Bacon and John Wilton, reflecting the status and wealth of the colony during the eighteenth century.

The **Blessed Sacrament Chapel**, to the left of the altar, holds a memorial to Basil Keith, governor of Jamaica during the 1770s; the sculpture by Wilton was the first monument in the country to be built with public funds. The **Lady Chapel**, on the other side, has a cherubic monument to another governor, Thomas Effingham, sculpted by Bacon. Slightly differing versions of the Jamaican coat of arms, with its Taino figures, crocodile and pineapples (once a sign of great wealth), can be seen on the Effingham monument and on the stained-glass window behind the altar. Also in the Lady Chapel, the memorial to one Hugh Lewis on the south wall features the only **death mask** in the Caribbean.

Throughout the cathedral are eloquent memorials to former governors, bishops and other leading figures of Jamaican society. William Chadwick was the only principal of Jamaica's first university – the Queen's College – which opened in 1873 for seven students but survived for just one year. Matthew Gregory established a benevolent fund for poor whites in 1765, aimed at finding a trade for the boys and a husband for the girls. John Colbeck, whose tomb is by the south door, was a soldier with the original English invading force in 1655 and is believed to have been the designer of Colbeck Castle, a few miles west of Spanish Town. Other tombs were mass burial sites for victims of cholera epidemics, or those who died on ships en route to the colony.

Outside, you can spend an hour exploring and deciphering the ancient gravestones under the mango trees. Note the **gargoyles** with African features

– considered to be unique anywhere – standing guard over a south window. Below them, a number of early governors, including Modyford and Lynch, found their final resting place, as did Martha Ducke, an early settler "most barbarously murdered by one of her own Negro slaves" in 1678.

Other sights

The old **iron bridge** spanning the Rio Cobre near where you drive into Spanish Town was erected in 1801 after being cast in England, and was the first of its kind in the Americas. In town, the attractive old English **barracks** building, west of the cathedral along Barracks Street, dates from the late eighteenth century. Before this the soldiers had been based in private houses dotted around town, which was seen as a threat to discipline. Cannons stand at the entrance to the barracks, as they once did at each of the public buildings, as a place to hitch up your horse.

A short walk from Parade Square down Constitution Street brings you to **Mulberry Park**. Formerly the site of a monastery where mulberry trees were grown to produce silk, today it is an infirmary for the indigent. It has also been a Jewish cemetery, and though now overrun with banana trees, the old headstones – some in English, others in Hebrew – have been propped up around the park's perimeter.

North of the square, on the corner of French and William streets, is an unremarkable Baptist church, first built in 1827 but badly damaged by the 1951 and 1988 hurricanes. It is popularly known as **Philippo's Church** for its associations with James Philippos, a missionary who campaigned for the abolition of slavery and the establishment of "free villages" for emancipated slaves, and who set up the first such community at **Sligoville** (see p.124). These free villages were an important part of the development of Jamaican society after emancipation. The plantation owners were strongly opposed to allowing slaves to set up their own communities, hoping that they would be forced to return to semi-serfdom on the plantations. They didn't reckon on the missionaries, mostly Baptists like Philippo, who bought up old estates, subdivided them and sold them off to the former slaves on generous terms. A church and a school were usually the first buildings erected in these new villages, with the houses going up around them, and this pattern of development can still be seen in parts of the country.

Practicalities

There are no good **hotels** or guesthouses in Spanish Town (those that exist are "love hotels" used by couples seeking a discreet rendezvous), and it's best to visit as a half-day trip from Kingston. A smattering of **restaurants** around the town centre serve typical if unexciting chicken and fish meals, and there are a couple of snack bars on Bourkes Road near the bus stop. The market, on Old Market Street, is good for a wander, and is busiest from Thursday to Sunday.

Around Spanish Town

A handful of places near Spanish Town merit a quick stop, particularly if you're driving. Two miles east is the **White Marl Taino Museum**, located at an important Taino archaeological site. Eight miles to the northwest, **Mountain River Cave** – home to some rare Taino cave paintings – takes quite a lot of effort to reach, but rewards the trouble. The route north from Spanish Town passes through the dramatically scenic **Bog Walk Gorge**. Ten miles to the north, and a few thousand feet above, the historical settlement of **Sligoville**, one of the first "free villages" established after the abolition of slavery, provides a cool perspective on the area. If you're heading west, you'll pass through the bustling little town of **Old Harbour**. If you're in a car, the ruins of nearby **Colbeck Castle** invite a quick detour.

You can of course explore Spanish Town's surrounds independently, but given the rich history of the area, you may find it more rewarding to arrange a tour with Our Story (see p.108).

White Marl Taino Museum

Two miles east of Spanish Town on the main A1 highway, the **White Marl Taino Museum** (Mon–Fri 9am–4pm; J$100) is located in a round thatched building built along the lines of a Taino *cacique*'s (or chief's) hut. It sits on top of a former Taino midden that's considered one of the most important in the Caribbean. Excavations of the hill have turned up burial grounds containing Taino skeletons ranging from seven hundred to a thousand years old, as well as pottery, woodcarvings, jewellery, amulets and cooking and eating utensils. Some of them are on display inside, but the majority were taken out of the country long ago. Many of the best, commandeered by Sir Hans Sloane, reside in the British Museum, so some of the artefacts are reproductions. Nonetheless, the museum makes a valiant and successful effort to portray the Taino people and their way of life. Well-labelled panels around the walls describe everything from the Tainos' complex social structure to their fishing and hunting techniques, burial customs and religion; check out the spatulas used to induce cleansing vomiting before worship. The museum is on the Kingston-bound side of the highway, and the turn-off for White Marl is signposted.

Mountain River Cave and Guanaboa Vale

Although Taino petroglyphs or stone-carvings have been found throughout the Caribbean, very few instances of their **paintings** survive. Accordingly, the flat roof of **Mountain River Cave**, adorned with fifty or so black drawings – human figures, a turtle, lizards, fish, frogs – is a significant historic relic. The emphasis on food suggests that the cave might have been used for religious rites intended to ensure successful hunting. Don't expect anything spectacular - the figures are small, and it's not always easy to make out what they are supposed to be. The real pleasure of this isolated spot is the tiny glimpse offered by the paintings - among the few visible markers left by the island's first inhabitants – into Jamaica's pre-Columbian history.

First uncovered in 1897, the small cave has been thoroughly documented by the Smithsonian Institution in Washington DC and is now a National Trust site. To reach it, drive northwest from Spanish Town towards Lluidas Vale, where a monument commemorates **Juan Lubolo**, a slave turned maroon turned guerrilla who assisted British forces in the fight against the Spaniards. You'll pass through the pretty and ancient village of **Guanaboa Vale**, childhood home of Jamaican National Hero and former political leader Norman Manley. A **church** has stood here since 1675 – very early in the period of English rule – although the present structure mostly dates from 1845, after repeated hurricane damage to the original. A couple of miles uphill beyond Guanaboa in Macka Tree district, *Cudjoe's Cavern* restaurant (good for drinks and basic Jamaican meals) and a small signpost on your right mark the entrance to the site; ask at the adjoining house for a guide to take you to the cave. It's a fairly tough half-mile walk, involving a couple of steep slopes through cocoa, coffee and jackfruit trees. You'll also cross the narrow Thompson's River, which, a hundred yards downstream, has a small **waterfall** and a refreshing swimming spot.

Bog Walk Gorge, Sligoville and the road to Ocho Rios

The smooth but busy main road from Spanish Town to Ocho Rios, a couple of hours' drive away, runs north past Bog Walk and Ewarton. The first part of the drive is very scenic, the road cutting through the deep **Bog Walk Gorge**, a towering limestone canyon carved out of the rock over the centuries by the deep green waters of the Rio Cobre. Cars cross the river at **Flat Bridge**, an eighteenth-century stone bridge that has no sides and loses reckless drivers into the eddying river with alarming frequency. Just past Flat Bridge, a Jamaican companion may be able to point out "Pum Pum Rock," a very vagina-like cavity in the Rio Cobre's rocky banks. All along the route you'll see farmers selling their colourful crops – bananas, oranges, sweet potatoes and, in season, fabulous mangoes and luscious naseberries. If you're passing on a Saturday, **LINSTEAD**, eight miles north of Flat Bridge, still has a traditional weekend market, immortalized in the folk song *Linstead Market*: "Carry me ackee go a Linstead Market/Not a quattie would sell".

SLIGOVILLE, six miles east of Bog Walk and several hundred feet above, was the first free village in Jamaica. It was named in honour of the pro-emancipation Marquis of Sligo, Howe Peter Browne, who arrived from Britain as Jamaica's governor in 1834 to supervise the six-year "apprenticeship" (in effect, semi-slavery) period that followed the initial abolition of the trade in the same year. Browne bestowed land at Sligoville to the Reverend James Philippo so that he could establish a settlement for ex-slaves. Unsurprisingly, Browne's stance on emancipation didn't go down too well with the white planters in Jamaica, who regarded their governor as an "annoying" man who "interpreted the law in favour of the Negro". Exasperated by his opponents, Browne resigned two years later and returned to Britain to press for full emancipation, testifying in the commission of enquiry that led Queen Victoria to grant full freedom to Jamaica's former slaves.

Sligoville is a peaceful, serene place today. There's not much to it – turn left just before the police station to reach the Marquis' former **summer house**, Highgate, built to take advantage of the cool mountain climate. It's now occupied by the US Peace Corps, which has developed the building into an environmental education centre. Highgate affords utterly fabulous views of shimmering Portmore below, and makes a pleasantly different place to **stay** for a night or so, though you need your own transport. Currently there are only hostel-type bunks (US$20) and shared facilities in the Peace Corps building. To reserve a space, call ahead or email (T749 1845, Esligoville1 @hotmail.com). Meals are available.

On a ridge opposite Highgate is the boxy **Mount Zion Church**, originally established by black Baptist George Lyle (see p.401) but rebuilt after hurricane damage. Inside is a plaque presented to the church by Jeremy Ulick Browne, the eleventh Marquis of Sligoville and a descendent of Howe Peter Browne, when he visited Sligoville in 1996 to attend a service commemorating the end of slavery in Jamaica.

West to Old Harbour

West of Spanish Town, the main A2 road divides at Bushy Park; left takes you along the old main road to Old Harbour, while going straight ahead takes you onto the spanking new first portion of the Highway 2000, which will eventually run the length of the south coast. The old Old Harbour main road is lined by hole-in-the-wall shops, multiple go-go clubs and bars decorated with some gaudily gorgeous exterior paintwork – the *No To The System* bar is particularly psychedelic. Four miles or so from Spanish Town, a Texaco garage on the

Indians in Jamaica

In 1845, just over a decade after slavery was ended in Jamaica, *The Blundell* landed at Old Harbour Bay. The event marked the start of a new bout of colonial social engineering in Jamaica, for the ship carried the first load of indentured Indian labourers. The abolition of slavery and the subsequent refusal of many ex-slaves to work for their former masters provoked a drastic need for cheap labour on the sugar estates. The estate owners, having failed to import the required workers from Europe, China and Africa, turned instead to the poverty-stricken states of northern India.

Thirty-five thousand Indians came to Jamaica before the Indian government put a stop to it in 1917. In theory, the labourers were to work on the estates to pay the cost of their passage from India, and would have the chance to earn money to send home before returning themselves at the end of their contracts (generally five to seven years). In fact, almost all were forced to work under appalling conditions of semi-slavery for miserly pay (if any) and the majority remained and died in Jamaica, establishing close communities and continuing to celebrate traditional Hindu festivals like Diwali, Holi and Hosay. Indians still constitute what is probably the largest ethnic minority in the country (although on nothing like the scale of Trinidad and Guyana), but in recent decades their separate identity has begun to disappear as they have been assimilated into the wider community. Today their most potent legacy is a taste for curry and for ganja, introduced to Jamaica by the first wave of Indian labourers.

right marks the turn-off for the **Serenity Fishing and Wildlife Sanctuary** (Thurs–Sun 10am–6pm, call ☏708 5515 to visit on other days; J$200). If you pass the Serenity sign on the main road, you've gone too far. Owned and operated by the Guardsman security company (the frenzied barking that echoes around the place emanates from the guard dogs that are reared and trained here), Serenity is a neatly landscaped complex of **fishing ponds** stocked with tilapia. There's also a small **zoo**, inhabited by ostriches, ponies, llamas, monkeys, tropical birds (many with a well-developed vocabulary), and reptiles in a long row of cages. Less exotic are the "frizzle" chickens, also known as "peel neck" fowl for their scrawny, featherless necks and rumpled plumage. The zoo is generally the preserve of school groups, who come for educational days out, while the ponds are popular on the weekend when locals descend to fish for their suppers or cool off at the bar. Rods and lines are included in the entrance fee, and you pay for your catch by the pound; you can either have it cooked up here at the restaurant/bar area or take it home. Boat and horseback treks are also available, and it's a nice, breezy spot to break your journey.

Past Serenity, and just before the road swings into Old Harbour proper, look out for the banner on the left of the road for the Mighty Gully Youth Project. Behind it is the simple studio and shop of accomplished woodcarver **Lancelot Bryan**, a former tractor driver who won a scholarship to the Jamaica School of Art after coming second in a national art competition. Working only in lignum vitae roots, which must be seasoned for ten years before being set upon with a chisel, Bryan produces exquisite, delicate figures, deemed good enough to have been presented to Desmond Tutu and Queen Elizabeth by the Jamaican government. If you're considering bringing carvings home, this is an excellent place to buy. Bryan also runs a training school for young local artists.

From Bryan's studio, it's a short hop to the busy little town of **OLD HARBOUR**, nine miles west of Spanish Town. Crowded, noisy food markets spill over onto the road near the town centre, and traffic always seems to get clogged up around the central square. The delay will give you time to admire the **clocktower**, which has kept pretty much perfect time since it was first installed here in the seventeenth century.

Three miles south (take the left turning from the square), the fishing village of **OLD HARBOUR BAY** was, four hundred years ago, an important harbour for the Spanish as they settled in and around Spanish Town. Columbus stopped here to meet with Taino leaders in 1494, and in 1845 the first wave of Jamaica's Indian indentured labourers docked here (see box, page 125). Columbus named the area Cow Bay, after the **manatees**, or sea cows, that once proliferated offshore. Few of the gentle creatures have survived centuries of slaughter at the hands of local fishermen, and the only things you'll find here now are fishing boats, shacks and a few stalls selling fresh fish and lobster. As you'd expect, it's a good place to stop for a tasty fish lunch. Try *Aunties*, some way back from the sea, with a shaded outdoor dining area – the conch soup is excellent. Just offshore from the fishing beach, the virtually uninhabited **Great Goat Island** was used as a US Navy base during World War II, and is now home to a few fishermen who shelter in the crumbling barracks.

Two and a half miles from Old Harbour lie what's left of **Colbeck Castle** (unrestricted access). These are among the oldest ruins in the country and, like Fort Charles at Port Royal, speak of the constant fear of invasion felt by the early English settlers. The castle was built on land granted to John Colbeck, an officer with the English invasion force that captured Jamaica from the Spanish in 1655, and strategically placed within ten miles of both the coast and the capital Spanish Town. Though the date of construction is uncertain (it's estimated at 1680 by the Jamaica National Heritage Trust), it is probable that Colbeck himself had the castle fortified with the massive walls of imported brick and local cut stone. A perimeter wall had a smaller guardhouse – probably a combination of living quarters and a defensive position – at each corner.

No records have been found detailing the identities of the workmen, but it seems likely that the work was done by slaves under the guidance of skilled artisans from England. The circular brick windows on the ground floor are unusual, and the brick arches that front the main building are equally striking, suggesting that decoration, as well as defence, was important to the architect. The rest of the castle is rather dilapidated, with collapsed staircases and exposed timbers hinting at a grand design.

It's a bit of a palaver to get to Colbeck. Turn inland at the clock tower in Old Harbour and continue until the road splits in three; take the centre route and follow the winding road lined with fields of tobacco plants (the ruins loom up on your left after a while) until you cross a bridge. After about four hundred yards, take the first left down a gravel road/dirt track. Follow this for just over half a mile to the castle. If it has been raining you may want to walk rather than risk getting your vehicle stuck.

North of Kingston

The main A3 artery shoots north from Kingston, shearing first through the affluent Stony Hill suburbs, all electric gates, expansive driveways and barking guard dogs. First stop, fourteen miles along, is **Castleton Botanical Gardens** (daily 9am–5pm; free), which occupy fifteen acres adjacent to the Wag Water River. Established in 1862, with support from London's Kew Gardens, Castleton quickly became the best-stocked garden in the Caribbean, and many of the plants that now dominate the island – the ubiquitous **poinciana** for example – were first introduced here. Despite the damage caused by recent hurricanes (and by official neglect), the gardens are still an important research station and well worth a stop if you're passing. The guides, who are no longer paid and survive only on tips from visitors, are quite excellent; chief guide Roy Bennett has been here for over sixty years, and his tours are a delight.

The gardens are well set out and easy to explore. There is a bewildering variety of palm trees, as well as coffee, cocoa and ebony, all of the island's perfume and spice plants, and a diverse collection of foreign plants and trees, including the startling cannonball tree. You'll also be offered the opportunity to taste fruits in season, such as the unusual African velvet apple. The peace and quiet attracts a lot of bird life. You may well spot Jamaica's national bird – the streamer tail hummingbird, also known as the "**doctor bird**", supposedly for its resemblance to a doctor in Victorian costume – and the tiny bee hummingbird, one of the smallest birds in the world. When you've finished your tour, there is a small **bar** on the other side of the road, where you can also buy Mr Bennet's accomplished bamboo carvings. Further down there's more open space with access to the river, where you can swim or take a picnic.

Beyond Castleton, the A3 winds a beautiful – but demanding if you're driving – route to Annotto Bay on the north coast (see Chapter Two, p.183). The road runs parallel to the Wag Water River and offers occasional marvellous views of the rocky river bed below. About halfway to the coast, the tiny community of **Friendship Gully** – better known to all as Junction – offers a couple of places to break your journey with a snack at a fried chicken/Chinese food joint or a small Jamaican eatery.

Travel details

It is impossible to predict accurately the frequency of buses and minibuses in the Kingston region, so the figures below are only general guidelines. However, on the most popular routes you should be able to count on getting a ride within an hour if you travel in the morning; things normally quiet down later in the day. On less popular routes, you're best off asking for probable departure times the day before you travel.

Buses and minibuses

Kingston to: Black River (4 daily; 4hr); Mandeville (6 daily; 3hr); Montego Bay (3 daily; 5hr 30min); Negril (2 daily; 6hr); Ocho Rios (4 daily; 3hr 30min); Port Antonio (via Annotto Bay, 4 daily, 4hr; via Morant Bay, 3 daily, 4hr 30min); Port Royal (7 daily; 25min); Spanish Town (12 daily; 30min). **Spanish Town to:** Black River (2 daily; 4hr); Mandeville (6 daily; 2hr 30min); Montego Bay (3 daily; 5 hr); Negril (2 daily; 5hr 30min); Ocho Rios (3 daily; 2hr 30min).

Ferries

Kingston to: Port Royal (Mon–Sat 7 daily, Sun 4 daily; 30min).

Flights

Kingston to: Montego Bay (Mon–Fri 8 daily, Sat & Sun 5 daily; 35min); Negril (1 daily; 1hr); Port Antonio (1 daily; 40min).

2

The Blue Mountains and the east

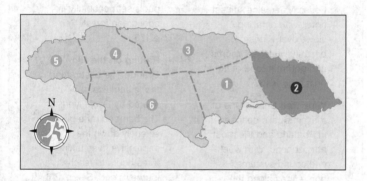

CHAPTER 2

Highlights

✳ **Climbing Blue Mountain Peak** Start at midnight and arrive at Jamaica's highest point in time to see the sun rise over the spectacular Blue Mountain range. See p.137

✳ **Strawberry Hill Hotel** Possibly Jamaica's finest hotel, with amazing views over Kingston, beautifully elegant rooms and gourmet food at its best. See p.137

✳ **Winnifred Beach** One of the last public beaches in Portland and the most atmospheric, with weekend sound systems, horse rides along the sand and little shacks serving up cold beer and fresh fried fish. See p.169

✳ **Port Antonio** Small historic town with lots of character set around two pretty bays. *Jamaica Heights,* right above the town, is one of the best guesthouses on the island. See p.161

✳ **Reach Falls** Low-key tourist attraction with a lovely waterfall and series of upstream river pools set peacefully in cool green forest. See p.175

✳ **Rafting on the Rio Grande** The best rafting trip in Jamaica, pioneered by Errol Flynn. The bamboo rafts glide serenely down the impressive river, taking three hours to reach journey's end. See p.176

✳ **Jerk Pork at Blueberry Hill** Better even than Boston Bay's, the jerk pork sold at this scruffy roadside stall is the most succulent in Jamaica. See p.183

△ Long Bay Beach, Portland

2

The Blue Mountains
and the east

Towering behind Kingston and enticingly visible from anywhere in the island's eastern third, the **Blue Mountains** conform with few people's mental image of Jamaica, land of sand, sea and reggae. At 28 miles, the mountains form one of the longest continuous ranges in the Caribbean, and their cool, fragrant woodlands, dotted with coffee plantations and often shrouded in mist, offer some of the best hiking on the island and a welcome break from the heat of the coast. The most popular hike is to **Blue Mountain Peak** – at 7402ft, the highest point in Jamaica – but there are dozens of other trekking possibilities, and more relaxed options for non-hikers, including a lovely undeveloped **waterfall** at Fishdone, down towards the north coast, the **botanical gardens** at Cinchona and a chance to visit the estates producing some of the most expensive **coffee** on earth.

Bisected by the mountains, the island's two easternmost parishes are relatively unknown outside Jamaica. Spreading back from the coast south of the range, **St Thomas** is historically one of the country's poorest and least developed regions, despite its rich history, remote beaches and stunning scenery; tourist development remains negligible here, but there's plenty to do if you're willing to get into explorer mode. A handful of hotels are slowly springing up on the south coast's best beaches, particularly at **Lyssons** and **Retreat**, where you'll find small swathes of deserted golden sand. These are good bases for trips to the delightful mineral springs and botanical gardens at **Bath**, an attraction for several centuries but neglected since Hurricane Gilbert ravaged the area in 1988, or to the deserted beaches around **Morant Lighthouse**, Jamaica's most easterly point.

On the other side of the Blue Mountains (here officially known as the **John Crow** range), the northeastern parish of **Portland** is justifiably touted as one of the most beautiful parts of Jamaica, with jungle-smothered hillsides cascading down to postcard-perfect Caribbean shoreline. However, abundant rainfall and a longish, bumpy drive from the island's main airports mean that the tourist presence is less conspicuous than in other main resorts. All the more reason to come – the wetter climate supports some truly stupendous natural scenery, and if you stay in the parish capital, **Port Antonio**, you'll be close to the lovely waterfalls of **Reach** and **Somerset** and fabulous swimming at the magical **Blue Lagoon**. Inland, you can hike in pristine tropical **rainforest** or

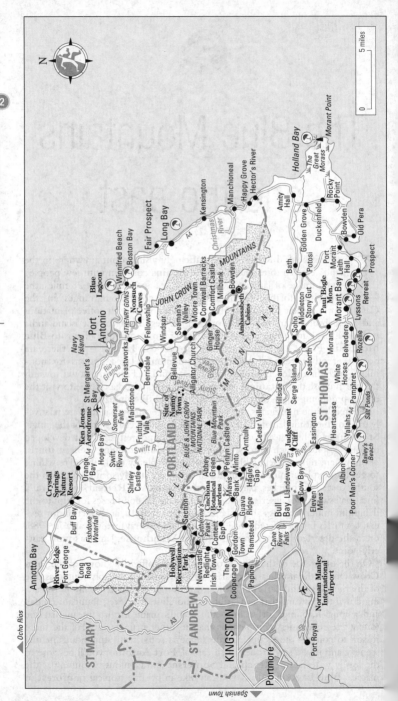

take a more gentle rafting trip on the **Rio Grande**. The **beaches** are equally spectacular as those further west, and they're far less crowded. There are some lovely places to stay to boot: the idyllic, surf-pounded stretch at **Long Bay** is fast developing into a haven for younger visitors, who come for the waves and the chilled-out atmosphere.

The main **A4 highway** runs all the way around the coastline of Portland and St Thomas, and most points along it are reachable by bus, but you'll need a car to explore much of the interior.

The Blue Mountains

The **BLUE MOUNTAINS** begin where Kingston ends, and a starker contrast would be hard to imagine, with the chaos of the city fast replaced by a tranquillity and a gentle beauty that, at its best, is truly staggering. The mountains are named for the mists that colour them from a distance, and their craggy slopes form an unbroken, undulating spine across Jamaica's easternmost parishes, a fabulously fertile tropical wilderness with a cool, wet climate found nowhere else in Jamaica.

The northern slopes of the mountains, the John Crow range, are covered by a huge quilt of dense, primary forest – easily the largest on the island. But deforestation has badly affected the southern side, where great chunks have been cleared by coffee planters, farmers, squatters and (catastrophically) Hurricane Gilbert in 1988. To try to protect the wilderness from further devastation, 200,000 acres of the Blue and John Crow mountains were designated as a **national park** in 1993, with the stated aims of managing natural resources for long-term sustainable use and generating income opportunities through eco-tourism. To help in the latter, great **hiking trails** have been carved into the interior of the forest, often following ancient mule trails over the mountains.

Most visitors to the park come here to hike up **Blue Mountain Peak** (see p.137) or follow the well-maintained trails around **Holywell** (see p.139); though exceptionally beautiful, the northern reaches are too remote and tough-going to be attempted by anyone except the most determined hikers. Elsewhere in the mountains, the botanical gardens at **Cinchona** (see p.142) are another delightful spot, a magical splash of colour 5000ft up, while the coffee factory at **Mavis Bank** (see p.144) is the place to go for the lowdown on production of the world's best coffee.

In population terms, though the dense forest provided perfect cover for the Windward Maroons during the seventeenth and eighteenth centuries (see box on p.178), the mountains have historically proved largely inhospitable. Even today, the population remains low, concentrated in small settlements like **Gordon Town** and **Newcastle**, or scattered around the edges of the national park, where people farm and raise cattle on the denuded slopes. Many visitors find mountain residents more gentle and welcoming than Jamaicans elsewhere – particularly compared to the residents of the heavily touristed north coast – despite the evident poverty and grinding workload many of them face. If

THE BLUE MOUNTAINS

ACCOMMODATION
Barbecue Heritage	4
Gardens	
Blue Mountain View	12
Guesthouse	
Dennis Family House	1
Forres Park	11
Gap Café	2
Hollywell Cabins	2
Jah B's	10
Mount Edge	5
Portland Gap Cabins	6
Starlight Chalet	3
Strawberry Hill Hotel	7
Whitfield Hall	8
Wildflower Lounge	9

RESTAURANTS
Crystal Edge	B
Gap Café	2
Seven Stars	A
Starlight Chalet	3
Strawberry Hill	7

0   2 miles

you're driving around, you'll pass some of the women who walk miles to pick coffee beans on the main estates, and a lift will be much appreciated.

   Tourism in the mountains remains small-scale. There are a few hotels, some of them quite spectacular, and a couple of backpackers' hostels (detailed throughout the text), but **coffee** is the mainstay of the local economy. Dark and earthy, Blue Mountain coffee is considered one of the world's best by experts, and prices reflect that assessment, though you can usually find it cheaper here – at the hotels or coffee factories or direct from the farmers – than anywhere else on the island. There are also several moderately diverting **coffee estate tours** for those keen to see how the stuff is produced.

Getting around

You'll need a **car** to get the most out of the mountains. Resurfaced in recent years, the principal access road, the **B1**, cuts straight through the slopes, connecting Kingston with Buff Bay on the north coast; a right fork at the small village of **The Cooperage** leads to Mavis Bank, the main access point for Blue Mountain Peak. Though the upgrade has improved the weather-battered tarmac considerably, landslides are inevitable in the wet season, when the roads come in for heavy assault; expect some bone-rattling. If you plan to head off these main routes, particularly to Cinchona or Abbey Green, you'll need a four-wheel-drive, otherwise, a regular rental car should suffice. Whatever you drive, though, you'll need to be extra-attentive when behind the wheel here. Though the roads appear wide enough only for a single vehicle, snorting delivery trucks loaded with precariously balanced crates of Red Stripe frequently barrel up the slopes, sounding their presence with mighty blasts on the horn. It's wise to turn off the radio here and listen out for oncoming traffic. Be sure to announce your presence with regular toots as well.

   Public transport will only take you as far as the main settlements. From Papine in northeast Kingston, **buses** (roughly J$50) go to Newcastle via Irish Town (with the occasional minibus managing to get up as far as Holywell), to Mavis Bank, and less frequently to Hagley Gap via Gordon Town. Ask around in Papine Square the day before you plan to travel, and avoid starting out on a Sunday. **Cycling** is an attractive option if you've got your own mountain bike (finding one to rent can be difficult). Several hotels run daylong biking expeditions, among them the *Mount Edge Guesthouse* (℡944 8151, Ⓦwww.jamaicaeu.com; US$40; see p.139), calling in at small coffee farms and private homes. Blue Mountain Tours (℡974 7075; US$89 including transfer, brunch, lunch and refreshments) picks you up from Port Antonio or Ocho Rios, drives you up into the mountains and lets you freewheel eighteen miles or so down to Fishdone waterfall near Buff Bay (see p.141).

Hiking

Extreme weather conditions, ecological protection projects and lack of funding mean that of the thirty recognized **trails** in the park, only twenty or so are open at any given time; any ranger station will provide a current update. If possible, avoid hiking in the rainy season (May–June & Sept–Oct), when you're almost guaranteed to get drenched.

   All the usual common-sense guidelines apply to mountain hiking. Bring the standard equipment (see p.55), including **drinking water**. (Wild pine bromeliads hold over a pint of water between their leaves, but as they're home

The mountain environment

The Blue Mountain range is Jamaica's oldest geographical feature, formed in the Cretaceous period (between 144 and 65 million years ago). Though the peaks are named for their cerulean tint when seen from afar, some of the rock actually is coloured blue by crossite minerals.

Categorized as montane (the technical term for high-altitude woodland), the **forests** are mostly native cedar, soapwood, sweetwood and dogwood evergreens, with a few blue mahoe, mahogany and teak trees, but the eucalyptus and Caribbean pines introduced in the 1950s are starting to dominate even in the primary forest above Holywell. The primeval-looking cyathea (**tree fern**), with its diamond-patterned trunk and top-heavy fronds is particularly distinctive; the tallest are more than 150 years old. Below the dense canopy is a layer of **shrubs**, of which the red tubular flowers of the cigar bush are the most identifiable. Every tree trunk or exposed rock is festooned with brightly coloured epiphytic ferns, mosses and lichen; most common are the inexhaustible swathes of dirty lime-coloured old man's beard. Wild strawberries, raspberries, blackberries and rose apples provide a free feast at middle altitudes, and you'll doubtless encounter the prickly vines of climbing bamboo, the only variety native to Jamaica. The tiny white flowers appear only once every 33 years, when each and every one blossoms simultaneously – but as they last bloomed in 1984, your next chance to see them is 2017. The mountains support over five hundred species of **flowering plant**, including around 65 varieties of orchid. Begonias, blue iris, agapanthus, lobelias, busy lizzies and fuchsias proliferate, while wild ginger lilies lend a delicate perfume to the fresh mountain air.

Other than mongooses, coneys and the wild pigs that roam the northern slopes, there are few **mammals** in the mountains. You may hear the scuffles of feral cats, mice and rats in the undergrowth, and Jamaican yellow boas inhabit the lower slopes in small numbers. The presence of bats is poorly documented; you're most likely to see them around the limestone slopes of the John Crow Mountains. By contrast, **bird life** flourishes; the forests ring out with the evocative whistle of the rufous-throated solitaire, and mockingbirds, crested quail doves (known as mountain witches), white-eyed thrushes, blackbirds and Jamaican todys add to the cacophony, backed by the squeaking mating calls of tree frogs.

The mountains are the sole habitat of one of the rarest and largest **butterflies** in the world, the six-inch **Giant Swallowtail**, but its distinctively patterned dark brown and gold wings rarely flutter into view – again, the warmer John Crow range yields the most sightings. Insects, on the other hand, are multitudinous, particularly during the summer months when it's common to see thousands of **fireflies** (locally known as peenie-wallies) clustering on a single bush and lighting it up like a Christmas tree.

to insect nymphs and tree frogs, you'll only be tempted to sup in an emergency.) Bins are rare, so carry a plastic bag to take every scrap of your rubbish home.

North to Newcastle

At Papine in northeast Kingston (see p.98), the city slams to an abrupt halt as it meets the southern edge of the Mona Valley. From here Gordon Town Road (B1) winds slowly upward into the riverine hills; the contrast between the lush, seemingly impenetrable countryside that leaks onto the battered tarmac to the concrete maelstrom you've left behind couldn't be more stark. Passing the Hope River, its banks reinforced with high concrete walls that carry floodwater into the Mona Dam, the first place you reach is the tiny village of **THE**

COOPERAGE, which is wrapped around a road junction and named for the Irish coopers who worked here in the early nineteenth century, making the wooden barrels in which Blue Mountain coffee was shipped abroad. The right fork leads toward Mavis Bank, and ultimately, Blue Mountain Peak (covered on p.144), while the left fork leads up a winding road for three miles to **IRISH TOWN**, where the coopers lived. Just over 3000ft above sea level, the town is now a small farming community, dominated by one magnificent **hotel**, *Strawberry Hill* (℡944 8400, ℻975 8408, ⓦwww.islandoutpost.com; ●). The brainchild of Island Records magnate Chris Blackwell, this former plantation opened as a hotel in 1994. Winner of a host of architectural awards, it's one of the most attractive places to stay in all Jamaica, with beautifully landscaped

Hiking in the Blue Mountains

Park practicalities

There's no charge to enter most parts of the Blue Mountains; however, since 1999, visitors pay US$2 to enter the managed Holywell Recreation area, and an additional US$3 to walk its orderly, waymarked trails. Park information is available from the park's main **ranger station**, located at **Holywell**; though there are smaller ranger stations at **Portland Gap** and **Millbank**, these are not always manned. Rangers can provide advice on weather conditions and trail access, and ordnance survey maps are on display in the stations for reference. None of the ranger stations has a phone, but you can make prior contact through the Jamaica Conservation and Development Trust in Kingston, which runs the park (℡920 8278-9, ⓦwww .greenjamaica.org).

Guides and organized groups

No matter where you're walking in the Blue Mountains, it's almost always advisable to use a **guide**; given the changeable weather conditions and poor hiking maps (in a terrain with few obvious landmarks), it's very easy to get lost. Security can also be a problem for unaccompanied hikers, particularly on the Kingston side of the mountains. A guide will ensure your safety, clear overgrown paths and provide an informed commentary. Most of the hotels in the mountains are a good starting point for an exploration of the area and offer guided tours and information on local hiking.

Forres Park Mavis Bank ℡927 8275 or 5957, ℻978 6942, ⓦwww.forrespark.com. This small hotel and farm isn't an official tour operator as such, but it can set up hiking tours and organize guides and transport all over the mountains. It also has its own accommodation in Abbey Green.

Mount Edge Just south of Newcastle ℡ & ℻944 8151, ⓦwww.jamaicaeu.com. Guesthouse with a limitless range of customized tours, standard trips to the Blue Mountain Peak (US$55 per person) and cycling tours (US$40, 4hr).

Strawberry Hill Irish Town ℡944 8400, ℻975 8408, ⓦwww.islandoutpost.com. The hotel offers a variety of short hikes and and nature tours to both guests and non-guests, from US$35 per person. Options include the Gordon Town Trail, which passes through small villages accessible only by foot, and the Copper Gully Trail to the attractive residential community of Greenwich. Both are steep, 2–3hr hikes.

Sun Venture 30 Balmoral Ave, Kingston 10 ℡960 6685, ℻920 8348, ⓦwww .sunventuretours.com. By far the best option for Blue Mountain hikes, including various daylong mountain walks (US$75–80) as well as treks to the peak, with a night at *Wildflower Lodge* in Abbey Green (US$110). Customized trips, including an overnight tour of the Grand Ridge, a mighty range of peaks that forms a boundary between Portland and St Thomas, are also available. These prices are based on groups of two to four people, and transport is included.

gardens (look out for the jade vine, with its unusual green flowers), a glorious pool and deck affording panoramic views, and a state-of-the-art spa. *Strawberry Hill* has a strong rock-and-roll pedigree – the Rolling Stones and U2 are regular visitors, and Bob Marley was brought here to convalesce after being shot in 1976 – but the stunning setting is far more absorbing than the celebrity credentials. Perched on the hillsides and offering fabulous Kingston or mountain views, the twelve luxury cottages – from studios to two-bedroom villas with full kitchens – are all made from local materials and imaginatively designed with Jamaican heritage in mind. The cottages boast hand-carved fretwork, louvered windows, muslin-draped mahogany four-poster beds with heated mattresses (it gets cold at night) and antique furniture; some feature private jacuzzis.

Even if you can't afford to stay here, **eating** at *Strawberry Hill* is a must. Set on the Great House terrace, the restaurant is the ultimate spot for a romantic dinner. The sublime fare is an eminently successful combination of fresh local ingredients and sophisticated international-style cooking, from baked crab backs with tropical remoulade, angel-hair pasta with tomato concasse and gorgeous salads to more conventional meals of jerk chicken roti or plantain crusted snapper. The restaurant's Sunday brunch, at US$53 per person, is an unmissable institution.

If you're after a less formal meal in Irish Town, the friendly *Crystal Edge*, at the roadside just south of the village, has an outside terrace with great views. It serves up a lovely janga or red peas soup and delicious jerk chicken and pork cooked in the open air.

Beyond Irish Town, the B1 passes the near-vertical driveway for **Craighton Coffee Estate**, a private Japanese-owned coffee plantation. The estate which previously offered low-key tours, is now closed to visitors.

From Craighton, the road passes the ridiculously high boundary walls of a private house (known locally as the Great Wall of China) built by the owner to protect his property from landslides and subsidence, and continues through the tiny village of **REDLIGHT**, named for the former brothels that kept the Irish coopers entertained. It's a charming, laid-back place with a couple of basic rum/provision shops and an attractive Ital restaurant and craft shop, the *Seven Stars*, which you can't miss – a double-storey building, it's boldly painted in Rasta colours of red, green and gold. The owners, a couple of friendly Rastafarians, are committed to their community and environment and are happy to help visitors with local information and finding accommodation in private homes.

The **Gordon Town Trail** loops downhill from Redlight, passing through small coffee plantations and precipitous fields of broccoli and scallion. The trail offers lots of opportunities for river swimming, with plenty of mini waterfalls and deepish pools; it's easy to follow once you get on to it – ask anyone in Redlight to direct you to the start, from where it'll take about two and a half hours to get to Gordon Town.

Newcastle

Four thousand feet up from Redlight is **NEWCASTLE**, an old British military base established by Major William Gomm in 1841 to escape the yellow fever raging on the hot, swampy plains below. The main road cuts across the **parade ground**, now a training ground for the Jamaica Defence Force, which still features old cannons and the insignia of the various regiments stationed here during the past century or so. The nearby military graveyard remembers the dead of that period with its neat, white crosses. Rather bizarrely, Newcastle soldiers operate a small, sporadically opened tuck shop in a far corner of the parade ground where you can buy beers and basic snacks. The views from the base across the mountains and down to Kingston are dazzling and almost vertiginous, while behind you, immediately above Newcastle, **Catherine's Peak** (5060ft) – named after Lady Catherine Long, the first woman to climb it, in 1760 – marks the highest point in the parish of St Andrew. You can make the steep, misty hike to the pylon-topped summit of Catherine's Peak via a concrete road that branches off the B1 just north of Newcastle and winds its way up, affording excellent views of Kingston when the mist clears.

For **accommodation**, a mere half mile from Newcastle is a delightful two-bedroom house to rent, marked by a sign for the *Barbecue Heritage Gardens of Cold Spring* (☎944 8411; ❸). Set on the grounds of a former coffee plantation, established by Irish naval officer Matthew Wallen while he was posted to the Newcastle barracks, the two-hundred-year-old house is eclectically furnished and boasts a long, shady verandah and a large bathroom with tub. Its caretakers, brothers Shawn and Chris Finnegan, live in a separate building on the property, take good care of the landscaped gardens and are friendly and welcoming hosts. Several miles further down and clinging to the side of the valley, *Mount Edge* (☎ & ℱ944 8151; ⓦwww.jamaicaeu.com; ❶–❸) is a laid-back guest-house-cum-restaurant run by wily local personality Michael Fox. The simple rooms inside the main house, and separate but small units just outside, are perfect for backpackers, while the bar is a great place to chill out. Meals (cooked to order; call ahead for dinner) are also available, ranging from crab in coconut milk to crayfish.

Holywell Recreational Park

A couple of miles past Newcastle, the mountain pass 4000ft up at **Hardwar Gap** is named for a British army captain who supervised the construction of the road from here to Buff Bay. On the left is the atmospheric **Gap Café** (☎997 3032; 10am–5pm), constructed in the 1930s and originally designed as a way station for those traversing the mountains by horse and carriage. American or continental breakfasts, and lunches or dinners of pizza, sandwiches, smoked marlin, escovitched fish, steaks or pasta are excellent here, costing J$300–500; the charming garden terrace and snug dining area are also perfect places to sink a cocktail or a beer. The café also has just one attractive **room to rent**, with its own kitchen; after dark, you'll have the place entirely to yourselves (❺ with continental breakfast).

Just beyond the café is the entrance to the **Holywell Recreational Park**, where you pay your US$2 entry fee (US$5 including guided walks of the trails within). The park is over 4000ft above sea level, and the deliciously fresh, fragrant mountain air here is always cool. Holywell is often bathed in mist; when it clears, you get a spectacular unbroken view over the shimmering streets of Kingston, Port Royal and Portmore below. This three hundred-acre "park within a park" is the gateway to the mountains proper and had protected status before the rest of the area. Easily accessible from the city, it's the busiest part of the mountains and is latticed with enjoyable, well-maintained hiking trails. Call at the ranger station – a hundred yards beyond the *Gap Café* – if you plan to hike further afield than the basic trails in the immediate area, best of which is the gentle Oatley Mountain jaunt (see below). On the opposite ridge you'll find a picnic spot with tables, covered gazebos, water faucets and a toilet.

Extensively replanted with Caribbean pines after Hurricane Gilbert, and a sanctuary for a wide variety of birds, the forest rising up sharply behind the ranger station is **Oatley Mountain** itself, while to the east is Mount Horeb and the ecologically sensitive (and so off-limits) Fairy Glades Trail, where pines are outnumbered by the twisted trunks of soapwood and dogwood trees laden with clusters of orchids and wild pines.

The popularity of **trails** around Holywell, detailed on boards dotted around the area, means that most are well maintained, but as rain can wreak havoc overnight, check in at the ranger station before you set off; you'll also need to be accompanied by a ranger for many of them. The best Holywell hike is the **Oatley Mountain Trail** (two miles; 40min) an easy, varied circular hike through the tunnel-like jungle. There are a couple of lookout towers and viewing platforms from which to enjoy the views, and several information boards explaining the flora and fauna found in the area. You can continue on to the **Waterfall Trail** (one and a half miles; 1hr 30min) – a mildly testing scramble along a river bed to the Cascade Waterfall; however, landslides have reduced the icy waters and swimming hole to a trickle.

If you want to **stay**, there are three **cabins** (❸), which are always full at weekends. You'll need to book well in advance through the Jamaica Conservation and Development Trust, 29 Dumbarton Ave, Kingston 10 (☎920 8278-9, ⒺJcdt@greenjamaica.org). The cabins sleep four to six people and are attractively rustic, with fireplaces and kitchenettes. But their interiors take second place to the marvellous setting, a Kingston view from your balcony, complete seclusion and plenty of pure mountain air. You can also **camp** at one of two picturesque campsites in the park (US$4 per person).

The park is host to an annual festival called "Misty Bliss – Mixing Mountain Pleasures and Treasures." Held on the last Sunday in February (10am–5pm; J$200), it celebrates Jamaica's unique mountain environment and culture. Traditional food and crafts are sold and entertainment includes Maroon drumming and dancing, storytelling and nature tours. Visitors are advised to take the special shuttle bus from the University of Technology in Kingston, and should call the JCDT (see above) for additional information.

Old Tavern Coffee Estate

A mile or so beyond Holywell at **Green Hills**, and stretching right up to Section, is the 120-acre **Old Tavern Coffee Estate** (☎ & ⒻJcdt924 2785). It's run by Alex and Dorothy Twyman from their unmarked cottage, which hangs vertiginously just below the mountain road. (Look out for Alex's battered Land Rover outside.) Due to archaic laws that insist all coffee beans grown in the Blue Mountains be processed at the JABLUM factory in Mavis Bank (see p.144), the Twymans were forced to fight long and hard for the right to process their own crop. In 1997, they became the only growers in the country to be awarded a licence to self-process, and the result is unquestionably the best Blue Mountain coffee you'll find anywhere in Jamaica, roasted to perfection right here. You can buy any of the Old Tavern blends directly from the source at a far lower price than in the resorts, or have it shipped right to you door; call the number above or visit ⓦwww.exportjamaica.org/oldtavern. If you call ahead, you should be able to arrange to tour the farm and learn a little of the incredibly tricky progression from plant to bean to pot. The estate is also laced with hugely enjoyable trails, and there's an appealing waterfall for swimming; you're welcome to use them, but it's best to phone in advance.

Section and around

Two miles past **Old Tavern**, **SECTION**, a friendly little settlement straggled around the road, is home to several small-scale coffee farmers and is a great place to both enquire about a hiking guide and buy some coffee (a pound of beans should cost about JS$500). The Dennis family, local coffee growers, offer cheap and very basic **accommodation** (☎423 6975; ●) in a large concrete house right on the road; there's usually someone hanging around outside to show you the traditional processing and roasting methods on display in out-buildings behind the house. There's a small, heavenly scented (of coffee, naturally) bar and café on site, too.

At Section, the road forks; turning left carries you toward the coast at Buff Bay (see below), while turning right and to the east takes you toward **Silver Hill**. As the road negotiates switchback turns, it then passes the signposted entrance to the *Starlight Chalets* (☎ & Ⓕ969 3116 or 985 9830, Ⓕ906 3075, Ⓦwww.jamaicamarketplace.com/starlight; ❸), an isolated and extremely appealing hotel on a gorgeous flower-filled bluff overlooking Silver Hill Gap. The carpeted rooms are modern and comfortable, with balconies and private, hot-water bathrooms. Guests enjoy access to a shared TV lounge as well as a sauna and small gym. You can use the kitchen, too, but after a day of mountain air, you'll probably prefer to eat the good, inexpensive Jamaican meals served up in the **restaurant**. This, and the attached bar, are also open to non-guests; call ahead if you plan to eat. There are a couple of bicycles available for guests to use, and several short trails surround the property, one leading down the valley to a swimmable river; guides are available.

Back at Section, the B1 begins its attractive seventeen-mile descent to Buff Bay on the north coast (see p.182), with fantastic clear views over the mountain gaps planted with neat rows of coffee. Other than the odd rum shop or farmers' cottage tucked into the jungle, there's little of specific interest to see, but the one essential stop is for a dip at **Fishdone Waterfall**, about nine miles before Buff Bay – turn left just before the white Silver Hill bridge at a sign for the Avocat Primary School. The fat, gushing cascade offers opportunities for a natural power shower, and the wide, clear pool of cool water is a fabulous place for a secluded swim.

Gordon Town and around

Back at the Kingston foothills of the Blue Mountains, the right fork off the B1 at The Cooperage heads past the tiny riverside village of **Industry**, where the Gordon Town River provides lots of swimming spots, to undistinguished **GORDON TOWN** itself. The only sizeable settlement in the Blue Mountains, it's built around a neat central square with a couple of small snack bars and the usual giggling gaggles of smartly turned-out schoolchildren. Crossing the bridge here and heading three miles east brings you past the colourful mural-painted walls of what was once the **Sangster's World's End liqueur factory**, the production centre for one of Jamaica's smallest rum makers until it went into receivership in 1999. The factory is permanently closed.

Flamstead, Clydesdale and Cinchona Botanical Gardens

Heading east from World's End, the road splits at the hilltop junction of Guava Ridge. Left takes you toward Section, while two consecutive right turns will take you past **Nyumbani** – the late Michael Manley's mountain home and coffee estate – to the **Flamstead plantation** (℡926 8257 or 960 0204, ⓦwww.flamstead.com). It was once the site of a magnificent great house that was home to Governor Edward Eyre (see box on p.152), British Admiral Horatio Nelson and subsequent naval captains, but the house has since been turned to rubble by a series of hurricanes. Today the plantation grows Blue Mountain coffee, and in an area where every turn you make offers jaw-dropping vistas, the panoramic view over Port Royal and the Caribbean Sea is unsurpassed. The plantation is open to the public: there's no charge if you just want to meander through the ruined house and gardens, but call ahead if you want to tour the small on-site museum – there's a modest fee depending on the size of the group. The road to Flamstead is pretty dire; it's probably best to take a tour with one of the hotels or tour operators listed on p.108. Alternatively, JUTA buses make the journey from Kingston for US$300 for fourteen passengers.

The northern fork of Guava Ridge takes you into the heart of coffee country. Two miles further north of the tiny hamlet of **Content Gap**, tucked into a remote pocket of the mountains and accessible only by foot or four-wheel-drive, is **Clydesdale**, an old coffee plantation converted into a nursery in 1937 by the Forestry Department. It's the last commercial tree plantation remaining in the mountains, with row upon row of Caribbean pines neatly arranged up the hillsides, networked by several paths that make for a pleasantly shady walk. Sadly, the plantation is now barely functioning as a financial enterprise; its buildings have long been abandoned and are in an advanced state of disrepair. It's still a lovely, tranquil spot though, and usually completely deserted so you'll need to bring a guide: *Forres Park* hotel in Mavis Bank run day-trips up to Clydesdale and on to Cinchona (US$45 for two people). It's also possible to camp here, though there are no facilities and you'll need written permission from the Forestry Department, 173 Constant Spring Rd (℡924 2667–8). There are also a couple of marked hiking trails through the grounds. Just before you reach the plantation, the road passes a small, icy-cold waterfall and river pool, known locally as the **Fountain of Life** for its supposedly healing properties. This was once a picnic and swimming spot, popular among locals and Kingstonians, a fact attested to by the now-derelict changing rooms; some people still make the tough journey up from Kingston.

Cinchona Botanical Gardens

From Clydesdale, you can drive within a mile of **Cinchona Botanical Gardens** (no set hours; free), bearing left up the steep path that snakes through the precipitous vegetable patches and coffee groves that cover Top Mountain. The road is abysmal, however, and you'll need a 4WD and a guide (see box on p.108). The gardens are at the summit, and their orderliness is a surprise after the rugged and wild hillsides below. Clinging to the ridge opposite Blue Mountain Peak and overlooking the Yallahs River valley, the ten-acre maintained gardens were initially a commercial venture, planted with Assam tea and cinchona trees – which produce quinine, used as an anti-malarial before the advent of modern drugs – in 1886. However, the inaccessibility of the site and competition from Indian plantations led to the project's decline, and it became a government-run public garden in 1968. It's still an important centre for botanical research.

The cinchona trees have all died out now, battered by the hurricanes, but the gardens are magical nonetheless. Several varieties of eucalyptus whistle in the breeze, and Norfolk Island pine, Japanese cedar, weeping cypress, rubber and camphor trees flourish in the mist. The vivid walled flower beds are bursting with blooms, and wild coffee smothers the slopes. You can see it all on the **Panorama Walk**, preferably accompanied by one of the gardeners (leave a tip). The walk takes you through a tunnel-like thicket of Holland bamboo, past a broken-down old caretaker's house and back to the main house, an ancient oblong of stone that still contains most of its original fittings. There are several other trails to enjoy around Cinchona; the garden supervisor will rustle up a guide for a nominal fee. Among the most rewarding paths are the sticky six-mile hike down to Mavis Bank, and the historic, ten-mile **Vinegar Hill Trail** to Buff Bay, an old trading route that the British used to transport supplies from Kingston to the north coast.

If you want to **stay** in Cinchona, US$6 will buy you floor space in the main house, but you'll need to bring food and bedding with you; you can also camp in the grounds.

Mavis Bank, Abbey Green and Blue Mountain Peak

Heading east from Guava Ridge, the next settlement along is **MAVIS BANK**, nestled in the Yallahs River valley. Accessible by bus from Papine, neatly arranged Mavis Bank is the last full-scale village on the route to Blue Mountain Peak. If you're driving, this is the place to park – in the lay-by opposite the police station – as only the sturdiest Land Rover can tackle the terrain beyond. There's little to the village itself, though it's very picturesque: the town's single street consists of a police station, several no-frills rum shops that also sell basic foods (Miss Jack's is the nicest of these), a couple of churches and a smattering of homes. The main organized attraction is the privately owned **Mavis Bank Central Factory** (Mon–Fri 10am–2pm; US$8; tours by appointment in advance, ☎977 8015) on the west side of the village. In business for around a hundred years and handling some 70,000 bushels of coffee per year, the factory is Jamaica's main Blue Mountain coffee processing plant, and it is here that the precious beans are graded, roasted and packaged under the **JABLUM** consortium name. Beginning with the obligatory infusion of steaming caffeine, the tour takes you through the entire process "from the berry to the cup". It's an engaging journey, particularly as the place is very much a working factory, and well worth an hour or so of your time. At the end, you can buy bags of beans far cheaper than in the shops.

Coffee aside, though, the main motivation for visiting Mavis Bank is undoubtedly hiking; with the peak temptingly close and legions of fabulous walks nearby, you'd be crazy not to test out some of the trails.

If you want to linger in Mavis Bank, the best place to **stay** is *Forres Park* (☎927 8275 or 5957, ℱ978 6942, ⓦwww.forrespark.com; ●–●), a delightful

Blue Mountain coffee

The story of **Blue Mountain coffee**, rated as one of the world's finest, is a long and turbulent one. Coffee trees from Ethiopia were introduced to Jamaica in 1728 by Governor Sir Nicholas Lawes, and they flourished on the cool slopes of the Blue Mountains. Cultivation of the crop reached new heights of excellence in 1801, when expert coffee growers flooded into Jamaica from revolution-torn Haiti. At the same time, the craze for coffee houses in Europe fuelled a massive demand for the beans. During the first half of the nineteenth century, Jamaica was among the world's main coffee exporters, producing up to fifteen thousand tons of beans per year.

The industry suffered its first crushing blow with emancipation in 1838, as streams of former slaves left the plantations to set up their own small farms. Soon afterwards, Britain abolished preferential trade terms for its colonies; under free trade, direct competition from the excellent coffees of South America crippled the small Jamaican farmers. The industry's decline continued into this century, with periodic hurricanes wiping out entire plantations.

After World War II, the Jamaican government took belated steps to save the Blue Mountains plantations. It established quality guidelines for both cultivation and processing, stipulating that only coffee grown at a certain altitude could claim the Blue Mountain name (you'll see other Jamaican coffee around the island called High Mountain or Low Land). This exclusivity heightened the coffee's cachet and helped to underpin its reputation worldwide. The biggest boost for the industry came during the 1980s as Japanese companies, with a big domestic market for Blue Mountain coffee, invested huge amounts in the best of the plantations. More than ninety percent of the stuff is now sold to Japan, reducing the amount available for export elsewhere and contributing to the extremely high price that you'll pay for Blue Mountain coffee in Europe and North America.

---

collection of self-contained wood cabins set around a large house that holds simple, comfortable rooms with private bathrooms. The staff are extremely friendly, and **meals** are available on request (non-guests are also welcome). It's also possible to arrange walks (both guided and self-guided) in the surrounding countryside and longer hikes to Blue Mountain Peak, Flamstead and Cinchona Botanical Gardens. The owners of *Forres Park* have plans to develop eco-tourism in the area and to turn the main house on their small coffee plantation in Abbey Green into a hostel for hikers; check their website for updates. They already operate specialist mountain-cycling excursions and bird-watching holidays led by expert birders – there are more than 33 endemic and migrant species in the area.

Abbey Green

You can start the hike up to Blue Mountain Peak from Mavis Bank, along the steep and strenuous Farm Hill Trail from the church, but most people prefer to begin from **ABBEY GREEN**, just over five miles northeast. At some 4500ft above sea level, it's a completely different world, where wind whistles through eucalyptus trees and seemingly impenetrable mists billow over the mountainside only to evaporate after a few rays of sun. It's a magical, intensely beautiful place, and you're unlikely to meet anyone save the odd coffee grower or scallion farmer. Three rustic **hostels** in Abbey Green (call ahead; see below) act as bases for peak hikers and offer Land Rover pick-up from Mavis Bank for US$30-40 per carload (maximum six people). On the way up, you'll turn left through **Hagley Gap** – a steeply inclining one-street village where you can buy last-ditch provisions and get a hot meal from a couple of small-scale cook shops – after which you'll traverse one of the least road-like roads in Jamaica, with huge gullies carved through the clay by coursing water and a constant scree of small boulders in your path.

Shortly after embarking on this tortuous route, you pass through pretty **MINTO**, a drawn-out roadside community where proud locals have decorated their gardens with brightly coloured flowers and shrubs. You can stay here at the *Blue Mountain View Guesthouse* (☎375 4588; ●), which has four simple bedrooms, a communal kitchen and stupendous views. The guesthouse's genial Rastafarian owner will prepare vegetarian meals and organize pick-ups from Mavis Bank (US$14 round-trip).

Of Abbey Green's hostels, *Whitfield Hall* (☎926 6612 or 927 0986; ●) is by far the most atmospheric, set in an old stone planters' house, with a huge communal sitting room with yellowing books lining the walls and a large blackened fireplace. The low ceilings and pre-war kitchen add to the archaic feel, as do the flickering oil lamps come nighttime. You sleep in bunks in the main house or in a self-contained cottage just down the hill, and you should be able to arrange to camp (US$5). The house sits at the centre of a working coffee plantation and farm; you can buy its own coffee and canned peaches. *Whitfield Hall* operates on a strictly no-ganja policy; if you're determined to light up you'll have to stay elsewhere.

A few hundred yards down the road is *Wildflower Lodge* (☎929 5395; ●), a modern two-storey house set in gorgeous flowered gardens. Bedding choices are similar, though there are private double rooms as well as bunk beds and a self-contained cottage; there's also a gift shop, cavernous kitchen and dining room. Whichever lodge you choose, it's a good idea to arrange to have a **hot meal** prepared ready for your return; you'll need it. Another option, on the hillside just below *Wildflower*, is the simple, friendly guesthouse run by local Rasta Jah B (c/o ☎977 8161), where bunk beds cost US$12 and meals are available. All the hostels can provide guides for the peak hike for around US$30.

Blue Mountain Peak

Undeniably the most rewarding hike in all of Jamaica, **Blue Mountain Peak** (7402ft), the highest point on the island, seems daunting but isn't the fearful climb you might imagine – though it's hardly a casual stroll, either. It is magnificent by day, when you can marvel at the opulence of the canopy, the thousands of orchids, mosses, bromeliads and lichens, the mighty shadows cast by the peak, and the coils of smoke from invisible dwellings below. It's also thrilling by night, when after a magical moonlit ascent, Kingston's lights occasionally twinkling in the distance, you find yourself at Jamaica's zenith as a new day dawns – a completely heart-stopping experience.

From Abbey Green, the climb to the peak is around eight miles, and can take anything from three to six hours depending on your fitness level. If you're staying at one of the hostels, you can start at around 1am and catch sunrise at the peak (at around 5.15 to 6.15am, depending on the time of year). If you synchronize your walk with a full moon, you'll get beautiful natural floodlighting – otherwise, take a flashlight. Regular signposts make the route easy to follow without the aid of a guide, but in this remote area it's sensible to go with someone who knows the way. Don't stray onto any of the tempting "short cuts" – it's illegal, you'll damage the sensitive environment, and you'll almost certainly get hopelessly lost. Rescue patrols might take days to find you, by which time you'll be in serious trouble.

The first stretch of the trail, a steep series of switchback turns through thick forest aptly named **Jacob's Ladder**, is said to be the most arduous (though you might disagree after a few hours more of tramping without a peak in sight). The halfway point – around 4.5 miles, or two hours' walking – is **Portland Gap Ranger Station**, where you can rest at the gazebo, fill up water bottles and let the rangers know that you're walking the trail (leave a note if you arrive in the early hours). A coffee shop is planned, but for now there's just a tuck shop, some pit toilets, a water pipe, a barbecue and two very basic cabins (**①**) where you can rent a bunk or some floor space – bring your own bedding and cooking utensils. Tent sites cost J$80. The cabins must be booked in advance via the Jamaica Conservation and Development Trust on ☎ 960 2848.

Once past Portland Gap, it's another three and a half miles to the peak. You'll hike through twisted montane and eventually low-lying elfin forest, in which the gnarled soapwood and dogwood evergreens are so stunted by low temperatures, exposure and lack of nutrients that they grow no higher than 8ft. You're still only about 6000ft up, but you might already be feeling dizzy or faint from the rising altitude; if so, go slowly and eat a high-energy snack. At around 7000ft, the plateau at **Lazy Man's Peak** is where many hikers call it a day, but it's worth struggling on for another twenty minutes, as a far more spectacular panorama awaits you at the peak.

If you've arrived before dawn, you'll be completely bowled over. The inky black slowly melts into ever-intensifying pinks, oranges and purples until finally a hint of wispy blue heralds the sun and reveals ranges unravelling like a sea of crumpled corrugated cardboard. It's quite possible you'll be here alone, the highest person in Jamaica and feeling – literally – on top of the world. As the sun burns off the mist, the panorama becomes recognizable; you can make out Cinchona and, on a good day, Buff Bay and Port Antonio's Navy Island to the north and Kingston, Portmore and coastal St Thomas to the south. If visibility is especially good, you may even catch a glimpse of Cuba, seventy miles away to the north. You get a heady perspective of the ranges you've crossed to get here, although a rather depressing view unfolds of the deforestation towards Kingston.

This is the furthest you can go into the Blue Mountains, as thick forest and treacherous, unexplored terrain means that even the burly pig hunters seldom venture further east, preferring to enter the John Crows from Millbank in Portland (see p.180).

St Thomas

ST THOMAS, nestling below the Blue Mountains, is probably the most neglected of Jamaica's parishes. Historically volatile, it has traditionally suffered from lack of government support. As a result, most of the villages you'll pass through are pretty impoverished, and tourist facilities remain meagre throughout. For some, however, this is the area's draw: a slice of the "real" Jamaica, untouched by the demands of tourism and boasting plenty of historical intrigue as well as some fabulous little-visited beauty spots.

Largely due to the presence of the descendants of free Africans, who were brought to the island after the abolition of slavery, St Thomas is also the cradle of Jamaica's African-based religions (see *Contexts*, p.401). Traditions from the mother country are more a part of daily life here than anywhere else in the island; it's not uncommon to see a Kumina session taking place right by the roadside. The region is also a favourite retreat for Kingstonians, who head for the beaches at weekends and stage large-scale sound-system parties and stageshows during holiday periods. Though the St Thomas coastline is served by buses barrelling between Kingston and Port Antonio, it's difficult to reach the more remote attractions without a car. But if you have your own transport or hire a driver for the day, they're well worth the effort.

The coastline between Kingston and **Morant Bay**, the parish capital, is mostly scrubby and less attractive than the north coast, despite the backdrop of the Blue Mountains, and there is little to Morant Bay itself. East of here, though, the scenery improves, becoming quite spectacular in places, while inland, sweeping vales and lush pastures are as pretty as any in Jamaica. **Lyssons** and **Retreat** are a couple of good beaches, and the rambling old spa town of **Bath**, up in the foothills of the mountains and close to the historic village of **Stony Gut** – birthplace of National Hero Paul Bogle – merits a visit in its own right. The romantically inclined can make for the deserted **Morant Point**, where a candy-striped lighthouse overlooks a stunning beach that marks Jamaica's most easterly point.

Kingston to Morant Bay

Heading east from Kingston, past the Palisadoes turn-off to Port Royal (see Chapter One), the A4 hugs the coastline, sweeping past the unappealing, litter-strewn Cable Hut beach, used more for sound-system parties than for swimming. Beyond the beach, the road barrels past the tiny settlements of **BULL BAY** and **COW BAY**. Named for the manatees that were caught and slaughtered here in the seventeenth and eighteenth centuries, they are more notable these days for the red-gold-and-green-painted buildings of the Bobo Shanti Rastafarian camp in the hills above Bull Bay, populated by orthodox followers of the late Prince Emmanuel Charles Edward. Unless you're serious about learning something of Bobo Shanti ways and are willing to dress appropriately modestly, it's not really a place to visit, particularly without someone to introduce you. Bull Bay itself is a rather intimidating place, and there's no reason to stop here unless you want to visit the **Cane River Falls**. The falls offer freshwater swimming, but they're little-visited by tourists, and you're best off going in local company. To reach the falls, turn off the A4 just before Bull Bay (it's marked by a hand-painted sign) and follow the marl-covered road for a mile or so. Just before a small Bailey bridge, a path leads down to the thin-but-strong cascade, said to have been Bob Marley's favourite place to wash his locks.

Back on the A4, the village of **ELEVEN MILES** holds a roadside marker that recalls **Jack Mansong**, a nineteenth-century Jamaican Robin Hood figure (see box p.149). North off the main highway here (turn inland at the Eleven Miles community notice board), a road leads up into the scrubby, forested hills towards the tiny village of **Llandewey**. (Look out for good Blue Mountain views around the sixteen-mile marker.) Turn right at Llandewey's Bethlehem Church, and you can take in the thousand-foot wall of **Judgement Cliff**. It was created by a massive landslide in 1692, caused by the same earthquake that flattened Port Royal a few miles west (see p.111). Local legend claims that its fall buried a particularly cruel and rapacious local planter and his estate – hence the name. As the cliff is smothered in vegetation these days, it's not exactly a startling sight. Heading back down towards the coast, the road runs parallel to the **Yallahs River**, one of Jamaica's longest waterways, now partially diverted to provide the capital with water, and passes the still-sturdy stone buttresses of Easington Bridge, which looks unfeasibly large in the dry season, when the river slows to a trickle. Just past the buttresses, you can either continue on to rejoin the coast at **Albion**, or cross the new bridge and head towards the sea via **Heartsease**. A string of rum bars and jerk vendors stand sentry at Heartsease, as if in wait for the regular spells of activity they see when the Yallahs River turns into a raging torrent during the rainy months. The river often floods the A4, forcing coastal traffic on an inland detour.

Yallahs and around

Back on the highway, the arid landscape is broken at **Poor Man's Corner**, the wide, boulder-strewn mouth of the Yallahs River, where a large new ford has been built in a not-altogether-successful attempt to keep the road passable when the river floods. Yet more rum bars herald your entrance into busy little **YALLAHS**, best known for its **twin giant salt ponds**, divided from the sea by a narrow spit of land and said to have been created by the tears of an English estate owner, distraught when his brother married the woman he loved. Up to eight times saltier than the ocean, the larger of the two ponds (and the second one you pass if driving east) has the highest saline levels; however, though it's a source of rock salt, it's not suitable to be made into table salt, as demonstrated by the scummy foam that laps the banks. Bacteria occasionally go on the rampage, turning the ponds a reddish colour, and scientists reckon that some of the micro-organisms are actually archeo-bacteria, among the earliest of the earth's life forms. A UWI research team, based at the lagoon edge, are currently studying the ponds, concentrating on artemia, a shrimp-like creature that's one of the few animals able to survive in such harsh surroundings.

Yallahs is known for its jerk stands, which line the main street, with large speakers blaring out the latest dancehall tunes. If you're travelling round the coast from Kingston, it's a much friendlier place to break your journey than Bull Bay (see above). *Thelma's,* on the eastern edge of town, is a good local restaurant serving standard Jamaican fare, as is the more centrally located *A&1* – both restaurants are on the main street. The *Links Seafood Lounge* is a more up-market fish restaurant on the ocean's edge with a swimming pool and regular sound-system parties and live music events. If you get stuck in Yallahs, there's a basic but serviceable hotel, the *Bailey's Beach Resort* (☎982 5056; ❶), set on an unappealing piece of grey fisherman's beach. It hosts popular Friday night karaoke sessions in its bar.

Continuing east of Yallahs, the A4 slips into the village of **WHITE HORSES**, named for its white limestone cliffs (though some say the moniker stems from the white-tipped waves of the choppy waters hereabouts). It's a relaxed, easy-going place to break your journey, with fruit sellers constantly present, and an opportunity to swim at **Rozelle Beach**, a pebbly, brown-sand strip paralleled by the tarmac that gets busy at weekends, when Kingstonians pile in for a day on the beach, queuing up to shower under the mini waterfall that gushes from the rocks on the inland side of the road. **Food** is available from a couple of beach shacks, and fried fish stands set up at weekends. If only for the name (though the food is fine), check out the *HotTaurant* restaurant in White Horses.

Three Finger Jack

Named **Three Finger Jack** for his battlescars, **Jack Mansong** was a runaway slave turned bandit, the scourge of British soldiers and travellers but, in the best tradition of the romantic nineteenth-century highwayman, unfailingly courteous to women and children. A formidable figure of nearly seven feet tall, Mansong's criminal activities began with the bungled attempted murder of one Captain Henry Harrop, the slave trader who'd transported Mansong's parents from Africa to Jamaica. Harming a white planter ensured a particularly grisly death sentence, but the night before his execution, Mansong escaped from his cell, capturing Harrop and carrying him to a cave deep in the St Thomas interior where, with delicious irony, he forced his former master to become his slave, eventually leaving him shackled to the cave wall where his remains were found years later. Using various hideouts – including caves near the Cane River Falls – Mansong then embarked on a reign of terror, gaining an almost mythical reputation in the process. By 1870, the House of Assembly had offered a reward of £100 and freedom to any slave who could capture him; a year later, with Jack still at large, the reward had been raised to £300 – a massive sum at the time. Fuelled by the promise of such riches, Quashie, the Maroon who had relieved Mansong of his fingers, managed to track him to his hideout. After a bloody battle, Mansong was shot in the stomach. Cutting off his head and hands and preserving them in a bucket of rum, Quashie proceeded to Spanish Town to claim his reward – reputedly, he was still receiving a generous pension from the state some sixty years later. Back in England, Three Finger Jack's legend was equally persistent – contemporaneous fascination with a man seen as a romantic hero inspired several plays and a West End musical.

Just beyond the beach, you'll pass the fertile **Rozelle** and **Belvedere** districts. The family of Captain Dow Baker (see box on p.157) once owned much of this land; today, it's still made up of large sugarcane, coconut and papaya plantations.

Morant Bay

Some two miles east of Rozelle, the lengthy span of the Bustamante Bridge over the Morant River takes you into the dusty town of **MORANT BAY**. Parish capital of St Thomas, Morant Bay is best known for having witnessed some of the ugliest moments in Jamaica's post-emancipation history. Edna Manley's grim-faced, life-size (but not that lifelike) statue of National Hero **Paul Bogle** stands in front of the courthouse in the town square, where he was hanged after leading the 1865 **Morant Bay Rebellion** (see box on p.152); a plaque honours the "patriots" who died alongside him. With a wide, double-spiral stone stairway leading up to a columned portico, the courthouse you see today was built as a replacement after the original building was razed in the rebellion. Bogle is buried behind it, alongside those who were tipped into a mass grave here after the uprising, and who were only afforded a proper burial when their remains were dug up by chance in 1965. Today, a memorial erected "in gratitude from the generation who now realize that they did not die in vain" marks the spot, poignantly dedicated to those "who fell because they loved freedom." Paul Bogle Day is celebrated yearly in Morant Bay on October 11, with a road race starting from his home village of Stony Gut, six miles away, and a big party in the town square. Nearby are three of the original nine 24-pound cannons that were installed here when the site housed a **British fort**.

There's not much else to the town. West across the square from the courthouse, past the attractive red-brick **Anglican church**, built in 1865, you're on Morant Bay's main street, home to the crowded **market** (Thurs-Sat), bursting

The Morant Bay Rebellion

A generation after emancipation, living conditions for Jamaica's black population remained abysmal. High unemployment and heavy taxation hit the poor hard, and the transition to a free society was hindered by the bias of the authorities. Courts invariably supported white landholders in cases of trespass or squatting against the small farmers, who struggled to find decent land to cultivate, and there were frequent dissenting outbreaks across the island. Some of these were over rumours of re-enslavement, others were protests at taxes, food shortages or lack of access to property. It was only a matter of time before black Jamaicans registered their grievances with a more organized, premeditated uprising.

In St Thomas, Baptist Deacon **Paul Bogle** – supported by **George William Gordon**, a wealthy mulatto member of the National Assembly whom Bogle had campaigned for (and who owed his seat to the support of Bogle's Native Baptists in St Thomas) – began to organize demonstrations against the inequity of the legal system. In August 1865, Bogle led a group that marched 54 miles from St Thomas to Spanish Town to protest to the island's governor, Edward Eyre – who refused to meet them. After being turned away, the group returned to St Thomas and made plans to create a "state within a state" at **Stony Gut**, Bogle's home village and the site of his church, with Bogle himself as priest, judge and chief. Getting wind of what they saw as seditious plans, the police had two of Bogle's supporters, Alexander White and Lewis Miller, arrested on trumped-up charges of assault and trespass. On October 7, Bogle and his men marched military-style to the Morant Bay courthouse where White and Miller were being tried, in an attempt to disrupt the proceedings against them (though only by surrounding the building). Despite the peaceful nature of the protest, the authorities saw their chance to arrest a "troublemaker" and issued warrants for Bogle's arrest. The police who tried to capture him were thwarted by the sheer power of numbers and forced to swear oaths that they would no longer serve public officials before they could escape.

On October 10, six policemen and two constables set out for Stony Gut in a bid to arrest Bogle and 28 of his followers. They underestimated his support, however, and were quickly overpowered and forced to swear allegiance to Bogle. Once back

out of its long-standing home and a good place to pick up fresh fruit and vegetables. Also on the main street is the Morant Bay library (Mon–Fri 9am–6pm, Sat 9am–1pm) which holds lots of tattered but interesting material on Paul Bogle and his rebellion.

The coastal road runs below Morant Bay's main street; to get to the square, turn uphill at the businesslike *Morant Villas Hotel* (℡ 982 2418, ℻ 982 1937; ❷), and the road leads up to South Street, where you can park by the courthouse. The **hotel** itself is fine, with a restaurant, bar and pool, and adequate, clean rooms and suites with fan, a/c and some with kitchenette, though there's not much reason to base yourself here when you can stay alongside the beaches further east. Morant Bay has several decent places to **eat** - the *Village Green* cafeteria, by the Esso petrol station as you head in from Kingston, serves particularly good fried chicken. The *Staff of Life* restaurant, in the Morant Bay Plaza, is a brightly painted Ital diner with tasty vegetable stews and natural juices.

If you've business to do, you'll find a small **shopping mall** on the lower coast road, with a branch of FX Trader for **currency exchange,** and there are several supermarkets on the town's main street. **Buses** and shared **taxis** en route to all parts of the island pull up at the car park next to the petrol station on the coast road.

in Morant Bay, the officers impressed the seriousness of the situation on the then-Custos Baron Von Ketelhadt, who promptly contacted his Kingston superiors for support; accordingly, one hundred soldiers set sail aboard the *HMS Wolverine*. On October 11, Bogle and his men again marched into Morant Bay from Stony Gut, raiding the police station for arms before attacking the courthouse where the local council was meeting. Eighteen soldiers and council members were killed as the crowd's frustration erupted; the courthouse was burned to the ground, and arms, gunpowder and foodstuffs were taken from the town's shops. The unrest quickly spread throughout St Thomas, but the government troops aboard the *Wolverine* were too late to quell the disturbance in Morant Bay when they put to shore on the morning of October 12. Fearing that the whole country would soon be engulfed, the authorities gave free rein to the army, and the protesters were crushed with brute ferocity. A staggering 437 people were executed; another six hundred men and women were flogged; and over a thousand homes were razed to the ground. Paul Bogle evaded capture and fled to the hills, where he remained undetected for several days. In Kingston, Governor Eyre declared martial law in the then-parish of St Thomas in the east and hand-wrote a warrant for the immediate arrest of his chief political opponent, George William Gordon, who was transported to Morant Bay for trial and was hanged outside the courthouse on October 20. With his chief advocate silenced, there was nowhere for Bogle to hide; he was captured at Stony Gut on October 23 and went to the gallows two days later.

The rebellion marked a key political and social watershed for Jamaica. Governor Eyre, the man behind the repression, was immediately recalled to England and stripped of his position. Jamaica's constitution was suspended and replaced with direct rule from the home country, allowing British governors to impose reforms, for example in education and the legal system, that would never have got past the local elite under previous governments. Although progress for the poor was still painfully slow, Bogle's defiant legacy ensured that Jamaica remained relatively peaceful until well into the next century. The Jamaican government eventually recognized Paul Bogle as a National Hero, and a monument to him stands in Heroes Circle in Kingston (see p.90).

Hillside Dam and Stony Gut

From the roundabout at the western outskirts of Morant Bay, a pockmarked road winds inland through luxuriant cattle pastures to a couple of little-visited attractions. Just past the Paul Bogle Junior High School are the tattered fronds of what was the Morant Banana Farms plantation, closed during the restructuring of the Jamaican banana industry following the WTO ruling against preferential prices paid by EU countries for Caribbean bananas. Another minor road forks off to the right here, leading toward Paul Bogle's birthplace, **Stony Gut.** Carrying straight on takes you into residential **Seaforth**, where the roadside is sprinkled with small-scale shops, bars and restaurants. From here, bear left and cross a bridge over the Morant River toward the pastoral surrounds of **Serge Island**, a dairy farm based on the site of an old sugar plantation, where the Blue Mountain views are fabulous and the fields of fat Jamaica Hope and Jersey cattle munch idly. A rough track to the right of the factory gates (in rainy season you'll need to walk it unless you have a 4WD) leads towards the Johnson River, where the shallow but fast-flowing waters meander along the centre of an improbably wide, boulder-strewn river bed, with the foothills of the Blue Mountains shelving off behind. Proceed left along the river bank and you'll reach **Hillside Dam** after a few minutes' walk. The dam was once a hydroelectric plant (closed after floods swept away most of the machinery); these days the water cascades over the dam's concrete lip, creating a deep swimming pool at its base. You can climb the huge rocks at the side to get to the top of the dam. It's a fabulously secluded place to spend a day, and you're unlikely to meet another soul – for that reason, you're probably best-off going in a group.

Stony Gut and the Paul Bogle Monument

Back on the inland road from the Morant Bay roundabout, the first right fork, at the hamlet of Morant, heads up into the hills towards **STONY GUT**, a half-hour drive from the coast and the former home of **Paul Bogle**, National Hero and leader of the Morant Bay Rebellion (see box on p.150). Though Stony Gut looks no different from the other communities you've passed through on the way up, with neat houses and flower-filled gardens lining the roadside, chickens pecking around on tarmac and curious eyes following any vehicle that makes it up this far, the village is central to the history of St Thomas and of Jamaica as a whole. From here, Deacon Bogle built the rockbed of support that enabled him to lead his rebellion, and it was also here that he was eventually captured by the authorities. Opposite the Methodist church, a large sign for the **Stony Gut Monument** points downhill to Bogle's simple stone memorial, shaded by Otaheite apple trees and bearing a plaque that outlines his deeds. Bogle's late great-grandson was caretaker of the site for many years and was interred behind the monument in 1995 at the request of the Jamaica National Heritage Trust.

Even if you've no interest in seeing Bogle's memorial, it's worth taking the trip for the scenery alone, with constant vistas of the Blue Mountains over verdant, fruited vales. From Stony Gut, you can drive further into the mountains via Middleton and Soho, looping back to the coast by way of Bath Mineral Spa (see opposite) or Serge Island.

Lyssons and around

Back on the coast, and a mile or so east of Morant Bay, the road swings into **LYSSONS**, a pretty residential community notable chiefly for its palm-fringed **beach**, easily the best in the area. Presiding over the beach is the aptly named but unobtrusive *Golden Shore Beach Resort* (T734 0923; ❷), at the end of the track opposite a small supermarket. With cool tile floors, a/c and cable TV, rooms are practically on the sand, and there's a restaurant and a small gazebo bar on site.

Lyssons slides imperceptibly into **RETREAT**, an unassuming sort of place that holds the majority of St Thomas's **accommodation** options. At the bottom of Crystal Drive, a right fork off the main road and right at the sea's edge, is the elegant *Whispering Bamboo Cove* (T982 2912, F734 1049, Wwww .go-jamaica.com; ❸-❺ breakfast included). It has a restaurant, a flower garden with a gazebo overlooking the sea, and rooms ranging from rather cramped but spotless doubles with private bathroom, cable TV and fan, to spacious suites. Back on the main road and a few hundred yards east, the wide lawns of the supremely friendly *Brown's Guesthouse* (T982 6205; ❷) sweep down to the sea; rooms are immaculate and home-style Jamaican, and meals are available. Set back from the main road in the East Prospect housing development, the *Bluemah Palace* (T & F982 6250; ❷) is a cavernous hotel, restaurant and bar. Rooms have huge beds, cable TV, a/c and the odd balcony, and the atrium area serves as a venue for occasional **Friday night jams**, with oldies reggae and plenty of food. Behind the *Bluemah Palace* on Blue Mahoe Road, heading straight down to the sea, is *Drakes Cove Guest House* (☎982 6244; ❷), a large concrete structure with simple but comfortable rooms set in a large garden right on the water. The friendly Jamaican owners can arrange fishing or boat trips with locals. All of Retreat's hotels are steps away from a pretty, unadorned strip of brown-sand beach.

The only other facilities are slightly further on at **PROSPECT** itself, which merges with Retreat. The **Hymans Bathing Beach** at Prospect boasts a simple bar and rudimentary changing rooms. On weekend nights the bar, which doubles up as the local go-go club, gets packed out.

For **food**, the enormous *Chef's Sea View* on the Lyssons road just east of Morant Bay is decent enough, serving Jamaican breakfasts, lunches and dinners daily; the restaurant is occasionally used to stage parties and the odd reggae show. Best of all in the area is the *Fish Cave* restaurant in Leith Hall, a small fishing community between Prospect and Port Morant. You choose your fish from a cool box and it's cooked one of several ways, including fried and stewed with vegetables. Conch soup and other seafood dishes are also on the reasonably priced menu. Shaded tables are set out in a peaceful grassy lawn, and the staff are supremely friendly. If you fancy a **drink**, head for one of several rum shops that line the main road or, better still, the mural-covered *Jack Palance Palace*, a friendly rum shop just east of Morant Bay, where the white rum flows, the owner's collection of oldies hits is a treasure and delicious fried chicken is served up.

Bath

Heading east from Morant Bay, a road cuts inland at Port Morant. Six miles from the coast, and right on the edge of the John Crow Mountains jungle, the little-visited village of **BATH** was born when a runaway Spanish slave stumbled across some hot mineral springs here in the late 1690s. He found that the springs cured wounds he had incurred during his escape, and slowly the word spread. Ironically, though, the slave's "master" claimed the spring and some 1130 acres of land that surrounded it, and sold it to the British government in 1699 for £400. The British swiftly carved a road through the hills from the coast (still an exceptionally pretty drive today) and erected a spa building here in 1747.

Colonists came from all over the island to treat their various ailments; the wealthy built their fashionable summer homes nearby; and for a while in the early 1700s Bath glittered in the spotlight. However, the atmosphere was soon soured by disputes between political factions (specifically, supporters of the Stuart and Hanoverian dynasties competing for the throne back in England). Hurricane damage also took its toll, and Bath fell from favour. By the late eighteenth century, it had become a ghost town, with only ten residents. Today, it's a quiet and rather backward country village, surrounded by jungle, with a straggle of visitors coming to take the waters. You may run into the odd tourist or someone up from Kingston taking treatment for rheumatism or arthritis, but it's just as likely that you'll have the place to yourself.

Hurricane Gilbert

In September 1988 **Hurricane Gilbert** pulverized Jamaica. By the time the carnage had stopped, 45 people had died, 500,000 were left homeless – their tin shacks went down like ninepins – and agriculture was laid waste, with US$50 million worth of damage to banana, coffee, sugarcane and other crops. Sections of the Blue Mountains were denuded as the winds uprooted trees and hurled them down the slopes. With electricity out for days, looting was widespread, particularly in Kingston. Aid poured into the island – US$125 million from the USA alone – and, in many parts of the island, particularly the main tourist areas, life returned to normal with remarkable speed. However, in the hardest-hit eastern parishes of Portland and St Thomas, it has taken a lot longer to repair the damage. Even today you can still find traces of Gilbert, as at the *Bath Fountain Hotel* (see opposite), which is still coping with the hurricane's consequences more than fifteen years later.

The spa

Reached along a signposted one-mile road from the town centre, opposite the church, the **spa** (daily 8am–9.30pm; J$150 for a single-person bath, J$250 for a two-person bath) now adjoins the rambling old *Bath Fountain Hotel* (see opposite page), with ten small cubicles each housing a sunken tiled bath. The water is high in sulphur and lime and, like most mineral baths, slightly (though not, they insist, dangerously) radioactive. The charge covers use of a towel and a twenty-minute bath (any longer is not recommended because of the risk of dehydration). The private cubicles, which have been immaculately refurbished, provide a secluded soak, but for a prettier bathe in the open air, surrounded by a thick forest of trees, vines and lianas, head up the path to the left of the hotel/spa building (cross the small bridge first and turn right). The path follows the "Sulphur River" to the point where the natural hot and cold springs gush out from the rocks. (Water from the two springs is diverted to the spa and mixed to provide you with a bath of a more even temperature.) Just beyond the spot where the hot water is piped as it comes out of the rock, you can scramble down the bank to swim in the river and partake of the thermal springs. Waterfalls tumble prettily through the trees, and hiking trails lead from here for miles across the Blue Mountains and into Portland. If you'd like to hike from here, the hotel may be able to help out with a guide; otherwise, contact Sun Venture Tours (see p.108) or Free-I at *Zion Country Cottages* in Manchioneal (see p.175). Before you start to head up to the spring mouth, though, you'll probably be accosted by a group of Rasta hangers-on offering a completely unnecessary, unofficial "guide" service to the spring. If you're female, they'll also proffer amateur massages and so-called spa treatments (having your towel dunked in the water and wrapped around you). Rates for such services are inevitably exorbitant; if you take up any offers, make sure you agree on a reasonable price first. Otherwise don't be put off heading up to the river mouth alone: it's easy to find and the track is safe.

Bath Botanical Gardens

At the bottom of the road to the spa, and adjacent to the cut-stone Bath Anglican Church, are the **Bath Botanical Gardens** (daily dawn to dusk; free). The gardens were established in 1779, a small patch of land where many plants – including cinnamon, jacaranda, bougainvillea and mango – were first introduced to the island. For a century or more this was a thriving little spot, but the ravages of time and Hurricane Gilbert have ensured that little remains of the original, carefully ordered scheme. None of the trees are labelled anymore, but you'll see descendants of the **breadfruit trees** first brought from Tahiti by Captain Bligh of the *HMS Bounty* in 1793 (see the box on p.165). The gardens also house guava trees, royal palms, bamboo and crotons, and it's a pleasant and shady spot to stroll for fifteen minutes or so and test your botanical knowledge.

If you're in no hurry to get back to the coast, and you have your own transport and an eye for scenery, it's worth taking an inland detour. Double back on the road to Port Morant from Bath, then turn off at tiny Potsoi, where two pretty rugged roads weave through the luscious interior, both passing the Paul Bogle Monument at Stony Gut (see p.151) and returning to the coast at Morant Bay.

Practicalities

If you want to **stay**, the *Bath Fountain Hotel* itself (℡703 4345, Ⓕ703 4405, Ⓔbathmineralspahotelja@yahoo.com; ❷) is old-fashioned and supremely quiet, and rates include free access to the baths. The dining room of the hotel offers tasty Jamaican **meals** and some excellent fruit juices, and the town also holds a couple of tiny rum shops and snack bars. Bath is also the scene of a **Breadfruit** festival, held every September.

There are several daily route taxis running to Bath from Kingston; buses from Port Antonio will only get you as far as Morant Bay, from where you can swap to a route taxi going to Bath.

The southeastern corner

About five miles east of Morant Bay, the tiny fishing village of **PORT MORANT** was a key harbour and banana-shipping point during the eighteenth century, protected in its heyday by several bristling forts that dotted the coastline. These are now long gone, and except when the fishing boats are unloading their catch, the place has a sleepy and somewhat melancholy feel. A mile or so on from Port Morant itself, a minor road swings off the A4 along the coast towards **Bowden Wharf**, though the water is masked by vegetation and the odd house. As you reach the water, a pair of large red gates mark the impromptu headquarters of an **oyster-farming** operation – the only commercial operation here since bananas ceased to be exported. Attached to pieces of tyre suspended in the water from wooden poles, the molluscs take around three months to grow to maturity. Oysters are as much a delicacy in Jamaica as anywhere else; here they are most often enjoyed gulped down with a fiery sauce of Scotch bonnet peppers, scallion, thyme, pimento, sugar and vinegar. If any of the workers are around, they'll usually let you poke about.

East of Port Morant, the main highway skirts the far southeastern corner of the island. It's a gorgeous six-mile drive, a seamless feast of banana, sugar and coconut plantations. Look out for the neat but dilapidated rows of roadside homes, built on stilts to accommodate cane cutters working at the still-operational Duckenfield sugar plantation. The next sizeable village is the rather shabby **Golden Grove**. You won't want to stop here, but a quick detour south, past the dishevelled-looking Duckenfield sugar factory, will bring you to **Rocky Point Bay**, one of the best and most secluded beaches in this part of the country. A sizeable fleet of small fishing boats is based here, normally out from dawn until the early afternoon, when some of their catch starts frying at the bar. Another detour, a direct and extremely scenic road to Bath Spa, swings inland from Golden Grove.

Also starting at Golden Grove, innumerable tracks weave through the Duckenfield canefields, and then the swampy mangroves of the Great Morass, out to the serenely isolated hundred-foot **Morant Point lighthouse**, cast in London in 1841 and put up here by Kru men from Sierra Leone, among the first free Africans to be brought to the island after the abolition of slavery. It's a deserted and windswept spot, with the sea crashing onto the rocks and sand; climb the lighthouse and look out over the bay and back to the Blue Mountains. As you approach the lighthouse (and on the other side of the lighthouse promontory to Rocky Point), you'll pass the utterly gorgeous **Holland Bay**, a deserted swath of fine white sand and pellucid water overlooked by a few ragged palms – the perfect place to live out your Robinson Crusoe fantasies. During the cane-cutting season, the muddy tracks to the lighthouse are completely undriveable, churned up by large industrial vehicles; even at other times of the year you'll need a four-wheel-drive. A much more scenic route here is by boat; ask one of the fishermen at Leith Hall or Port Morant to take you, or organize the trip through the *Drakes Cove Guesthouse* (see p.151) in Prospect.

Back on the A4, and continuing north from Golden Grove, the road leads uphill, with a magnificent panorama behind you over Holland Bay and the mangrove swamps of the Great Morass. A little further on, **Hector's River**, halfway up Jamaica's eastern tip, marks the boundary between Portland and St Thomas.

Portland

PORTLAND, north of the Blue Mountains, is generally considered the most beautiful of Jamaica's parishes – a rain-drenched land of luscious foliage, sparkling rivers and pounding waterfalls. Eastern Jamaica's biggest resort, the small town of **Port Antonio**, is your most likely destination, a good base for sightseeing with a couple of fabulous **beaches** a short ride away. The waterfalls at **Somerset Falls** and (a bit further afield) the gorgeous **Reach Falls** are within striking distance, while, if you head into the interior, you can be poled down the **Rio Grande** on a bamboo raft or hike through the rainforest along the centuries-old trails of the Windward Maroons. An increasing number of visitors are venturing east of Port Antonio for the more laid-back pleasures of **Long Bay** – with a growing young travellers' scene, a great swathe of unspoilt beach and good surfing – while the roadside vendors in **Boston Bay** continue to offer some of the most authentic jerk pork in the country in a dazzling oceanside setting.

Some history

Even after the conquest of Jamaica by Britain in 1655, Portland was one of the last of Jamaica's parishes to be settled. Although its obvious capital-to-be, Port Antonio, blessed with two natural harbours, was superbly located for trade and defence, reports of the difficult terrain and the constant threat of Maroon warfare deterred would-be settlers. Eventually, the Crown was obliged to offer major incentives, including land grants, tax exemptions and free food supplies, before the parish was officially formed in 1723.

As in the rest of the country, Portland's early economy was dependent on sugar, with large estates scattered around the parish. However, as the sugar industry declined in the nineteenth century, Portland's fertile soil proved ideally suited for the surprise replacement crop – **bananas** (see box below). As the country's major banana port, Port Antonio boomed, ushering in a golden era of prosperity for the town and the region. Steamer lines and businessmen poured in from Europe and North America, and in 1905, the town's first **hotel** was built on the Titchfield peninsula. Cabin space on the banana boats was sold to curious tourists, who found themselves rubbing shoulders with the rich and famous – publishing magnate William Randolph Hearst, banker J.P. Morgan, actress Bette Davis et al – swanning in on their private yachts.

The reign of the banana was to prove relatively short-lived – blighted by hurricane damage and Panama disease from South America – but the high-end tourism it had helped to engender soon became a key revenue-earner. With the enthusiastic patronage of movie stars like Errol Flynn (see p.173), Port Antonio's place in the glitterati's global playground was assured. The first luxury hotel in Jamaica, *Frenchman's Cove*, was built here and remains a testament to faded glamour to this day.

Bananas

First brought to Jamaica from the Canary Islands as early as 1520, the **banana** was long considered an unpalatable vegetable, fit only for animals and slaves. The turning point in its popularity came in 1871, when sea captain **Lorenzo Dow Baker** took a shipload of bananas from Port Antonio to Boston to see whether he could drum up any interest in the fruit in the United States. His gamble paid off handsomely – he had barely unloaded the crates before the entire stock was sold for a healthy profit, setting off a mass demand for the "new" fruit that would bring him (and others like him) colossal fortunes over the next couple of decades.

With sugar already in decline by the second half of the nineteenth century, Jamaica's farmers rushed to plant the new crop of "green gold", and Portland's high rainfall and fertile soil secured its position as the island's leading production centre. Banana production went ballistic, with output hitting highs of around thirty million stems per year. With little employment available elsewhere, armies of workers arrived from all over the country to earn the pitiful sustenance wages available to planters and pickers, who lived in wretched conditions on the edge of the plantations.

The arrival of banana ships at the wharves was signalled by blasts on a conch shell throughout the interior, followed by frenetic activity as the labourers cut the stems and carried the fresh fruit off the estates and onto the waiting trucks. At the dock the bananas were unloaded from the trucks and taken to the checkers, who ensured that the stem had the nine hands of bananas required for it to count as a bunch – hence, in the banana boat song, *Day O* "six hands, seven hands, eight hands, bunch!". Once the stem was carried aboard the ship, the tallyman gave the carrier a tally to redeem for pay later, and the workers made their weary way back to the plantation or to the nearest bar.

Sadly for Portland, the banana boom didn't last long. By the 1920s, a combination of disease and hurricane damage had decimated Jamaica's banana crops, and the decline was compounded by the disruption of shipping during World War II. Nevertheless, the precious banana remains the country's second most important official agricultural commodity (behind sugar) and still accounts for around four per cent of Jamaica's total exports.

Celebrities still sequester themselves in Portland, and there's a burgeoning backpacker scene at Long Bay, but the area can't yet compete for the mainstream vacationer, losing out to the more accessible and better-marketed resorts of Montego Bay, Negril and Ocho Rios. Agriculture is still important, though, and the region's lush vegetation provides vast amounts of fruit and vegetables for domestic and export markets. The movie business, too, periodically injects much-needed cash into the economy – films shot here include *Cocktail*, *The Mighty Quinn*, *Club Paradise* and *Lord of the Flies*. Although Portland is a long way from the prosperity of its heyday, there are now positive moves to revitalize the tourist potential of the area.

Port Antonio

A magnet for foreign visitors during the 1950s and 1960s, the quiet town of **PORT ANTONIO** feels more like an isolated backwater these days. However, things are stirring in the sleepy little town and it may well become a popular tourist resort once more. A smart new marina has been built to accommodate luxury yachts and small cruise ships, the waterfront has been expensively landscaped, and there are plans to develop both Navy Island and the Titchfield peninsula. There's still not a huge amount to see here, and there is little in the way of watersports or shopping, but 'Portie' is a friendly and beguiling place with a bustling central market and a couple of lively clubs and bars. The real highlight of this area is the great **outdoors** – waterfalls, river trips, hiking, splendid tropical scenery and some lovely beaches – and Port Antonio is the perfect base for exploring it all.

Arrival and information

Flights arrive at **Ken Jones Aerodrome**, six miles west of town in St Margaret's Bay, from where a taxi into town costs around US$20. **Buses** and **minibuses** from Kingston (3hr 30min) and Montego Bay (5hr) pull in at the main terminus by the seafront on Gideon Avenue, or by the town's central square on West Street (which also serves as the main **taxi rank**). If you're **driving**, the A4 highway runs straight into and through the town, whether you're coming from the east or the west. The Port Antonio Marina offers **boat mooring** and excellent maintenance facilities.

The **Jamaica Tourist Board** office (Mon–Fri 8.30am–4.30pm; ☎993 3051) is upstairs at the City Centre Plaza on Harbour Street, although it doesn't have much in the way of local information, just a few scant brochures on hotels and attractions.

The **Portland Parish Library** (Mon–Fri 9am–6pm, Sat 9am–1pm; ☎993 2793) is situated in a section of the new **marina park** opposite the Village of St George shopping centre. It has the cheapest and most reliable Internet connection in town.

Getting around

Sandwiched between the mountains and the sea, Port Antonio is small and easily navigable. Two main streets dissect the town: **West Palm Avenue**, which becomes **West Street**, runs from the western entrance of Port Antonio to the clock tower at the centre of town. From there, **Harbour Street**, the other commercial thoroughfare, cuts across the town. To really get your bearings,

PORT ANTONIO

THE BLUE MOUNTAINS AND THE EAST

Blue Lagoon & Boston Bay

Woods Island

Folly

Folly Oval

Folly Point Lighthouse

CARIBBEAN SEA

Navy Island

West Harbour

East Harbour

Titchfield Peninsula

Titchfield High School (Fort George)

Folly Beach

Boundbrook Wharf

Port Antonio Marina

Musgrave Market

Ferry Terminal

Carder Park

Bonnie View Hotel

Hospital

Amatto River

ALLAN AVENUE

EAST PALM AVENUE

EVELEIGH PK RD

RED HASSELL ROAD

SUMMERS TOWN ROAD

MANNINGS AVE

BONNIE VIEW ROAD

W BAPTIST AVE

EAST BAPTIST AVE

HALL'S AVE

PALM AVENUE

RICE PIECE ROAD

WEST PALM AVENUE

BOUNDBROOK ROAD

SWINGBANK ROAD

GIDEON AVENUE

HARBOUR ST

WILLIAM ST

WEST ST

LOVE LANE

FORT GEORGE ST

QUEEN ST

KING ST

TITCHFIELD ST

BRIDGE ST

Nonsuch, Berridale & Moore Town

N

0   500 yds

Airport, Somerset Falls & Buff Bay

ACCOMMODATION
De Montevin Lodge	
Holiday Home	
Inn and on the Lake	
Ivanhoes	
Jamaica Heights Resort	10
Little Reef Guesthouse	5
Ocean Crest Guesthouse	3
Shadows	7
Sunnyside Hotel	6
Triffs Inn	9

RESTAURANTS
Anna Bananas	F
Barracuda	9
Blue Marlin	C
Dickie's Best Kept Secret	A
Dixon's Food Shop	J
Gallery Café	K
Golden Happiness	D
The Hub	B
Miss Shine-Eye	H
The New Debonaire	G
Pier View Jerk Centre	E
Survival Beach	
Try Me	L

PORT ANTONIO (inset)

Village of St George

Huntress Marina

Musgrave Market

Ambokile Gallery

Courthouse

Clocktower

Scotia Bank

Pharmacy

Jamaica Tourist Board

Police Station

Bus Terminal

Christ Church

Bonnie View Hotel

GROSSETT RD

LOVE LANE

WEST ST

WILLIAM ST

HARBOUR ST

GIDEON AVE

ALLAN AVE

BRIDGE ST

BONNIE VIEW

BOUNDBROOK ROAD

159

Safety and harassment

Most people find Port Antonio something of a relief after the harassment of the north coast, and any hassle you do encounter tends to be fairly half-hearted. There is also a relatively low crime rate, despite the odd night-time robbery on the Titchfield peninsula. Even so, it is worth taking the normal precautions: don't flash wads of cash around or wander off the main streets after dark. The local police often set up roadblocks east of town, and it's not unusual for tourists to have their cars thoroughly searched for drugs. If this happens to you, be helpful and friendly and you shouldn't be detained long.

head up to the *Bonnie View Hotel* on Bonnie View Road, a steep climb from the town centre. The hotel's terrace bar overlooks the entire town and provides great views of the area. You can comfortably **walk** between the handful of sights in a couple of hours, while most places of interest outside town (and all of the beaches) can be reached by **public transport**. Shared taxis run along the main road as far as Long Bay; you'll pay J$40 to Dragon Bay/Frenchman's Cove, J$50 to Boston Bay, and J$60 to Long Bay.

Because you'll want to get out of town a lot, renting a **car** is a tempting option. As rental rates are slightly higher here than in the capital or the resorts, you'll probably get a better deal with a Kingston- or Ocho Rios-based company (see p.192). If you're just planning a single day-trip – say to Reach Falls or the Rio Grande – it can work out cheaper to use a **taxi**. The main rank is in the central square; alternatively, call the cheerful Mr Palmer on ☎993 3468 or 707 4276, the Port Antonio taxi co-operative (☎993 2684), or JUTA at 7 Harbour St (☎993 2684). If you want an easy life, and are prepared to pay for it, you can enjoy all of the area's main draws – Reach Falls, Nonsuch Caves, Rio Grande rafting, the John Crow Mountains – with Attractions Link, a tour company based at Travel Express in the City Centre Plaza on Harbour Street (☎993 2102 or 4828, Ⓔattractionslink@cwjamaica.com). For hiking trips in the Rio Grande valley, contact the excellent Valley Hikes or Grand Valley Tours (see p.177). Independent guide Joanna Hart (☎831 8434) takes people on guided tours of Port Antonio's highlights, including local beaches and villages for US$38 per person for a three-and-a-half-hour trip, and also offers specialist tours on request. If you're interested in a serious fishing trip or a sunset cruise, Captain Paul Bohnenkamper (☎909 9552, ⒺCaribbeCapt@aol.com), based at Port Antonio Marina, rents out his fully-equipped sports-fishing boat, *La Nadine*.

Accommodation

Port Antonio has a decent amount of good **accommodation**, much of it far cheaper than in more heavily visited north coast resorts. If you're on a budget, you'll make significant savings by staying here rather than the more glamourous hotels to the east of town.

From her *Drapers San* guesthouse east of Port Antonio (see p.170), the supremely friendly Maria Carla Gullotta runs the Port Antonio Guesthouse Association (☎ & Ⓕ 993 7118, Ⓦwww.go-jam.com), which represents some of the most appealing properties in the area. She will book rooms for you, and can also provide tours and accompanied forays to the *Roof Club* and nights of traditional African drumming.

De Montevin Lodge 21 Fort George St ☎993 2604, Ⓕ715 5987, Ⓦwww.demontevin.com. Good value in a lovely old gingerbread house, a relic from colonial days. Clean, cool and simple rooms, each with a balcony and shared or private bathroom. ❸

Holiday Home 12 King St ☎ 993 2066, ⓦ www.go-jam.com. Comfortable, friendly guesthouse set in an old wooden house on the Titchfield peninsula. Rooms are clean and inviting, with fans. ❶

Inn and on the Lake 17a West Palm Ave ☎ 993 3468, ⓕ 993 3332. Cheerful place offering clean, appealing rooms with fan and private bathroom, at the back of the owner's home. A separate apartment has a private entrance, two bedrooms and a kitchen. Clothes-washing facilities are available, and there's a sun deck on site. ❸

Ivanhoes 9 Queen St ☎ 993 3043, ⓕ 993 4931, ⓔ lornamburke@hotmail.com. Scrupulously clean and tidy no-frills guesthouse opposite the ruins of the old *Titchfield Hotel*. Each of the appealing, reasonably priced rooms has a fan and a private bathroom with hot and cold water. Meals are available. ❶–❸

Jamaica Heights Resort Spring Bank Rd ☎ 993 3305, ⓕ 993 3563, ⓦ www.jamaicaheights.net. Mellow guesthouse in a great location, high up in the hills. It's easily the best in Port Antonio. Beautiful and spacious rooms are excellent value, and views over the town are staggering. Facilities include its own "private" river and waterfall, as well as a pool and Ping-Pong table. ❹

Little Reef Guesthouse 1 Queen St ☎ 993 9743. Extremely friendly place. The homely rooms have double beds, some also have private bathrooms. Guests may use the communal kitchen. The genial owners usually throw in local tours as well. ❶

Ocean Crest Guesthouse 7 Queen St ☎ 993 4024. Small, simple guesthouse with six rooms, all with private bathroom and hot water. There's also a large dining area and sunny terrace; guests can use the kitchen. ❷

Shadows 40 West St ☎ 993 3823. Conveniently located in the centre of things and set back from the road, these small rooms have a/c, fan and cold water only in the private bathrooms, but they're excellent if you're on a budget. ❷

Sunnyside Hotel 18 Fort George St ☎ 993 9788. Extremely basic (and equally inexpensive) place opposite the *De Montevin Lodge*, just above the ocean. Rooms vary greatly – several look out to sea – but all are pretty bare, with a fan and shared or private bathroom; the most expensive has cable TV. ❶

Triffs Inn 1 Bridge St ☎ 715 6890, ⓔ tiahuslin@hotmail.com. Good mid-range option in the centre of town, popular with Jamaican business travellers. Rooms have a/c, cable TV and private bathroom with hot and cold water. There's a decent restaurant attached. ❷

The Town

The obvious starting point for a stroll around Port Antonio is its **central square**, with a landmark **clock tower** opposite the red-brick, two-storey Georgian **courthouse**, built in 1895 and fronted by an elegant fretworked veranda supported by cast-iron columns courtesy of the William MacFarlane Company in Glasgow, Scotland. The area is always milling with people on court business or visiting the post office below. Looking to the other side of the road, your eyes can't help but be drawn to the **Village of St George** shopping mall, a mishmash of architectural styles from medieval to Tudor and Renaissance built over the old Delmar Theatre. Some like it, many hate it, but somehow its opulent exterior, richly embellished with murals and sculptures, manages to complement the surrounding buildings. The brainchild of the locally infamous Zigi Fami, owner of the equally exuberant *Jamaican Palace* hotel and the woman behind Trident Castle (see p.168), St George's boasts a handful of rather ordinary stores, a small café and a couple of popular local hangouts.

Due north from here, the **Titchfield peninsula** juts out into the Caribbean Sea, dividing Port Antonio's **twin harbours**. The tip of the peninsula once held the British **Fort George**, whose ancient cannons and crumbling walls today form part of Titchfield High School, alive with noisy open-air lessons and frenetic games of football and netball. The short wander up from town takes you past the **De Montevin Lodge** hotel – high-Victorian gingerbread architecture at its best – and the ruins of the **Titchfield Hotel**, Port Antonio's first and once owned by Errol Flynn – although there's little to see there these days. Aside from the school, the whole peninsula is a somnolent and peaceful place. As you walk up Queen Street and head toward the ruins, which occupy a wasteland that parallels the street, you'll pass several of the large wooden houses that characterize the area, now rather dilapidated private homes and family-run budget guesthouses.

Back in the centre of town on West Street, which shoots off from the clock tower, compact **Musgrave Market** is the liveliest spot in town, friendly, easy-going and crammed with stalls. Fresh fruit and vegetables are the market's strong point, but there's also a busy trade in fish, meat and clothes, and a handful of crafts and souvenirs are sold – try woodcarver "Rock Bottom" at the back near the library. Further up West Street, past the grassy lawn where the **ferry** used to leave for Navy Island, **Boundbrook Wharf** is still the loading point for bananas being shipped to Europe and the United States. This is the place that inspired the banana boat song *Day O* – "Work all night for a drink of rum, daylight come and me wanna go home". Today the back-breaking work is much simplified, with the bananas packaged centrally and mechanically loaded at the wharf.

Back in town, the red-brick Anglican **Christ Church** on Bridge Street, Romanesque in design, is the most prominent of Port Antonio's many houses of worship. Built on the site of an earlier church in 1840, its numerous memorials date as far back as the late seventeenth century. The eagle lectern was donated in 1900 by the Boston Fruit Company, a firm owned by Captain Dow Baker (see box on p.157), which owed its foundation and much of its profits to the trade in bananas between Port Antonio and North America. You'll probably be grabbed by one of the ancient assistants who guard the church and dish out nuggets of local history to visitors – you might want to leave a donation.

Across the road from the church, a stiff half-mile walk up Bonnie View Road takes you to the **Bonnie View Hotel**. A long-established, though rather run-down hotel, this is a great place to head to on arrival, as the views are magnificent. From the front you look over the town and the twin harbours, while from the lovely back garden you can see into the heart of the Blue and John Crow mountains. Hiking trails into the hills start from here, and with a bit of advance notice, the hotel can organize half-day horseback tours of the area (from US$30 per person).

Port Antonio Marina and Navy Island

Port Antonio has long been recognised as having one of the loveliest natural harbours in the world, and in recent years the entire waterfront of the town has undergone a massive multimillion dollar redevelopment project. The first phase of the project, the brand-new Port Antonio Marina and Ken Wright Ship Pier on the West Harbour (☎715 6328, ⓦwww.themarinaatportantonio.com), was opened by Jamaican Prime Minister P.J. Patterson in September 2002 to great critical acclaim. Designed to appeal to mega-yachts and small cruise ships, the elegant, state-of-the-art **marina** features landscaped gardens, a pool and extensive facilities in pastel-colored wooden buildings, including a well-stocked chandlery, washrooms and its own police station. Controversially, though, Port Antonio's entire waterfront is now secured behind enormous gates, including the towns' only proper strip of sand, **Folly Beach**, which has been tidied up, planted with palms and is no longer public. Quite how much the marina and the waterfront become part of the town's life rather than a wealthy visitors' ghetto remains to be seen. For the moment though, it's an attractive spot for an evening drink or meal with great views across the bay to Navy Island.

The largest of the small islands that dot the Portland coast, **NAVY ISLAND** is a five-minute boat ride from the mainland. The British Navy used it for storage and barracks in the early eighteenth century – hence the name – and

△ Veranda at Strawberry Hill hotel, near Irish Town

Captain Bligh landed here in 1793, bringing breadfruit plants from Tahiti. A later adventurer, Errol Flynn, came to Port Antonio in 1947 and, taken with the beauty of the island, immediately bought it as a private retreat for entertaining Hollywood starlets. Local legend – one of the myriad Flynn myths – says that he lost it in a poker game less than a decade later. The 64-acre island, which is covered in lush vegetation, walking trails and has several good beaches, now belongs to the Port Authority, which has closed it to the public; there are no longer passenger ferries making the crossing and no immediate plans to re-instate them. It's rumoured that an up-market resort will be built on the site, part of Port Antonio's extensive development project.

The Folly

At the end of Allan Avenue (or Folly Road, as it's known to the locals), which runs east along the coast out of Port Antonio, is the second of the town's peninsulas, **Folly Point**. Largely covered with low-lying scrub, the area is home to a cricket ground and at its end, down a mud track, Port Antonio's **lighthouse**. You'll need to attract the attention of the keeper and his family to let you into the rather pretty garden planted with flowering shrubs that surrounds the lighthouse – they'll expect a donation. You can't climb the lighthouse but you're free to walk over the rocks in front of it, a favorite fishing spot for the locals.

Before you reach the lighthouse, a right fork brings you to the **Folly**, the sorry ruin of what was, briefly, one of the grandest houses in Jamaica. Built in 1902 for American banker Alfred Mitchell and widely applauded as a model of mock-Grecian architecture, the concrete house was a model of ostentation – until the roof collapsed in 1935, a victim of shoddy construction and the short-sighted use of salt water in the cement mix. The place was left to decay, and only the pillars and half a staircase remained standing today; graffiti-daubed and strewn with litter, they form a grim testament to lost glamour. Quirky and evocative, the shell's dramatic presence is not lost on film makers. It has been featured in many movies as well as pop music videos by the likes of Shabba Ranks and Lauryn Hill.

Just across the water, tiny **Woods Island** was once joined to the mainland by a stone causeway, and Mitchell had a small zoo built on it for his pet monkeys. Nothing remains from that time, but swimmers can cover the short distance to create their own private retreat. Take care if you're swimming – undercurrents can be strong.

Eating

A number of inexpensive **restaurants** in Port Antonio offer a standard Jamaican menu, and there are cheap vegetarian and Chinese options, too. If you're after something much more sophisticated, you'll need to head east of town to *Mille Fleurs* at the *Mocking Bird Hill Hotel*, by far the best place to eat in the area (see p.171).

CC's Bakery, at 1 West Palm Ave on the outskirts of town, is famous for its "**holey bulla**", a smaller and far more toothsome version of the traditional pastry, with (unsurprisingly) a hole in the middle. For delicious wholemeal bread, head for *Dixon's Food Shop* (see opposite page), which has freshly baked garlic and raisin loaves every Friday. Snacks, cakes and ice cream are served at *Cartoons* on West Street. Jerk barbecues set up outside the market and at both ends of town once the sun sets; look out for those with silver-foil parcels of spicy curried conch with okra, an East Portland speciality.

Anna Bananas Allan Ave. Fetching seaside restaurant on a raised wooden boardwalk over-

looking the bay. It's one of the best inexpensive places to eat in the area, with friendly service. The

The breadfruit and the *Bounty*

Up until the late eighteenth century, Jamaica – like most of the West Indian islands – was not self-sufficient in food, relying on imports (particularly from North America) to feed the ever-increasing slave population. As a result, the American War of Independence (1775–81), which severely disrupted food supplies, brought tragedy to the islands, with thousands of slaves dying of malnutrition and related disease. To eliminate this catastrophic dependence, planters lobbied the British government for a source of cheap food that could be grown in the islands. The starchy, nourishing **breadfruit** – about which the great explorer Captain Cook had rhapsodized, "if a man plants ten of them... he will completely fulfil his duty to his own and future generations" – was at the top of their wish list. In due course, the British designated *HMS Bounty* to bring breadfruit plants from their native Tahiti, and appointed one **Captain William Bligh** to command it.

Setting sail from England in 1787, the *Bounty* arrived in Tahiti the following year after a long and dangerous journey around Cape Horn, and captain and crew were treated as royalty by the islanders, garlanded with flowers and showered with gifts and hospitality. But Bligh had little time to waste and insisted on loading up the breadfruit plants and moving on. Three weeks later, facing another arduous crossing under a captain who seemed to care more for his plants than for his men, the ship's crew, led by second-in-command Fletcher Christian, mutinied. Bligh was cast adrift in the middle of the Pacific Ocean with a handful of loyal followers, while Christian and his acolytes made for Ascension Island and their place in history.

Incredibly, Bligh survived. He eventually found his way back to England, where he was cleared of any blame for the loss of the *Bounty* and entrusted with command of another ship, *HMS Providence*, to complete his mission. The Jamaican House of Assembly voted him a substantial gift of 500 guineas to encourage his endeavours on their behalf, and the *Providence* left England in 1791, finally delivering the breadfruit to the island in February 1793. The plants were sent on to Bath Botanical Gardens (see p.154) for propagation and eventually spread throughout the island, an important step towards Jamaican self-sufficiency.

food is reliable Jamaican; breakfast, lunch and dinner are served daily. There's a pool table, too.

Barracuda 1 Bridge St. Sophisticated restaurant with attractive decor, located underneath the *Triffs Inn*. The menu offers steak, seafood and traditional Jamaican dishes such as stamp-and-go and saltfish fritters, at moderate to expensive prices. Continental and Jamaican breakfasts are also served.

Blue Marlin Port Antonio Marina ☎ 993 3209. An atmospheric restaurant right on the water overlooking Navy Island, frequented by boat people, sports fishermen and town dignitaries. The menu features moderately priced fare, including fried chicken, lobster, pizza and club sandwiches. A good place for Sunday brunch in the high season.

Dickie's Best Kept Secret On the A4, just west of Port Antonio. Nestled on a knoll as you round the far bend of Port Antonio's West Harbour, this simple wooden shack is easily missed, but is one of the best – and most unusual – choices around. Cooked by owner Dickie and served in his kooky lounge, the beautifully presented, moderately

priced, four-course dinners are fabulous and include dishes such as ackee on toast, garlic lobster and steamed fish; order the morning before you want to eat. You can also drop by for breakfast, lunch or afternoon tea.

Dixon's Food Shop Bridge St. Takeout lunch joint with delicious home-made vegetarian food – including curried tofu stew, stir-fried veg and salads – at rock-bottom prices. There's an airy upstairs room if you want to eat in. Closed at weekends.

Gallery Café Village of St George. Cool upstairs diner that's good for breakfast (omelettes, pancakes) or lunch (quiche, pizza, sandwiches, Jamaican hot meals).

Golden Happiness corner of Harbour and West streets. The best Chinese food in town, with a huge menu of chop suey, sweet and sour dishes and masses more. Very cheap to boot.

The Hub 2 West Palm Ave. Just west of the main drag and tucked off the main street near the old train station, this is a popular place for inexpensive Jamaican food: rundown, liver or callaloo for breakfast; stew beef, stew peas, cow foot, and fried and baked chicken for lunch and dinner.

Miss Shine-Eye Boundbrook Wharf. Simply the best jerk chicken in town is served in this little restaurant on the approach road down to the wharf.

The New Debonaire 22 West St. Hole-in-the-wall eatery, serving up inexpensive local fare daily from 7am to midnight. Jamaican breakfasts, and lunches and dinners of JA-style roast pork and beef, curry goat and chicken, brown stew, and escovitched, steamed or sweet-and-sour fish.

Pier View Jerk Centre 21A West Palm Ave. Large, pleasant garden restaurant with a proper jerk pit; serves moderately priced pork, chicken or fish, cooked over charcoal.

Shadows 40 West St. Excellent omelettes for breakfast and good Jamaican and Chinese meals, served at a pleasant bar with gazebo or in the smarter, less atmospheric restaurant.

Survival Beach Allan Ave. Inexpensive Ital and fresh seafood dishes are served at this easy-going little restaurant with outdoor tables and a neat strip of sand by the water.

Try me 29 West St. Friendly family-run Jamaican place with local staples – curried goat, chicken foot and red peas soup – at local prices.

Drinking, nightlife and entertainment

Port Antonio isn't exactly bursting with good places to **drink**, and the few places that exist are often very quiet. If you want to join in with the locals, Allan Avenue (more commonly known as Folly Road) is a great spot to go for a drink right on the water's edge. Follow the coast road east; fifteen minutes' walk from the centre of town brings you to a series of lively rum bars, strung with fairy lights and blasting out the latest dancehall and reggae tunes.

The fluorescent-streamer-bedecked UV palace of the *Roof Club* at 11 West St (daily; J$150) is the only proper **nightclub** in Port Antonio and one of the most relaxed places to have a serious night out in Jamaica. It's busiest at the weekends (though rarely before midnight). DJs pump out the latest dancehall, reggae, soca, hip hop and R&B, with the occasional oldies night. Women get in free for the popular Thursday "Ladies' Night". The *Pier Lounge* (see below) on West Palm Ave has **live music** on Fridays and Sundays and an **oldies hits** night every Saturday.

If you're interested in **African drumming**, visit the Lioness shop (see "Shopping" on opposite page). Its formidable owner, Sista P, has all kinds of links to West Africa, runs annual trips to Ghana and has her own **nyabingi** drumming group who rehearse on Friday evenings – you're welcome to attend rehearsals. Sista P also organizes an annual festival to celebrate Jamaica's African heritage, **Afi wi Sinting**, which takes place every February on the Sunday closest to the full moon at Accompong Lawn in Boundbrook (J$200). Fashion shows, crafts and food stalls, music, storytelling and dub poetry are all part of the day, which packs in crowds from miles around.

In late September/early October, the prestigious **Port Antonio Blue Marlin Tournament** attracts serious anglers from all over the world, who carouse the streets in the evenings. For more information, contact the JTB on ☎ 933 3051.

Bars

Blue Marlin West Palm Ave. A breezy but fairly up-market bar on the waterfront offering cocktails and occasional live music.

The Hub 2 West Palm Ave. A good, if rather testosterone-charged choice, with late-night drinking on Friday and Saturday. Popular with the local officers of the law.

K-S Kozy Knook Allan Ave. The archetypal Jamaican drinking hole, with a circular bar and lots of white-rum drinkers fuelling the chitchat.

Pier Lounge 21 West Palm Ave. Friendly upstairs bar with balcony and late hours (open daily until 3am).

Roc Village of St George. This rather swanky lounge bar at the top of the shopping centre has sofas in a back room and an local, uptown crowd. Open Wed, Fri & Sat (8pm–1am).

Shadows 40 West St. There are bars upstairs and down, and a weekend disco, where the reggae, soca and hip hop draws a mixed but mellow older crowd. The outdoor bar is good for a drink at anytime.

The Vibes Sports Bar Village of St George. Pool and slot machine hall popular with the town's youths. Open until 2am on weekend nights.
Willy's Musgrave Market. This tiny hole-in-the-wall bar at the back of the market is *the* meeting place in Port Antonio – if you don't mind mixing with the local riffraff, ganja dealers and boozy market types. Great for people-watching and catching up on local gossip.

Listings

Airlines Air Jamaica Express, Ken Jones Aerodrome ☎913 3692.

Airport enquiries The information number for Ken Jones Aerodrome is ☎993 2405.

Banks and money There are plenty of banks along Harbour and West streets. Better exchange rates are available at the town's cambios; FX Trader is in the City Centre Plaza on Harbour Street, but Kamal's supermarket, 12 West St, has longer opening hours (9am–7pm, including Sundays).

Car and bike rental Eastern Car Rentals, at 16 West St (☎993 3624), will deliver to your hotel, as will Derron's, east of town at Drapers (☎993 7111, ⓕ993 7253). High-season prices start at US$80 per day, plus insurance.

Doctors Dr Daniella Speed in Boundbrook (☎993 3564) is recommended; Dr M Valenti, 38 West St (☎715 6486), is a holistic practioner.

Hospital The public hospital is on Nuttall Rd (☎993 2646).

Internet access The Portland Parish Library, in the marina park, has the cheapest and most reliable connection in town; J$100 per hour. Don J's Computer Centre, Shop 10, Village of St George (☎715 5559; Mon–Sat 9am–5pm), offers net access at J$150 per hour.

Laundry The Ever-Brite Cleaners and Laundromat has two branches: 55A West Palm Ave (☎715 3613) and 30 Harbour St (☎715 1851). A machine load costs J$200 with soap, an extra J$100 for a service wash; opening hours are 9am–pm daily

except Sundays.

Pharmacy City Plaza Pharmacy (Mon–Sat 8am–6.30pm) is opposite ScotiaBank on Harbour Street.

Police The main station is on Harbour St (☎993 2546). Call ☎119 in an emergency.

Post Office The main branch is on Harbour St opposite the clock tower (Mon–Fri 9am–5pm).

Scuba diving Lady G'Diver (☎993 8988, ⓦwww.ladygdiver.net), based at the *Blue Lagoon* to the east of town (see p.169), is the only scuba operator in the area, offering dives, certification courses and equipment rental.

Shopping Sista P's shop, Lioness, 10 Matthews Ave (round the corner from Dixon's Food Shop on Bridge St) sells an interesting range of West African wraps, clothes, carvings and jewellery as well as natural beauty products. Crafts and souvenirs are sold in Musgrave Market and in the small arcade near ScotiaBank. Pieyaka Muzik, a shack in the Love Lane car park, sells CDs and oldies hits on vinyl. The best supermarket is Kamal's, at 12 West St (daily 9am–7pm), and three or more of the same item are sold at budget prices by G&L Wholesale, 5 Harbour St (Mon–Thurs 8.30am–5pm, Fri & Sat 8.30am–7pm).

Taxis The main rank is in the central square, or call the Port Antonio taxi co-operative (☎993 2684) or JUTA (☎993 2684).

Telephone Eastern Communication at 28 Harbour St (Mon–Sat 8am–10pm, Sun 10am–10pm) offer inexpensive international calls.

East of Port Antonio

Made all the more alluring for its delicious sense of faded glamour and relative lack of visitors, the rugged stretch of coast east of Port Antonio is one of the most attractive parts of Jamaica. It's a fairy-tale landscape of lush, jungle-smothered hills rolling down to a coastline studded with fantastic beaches, such as **Frenchman's Cove**, **San San** and **Winnifred**, and swimming inlets such as the **Blue Lagoon**, a fabulous aquamarine pool of salt- and fresh water made famous by the eponymous 1980 movie. A series of smart hotels vie for business with a handful of less expensive guesthouses, and you can plump for dinner-jacketed feasts at their salubrious restaurants or for more authentic jerk cooking at **Boston Bay**.

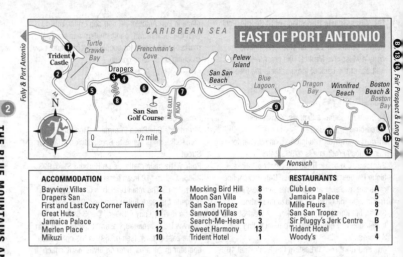

EAST OF PORT ANTONIO

ACCOMMODATION				RESTAURANTS	
Bayview Villas	2	Mocking Bird Hill	8	Club Leo	A
Drapers San	4	Moon San Villa	9	Jamaica Palace	5
First and Last Cozy Corner Tavern	14	San San Tropez	7	Mille Fleurs	8
Great Huts	11	Sanwood Villas	6	San San Tropez	7
Jamaica Palace	5	Search-Me-Heart	3	Sir Pluggy's Jerk Centre	B
Merlen Place	12	Sweet Harmony	13	Trident Hotel	1
Mikuzi	10	Trident Hotel	1	Woody's	4

Trident Castle, Frenchman's Cove and San San

Several miles from Port Antonio and looming up suddenly as you make your way east, the fantasy **Trident Castle** is the most prominent landmark for miles around – a huge, white Disney-like edifice with each of its gleaming towers topped by a pointed roof. The castle began life in the 1970s as a relatively modest home for European baroness Zigi Fami, who has big land holdings in the area, including the *Jamaica Palace* hotel. She was forced to sell after running into financial trouble, and the new owners got increasingly carried away with elaborate additions. Robust enough to have survived Hurricane Gilbert with barely a lost slate, the castle is occasionally rented out for private functions (contact *Trident Hotel;* see p.171) but is otherwise not open to the public.

Continuing three miles east from Port Antonio, you arrive at **Frenchman's Cove** hotel (℡ 993 7270, ℻ 993 7404, ⓦ www.frenchmanscove.com; ❾), with its lavish tropical gardens and stunning beach. It was once one of the area's most famous hotels, home away from home to royalty and A-list celebrities during the 1950s and 1960s. The formerly sumptuous hotel villas have deteriorated, but the grounds are still beautifully maintained, and the **beach** (daily 9am–5pm; J\$200), though small, is one of the most splendid in Jamaica, with a curve of fine sand enclosed by verdant hills, and a fresh-water river, its bottom alluringly lined by white beach sand, running straight into the sea. Food and drink are usually available, and you can rent loungers or take a boat tour to nearby beaches or the Blue Lagoon (US\$10 per person). At the end of October, *Frenchman's Cove* hosts an all-day all-inclusive beach party, popular with Kingstonians – look for posters slapped up around Port Antonio. On a daily basis the resort offers guided horseback riding on and off the property (US\$24 per hour) and bike rental (US\$10 per day). The easily missed entrance is opposite the eighteen-hole San San Golf Course (℡ 993 7645).

Two miles east, **San San** is a narrow but gorgeous strip of white sand beside a wide crescent bay, with rich reefs a few yards from the shore that provide some of the best snorkelling around. These days, though, San San has fallen to the more unsavoury demands of the tourist industry. Once a lively spot, popular with Jamaican bathers, it's now fenced-off, presumably to stop "undesirables" (in other words, regular Jamaicans) from getting anywhere near foreign guests. You'll be charged US$5 to go in. Just across from the beach is the tiny but beautiful **Pelew Island**, also known as Monkey Island despite a lack of primates. It's great for snorkelling or lazing if you're up to the swim out there.

The Blue Lagoon

The **Blue Lagoon** is where fourteen-year-old nymphet Brooke Shields (and the now-obscure cherub Christopher Atkins), playing child castaways on a deserted island, frolicked naked in the movie of the same name. Enclosed by high cliffs that give a deep green tint to the noticeably turquoise depths, the lagoon is a result of several underwater streams running down from the mountains. Surrounded by rocks, trees and flowers, the whole effect is very picture-postcard. The water, a remarkable shade of blue, drops to 198ft at its deepest spot. It's a peaceful place to swim, made more unusual by the thermal waves as warm sea water mixes with chilly gushes of fresh.

You can swim for free from a pebbly "beach" straddled between the high green walls of the purpose-built Blue Lagoon complex, although the J$200 entry fee gives you access to its facilities – changing rooms, gift shop and diving platform. A wooden **restaurant** area hangs over the water. Lady G'Diver (☎993 8988, ⓦ www.ladygdiver.net), a comprehensive watersports and scuba-diving operator, is also on site. Snorkelling equipment costs US$9 to rent, kayaks are US$12 per hour, and there are several boat trips on offer (US$15–20; 1 hr). A water taxi offers pick-up and drop-off service at private/public piers and beaches from Boston Bay to the *Trident Hotel* (US$6–18 per person). Scuba-diving courses and dive packages are also available (from US$61 for one dive), and since the lagoon is the training site of World Freediving Champion David Lee (his parents run the dive shop), specialist courses in freediving can be booked in advance. In 2001 David Lee set a new world record at the Blue Lagoon when he dived without assistance to a depth of 147 feet.

Dragon Bay and Winnifred Beach

There's more marvellous swimming a couple of miles east at **Dragon Bay**, a protected sandy beach where Tom Cruise juggled his bottles in *Cocktail*. Currently closed to the public while the *Dragon Bay Hotel* is refurbished by its new owner, the Sandals hotel chain, the beach may be accessible to non-guests for a fee once the work is completed.

A mile or so on, **Winnifred Beach** is one of the biggest and most appealing beaches on this side of the island; confusingly, **Fairy Hill** is the name of the surrounding community. Used as the setting for the Robin Williams movie *Club Paradise*, the wide, golden crescent of sand is justly popular with Jamaicans. The small reef just offshore is perfect for snorkelling (you'll probably need to bring your own gear) and protects the bay from the waves, ensuring clear, calm, bright-blue water that shelves gently from the sand. At the western end, a small mineral spring offers a fresh-water rinse (the changing facilities are best avoided).

In keeping with its supremely laid-back atmosphere, Winnifred has good, unobtrusive food and drink facilities. Near the ramshackle changing rooms in the centre of the beach, *Roots Man Corner* sells beer and soft drinks as well as Ital or fish meals at weekends. Tucked into the beach's eastern corner, the larger *Painter and Cynthia's* offers delicious, delicately seasoned platefuls of ackee and saltfish or grilled chicken and fresh fish – food is cooked to order, so you're best off putting in lunch requests when you arrive. At weekends, local operator Scotty offers childrens' horseback rides along Winnifred Beach's sands (J$150); fishermen will provide boat trips to nearby Monkey Island (1hr; US$10). Unfortunately, in recent years an aggressive gang of locals has taken to roping off the entrance to the beach and trying to charge a "voluntary fee for cleaning". Winnifred is one of the last public beaches in the area, and you're under no obligation to pay (most Jamaicans refuse to), though there's no harm in giving a tip to anyone you see genuinely tidying up the place.

The coast road swings away from the sea parallel to Winnifred; to get to the beach, take the road opposite the *Jamaica Crest Resort* and follow it for half a mile or so through a neat housing scheme. If you're driving, you can park and walk down to the sand where the tarmac ends; if it hasn't been raining recently, you should be able to drive right down onto the beach.

Boston Bay

The once-pretty public beach at **BOSTON BAY**, further east along the A4, is now largely eroded as a result of damage caused by Hurricane Gilbert. There's barely any sand to speak of, and the water is frequently choppy. In any case, the place has long been better known for its collections of **jerk stands**. Jerking of meat originated in this part of the country – the Maroons hunted wild pigs here and smoked the meat to preserve it – and the pork and chicken on sale here is reckoned by many to be the best in Jamaica (though there have been recent reports that the meat is not always as tasty and succulent as it ought to be). It is still authentic, though, cooked for hours over large charcoal pits. You'll pay around J$150 for half a pound of chicken, and J$200 for half a pound of pork; both are best eaten with roast yam, breadfruit or a hunk of fresh hard-dough bread. Take your picnic down to the beach below. If you've room in your bags, buy a jar of the fiery home-made jerk sauce – you won't find better anywhere.

Boston Bay is reportedly the best place to surf in the area – some claim the best in Jamaica - and it's possible to hire boogie and surf boards (US$5–10 per day) from Alton, a friendly Rasta who has a shack on the beach. **Buses**, minibuses and shared taxis run to Boston Bay from Port Antonio.

Accommodation

The coastline east of Port Antonio is crammed with good **places to stay**, though none is as cheap as you'll find in town. Bear in mind, too, that transport links around here are poor, and if you don't have a car, you'll be reliant on taxis. Expect to pay J$200–300 for a charter to Port Antonio from any of these places, and around J$30–50 for shared taxis. All the hotels listed here are marked on the map on p.168.

Bayview Villas Just east of Port Antonio ☎ 993 3118, ☏ 715 5779, ⓦ www.bayviewvillas.com. Owned by Caribic Vacations and just east of Port Antonio, this small hillside hotel has attractive wood-panelled rooms with fans and a/c. There's also a pool with great views and a lovely flower garden. Breakfast included in rates. ❸

Drapers San Drapers ☎ & ☏ 993 7118, ⓦ www.go-jam.com. Funky, friendly, Italian-run guesthouse with an eclectic collection of rooms, some with kitchen, some with shared bathroom. Breakfast is included in the rates, and tasty Italian or Jamaican evening meals are also available. ❸

First and Last Cozy Corner Tavern Boston Bay ☎ 993 8450. Comfortable two-bedroom apartment with shared bath, kitchen and hot water. Ask for Mr West in the shop – the apartment is several hundred yards away. ❷

Great Huts Boston Bay ☎ 202/251 2558 in US, ⓦ www.greathuts.com. Located at the end of the track lined with jerk food stalls, this is a truly amazing resort run by dynamic American doctor Paul Rhodes. The "rooms" are a collection of beautifully designed tents and huts perched on top of cliffs and connected by winding paths; all have hand-carved bamboo or driftwood beds. Breakfast and dinner are included in the room rate, twenty percent of which goes to a local charity. ⑤

Jamaica Palace Just east of Port Antonio ☎ 993 2020, ℱ☎ 993 7759, ⓦ www.jamaicapalace.com. Quirky fantasy hotel, designed to resemble a European chateau with a huge black-and-white tiled patio and a swimming pool in the shape of Jamaica. Rooms are comfortable, with large beds, a/c and marble bathrooms. ⑥

Merlen Place Fairy Hill ☎ 838 9708 or 839 9372. Two large rooms, each with private bathroom, fan and fridge, in family home opposite the supermarket in Fairy Hill. Comfortable enough and very cheap. ①

Mikuzi Winnifred Beach ☎ 973 4859. Gorgeous two-bedroom cottage with funky decor and kitchen, and a smaller, one-bed studio at the top of a badly rutted track down to Winnifred Beach. US$35 for studio and US$75 for cottage. ②/⑤

Mocking Bird Hill San San ☎ 993 7267, ℱ 993 7133, ⓦ www.hotelmockingbirdhill.com. Eco-friendly hotel, set in a peaceful location in the hills above San San and filled with sculptures and paintings by artist and co-owner Barbara Walker. The airy rooms feature bamboo furniture and balconies, and there's a pool and a superb restaurant. ⑥

Moon San Villa Blue Lagoon ☎ 993 7600, ⓦ www.moonsanvilla.com. Gorgeous airy villa 300ft from the Blue Lagoon. With lovely, clean decor, mosquito nets and fans, the four bedrooms can be rented separately, in which case you get

access to the kitchen and living room. Passes to San San beach and the lagoon are included in the with surprisingly reasonable rates. Meals are available. ⑥

San San Tropez San San ☎ 993 7213, ℱ 999 7399, ⓦ www.sansantropez.com. This genial Italian-run property, best known for its restaurant, also offers spacious rooms that sleep four (for the same price per room as for two people). The rooms have king-size beds, a/c, cable TV and private bathrooms with hot and cold water. ④

Sanwood Villas San San ☎ 995 5788, ⓦ www.geejamstudios.com. Hip recording studio with very classy accommodations (only available if they're not being used by musicians). Main house and several eco-huts are beautifully furnished with bamboo and batik, and extensive facilities include gym, outdoor pool table, jacuzzi and pool. ⑥/⑦ with all meals and drinks.

Search-Me-Heart Drapers ☎ 807 0233, ⓦ www.searchmeheart.com. Pretty Italian guesthouse with three airy bedrooms, large verandah and tropical garden. Rates include breakfast. ③

Sweet Harmony Boston Bay ☎ 993 8779, ℱ 993 3178. Small cosy French-Spanish-owned guesthouse with sweet rooms, attractive rooftop terrace and European cuisine available. Turn off the main road by the large Anglican church and follow signs. ③

Trident Hotel Just east of Port Antonio ☎ 993 2602, ℱ 993 2590, ⓦ www.tridentvillas.com. Still the epitome of tasteful luxury, though it's seen better days. There are lawns (including one set up for croquet), topiary, peacocks, delightful cottages by the sea, a small private beach, a pool, tennis courts and a suitably elegant restaurant. Rates include breakfast. ⑦

Eating

On this side of Port Antonio there's a dearth of good **places to eat** – many visitors eat in their hotel restaurants come night-time. The area does, however, boast a couple of the finest restaurants for miles around: *Mille Fleurs* and *San San Tropez*. The renowned jerk stands at Boston Bay (see previous page) offer excellent, inexpensive fare.

Club Leo Boston Bay. Simple, homely restaurant at the back of the beach serving standard Jamaican food at local prices.

Jamaica Palace Just east of Port Antonio ☎ 993 2020. Elegant, expensive European-style restaurant. The menu is big on steaks, with some German dishes.

Mille Fleurs *Mocking Bird Hill Hotel* ☎ 993 7267. A soothing terrace setting and imaginative – and often delicious – concoctions based on Jamaican staples. There's a daily vegetarian option, and pud-

dings are sublime.

San San Tropez San San ☎ 993 7213. Flavoursome, authentic Italian cooking: homemade spaghetti and fettucini with tomato, seafood or pesto sauce; fantastic thin-crust pizzas; and Italian-style grilled fish with tomatoes. The crème caramel, made on site, is delightful.

Sir Pluggy's Jerk Centre Fair Prospect. Simple little bar in the village just before Long Bay; some say it makes the best jerked meat in the area. Cooked by amiable local character Sir Pluggy himself, chicken and pork are served with bread or rice.

Trident Hotel Just east of Port Antonio ☎ 993 2602. Excellent haute cuisine Jamaica-style is served at the poshest and priciest option on this coast. White-gloved waiters and a smart dress code go with the genteel atmosphere.

Woody's Drapers. Inexpensive and friendly family-run café, a little way east of *Jamaica Palace*, with great burgers (including veggie burgers) and sandwiches. Jamaican staples such as fish with pumpkin rice, pepperpot soup, jerk and curries have to be ordered a day in advance.

Drinking and nightlife

The area east of Port Antonio is perfect for a quiet sunset **drink**, but otherwise it's pretty sleepy. If you're after serious nightlife, you'll need to head into Port Antonio.

You can have a sophisticated evening beer or rum in the attractive upstairs bar at *Mocking Bird Hill Hotel,* or at the *Blue Lagoon* restaurant, right on the Blue Lagoon and an excellent spot for a sunset cocktail. There are several basic rum joints in the friendly little community of Drapers, though *Woody's* (see above) is most favoured by visitors for a lively evening drinking session. The *Bayview Villas* complex have a poolside **fish fry** party on most Fridays, with live music and fresh fish cooked to order. In Boston Bay, *Club Favorita,* just past the beach on the main road, hosts a similar though somewhat rowdier event, also on Fridays, with drinking and dancing until the wee hours. The *Great Huts* resort has a Sabbath ceremony on Fridays, a fusion of Jewish and Jamaican cultures with local children singing and traditional African chanting and drumming.

Long Bay to Manchioneal

The rolling pasturelands below Boston Bay are **Errol Flynn country**. The erstwhile screen idol bought much of the land between Boston Bay and Fair Prospect in the 1950s, and his widow, Patrice Wymore, still manages the 2000-acre estates, growing coconuts and guavas and raising beef cattle. At the time of writing the land was up for sale, however (at a whopping US$52 million). Both locals and ex-pat residents were anxiously waiting to discover the nature of any buyers' plans, which could radically alter the unspoilt area forever.

Past the ranch, **Long Bay**, with its gorgeous swath of surf-pounded honey sand and laid-back counter-culture atmosphere, is a marvellous place to get away from it all, and conveniently close to the fabulous **Reach Falls**, where Tom Cruise got amorous in the movie *Cocktail*. Past the falls, Jamaica's eastern tip is pretty much indifferent to tourism, and a couple of simple accommodation options near the fishing village of **Manchioneal** are perfect if you're after some unaffected charm.

Long Bay

East of Boston, the main road cleaves to the coastline, offering great views of the surf pounding in on this unprotected side of the island. After five miles of bumpy, potholed tarmac, the road swings into **LONG BAY**, where a mini tourist industry – unusual on the barely developed east coast – is swiftly growing. A wide crescent of sand with a laid-back atmosphere and the best surf in Jamaica, the bay has been attracting a smattering of European backpackers for the last decade. Some have settled here and opened guesthouses.

It's a far cry from the developed resorts on the north coast. Simple, friendly beach bars cater to the demand for entertainment, and tourists are outnum-

Errol Flynn

By the time he arrived in Jamaica in 1947, **Errol Flynn**'s movie career was already in decline. The era of the swashbuckler was drawing to a close, and the Australian actor – star of classic Hollywood action movies like *The Sea Hawk* and *Captain Blood* – had begun to fall from favour with the studios. Nonetheless, sailing ashore at Kingston in his yacht *Zaca* (now owned by the Superclubs hotel chain), Flynn quickly worked his way into local legend. Even today, you'll occasionally find people recounting (increasingly improbable) stories of his strength, powers of seduction, formidable drinking and addiction to gambling – he reputedly lost Navy Island, just off Port Antonio, in one particularly unfortunate poker bet.

Flynn loved Jamaica. Soon after his arrival, he bought the *Titchfield Hotel* in Port Antonio as well as Navy Island; later, with his third wife, Patrice Wymore, he set up a ranch near Boston Bay and planned a castle-like home up in the John Crow Mountains. For a while, he threw wild parties at his hotels – pulling a string of celebrities to the island – but unsuccessful efforts to resurrect his movie career and continuing bouts of heavy drinking and ill health were already taking their toll.

During his final years, Flynn spent much of his time in Jamaica, living at Titchfield with the teenage actress Beverley Aadland. After his death in 1959, Aadland asked that Flynn be buried in Jamaica, but Wymore insisted that his body go to Hollywood. Today, despite the tarnishing of Flynn's reputation over the years, the people of the area remember the one-time heart-throb with considerable affection.

bered on the beach by local people. The whole place feels a bit like Negril must have in the 1960s – good-natured and vaguely alternative, with a lot of ganja-smoking and general hanging out.

There isn't much to the village, which has grown up piecemeal on either side of the main road. The north end of the beach is where you'll find a small **surf** scene, though Boston Bay further west is rated better by professionals. Locals propping up the beach bars should be able to help find a board, and they'll also know of anyone who'll take you out **fishing**. **Swimming** is excellent here, too, particularly if you're feeling a little jaded toward the usual placid Jamaican shores. But watch out for a dangerous undertow and riptides; it's best not to swim out further than you can stand. If you stay in Long Bay, try to get up early to catch the **sunrise** over the ocean – it's staggering.

At the south end of the bay, by the Seven Day Adventist church, a steep rutted track winds uphill to the quiet community of Rose Garden, which has a fair proportion of Long Bay's accommodation.

Arrival and information

Buses and **minibuses** run daily to Long Bay from Port Antonio and, less frequently, from Kingston. A shared taxi from Port Antonio will cost about JS$60. If you're driving, be aware, there's no petrol station between Port Antonio and Long Bay – the first you'll reach is just as you enter the village. The small Ocean View Supermarket, at the southern end of the community, sells basic supplies, ice cream and alcohol. A good place to head for in Long Bay is the popular *Cool Runnings Bar*, situated halfway down the beach, whose welcoming owners, Skanka and Junie, will help you find somewhere to stay, guard your bags while you look around, and generally point you in the right direction.

Accommodation

There's an increasing wealth of budget accommodation in Long Bay, possibly more so here than in any other part of Jamaica. If you're after luxury and comfort, however, you should stick to the hotels between the bay and Port Antonio (see p.170).

(see p.170)

Blue Heaven Resort Long Bay ☎ 913 7014, ⓦ www.blueheaven-jamaica.com. Two rooms in a concrete house, plus a basic bamboo hut at a simple but funky property with a clifftop setting and a creek running through the garden. ❷

Fisherman's Park Long Bay ☎ 913 7482. Several homely and immaculate rooms, with private bathrooms and hot water, in an atmospheric Jamaican home. Great value. ❶

The Glass House Long Bay; ask for Miss Lou at the *Sweet Daddy* restaurant. Five-bedroom house right on the beach, with eclectic, homely decor. Services of a cook/cleaner are included in the rates. US$100 per night. ❺

Likkle Paradise Long Bay ☎ 913 7702. Just one room in the home of ever-gracious local Herlette Kennedy, this is perhaps the most appealing place to stay in Long Bay. It offers attractive decor, a private bathroom, sole use of the kitchen, and a lovely, peaceful garden. ❷

Rose Garden Guesthouse Rose Garden ☎ 913 7311, ⓔ rosshirt@cwjamaica.com. A pretty, flower-wreathed, child-friendly place, with small rooms in the main house. All rooms have fans and mosquito nets, and there's a shared hot-water bathroom. ❷

Rose Garden Pool Villas Rose Garden ☎ 913 7431. Situated right at the end of Rose Garden, the two villas vary enormously in quality. One is a standard three-bedroom house (US$50 per room per night) and the other is a gorgeous, romantic one-bedroom studio with its own pool (US$100 per night). ❺

Rose Hill Cottage Rose Garden, no phone. Self-contained cottage on the road up to Rose Garden (signposted from the main road), owned by famous German author Peter-Paul Zahl. Simple interior with two bedrooms, kitchen and a sea-facing verandah. Dinner included in rates. US$350 per week with two sharing. ❹

Skanka Heights Rose Garden ☎ 422 6576, ⓔ skankaheights@hotmail.com. A perfect back-packers' hangout with gorgeous views. Rooms are in the main house or private cottages; all have fans, mosquito nets and access to the kitchen. ❶

Seascape Long Bay ☎ 913 7762 or 425 6993, ⓦ www.jamaica-beachvillas.com. This is the most up-market and comfortable place to stay in Long Bay. The property includes two three-bedroom villas on the beach; rooms can be rented separately. The manager, David Escoe, is helpful, friendly and a great cook. Rates include breakfast. ❸

Yahimba Long Bay ☎ 913 7067, or ask for Lolita in the white house opposite. Two attractive wooden cabins midway down the beach, with verandahs, private bathrooms and hot water. Right in the middle of Long Bay's "action" – which means not much privacy but great convenience. ❸

Eating, drinking and entertainment

Evenings in Long Bay are usually centred around *Cool Runnings,* an excellent bar and restaurant with cheap beer and reasonably priced fish, pizza and salads. There are regular full-moon parties with dub poetry sessions and every other Saturday sees a talent show with live music. At the north end of the bay is *Sweet Daddy,* a local cook shop serving tasty home-cooked Jamaican food. Further down the beach, at its southern tip, is the *Mid-Way* bar, a friendly place for a drink. It's popular with locals, as is the unnamed Rasta-striped bar just beyond it. There's a well-organized round robin-type agreement among bars in Long Bay and other communities in East Portland for Sunday night gatherings, with everyone heading for a different place each week. Just ask around or look out for posters – you'll have no trouble finding the action.

Reach Falls and Manchioneal

South of Long Bay, the road passes by some marvellously rugged coastline, with waves crashing against the cliffs. Before crossing the Christmas River, you'll pass the tiny village of **Kensington**, four miles on from Long Bay. It's the birthplace of Father Hugh Sherlock, who composed Jamaica's national anthem in 1962. Enclosed by a thick covering of trees and utterly pitch black at night, the tunnel-like, hairpin-bend punctuated stretch of road near Kensington is locally known as "see me no more". Just over the river, the *Ranch Bar* (☎ 993 6138; ❷) is a peaceful, rootsy place with basic **rooms** and shared bathrooms in a lovely grassy garden beside the water. A rugged slip of beach is steps away (though the water gets pretty rough). If you've a tent, you can camp for US$10.

Halfway along Jamaica's eastern edge, and a mile or so on from the *Ranch Bar*, a road swings left off the main to **Reach Falls** (9am–5pm; J$170). It is one of the loveliest spots on the island, with the Drivers River running through some sumptuous rainforest before cascading over the falls into a wide, green pool. The thirty-foot waterfall itself is pretty spectacular, and you can stand right underneath it for an invigorating water massage. From the base of the falls, tour guides will take you on a thirty-minute trek upriver through the rainforest – climbing up beside the waterfall, picking your way across slippery rocks, swimming through deep pools and wading along the riverbed. There's no official charge, though you're expected to leave a tip (less than US$5 will be scoffed at). You can ask to be taken to the base of **Mandingo Cave**, though it's quite a tricky climb. You follow the same route returning downriver, ending (if you can muster the courage) with an exhilarating jump into the pool at the base. Movie fans might recognize Reach Falls as the place where Tom Cruise cavorts with his lady love in the film *Cocktail*.

The side road from the main A4 coast road to the falls winds for a little over three miles through some dazzling countryside. If you have time, stop at Jah Priest's wood-carving shack by the side of the road. Just before the falls themselves is an arrival point with a car park, small bar and unusual crafts stall with bamboo instruments and games made by sweet-natured Rasta Rennie. On weekends, stalls selling excellent janga soup and roast corn set up; further back from the car park are clean changing rooms and toilets. A round-trip taxi from Port Antonio to the falls costs around US$40; if you're short of funds you could take a route taxi for J$70 to the signposted turn-off from the A4 and walk or hitch the rest of the way.

Manchioneal

Half a mile before the turn-off for Reach, if you're coming from Long Bay, the coast road inches into the pretty fishing village of **MANCHIONEAL**. Here brightly painted stalls selling roast fish and conch soup border the road, and canoes line up on the sand; there's also a petrol station, and you can sup a Red Stripe at the diminutive *Titus Bar*. The best place in town to eat fresh fish is the *B and L* restaurant, on a breezy terrace above the local grocery store. Protected by the headlands, Manchioneal Bay is frequented by a family of **manatees** (locally known as sea cows); the four-strong brood can often be seen gambolling in the water.

Across the bay, and offering gorgeous views of the harbour, there's a wonderful **accommodation** option, *Zion Country Cottages* (☎993 0435, ⑤993 0551, ⓦwww.zioncountry.com; ⓸), well-signposted and a hundred yards down a dirt track off the main road. Run by an enthusiastic Dutchman, Free-I, who has built Rasta sensibilities into his eco-friendly outlook, the complex spreads down the cliffs to a small shingle beach complete with hammocks for catching the evening breezes, while lovingly tended flowers and plants wreathe the pathways. The four simple, bright cabins share showers, and meals are available. Free-I runs excellent informal **tours** of the surrounding area, including hikes along the volcanic rocks of the local coastline to impressive blowholes and natural swimming pools, and also offers islandwide excursions.

The Rio Grande valley

Portland's interior – the **Rio Grande valley** – is a fantastically lush and partially impenetrable hinterland of tropical rainforest, rivers and waterfalls. The **Rio Grande** – one of Jamaica's major rivers – pours down from the John Crow Mountains through the deep and beautiful valley of real virgin forest, with none of the soil erosion and deforestation found on the south side of the Blue Mountains.

Despite its beauty, the area is little explored; many people only get as far as the **Nonsuch Caves** on its outskirts. Those tourists who do venture in are here to **raft** the river, though visitors are starting to discover the superb **hiking** options, which range from gentle riverside walks to strenuous overnight pilgrimages up into the mountains. This is Maroon country, and many of the rivers and springs are named after local leaders – Nanny, Quao, Quashie and Quako. The major remaining Maroon settlement is **Moore Town**, though its past is more of a draw than its present, and while some of the other **villages** have lovely settings and fascinating names – Alligator Church, Comfort Castle – you'll only want to visit if you're craving rustic isolation.

Nonsuch Caves and Athenry Gardens

Four miles south of Port Antonio, on the outer fringes of the Rio Grande valley, the **Nonsuch Caves and Athenry Gardens** (daily 9am–5pm; US$6 with complimentary rum or fruit punch) are an obvious and mildly entertaining first stop in the interior. The fourteen ancient subterranean chambers were used by Taino Indians in pre-Columbian times (although their relics were removed to the University of the West Indies long ago) and now house some impressive stalactites and plenty of bats. The guides who shepherd you through the well-lit passages deliver a well-oiled patter. They'll point out fossils of fish, coral and sea sponges from the days – around one and a half million years ago – when the whole of Jamaica was still underwater. Once you've emerged back into the sunshine, take a stroll around the expansive **gardens** adjacent to the caves; they command a magnificent view over the coastline and are packed with ginger lilies, bougainvillea, royal poinciana trees and the like.

The road up to the caves, once in a dreadful condition, is now one of the smoothest in Jamaica. But you shouldn't race up it. Driving – or being driven - slowly will allow you to appreciate some spectacular views of the John Crow Mountains.

Rafting the Rio Grande

Once just an easy way to transport bananas to the loading wharf in Port Antonio, **rafting** down the majestic Rio Grande has been Portland's most popular attraction ever since Errol Flynn began organizing rafting races for his friends in the 1950s. Today, it's a delightfully lazy way to spend half a day, although the sun can get fierce, so take a hat or umbrella.

From the put-in point at **Berridale**, six miles southwest of Port Antonio, thirty-foot rafts – made of lengths of bamboo lashed together, with a raised seat at the back that can hold two people and a small child – meander down the river on a three-hour journey through some outstanding scenery before terminating at Rafters' Rest at St Margaret's Bay (see p.181). The raft captain stands at the front and poles the craft downstream, stopping periodically to let passengers swim or buy snacks from vendors positioned along the route.

Tickets are sold at the put-in spot by Rio Grande Attractions Ltd (daily 9am
–4pm; US$45 per raft; ☎993 5778), or occasionally by hotels and tour groups
in Port Antonio. Because it's a one-way trip, **transport** can be a problem. If
you're driving, you can leave your car at Berridale and have an insured driver
take it down to Rafters' Rest for around US$15. A taxi to Berridale and back
to Port Antonio from Rafters' Rest costs around US$16. If you're desperate to
save cash, the Berridale route taxi from Port Antonio (J$50) runs close by the
put-in point, and route taxis to Port Antonio from Kingston and Buff Bay pass
the entrance to Rafters' Rest approximately once an hour.

You'll occasionally find people touting **unofficial rafting trips** for a lower
price. Don't hand over the cash until you've finished the journey at Rafters'

Rio Grande valley hikes

The hikes listed here are merely the most popular, pleasant or spectacular, but there
are many more to explore. One or two of the peripheral hikes, such as Road End,
can be done on your own, but a **guide** is essential if you're heading deep into the
valley. You can easily find someone to guide you once you're up in Millbank; ask at
Ambassabeth Cabins in Bowden (see p.180) or *Sister Ivelyn* in Cornwall Barracks.
There are also two official organizations based in Port Antonio offering reasonably
priced tours with well-trained local guides who really know their stuff: Valley Hikes
(Unit 41, Village of St George, ☎993 3881, ©valleyhikes@cwjamaica.com) and
Grand Valley Tours (12 West St, ☎993 4116, ⊛www.grandvalleytoursja.com). Rates
range from US$35 per person for two- to four-hour Lower Rio Grande treks, to
US$150 for a trek to Nanny Town, high up in the hills. Both organizations can
arrange home-stay accommodation with local families in the valley and opportunities to meet members of the Rio Grande communities.

The only other reputable organization offering guided treks in the Rio Grande valley
is Kingston-based Sun Venture Tours (☎960 6685, ☎920 8348, ⊛www.sunventure-
tours.com), which can arrange hikes on request along pig hunters' trails in the area;
contact them in advance for rates.

Trails

Guava River Trail (7 miles; 7hr) A difficult trail that's well worth the effort. From
Bellevue head straight into the jungle and follow the Guava River for most of the
way. Opportunities abound for swimming and waterfall-spotting, and there are even
some hot springs if you fancy a dip.

Nanny Town (10–15 miles; 2 days) Once a sizeable village, Nanny Town is today a
scattering of crumbling and overgrown ruins. But it remains an important symbol of
Maroon history, allegedly haunted by the ghosts of vanquished British soldiers. This
is a two-day excursion from Coopers Hill through untouched forest of unparalleled
beauty to the site of the eighteenth-century hideaway. The extremely difficult hike
demands determination, a love of nature and a tent; enlist a trained guide.

Scatter Water Falls (0.75 miles; 20min). The shortest, easiest and most popular
hike in the area, usually done from Berridale (see previous map). From there, a raft
takes you across the Rio Grande, and it's then a twenty-minute walk to the falls,
where there are swimming pools and a bar. A further fifteen-minute hike up the falls
leads to the Foxes Caves, which you'll need a flashlight to explore properly. This trip
is only offered by Grand Valley Tours.

White River Falls (4 miles; 7hr). Starting from Millbank, this tough climb traces the
beautiful White River through virgin rainforest to a series of fabulous high waterfalls.
The trail is strenuous and slippery, with lots of uphill scrambling, but at the first cascade you get your reward – a swim in the freezing froth. There are seven falls in all,
but most people go only as far as the first two or three.

Rest, and don't go with anyone unless you feel completely comfortable with them.

Hiking in the Rio Grande

Although some of the villages they once connected are long gone, the old parish council "roads" provide the basis for a number of **hiking trails** into the Rio Grande valley; others follow traditional pig hunters' routes. Many of them feature occasional reminders of Maroon occupation, from half-buried sugar pans to the remains of a deserted village above the Quako River.

Hiking in the valley is an entirely different experience to hiking in the Blue Mountains. The lower limestone John Crow Mountains are hotter and wetter – a waterproof is essential – and the humidity can make walking uncomfortable, though the proliferation of mineral springs and Rio Grande tributaries means that you're never far from somewhere to cool off.

Moore Town

Eleven miles inland from Port Antonio, **MOORE TOWN** is Jamaica's principal Maroon settlement, founded, so the legend goes, by **Nanny** (chieftainess of the Windward Maroons and now a National Hero) in the mid-eighteenth century. Today, it's a small, quiet place at the end of a winding rocky road, with few signs and little apparent sense of its historical importance. The road, a left fork downhill from the main route from Port Antonio, goes straight into the heart

The Windward Maroons

When the Spanish left Jamaica in 1660, they armed and freed most of their African slaves and encouraged them to fight a guerrilla war against the new British colonists. The Spanish called these guerrillas *cimarrones* (meaning wild or untamed), a word corrupted by the British to **Maroons.** Over the years, the ranks of the Maroons were boosted by runaway slaves from the sugar plantations. They set up small communities in inaccessible parts of the island, with the **Windward Maroons** establishing themselves in the Blue and John Crow mountains and the Trelawny Maroons making a base in Cockpit Country (see p.281). As they grew in confidence, the Maroons raided British settlements for weapons and supplies. By the 1720s, they had become such a serious threat that the British decided to send the troops in.

The Windward Maroons had their headquarters 2000ft up in the mountains at **Nanny Town**, virtually inaccessible to the British soldiers, who were unfamiliar with the area. They only discovered it after a black slave led them there in 1728, and were periodically slaughtered on their forays into the rainforest to destroy the settlement. Eventually, in 1734, British army captain Stoddard dragged swivel guns up the south side of the John Crow Mountains and bombarded Nanny Town, destroying most of the 140 homes and scattering the Maroons, forcing many of them to move south. Still the British couldn't flush them out completely. Five years later a peace treaty was signed, giving the undefeated Maroons a semi-independent status that they retain today, as well as five hundred acres of land in the Rio Grande valley, on which they established their new base at Moore Town (see above).

Today, the Windward Maroons have been virtually assimilated into the wider Jamaican population. Though some of the elders remain fiercely proud of their heritage – and a handful still speak the traditional Coromantee language – most young Maroons see little opportunity in their mountain villages and move to the cities for work, intermarrying with other Jamaicans. Within a generation there are likely to be few pure-blood Maroons left.

of the village, with houses and small shacks scattered beside it and across the adjacent fields. You should, as a matter of protocol, check in by saying hello to the Maroons' **colonel** or chief. The present chief, Colonel Stirling, to whom leadership was officially passed in 1995, lives some way up the village, though you'll learn more from his charming predecessor, Colonel Colin Harris, a knowledgeable elder whose house is the first on the right after the post office. There's no charge for looking around, but you may be asked for a donation to a planned (though probably far-off) Maroon museum.

Bump Grave, a monument to Nanny and supposedly the place where she's buried, is in the town's small central square, and is pretty much the only thing to see. It's a stone tomb, with a plaque to the "indomitable and skilled chieftainess", and the Maroon and Jamaican flags fly side by side overhead. Otherwise, apart from the usual profusion of schoolchildren, Moore Town feels deserted. Many villagers live scattered around the nearby hills, and you'll see houses perched in the most unlikely places.

If you're lucky, you'll catch a **cricket game** in the grassy square across from the monument. Given the precarious position of the pitch at the edge of the Wildcane River, several fielders normally stand up to their ankles in water to catch any well-struck balls before they disappear downstream.

Alternatively, you can hike up to **Nanny Falls**, following the track north through town for around forty minutes. A guide will help you to find the best places to swim and can take you on a longer hike through the jungle if you wish; ask around for a suitable person and arrange a fee (approx US$10). Both **Valley Hikes** and **Grand Valley Tours** (see p.177) will also provide a guide to Nanny Falls. The guide will pick fruits for you to sample and point out medicinal plants along the way (US$25 per person); longer walks along trails around the town are also available (US$30 per person).

Moore Town is also renowned as the home of Mother Roberts, a spiritual healer practised in the art of *pukkumina* (a syncretised religion whose leaders link the earth and spirit worlds and speak in tongues) with legendary powers. People come from all over Jamaica to visit her at the rather splendidly named *AME (African Methodist Episcopal) Zion Deliverance Centre*, a small flower-decked church on the left-hand side as you enter the village. Healing sessions are held every Monday (apart from the first in the month), Tuesday and Wednesday between 9am and 6pm. Although Mother Roberts doesn't officially charge, you'll be expected to give a hefty donation if you're seen by her.

Moore Town is served by frequent **route taxis** from Port Antonio most of the week, but there are few if any on Sundays. Take a **picnic,** as there are no restaurants. There's also no official accommodation - if you're planning to stay overnight, contact one of the tour organizations above to see if it's possible to lodge with a local family.

Further into the valley from Moore Town is **CORNWALL BARRACKS** – continue straight on the main road, which winds up into the village and comes to a meandering halt. The surroundings here are as picturesque as any in the area. Though tourist facilities are otherwise minimal, the village is home to the formidable Ivelyn Harris, who rents out a pretty one-room cabin (☎806 0161, ⓦwww.portantoniojamaica.com; US$50 per night for one person or US$100 for two) in her lushly planted garden. Known locally as "Nanny of the Maroons", or Sister Ivy, Ivelyn is an expert herbalist and alternative-medicine practioner and craftswoman. She conducts purifying herbal baths (US$45), serves up excellent Maroon food and takes guests on bird-watching and adventure hikes in the area.

Millbank

Little-visited **MILLBANK** – the last sizeable town in the Rio Grande valley – nestles deep in the John Crow Mountains, five miles south of Moore Town. "Sizeable" in this case means a couple of basic shops, a playing field and a community centre, but the town also contains one of the three Blue and John Crow Mountains National Park **ranger stations** (see box on p.137). The station acts as an unofficial information centre – when there's a ranger on the premises (they're often out on patrols). You're in prime Maroon country here, and many of the town's older inhabitants – a healthy diet and clean mountain air mean that many residents are pushing 100 – will happily tell you tales of Maroon history, while the younger locals can escort you to derelict settlements that don't appear on the maps.

Millbank's setting is spectacular: rainforest rises up all around and the perfume of wild ginger lilies hangs heavy in the air. It's also the starting point for several good **hikes**, the most popular (detailed on p.177) heading to **White River Falls**, seven high cascades on the other side of the Rio Grande; ask around for a guide or prearrange with Valley Hikes (see p.177).

As the road stops just beyond Moore Town, getting to Millbank involves taking the right fork at Seaman's Valley via **Alligator Church**, where a rather perilous bridge crosses the Rio Grande. Here the river forms a large natural pool edged by smooth sun-warmed rocks, a popular bathing spot. If you're brave and the river is deep enough – follow local advice - you can jump right in from the bridge for a wonderfully exhilarating dip. On the way up to Millbank you'll pass the diminutive communities of **Ginger House** and **Comfort Castle**.

The only **place to stay** in the area is the wonderful *Ambassabeth Cabins and Campsite* (☎938 5036, ⓕ977 8565; ●) at **BOWDEN**, a half-hour walk southeast of Millbank. A regular car should be able to handle the road if there's been no rain; otherwise, you might be able to scrounge a lift in Millbank square or from the ranger station. The down-to-earth wooden cabins have no electricity or running water (though fresh water is readily available from mineral springs), but bags of atmosphere and ingenuity. Baths are taken in the Rio Grande or at a small spring nearby, and traditional Maroon meals are prepared on an open fire. If you're on a budget, you can rent floor space in one of the larger cabins for US$5; beds cost US$12. Camping is also possible for a nominal fee. Guides are available for walks in the area. As *Ambassabeth* is so remote, it's best to arrange your stay in advance; the owners can also arrange transportation from Kingston or Port Antonio.

Between Millbank and Bowden, a rope and board **suspension bridge** provides the only dry means of crossing the Rio Grande for miles around and is an important link for locals – crossing the river here brings you to Cornwall Barracks (see p.179). Once past *Ambassabeth*, the road widens into an improbably large thoroughfare, built in the late 1970s by British ex-servicemen granted large tracts of crown land. Harsh conditions and lack of modern conveniences prompted a swift exodus, and the now grassy track melts abruptly into the bush at Road End, less than a third of the way to its intended destination at Bath.

West of Port Antonio

The A4 winds west from Port Antonio, crisscrossing the old railway track torn up by Hurricane Allen in 1980 and threading through a series of tiny fishing villages, peppered with stalls selling local fruit and vegetables. You can stop for a fresh-water splash at **Somerset Falls**, head inland to **Swift River** or **River Edge**, or explore the towns of **Buff Bay** and **Annotto Bay**, both bursting with small-town character.

Buses run between Port Antonio and Annotto Bay every hour or so in both directions and will stop wherever you ask.

St Margaret's Bay and Somerset Falls

About five miles west of Port Antonio, the first settlement of note is tiny **ST MARGARET'S BAY**, where the Rio Grande empties into the sea underneath an iron bridge dating back to 1891. Just by the bridge, a side road leads towards **Rafters' Rest**, a pretty colonial-style building that serves as journey's end for Rio Grande rafting excursions (see p.176). You can also book a trip here, and a posse of raft operators usually hang out by the bridge touting for business.

Past Rafters' Rest, you enter St Margaret's Bay proper, an appealingly neat settlement spreading back from the roadside. St Margaret's Bay was the last stop-but-one of the Jamaica Railway until Hurricane Allen dispensed with most of the track here in 1980, ten years before the railway was shut down islandwide. The railway buildings now serve as homes, and the old station itself operates as a simple restaurant/bar.

If you want to **stay** in the area, *Rio Vista* (T993 5444, F993 5445, Wwww.riovistajamaica.com; ❻) is beautifully situated on a bluff that affords fantastic views of the Rio Grande and foothills of the Blue and John Crow mountains. You can stay either in a room in the main house (rates for these include breakfast), or a self-contained one-bedroom villa with a kitchen. There's a pool, and delicious gourmet meals can be arranged. A little further west, the friendly *Paradise Inn* (T993 5169, F993 5569, in the UK T020 7350 1009, F020 7228 3536, Eparadiseinn295@hotmail.com; ❷–❺) has simple rooms and a grander selection of studio apartments with a/c, fan, phone and a kitchen. Otherwise, the hills above town hold the quiet *Pleasant View Guesthouse* (T913 3058; ❷), where the spacious rooms have private hot-water bathrooms, two double beds, fans and TVs, and the pool faces verdant mountain slopes. St Margaret's Bay has a couple of roadside shacks selling cheap **meals**, and at its western end, the *Seaview Jerk Centre*, a friendly local joint with a shady garden backing onto the sea.

Just outside St Margaret's Bay, lush landscaping and sizeable signs mark the entrance to the concrete complex built around **Somerset Falls** (daily 9am–5pm; US$5), part of the cascading Daniels River. Guides lead you through to the main falls, passing a stairway that provides access to the "cool pool" – a refreshing place to have a dip and slide over the rocks. Your entrance fee also buys you a boat ride through a chink in the gorge-like rocks to the spectacular "hidden falls" beyond, cascading into a 20ft deep pool and perfect for a natural power shower. There's a simple **café** serving cold drinks.

Hope Bay and Swift River

West of St Margaret's Bay, past the turn-off to Ken Jones Aerodrome, the road swings into the busy little village-cum-fishing-community of **HOPE BAY**, home of a string of shops and rum bars. At the police station, you can turn inland for some marvellous **river swimming** in the upper reaches of the Swift River, a half-hour drive through cocoa groves and mountain valleys. Follow the road signs and keep bearing left to the tiny and supremely friendly settlement of **SWIFT RIVER** itself, where you turn left off the main road at a small suspension bridge and follow the path of the river. The further you go upstream, the quieter it gets, and there are innumerable deep pools for a dip.

There are several decent places for **food** in Hope Bay – the best is *Total Satisfaction*, a simple white and blue hut close to the PNP's regional office on the eastern edge of town. At the other end of the village is an unnamed seafood restaurant right on the black sand beach, with very cheap Jamaican staples and a cheerful local atmosphere. The *Railway Drive-In Bar*, in the old clapboard train station, makes a pleasant spot for a drink.

Should you wish to stay in the area, there are several budget options. *Crystal's* (T913 0501; ●) is a large Jamaican home set back from the road as you enter Hope Bay from the west. It offers several basic but homely rooms upstairs and a rather kitsch bar/restaurant on the ground floor. Opposite *Total Satisfaction*, friendly local Dyce rents out two no-frills bedrooms in his wooden shack (●) – there's no running water or electricity, but it's clean and safe enough. Close by, Linton's **crafts shop** sells woodcarvings, jewellery and handmade drums at cheaper prices than in Port Antonio.

Crystal Springs, Buff Bay and Annotto Bay

Heading west from Hope Bay, the main road winds up and over **Black Hill**, a tiny community with one tranquil and rather funky Italian-run guesthouse, *Ital Village* (T913 0917, Wwww.italvillage.com; ❸ with breakfast) hidden away down one of its side tracks. Follow the sign at a right fork on the peak of the hill. If you're driving you'll need a four-wheel-drive vehicle, otherwise it's an arduous two-mile walk before you reach the attractive wooden house, surrounded by fruit trees and clinging to the side of a hill. Rooms are simple but comfortable, with a shared cold shower.

Continuing round the coast westards, **Crystal Springs nature resort** (daily dawn to dusk; J$100) is a quasi-botanical garden on the site of a seventeenth-century sugar plantation; it's signposted off the main road just before Buff Bay. A river runs through the rambling gardens, where there's a fine collection of orchids and an old water wheel. The **mongoose** was introduced to Jamaica here in 1872, in an attempt to wipe out the cane rats that were wrecking the local sugar harvest. The plan backfired badly, as the mongooses, showing more catholic taste than had been anticipated, turned their attention to the island's harmless coneys and iguanas and devastated their respective populations. Mongooses are still all over the place; if you're driving around the country, you'll often see them legging it across the road with gay abandon. There are wooden cabins at Crystal Springs though they've long been closed for "refurbishment"; you can call T993 1400 to see if they're open again.

Beyond Crystal Springs, the road affords some awesome views of the Blue and John Crow mountains. The peaks poke up above the endless fields of coconut palms and banana groves that were planted as part of the United Fruit Company's Kildaire Estate, itself occupying land that was previously a colonial-era sugar plantation.

It's another half-mile along bumpy, potholed tarmac before you get to the easy-going market town of **BUFF BAY**, where Blue Mountain farmers come to sell their wares in the dingy covered market. Aside from the piles of produce and a rickety metal arch over the main street – a relic from the 1962 independence celebrations – there's not a lot to see, but you might want to poke around **St George's** Anglican church, the oldest building in town. There's been a church on this site since 1681, although most of the present structure dates from 1814.

The Kildaire estate's former great house, on the edge of town, serves as an efficient rest stop these days, with a good restaurant, a well-stocked gift store and sparkling bathrooms, which are quite a rarity in these parts. Aside from Kildaire, the best place to **eat** in Buff Bay is the excellent *Pacesetter*, almost opposite the church, with great curry goat and rice and peas, and a lovely selection of cakes and pastries. If you're a jerk pork fan, though, the *Blueberry Hill* jerk centre, just outside the town on the knoll of a hill, offers meat that some say is better than Boston Bay's. And if you're looking for somewhere to spend the night, the *Blueberry Hill Guesthouse* (☎913 6814, ⓕ996 1339; ●), signposted from the main road, has clean rooms with cable TV and hot water.

Ten miles west of Buff Bay, the road enters **ANNOTTO BAY**, a busy, tatty little one-street town named after the red annatto dye once produced here from the pulp of indigenous trees (though locals argue that the name comes from the colour of the bay after rain). The town serves as a commercial centre for surrounding communities; at one time produce was loaded from its wharves. Since the scaling-down of local banana and sugar industries, however, it has become a lot quieter. The town boasts a police station, courthouse and a market behind the main square. The market's main days are Friday and Saturday; in March and April this is the place to pick up some of the small but coveted **long mangoes**, which are grown in the fertile pastures inland of Annotto Bay. Pause to admire the red and yellow **Baptist church**, built in 1892, its entrance guarded by old cannons, the meagre remains of British Fort George.

For **food**, there are several basic cook shops serving up standard Jamaican dishes. Better by far than these is the *Human Service Station*, just east of town, serving delicious fish, fried chicken and natural juices on a breezy outdoor terrace right on the sea. A tight corner in the road just beyond the outskirts of town causes drivers to slow down and offers vendors a prime opportunity to flog Irish Moss seaweed and peppered shrimp, the latter freshly caught in the rivers of the Blue Mountains above.

The countryside **inland of Annotto Bay**, sheltering under the eaves of the Blue Mountains, makes a welcome change from the endless coastal vistas of the A4; turn in at the Annotto Bay All Age School and follow the signs to **River Edge** (☎944 2673, ⓕ944 9455), twenty minutes' drive from the coast. On the way, you'll pass grove upon grove of bananas, and a commercial palm and flower farm nestled at the bottom of a pretty valley. Built around the cool, clear waters of the Pencar River, *River Edge* is a friendly, family-run combination of restaurant, swimming spot and guesthouse. Shallow swimming pools offer a refreshing dip (or a natural jacuzzi), and you can have a drink, a tasty Jamaican meal or even a massage in the shady waterside gazebo. If you want to **stay** here, you have your choice of pleasant, airy dorm beds (U\$20) or private studio apartments with bathrooms and cooking facilities (●). If you fancy camping, pitches hooked up to electricity, with showers and bathrooms nearby, cost U\$6 per person if you have your own tent, U\$10 per person if you need to rent one.

Travel details

Buses and minibuses

It is impossible to predict accurately the frequency of buses and minibuses in the Blue Mountains and the east. Service is often chaotic and delays and cancellations are frequent, so the figures provided here are only general guidelines. However, on the most popular routes you should be able to count on getting a ride within an hour if you travel in the morning; things normally quiet down later in the day. On less popular routes, you're best off asking around for probable departure times the day before you travel.

Bath to: Kingston (1 daily; 2hr 30min).

Morant Bay to: Kingston (3 daily; 2hr); Port Antonio (2 daily; 2hr 30min).

Papine to: Mavis Bank (2 daily; 1hr 20min); Newcastle (2 daily; 1hr 10min).

Port Antonio to: Boston Bay (4 daily; 20min); Buff Bay (4 daily; 1hr); Kingston (via Buff Bay, 4 daily, 3hr 30min; via Morant Bay, 2 daily, 4hr 30min);

Long Bay (4 daily; 50min); Montego Bay (1 daily; 5hr); Moore Town (2 daily; 1hr 30min); Morant Bay (2 daily; 2hr 30min); Ocho Rios (1 daily; 3hr).

Flights

Port Antonio to: Kingston (2 daily; 15 min); Montego Bay (3 daily; 35min); Negril (2 daily; 45min), Ocho Rios (2 daily; 20min).

Ocho Rios and the north coast

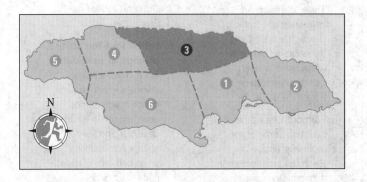

CHAPTER 3   # Highlights

✳ **Cranbrook Flower Forest** One of the loveliest gardens in Jamaica, with its own large river pool, grassy lawns to picnic on and a fine collection of orchids and other tropical plants. See p.219

✳ **Time 'n' Place** An extremely laid-back beach "resort", it has three cabins set on fine white sand, a funky beach bar and a genial host. See p.236

✳ **Falmouth** As well as boasting some of the most impressive Georgian architecture in Jamaica, this small market town has a lively but unhurried atmosphere. See p.232

✳ **Reggae Beach** Just outside Ocho Rios and a world away from its crowded streets, Reggae Beach is a peaceful stretch of sand with a funky vibe. See p.201

✳ **Firefly** Noel Coward's modest home has one of the best views on the island, over the bay of Port Maria and as far as Cuba on a clear day. See p.214

✳ **Faith's Pen** This string of roadside stalls dishes out all the Jamaican favorites – jerk chicken, conch soup, curried goat, roast fish – each delicious and very cheap. A matchless Jamaican eating experience. See p.199

✳ **Wilderness Resort** In the rolling green hills of St Ann, this working farm offers properly organized ATV tours, fishing and riding. See p.201

△ Beach ride, St Ann

3

Ocho Rios and
the north coast

The north coast road is the busiest tourist route in Jamaica and, once the section of the extensive Highway 2000 road-building project between Montego Bay and Ocho Rios is completed, may become even busier – though much more streamlined. In the meantime, traffic belts round the potholed curves between the most commercial of Jamaica's resorts, and hundreds of hotels, bars, jerk stands and craft shacks line up to catch the possible trade that passes by but rarely stops. The attraction of the north coast is obvious: barrelling through the diverse parishes of St Mary, St Ann and Trelawny, the road passes sparse mangrove coastline, luscious farmland and sweeping cane and coconut plantations and runs parallel to miles of white-sand beaches with reefs less than a hundred feet out to sea. Yet the "touristy" coast can seem like Jamaica at its most forlorn – many of the sights appear contrived, much of the accommodation is in fenced-in all-inclusive resorts, and the ingrained practice of tourist hustling in the resorts can make every interaction feel like a sales pitch. Nonetheless, the area does offer Jamaica's highest concentration of things to do and boasts an energetic atmosphere that's noticeably absent in more tempered parts.

Much of the tourism development is centred on the "garden parish" of **St Ann**, so called because of the area's immensely fertile soil. St Ann has also spawned luminaries such as **Marcus Garvey**, **Bob Marley** and **Winston "Burning Spear" Rodney**, and is considered the spiritual centre of the island. The nucleus of the parish and the home of the famous **Dunn's River Falls**, **Ocho Rios** is fast becoming Jamaica's most popular holiday destination, with all the high-rise blocks, buzzing jet skis and thumping nightlife you could ask for. But just a few miles to the east, the quiet coastal villages of **Oracabessa** and **Port Maria** are disturbed by little other than birdsong, with miles of deserted coastline nearby and lots of possibilities for hiking and waterfall hunting. West of Ocho Rios, **St Ann's Bay**, parish capital and site of ruined Spanish settlement **Sevilla Nueva**, makes a refreshing change to the glitz of its neighbour, while the dusty resort towns of **Runaway Bay** and **Discovery Bay**, where tourism is largely restricted to all-inclusives, maintain communities relatively unaffected by the influx of foreigners. Small villages and brashly advertised rest stops punctuate the scenery as far as the windswept market town of **Falmouth**.

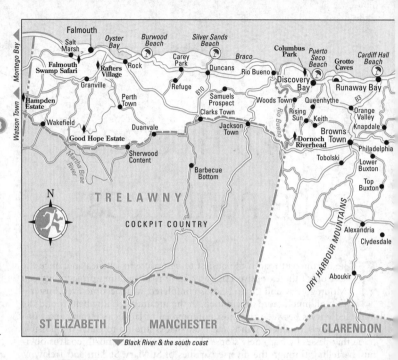

Falmouth
Salt
Marsh
Oyster
Bay
Burwood
Beach
Silver Sands
Beach
Columbus
Park
Puerto
Seco
Beach
Grotto
Caves
Cardiff Hall
Beach
Falmouth
Swamp Safari
Rafters
Village
Rock
Carey
Park
Braco
Rio Bueno
Discovery
Bay
Runaway Bay
Granville
Refuge
Duncans
Woods Town
Queenhythe
Orange
Valley
Hampden
Estate
Perth
Town
Samuels
Prospect
Clarks Town
Rising
Sun
Keith
Knapdale
Wakefield
Duanvale
Jackson
Town
Rio Bueno
Dornoch
Riverhead
Browns
Town
Philadelphia
Good Hope Estate
Sherwood
Content
Tobolski
Lower
Buxton
Martha Brae River
Barbecue
Bottom
Top
Buxton
N
TRELAWNY
Alexandria
Clydesdale
COCKPIT COUNTRY
DRY HARBOUR MOUNTAINS
Aboukir
ST ELIZABETH
MANCHESTER
CLARENDON

▼ Black River & the south coast

◀ Montego Bay
◀ Watson Town

Inland, smack in the middle of St Ann, is **Nine Mile**, Bob Marley's birthplace and site of his mausoleum, where an obligatory cache of Rasta guides welcome hordes of reggae disciples. Away from this star attraction, though, you can drive for hours through the mostly undeveloped **interior** with only cattle for company and some marvellous scenery to distract you from the wheel.

Ocho Rios and around

Light years away from the "sleepy fishing village" of a few decades ago, **OCHO RIOS** (usually just called "Ochi") has long been overtaken by the tourist industry. These day, though, the town (like Montego Bay) has suffered from the general decline in the number of visitors to Jamaica and looks slightly down at heel. The first town in Jamaica to be developed specifically as a resort, Ochi has seen rapid growth, and in some places, the planners have overlooked aesthetics in the chase for foreign dollars. The town depends on the spending power of the thousands of cruise-ship passengers who disembark each week – up to a staggering six thousand a day in the Caribbean cruising season from December to March – and is fully geared up to cater to easy-access tourism. The streets

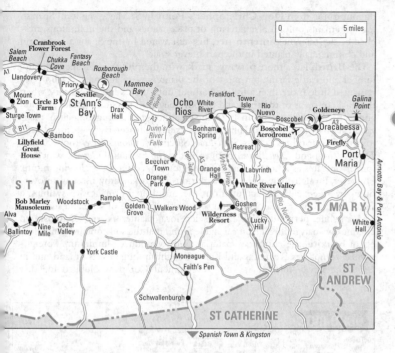

Spanish Town & Kingston

abound with neon-fronted in-bond stores, fast-food chains and visitor-oriented restaurants, while several slickly packaged attractions are within a few minutes' drive. Local culture takes a bit of a back seat to the tourist trappings, though, and Ochi is not a place to get an authentic flavour of Jamaica. Nor is it the best choice amongst the island's "big three" resorts for the classic Caribbean beach holiday – the meagre strip of hotel-lined sand just can't compete with the beaches of Negril and Montego Bay, and the club and bar scenes are less vibrant. In spite of its scenic deficiencies and noisy, polluted streets, Ochi does have a certain infectious energy. Harassment has become only a minor irritation since resort police became a permanent presence, and as Ochi's town and tourist area are one and the same, there's less of the "sitting duck" atmosphere of the Montego Bay strip.

Some history

"Ocho Rios" is a corruption of the Spanish name *chorreros* or *chireiras*, referring to the "gushing water" of the many local waterfalls. While the name literally means "Eight Rivers", in fact there aren't eight rivers here. In contrast to its poetic name, the town has a somewhat violent history. Its surrounds were the site of several bloody battles, which took place when local Spanish governor **Don Christobel Arnaldo de Yssasi** – whose family had been in Jamaica for over a hundred years – refused to give in to the British after their capture of the island in 1655. Major skirmishes took place at Dunn's River in 1657, Rio Nuevo in 1658 (see p.201) and Shaw Park in 1659, when Yssasi's men were attacked by a group led by his erstwhile ally, **Juan De Bolas**, a former slave who had defected to the British. In April 1660, Yssasi fled the island in a dugout canoe from **Don Christopher's Point** in St Mary. The local Spanish legacy remains only in a smattering of place names and the ubiquitous presence of the fragrant **pimento** tree, first discovered by the Spanish in St Ann and commercially planted in the parish ever since.

The **British** left a more pervasive mark, with their huge sugarcane, pimento, lumber and cattle farms, but most of the planters were absentees. Ocho Rios remained little more than a fishing harbour until the twentieth century, when the dual concerns of **tourism** and **bauxite** began to physically sculpt the land and secure local prosperity. In 1923, the great house of a struggling citrus plantation at Shaw Park became Jamaica's first exclusive **hotel**. By 1948, it had been joined by four others – *Sans Souci Lido, Silver Seas, Dunn's River* (now *Sandals Dunn's River*) and *Eden Bower* (until recently *The Enchanted Garden,* which no longer operates as a hotel) – and Ocho Rios looked set for a glowing future. However, though there were a few glorious beaches nearby, most were overhung by steep cliffs or cut off from the mainland by mangrove swamps, a significant problem in a destination sold on the premise of sand and sea.

Meanwhile, perpetual crop failures led local planter **Alfred DaCosta** to chemically analyze the St Ann earth. He found that the soil contained high levels of **bauxite**, the chief raw material used to produce aluminium. Foreign-owned companies Reynolds and Kaiser bought up huge tracts of land, and in 1968, the newly formed St Ann Development Company clubbed together

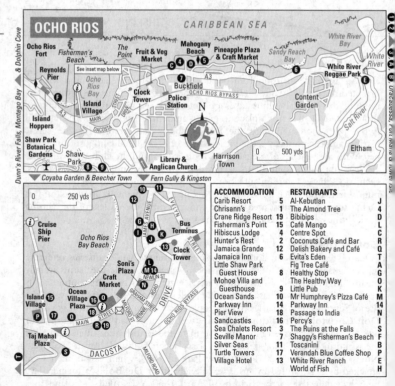

ACCOMMODATION		RESTAURANTS	
Carib Resort	5	Al-Kebutlan	J
Chrisann's	1	The Almond Tree	4
Crane Ridge Resort	19	Bibibips	D
Fisherman's Point	15	Café Mango	L
Hibiscus Lodge	4	Centre Spot	C
Hunter's Rest	2	Coconuts Café and Bar	R
Jamaica Grande	12	Delish Bakery and Café	Q
Jamaica Inn	6	Evita's Eden	T
Little Shaw Park		Fig Tree Café	A
Guest House	8	Healthy Stop	G
Mohoe Villa and		The Healthy Way	O
Guesthouse	9	Little Pub	K
Ocean Sands	10	Mr Humphrey's Pizza Café	M
Parkway Inn	14	Parkway Inn	14
Pier View	18	Passage to India	N
Sandcastles	16	Percy's	I
Sea Chalets Resort	3	The Ruins at the Falls	S
Seville Manor	7	Shaggy's Fisherman's Beach	F
Silver Seas	11	Toscanini	B
Turtle Towers	17	Verandah Blue Coffee Shop	P
Village Hotel	13	White River Ranch	E
		World of Fish	H

with Reynolds Jamaica Mines and the Urban Development Corporation to reclaim forty acres of land behind what is now Ochi's Main Street. The harbour was dredged, and Reynolds built a deep-water pier to load purified bauxite for export, while the UDC imported sand for the beach and built another jetty to accommodate cruise ships. More than three decades later, their efforts have brought about the firmly established resort town of today.

Arrival and information

All **buses** pull in at the disorganized transport terminus adjacent to the town's police station, which backs onto the bypass road running behind Main Street. You're within walking distance of most hotels, but taxi drivers usually hang around plying for fares. If you're **driving** in from Montego Bay, the coast road forks as you enter town; left takes you onto the one-way section of Main Street, where the majority of hotels are located, while right takes you along DaCosta Drive, which connects with the bypass (the route to hotels east of town), and with Milford Road, which leads to Fern Gully and, eventually, Kingston. If you drive in from the east, you enter town via the bypass and there are numerous signposted exits onto Main Street. Domestic **flights** touch down at Boscobel Aerodrome, a thirty-minute drive from town; a cab should cost about US$25.

The main **JTB office** (Mon–Fri 9am–5pm, Sat 9am–1pm; ℡974 2582 or 2570) is in Ocean Village Plaza on Main Street (go up the staircase at the side of the building, and it's the first door on the left). It has flyers on activities and hotels and dispenses useful local maps as well as general information. There are smaller **information booths** on Main Street, one by the turn-off leading to the *Jamaica Grande* hotel and another opposite the Taj Mahal Plaza shopping centre. *The North Coast Times*, a local weekly newspaper, is a valuable source for one-off entertainment events.

Orientation and getting around

The clock tower, the car park next to Ocean Village Plaza, and the road leading to the cruise-ship pier are all unofficial **taxi ranks**; if you want to call a taxi, see p.207 for a list of reliable firms. The abundance of tourist dollars can mean unreasonably inflated fares – haggle, as there is always another taxi waiting. As a rule of thumb, expect to pay about J$500–750 to charter a taxi from downtown to the Tower Isle area or Dunn's River Falls. **Shared taxis** running along Main Street can be flagged down anywhere at the roadside. For most drives around town, you'll pay around J$30; trips to Boscobel or Oracabessa will cost about J$50. **Car-rental agencies** abound, and rates are as you'd expect for a major tourist destination. If you're spending most of your time in town, you'll probably find it's easier to walk. Centrally located hotels are all within walking distance of Ochi's beach, shopping and nightlife.

Accommodation

The fashion for **all-inclusive resorts**, particularly on the north coast of Jamaica, has led to the demise of several long-established hotels in Ocho Rios.

Organized tours from Ocho Rios

In terms of quality and choice, the Ocho Rios roster of **organized tours** is second to none in Jamaica. Scores of comparably priced operators (most with in-hotel desks) will whisk you off to Dunn's River Falls or Nine Mile, though it's often more interesting to go without the company of twenty other camera-toting tourists. Of the more conventional operators, the best is **Chukka Cove Adventure Tours** (T972 2506, W www.chukkacove.com), an efficient and well-staffed tour company based at the Chukka Cove polo ground several miles west of Ocho Rios; it operates free pick-ups for all tours from your hotel. Excursions include a mountain-bike tour from the picturesque village of Mount Zion to a secluded snorkelling spot (3.5hrs; US$50); tubing along the White River from Spanish Bridge (3.5hr; US$49); a lively "reggae bus" tour to Nine Mile (see p.228 for further details); and several jeep safaris (3.5–5 hrs; from US$55), which combine trips to the highest local viewpoint at Murphy Hill and scenic parts of inland St Ann with major attractions Coyaba Garden or Dunn's River Falls.

Among the more adventurous possibilities, try the exhilarating ATV (or **quad bike**) tours offered by Wilderness Resort in the St Mary interior (T974 5189 or 381 FISH; see p.201). Their valley tour (1hr; US$45) goes through the lush landscape that surrounds the Wilderness farm, while the country tour (2hr; US$80) takes you to the Spanish Bridge Blue Hole, with stops for swimming and photos. All trips can be organized by your hotel tour desk to include transport to and from the hotel at a further charge. Trips combined with other Wilderness activities such as fishing, hiking and horseback riding work out cheaper – for example, fishing, lunch, a half-hour horseback-riding tour and an hourlong ATV tour costs US$81. (Note that Wilderness Resort should not be confused with similarly named Wilderness Tours, a cowboy operation that operates unsafe ATV tours from a small enclosure opposite the bauxite factory in downtown Ocho Rios.)

One of Ochi's most popular tours is the exhilarating "no pedalling" downhill bike trip run by Blue Mountain Tours (US$89 for a whole day's outing; T974 7075, E bmbike@cwjamaica.com). Hooves (T972 0905; W www.jamaica-irie.com/hooves /index.html) offer **horseback trail rides** around the Seville Great House at St Ann's Bay (see p.217); they also offer inland hacks and can do private rides on request. Closer to Ochi, Tourwise (T974-2323, W www.ochoriosonline/tourwise) operates various horse rides through the grounds of Annandale Great House, its neighbouring countryside and small villages in the hills of St Ann. Finally, Island Hopper Helicopter Tours, 120 Main St (T974 9756), offers expensive but unforgettable **helicopter** jaunts – call a day ahead to book. The one-hour "Jamaican Showcase" tour takes in Linstead, Bog Walk Gorge, Spanish Town, Port Royal, Kingston, the Blue Mountains and Port Maria; it costs US$220 per person. A half-hour tour over Ocho Rios and down the coast to Port Maria costs US$110 per person, and the cheapest option is twenty minutes above Ochi for US$65 per person. The whole helicopter, which accommodates four passengers, can be chartered for US$600 per hour.

An alternative to taking an organized tour is to hire a local driver and do some independent sightseeing; try Clifton Riley (T375 8174), Horace Hoilett (T797 1739) or Dawn Clarke (T774 1202). 'Cool Marco' Kura (T784 3099) specializes in off-the-beaten-track days out and charges US$100–150 per day.

While there are still plenty of places to stay in the town, there is a decided lack of attractive, reasonably priced accommodation. All-inclusives tend to be sited on the eastern end of town and include several Sandals (W www.sandals.com) resorts, one right by Dunn's River Falls, and a distinctive Superclubs(W www.superclubs.com) property, the supremely luxurious *Grand Lido San Souci.*

Particularly popular in Ochi are condomium resorts – blocks of self-catering apartments grouped around a swimming pool and an on-site bar. These are usually comfortable, if not beautiful, and convenient for families. Backpackers and budget travellers are not well catered for here; there are very few rooms available in the town for less than US$50 per night.

There are hordes of self-contained **villas** in and around Ocho Rios. The more luxurious units can rent for more than US$10,000 per week, others go for as little as US$1750 a week – not bad considering some sleep up to eight and many are fully staffed. Most villas are bookable via JAVA, the Jamaica Association of Villas and Apartments, PO Box 298, Ocho Rios (☎974 2508, ⓕ974 2967, ⓦwww.villasinjamaica.com). Good choices include *Scotch on the Rocks,* which has its own pier (four bedrooms; US$3500 per week), and the more modest *Valhalla* (four bedrooms; US$2000 per week). The *Prospect Plantation,* which hosts a popular jitney tour (see p.201) rents out five luxurious seafront villas (☎994 1373, ⓕ994 1468, ⓦwww.prospect-villas.com; US$2500–12,000 per week). *The Cottage at Te Moana* (☎974 2870, ⓕ974 2651, ⓦwww.harmonyhall.com; US$100 per night) is a more unusual ocean property, owned by the proprietors of Harmony Hall art gallery and funkily designed with one loft-style bedroom. If money is no object you can rent *Rio Chico* (in the US ☎1-800/372-1991, ⓦwww.riochico.com; US$25,000 and above per week). It sits in an extravagantly beautiful garden below Dunn's River Falls, has its own on-site waterfalls, and offers plenty of amenities, including six bedrooms, a tennis court and a swimming pool.

Carib Resort PO Box 78, Ocho Rios ☎974 0305. Quiet and quaintly furnished apartments in a well-situated two-storey building overlooking Mahogany Beach, with manicured gardens and access to the sea. All units have small balconies and ocean views; some have a/c and TV. ❷

Chrisann's PO Box 11, Tower Isle, St Mary ☎975 4467, ⓔchrisannsresort@hotmail.com. Attractive resort in the eastern suburb of Tower Isle. Clean, well-maintained studios and one- to three-bedroom apartments with a/c, cable TV, fully equipped kitchen and access to the pool and mini private beach. ❹

Crane Ridge Resort 17 DaCosta Drive ☎974 8051-69, ⓕ974 8070, ⓦwww.craneridge.net. Overlooking the town, each of these agreeable self-contained units has a/c, satellite TV, phone, balcony and kitchenette. A large pool, a restaurant and tennis courts are on site. ❺

Fisherman's Point PO Box 747, Ocho Rios ☎974 5317-18, ⓕ974 2894, ⓦwww.fishermanspoint.net. In a centrally located low-rise building, these apartments are clean and comfortable, with private balconies, a/c, cable TV and kitchenettes. Friendly staff, Jamaican restaurant and a small pool are nice extras. ❺

Hibiscus Lodge, 83–87 Main St ☎974 2676, ⓕ974 1874, ⓔmdoswald@cwjamaica.com. Set back from the road in beautiful gardens, this is one of Ochi's most attractive hotels. The clean, pleasant, cliffside rooms all have balconies. Other highlights: a pool, jacuzzi, tennis court, sun deck, sea access, excellent restaurant and a bar with swing-

ing seats. Rates include breakfast. ❻

Hunter's Rest B&B Tower Isle, St Mary ☎975 5490, ⓔjonsson@cwjamaica.com. Small guesthouse, close to the Rio Nuevo battlesite, on the land side of the busy main road. It offers clean, pleasant rooms with en-suite bathrooms, a small pool, and a friendly, low-key atmosphere. ❸

Jamaica Grande PO Box 100, Ocho Rios ☎974 2201, ⓕ974 2162, ⓦwww.offshoreresorts.com. Jamaica's largest hotel features 720 amenity-packed rooms, a man-made waterfall in the lobby, four restaurants, eight bars, a private beach, a fitness centre, three pools, a gym, tennis courts, a disco, a mini-casino, a children's activity programme and the atmosphere of a ritzy shopping mall. ❼ All-inclusive deals are available.

Jamaica Inn PO Box 1, Ocho Rios ☎974 2514, ⓕ974 2449, ⓦwww.jamaicainn.com. The most attractive (and expensive) hotel in Ochi, tasteful and elegant, with a gorgeous private beach, pool and sophisticated oceanfront spa. Rooms have a/c, beautiful blue and white decor and ocean-facing balconies. No children under 14; jacket and tie required for dinner. ❽ All-inclusive deals available.

Little Shaw Park Guest House 21 Shaw Park Rd ☎974 2177, ⓕ974 8997. Easy-going, family-owned place set in gardens overlooking town, with space for camping (US$25). Homely rooms with cable TV, fan, and hot and cold water; some share bathrooms, others have kitchen facilities. Meals are available. Friendly owners offer local tours for guests. ❸

Mohoe Villa and Guesthouse 11 Shaw Park Rd
T 974-6613. Eleven immaculate, though spartan,
rooms in a large old house near Shaw Park Garden.
Some bathrooms are shared, other are en suite. ❸
Ocean Sands 14 James Ave T 974-2605, F 974-
1421, W www.oceansandsresort.com. Simple,
comfortable rooms with sea-view terraces. Other
pluses include a small private beach, pool, and a
charming restaurant on a wooden jetty. Rates
include continental breakfast. ❻
Parkway Inn 60 Main St T 974 2667. Centrally
located, these clean, serviceable rooms come with
a/c or ceiling fan. There's a good Jamaican restaurant and atmospheric bar on site. ❸
Pier View PO Box 134, 19 Main St T 974 2607,
F 974 1384. Busy, friendly and laid-back apartment development, next to the beach and popular
with younger travellers. Rooms or self-catering
units with kitchenettes; all have refrigerators,
cable TV, fan or a/c, and access to the pool and
sun deck. Discounted rates for longer stays.
❸–❺
Sandcastles 120 Main St T 974 2310, F 974
2247, E sandcastles@cwjamaica.com. In front of
the beach (guests get a pass), these airy studios
and one- or two-bedroom apartments have a/c,
cable TV and kitchenettes. Good for families – the
pool has a slide and a children's area. ❺
Sea Chalets Resort Boscobel, St Mary T 975
3265, F 960-4204, E exclusiveresorts2002

@yahoo.com. Four self-contained villas opposite
Boscobel Aerodrome, with rooms also rented as
single units. Comfortable en-suite bedrooms with
a/c, friendly staff and two pools in pretty gardens.
❻
Seville Manor 84 Main St T 795 2900, F 974
4045. Friendly small hotel popular with holidaying
Jamaicans. All rooms have a/c and cable TV and
are very spacious, immaculate and great value. ❸
Silver Seas Main St T 974 2755, F 974 5739,
W www.silverseas.com. Slightly faded and wonderfully atmospheric hotel, popular with backpackers. Rooms are simple, though comfortable, and all
have sea views and private verandahs. Large garden, pool and bar on site. The most attractive
"budget" option in Ocho Rios. ❸
Turtle Towers PO Box 73, Main St T 974 2760,
F 974 4345, W www.turtlebeachvacations.com.
Centrally located high-rise condominiums, opposite Island Village, with full self-catering facilities,
a/c and cable TV. A pool and restaurant are on site.
Popular with holidaying Jamaicans. ❻
Village Hotel 54 Main St T 974 9193, F 974
8894, W www.geocities.com/villagehotel. Friendly
property slap in the centre of town and five minutes' walk from the beach. Rooms have queen-
size bed, cable TV, a/c and phone; some also have
kitchenette. There's a pool, restaurant and bar.
Internet café and spa are located in the hotel's
ground-floor mall. ❺

The Town

Apart from trawling the shopping malls or hanging out in a bar, activities in
Ocho Rios are limited. Although compact enough to explore on foot, the permanently busy streets hold little interest for sightseers. Unless you're heading
out to one of the nearby attractions, days in Ochi are best spent lazing on the
beach. Running parallel to the sea (but hidden from it by all the concrete),
Main Street houses the majority of hotels, bars, banks, shopping plazas and
restaurants, as well as the craft markets and the post office. **DaCosta Drive** is
Ochi's quieter back entrance and a slip road for fast traffic. Opposite the clock
tower and forking off toward the sea from Main Street, **James Avenue** has a
somewhat seedy feel and is home to plenty of low-key, Jamaican style eateries,
the odd ganja hustler and several no-frills clubs.

During the day, most of the town's tourist activity centres around the main
beach – variously known as Mallards, Turtle and Ocho Rios Bay (daily
8.30am–6pm, with last entry to the beach at 4.30pm; J\$50, children J\$25).
Tucked under the high-rises and accessible from the western end of Main
Street near the *Pier View* and *Sandcastles* hotels, the white-sand beach is wide,
fairly attractive and well maintained, with showers, changing rooms, bars and
plenty of general hanging-out and activity. However, the water is prone to
patches of sea grass, and occasional reports of unacceptable pollution levels
mean that this isn't one of the north coast's most appealing beaches, particu-

Although there isn't that much to see underwater at the main beach in Ocho Rios – you'll find much richer pickings east of the harbour or at the reef at the bottom of Dunn's River (see p.196) – there are several long-established **watersports concessions** based there. Garfield Diving Station and Water Sports (☎395 7023) offers the whole gamut of water-based activities: jet-ski rides (US$50 per half-hour), snorkelling (US$25 each for 1hr), and deep-sea fishing (US$350 for a half-day). Watersports Enterprises Ltd is based on the section of the beach used by the *Jamaica Grande* hotel, but non-guests are welcomed; as well as the usual options, it's possible to parasail (US$55 per hour) or take a ride under the sea in a semi-sub (US$45 per hour). You can also take a glass-bottom boat ride (US$15 per person for 1hr) from the beach; most boats, which are moored at the small pier opposite the entrance to the beach, will also go along the coast to Dunn's River Falls, at a cost of around US$25 per person. For **scuba diving**, try Garfield (see above) or Resort Divers at 2 Island Plaza (☎974 5338, ⊛www.resortdivers.com); one dive costs approx US$50.

The tiny strip of sand by the cruise-ship pier, until recently part of the town's public beach facilities, has been appropriated by the new Island Village complex. Under its new name, Beach World, it now charges entrance fees (US$5 with beach chair, or US$15 with all activities included). A range of watersports equipment is available for rent, including kayaks (US$5 per half-hour), water beetle/pedalos (US$10 per hour), and windsurfers (US$40 per half hour). From here it's also possible to take a guided jet-ski tour along the coast (US$60 per half hour).

The coast reverberates to the sound systems of the many private boats offering **pleasure cruises**. Day-trips go to Dunn's River for snorkelling and climbing the falls and include an open bar and lunch or snacks; sunset cruises include drinks only, but most operators offer dinner cruises, too. Among the better-organized operators are Red Stripe (☎974 2446) and Heave-Ho (☎974 5367, ⊛www.heaveho.net); both offer a day cruise (3–4hr; US$50), a sunset soca cruise (2hr; US$25) and private charters. All prices are per person.

larly when it's overshadowed by the bulk of docked cruise ships across the bay. It's also a lot smaller than it used to be, as a prime section at the eastern end has long been appropriated by the immense *Jamaica Grande* hotel.

Island Village

For visitors not interested in lounging on the beach or taking an organized tour, the **Island Village** complex, which bills itself as "Jamaica's first theme park", is an increasingly popular place to spend a few hours. Not actually a theme park but rather a combination of shopping mall and entertainment centre, the village has been carefully designed to imitate the prettiest aspects of Caribbean architecture. Wooden shacks in washed-out ice-cream colours line the edge of the complex, selling a variety of classy holiday souvenirs, clothes and jewellery. The large central square is a grassy plaza with a striking bronze statue of Bob Marley, guitar in hand, and a covered stage that hosts musical events and free cultural entertainment – dance, poetry speaking, drumming – at sporadic points throughout the day. The entrance hall contains a 200-seat cinema, The Cove (US$7, children US$5; ☎675 8884), which shows all the latest features; The Eight Rivers Casino, with slot machines and touch-screen poker; and **Reggae Explosion** (9am–5pm daily; US$7; ☎974 8353), Jamaica's only museum devoted to reggae and other forms of Jamaican music. The museum is an illuminating collection of photographs, music and video clips of all of the island's musical heros, from Prince Buster through to Bounty Killer. Presented historically, the collection covers mento, ska, roots reggae, dub and dancehall. Understandably, the section devoted to Bob Marley is the largest, with the inclusion of several never-before-seen photos of the young musician. The re-creation of legendary music producer Lee "Scratch" Perry's Black Ark Studio is another of the museum's highlights. Next to it, in a series of white-walled rooms, is an offshoot of the Kingston's Jamaica National Gallery, which displays a rotating selection of paintings from the biggest collection of native art in the country.

Ocho Rios Fort and Dunn's River Falls

If you head west of town along Main Street, past the bauxite factory gates, you'll reach the town's only historical feature, **Ocho Rios Fort**, sandwiched between the cruise-ship terminal and a former slaughterhouse. The fort was built by the British in the seventeenth century and restored in 1780 to defend against a feared French attack, but there's little to see other than two cannons, taken from the now derelict Mammee Bay Fort and placed here by the Reynolds bauxite company in the 1960s.

Just past the fort and the Island Hopper helicopter landing pad is the beginning of the **"One Love Trail"**, a pretty three-mile seaside path lined on either side with well-maintained tropical shrubs and trees, among them hibiscus, plumbago and june rose. The trail gives easy access to two of Ochi's busiest tourist attractions, Dolphin Cove and Dunn's River Falls (see below). There are clean toilets en route, along with several tidy shacks selling snacks and cold drinks, and a manned information point. Clarke's Art Studio, a flower-wreathed, green-painted wooden house on the cliff side, makes a nice stop even if you don't want to buy any crafts. It offers gorgeous views of a small waterfall cascading down to the beach below, itself accessed via a dirt track from the roadside.

Just beyond the end of the trail is **Dolphin Cove** (daily 8.30am–5.30pm; ☎876/974 5335, ⓦwww.dolphincovejamaica.com). The main draw at the landscaped, theme-park style complex is the chance to interact with the trained bottlenose dolphins kept in a fenced-off section of the bay. There are three choices of "interactive programme": the "Touch Encounter" (US$35), in which you stand in knee-high water and get to stroke a dolphin and have your photo taken (US$12); the "Encounter Swim" (US$79), which gets you into the water to kiss and play with the animals; and the "Swim with Dolphins" (US$145), in which you spend a bit more time in the water, and get a dorsal pull. The dolphin programmes start daily at 9.30am, 11.30am, 1.30pm and 3.30pm. You'll need to book at least two weeks ahead, and you must arrive half an hour before the programme starts. While it's all very organized, nothing much can detract from the delight of being so close to the dolphins.

Elsewhere in the complex, there's a pool containing sharks and rays; a nature trail with stops for petting macaws and touching starfish and snakes; a small beach where you can rent snorkel equipment and canoes; a restaurant; and a great gift shop. There are changing facilities and lockers on site, but most people arrive in their bathing suits. The entrance fee of US$15 allows you to stay and explore all day.

From Dolphin Cove, a ten-minute stroll along the boardwalk brings you to **Dunn's River Falls** (daily 8.30am–4pm, beach closes 6pm; US$10, plus a tip for the guide; ⓦwww.dunnsriverja.com). Jamaica's best-loved waterfall and a staple of tour brochures, the falls are overdeveloped but still breathtaking, and remain the area's major tourist honeypot. Masked from the road by restaurants, craft shops and car parks, the wide and magnificent 600ft waterfall cascades over rocks down to a pretty tree-fringed white-sand beach that's far cleaner than the one in town. There's a lively reef within swimming distance, and snorkel gear is available to rent from several touts.

Impressively proportioned, with water running so fast you can hear it from the road below, the falls are surrounded by dripping foliage and more than live up to their reputation, despite the concrete and commerciality. The main activity is climbing up the cascade, a wet but easily navigable hour-long clamber. The step-like rocks are regularly scraped to remove slippery algae, and the done thing to prevent a stumble is for visitors to form a hand-holding chain led by one of the very experienced guides. It's thoroughly exhilarating, as you're showered with cool, clear water all the way up – wear a bathing suit. There's a restaurant and bar, craft and hair-braiding shacks and full changing facilities at the beach and at the top of the falls. This is a very popular attraction – frequently hundred-strong queues form along the beach. To avoid the crowds, arrive at the falls late in the afternoon (the last climb leaves at 4pm), when cruise passengers are safely back on board their ships.

An alternative to the crowds and the admission price of Dunn's River Falls are the unmaintained waterfalls above the enclosure. To get to them, take the main route to Dunn's River but carry on up past the car park to where the tarmac ends. Follow the dirt path into the bush to your right for five minutes. There are several more waterfalls further up the road, which you can drive or walk to, but you may need a local companion to find them. Alternatively, Kingston-based Sun Venture Tours (☎960 6685, ℻920 8348, Ⓦwww.sunventuretours.com) offers a six-hour tour of the area (US$65 per person, minimum group of four) with local guide and forest ranger "Brother Mike"; it explores the surrounding limestone forest and smaller waterfalls as well as Dunn's River Falls.

Shaw Park and around

From the main roundabout at Ochi's western outskirts, a twenty-minute drive starting along Milford Road takes you to two of Ochi's better-known pastoral attractions. Both are on the ill-maintained Shaw Park Road (turn right from Milford Road 100ft from the junction at the Shaw Park signpost). About a hundred yards from the main roundabout, Shaw Park Road forks; a left turn and a steep twenty-minute drive brings you to the 1922ft peak of **Murphy Hill** (sometimes called Governor's Hill), which provides handsome views over Ocho Rios Bay. A right turn from the fork brings you past some swanky private homes to the **Shaw Park Botanical Gardens** (daily 8am–5pm; US$4, plus a tip for your guide), a mere 550ft above sea level but boasting stunning aerial views of town nonetheless. The former grounds of a long-gone hotel, Shaw Park is a much less visited attraction these days, which means you might get the place almost to yourself. The creatively planted 25-acre gardens are resplendent with unusual flowers, plants and trees – including a huge banyan – set amidst grassy lawns. There's also a near-perpendicular (but non-swimmable) waterfall. You can walk unaccompanied, but the knowledgeable gardeners-cum-guides will initiate you into the wonders of tropical horticulture. There's an on-site bar, and crafts and jewellery are sold at the gift shop.

About five minutes further up Shaw Park Road, the more intimate **Coyaba River Garden and Museum** (daily 8am–6pm; US$5; ☎974 6235, Ⓦwww.coyabagardens.com) is much more packaged an attraction than Shaw Park. While nowhere near as impressive, the small well-maintained site is well worth an hour of your time. Wooden walkways allow easy viewing of the heliconias, anthuriums, hot-pink ginger lilies and rampant vines, and the flower beds are bisected by streams teeming with mullet, koi, crayfish and turtles, with occasional glass panels embedded into the banks to provide a view of the underwater goings-on. Housed in an elegant cut-stone building, the museum has a limited but thoughtful collection of exhibits spanning Jamaican history, from Taino *zemis* (talismans used to ward off evil spirits) to a nineteenth-century man trap and photographs depicting post-emancipation Jamaican life; special weight is given to St Ann's own Marcus Garvey and Bob Marley. There's a good café and gift shop on the premises as well as a small spa offering facials and massage.

Fern Gully and beyond

Carrying on along Milford Road past the Shaw Park Road turn-off brings you into **Fern Gully**, a densely vegetated and steeply inclining three-mile stretch of the A3/A1 road to Kingston, made famous by the arboreal splendour of the five hundred or so varieties of fern that smother the roadside banks. First planted in the 1880s, the ferns are overhung by tall trumpet and mahoe trees that meet overhead, filtering the sunlight to create a cool, green-tinged tunnel. Moist and sheltered, the gully environment is ideal for ferns, but exhaust fumes from the heavy traffic have damaged and even wiped out some of the species, and there are regular calls for Fern Gully to be closed to traffic and redeveloped as a beauty spot. This proposition makes even more sense in bad weather – after heavy rains the gully is reduced to an impassable series of potholes, causing traffic jams that stretch right back into town. You can walk up from Ochi in about twenty minutes, but the whizzing traffic, lack of pavements and persistent roadside vendors make pedestrians vulnerable.

While you're in the area, the **Wassi Art pottery works** at Great Pond (Mon–Sat 9am–5pm; free) make an interesting distraction; turn off Milford Road at the colourful signposts just before Fern Gully. The small, family-owned commercial factory produces some of the island's better ceramic pieces. Wassi's tours take you through each stage of production, from clay processing to pot throwing, painting and firing, and you can buy the works at cheaper prices than at local gift shops.

Once you're at the top of the Fern Gully hill and beyond its leafy canopy, the landscape opens up, with eye-popping views across the pastures and hillocks of the eastern interior, and the misted Blue Mountain peaks just visible in the distance. The first community that you'll come to is **WALKERS WOOD**, home of the fiery Walkers Wood jerk sauce, which is not only excellent but is now sold all over the world. It's made in a brand new, state-of-the-art factory. The village is also home to artist Nancy Burke, aka Inansi, who makes wonderfully quirky bags, earrings and mobiles. You'll find her workshop and **craft gallery** in the main square opposite the post office.

Continuing along the A3, through emerald fields dotted with dilapidated gingerbread houses and restored plantation homes, you eventually reach **MON-EAGUE**, a quiet roadside town that's worth a stop for its sole **restaurant**, the elegant *Café Aubergine* (☎973 0527; Wed–Sun noon–9pm), set in a beautiful colonial-era building. The linen tablecloths and tastefully rustic decor here come as a bit of a surprise after all the roadside cook shops you've passed. The fare is as sophisticated as anything you'll find in Ochi and is well worth the forty-minute drive from town. The menu offers starters such as conch in lemon vinaigrette and mains like lamb chops marinated in provencal herbs, and linguine with shrimp and scallops in a garlic sauce. The cooking is complemented by a decent wine list and a supremely soothing atmosphere. Easily missed, the restaurant is marked by a nondescript sign on the left of the road just as you enter town. When you leave after your meal, one of the efficient staff will invariably guide you out – the entrance/exit is a bit of a blind spot and traffic on this section of road is invariably fast.

If *Café Aubergine* is beyond your budget or time constraints, a ten-minute drive along the A3 north of Moneague brings you to one of Jamaica's best-loved street-food institutions, **Faith's Pen**, a string of smoking food stalls housed in a purpose-built layby. Blackened by years of barbecue cooking, the stalls do a cracking trade with the steady stream of traffic passing between Kingston and Ochi. Though some are more popular than others (go for the cook with the longest queue), each stall sells a variation on the same theme: roast yam and saltfish, jerk chicken or pork, ackee and saltfish, roast corn, curry goat, mannish water or fish/conch soup, alongside the usual array of cold beers and natural juices. You eat at a bench by the stall, with whizzing cars and the strains of Irie FM blaring from the vendors' ghetto blasters serving as background music. Though not the most picturesque place for a meal, Faith's Pen is the consummate on-the-road eating experience.

East of town

The clamour of Ocho Rios's Main Street recedes as you head east of town, but one place you shouldn't pass by is **Mahogany Beach**, a quiet, secluded beach (free admission) just off Main Street past the *Hibiscus Lodge* hotel. Occupying a pretty strip of sand with good snorkelling, swimming and watersports, and boasting an excellent beach bar and grill, large natural spring pool and even a massage hut (US$60 per hour), all set in beautiful landscaped gardens, Mahogany is Ochi's most attractive chill-out spot, worth a visit by day or night. On weekend nights, jerked meat and fish is grilled outside on barbecues and there's an uptown party atmosphere. Although noise restrictions have been successfully imposed by neighbouring residents, which means that all sound systems must end by midnight, Mahogany Beach hosts occasional daytime music events at weekends.

Beyond Mahogany, in amongst the glamorous frontages of the all-inclusive hotels, the studios of **Irie FM** are marked by a colourful billboard and set back from the road opposite the Coconut Grove shopping centre. Jamaica's most popular radio station, Irie was the island's first reggae-only station – the airwaves were previously dominated by American soul, gospel and country and western. Since its first transmission in June 1990, Irie has championed the artistic and cultural legitimacy of a musical genre branded subversive until the early 1970s. Today, the station provides the soundtrack for the nation. Wherever you go, you'll hear the music, the massively popular talk shows, and the patois jingles: "Irie FM – a fi wi station" or "My radio dial stuck pon Irie FM, and guess what – me nah bother fix it". Steel Pulse, Burning Spear, Aswad and Third World, among others, have recorded at Irie's Grove Studios, and the station has brought a bit of Kingston-style culture to the town.

Past Irie FM, Main Street merges into the A3 coast road and crosses the bridge over the wide but sluggish **White River**, which marks the parish boundary of St Ann and St Mary. Several tour operators offer tubing on the White River (see box on organized tours, p.192) or you can take a more relaxed trip on bamboo rafts with Calypso Rafting (☎974 2527; 45min; US$45 per raft). Just before the bridge, Bonham Spring Road winds inland, taking you through Ochi's satellite communities and past the sumptuous Sandals Golf and Country Club at Upton. The eighteen-hole golf course is rated as one of Jamaica's finest (see p.54 for details). This is also the route to

△ Bob Marley's Mausoleum, Nine Miles

the fabulous **Irie Beach**, a landscaped portion of White River banks with a deep swimming pool. Unfortunately it's currently closed and its private owners have no plans to re-open it – though locals have long been sneaking through the fence to take a dip. You might be able to persuade one of them to take you along for the ride.

Back on the main road and half a mile into St Mary, the former haunt of British planter Harold Mitchell has been reincarnated as a tourist attraction, **Prospect Plantation** (1hr 15min guided tours Mon–Sat 10.30am, 2pm & 3.30pm, Sun 11am, 1.30pm & 3pm; US$12; ☎994 1058, ⓦwww.prospect-villas.com). Designed to introduce the more sedentary visitor to the delights of tropical farming, the tour consists of sitting with 38 others on an open trailer and listening to an inaudible commentary while trundling through sugarcane patches and groves of coconut palm, pimento, lime, ackee, breadfruit, mahoe and soursop trees, stopping only to sample fruits, admire the bay views from Sir Harold's lookout, and potter around a stone church. You'll feel less like a member of a cattle herd if you do the tour aboard a **mountain bike** (1hr 15min; US$12), or on **horseback** (1hr; US$20). Other **trail rides** cover the property and go down into White River gorge (1hr 30min; US$35), the site of Jamaica's first hydroelectric plant, while the "View Jamaica" trek goes down to the river and up into the hills (2hr 15min; US$50). You'll need to book all rides one day in advance, and the horses rest on Sundays.

A few minutes' drive east of Prospect along the A3 is **Reggae Beach** (Mon–Fri 9am–5pm, Sat & Sun 9am–6pm; J$200). A pretty curve of yellow sand backed by shady palm tree groves, it's a world away from the beach in town, with no hotels, no hustlers and just one laid-back bar and restaurant serving up deliciously fresh fish grilled over an open fire. As it's a fair drive from town, you'll usually have the place to yourself during the week. At weekends, Reggae Beach is occasionally the venue for immensely popular music events.

Beyond the beach, the coast road is intermittently lined with clumps of hotels and condos that have sprung up in the hope of capitalizing on Ochi's resort status. One of these new developments has almost obscured **Rio Nuevo Park**, a rather nondescript monument at the ocean side of the road commemorating the final skirmish that made Jamaica a British rather than a Spanish territory. The area was donated to the Jamaica National Heritage Trust by its owners, the Beckfords; their efforts have ensured that the rather decrepit memorial plaque and gazebo remain despite the new building.

Inland to Wilderness and White River Valley

Just past Prospect Plantation, the coast road whips past a narrow inland turn at Frankfort, where you'll see the signposts for **Wilderness Resort** (Tues–Sun 10am–5pm; ☎974 5189 or 4613, ⓔwildlani@yahoo.com), a 447-acre commercial cattle and fish farm that's been opened up to the public. From the coast, the narrow road winds a snakelike parallel of the White River Gorge – you can hear the gushing water far below – before the overhanging trees recede and the stunning views of the rolling St Mary countryside open up: cattle pastures, banana plantations, citrus orchards and banks of yam plants are broken only by the tiny settlements of Cascade, Labyrinth and Goshen. Signs directing you to Wilderness are present at all of the junctions. In the late nineteenth century, the entire area was part of a 40,000-acre estate owned by one Judge Roper, who converted what had formerly been a vast sugar plantation into a successful cattle and horse-rearing farm. At Gayle, the site of today's

Wilderness Resort, he built a racetrack, a polo field and a showground, which became a favourite haunt of the St Ann planter elite, who came to lay their bets and parade their prize cattle and horses. Judge Roper bestowed portions of his property to each of his nine children, but as bauxite began to eclipse agriculture as the area's main industry, only two of the farms remained in the family, run by his sons, Leicester and Harold. The Roper connections persist today, though: these days Wilderness is owned and run by the judge's grandson, Alex Lanigan.

Wilderness is easily the most appealing of the managed attractions that surround Ocho Rios. Ensconced in a wonderfully lush, riverine valley a thousand feet above sea level (it's usually about ten degrees cooler here than on the coast), it boasts 37 **fishing ponds** stocked to bursting with fresh water snapper, as well as hiking trails, kayaking, paddle-boating, a stable full of **horses** for country hacks, and a garage filled with well-maintained ATV **quad bikes**. If you simply want to see the property and hang out at the clubhouse/restaurant, you'll pay US$3 per person, US$2 for children. But there are all kinds of combination activity packages available at Wilderness – some of which include transport to and from your hotel: catch-and-release fishing and lunch (US$21, US$14 for children); hiking (90min, US$20); horseback riding (1hr, US$40); and guided ATV tours in the Wilderness valley (1hr, US$45; US$70 with round-trip transport). Perhaps the best of the bunch is a two-hour ATV tour to Spanish Bridge, a fabulous, deep swimming pool on the White River (US$80; US$103 transport to and from your hotel). Combinations of all the activities work out much cheaper: fishing, lunch and an hourlong ATV tour, for example, costs US$81.

Fifteen minutes after the turn off from the main coast road and before you reach Wilderness, a large sign at a right fork in the road points you in the right direction for a new leisure park, the **White River Valley** (8am–6pm; US$8; ℡929 9403). Situated in the tiny hamlet of **CASCADE**, it comprises almost four hundred acres of verdant flatlands, fruit orchards and river valley. Although White River Valley lacks the patrician charm and tranquillity of Wilderness, it's impossible to deny the stunning beauty of its surroundings. No expense has been spared in the construction of the park. The arrival point for all visitors boasts a rather swanky "village" of brightly painted wooden buildings housing a restaurant and gift shop, amidst very pretty though manicured flower gardens. From here you can choose either to just hang out on the expansive property, enjoying your own picnic if you wish, or partake in one of several activities. These include tubing on the White River (45min–1hr; US$40), horseback riding (60-90min, US$50), and hiking (1hr, US$30); combination packages are also offered.

Eating

As many of Ochi's **restaurants** aim to please the foreign palate, Italian, Indian, Chinese and American cuisine vie for your custom alongside the Jamaican staples, and there are a couple of decent vegetarian options. Most places here stay open late, so you'll rarely be stuck for a midnight feast. There are several cheap eateries in the market – the best of these is *Winston's*, though you shouldn't go there after dark. The best place to find delicious and inexpensive jerk chicken is around *Mother's* on Main Street. Once the sun has set, the local vendors wheel out their oil-drum barbecues and the air fills with the heady smell of charcoal smoke and spicy grilled meat. For a truly tasty – and inexpensive –

Jamaican meal, try the fisherman's beach just west of the Island Village complex. There you'll be invited to choose freshly caught fish or lobster from large cool boxes, and your selection will then cooked up over an open fire. If not otherwise indicated, the places listed serve both lunch and dinner.

Inexpensive

Al-Kebutlan 1 James Ave. Colourful Rasta-oriented indoor diner offering good, Ital-style breakfasts (including cornmeal, plantain and oats porridge) and various vegetarian delights for lunch and dinner, as well as the full array of natural juices.

Centre Spot 75 Main St. Close to the *Hibiscus Lodge* hotel, this small lunchtime joint is the best value in town. It serves strictly Jamaican food, very tasty and dirt cheap. Closed after 5pm.

Delish Bakery and Café 16 Main St. Funky café with good on-site bakery. It serves natural juices and tasty good-value Chinese and Jamaican lunches (no dinner). The café walls act as a small art gallery and are hung with paintings by local artists.

Fig Tree Café On the A3 to Oracabessa, just before the entrance to Prospect Plantation. Excellent vegetarian café with salads, grilled veggies and falafel, amongst other imaginative options. Great cakes and ice cream also. Open Mon–Sat 7am–7pm.

Healthy Stop 28 James Ave. Pleasant upstairs restaurant with wide range of natural juices, excellent soup and an emphasis on vegetarian food.

The Healthy Way Ocean Village Plaza. Energetic and efficient vegetarian take-away, with a couple of tables, offering veggie/tofu burgers and patties, soups, Ital juices, fruit salad, cakes and a different main dish each day. Open daytime only.

Mr Humphrey's Pizza Café 10 Evelyn St, off Main St ☎974 8319. Fast and tasty pizzas, sub sandwiches, jerk chicken and pitta pockets. Free delivery.

Parkway Inn 60 Main St, entrance on DaCosta Drive. Popular, unpretentious restaurant serving up large portions of tasty Jamaican food to a predominantly local clientele. Breakfast is particularly good.

Percy's 6 James Ave. Excellent homely local restaurant specializing in seafood and fish. Food is cooked to order and is very good value.

Shaggy's Fisherman's Beach. The only place on this beach that offers a proper seat. Genial Rasta Shaggy serves up excellent steamed fish with vegetables at lunchtime only. It's popular with local taxi drivers, which is always a good sign and means you might pick up some useful info while you eat.

White River Ranch White River. Busy, late-opening jerk joint with tables outside, cooking up sizzling chicken, pork and fish for an enthusiastic

crowd. The conch soup and roast or steamed fish are pretty good, too.

World of Fish 3 James Ave. Popular place for a late supper (lunch is served, too). Fish is prepared any which way, with bammy, festival or rice and peas. Open Mon–Sat until 2am.

Moderate

Bibibips 93 Main St. Set back from the road, with tables overlooking the sea, this is one of the best choices in town. The menu includes devilled jerk chicken, coconut curry chicken, seafood crepes, vegetable stir-fry, Rasta pasta, Red Stripe shrimp and all the usual Jamaican favourites – fish is a definite winner. The service is excellent. There is another branch of Bibibips by the Taj Mahal shopping centre, which catsers mostly to passing cruise-ship passengers, and has excellent jerk chicken.

Café Mango Main St, opposite the entrance to *Jamaica Grande*. Semi-open-air diner in a shady, central location. Jamaican and American breakfasts are served, and there's an interesting variety of lunch options, including calamari, nachos, chicken wings, salads, some Mexican dishes, pasta and pizza.

Coconuts Café and Bar 10 Main St. Attractive tourist spot with an imaginative mixed menu of Tex-Mex dishes (fajitas, potato skins, etc), salads and traditional Jamaican fare. Staff are very friendly and know how to make a mean cocktail. A seat at the bar is a great place to while away the evening if you're alone. Open late.

Little Pub 59 Main St ☎974 2324. American and Jamaican breakfast and lunch are served in a roadside café with a juice bar on site. Dinner – from filet mignon to lobster thermidore – is dished up in the "entertainment area".

The Ruins at the Falls 17 DaCosta Drive. Newly renovated restaurant on a terrace at the foot of a largish waterfall. It offers an extensive Chinese menu, but the unusual setting alone makes it worth a visit.

Verandah Blue Coffee Shop Island Village. Attractive wooden building at the back of Island Village. Distinctly non-Jamaican snacks on offer include panini sandwiches, filled bagels and cakes. There's also Blue Mountain coffee in various forms – espresso, cappuccino, latte – and wine by the glass.

Snacks

The recent influx of international **fast-food chains** divides office workers between those who opt for *Burger King* or *KFC* (both on Main Street) and those who stick with the traditional callaloo loaf, patties and coco bread. The best places for the latter are *The Golden Crust Baking Co*, at 72 Main St. and *Delish Bakery and Café*, 16 Main St; for vegetarian patties, try *Juici-Beef Patties*, at 61 Main St, or *The Healthy Way* (see p.203). The ubiquitous *Mother's* has a 24-hr branch at 17 Main St, serving patties, burgers, chicken and ice cream, and there's a branch of *Island Grill* at 12 Main St, good for jerked chicken, pork and fish. If you've a sweet tooth, the *Baskin-Robbins* ice-cream chain has a branch in Ocean Village Plaza, but the far-superior Devon House I-Scream is sold at various outlets along Main Street and in Island Village.

Expensive

The Almond Tree *Hibiscus Lodge Hotel* ☎ 974 2813. Romantic clifftop setting, friendly service and a great gourmet menu, featuring superb seafood.

Evita's Eden Bower Rd ☎ 974 2333. The best-advertised pasta on the north coast, served on a gingerbread verandah overlooking the bay. Huge choice of starters, salads and soups; main courses include fettuccine bolognaise, linguine with pesto, seafood, and "Lasagne Rastafari" with ackee, callaloo and tomatoes. Calorie-packed desserts, too.

Passage to India Soni's Plaza, 50 Main St ☎ 795 3182. Attractively decorated rooftop restaurant serving excellent Indian cuisine. The menu is pretty comprehensive: tandoori meats, chicken jalfrezi or masala, rogan josh, lots of seafood and a vast array of vegetarian dishes. Breads are particularly good, as are the lassi yogurt drinks and desserts.

Toscanini Harmony Hall ☎ 975 4785. Under the eaves of pretty Harmony Hall, a ten-minute drive east of the centre, this is easily one of Ochi's best restaurants. Service is great and the menu features all the Italian classics, from carpaccio to home-made pasta and meat dishes such as veal escalope with prosciutto and parmesan. Vegetarians are well catered for, too. Daily specials are displayed on the blackboard, and the puddings are sublime. Closed Mon.

Nightlife and entertainment

Though it's not Kingston or Negril, Ocho Rios does have **bars** and **clubs** open every night of the week. The most popular, by far, is **Jimmy Buffet's Margaritaville** in Island Village (see p.195), which, despite high prices, attracts hordes of locals as well as tourists. **Amnesia**, on Main Street, is a more Jamaican dancehall, though it, too, has a fairly uptown crowd and atmosphere. James Avenue is host to several of the seediest joints in town. Though they're actually pretty harmless, the street is the town's red-light district and you might not want to walk down – or back up it – late at night. Jack Ruby's lawn, behind the restaurant of the same name on James Avenue, is a regular venue for sound-system dances and concerts, as is **Reggae Beach**, several miles east out of town. **Mahogany Beach** is a good place for a classier evening out, with low-key music and candlelit tables on the beach. *Evita's* restaurant (see above), holds occasional theme nights (Latin and the like) with dancing. If you fancy taking in a standard Caribbean-themed **floor show**, try the *Little Pub* (see opposite page), which also hosts a popular karaoke night every Tuesday. Another possibility is an evening pass to one of the all-inclusive hotels. These cost from US$25 and cover a meal and unlimited drinks as well as entertainment – call individual properties for details.

Finally, the stellar **Ocho Rios Jazz Festival** brings Ochi to life every June, with concerts at venues around town. For more information call the tourist board or the Jazz Hotline (☎927 3544). The Jazz Festival website (W www.ochoriosjazz.com) posts line-ups and information prior to the event.

Bars

Bibibips 93 Main St. Laid-back clifftop bar popular with upscale Jamaicans, and one of the best places in town for a drinking session. Live reggae on Wed.

Coconuts Café and Bar 10 Main St. Attractive, friendly and safe, with late hours ("until whenever") and mellow, adult-oriented rock on the sound system.

Jamaican Hard Rock Café Coconut Grove Shopping Centre. Not part of the international chain, but a Jamaican version of an American bar. Popular with guests from the all-inclusives at Ochi's eastern outskirts. Occasionally has live music at weekends.

Jimmy Buffet's Margaritaville Island Village. The latest incarnation of the hugely popular bar and club, which has its own swimming pool and water slide. Open from 8am to 5am daily, the bar specializes in margaritas and other potent cocktails and has themed nights with drinks promotions. Wednesday is the busiest night, with a pool party. The US$20 entrance fee covers all drinks and access to the small beach, torchlit for the occasion; the fee is only US$10 if you arrive in swimwear.

Glenn's Jazz Club and Cocktail Lounge Tower Isle. Out of town steak restaurant with cheesy 1970s decor, tinkly jazz as background music and occasional live performances.

Little Pub 59 Main St. Right in the centre of Ochi and one of the town's most enduring nightspots. Football games and boxing via satellite TV provide diversion in the busy bar area (also great for people-watching). There's different entertainment each night of the week in the stage/dance-floor area: everything from karaoke to comedy, discos and the spangly-costumed "Jamaica Farewell" cabaret. Details are posted on a board outside and entrance fees vary.

Ocho Rios Village Jerk Centre Just before the roundabout on DaCosta Drive. Well-patronized jerk centre with good food and lots of rum bar-style banter.

White River Ranch White River. Busy, open-air circular bar of a popular restaurant, five minutes east of the centre. Good for white rum drinking alongside the predominantly local clientele.

Clubs

Amnesia Disco 70 Main St, above the Mutual Security building. The town's only proper nightclub, with an indoor, air-conditioned dance floor and an outdoor bar area. Wednesday is the quiet "warm-up night"; women get in free on Thursday for the ever-popular "Ladies' Night"; Friday is "After Work Jam" with drinks promotions; on Saturday, everyone dresses up for the "Marathon Dance Party"; and Sunday is quieter "oldies night". Music policy is dancehall, R&B, hip hop and dance. Cover J$200. Open Wed–Sun.

Jamaika-Me-Krazy Jamaica Grande. Popular in-hotel disco with good sound and lights and a happy holiday crowd taking advantage of the all-inclusive bar. Cover US$25, includes all drinks. Closed Tues.

The Roof Club 7 James Ave. No-frills local disco. Music policy is dancehall and more dancehall, with some R&B thrown in. Women get in free most nights, but it's a place to avoid if you're feeling fragile or want to be left alone. Open nightly, but best at weekends. Cover J$100.

Shades A3, opposite the turn-off to the Jamaica Inn hotel. Enduringly popular go-go club with "Freaky Tuesdays", when women perform live sex with other each on stage. Not for the faint-hearted.

Strawberry Night Club 6 James Ave. Modest and unthreatening local disco with Ladies' Night (free entrance and wine for women) on Sundays.

Shopping

Shopping is big business in Ocho Rios. The town's three **craft markets** (daily 7am–7pm) have enticed many a hapless soul to leave Jamaica laden with "Yeh mon it irie" and "Same shit, different island" T-shirts or Rasta hats complete with "comedy" fake dreadlocks. A frantic free-for-all on cruise-ship days, these are otherwise great places to shop – among the dross you'll find really nice T-shirts and sculptures, and vendors have a wicked line in sales banter. The main market is to the right of Ocean Village Plaza, while the much smaller Pineapple Place and Coconut Grove markets are further east towards *Hibiscus*

Lodge and the all-inclusive hotels.

As well as the craft markets, Main Street houses no less than eleven **shopping malls**, open-air courtyards set back from the road and lined with near-identical **in-bond shops** selling imported jewellery, watches and china, as well as up-market craft shops. The latter are the scourge of market vendors, who claim that deals struck with cruise-ship companies ensure that prospective souvenir buyers are ferried straight into the air-conditioned calm rather than making their purchases on the street. Prices in the stores are higher than in the markets, but the quality of merchandise is reliable. Alternatively, go directly to the source at Clarke's Art Studio, a tiny, green-painted wooden shack just west of town – the sculptures, carvings and acrylic paintings are beautiful. **Ceramics** and various other creative souvenirs are sold at the Wassi Art Factory Outlet at Great Pond, in the hills above town (see p.198), though you can buy the products in most local craft stores and the markets. There's also a gorgeous **art gallery** and shop at Harmony Hall (☎975 4222, ⊛www.harmonyhall.com), ten minutes' drive out of Ochi on the way to Tower Isle. Set in a beautifully restored great house, the gallery features small but comprehensive and ever-changing collections of work by renowned contemporary Jamaican artists, along with a variety of crafts, Caribbean books, aromatherapy oils and women's clothing. The site hosts excellent monthly art and craft fairs, held on Sundays. A mile or so east of Tower Isle, local artist Henry Simms sells his unique flat tin figures, fish and horses by the side of the road. You'll see them hanging from rails on the right-hand corner just before you pass *Beaches Boscobel* all-inclusive resort.

Island Village, by the cruise-ship pier, has become one of Ochi's most popular places to shop. Prices are not cheap, the goods on offer are not especially Jamaican, and it's nowhere near as atmospheric as the craft market, but the range of products is eclectic and quality is consistently high. Both Cool Gear and Island Leisure have a selection of attractive holiday clothing and accessories; Silvermine sells classy pieces of silver jewellery; and Tallawah Arts displays and sells innovative Jamaican art and crafts – batiks, ceramics, prints and paintings.

For **books**, try Bookland in Island Village, which has an excellent selection of Caribbean titles as well as international novels and magazines. Everybody's Bookshop in Ocean Village Plaza carries a smaller selection, some titles published only in Jamaica, plus magazines and foreign newspapers. For **music**, Reggae Yard in Island Village has the largest selection of reggae and other CDs outside Kingston. Disc and Dat in Island Plaza stocks the latest dancehall, reggae, R&B and hip hop, as does Vibes Music Shack in Ocean Village Plaza.

Listings

Airlines Air Jamaica has a local office (☎974 2566) for flight confirmations and information; for other airlines see Montego Bay listings, p.268. Air Jamaica Express (☎975 3254 or 922 4661) runs internal flights to and from Boscobel Aerodrome (☎975 3101).

American Express at Great Vacations Ltd, Ocean Village Plaza.

Banks and money Most of the banks are on Main St opposite Ocean Village Plaza, and there are several ATMs on Main St – run by NCB next to

Mothers and Scotiabank opposite the market. The best rates in town for currency exchange are offered by Cambio King, 12 Ocean Village Plaza (Mon–Sat 9am–5pm), while Cambio Express, 19 Main St, is open late (Mon–Fri 9am–7pm, Sat 9am–8pm). Cool Card (⊛www.coolcorp.com) has an air-conditioned cambio at 11 Main St (Mon–Sat 9am–4pm), with ATMs dishing out both US and Jamaican dollars. Wire transfers are available through the Western Union outlet at *Pier View* hotel or Vintage Retailers, 3 Ocean Village Plaza.

Car rental Many of the international firms have in-hotel branches in Ochi. Otherwise the following local companies are recommended and may give you a better deal: Bargain, Pineapple Place Shopping Centre (℡ 974 5298, ⓦ www.bargainja.com); Caribbean Cars, 99A Main St (℡ 974 2513, ⓕ 974 5760, ⓦ www.caribbean-carrentals.com); Island, 4 Carib Arcade, Main St (℡ 974 2666, ⓦ www.islandcarrentals.com); and Sunshine, 154 Main St (℡ 974 2980, ⓔ sunshine-office@cwjamaica.com).

Doctors Dr Prakash Kulkani, 16 Rennie Rd (℡ 974 2012), offers a 24-hr service. For a paediatrician, call Dr Horace Betton at 14 Carib Arcade on Main St (℡ 974 2005 or 5413) or the Allied Physicians Family Health Centre, 74 Main Street (℡ 795 2484). The Holistic Medical Centre, 40 Ocean Village Plaza (℡ 974 6403–4), offers homeopathic and chiropractic therapy alongside regular medical care and also have a link to an air ambulance (℡ 974 6403–4; 24hr).

Hospitals The nearest is at St Ann's Bay (℡ 972 2272), a fifteen-minute drive from Ocho Rios. In an emergency call ℡ 119 or 974 7035 for a private ambulance.

Internet The most efficient service – but very pricey – is at Internet Jungle in Island Village (Mon–Fri 8am–8pm, Sat 9am–8pm, Sun 10am–7pm), which charges US$4 for 15min. A cheaper option is Cyber Spa in the Village Hotel mall (Mon–Sat 10–7pm).

Laundry Mr Kleen Laundromat, 43 Ocean Village Plaza (Mon–Sat 8am–6pm), charges US$7 per load. Travellers Rest, 1a Da Costa Drive (Mon–Sat 9am–5pm; ℡ 974 8436), charges a more reasonable US$3.50 per load and also does dry-cleaning.

Pharmacies Ochi pharmacies are plentiful, well-equipped and often open late; most useful are the Ocho Rios Pharmacy in Ocean Village Plaza (daily 8.30am–8pm) and Pinegrove Pharmacy at Pinegrove Plaza on Main St (Mon–Sat 9am–8pm

Sun 10am–3pm).

Photography Pugh's Photo Lab in the Mutual Security Building, 70 Main St, and Hot Shots, with outlets in the Ocean Village Plaza and Island Village, both offer Kodak film, photographic supplies and 1hr developing.

Police The police station (℡ 974 2533 or 4588) is on Evelyn St behind the Texaco garage that faces the clock tower; in emergencies call ℡ 119.

Post office The permanently busy post office is on Main St opposite the main craft market (Mon–Fri 8am–5pm, Sat 8am–noon).

Spas Several places in Ocho Rios offer massage, facials and other beauty treatments. The most impressive is the fabulous Kiyara Ocean Spa at the *Jamaica Inn* hotel (℡ 974 2380); it uses solely natural ingredients – aloe, pineapple, coffee beans – for its treatments, which take place on breezy seaside terraces. Veroniques, at the Village Hotel on Main St (℡ 795 3425), offers reasonably-priced manicures, pedicures and reflexology.

Supermarkets General Foods in Ocean Village Plaza is Ochi's largest and carries a wide range of imported food alongside Jamaican staples. Fruit and vegetables are cheaper and better at the market, which is located off the bypass and adjacent to Evelyn St.

Taxis Reliable operators include Eight Rivers Taxi Service (℡ 974 3063), JUTA (℡ 974 2292), Maxi Taxi (℡ 974 2971, ⓦ www.maxitoursochorios.com) and Rising Bird (℡ 974 7339).

Telephones Pay phones are dotted around town. Local phonecards are available from *Mother's* on Main St, the post office and pharmacies. Worldtalk cards are available from most gift shops. If you're going to be on the island for a while, Digicel, 70 Main St, sells local network SIM cards or you can rent a phone from Internet Jungle in Island Village. Inexpensive overseas calls can be made from the Call Direct Centre, 85 Main St. You can send faxes from the Xerox Centre in Ocean Village Plaza.

East of Ocho Rios

As the clamour of Ocho Rios recedes, the A3 coast road narrows as if to make way for some of the most beautiful scenery on the north coast. Lushly vegetated cliffsides almost overwhelm the tarmac, and the region's languid allure is markedly different to the in-your-face glitz of Ochi. The main settlements,

Oracabessa and **Port Maria**, are slow, close-knit communities where tourism is only just starting to take hold, and the small guesthouses and excellent little restaurants that pepper the roadsides are generally overlooked by those who prefer sports bars and jet skis to peace and quiet exclusivity. Low-key glamour has a lengthy history here, however. Though ostensibly quiet, the area has long been a favourite haunt of the rich and famous. Noel Coward and James Bond creator Ian Fleming both lived here in the 1950s and 1960s, and their old homes, **Firefly** and **Goldeneye**, are still standing. Firefly has been transformed into a prime tourist site, and *Goldeneye* is the centrepiece of a luxury villa complex.

The presence of small-scale tourism extends about as far as pretty Port Maria. Beyond the town, the road swings inland and the coastline extends in an unbroken series of forested outcrops interspersed by deserted, volcanic-sand miniature beaches reachable only by foot or boat. Hikes or drives around here uncover breathtaking vistas as the peaks of the Blue Mountains (see p.133) shimmer into view. If you're interested in really exploring the area, Libby and Clarence "Chef" Thompson, the friendly couple who run *Sea Lawn Coral Beach* (see p.210) offer rootsy local tours tailor-made to your requirements.

Accommodation

In addition to a large new **all-inclusive**, the family-orientated *Beaches Boscobel Resort and Golf Club* (ⓦ www.beaches.com), there are some really lovely small-scale **guesthouses** and **rental villas** around Oracabessa and Port Maria, which range in price and facilities from the very cheap and simple to the extremely expensive and plush.

Belretiro Inn PO Box 151, Galina ☎ 994 0035, ⓔ winior@cwjamaica.com. Lovely, breezy property on the cliffside in Galina, with various standards of clean, basic rooms with private bathrooms; some have a TV or a verandah. All guests can use the kitchen. There's a saltwater pool, good snorkelling and sea swimming, and the best rates in the area. ❶-❷

Blue Harbour PO Box 50, Port Maria ☎ 725 0289, ⓦ www.blueharb.com. Built in the 1950s by Noel Coward, and pretty much as he left them, these three seaside villas may be rented whole or room by room. Overlooking Port Maria bay, the villas offer the best views in the area, and the whole place is wonderfully atmospheric. There's a saltwater pool, a small beach and plenty of seclusion. Rates include all meals. ❺

Bolt House Galina ☎ 994 0303, ⓕ 975 3620, ⓦ www.islandoutpost.com. Built by Blanche Blackwell (mother of Island Records impresario Chris), this gorgeous villa on a bluff below Firefly affords the same stunning views of Port Maria bay. The place is beautifully furnished, its walls hung with the best in contemporary art. It's the epitome of classy, secluded luxury, with two bedrooms, dining and living rooms and a lovely pool, all set in landscaped gardens. ❽

Caribbean Pearl PO Box 127, Port Maria ☎ & ⓕ 725 0261, ⓦ www.caribbeanpearl.com.

Spotlessly clean guesthouse, geared to German travellers, on a hillside just west of town. The spacious rooms have rattan four-poster beds, and there's a lovely pool and bar with views of the bay. Breakfast is included in the rates. ❺

Casa Maria Hotel PO Box 10, Port Maria ☎ 725 0156, ⓦ www.nwas.com/casamaria. Plenty of very faded grandeur, with simple though spacious rooms at decent rates. There's a pool, bar and restaurant on site. ❸

Dream River Castle Garden, near Port Maria (ring first for directions) ☎ 725 0893, ⓕ 994 9150, ⓔ dreamriver@cwjamaica.com. Lovely four-bedroom house in gorgeous, secluded setting, with a large pool, tropical woods and a river running through the grounds. There's even a recording studio built by Rita Marley, who once lived here. Rooms can be rented individually, and rates include continental breakfast. ❺

Goldeneye Oracabessa ☎ 975 3354 ⓕ 975 3620, ⓦ www.islandoutpost.com. Understated class is the hallmark of this, one of Jamaica's most exclusive hotels, a regular haunt of the rich and famous. Centred on Ian Fleming's beautifully restored Jamaican home, the one- to three-bedroom villas are secluded and indescribably inviting, with outdoor showers and all the delightful extras you'd expect. Each has access to the private beach where Fleming cooled his toes. Rates include all

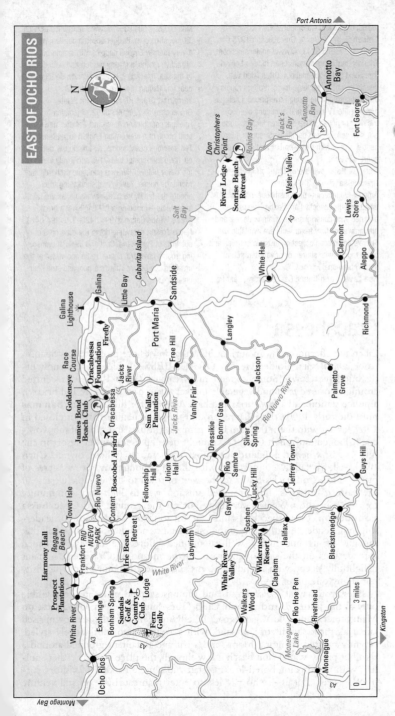

N

Port Antonio

Annotto Bay

Fort George

Don Christophers Point
River Lodge
Sonrise Beach Retreat

Robins Bay

Jack's Bay

Annotto Bay

A4

Water Valley

Lewis Store

Clermont

Aleppo

Salt Bay

Cabarita Island

White Hall

Richmond

Galina
Galina Lighthouse
Little Bay

Sandside

Firefly

Port Maria

Langley

Oracabessa Foundation

Free Hill

Jacks River

Jackson

Goldeneye
Race Course

James Bond Beach Club

Oracabessa

Sun Valley Plantation

Vanity Fair

Bonny Gate

Dressikie

Rio Nuevo River

Palmetto Grove

Jacks River

Silver Spring

Boscobel Airstrip

Rio Nuevo

Fellowship Hall

Union Hall

Rio Sambre

Lucky Hill

Jeffrey Town

Guys Hill

Content

Gayle

Goshen

Tower Isle

Harmony Hall

Reggae Beach

Frankfort

RIO NUEVO PARK

Irie Beach Retreat

Labyrinth

White River Valley

Halifax

Wilderness Resort

Blackstonedge

Prospect Plantation

White River

Exchange

Bonham Spring

Sandals Golf & Country Club

Fern Gully

White River

Lodge

Clapham

Walkers Wood

Rio Hoe Pen

Riverhead

Ocho Rios

A3

Moneague Lake

Moneague

A3

Kingston

3 miles

0   3 miles

209

Montego Bay

meals, drinks and watersports. ⑧

Golden Seas PO Box 1, Oracabessa ☎975
3540–41, ℱ975 3243, ⓦwww.goldenseas.com.
Friendly Jamaican-owned resort hidden behind
trees next to the roundabout. Often filled with
guests on cheap package tours, it offers rooms
that are comfortable though overpriced. Each has
a/c, satellite TV, phone and a balcony overlooking
the river or ocean. Other features include a medium-size yellow-sand beach, watersports, fitness
centre, a pool with swim-up bar and a tennis
court. ⑤

Nix-Nax Rainbow Isle of Light off Main St,
Oracabessa ☎975 3364. Small
American/Jamaican-run guesthouse with an
unashamedly collective ambience – walls are
adorned with consciousness-raising adages, and
alternative medical treatments are available.
There's an eclectic collection of basic but nice and
clean rooms, with shared or private bathrooms,
and a communal kitchen. ①

Sea Lawn Coral Beach Castle Garden, near Port

Maria ☎ & ℱ994 9367, ⓦwww.sealawncoralbeach
.20megsfree.com. Budget accommodation, run by
a very friendly English couple, with simple but
attractive rooms, a grassy garden and path down
to the sea. Interesting local or islandwide tours,
boat and fishing trips are available. ①

Tamarind Great House Crescent Estate,
Oracabessa ☎ & ℱ995 3252, ⓦjamaica
-gleaner.com/gleaner/tamarind. Palatial, newly-
built home of a welcoming English expat family.
Ten spacious guest rooms, all luxuriously decorated, have four-poster beds, TVs and lovely views of
the valley below. There's a pool, and orchards surround the house. Sailing and snorkelling trips
aboard the family yacht are available, as are fabulous meals – including a full English-ish breakfast.

Trade Winds Galina ☎994 0420–2, ℱ994 0423.
Newish resort sprawling down the cliffs on the
outskirts of Port Maria. Cool and clean, if uninspiring, rooms have a/c, phone, radio and views of the
crashing sea below. There's a pool and small bar
on site. ③

Oracabessa

Lit in the afternoons by an apricot light that must have prompted its Spanish
name, *Orocabeza* ("Golden Head"), **ORACABESSA** is a leisurely, friendly little one-street town. Some sixteen miles east of Ocho Rios, it is centred
around a covered fruit and vegetable market (main days Thursday and Friday),
a police station and a few shops and bars. A centre for the export of **bananas**
until the early 1900s, the wharves around the small natural harbour closed in
1969, taking with them the rum bars, gambling houses and most of the workers. It looked as though Oracabessa might develop as a low-key resort in the
mid-1990s, when the **Island Outpost** corporation (whose owner, Chris
Blackwell, has family connections with the area) bought up seventy acres of
prime land – from Jack's River to the west of town to the *Goldeneye* estate at
the eastern outskirts. The proposed mission was to kick-start community
tourism, but the project never really got off the ground. The **Oracabessa
Foundation**, established by Island Outpost to foster a local sense of leadership, independence and community responsibility, no longer exists, and all that
remains of its undeniably well-intentioned efforts are the Rasta-striped
garbage bins on the side of the road. In the meantime Oracabessa remains
delightfully sleepy, with friendly citizens and a mere handful of tourists visiting at any one time.

Unless you stay at *Goldeneye*, Island Outpost's grand plans are now visible
only at the **James Bond Beach Club** (Tues–Sun 9am–6pm; US$5), just off
Main Street along Old Wharf Road. Briefly, in its infancy, the area comprised
Jamaica's most stylish strip of sand, with a collection of distinctively styled,
brightly painted changing rooms, and a bar and restaurant grouped around a
slim but pretty white-sand beach. Now though, the place is really rather soulless, with faded paint, bored-looking staff and a mere handful of visitors during the week. Locals – who pay less to enter than tourists - do still venture

down at weekends, and the expansive oceanfront lawns, often used to stage large-scale concerts such as Sashi in August, make a wonderfully breezy outdoor venue. For adrenaline junkies the beach also offers guided jet-ski safaris along the coast (US$55 for half an hour).

If you prefer to stay away from the glitterati, the small adjacent **fisherman's beach** is an equally appealing place to swim (though the showers and

007's Jamaica

From Errol Flynn to Ralph Lauren, Jamaica has always attracted the rich and famous, but the island has also served as inspiration for the ultimate (albeit fictional) symbol of glamour – **James Bond**. As a commander in the Naval Intelligence Division of the British army, Bond's creator, Ian Fleming, first visited Jamaica in 1943 on military business. Staying in the Blue Mountains, he was immediately taken with the island's sensual pleasures and declared that he'd be back to put down permanent roots as soon as the war ended. By 1947, he'd paid £2000 for a plot of land on Jamaica's north coast that had once served as Oracabessa's racecourse, and engaged local workers to build the simple, elegant beach house that he'd designed himself. Naming it after a bungled NID anti-German operation that he'd been involved in, **Goldeneye** became his winter retreat and a source of competition with neighbour **Noel Coward**, who insisted that his Blue Harbour (see p.208) was far superior to Fleming's spartan bachelor pad. A series of magazine articles penned by Fleming on the joys of his island paradise soon began to lure a glamorous, fashionable set to Jamaica. Goldeneye played host to such luminaries as Sir Anthony and Lady Eden, Truman Capote, Lucian Freud, Graham Greene, Evelyn Waugh and Cecil Beaton. Cocktails by the pool and snorkelling expeditions with his "Jamaican wife" Blanche Blackwell (mother of Island Records' Chris Blackwell) soon began to take up most of Fleming's time. It wasn't until his other long-term lover and soon-to-be wife, Lady Anne Rothermere (ex-wife of the British newspaper baron), became pregnant in 1952 that he got down to any serious writing. He cracked out *Casino Royale* on a rickety old Remington typewriter with the jalousies shut to block out the distracting sea view.

Fleming took his hero's name from the author of the classic book *Birds of the West Indies,* and many of his characters were inspired by various Jamaican friends. Pussy Galore, in the *Goldfinger* novel, was said to be a tongue-in-cheek representation of Blanche Blackwell. Clearly besotted with the island, Fleming exploited the Jamaica connection in his writing wherever possible. Two novels, *Doctor No* and *The Man with the Golden Gun,* were set here (scenes for the movie versions were filmed in Kingston and Westmoreland respectively), and the island served as the fictional San Monique in *Live and Let Die.* And of course 007 wouldn't have dreamed of drinking any other coffee than his favourite Blue Mountain brew. Fleming later wrote "Would these books have been born if I had not been living in the gorgeous vacuum of a Jamaican holiday? I doubt it."

A regular routine developed, with Fleming returning to Goldeneye each January, spending a couple of months writing, and returning to England in March. However, the years of hard drinking and partying began to take their toll, and by the late 1950s, his health had seriously deteriorated. Fleming survived long enough to supervise Cubby Broccoli's movie version of *Dr No,* filmed in Jamaica with Chris Blackwell as location manager. In the first few months of 1964, Fleming returned to Goldeneye and wrote his last 007 novel, *The Man with the Golden Gun,* infusing the pages with a strong sense of nostalgia for Jamaica. His strength was waning, however. Though his Bond novels had by then sold some forty million copies, Ian Fleming died on August 12, 1964, without ever really knowing what a sensation he had created. Four months after his death, the release of the movie version of *Goldfinger* signified the beginning of a worldwide Bond mania that continues to this day.

changing rooms are rather less so). The Rasta carvers who've built a shack on the sand sell seafood meals and drinks as well as putting on the odd sound-system dance.

East of the turn-off for James Bond Beach and the town's petrol station, Oracabessa merges into the residential community of **Race Course**. Here, gates, walls and trees mask **Goldeneye** (see also p.208), the unassuming white-walled bungalow designed and purpose-built by Ian Fleming, sometime military man and creator of James Bond, who wrote almost all of the James Bond novels within its walls.

Right on the other side of town and before the market, a roundabout crowded with fruit vendors (and serving as an unofficial **taxi rank**) forms the junction of the coast road and the B13 inland road. The latter wreathes through attractive residential communities towards the well-signposted **Sun Valley** (daily, 1hr 30min tours at 9am, 1pm & 2pm; US$12), one of the north coast's most attractive plantations, though one of its smallest. This working, family-owned estate concentrates on bananas and coconuts. The charming low-key tour explains the growth processes of the two fruits; takes in some interesting trees, flowers and bushes; and includes drinks, a light meal and some fruit tasting.

If you're interested in art, it's worth stopping by the Wilderness House of Art, a large striking house set back from the road in Race Course. It's home to two genial Rastafarian artists, known simply as Akete and Ireko. The front of the property is a small shop selling their distinctive hand-printed silk scarves, wraps and T-shirts. Each January the house plays host to *Kwanzaa*, a black-consciousness festival that celebrates African roots with drumming, herbal healing and traditional food and crafts on sale.

Eating, drinking and entertainment

There is a marked shortage of decent **places to eat** in and around Oracabessa. The town itself has little other than a friendly local cook shop adjacent to the market, *Oracos,* which serves up home-cooked Jamaican staples such as curried goat and fried chicken. Perched atop a cliff on the other side of town and one of the most popular options in the area, jovial and friendly *Dor's Sea Cliff Fish Pot* in Race Course has juicy fresh fish or lobster dinners, superlative conch and fish soups and a nice circular bar for lounging and chatting (daily; 24hr). The brilliant – though now faded – murals of 1970s' style north coast scenes are also pretty good. Also in Race Course is *Club Tan Jan,* behind the variety store of the same name. It's a surprisingly spacious and attractive backroom bar with a pool table and a simple lunch menu of tasty fare, including a veggie (tofu) choice. If you're looking for proper gourmet food, your best and only real option is to head up to *Tamarind Great House* in nearby Jacks River (see "Accommodation", p.210). Host Gillian Chambers cooks up delicious three-course meals, which are served on the hotel's pretty and elegant verandah. You'll need to book in advance (⊕995 3252; dinner costs approx US$25) and take a charter taxi from Oracabessa if you don't have your own transport.

Unless you visit a hotel or head into Ochi, your **drinking** choices are limited to hole-in-the-wall rum shops such as noisy *Cheers Bar* in Oracabessa town or the *Cozy Corner,* a tiny but very welcoming local haunt in Race Course. If you really want to sample Jamaican village nightlife, head for the small rural community of Jacks River (take the signposted right fork as you enter town), where there are several lively bars – including the *Frontline* and the *New Success No 1 Jerk Centre.* They occasionally bring in sound systems on Friday and Saturday nights. *Nix Nax,* a large concrete building in Oracabessa (opposite the hotel of the same name), is a roomy indoor bar with video games, frequented by the local teenage boys. The only place to **dance**, although it's considerably less lively than it used to be, is *Tropical Hut*, a fairy-light-strewn bar set back from the road in Race Course. The "lawn" is occasionally fenced-off to provide a venue for oldies parties and more raw dances with the likes of Stone Love. James Bond Beach (see p.210) hosts live music events from time to time; the annual **Sashi concert**, held at the end of August, is a highlight.

Port Maria

The diminutive capital of St Mary, **PORT MARIA** was once one of Jamaica's most picturesque towns, nestled around a crescent bay with lots of cut-stone and faded gingerbread fretwork alluding to more auspicious times, and far more in the way of shops and offices than Oracabessa. However it's rather a scruffy and crowded place these days, and once you've taken in the bay view and strolled the few shopping streets, there's little to keep you here.

The town's main attractions are all on its outskirts. As you round the twisting outcrops that protect the natural harbour, a stunning view of tiny and forested **Cabarita Island**, right in the middle of the bay, is revealed. Around the next outcrop and marked by two sizeable royal palms at its gates is the beautiful cut-stone **St Mary Parish Church**, dating back to 1861. The cemetery extends down to the sea, and its weathered gravestones stand testament to the abrasive properties of salty air. To the right of the church is a playing field, which fronts the parish library; in the middle of the grass is a monument to black freedom fighter **Tacky** (see box). Opposite is the old police station, gutted by fire in 1988 and now refurbished. Just beyond, the attractive clapboard building housing the Office of Health Department faces the covered fruit and veg **market** (main day Friday), a maze of dingy paths winding through the piles of yams,

The Tacky Rebellion

In the late eighteenth century, Port Maria saw one of Jamaica's bloodiest rebellions against slavery, an uprising that sowed the seeds for emancipation eighty years later. Led by a runaway slave known as **Tacky** (a European spelling of the Ghanaian name Tekyi, meaning "the great"), who was said to have been a chief of Coromantee descent, the rebellion sparked violent protests throughout the island. It aimed at a complete cull of whites and the creation of an all-black colony. The revolt began on Easter Sunday 1760, when Tacky and a small group of slaves from local estates murdered their overseers and marched to Port Maria, killing the storekeeper at Fort Haldane and seizing arms and ammunition. Five months of fighting ensued, with £100,000 worth of damage done to nearby plantations. However, the thousand-strong slave army could not compete with the military force of the British, who utilized loyal slaves and Maroons (in accordance with the 1739 treaty) in the guerrilla warfare. The rebellion was savagely quashed and severe punishments meted out to the freedom fighters. Tacky was captured by Maroon marksmen and killed, his head cut off and displayed on a pole in Spanish Town. Others were chained to stakes and burned alive, gibbeted or hung by irons and left to die as an example to others contemplating sedition. It's said, however, that in one last gesture of defiance, Tacky's sympathizers removed his body under cover of night and gave their leader a proper burial. After Tacky's death, many of his followers committed suicide rather than live enslaved. In all, three hundred Africans died fighting, fifty were captured and executed and three hundred transported abroad, but only sixty whites lost their lives.

bananas and assorted local produce. A bridge crossing the murky Ochom River brings you into the town centre, where the streets of yellow stone and clapboard buildings are laid out in a rough grid formation.

At the eastern end of town is Pagee Beach, where you can arrange a combined fishing trip and visit to Cabarita Island (approx US$20) with one of the local fishermen. They moor their boats at one end of the stretch of greyish sand, which, although strewn with sea grass and washed-up debris, nevertheless extends in a long picturesque sweep and is backed by shady palm trees.

Firefly

Perched on a hilltop about two miles west of town, Port Maria's only organized attraction is **Firefly** (daily except Fri and Sun and public holidays 9am–5pm; US$10 for guided tours), the Jamaican home of Noel Coward and his partner Graham Payn, from its construction in 1956 to Coward's death in 1973. The house was built on the site of a former Taino settlement (many artefacts have been found here). The spot was later the stamping ground of pirate extraordinaire Sir Henry Morgan (see p.112), who used it as a vantage point during his reign as governor three hundred years ago; gun slits in what is now the on-site bar recall the buccaneer days. Coward stumbled upon the site during Jamaican holidays, when he stayed at his **Blue Harbour** beach house on the coast below, and bought it from local politician Roy Lindo for £150.

Acquired by Island Outpost in 1992, the house remains much as Coward left it: his studio set up with a painting on the easel; the drawing room – where illustrious guests from Sophia Loren to Audrey Hepburn and Joan Sutherland were entertained – complete with two polished pianos; kitchen cupboards full of yellowing bottles and packets; and the table freshly laid as it was on the day the Queen Mother came to lunch in 1965. Coward died here in his bedroom and is buried on the property. A statue of him by UK-based artist Angella Connor still overlooks his favourite view. Even if you're not a Coward fan, it's worth coming up to Firefly for the view alone. One of the best on the island, the panorama takes in Port Maria bay and Cabarita Island to the east, with the peaks of the Blue Mountains poking through the clouds, while to the west lies **Galina Point**, the most northerly tip of Jamaica, where there's a **lighthouse**. You can even see Cuba on a clear day. Firefly is occasionally the venue for lavish private parties and special events.

Eating, drinking and entertainment

Port Maria has plenty of small **restaurants** serving simple, cheap Jamaican fare. Among the more reliable are *Essie's Faith*, in the town square next to Courts furniture store, and S*onia's E Spot* on Warner Street, which serves up traditional food with delicious fruit juices. *Solos*, a long-standing no-frills bar and restaurant, is situated in front of the fishing boats on Pagee Beach at the east end of town, and has the freshest cooked-to-order fish around. There are several other small shacks selling food and drink along the beach itself. Port Maria has **rum bars** aplenty; a few play rocksteady into the night on Saturdays and Sundays. Particularly popular is the open-air *Roof Club*, which gets going late. The weekend "ben-dung" (literally, "bend down", with items spread out on the ground) **market** adds a bit of bustle.

Robins Bay and around

Past the strip of bars and restaurants on the eastern outskirts of Port Maria, the potholed A3 swings away from the coast. It travels over a series of clattering Bailey bridges and through tiny settlements where kids play at the edge of the ever-frayed tarmac and chickens pick through the dust. Keep an eye out for the roadside stall bedecked in all shapes and sizes of aluminium saucepans, including the ubiquitous Jamaican favourite, the squat "Dutch pot", used for cooking on open fires. About four miles from Port Maria, signs for *River Lodge* and *Sonrise Beach Retreat* marks a re-covered road towards the sea at **ROBINS BAY**. The coastline here is fabulous, with cattle pastures on one side of the road and a series of deserted **white-sand coves** on the other; further east, development tails off completely, and there are scores of gorgeous, little-visited black-sand beaches and **waterfalls** to explore. The area's idyllic aspect was first exploited in the 1970s, when the free-love shenanigans of American hippies at the long-gone *Strawberry Fields* campsite drew sighs of consternation from local people.

These days, the campsite has been re-opened as *Sonrise Beach Retreat* (℡999 7169, Ⓦwww.in-site.com/sonrise; ❹–❺), a Christian-oriented hotel centered around the pretty white-sand cove from which Spanish governor, Don Christobel Arnaldo de Yssasi, fled the island in 1660. Cabins are scattered throughout the extensive grounds; some have a shared bathroom, others a kitchenette, and a deluxe two-bedroom cottage comes with its own private beach. There's also a gazebo on the cliffs for chilling out or watching the sun come up. *Sonrise* is popular amongst local church groups, many of which attend the weekend Family Fun Days. Owner Bro' Bob conducts various eco-oriented **tours** of the area, which cost US$25–75. Among the offerings is the invigorating River Water Therapy Experience, a day of river gorge hiking, natural whirlpool massage and rock climbing. Day passes (9am–5pm) to the *Sonrise* property cost US$4, which covers use of the showers and changing rooms as well as volleyball, table tennis and a bounce on the trampoline.

Past *Sonrise*, the tarmac gives way to dirt and stones, and the atmosphere lightens as you pass through a friendly Rasta-oriented community. It's home to a couple of small bars – the first, *Bobby's Place*, is decked with fairy lights, while the second, *Wackie Lawn*, has a quieter vibe and good Jamaican food. A few minutes' walk further west along the road takes you to *River Lodge* (℡ & Ⓕ995 3003, Ⓦwww.river-lodge.com; ❸ with breakfast and dinner included), the most alluring place to stay for miles. Owned and run by German expat Brigitta Fuchslocher, this restful complex on the inland side of the road is built around the restored ruins of a seventeenth-century Spanish fort. Rooms make full use of the stone walls, with attractively minimal decor; shared and private bathrooms are available. A river running through the grounds has swimming possibilities during the wet season, and the beach is steps away. Serving mostly vegetarian food and set under an open-sided, thatched-roof gazebo, the restaurant and bar are delightful, particularly after a day spent walking along the coast. Excellent low-key boat trips along the coast to a black-sand beach, followed by hikes through the bush to one of several impressive – and deserted – waterfalls, can be arranged with the staff at *River Lodge* (US$10 per person).

Rio Sambre and inland St Mary

Firmly off the tourist track, the gorgeous scenery of the **St Mary interior** is well worth exploring if you have a car or can hire a driver for the day, and there are several opportunities for a fresh-water **swim** if the going gets too hot. A mile or so east of Port Maria, turn inland at the tiny community of **SANDSIDE**, and right again at a sign for the *Rio Sambre* resort. The road clambers up a steep hill, which provides eye-catching views of the rolling St Mary countryside and the Port Maria coastline below, and passes a waterfall at Preston Land and orange groves at New Road. You'll hardly notice the hamlets of Langley, Bonny Gate and Silver Spring, but the slightly more substantial **DRESSIKIE** has a friendly roadside bar, the *D&B Groove Scene Pub*, opposite a popular local swimming spot, the Zennor Hole. From here, continue towards Gayle and follow the signs for a couple of miles to *Rio Sambre* (☎975 8146, ℱ975 8967; entry US$4, camping US$12 per person; ❸). A campsite-cum-lido centred around the clean, fast-flowing river from which it takes its name, *Rio Sambre* is popular with Jamaicans. Islanders come to swim in the wide, deep **river pool**, play cricket and volleyball, ride go-karts, and then settle down for drinking and dominoes or a meal at the restaurant. If you want to **stay**, there are two hexagonal cabins to rent, each with kitchen, hot water, fans, satellite TV, VCR and a balcony overlooking the property. You can also hire a good-quality tent that sleeps three to twelve people and comes equipped with air beds (tent and beds are included in the rates). Guided **hikes** of the surrounding area are included in the entry fee (which also covers use of the changing rooms and showers).

West of Ocho Rios

Though the coast between the top resort towns sees plenty of tourist traffic, the craft stalls, "Welcome to Jamaica" billboards and fruit vendors are generally restricted to the coast. Even in the established resort neighbours of **Runaway Bay** and **Discovery Bay**, tourism is pretty low-key and much less invasive than in Ocho Rios or Montego Bay. With its thriving market and Georgian architecture interspersed with gently weather-beaten clapboard houses, **St Ann's Bay**, just west of Ochi, is the small, unpretentious capital of St Ann. The ruined Spanish capital **Sevilla Nueva**, today called Seville, is a few minutes' walk away. As you work your way west along the coast, historic but unkempt **Rio Bueno** marks the boundary of St Ann and Trelawny parishes and a distinct change in the landscape, from languid hills to rugged hillocks. Unexpectedly energetic interior villages, such as **Brown's Town**, perch on the fringes of Cockpit Country (see Chapter Four), and the panoramic views over deep valleys are constantly spectacular. The interior remains largely undeveloped, save for the **Bob Marley Mausoleum** in central St Ann, and a couple of tourist-orientated attractions around **Falmouth**, capital of Trelawny and an architectural gold mine.

St Ann's Bay and around

If you're a James Bond fan, you might be interested to know that halfway along the eight miles between Ochi and St Ann's Bay, behind the Roaring River generating station, is the now-private beach where Ursula Andress emerged from the sea as Honey Ryder in the 007 movie *Dr No*. Otherwise there's little worth stopping for on this stretch of road before reaching the town of **ST ANNS BAY**. (Although on a prosaic note, the Cool Oasis petrol station boasts the cleanest bathrooms on the north coast.) The town stretches up the hillside from the coast and is characterized by its porticoed shop-fronts, sloping streets and old-fashioned atmosphere. Small enough to cover on foot in an hour, it consists of two central thoroughfares, Bravo and Main streets, which meet in a crossroads. Main Street hogs all the action, lined with shops and a **market** that spills out onto the street on Fridays and Saturdays, selling everything from reggae tapes to string vests.

The town's distinctive 1860 **courthouse** dominates from its perch at the top of Main Street. You can enter as an observer during trials, though the bureaucratic rigmarole of the Jamaican court system is often more arresting than the cases themselves. Down Main Street, in the middle of a roundabout, sits an ornate monument to Christopher Columbus by Spanish artist Michele Geurisi. The adventurer strikes a noble pose above his sunken ships. Just before the road forks, the church of **Our Lady of Perpetual Help** is one of the few remaining Catholic houses of worship in Jamaica. It's constructed of stone that was reclaimed from an earlier structure on a different site – Peter the Martyr Church, the first stone church in Jamaica, built in 1524 by the Spanish in Sevilla Nueva.

The quieter left fork of Main Street holds the **library** (Mon–Sat 9.30am–6pm), with its **Marcus Garvey memorial statue** on the front lawn. The outsize bronze stands before the words "We Declare to the World – Africa Must Be Free". Other than a parade in the town centre every August 17, the statue is the only distinctive evidence of Garvey's local connection (the house where he was born – 32 Market St – is a private residence). But the library itself is a good source of information on Garvey's life and work. For more on the great man, see box overleaf.

Seville

St Ann's Bay is bordered to the west by the old Spanish village of **SEVILLE**, Jamaica's first Spanish settlement (see box on p.220), but now an overgrown wasteland dotted with the crumbling remains of once-impressive buildings. Across the road from the site of old Seville village is **Seville Great House and Heritage Park** (daily 9am–5pm, 45min tours; US$4). Managed by the Jamaica National Heritage Trust, this is one of the few true heritage sites on the island, focusing on the lives, customs and culture of Tainos and Africans rather than celebrating plantation owners or "discoverers". A video presentation gives a detailed overview of Seville's history, and the museum displays intricately crafted Taino *zemis* (talismans used to ward off evil spirits) and other artefacts. Hidden in cattle pastures and woods, the ruins of Seville itself are not visible from the main road. But staff at the great house may be persuaded to accompany you on a walking tour of what remains: a water wheel, parts of Peter the Martyr Church, built by the Spanish, a sugar mill and the governor's castle, as well as the sites of Taino villages and slave settlements.

A better way to see the site is on a **horseback trail ride** courtesy of Hooves (2hr 30min Beach Ride; US$60; ☎972 0659, ⓦwww.jamaica-irie .com/hooves/index.html). The Beach Ride, as it's called, meanders through the bush from the great house to Seville, winds past what's left of the buildings and finishes up at the sea, where you can ride your mount in the water. Hooves also offer the Bush Doctor Mountain Trail (3hr 30min; US$70) into the hills toward Higgin Town.

Marcus Garvey

Born at 32 Market Street in St Ann's Bay on August 17, 1887, the **Right Excellent Marcus Mosiah Garvey** was one of the most powerful black rights activists of the twentieth century. His outspoken denunciations of colonialism and racism and his concrete efforts to unite and empower the African diaspora influenced politicians, musicians and academics alike. His legacy remains one of the most significant in Jamaican history – Rastafarians call him a **black prophet** and his philosophies form the basis of their faith (see "Religion" in *Contexts*, p.406).

Reputedly of Maroon descent, Garvey was the son of a master stonemason, a man with an uncompromising attitude, who earned enough to pursue multiple lawsuits against those he felt had slighted him on racial grounds. Though lack of funds ended the young Garvey's formal education at fourteen, he continued to be tutored privately and spent long hours in his father's extensive library. Prodigious from an early age, Garvey was made foreman of his uncle's Eclypse Printery at eighteen. But small-town living offered scant opportunities, and in 1906 he moved to Kingston and found work as a printery foreman – a significant coup at a time when supervisors were usually white. He soon became an activist in the fledgling trade union movement. Disturbed at the institutionalized injustice meted out to black workers, Garvey left Jamaica in 1910 to search for better prospects in Costa Rica, where he worked as a timekeeper on a banana plantation and set up two workers' newspapers to publicize the deplorable conditions for West Indian migrants. During a stint in England in 1912, he took classes at Birkbeck College and read up on other black nationalists such as Booker T. Washington, whose seminal text *Up From Slavery* was highly influential in fostering Garvey's ever-increasing militancy. In 1914, he returned to Jamaica and formed the **Universal Negro Improvement Association** (UNIA) "to champion Negro nationhood by redemption of Africa; to make the Negro race conscious, to advocate self determination, to inspire and instil racial love and self respect". But Jamaica's middle classes weren't ready to embrace such radical

Around St Ann's Bay: Priory to Chukka Cove

The short coastal stretch west of St Ann's Bay is dotted with minor roadside communities. A mile and a half along is tiny **PRIORY**, little more than a roadside strip but a favoured selling spot of jerk vendors, who set up reams of smoking oil-drum barbecues each evening. Running parallel to the main strip are the appealingly deserted, clear waters of **Fantasy Beach** (more simply known as Priory beach to the locals), a favoured swimming spot and much the most attractive public beach for miles around. The beach's circular bar is a nice place for a drink and the venue for occasional sound-system dances as well as a lively daytime beach party most Sundays.

Inland of Priory – take the final left fork out of the village onto Tanglewood Road and drive for ten minutes or so – **Circle B Farm** (daily 10am–5pm; US$12, US$24 with lunch; ☎913 4511) offers interesting, low-key walking tours of a working plantation. Several miles further along the same road, **Lillyfield Great House,** (9am– 5pm daily) which is set in the hills behind St Ann's Bay, offers guided tours (US$10; call ahead to reserve, ☎972 6045).

Half a mile or so west of Priory, the mountains recede back from the coast and the road cuts through the cattle pastures and sugarcane flats of **Llandovery**, once home to a huge sugar plantation, the Llandovery-Richmond estate, established in 1674 by the English. You can just make out the factory chimneys from the road. Just west is **Chukka Cove**, the most prestigious equestrian facility and polo ground in Jamaica. Matches are open to

ideas, and Garvey immigrated to the USA in 1916 to seek a more sympathetic audience. Black Americans identified so strongly with his message that by 1920 the UNIA had become the largest black pressure group ever to exist in the US, with a membership estimated from two to six million. Despite being outlawed in most of the colonies, Garvey's self-published *Negro World* newspaper achieved the largest circulation of any black paper in the world. With the financial backing of thousands who bought shares, Garvey formed the Black Star Line Shipping Company to foster trade links between black nations and enable repatriation to the African homeland.

Though known principally as a "Back-To-Africa" advocate, Garvey was equally concerned with improving the cultural and economic situation of blacks wherever they found themselves. His assault on post-colonial nihilism was his greatest achievement. Eschewing the sense of inferiority and powerlessness fostered during enslavement, he advocated black pride and self-determination, using the historical achievements of Africans to animate blacks: "Up you mighty race, you can accomplish what you will".

Marcus Garvey was regarded as a subversive by white America, and his supporters saw his 1922 imprisonment on a trumped-up mail-fraud charge as an attempt to muzzle the message. After Garvey spent two years in Atlanta Federal Prison, pressure from UNIA members secured his release. In 1927 he was deported back to Jamaica on a wave of publicity. However, Garvey's imprisonment had caused a loss of campaign momentum. The Black Star Line had foundered, and he never recaptured his early success. Tiring of constant battles with authority, he moved the struggle to the UK, where he died in obscurity in 1940. His importance was only recognized posthumously – in 1964 his remains were returned to Jamaica by the state and interred in Kingston's National Heroes Park. In the 1970s, music inspired a resurgence of Garveyism in Jamaica, with Rastafarian musicians like Burning Spear immortalizing his life and work in song. Today Marcus Garvey's ideas remain central to the Jamaican national consciousness.

observers most weekends; call for schedules (☎972 2506, ⓦwww.chukkacove .com). The immaculate stables are the home base of the excellent **Chukka Cove Adventure Tours**, which offer a fabulous three-hour beach ride (US$65 with return transportation and drinks; see p.192 for further details of various tours). After a gentle hack through cattle pastures, you swim your snorting mount in the sea below the barren volcanic cliffs, which were used as a backdrop for scenes from the cinematic epic *Papillon*. Chukka Cove also serves as the main north coast venue for Carnival celebrations each April – for more details, contact the JTB in Ocho Rios (see p.191).

A mile or so past Chukka Cove, a tiny paved road cuts inland toward the signposted **Cranbrook Flower Forest** (☎770 8071; daily 9am–sunset; US$6), an exquisitely landscaped, 130-acre nature park with several grassy lawns, a fishing pond, a family of resident peacocks and a swift-running river with plenty of marvellous swimming spots. Run by a friendly Jamaican family, who wanted to create a space where visitors and local people could retreat from urban clamour, Cranbrook is an overwhelmingly peaceful spot. No ghetto-blasters or vendors are allowed, and it's the perfect place for a quiet picnic and river swim. It's best to bring your own food and drink, though you can buy snacks from the tuck shop and bar, housed in a pretty cut-stone building that was originally an outbuilding of the sugar estate that flourished here. To the right of the tuck shop is the **fishing pond**, a flower-wreathed man-made pool that's well stocked with tilapia. Caught with the aid of a customized bamboo pole, your fish can be scaled, seasoned, roasted and served with roast yam or

Christopher Columbus and the Tainos at Seville

The north coast is often referred to as "**Columbus Country**" – and though a little jaded, the title is certainly apt, as the conquistador got his first sight of Jamaica at St Ann's Bay. Sailing into the bay during his second voyage in 1494 to claim new territories on behalf of King Ferdinand and Queen Isabella of Spain, Christopher Columbus was so impressed by its beauty that he named it **Santa Gloria**. He was rather less enamoured during his fourth and final voyage in 1503, when the unsea-worthy state of his worm-eaten, weather-beaten caravels forced him and his crew to spend an unhappy year marooned here in makeshift shacks, awaiting rescue from Spanish compatriots in Hispaniola. Plagued by illness and worried by the partial mutiny of his men, Columbus used a mixture of bribery and superstition (his predic-tion of a solar eclipse led them to believe he was a god) to coerce Taino Indians into providing food for him and his crew. They were eventually rescued in 1504, after a year and a day on the beach.

Columbus died in Spain in 1506, but his son **Diego** was appointed Governor of the Indies. He directed **Juan de Esquivel** to establish the first Spanish colony on the island, **Sevilla Nueva** – today called Seville – in 1510. Situated on the site of the Taino (or Arawak) village of **Maima**, Sevilla Nueva eradicated Jamaica's Indian pop-ulation in fifty years. The *encomienda* system of serf labour – the antithesis of the previously unfettered Taino lifestyle – was introduced and brutally enforced, and Caciques (Taino chiefs) selectively murdered. With their society in tatters and their forms of authority destroyed, the confused Indians were easily branded and enslaved. Along with Africans, who were transported to the island by the Spanish for the purpose, the Tainos were conscripted to build the new city. Less robust than the Africans, the Amerindians were unable to bear a life of slavery; ill-treatment and European diseases soon eradicated those who didn't commit suicide. But while the Tainos expired, New Seville rapidly developed into a sizeable town, with churches, castles, irrigation and drainage sites and a wharf. However, its occupation lasted only until 1534, when the marshy, disease-inducing environment was abandoned in favour of Villa de la Vega, or Spanish Town (p.118).

rice and peas for just US$4 (order before 10am). The stretch of river next to the pond has several shallow pools ideal for splashing children. Beyond the pond is the largest of the lawns, and past here pathways overhung with enor-mous tropical flowers, tree ferns, philodendrons and sheaves of giant bamboo run parallel to the riverbank. Strategically placed steps lead down to the deep-er pools, but for Cranbrook's best swimming, you'll need to walk half a mile to the **riverhead**, a gorgeous 20ft-wide pool where the river gushes up from the rocks. Overhung with lush greenery, the deep turquoise water is cool, refresh-ing and absolutely clean, having been freshly filtered through the limestone. Sadly Cranbrook's extensive collection of **orchids** is no longer on open dis-play due to their regular theft by visitors; there are plans to create a more secure orchid house on another part of the property.

Accommodation

Though **accommodation** choices are few around St Ann's Bay, staying here has its advantages: you escape the dust and bustle of Ochi while being close enough to enjoy its good points, and you can relax in less restricted surround-ings.

.**Chukka Cove Villas** PO Box 160, Ocho Rios ☎ 913 4851. Luxury two-bedroom villas, each with a/c, full kitchen, living room and large verandah. All are dotted around lush gardens with fruit trees and a mineral pool, and have access to deep-sea swimming and excellent snorkelling. Rates include the services of a cook and maid. Paradise – if you can afford it. ❻

High Hope Estate PO Box 11, St Ann's Bay ☎972 2277, ℱ972 1607, ⓦwww.highhopeestate.com. A ten-minute drive inland from the town up into the hills – phone ahead for directions – this eclectically furnished seven-room hotel is both intimate and luxurious. It offers fantastic views, a pool, gorgeous and extensive gardens, excellent food and free access to a private beach club. Rates include breakfast. ❻

Lion's Rest Circle B Farm, Priory ☎995 3580, ⒺIionsrest@cwjamaica.com. Small, friendly hostel on a working plantation with simple, four-bed dormitory accommodation, a couple of private rooms, a communal kitchen and camping at US$10 per night, per person. ❶

Seacrest Beach Hotel PO Box 324, Priory ☎972 1594, ℱ972 8973, Ⓔseacrestresort@cwjamaica .com. Quiet and friendly Jamaican-run hotel with 24 comfortable rooms, a restaurant and a pool. ❹

Seascape Hotel Priory ☎ & ℱ972 2753. Laid-back budget hotel set in lush gardens at the sea's edge, with simple rooms, comfortable villas and camping. Meals are available and guests may use the communal kitchen. There's a small pool on site. To get there, go down the slip road for the Seacrest Beach Hotel – it's the last property on the right-hand side. ❶ ❸

Eating and entertainment

Patty shops and small **restaurants** line Main Street in St Ann's Bay. *Square One* on Bravo Street is especially good for cheap Jamaican meals or snacks – chicken, patties, callaloo loaf and pastries – while the *Sunshine* restaurant on Main Street serves up cheap beer and steamed fish in a peaceful courtyard set back from the road. Fabulous sit-down meals are served at *The Mug* (☎972 1018), on the coast road opposite the turn-off to St Ann's bay, one of the north coast's best seafood restaurants; Jamaicans come from miles around for the excellent conch, fish, lobster and shrimp, served with sublime bammy, rice or chips. Elsewhere, check out the *Seafood Specialist*, a breezy, enduringly popular eatery just off the road between St Ann's Bay and Priory. It specializes, unsurprisingly, in seafood, and it's some of the best around. The menu offers sublime conch soup, fish tea, fried fish, fish and chips and "crack conch" – marinated, deep-fried pieces of tender meat so named because, like the drug, it keeps you going back for more. Chicken and brown stew are served, too. *Jus' Cheers* jerk centre, on the coast road just west of St Ann's Bay, is a popular jerk joint and a nice place for a drink. On Thursdays the place is crowded with locals from miles around for noisy **karaoke** sessions; they often set up a sound system at weekends, too. For **entertainment**, sound-system dances and stageshows are regularly held at the open-air *Windsor Lawn* in St Ann's Bay (☎972 2940), and occasionally at Fantasy Beach in Priory. Look out for promotional posters at the roadside or listen out on Irie FM.

Just east of St Ann's Bay, Drax Hall is the venue for the huge Easter Monday **kite festival**. The annual event attracts amateur and professional kite flyers from all over the world and draws thousands of spectators; for more information call ☎972 9607.

Runaway Bay and Discovery Bay

Sitting halfway between Ocho Rios and Falmouth, two mini-resorts stretch one into another along the busy coast road. Both are rather uninspiring places, indolent to the point of inertia aside from the constant roar of traffic, with little to offer visitors in the way of natural beauty or manufactured attractions. Both places, though, have attractive public beaches – Discovery Bay's is particularly fine. Dominated by lavish all-inclusives, **Runaway Bay** is the more developed of the two, although beyond the razor-wire fences and Italianate marble lobbies of the resorts, town life is low-key, organized around a small square and a series of basic commercial centres and no-frills rum joints. Even more pacific than its neighbour, the crescent harbour of **Discovery Bay** is dominated by the red-stained sphere of the Kaiser Bauxite plant, with fewer hotels that Runaway Bay but a fantastic public beach. Contrary to popular belief, Discovery Bay does not hold the dubious honour of being the place where Columbus first stepped onto Jamaican shores; that accolade goes to Rio Bueno a few miles down the road.

Theories abound as to the **naming** of the twin bays. While it's usually assumed that the "runaways" were Spanish troops fleeing the strong arm of the British in the late seventeenth century, it's more likely that the name refers to Africans who made the risky ninety-mile canoe trip to Cuba and freedom from slavery. Survivors were baptized into Catholicism, and calls for their return were denied on the grounds that Catholics couldn't be expected to live among sectarians.

Arrival and getting around

As both communities spread out from the coast road, getting lost is practically impossible. Rather confusingly though, the **eastern** end of Runaway Bay is actually known as **Salem** to the locals and continues as such for a mile or so before blending seamlessly into **Runaway Bay** proper, which is marked by a post office, small square and the inland road to Browns Town. Most things you'll want to do are within walking distance, but you may find it easier to jump in a shared taxi for the ride to lovely Puerto Seco beach in **Discovery Bay**, which is several nondescript miles to the west; these taxis run constantly along the coast road. **Buses** from Montego Bay and Ocho Rios arrive and depart from points all along the main road through Runaway Bay, and from the A1/B3 intersection in Discovery Bay. Regular **taxis** are available from any of the larger hotels, while shared taxis shuttle constantly between Discovery Bay, Runaway Bay and Ochi. **Car rental** is available from Caribbean Car Rentals in Runaway Bay (☏973 3539) or from Salem Car Rental, in (of course) Salem (☏973 4167, ⓦwww.salemcarrentals.com). Petrol stations are located on the main A1 road, opposite Cardiff Hall beach in Runaway Bay and Puerto Seco beach in Discovery Bay.

Accommodation

All-inclusives dominate the bays, notably two Superclubs (ⓦwww.superclubs) resorts: *Breezes* which has every facility possible including its own eighteen-hole golf course, and *Hedonism III,* the second branch of the infamously "adult" resort, with a nude beach and an intentionally risque ambiance. The *Franklyn D Resort* (ⓦwww.fdrfamily.com) is specifically family-orientated, with around-the-clock childcare on offer. Otherwise there is a marked lack of attractive **hotels** and **guesthouses** in Discovery and Runaway bays, though rates in both places are a little more competitive than rates in Ocho Rios. There are, however, lots of luxury **villas** in the area, which can be cost-effective for large groups – a four-bedroom place rents from around US$2000 per week. For further information, contact JAVA (☏974 2508, ☏974 2967, ⓦwww.villasinjamaica.com). *Sunflower Resort* has some reasonably priced villas in the hills above Runaway Bay; *Cindy Villa* (☏973 2584) is a comfortable four-bedroom house with a pool, maid and gardener. The three- and four-bedroom villas operated by *Portside Villas* (see opposite page) are more luxurious, with pools, all mod cons and fabulous views of Discovery Bay from their hilltop perches.

Accommodationer Discovery Bay ☎973 2559. Friendly, low-key Jamaican guesthouse close to the post office. The homely rooms have hot water and huge beds; guests may use the communal kitchen. ②

Caribbean Isle Hotel PO Box 119, Runaway Bay ☎973 2364, ℱ974 1706. Quiet, friendly resort between the bays and close to the Green Grotto, with its own beach, pool and restaurant. ④

Goldflower Apartments Salem ☎973 6814. Cosy self-catering apartments with kitchenettes, centred around a swimming pool, garden and small, German-owned bar. In front of the Sunflower resort. ③

Hampton View Runaway Bay ☎973 4337. Self-catering apartments in a characteristic Jamaican abode on Hampton Road – not flash, but comfortable and homely, with kitchen and shared verandah. ②

House Erabo Runaway Bay ☎973 4813, ℮erabo@anngel.com.jm. Attractive and spotless three-bedroom house on the western edge of town. All rooms are en suite and can be rented separately. Steps lead down to a small private beach. ②

Piper's Cove Runaway Bay ☎973 7156, ℱ973 7714, ℮daisy@wtjam.net. Newly-built complex of one-bedroom apartments in a prettily landscaped garden next to Hedonism III. Each unit is attractively decorated with rattan fittings, fully equipped kitchen, living room, a/c, fans, cable TV and balcony. The property offers a pool and access to the sea, but no beach. Meals are available. ④

Portside Villas and Apartments PO Box 42, Discovery Bay ☎973 2007 or 3135, ℱ973 2720, ℮portsidevillas@hotmail.com. Characterful, popular complex of rooms, studios and one- to three-bedroom apartments that straddles the main road. Some rooms overlook the sea and all have kitchenette, a/c and satellite TV. There are two pools, a jacuzzi, tennis court, a bar and restaurant and a small beach with watersports equipment. ④

Reef Wind Villa Runaway Bay ☎973 7737. Large grand villa next to the Sunflower resort, with three spacious bedrooms, a swimming pool and well-manicured lawns. Individual rooms or the entire villa (US$120 per night) may be rented. Rooms ③, villa ⑥

Runaway Bay HEART Hotel, Cardiff Hall, Runaway Bay ☎973 6671, ℱ973 2693, ⓦwww.runawayheart.com. Outstanding service at reasonable rates in a government-sponsored hotel training school. Highlights include immaculate gardens overlooking the golf course, a great patio restaurant, a pool, daily beach shuttle and good rooms with balcony, a/c, cable TV and phone. ④

Sunflower PO Box 150, Salem, Runaway Bay ☎973 4809–10, ℱ973 4650, ℮sunflowervi@anngel.com. Inexpensive, friendly and popular with Europeans, the one- to three-bedroom apartments on this sprawling complex have kitchenettes, fan and balcony; a/c is on request. There's a pool and a shuttle to the beach. All-inclusive meal plans are available. ③

Tamarind Tree PO Box 235, Runaway Bay ☎973 4819 or 4106–7, ℱ973 5013. One of the few remaining "old school" hotels in the area, this place is struggling to keep up with the all-inclusives. It offers a quiet, friendly atmosphere, restaurant, large pool and a choice between rooms and three-bed cottages. Not far from some public beaches. ④

Village Resort Suites Salem, Runaway Bay ☎973 6368 or 973 2156 after 6pm. Between the Salem Car Rental outlet and the H&H shopping plaza, this small building has seven clean, comfortable self-catering apartments with a/c and TV, attractive cane furniture and white tiled floors. ③

Villa Rose Runaway Bay ☎973 3216. Basic, clean rooms in a building behind the owner's bar on the west side of town. Each has a large bathroom, ceiling fan, fridge and TV (you pay $5 extra for a set hooked up to cable); all overlook a small slip of beach. Be warned that rooms are often rented by the hour. ①

Runaway Bay

Little more than a roadside strip, **RUNAWAY BAY** stretches lazily along the coast for three miles or so, a sun-bleached and lackadaisical melee of bars and hotels running from the satellite community of **SALEM** to the east, where you'll find the majority of shops and restaurants. The **all-inclusive hotels**, which have fenced in the best stretches of beach, are spread throughout the town, although all you'll see of them from the main road are high walls and large patrolled gates. Runaway Bay is not a resort on the scale of Ocho Rios or Montego Bay, and as most holiday business takes place inside the all-inclusives, the place appears pretty somnolent and easy-going.

Other than the flurry of activity as buses come to a honking halt and vendors hawk their piles of cane and fruit around the open space in front of the post office, there is little going on in town. For swimming, sugary-sanded **Cardiff Hall public beach**, opposite the Texaco petrol station, is popular with locals, who congregate under the tree for dominoes and a beer. The **fisherman's beach**, at the Salem end of town, is less pristine but full of atmosphere – at weekends deafening sound systems sometimes set up on the narrow strip of sand. If you're a golfer, you may want to check out the lavish Superclubs **golf course** opposite *Breezes* (☎973 2436; US$35 greens fee for eighteen holes), which is open to non-guests; there's also a restaurant, bar and clubhouse on site.

For those in self-catering accommodation there are several **supermarkets** in the area. The best stocked are Taylor's, in the small square by the post office, and L & M Meats, by the *Sunflower* resort in Salem, which has a takeaway deli counter; both have Scotiabank **ATMs**. Northern Laundromat at Northern Plaza, Salem (daily 7am–11pm; ☎973 7365), has self-service machines and a pick-up and delivery service. Should you need a **doctor**, Patrick Wheate has a surgery in the H&H shopping plaza (Mon–Sat 10am–6pm, Sunday 12–5pm with appointments; ☎973 7587). Johnny's **pharmacy** is next door and opens daily (Mon–Sat 9am–6pm, Sundays 2–6pm).

Midway between the two bays are the **Green Grotto and Runaway Caves** (daily 9am–4pm), the area's sole managed attraction, once privately owned but now in the hands of government body, the UDC. So far grandiose plans to develop the site by adding a nature park with fishing and canoeing facilities haven't materialized. The only discernible upgrade is the entrance fee, which is now a whopping US$20 per person for the 45-minute guided tour (although locals pay only US$1).

The limestone caves may have been used as a hideout by fleeing Spanish troops and possibly as a Taino place of worship. They're expansive and well lit,

Plantation culture and the story of sugar

When the British took control of Jamaica in 1655, they found three ramshackle **sugarcane plantations** recently deserted by the Spaniards, who had brought the plant to the island from southeast Asia but failed to develop it. A hundred years later, there were well over four hundred plantations on the island. Having already established successful plantations in Barbados, the British were eager to transform Jamaica into a giant sugar-producing factory, offering thirty acres of land to any Englishman settling on the island. Hundreds took up the offer and the commercial cultivation of sugarcane began in earnest. Small concerns were quickly bought out, and by the early eighteenth century, huge plantations covered practically all of Jamaica's most fertile land, with African slaves shipped in to do the dirty work and absentee owners reaping tremendous profits.

By the mid-eighteenth century, tax and trade incentives made Jamaica the largest sugar producer in the world and the richest of England's colonies. The planters celebrated their wealth by building the lavish **great houses** that still overlook cane flats from breezy hilltop perches. However, the abolition of the slave trade in 1834 and full emancipation in 1838 left a labour gap and marked the decline of the sugar trade. The Sugar Equalization Act of 1846 ended preferential treatment for sugar produced in the colonies, and despite the influx of indentured workers from Africa, India and Europe, the industry could no longer compete with cheaper sugar produced in Cuba and Brazil. Nonetheless, the sugar industry is still Jamaica's single largest employer today and accounts for nearly twelve percent of its overall exports. But poor rates of pay make industrial action a regular occurrence, and inadequate technological advancement has seen a slide in productivity.

Watersports in Discovery and Runaway bays

There are more than twenty luxuriantly lively **dive sites** in the area, including sunken ganja planes and a Mercedes car. All are visited on dives run by the Jamaqua dive shops at all-inclusive resorts *Club Ambiance* and *Club Caribbean* (℡973 4845, ⓦwww.jamaqua.com). Jamaqua rents equipment and offers "taster dives", PADI certification courses and guided night and day dives. They also operate Discover Snorkelling tours (2hr 30min; US$35). Other reliable scuba operators in the area are Resort Divers (℡974 5338 ⓦwww.resortdivers.com) and Reef Divers (℡973 4400, ⓔreefdivers@pagescape.com). If you're a watersports fan, the *Sunflower* resort has an all-inclusive package that costs US$499 per week and includes all meals and drinks, one dive per day, and other water activities such as boat rides and snorkelling trips.

with a crystal-clear underwater lake 120 feet below sea level. Until fairly recently the grotto was used as a nightclub. It may have been wonderfully atmospheric but a surfeit of gyrating people badly damaged the cavern's delicate limestone formations, fortunately now starting to grow back. Gone also is the small boat that used to ferry visitors into the middle of the lake at the heart of the site; it too was deemed destructive to the place's unique and fragile ecosystem. The guides are properly trained and informative, however, and they work hard at injecting plenty of humour into their tours, pointing out bats and vaguely discernible animal shapes in the rock formations as they relate a little of the cavern's history.

Discovery Bay

DISCOVERY BAY is more a coastal clutch of shops, snack bars and houses than a town. The **bauxite industry** is very visible here – the orange-stained wharf and dome-shaped storage chamber are even attractive in their immense ugliness. Jamaica exports more than two million tons of "red gold" to US refineries annually, much of it from the plant at Discovery Bay. Local big cheese Kaiser Bauxite pays its dues by financing all sorts of community projects, even sponsoring the pushcart derby held every August on the cricket pitch behind the plant (a good laugh if you're around). The plant is also notable for acting as "Crab Cay," the fictional base of Dr Julius No, in the first of the James Bond movies.

A Texaco gas station and its surrounding shopping complex is the main focus of Discovery Bay. Bang opposite, **Puerto Seco beach** (daily 9am–5pm; J$150) is the best swimming spot in the bay that's not attached to a hotel. The name is derived from the old Spanish title meaning "dry harbour" in reference to Columbus's reluctance to land in a bay with no fresh water (see p.220). Despite gleaming sand, crystal-clear water and a gently shelving shoreline that's good for children, it's relatively deserted on weekdays. There are full facilities and a good snack bar. The adjacent **Discovery Bay beach**, east down a rutted dirt track and separated from Puerto Seco by a fence, is free but has no facilities and is in need of a bit of a cleanup. Past here, the eastern curve of Discovery Bay's horseshoe is dominated by luxurious villas owned by the likes of Jamaican entrepreneur Gordon "Butch" Stewart, owner of Air Jamaica and the Sandals resort chain. On the opposite outcrop, the University of the West Indies Marine Research Laboratory (℡973 2241) houses the island's only **decompression chamber**.

The broken-down structure as you round the bay is **Quadrant Wharf**, built in 1777 by the British, fearful of possible French attack; its cannons have long since disappeared, and only the basic stone structure and some rusting ironware remain. **Columbus Park** (daily 9am–5pm; free), on the western curve of the bay, is a slick, well-signposted, yet rather dull open-air museum exploiting the local Columbus link. The colonial-era artefacts include a water wheel and cannon, and there's an expensive craft market on site. The needle-straight stretch of road beyond Columbus Park was used as an **illegal airstrip** by ganja exporters in the 1970s. In the still of the night, they'd set up impromptu roadblocks, land their small planes and load bales of ganja aboard with the motor still running. The government finally wised up and installed concrete bollards at the roadside, smashing the planes' wings and putting a halt to proceedings on this part of the road at least.

There is a large **supermarket** in Discovery Bay, in Columbus Plaza behind the Texaco petrol station, It's open daily, including Sundays, from 7am to 10pm, and has a pharmacy on site.

Eating

The bays' fancy **restaurants** are predominantly within hotels, and as most are all-inclusive you have to buy an expensive day or evening pass to eat there. However, there are several Jamaican eateries serving hearty fare at attractive prices, and you can buy cheap and delicious soup, jerk, fried fish and bammy or chicken and rice at any of the roadside stalls that set up along the main road in Runaway Bay. Particularly good fresh fish is served up at several joints on the fisherman's beach in Salem. Patties, coconut bread and pastries are available from *Bayside Pastries* near the Post Office in Runaway Bay, and from *Spicy Nice*, beside the gas station in Discovery Bay.

Blue Pearl Runaway Bay. Good old-fashioned Jamaican restaurant in clifftop garden, with steps down to the sea. Open for lunch and dinner and offering all the local staples, from curried goat to fried chicken.

Cardiff Hall Restaurant *Runaway HEART* hotel. Reliable Jamaican and international cuisine and wonderful service at the formal in-house restaurant of this hotel training school.

Cozy Dee's Browns Town Rd, Runaway Bay. Friendly local bar with some tables set outside in a shady garden. Delicious conch soup, stewed fish and chicken.

Mackie's Bar and Jerk Centre Off the A1 between the bays. Open-air circular bar and restaurant serving good, cheap jerk chicken and pork.

Nana Kofi Cardiff Hall Blvd, Runaway Bay. Set back from the main road, this well-signposted vegetarian restaurant and health-food store cooks up succulent and imaginative wholefood fare, from cornmeal porridge to soups and vegetable stews served with brown rice and peas, as well as great soya, vegetable and corn patties and delicious cakes. Closed Sun.

Northern Jerk and Steak Pit Northern Plaza, Salem. Super-efficient shiny-countered indoor jerk house, with a selection of soups and a confectionery counter for late-night munchies. Open daily till midnight.

The Rising Sun Runaway Bay. Reliable Swiss-run bistro opposite Cardiff Hall beach, serving salads, sandwiches, burgers, pizza, seafood, chicken, steaks and Swiss specialities.

Seafood Giant Runaway Bay. Breezy dining area under an open-sided thatched roof, with a couple of rope swings for kids to play on. The menu offers stuffed baked crab backs, shrimp, fish, lobster and conch cooked in every imaginable style. The seafood can be a little greasy, but it's mostly passable; the conch or fish soup is the highlight.

Sea Shanty *Portside Villas*, Discovery Bay. In An attractive, semi-open-air setting on the waterfront, it serves imaginative, varied meals: solid local and "international" breakfasts; lunchtime salads, burgers, sandwiches and a great fish chowder; dinners such as fettuccine Alfredo, steamed fish and okra and Jamaican staples.

Tek it Eazy Runaway Bay. Unassuming rooftop restaurant and bar serving inexpensive Jamaican food alongside the rum and beer.

Ultimate Jerk Centre On the A1 opposite Green Grotto. Lively and popular, this roadside jerk centre serves up spicy and delicious helpings of pork, chicken and sausage. Tables are scattered across the grounds, and it's usually open until at least 1am.

Drinking and entertainment

There are several **bars** at the Salem end of Runaway Bay, many of which serve as go-go clubs these days; with plenty of rude, semi-naked gyrating, these places are not for the faint-hearted. Of these, the *19th Hole Club* is popular and also has a pool table; *Classique Nite Spot* in Discovery Bay is equally well patronized. Also in Discovery Bay, by the bauxite plant, *Nancy's*, a breezy open-air shack is a nice local joint. At Runaway Bay, the suitably named rooftop bar *Tek it Eazy* has piped music most nights, **karaoke** every Tuesday and occasional live music at the weekends. Don't bother with the seafood at *Seafood Giant* at the far western end of Runaway Bay – it's far better for a leisurely drink under the huge circular thatched roof, and there's a reggae "party" each Wednesday and Saturday with special deals on lobster between 6 and 9pm. The seafront *Sea Shanty* bar, at *Portside Villas* in Discovery Bay, is also an appealing place for a few drinks. Midway between the bays and opposite the Green Grotto cave, the *Ultimate Jerk Centre* is good for a purely Jamaican night out, with plenty of white-rum drinking and oldies on the stereo.

As most people head into Ocho Rios for their nightlife, the twin bays are not exactly jumping at night, though occasional live shows and sound-system dances are advertised on roadside billboards. Most of the **entertainment** is centred on the all-inclusives. Non-guests can buy an evening pass (US$45–75), which covers dinner, drinks, some kind of floor show and access to the disco – *Breezes* and *Club Ambiance* are particularly lively, while *Hedonism* offers especially raunchy fun. The *Seaview Bar and Club* in Discovery Bay hosts occasional weekend sound systems, as does the *Cutting Edge Entertainment Centre* on the Salem fisherman's beach. Finally, if you're around in August, look out for posters advertising Kaiser Bauxite's **Family Fun Days**, an uproarious blend of children's activities, push-cart racing, live music, sound systems and amateur comedy/cabaret.

Brown's Town

High in the hills above the twin bays, bustling **BROWN'S TOWN** hums with the dynamism and industry absent from the coast below. Reached on the B3 from Runaway Bay, Brown's Town is a sizeable inland community with fantastic views and a booming central **market**. The stalls that line the main road overflow with fresh produce – six-foot pillars of sugarcane, yams and dasheens caked in red alluvial earth, and oranges tied into strings of ten – ferried in by small-scale farmers and sold by formidable-looking female higglers. The main market days are Wednesday, Friday and Saturday. The food sold here is much better than that which can be bought on the coast – quality improves once you near the source, and people are too busy to bother about ripping you off. Bootleg name-brand clothing and tawdry knick-knacks also sell by the bucketload – this is *the* place for china figurines and fake flower displays. Even the proper shops are worthy of a root – Charley & Son on Main Street is a treasure-trove of ancient books with yellowing covers, tacky postcards and intriguing miscellany.

The **restaurants** and **bars** along Main Street are good for plates of steaming Jamaican food or a few white rums; *Colbys*, a small hexagonal hut north of the market, is friendly and has a range of delicious natural juices. If you want to **stay** and soak up the atmosphere, try the basic but comfortable rooms at *Meditation Heights* (☎975 9180; ❶), which is situated at the top edge of town – take a signed left fork beside the Cool Oasis petrol station. Buses from Runaway Bay arrive two or three times a day; taxis are much more convenient.

Marley's mausoleum and the St Ann interior

Both the B3 from Runaway Bay and the inland road from Discovery Bay lead toward **ALEXANDRIA**, a tiny hamlet where you turn left for the only tourist attraction in the St Ann interior, Bob Marley's Mausoleum, at his former home of **NINE MILE**. Though the scenery here is stunning – the red-earthed pastures, distant Cockpits and sweeping hills and gullies of the Dry Harbour mountains are a photographer's dream – there are few specific points of interest, and the viciously potholed road will demand most of your attention. You'll need to have your own transport or charter a taxi to get here; a round trip in a taxi from Runaway/Discovery bays or Ochi should cost around US$100 – but bargain as you may be able to haggle down the rate. Alternatively, you could sign up for the entertaining *Zion Bus Line* trip (US$65;

Bob Marley – King of Reggae

The legacy of the original ambassador of reggae is impossible to overemphasize. Jamaicans tend to regard their most famous compatriot with an emotional and religious reverence, and his lyrics continue to strike a chord across every social stratum. Born February 6, 1945, **Robert Nesta Marley** was the progeny of an affair between 17-year-old Cedella Malcolm and 51-year-old Anglo-Jamaican soldier Captain Norval Marley, stationed in the Dry Harbour mountains as overseer of crown lands. Marley's early years in the country, surrounded by a doting extended family (particularly his grandfather and formidable "myalman" Omeriah Malcolm) and by the rituals and traditions of rural life, had a profound effect on his development. Unlike most Jamaicans of mixed parentage, Marley clung to the African side of his heritage and revelled in the solidarity, freedom and rich cultural life of downtown Kingston, where he spent most of his later life. Marley was known as an intensely spiritual individual, emanating an almost-tangible energy and charisma. He was also a lover as well as a thinker: Although his 1966 marriage to **Rita Anderson** lasted until he died, his appetite for women was great and he fathered eleven children by various women. Appropriately enough, his 1970s' membership of the influential Twelve Tribes Of Israel – a Rastafarian sect that divides members by birth month into "houses" with a name and a colour – gave him the name Joseph, "a fruitful bough" according to the Bible.

Fusing African drumming traditions with Jamaican rhythms and American rock guitar, Marley's music became a symbol of unity and social change worldwide. Between 1961 and 1981, his output was prolific. Following their first recording, *Judge Not,* on Leslie Kong's Beverley's label, Marley's band, The Wailers (Marley, Bunny Livingstone and Peter Tosh), went on to record for some of the best producers in the business – Joe Higgs, Clement "Coxsone" Dodd, Clancey Eccles and Bunny Lee. Most agree, however, that their finest material was recorded in collaboration with innovative and volatile musical genius Lee "Scratch" Perry. In 1963, the huge hit *Simmer Down*, a warning to Kingstonians to cool down the increasing tension, meshed perfectly with the post-independence frustration felt by young Jamaicans, and the group's momentum of success began in earnest. The Wailers' lyrics providing a script for the island's development from rude boy to Rasta (see "Music" in *Contexts*, p.413). International recognition came when the Wailers signed to the Island label – owned by Anglo-Jamaican entrepreneur Chris Blackwell, who Marley saw as his "interpreter" rather than his producer. The first Island release was *Catch a Fire* in early 1973, and the eleven albums that followed all became instant classics. With the help of Blackwell's marketing skills, reggae became an interna-

5hr with pick-up, drinks and lunch included) organized by Chukka Cove Adventure Tours (℡972 2506, ⓦwww.chukkacove.com). The excursion takes you to Nine Mile in a brightly decorated vehicle designed to look like a Jamaican country bus, with a pumping reggae-based soundtrack and guides dressed in Marley-style khaki fatigues and football socks.

Along the way, small communities such as **CLARKS TOWN** bear the names of European estate keepers and missionaries, and history is everywhere in a landscape strewn with the crumbling chimneys of unidentifiable sugar factories and stone churches built by Baptist missionaries. From Alexandria, the narrow road off the B3 to the **Bob Marley Centre and Mausoleum** (daily 8am–8pm; US$12; ℡995 1763, ⓦwww.bobmarleymovement.com) winds through the hills past **Alva** and **Ballintoy**. You know you're in Nine Mile when you see the red-gold-and-green flags flying high above a fenced-off compound stretching up a hillock to the side of the main road. If you're driving, you'll be directed into the compound car park, from where you proceed

tional genre. Differences with Blackwell – particularly over his obvious concentration on Marley – led to the departure of Livingstone and Tosh in 1974, but the group continued to tour the world with new musicians and a new name – Bob Marley and the Wailers.

Inevitably, the socially aware Marley became embroiled in the factionalized and violent confusion of Jamaican politics. In the run-up to a headline performance at the 1976 Smile Jamaica concert – staged by the government to quell rising tensions in an election campaign so dogged by violence that Prime Minister Michael Manley declared a state of emergency – gunmen burst into Marley's Kingston home and tried to **assassinate** him. The attempt was bungled, and most of the shots hit manager Don Taylor (who made a full recovery), though Bob and Rita incurred minor injuries. Undeterred, a bandaged Marley went on stage under heavy security. After the concert, Marley left Jamaica to recover and record in Britain and the United States, but as his international reputation grew, so did his popularity at home, and Jamaicans began to embrace fully their home-grown megastar. Two years later, Marley returned to the island for the first time since the shooting to perform at the historic **One Love Peace Concert**, the result of an unprecedented – and short-lived – truce between the political garrisons of the PNP and JLP. He was the headline act of a line-up that also included Peter Tosh singing solo and spitting vitriol at the politicians, and Marley ended his performance by enticing arch-enemies Michael Manley and Edward Seaga on stage to join hands in a show of unity – a huge coup. But Marley's call for unity and freedom was not restricted to Jamaica; one of his greatest triumphs was performing the protest anthem *Zimbabwe* at the independence celebrations of the former Rhodesia, the last African country to free itself from colonial rule.

In the midst of a rigorous 1980 tour, Marley was diagnosed as suffering from cancer, and despite treatments at an alternative clinic in Austria, he died a year later in Miami, honoured by his country with the Order of Merit. The Honourable Robert Nesta Marley OM died without making a will, and years of costly legal wrangles over his US$46 million estate ensued, with his widow eventually granted the lion's share. Rita Marley's Bob Marley Foundation continues to sponsor the development of new Jamaican artists, and many of the Marley children have forged their own musical careers: Ziggy, Cedella and Sharon have found success abroad as the Melody Makers; Junior Gong, his son by 1976 Miss World Cindy Breakespeare, is a respected DJ; and another son, the US-based Kymani, is fast becoming a national heart-throb. But in the hearts of Jamaicans, the master's voice can never be equalled.

directly to the ticket office, where all visitors must sign in. There's also a vegetarian restaurant here, as well as a small gift shop selling tapes and Marley memorabilia. Once you've paid your fee, you're assigned to one of the throng of Rasta guides and are taken up the hill and into the centre proper. There's a prayer space to the left at the first plateau, sometimes occupied by orthodox Rastafarians who come to worship and hold "reasoning" sessions. To the right is the wooden shack that Marley lived in between the ages of six and thirteen, complete with the "original" single bed he sang of in *Is This Love*. Opposite is an outdoor barbecue where Marley cooked up Ital feasts during rural retreats at the height of his career, and the Rasta-coloured "meditation stone" where he rested his head for contemplation with a marvellous view, immortalized in the song *Talkin' Blues*. You leave cameras and shoes outside before entering the **mausoleum**, a concrete building painted with Rasta colours and depictions of black angels that encases the marble slab that holds Marley's remains. A stained-glass window filters red, gold and green sunlight over the stone, while candles, incense, fresh flowers and scribbled tributes make the mausoleum one of the more uplifting aspects of a place that in celebrating Marley's death seems only to succeed in highlighting the yawning gap left by his passing. Many Rastafarians – who eschew the concept of physical death – argue that Nine Mile is not his final resting place and that, like Haile Selassie, Bob Marley's bones will never be found.

In some ways, the centre is a bit of a disappointment, particularly if you're expecting some kind of theme-park ambience; there's also an undercurrent of hustle to the whole thing (you'll doubtless be offered overpriced ganja). Nothing can detract from the beauty of the locale though, the home of the original "Natural Mystic".

If you want to linger in Nine Mile, you can stay in the relatively basic **hotel** opposite the complex, run by extended members of the Marley family; rooms cost around US$50 and you can have meals cooked for you or use the kitchen yourself. Campers with their own tents can pitch them for free in the complex. Otherwise, the place comes alive every **February 6**, when Marley's birthday is celebrated with a jump-up and sometimes a live show featuring the Melody Makers. For details contact the Bob Marley Foundation in Kingston (☎978 2991) or simply turn up on the day (see also *Basics*, p.`47).

Rio Bueno to Duncans

A Spanish-built stone bridge marks the St Ann–Trelawny border and the entrance to **RIO BUENO**. It's a destitute-looking village of crumbling eighteenth-century buildings, too many skinny dogs and a peeling police station, all cowering in the shadow of a towering silver animal-feed factory – fortuitously absent when the town was used as a set for *A High Wind in Jamaica*. Yet despite its unprepossessing appearance, the town has a place in the history books. Having spent a night anchored off St Ann's Bay during his so-called discovery of the island in 1494, **Christopher Columbus** sailed west along the coast seeking a bay to land and find fresh water. With its rapidly running river and horseshoe dimensions, Rio Bueno is popularly agreed to be the "crescent harbour" he decided upon and recorded in his diary account. Columbus made a lucky choice – despite its diminutive size, the bay is one of Jamaica's deepest harbours.

The town today is nothing to write home about, though the British presence is evident in a ruined **fort**, named after Henry Dundas, British secretary of war, and dating back to 1778, and the neat, blue- and white-painted **St Mark's**

Anglican Church, built at the sea's edge by the British in 1833. The original **Baptist church** was burnt to the ground in that same year by hostile Anglicans – the present incarnation on the hill above town was erected in 1901.

The town fell into decline following the abolition of slavery, though there are proposals for its development as a heritage site. Until this comes to fruition, the only reason to linger is to peruse the collection at Gallery Joe James, an **art gallery** set in a seventeenth-century warehouse on the western fringes of town. The gallery also serves as a hotel, restaurant and the studio of James himself, a well-known Jamaican artist who has lived in Rio Bueno for some years. Pieces on display – by both James and other local luminaries – include paintings, masks and a stunning cedar Medusa, a carved sculpture with flowing locks of men and snakes. An on-site museum with a collection of African arts and crafts is planned, and the knowledgeable Mr James is usually on hand to explain the work, most of which is for sale.

If you're after more pastoral delights, head for a swim in the rapidly running **Rio Bueno** – the best spot for a dip is at the **Dornoch Riverhead pool**, a deep, cliff-edged swimming hole surrounded by silk cotton trees and throngs of mosquitoes. It's reached from Discovery Bay via the B10 through Queenhythe and Rising Sun, but it's hidden from the road and you'll probably need local help to pinpoint it. Baptist missionary and anti-slavery activist William Knibb used to baptize converts here, and a spiritual, slightly spooky ambience lingers.

Practicalities

Although there is no earthly reason to **stay** in Rio Bueno, a vast all-inclusive has seen fit to open two miles down the road. *Grand Lido Braco*, Rio Bueno PO, Trelawny (☎954 0000, ℱ954 0020, ⓦwww.superclubs.com; ◎) is a sprawling complex that strives to recreate a "real" Jamaican town – it even has its own town square (though obviously minus the traffic, goats and dirt) and extensive facilities. In Rio Bueno proper, **Gallery Joe James** (☎954 0046, ℱ954 0047; ◎) offers an eclectic selection of atmospheric but overpriced rooms and suites overlooking the sea. Guests and non-guests alike can **eat** at the hotel restaurant, *The Lobster Pot*, where seafood lunches and dinners and solid Sunday brunches (US$12) are served in an open-air dining room right on the water. The breezy indoor bar is an inviting place to sink a few Red Stripes. Just out of town, *Yow's Jerk Centre* sells great jerk, fish, chicken, fish tea, conch soup and very popular breakfasts in an attractive oceanfront setting. Just further on, the *Rio Bueno Travel Halt* (daily 8.30am–5.30pm) has a desultory restaurant, but spotless bathrooms. In between Braco and Duncans, the *Plane Stop* (so-named for the carcass of a crashed ganja-smuggling plane that stands outside) is an open-air jerk centre that serves tasty jerk chicken and pork, with roast yam and saltfish added to the menu at the weekends.

Duncans and the beaches

A peaceful village huddled under the hills of Cockpit Country, **DUNCANS** consists of little more than a supermarket, a few small-scale restaurants and bars, a pharmacy and a clock tower with a timepiece that hasn't worked for more than fifteen years. There's a huge **villa complex** set back from the coast road just east of town, *Silver Sands*, PO Box 1, Duncans (☎954 2001, ℱ954 2630, ⓦwww.silver-sands.com; ◎–◎). The mostly privately-owned holiday homes are decorated in varying styles and degrees of luxury, and the sense of seclusion makes for a fantastic beach experience away from the resorts. Directly opposite, the *Sober Robin* (T & F 954 2202, Esoberrobin@cwjamaica.com; ②) has an eclectic selection of rooms with various combinations of fan, a/c, TV and fridge. The place also features a pool, a restaurant, an ageing jukebox and numerous written reminders that the great Harry Belafonte once lived here – allegedly. Just east out of town and suffering from its isolation, the dirt-cheap, dependable and friendly *Montgomery's Holiday House*, PO Box 36, Duncans PO, Trelawny (T 954 0263; ②) stands alone in a sparsely-developed pasture set back from the main road. The comfortable if spartan rooms are fantastic value, with tiled floors, ceiling fan and hot and cold water.

The **coastline** parallel to Duncans is sublime – powdery white sand and big waves, though as the area is quite sparsely populated, you'll need a car to see the best of it – most buses will flash by full. The best beach is attached to the *Silver Sands* resort, though non-guests can normally use it for a fee; enquire at reception. Wide and windswept, the beach has famously white sand and the swimming is superlative. Alternatively, there's Duncans' **public beach**, basically a facility-free fisherman's beach that's so rocky it's hard to imagine how the boats ever manage to leave the shore. If you don't mind the zero comfort factor, it's a good place to eat fresh fish and soak up the local atmosphere. The turn-off for *Montgomery's Holiday House* marks a series of completely deserted bays – the water is quite shallow with some sea grass, but they're ideal spots for a secluded day by the sea. When you get **hungry**, try the *Prestige Fish Pot* at the roadside in Duncans town or its equally decent neighbour, *Kiki Rouge*, which has a friendly local bar, the *HQ*, attached.

Falmouth and around

Trelawny's capital reflects the history of the parish; at the height of the plantocracy there were 88 **sugar estates** in the region worked by thousands of slaves, and **FALMOUTH** – named for the English birthplace of parish Governor Sir William Trelawny – became the main port of call for sugar ships. Slaves were traded on the wharves and goods for the plantations unloaded while planters snapped up land and built elegant townhouses in Georgian style. In the late eighteenth century, Falmouth boasted more than 150 houses and a cage where the market now stands (akin to the one still standing in Montego Bay's Sam Sharpe Square – see p.258), used for locking up drunken sailors found on the streets later than the 6pm curfew. Though slavery was almost at an end when the town was dedicated as parish capital in 1790, Falmouth's central location and natural harbour ensured Trelawny's prosperity, and the town thrived where others declined, even after emancipation in 1838. However, the advent of the steamship – the first docked at Jamaican shores in 1837 – spelled the first step in the town's declivity. The harbour wasn't deep enough to accommodate these larger vessels, and trade was diverted to bigger harbours. By the 1890s Falmouth became something of a ghost town – the planters and traders had left for Montego Bay or Kingston, and their houses began to rot slowly in the sun and salty air. In 1896, the Albert George Market was built at the edge of the square, and Falmouth instead became Trelawny's main **market town**, a status it still enjoys. Each Wednesday, a bustling "bend down" market spills out onto the streets. Traders set out fruit and veg, bootleg clothing and garish arrays of brightly-coloured plastic fripperies along the pavements, and customers pour in from miles around, causing a day-long traffic jam and a flurry of complaints from those who see the market as a safety hazard.

Falmouth is a somewhat forgotten but nonetheless compelling place these days, entirely unaffected by tourism and rich with architectural interest. The town boasts the highest concentration of **Georgian architecture** in Jamaica – possibly in the whole of the Caribbean – but many buildings are in a terrible state of disrepair. Two-hundred-year-old timbers crumble onto the tarmac, and once majestic buildings serve as dilapidated shelters for chickens and stray dogs – testimony to the decline of the sugar industry and the failure to develop new business. Despite periodic calls for Falmouth to be granted some kind of official protection as a "heritage town", there's been no noticeable effort to capitalize on its historic status so far, and as there are no easy-access managed "attractions", most visitors pass through without a second glance. However, a wander through the streets provides an unadorned – and sometimes chilling – glimpse into Jamaica's past, and the lack of touristic glitz just adds to Falmouth's easy-going charm.

The Town

The town centre retains its original grid formation, neatly bisected by the busy A1, the western continuation of the A3. Most of the activity is centred on **Water Square**, named in allusion to Falmouth's status as the first Jamaican town with access to piped water. The nonfunctioning central fountain marks the spot of a stone reservoir that once held fresh water pumped by water wheel from the Martha Brae River. Though marred by the lurid facade of a furniture

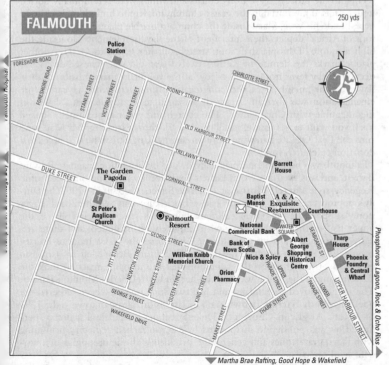

FALMOUTH

0   250 yds

N

Police Station

FORESHORE ROAD

FORESHORE ROAD

STANLEY STREET

VICTORIA STREET

ALBERT STREET

CHARLOTTE STREET

RODNEY STREET

OLD HARBOUR STREET

TRELAWNY STREET

DUKE STREET

The Garden Pagoda

CORNWALL STREET

Barrett House

Baptist Manse

A & A Exquisite Restaurant

Courthouse

St Peter's Anglican Church

Falmouth Resort

GEORGE STREET

National Commercial Bank

WATER SQUARE

Albert George Shopping & Historical Centre

Tharp House

PITT STREET

NEWTON STREET

PRINCESS STREET

William Knibb Memorial Church

Bank of Nova Scotia

Nice & Spicy

SEABOARD ST

Phoenix Foundry & Central Wharf

QUEEN STREET

KING STREET

Orion Pharmacy

UPPER PARADE STREET

GEORGE STREET

WAKEFIELD DRIVE

MARKET STREET

THARP STREET

LOWER PARADE STREET

UPPER HARBOUR STREET

233

Martha Brae Rafting, Good Hope & Wakefield

chain, the square has plenty of character, thanks to the antiquated aspect of the wooden shop-fronts that remain, combined with cane and coconut vendors and crowds of shoppers and people waiting for buses. Buses to Montego Bay and Ocho Rios arrive and depart outside Courts department store.

Some of Falmouth's most impressive constructions – the sagging **Tharp House**, the porticoed **post office** in the middle of Market Street, and the old **courthouse**, built overlooking the sea in 1895 – are still in commercial or municipal use, though badly in need of structural attention. Immediately striking as you enter or leave town to the east is the conical roof of the 1810 **Phoenix Foundry**. It's behind the locked gates of **Central Wharf** – where sugar, rum and slaves were shipped and traded during Falmouth's heyday – along with several dilapidated stone warehouses and the disintegrating remains of plasterboard set dressings from the filming of *The Wide Sargasso Sea*.

The stately **Baptist Manse** on Market Street is thought to have been inhabited by Baptist minister and anti-slavery campaigner **William Knibb**, whose efforts did much to facilitate emancipation. Once ruined, the manse is now being carefully and extensively restored. Slated to be completed by the end of 2003, the renovated structure will house a spacious and light-filled gallery upstairs, with various art-based community projects taking over the ground floor. The chunky **William Knibb Memorial Baptist Church** stands on the corner of King and George streets; it is named for the nonconformist preacher who lobbied for the abolition of slavery. On the momentous date of August 1, 1838, when Africans were given full freedom, crowds gathered outside the church to celebrate and to thank the man who had been so instrumental in the process. Slave irons, collars and whips were ceremonially buried under a raised memorial in the grassy churchyard; Knibb himself is also buried here, beside his wife, Mary. Inside the church, a marble plaque "erected by the sons of Africa" depicts their interment of the slave implements alongside the biblical quote "Ethiopia shall soon stretch out her hands to God". Another plaque marks the demise of Knibb's twelve-year-old son, whose "death was occasioned by fever from excess of joy" at the voluntary manumission of their slaves by the members of the congregation; members who, a year before emancipation was formally granted, managed to conclude that "slavery is incompatible with Christianity". The church and grounds are usually locked up. If you want to get inside, you'll need to ask church treasurer Mr Mac, who runs the Leaf Of Life hardware store on nearby King Street; he'll appreciate a donation to church funds.

Falmouth was built on land originally owned by plantation magnate Edward Barrett, and was even known as Barrett Town for a while. The once beautiful, Regency-style **Barrett House**, at 1 Market Street, was built in 1799. The family's appropriately fine domicile had a brick base and weatherboard upper storey supported by wooden columns. Long in a state of near-collapse, the upper half of the building has now completely disintegrated, and there are, sadly, no immediate plans to restore it. The house also has a tenuous literary connection. Having survived his three sons, Edward Barrett left his Jamaican estates to his daughter on the condition that the man she married took the Barrett name – the house was built by her husband, Charles Moulton Barrett. The family moved to England and had two sons, one of whom fathered the poet **Elizabeth Barrett Browning**. The last historical site in town is the 1791 **St Peter's Anglican Church** on Duke Street. It's a sepulchral structure, perfumed by wax polish and surrounded by a sun-bleached cemetery, brimming with faded gravestones and generously sprinkled with the droppings of a resident herd of goats.

If you're interested in learning more about the Georgian splendours of Falmouth, contact local resident and US ex-pat Jim Parent, who runs a company called Falmouth Historic Renewal Inc, 45 Trelawny St (℡ 617 1060), and takes visitors on well-informed walking tours of the town. The Georgian Society of Jamaica has produced an informative booklet complete with old photos, **Falmouth 1791–1970**. It is available from the society's headquarters, 18 Hillcrest Ave, Kingston 6 (℡ 927 9570).

Out of town

Several more attractions lie immediately outside Falmouth. The most visible is **J. Charles Swaby's Falmouth Swamp Safari** (daily 9am–5pm; US$10; ℡ 954 3065), a somewhat haphazard menagerie on the A3, five minutes' drive west of Falmouth. It belongs to the owners of the Black River Safari Boat Tours (see p.334), and like many small zoos, it's a bit depressing, though it's the only place on the north coast where you can see Jamaican **crocodiles**. Ranging from tiny babies to alarming twelve-footers, the crocodiles look fairly content, and there are various other indigenous animals on display. Incidentally, this is the place where James Bond used crocodile heads as stepping stones in *Live and Let Die*.

Half a mile east of Falmouth at **ROCK**, **Oyster Bay phosphorous lagoon** owes its name to the incandescent illuminations of microorganisms. After dark, the water shines bright green when agitated, and you can see the trails of fish darting about. *Glistening Waters*, a marina and restaurant right on the lagoon (℡ 954 3229), offers night-time boat trips costing US$10 for a twenty-minute jaunt; bring your swimsuit and plunge into the eerie depths. Local Michael Currie (℡ 348 1028) operates a similar trip to the lagoon in his glass-bottom boat, with a more relaxed attitude about how much time you spend in the water, and a reggae soundtrack blasting out. Ask for Currie at *Time 'n' Place,* a lovely laid-back hotel and restaurant (see p.236) set right on a stretch of white-sand beach, with crystal-clear sea, just east of the lagoon. Wide and wild **Burwood public beach** is two hundred yards further east. There are no facilities, but it's clean, with good swimming and snorkelling, and usually completely deserted. For those keen on souvenir shopping, **Bamboo Village** is a rather desultory collection of brightly coloured huts set in a circle at the back of the beach; the goods on offer are standard tourist fare but prices are more reasonable than in Ocho Rios or Montego Bay. If you're interested in a spot of serious fishing, *Glistening Waters* hires out fully equipped fishing boats from US$280 per half day.

Heading inland from Falmouth, a lone road threads from Water Square toward the **Martha Brae River**, Trelawny's longest waterway, notable chiefly for the popular **raft trips** that glide through its waters. If you want to have a go, follow the battered signs from Water Square for about three miles to the put-in point at Rafter's Village (daily 9am–4pm; 1hr 30min; US$42 per two-person raft; ℡ 952 0889, ⓦ www.jamaicarafting.com) which has a small swimming pool and decent gift shop on site. The leisurely trip begins with complimentary rum or fruit punch and takes you past banks overhung with silk cotton and mango trees, and under towering banyans festooned with vines. There are a few craft stalls on the riverbank, some floating bars and a constant mosquito offensive – bring repellent.

The Martha Brae road is also the route to **Good Hope Great House** (see "Accommodation", p.236) – follow the signed turn-off along a muddy and rutted road. The Tharp family home is a Georgian dream house overlooking a

2000-acre working plantation. Built in creamy English stone, beautifully furnished and set in gardens full of flowers and hummingbirds, it's a serene nod to colonial excess. The house is now let as an exclusive villa, so it's only accessible to those who rent it out. However, you can explore the grounds on **horseback**, and the estate offers some of the best riding around (as well as some very well-kept mounts). You go at your own pace, and it's a very different kettle of fish to the staid trail rides of the resorts – if you're lucky, it'll be just you and your guide. A hack (1hr 30min; US$40; call ☎1-610 5798 to book) takes you past original cut-stone estate buildings such as the aqueduct and water wheel – the old sugar-processing room is now used for the packing of Good Hope oranges, ugli fruit and papaya – and then on through citrus and coconut plantations, with a stop at a small waterfall on the Martha Brae where you can take a dip. You'll also pass, housed in one of the estate's picturesque outhouses, the **gallery** and workshop of on-site potter David Pinto, whose beautifully crafted plates, dishes and sculptures are very reasonably priced. In addition to offering locals weekly classes in clay pottery, Pinto holds popular twice-yearly ceramics workshops (see ⓦ www.andersonranch.org for details).

Accommodation

With Montego Bay so near, few people choose to **stay** in and around Falmouth. However, there's a fair spread of accommodation, and the area is certainly a more relaxing place to rest your weary head for a night or two while exploring the town and surrounding attractions. If you're planning on staying for any length of time, Elaine Stevenson (☎617 1213) rents out an eclectically decorated three-bedroom house at 9 King Street – rates are negotiable.

Bodmint Resort Rock ☎954 3551. A range of rooms and villas set in pretty gardens next to the phosphorescent lagoon. Rooms are clean with fan or a/c; the villas have fully equipped kitchens and screened porches. Tasty Jamaican food, baby-sitting and various water-based trips are available. ③

Falmouth Resort 29 Newton St ☎954 3391, Ⓕ954 3195. Managed by English returning residents, this quiet place is the only option in the centre of Falmouth. The small, basic rooms have a/c and TV, and a bar and restaurant are on site. ③

Fisherman's Inn Rock ☎954 3427, Ⓕ954 3078. Right on the phosphorous lagoon, these comfortable but vastly overpriced rooms have a/c, satellite TV and balconies overlooking the lagoon-side pool. Rates include continental breakfast, and there's a restaurant on site. ⑦

Good Hope PO Box 50, Falmouth ☎610 5798, Ⓕ979 8095, ⓦ www.goodhopejamaica.com.

Tastefully restored and utterly classy great house, rented as a private villa with space to sleep seventeen. The furnishings are mostly antique, and there's an unmitigated feel of grandeur about the place. The house overlooks the stunning estate below, itself ringed by the conical hillocks of Cockpit Country and best seen when the mists roll away at dawn. The estate also rents out an equally gorgeous three-bedroom cottage, right by a scenic river pool fringed by bamboo, for US$2900 per week in low season, US$4500 in high, including staff and all meals. ⑧++

Time 'n' Place PO Box 93, Falmouth ☎ & Ⓕ954 4371; ⓦ www.timenplace.com. Easily the most inviting choice in the area, just off the main road five minutes' drive east of Falmouth. It features Thai-style stilted wooden cabins right on a beautiful white-sand beach, with porches, a/c, and satellite TV; those with pull-out futons are good for families. The bar and restaurant are steps away, and the atmosphere is extremely friendly. ④

Eating and drinking

For **snacks**, try *Nice and Spicy* on Water Square, which sells pastries and patties. There are loads of **restaurants** around town – recommended is the *A&A Exquisite Restaurant* on Thorpe Street, which is clean and homely and serves tasty Jamaican and vegetarian food. There's also a decent Chinese restaurant, the

Golden Pagoda, on Duke Street. In Rock, the *Guango Tree* is set back from the main road in its own large lawn; it's run by charming, chatty Miss Annie and her daughter, who serve up delicious Jamaican food and fresh natural juices at budget prices. Also east of Falmouth, the fabulous beachside café/bar *Time 'n' Place* is the perfect place to hang out, despite the ugly resort that's sprung up on the doorstep. The food ranges from tasty burgers and fries to jerk chicken, steak, fish, key lime pie and fruit smoothies laced with rum. There are also hammocks, great swimming and snorkelling, boat trips on the phosphorous lagoon, domino tournaments and occasional parties. A little further east, the presence of the sprawling *Starfish Trelawny* all-inclusive has spawned a couple of eateries. Directly opposite the resort, the *Country Club* cooks up inexpensive Jamaican lunches and dinners but is better known as a hard-core **drinking** den with late opening hours and occasional **live music**. The nearby *Ponderosa* has tasty Jamaican and Chinese food.

Travel details

Other than the Air Jamaica Express (℡ 923 6664) internal flights to Boscobel Aerodrome near Ocho Rios, the only public transport along the coast is the haphazard bus system. Coasters, minibuses and the occasional old-style country bus ply the road between around 6am and 7pm, with a reduced service on Sundays, and little or nothing after 5pm. There are so many buses shooting along this stretch of the coast that we haven't put frequencies below – but you shouldn't have to wait any longer than thirty minutes for a bus; for pick-up points see relevant areas in this book. The interior is a different matter entirely; areas that are covered have only one daily service, usually departing at the crack of dawn and returning to base in the early evening.

Buses

Falmouth to: Duncans (20min); Montego Bay (30min); Ocho Rios (1hr 15min); Runaway Bay/Discovery Bay (40min); St Ann's Bay (55min).

Ocho Rios to: Duncans (55min); Falmouth (1hr 15min); Kingston (2hr); Montego Bay (1hr 45min); Oracabessa (30min); Port Maria (45min); Runaway Bay/Discovery Bay (30min); St Ann's Bay (20min).

Runaway Bay/Discovery Bay to: Brown's Town (30min); Duncans (20min); Montego Bay (1hr 15min); St Ann's Bay (20min).

Flights

Ocho Rios (Boscobel) to: Kingston (3 daily; 15min); Montego Bay (3 daily; 25min); Negril (2 daily; 35min); Port Antonio (3 daily; 15min).

Montego Bay and Cockpit Country

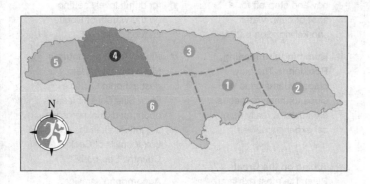

CHAPTER 4

Highlights

✳ **Doctor's Cave Beach**
Powdery white sand and
gin-clear waters make
this the ultimate place to
take a dip in the warm
Caribbean. See p.256

✳ **Boat trip** Jump on one
of the many party cata-
marans that cruise the
bay and stop off for a
spot of deep-water
snorkelling. See p.257

✳ **Hummingbird feeding,
Rocklands** The only
place in Jamaica to get
close to these gorgeous
creatures. A really magi-
cal experience. See
p.274

✳ **Tubing on the Great
River** The most exhilarating way to travel in
Jamaica, passing through
some lovely riverine
scenery. See p.274

✳ **Half Moon horseback
ride** A cut above other
riding excursions in
Jamaica, allowing you to
actually swim your
mount through the sea.
See p.270

✳ **Meal at the *Houseboat
Grill*** Gourmet Caribbean
food in a lovely setting
on the waters of Bogue
Lagoon. See p.263

✳ **Albert Town adventures**
Make the hair-raising
descent onto Quashie
River Sink Cave or learn
about medicinal herbs via
a gentle walk in the egg-
box foothills of Cockpit
Country. See p.278

✳ **Accompong** Jamaica's
most accessible Maroon
community, in a spectac-
ular hillside setting, is best
experienced during its
annual festival. See p.281

△ Doctor's Cave Beach, Montego Bay

Montego Bay and Cockpit Country

J amaica's second-largest city, the seaside settlement of **Montego Bay** is one of Jamaica's premier tourist honeypots. Planeloads of foreigners flood in every day, seduced by a heavily marketed Caribbean dream of swaying palm trees, lilting reggae and cocktails at sunset. In recent years, the flow of visitors has slowed down somewhat, with many heading straight for the more expansive charms of Negril. But Montego Bay still delivers in many ways: sitting pretty in a sweeping natural harbour boasting several fabulous **beaches** that are hemmed in by a labyrinth of protected offshore **reefs**, and framed by a cradle of hills, it's furnished with enough natural attributes to fill any brochure, and its tourism "product", designed to suite the commercial, easy-access tastes of cruise shippers, is as slick as anywhere in Jamaica. Montego Bay remains the reigning old madam of Jamaican resorts: gossipy, belligerent and overdressed, but also absorbing, spirited and lively, particularly during its world-renowned summer reggae festival, **Sumfest**.

Concentration upon the traditional pleasures of the Caribbean fantasy has left the surrounding countryside largely undeveloped, save for the public plantations and converted great houses on the fringes of town, most famously **Rose Hall**, site of Jamaica's massively embellished legend of voodoo and sexual intrigue. Inland, the landscape rises sharply toward the hillside retreats of **Montpelier** and **Kensington**, all once part of the huge **sugar estates** that were the backbone of the area before tourism took off in the 1920s. Sugar is still a part of the scenery here, and though they're fast being divided up as commercial lots to house shopping malls and the city's new sewage treatment plant, the cane fields on the outskirts of downtown Montego Bay are still worked, perfuming the air with the molasses tinge of burning cane during harvest season. Many of the estates further afield have opened their doors to visitors, and the magnificent settings are worth the trip alone. Otherwise, the verdant **Great River valley** to the west offers rafting through the silky green waters of the Great River from **Lethe**, or hand-feeding a hummingbird at the beautiful **Rocklands Bird Sanctuary**, an oasis of serenity high above the bay.

Less than two hours' drive from the centre of town lies an area so untouched by any kind of development that it's something of a parallel universe. The mainly uninhabited limestone hillocks of **Cockpit Country** are the antithesis

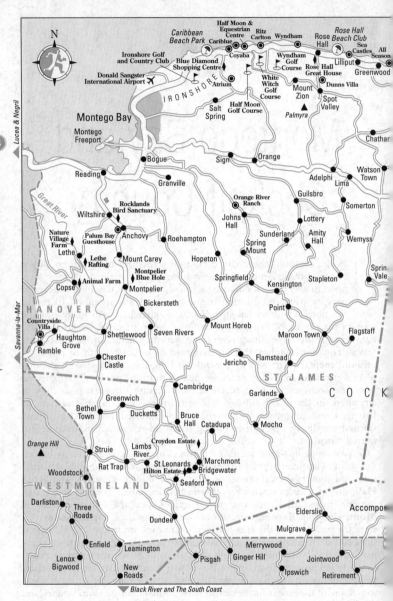

of the palm trees and concrete of the coast, and the few settlements that cling to the edges of this weird, almost lunar landscape are some of the most fascinating on the island. Some are still home to descendants of the once-mighty **Maroons**, escaped slaves who waged guerrilla war against the British from the depths of this impenetrable interior. Though **Accompong,** on the southern

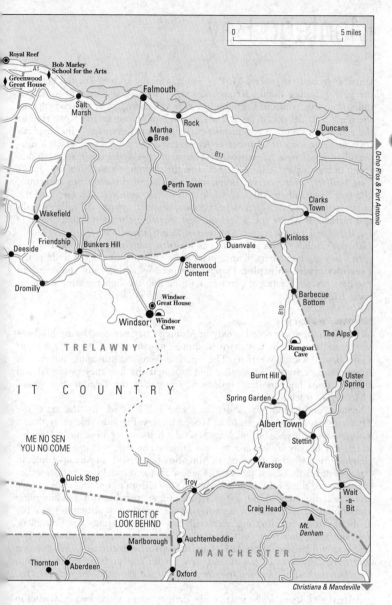

side of the Cockpits, is still a semi-autonomous state governed by a Maroon council, these Trelawny Maroons of western Jamaica welcome visitors and have been established on the tourist trail for much longer than the more secretive Windward Maroons (see p.178). As a result, the west is one of the better places to learn a little Maroon history first-hand.

Montego Bay

Jamaica's second-largest city, **MoBay** – as it is locally known – nestles between the gently sloping Bogue, Kempshot and Salem hills, and extends some ten miles from the haunts of the suburban rich at Reading at its western edge to the plush villa developments and resort hotels of Ironshore and Rose Hall to the east. It's made up of two distinct parts: the tourist-oriented "Hip Strip", as it's been christened, of **Gloucester Avenue**, and the city proper, which is universally referred to as "**downtown**". The split between the two is so sharp that many tourists never venture further than the dividing roundabout on foot. A long walkway of restaurants, hotels and bars, the Strip is the main attraction, and you'll certainly spend a lot of time in its bars and restaurants and on the public portions of its postcard-perfect beaches. But downtown, with its malls and markets, is where you'll find the best shopping, the most quietly rewarding sights and a more accurate picture of Montegonian life.

MoBay's holiday mask slips along its **western** stretch, an ugly sprawl of factories and gas containers, whose main concession to the tourist trade is the **Freeport cruise-ship pier**. Things don't get any prettier until you've passed the new sewage treatment plant and are cutting through the cane fields en route to Reading.

Some history

When Columbus anchored briefly in Montego Bay harbour during his 1494 voyage to the island, he was charmed enough to name it *El Golfo de Buen Tempo* (The Bay of Good Weather). The Spanish were less romantic, dubbing it *Manterias*, a derivation of *manteca* (pig fat), after the lard they produced and shipped from here in large quantities. Eventually, the English corruption, "Montego", stuck.

Spanish occupation was short-lived and half-hearted. By the time the Spaniards hastily fled the island in 1655, Montego Bay was little more than a village – a few haphazard buildings around a harbour. Its subsequent development was heavily influenced by two factors. The first was the presence in neighbouring Cockpit Country of **Maroons** (see p.374), an African-Jamaican band of militarily skilled rebel slaves whose frequent attacks on British settlements cowed the government and kept the town from prospering until a peace treaty was signed in 1739. By this time, **sugar production** was booming throughout Jamaica, and the turnover of the area's many plantations saw the harbour thronging with ships, and lavish cut-stone town houses and travellers' inns spreading back from the waterfront. Plantation culture built Montego Bay and nearly destroyed it; the 1831 **Christmas Rebellion** (see p.259), the first and most important of the violent slave revolts that prefaced emancipation, began in the foothills behind the town and burned almost all the estates to the ground.

After the collapse of the sugar trade, the city spent a hundred-odd years in limbo; many of the grander buildings were destroyed by fire or hurricanes. It was not until the early twentieth century that Montego Bay entered another period of growth, beginning when Sir Herbert Baker advocated the redemptive powers of the Doctor's Cave waters (see p.256) in the 1920s. Since then, Montego Bay has thrown full weight into its metamorphosis as the ultimate **tourist town**. Initially the trade was restricted to rich North Americans and

Europeans who built holiday homes around Doctor's Cave or arrived on a banana boat to stay in the town's first hotel, the currently closed *Casa Blanca*. Sangster International Airport grew from the original single airstrip built in the late 1940s, and the town was poised for development as a major resort. Its population increased four-fold between 1940 and 1970, with Jamaicans from all over the island moving in to work at the hotels that sprang up alongside the best of the beaches. In the 1960s, the Freeport peninsula was manually constructed on land reclaimed from the sea, and Montego Bay's position as a premier port of call on any Caribbean cruise was assured.

More recently, Montego Bay achieved fame as the base for Jamaica's **reggae festivals** – the first-ever Reggae Sunsplash took place here in 1978 and Sumfest is resident today – but overdevelopment and a reputation for aggressive hustlers led to a decrease in tourist arrivals in the 1990s. In a bid to lure back the visitors, the Urban Development Corporation have cleaned up the city, beautifying parts of downtown and constructing several new malls. Meanwhile, Gloucester Avenue has been largely cleared of street traders and hustlers; patrolled day and night by special resort police, it's now safer than ever. Doctor's Cave and Walter Fletcher beaches have both been attractively overhauled, and the *Margaritaville* restaurant and bar, with its waterslide and tropical high jinks, and Las Vegas-esque *Coral Cliff* restaurant, bar and gaming lounge have injected a bit of life into the scene. Cruise-ship arrivals are on the rise, college-age partyers inject a shot of raucous adrenalin during the debauched annual Spring Break, and the annual Air Jamaica Jazz and Blues and Reggae Sumfest music festivals keep things going in the slow seasons. These days, the town feels on the upswing, and with big plans for further redevelopment along the Strip, it looks likely that MoBay may well regain its status as Jamaica's top tourist town.

Arrival, information and getting around

Over eighty percent of visitors to Jamaica arrive at **Donald Sangster International Airport** (Ⓦwww.sangster-airport.com.jm), right by the sea three miles east of the town centre and a mile from the Gloucester Avenue Hip Strip. As you'd imagine, it's fully geared up for the newly arrived tourist, with a 24-hour **cambio** and a branch of the NCB bank, a tourist-board desk (daily, 9am–10pm) and numerous hotel, ground transport and car-rental booths. **Luggage trolleys** aren't permitted past immigration, but the official red-capped porters will carry your bags for a small charge (J$50 per bag).

Larger hotels provide free airport transfers (see below); alternatively you can charter a **taxi** from any of the omnipresent JUTA drivers. A taxi ride from the airport to Gloucester Avenue, Queens Drive or downtown should cost no more than US$20. If travelling *very* light, you can take one of the local **shared taxis** that leave from the petrol station past the airport's car park, which charge J$30 for the same journey. There is no public bus service from the airport.

If you're heading straight for Negril or Ocho Rios, check at the transport company and hotel booths in the arrivals area, which run **bus transfers** for guests in Negril and Ocho Rios hotels; space allowing, you may be able to jump in one for around US$20 per person to Negril, US$30 to Ochi. Otherwise, make for the downtown **bus station** (see p.248), from where buses run to destinations all around the island (see Travel Details, p.283). If you're headed for Negril, you'll probably have to change buses at Lucea or Savannah-la-Mar.

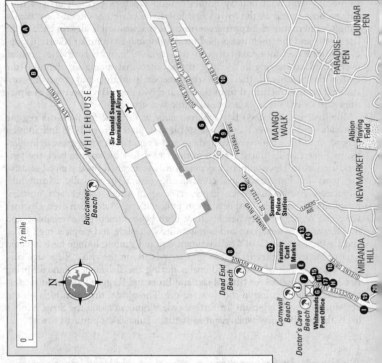

⊙ ⓓ ❶ ❷ ❸ ❹ ❺ ▲ Ironshore & Ocho Rios

WHITEHOUSE

Sir Donald Sangster International Airport

KENT AVENUE

Buccaneer Beach

Dead End Beach

Cornwall Beach

Doctor's Cave Beach

Whitesands Beach

Post Office

QUEENS DRIVE

CLAUDE CLARKE AVENUE

FORBES AVENUE

FEDERAL AVE

SUNSET BLVD

ST LISSER DRIVE

KENT AVENUE

LEADERS AVE

MIRANDA HILL

QUEENS DRIVE

GLOUCESTER AVE

DUNBAR PEN

PARADISE PEN

MANGO WALK

Albion Playing Field

NEWMARKET

Summit Police Station

Fantasy Craft Market

N

½ mile

0

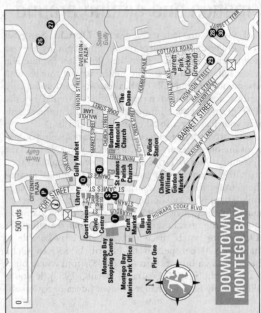

DOWNTOWN MONTEGO BAY

N

500 yds

0

CITY CENTRE PLAZA

FORT STREET

North Gully

South Gully

OVERTON PLAZA

UNION STREET

MARKET STREET

CHURCH STREET

DOME STREET

WALPOLE LANE

ORANGE ST

ST JAMES ST

STRAND ST

HARBOUR ST

FORT ST

Library

Gully Market

Court House

Civic Centre

Craft Market

Bus Station

Montego Bay Shopping Centre

Montego Bay Marine Park Office

Pier One

HOWARD COOKE BLVD

Burchell Memorial Church

St James Parish Church

The Dome

HUMBER AVENUE

COTTAGE ROAD

JARRETT TERR

Jarrett Park (Cricket Ground)

CORINALDI AVE

THOMSON STREET

HART STREET

JARRETT ST

BARNETT STREET

RAILWAY LANE

The Creek Street

PAYNE STREET

Police Station

Charles William Gordon Market

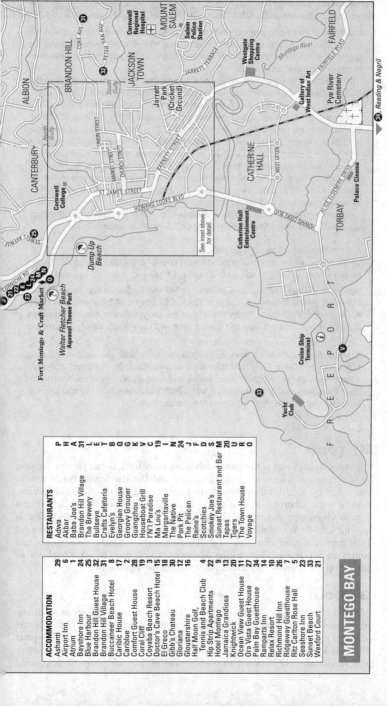

MONTEGO BAY

ACCOMMODATION	
Ashanti	29
Airport Inn	6
Atrium	1
Bayshore Inn	24
Blue Harbour	25
Brandon Hill Guest House	32
Brandon Hill Village	31
Buccaneer Beach Hotel	8
Caribic House	17
Cariblue	2
Comfort Guest House	28
Coral Cliff	19
Coyaba Beach Resort	3
Doctor's Cave Beach Hotel	15
El Greco	18
Gibb's Chateau	30
Gloriana	12
Gloustershire	16
Half Moon Golf,	
Tennis and Beach Club	4
Hip Strip Apartments	22
Hotel Montego	9
Jamaica Grandiosa	13
Knightwick	20
Ocean View Guest House	11
Ora Vista Guest House	27
Palm Bay Guesthouse	34
Ramparts Inn	14
Relax Resort	10
Richmond Hill Inn	26
Ridgeway Guesthouse	7
Ritz Carlton Rose Hall	5
Seashore Inn	23
Sunset Beach	33
Wexford Court	21

RESTAURANTS	
Adwa	P
Akbar	H
Baba Joe's	A
Brandon Hill Village	31
The Brewery	L
Bullseye	E
Crafts Cafeteria	T
Evelyn's	B
Georgian House	Q
Groovy Grouper	G
Guangzhou	K
Houseboat Grill	V
I'N'I Paradise	C
Ma Lou's	19
Margaritaville	I
The Native	N
Pork Pit	24
The Pelican	J
Raine's	F
Scotchies	D
Smokey Joe's	S
Sunset Restaurant and Bar	M
Tapas	20
Tigers	U
The Town House	R
Voyage	O

247

Organized tours

Hundreds of **tour companies** operate out of Montego Bay; most have booths at the airport and offices along Gloucester Avenue and offer similarly priced trips to the plantations and great houses in the area. For more on the activities available, visit ⓦwww.attractions-jamaica.com.

In addition to the standard **attractions** listed below, a few tour operators offer some different options. Glamour Tours, LOJ Shopping Mall (☏979 8207, ⓦwww.glamourtours.com), organizes bob-cart races, treasure hunts and trips to a Jamaican farm fair from US$40 per person; Marzouca (☏971 3859 or 952 8784, ⓦwww.marzouca.com) runs city tours from US$40 as well as trips to all the usual attractions. Barrett Adventures, Rose Hall (☏382 6384, ⓦwww.barrettadventures.com), puts together customized packages to waterfalls, plantations, beaches and Cockpit Country; horseback rides at Good Hope; and excursions to packaged attractions such as Rose Hall; prices start at US$60 per person per day. Caribic Vacations, 69 Gloucester Ave (☏979 3421, ⓦwww.caribicvacations.com), offers islandwide specialist and reggae tours and trips to Cuba.

Another alternative is to hire a **local driver** and do some independent sightseeing. Dale Porter, aka Rasta Shaka (☏806 8147 or 375 7918), is recommended.

Tour sites and popular excursions

Listed below are the best tour sites and most popular organized excursions. All can be seen independently or as part of a packaged tour with transport included.

Appleton Estate Siloah, St Elizabeth; ☏963 9215, ⓦwww.appletonrum.com; Mon–Sat; US$12 for entry. On edge of Cockpit Country in St Elizabeth, the orderly Appleton rum distillery in Siloah showcases the progression of cane to molasses and finally rum. Visitors view the ageing stills and taste every variety of rum and liquor in production.

Chukka Blue ☏979 6599, ⓦwwwchukkablue.com. Brilliant two-hour river tubing trips along the Great River (US$50), with a stop for lunch (not included) at Nature Village Farm. Swimming ability is necessary, and bring aqua shoes if you have them. Jeep tours into the St James interior (4hr; US$60) include swimming and lunch at Montpelier Blue Hole. Both trips include hotel transfers.

By road

All **bus** journeys end at the busy downtown **terminus**, behind the fire station at the corner of Howard Cook Boulevard and Barnett Street. Buses around town, run by the Montego Bay Metro Line (see p.250), run from the bus station to most suburban areas. If you're heading to an in-town hotel, charter a taxi to Gloucester Avenue or Queens Drive; the fare from the bus station is around US$10. You can take a **shared taxi** to anywhere in town for around J$30; trips to the suburbs (Ironshore, Reading, etc) are a little more. Shared taxi routes are set, and as they change frequently you'll need to ask somebody to show you the relevant departure point within the bus station.

By boat

Montego Bay's cruise-ship scene has undergone a recent renaissance, with visitor arrivals in the 2002–2003 winter season higher than ever before; some 200,000 passengers disembark here annually. Cruise ships dock at the **Freeport Pier** (ⓦwww.cruisemontegobay.com), centred in its own complex of shops and restaurants. Reps board the boats offering bus transport to designated

Croydon in the Mountains Catadupa, St James ☎979 8267, ⓦwww.montego-bay-jamaica.com/ajal/croydon; Tues, Wed & Fri; US$50. Half-day tour to Croydon Estate, a 132-acre working coffee and pineapple plantation in the foothills of the Catadupa mountains in the St James interior. Barbecue lunch and fruit tasting included in the price.

Hilton High Day Tour St Leonards, St James ☎952 3343, ⓦwww.montego-bay-jamaica.com/hilton; Tues, Wed, Fri & Sun; US$60. So-called because it once included a balloon ride, the tour is now a little short on thrills but still enjoyable. Visitors are bused up Long Hill through Montpelier and Cambridge to the diminutive Hilton Estate plantation house, whose small grounds contain a piggery and stables. Breakfast and lunch are included, as are a stroll around the village and local school, a bus ride to the German settlement of Seaford Town and its museum, and a drive back through the western outskirts of Cockpit Country.

Jamaica ATV Tours Rose Hall ☎953 9598, ⓦwwwatvtoursjamaica.com; daily 9am, 11am, 1pm & 3pm; US$45 including transfers from MoBay hotels. Popular with guests in the nearby all-inclusives, guided tours (1.5hr) on these robust three-wheelers take you 700ft above sea level into the mountains. No riding experience necessary, but you'll need to leave a credit-card imprint as deposit.

John's Hall Adventure Tour c/o *Relax Resort* ☎971 6958, ⓦwww.johnshalladventuretour.com; Mon, Wed, Fri & Sat; 5hr; $US50. A bit more than the usual plantation tour, with an informative stop at St James Parish Church and a primary school visit along the way to this small farm on the outskirts of MoBay. At the farm you get a look at local trees and plants as well as goats, pigs and mongoose and have a good Jamaican lunch.

Maroon Attraction Tours 32 Church St ☎979 0308; Tues, Thurs & Sat; US$50. The only tour company granted permission by Maroon officials to carry visitors to Accompong. Includes a stop at Kensington to view the Sam Sharpe monument, and a tour of Maroon Town, with introductions to "authentic" Maroons. Breakfast, lunch and live Maroon/mento band performance included. The views and countryside passed are spectacular.

in-bond shops and attractions, or you can negotiate a price with one of the many taxis that await ship arrivals; alternatively, shuttle buses run to Doctor's Cave Beach for US$4. If you're travelling on a private craft, full marina facilities are available at the nearby Montego Bay Yacht Club (☎979 8650).

Information

The main **Jamaica Tourist Board** office (Mon–Fri 8.30am–4pm, Sat 9am–1pm; ☎952 4425) is on the left as you go up the driveway to Cornwall Beach; there's also a nearby information kiosk on Gloucester Avenue and others at the Harbour Street Craft Market and the cruise-ship pier. All carry a limited selection of maps and flyers and can provide limited advice on hotels, restaurants and attractions. The twice-weekly *Western Mirror* and weekly *North Coast Times* both advertise local events. As in all other parts of Jamaica, musical events – concerts and special club nights – are usually announced by banners tied to trees and lampposts. For comprehensive online information on Montego Bay, check out ⓦwww.montego-bay-jamaica.com.

Getting around

Introduced in 2001, the **Montego Bay Metro bus company** runs several routes from the downtown bus station off Howard Cooke Boulevard out into the suburbs (Ironshore/Rose Hall, Reading etc) for a flat fee of J$20. The company was in financial trouble at the time of writing, however, and it looked likely that the services may cease. The only other public transport in town are the bevy of **shared taxis** that run set routes in the city centre, along Gloucester Avenue and out to the suburbs. They charge a flat rate of J$30 per person for anywhere in the city, and J$30–50 for trips out of town; bear in mind, though, that these rates are subject to change. Most shared taxis leave from the bus station or Gully Market (see p.258), but there are unofficial pickup/drop-off points along the Strip outside Walter Fletcher and Cornwall beaches.

If you want to charter a **private taxi**, you'll find there are legions of drivers along Gloucester Avenue, and you'll be assailed with offers. Be prepared to haggle and always settle the price before you get in; a taxi ride from Gloucester Avenue to the Harbour Street Craft Market should cost around US$6. The cheapest places to pick up a private taxi are the downtown taxi park at the intersection of Market and Strand streets, or by the bus station off Howard Cooke Boulevard (everything is less expensive downtown than on the strip), but there are also stands opposite Doctor's Cave and Cornwall beaches.

If you're staying on Gloucester Avenue, **walking** is your most convenient transportation option. You shouldn't experience any problems along the Strip even at night, but in the middle of town it's better to walk in company until you get your bearings.

Constant tailbacks during the daily rush hours (8–10am and 4.30–6.30pm) make **driving** a frustrating experience in town, and though you might want a car for independent sightseeing, you'll find that all the Strip attractions are reachable on foot. International **car rental** companies have booths at the airport, while most local operators are located along the lower section of Queen's Drive/Sunset Boulevard (listed on p.268). Rates are high, but most operators offer reductions for weekly rentals; expect to pay around US$50–70 per day. Motorbikes (from US$35 per day), scooters (from US$25 per day) and bicycles (from US$10 per day) are also available from most of the local companies.

Accommodation

As you would expect, the range of **accommodation** in one of Jamaica's top tourist cities is staggering. Most people stay adjacent to the beaches along the busy, buzzing **Gloucester Avenue** Hip Strip. Opting for a hotel on **Queen's Drive**, the road just above the Strip, reduces the likelihood of being accosted as soon as you step outside, and shared taxis run regularly down to the Strip. Hotels **downtown** are considerably cheaper, though you'll probably make up the difference getting taxis to and from Gloucester Avenue's nightlife. Many hotels include free airport transfers in their rates, and more distant properties throw in a free beach shuttle. As this is tourist territory, places are up to international standards; unless otherwise stated, rooms are equipped with air conditioning, TV and phone.

Although there are inexpensive options downtown and close to the airport, even the cheapest rates are pretty high in this tourist-oriented town. With so much to choose from, it's rarely difficult to find a vacancy, unless you hit town during Sumfest season (mid-July to mid-August) or around the Jazz Festival (Jan); it's a good idea to book ahead if you're planning on visiting during those months.

Montego Bay is prime **all-inclusive** territory, with the swankiest enclaves out at suburban Ironshore, just east of town. We've reviewed the more individual and interesting accommodation options below, but Montego Bay also is the site of several all-inclusive resorts run by major hotel chains (see Basics, p.35). Sandals (Ⓦwww.sandals.com) has several properties here – the diminutive *Sandals Inn* at the far end of the Strip, fun-oriented *Sandals MoBay* in Whitehouse and upscale *Royal Jamaican* in Ironshore – while Superclubs (Ⓦwww .superclubs.com) operates the charmless *Breezes*, hulking over Doctor's Cave Beach. Montego Bay's wealthiest visitors head for *Round Hill* resort, eight miles out of Montego Bay near Hopewell (see Chapter Five, p.289). It's the island's classiest hotel and literally swarming with the rich and famous.

Gloucester Avenue and around

Bayshore Inn 27 Gloucester Ave ⓣ952 1046, ⓔbayshorjm@yahoo.com. Cheerful gingham-swathed rooms above a great jerk restaurant at the less frantic end of the Strip. Reduced-rate weekly rentals available. ❸

Blue Harbour Sewell Ave ⓣ952 5445, ⓕ8930. Quiet small hotel perched above the Strip with good views, a nice pool and a restaurant serving breakfast and lunch. A range of rooms (some with kitchenette), all scrupulously clean; the cheapest are a bit gloomy. ❹

Buccaneer Beach Hotel Kent Ave ⓣ952 7658, ⓕ 6489. At the quiet end of the Strip opposite the free Dead End slip of beach, this place has a rather deserted air. But rates are reasonable for the location and the rooms are decent, with all mod cons and tile floors. ❹

Caribic House 69 Gloucester Ave ⓣ979 6073, Ⓦwww.caribicvacations.com. A small hotel slap in the middle of the Strip, it's popular with European backpackers. Clean a/c rooms (three categories), some with ocean views; all have fridge, cable TV and phone. ❸

Coral Cliff 165 Gloucester Ave ⓣ952 4130, Ⓦwww.coralcliffjamaica.com. Tucked behind the Disney-esque gaming lounge and restaurant, the rooms here are in the process of being transformed from shabby colonial to spanking-new resort chic. The older ones are the cheapest, with wooden furnishings. Pool and restaurant on site. ❺–❻

Doctor's Cave Beach Hotel Gloucester Ave ⓣ952 4355 or 4359, Ⓦwww.doctorscave.com. The best choice on the Strip, in a great location opposite (unsurprisingly) the beach. The communal areas have lovely funky decor and pretty tropical landscaping, and there's a pool, jacuzzi, restaurant, bar and small gym. The smart, modern rooms are comfortable, but the real draw is the very friendly atmosphere. ❻

Gloriana 1–2 Sunset Blvd, just off Gloucester Ave ⓣ979 0669–71, Ⓦwww.hotelgloriana.com. Cheap and cheerful hotel, popular with backpackers and Jamaicans. Rooms are basic but adequate, and there's a pool and poolside bar, jacuzzi, gym equipment, games room and a restaurant. ❷–❸

Gloustershire Gloucester Ave ⓣ952 4420, Ⓦwww.gloustershire.com. Opposite Doctor's Cave Beach, this MoBay stalwart is a bit 1970s in ambience. But the location is great and rooms are spacious and adequate; each has a private balcony and king-size bed. There's a nice pool with jacuzzi, and a bar and restaurant. Rates include full breakfast. ❻

Hip Strip Apartments Gloucester Ave ⓣ971 3859, Ⓦwww.marzouca.com. Appealing and inexpensive self-contained apartments adjacent to the *Brewery* complex. All have tile floors, big bathrooms and a separate living area with kitchenette. Tours are available. Rates include airport pick-up. ❸

Knightwick Corniche Rd ⓣ952 2988, ⓕ971 1921. Several large, comfortable rooms in the elegant hacienda-style building that houses the restaurant *Tapas*; conveniently situated above the *Coral Cliff* casino. Run by friendly live-in couple, with breakfast on the verandah included. Great rates and one of the best options on the Strip. ❹

Ocean View 26 Sunset Blvd ⓣ952 2662. Modest guesthouse situated between the Strip and the airport, with basic rooms but convivial atmosphere. Rates are good, so it's wise to book ahead. ❷

Seashore Inn 33 Gloucester Ave ⓣ940 6782, ⓔsyniverspencer@hotmail.com. Suffering from a lack of care and attention, the former *Belvedere* hotel has a rather forlorn air, though it's worth considering as a budget option. Rooms are basic and slightly shabby, and the a/c is ancient, so you should be able to do some bargaining. Good location opposite Walter Fletcher beach. ❸

Wexford Court Gloucester Ave ☎952 2854, ⓦwww.montego-bay-jamaica.com/wexford. Overlooking the only green space on the Strip, this reliable MoBay old-timer has recently undergone extensive restoration. With tile floors, tropical-style decor and king-size beds, rooms are bright and clean; some have sweeping ocean views. A pool, bar and restaurant are on site. ❹

Queen's Drive and around

Airport Inn Queen's Drive ☎952 0260, ☏929 5391. Two minutes from the airport, and clean and reliable. All rooms have kitchen facilities, and there is a pool and bar/restaurant. ❸

El Greco Queen's Drive ☎940 6116, ⓦwww.elgrecojamaica.com. Sprawling complex of self-contained apartments perched high above the Strip (access is via the lift of the adjacent *Montego Bay Club* resort), an excellent choice if you're driving and want independence. The modern one- or two-bedroom units are more like townhouses than hotel rooms, with balconies and fully equipped kitchens. The grounds feature a pool and tennis courts. ❺–❼

Hotel Montego Federal Ave ☎940 6009 or 952 3287, ⓔhotelmontego@cwjamaica.com. Big, friendly complex opposite the airport offering good value for its comfortable, mostly carpeted queen-bed rooms. Studios and suites with kitchens are also available, and there's a poolside restaurant and bar. ❹

Jamaica Grandiosa Queen's Drive, entrance on Leaders Ave ☎979 3205. There's something of a ghost-town atmosphere at this sprawling complex, but the rooms are pleasant and reasonably priced; go for one on the top floor with a high wooden ceiling. All have tile floors and queen-size beds, and there's a pool and restaurant on site. ❹

Ramparts Inn 5 Ramparts Close ☎979 5258. A quiet, friendly small hotel just off Queen's Drive (turn onto Leaders Ave) that's popular with English guests. Rooms are showing their age a bit, but all are comfortable and adequate. There are pretty gardens around the pool and restaurant. Excellent rates – book ahead. ❸

Relax Resort 26 Hobbs Ave ☎952 7218, ⓦwww.relax-resort.com. Run by a dynamic Jamaican family, this is a tranquil place on a side road above Sunset Boulevard. Highlights include pretty landscaping and spanking-new rooms and

apartments, plus a deep, large pool, small gym, shop, restaurant and bar. Free beach, airport and shopping shuttles available. ❹–❺

Ridgeway Guesthouse 34 Queens Drive ☎952 2709, ⓦwww.ridgewayguesthouse.com. Homely, eight-room place within walking distance of the airport (turn left at the roundabout). Lovely tile-floor rooms have wooden furniture, some are fan-only, others have a/c; those at the top afford sea views. Pluses: a restaurant, roof sun terrace and free beach shuttle. ❸–❹

Sunset Beach Montego Freeport ☎979 8800, ⓦwww.sunsetbeachjamaica.com. On the other side of the bay from the Strip, right at the end of the Freeport Peninsula, this is a very popular and friendly all-inclusive catering for singles, couples and families. Comprehensive facilities include disco, tennis, pool, watersports, spa and three sheltered beaches, one nude. ❼

Downtown

Ashanti 50 Thompson St, corner of Cottage Rd ☎952 6389. Thoroughly Jamaican-style rooms, all neat and tidy with tile floors, rugs, a/c, phone and fan; great value for the price. Communal veranda is great for watching the downtown world go by. ❷

Brandon Hill Guest House 28 Peter Pan Ave, Brandon Hill ☎952 7054, ☏940 5609. Quiet complex with a lovely mural in the lobby (though the eyes are more drawn to the enormous "No schoolgirls in uniform" sign by the front desk). It's a thoroughly respectable place, though, with airy, neat and spacious rooms, with ceiling fan or a/c, and a bar and pool. ❸

Brandon Hill Village 11 Coke Ave, Brandon Hill ☎952 7665, ☏940 7918. Eclectic collection of rooms and self-contained apartments, all with cable TV but no a/c (fans only), presided over by a genial Jamaican manager who provides free beach shuttles and lots of conversation and info. Used more by locals than visitors, the rooms are basic, clean and inexpensive. There's a great Jamaican restaurant, too. ❷–❸

Comfort Guest House 55 Jarrett Terrace, Barnett View Gardens ☎952 1238, ☏979 1997. Family-run place with a Christian slant – ideal for those seeking a reserved but friendly atmosphere. Comfortable rooms, TV lounge, sun deck and home-cooked meals, but rates are a bit on the high side. ❸

Gibb's Chateau 54 Jarrett Terrace ☎979 7861, ☏952 7189. Simple rooms, each with two double beds or one king-size, and a/c or fan; some have a balcony. There's a Jamaican restaurant on site. For the standard of the rooms, the rates are brilliant. ❷

Ora Vista Guest House Richmond Hill, off Union St ☎952 2576, ☏971 8897. A superb, friendly guesthouse overlooking downtown, with a great atmosphere and lovely bay views. Rooms are simple, with or without a/c, but clean and homely. There's a pool, bar, kitchen for guests' use, sun deck and communal lounge. Excellent Jamaican food available. ②–③

Palm Bay Guesthouse Bogue Crossing ☎952 1795, ☏940 0411. Busy guesthouse set back from the main road, on the shared taxi route into town. The clean, neat, tile-floor rooms range from basic fan-only to a/c, and all have phone and cable TV. There's a good Jamaican restaurant, and a shady bar/jerk centre outside that's a popular locals' drinking spot. Excellent value. ②

Richmond Hill Inn Richmond Hill, off Union St ☎953 3858, ⊛wwwrichmond-hill-inn.com. Easily the best views in town are from this lofty former planters' house. It also features lots of greenery in the open-plan communal areas and a great pool overlooking the bay. The guest rooms are in a separate building, not the plantation house. Though run-of-the-mill and a little dated, they're perfect if you're after peace and quiet. Service is rather hit-and-miss, though, and rates are rather inflated. ⑤

Ironshore and around

Atrium 1084 Morgan Rd ☎953 2605, ☏3683. Just off the main on the road to Blue Diamond Shopping Centre, this is a great option for those of an independent bent. The spotless, modern one- to three-bedroom apartments all have full kitchens and living areas, and fans and a/c in all rooms. There's a pool on site, too. ⑥

Cariblue ☎953 2250, ⊛www.caribluehotel.com. Right on the seafront, this scuba-oriented place (certification and dives available) is a good getaway if you're after peace and quiet. Rooms are spacious, with one king-size or two double beds,

but are showing their age a bit. Other amenities include a saltwater pool, sun deck, non-motorized watersports and an intermittently-open restaurant. Friendly atmosphere, and lots of deals available. ④

Coyaba Beach Resort ☎953 9150, ⊛www .coyabaresortjamaica.com. Classy resort with gorgeous landscaped gardens, a tranquil atmosphere and elegant, very modern rooms with balconies. Other pluses: a pool, free non-motorized watersports, three restaurants, bars, tennis courts (lessons are free), a spa and a good white-sand private beach with an offshore reef. Nightly entertainment is also on offer. ⑧

Half Moon Golf, Tennis and Beach Club Ironshore ☎953 2211, ⊛www.halfmoon-resort .com. One of the most exclusive properties on the island (Queen Elizabeth stays here on visits to Jamaica) and heavy with glitzy colonial-style atmosphere. Amenities are brilliant, including a shopping village, equestrian centre, 18-hole golf course, lovely half-mile beach with a brand-new dolphin lagoon, all watersports, three public and 54 private pools, tennis courts, croquet lawns, full spa centre, disco, six restaurants and various bars. Guests can stay in one of 220 luxurious rooms or a private villa. ⑨

Ritz Carlton Rose Hall ☎518 0100, ⊛www .ritzcarlton.com. Opened in 2000 as the most luxurious hotel in Jamaica, this huge property feels like a country unto itself, with 427 deluxe rooms in numerous categories and every imaginable amenity: golf course, spa, pools, legions of restaurants and bars. Even the sun loungers come equipped with flags to raise so that you can get a drink without moving more than your hand. There's a manufactured beach and a very manufactured atmosphere. ⑨

The Strip: Gloucester Avenue and the beaches

Though it stretches for less than two miles, Montego Bay's glittering ocean-front Hip Strip is the focal – sometimes only – point of many a Jamaican vacation. Occupying the whole of **Gloucester Avenue** and stretching north into **Kent Avenue**, this holiday highway builds to a bottleneck around Doctor's Cave Beach during the daytime, with hair braiders, taxi drivers and hustlers shadowing your every move and identikit gift shops competing for business. As night falls the action switches to MoBay's most happening joints, *Margaritaville* and *Coral Cliff*, and street vendors stake out jerk chicken stands and pushcarts selling sweets and snacks. Gloucester Avenue is where you'll find the majority

The constant tourist presence in Montego Bay has spawned a multitude of young **hustlers** trying to earn a living selling crafts, ganja, hair braiding or their services as a guide. Much of the heat has gone out of the hustle, however, due to the introduction in 1996 of a special tourist police force, the Resort Patrol, who pace the Strip day and night. But unless you're encased in an all-inclusive, you will at some point be accosted by someone trying to sell you something. It's can be tiring and irritating, and it's easy for visitors to lose perspective, bristling with tension and regarding every encounter as adversarial. You can't really blame the hustlers for trying, though, and whether or not the harassment becomes a problem depends largely upon your attitude. Resign yourself to being approached and learn how to deal with it. Hustlers play on guilt and use psychological trickery. Lines like "Don't you remember me from the hotel/car rental shop/airport/beach?" are designed to suck you into a dialogue. Of course you've never met them, but once you've stopped, the sales pitch begins. If you ignore the outstretched hand or catcall the response is often "Wh'appen, you too good to talk to a black man?". If you're white, don't fall into the liberal trap of buying things you don't want just to avoid looking racist. Don't try to avoid the issue by giggling or hinting that you may be interested another time; if you mean no, say no, in a friendly but straightforward manner. Keep your sense of humour and treat street sellers as people, and you'll minimize potential problems and maybe even make some friends.

of MoBay's tourist hotels and restaurants as well as the best beaches, bars and clubs, so even if you don't check into a Strip hotel, you'll find that you spend a lot of time here.

Starting at the roundabout that filters Howard Cooke Boulevard, Queens Drive and Fort Street traffic, the first stretch of Gloucester Avenue is a kind of no-man's land split in two by an elevated section of a one-way traffic system and bordered by the only sizeable undeveloped beach in town (see p.258). Easily missed on the upper section of Fort Street, which runs parallel to Gloucester Avenue, **Fort Montego** is an uninspiring hulk of stone with an even less impressive past. Dating back to the eighteenth century, the fort was built by the British to guard against foreign attack, but its cannons were fired only twice, both times with disastrous results. In a salute to celebrate the capture of Havana in 1760, one of the corroded guns misfired and killed its operator. In 1795 – in the fort's only recorded attempt at a defensive attack – it mistakenly opened fire on one of its own vessels, the schooner *Mercury*, carrying a cargo of dogs imported to hunt down Maroons; inevitably, the shots missed. Infinitely more absorbing, **Fort Street Craft Market** here is a relatively relaxed spot for a bit of bartering. Loosely arranged around steep steps that make a useful short cut to Sewell Avenue and Queen's Drive, stalls sell the usual array of carvings and T-shirts.

Though Gloucester Avenue runs parallel to the sea, the water is mainly obscured by the hotels and bars that carve the beach into private sections. The only place to fully appreciate the sweep of the bay is from the Strip's only **green space**, more of a thoroughfare than a public park, opposite the restaurants and bars at Miranda Ridge, just above the Strip. The former site of a long-gone hospital, today it's a favourite spot for football games, and there are a few benches at the edge of the cliffs from which to take in the views. The bucolic illusion is rudely shattered just past the park at **Margaritaville** (daily 10am–3am; Ⓦmargaritavillecaribbean.com), a mini-lido-cum-restaurant-cum-bar that's a mock-stone-clad, neon-flashing shrine to US kitsch and glitz. Look closely at the sign and you'll see the full name is *Jimmy Buffet's Margaritaville*. A regular visitor to Jamaica, the singer owns the well-known US chain of the same name; rather than face a copyright-infringement court battle, the Jamaican owners cut him in in 2000. *Margaritaville's* bar and outdoor eating deck are built right over the sea. Below there's a watersports area with boat berths and swimming platforms, while on the roof there's a jacuzzi, sun deck, and – best of all – a 110ft water slide (free to spending customers), which sluices down into the sea and draws hordes of tourists and locals alike. There are also water trampolines to bounce around on in the sea, and floating sun decks. *Margaritaville* is the epicentre of MoBay's Spring Break activities; come here in February, and it's wet T-shirts and beer-drinking competitions all round. On the other side of the road, sheltered under a thatched roof constructed by artisans shipped in from Africa, and with a waterfall cascading past faux-tropical ephemera toward the pavement, is **Coral Cliff**, a hotel, restaurant and gaming lounge with the outward appearance of a high-tech theme park. Inside, the slot machines and bar never close, and it's almost always a lively place to stop for a drink, with a small outdoor balcony overlooking the bay if the a/c gets too much.

The Strip builds in intensity as it approaches the magnificent Doctor's Cave Beach, becoming a seamless parade of bars, cafés and in-bond shops that doesn't slacken up until past Cornwall Beach. Beyond the entrance to Cornwall Beach and behind the last few stores is the diminutive **Fantasy Craft Market**, massively oversold by its vendors, who spend more time outside trying to induce you in than tending their stalls. The hotels peter out as Gloucester becomes **Kent Avenue** at the junction with Sunset Boulevard and continues to hug the coast. Locally known as Dead End Road, Kent Avenue passes tiny **Dead End Beach** (also known as Buccaneer or Sunset Beach; see p.258) before ending abruptly at the wall marking the distant section of the airport runway. The last of the Strip proper, **Sunset Boulevard** is home to a small complex of forlorn shops and bars, countless car-rental outlets and the rather grand **Summit Police Station**, the only one in Jamaica with its own pool (it was formerly a hotel). At the airport roundabout, the boulevard becomes part

Montego Bay Marine Park

Though offshore MoBay became officially protected in 1974, regulations were seldom enforced, and the reefs remained open to attack from plunderers, spear fishers, snorkellers, divers, boat anchors and industrial pollution. In an attempt to stem the destruction, **Montego Bay Marine Park** was created in 1991. It is Jamaica's first national park, with environmental regulations strictly enforced within its boundaries. Running west from Sangster Airport to Great River, just past Reading, the park comprises over nine square miles of coral reef, sea grass beds and mangroves, divided into watersports, fishing and fish nursery zones and patrolled by four rangers. Within the park it is illegal to mine sand; damage or move coral, shells and seaweed; fish without a permit; or drop litter. Mooring buoys have been introduced along the major reefs, spear fishing has been banned, and a larger mesh is being used in wire traps. With two days' notice, rangers lead educational diving and snorkelling expeditions; there's no charge but donations in cash or kind (particularly depth gauges) are gratefully accepted. Unfortunately, the Marine Park organization is desperately underfunded and in urgent need of financial support; if you're interested in helping out details are available from the Resource Centre at Pier One (☎971 8082, ◉www.montego-bay-jamaica.com/mbmp). For more on the conservation movement in Jamaica, see *Contexts*.

of **Queen's Drive**, an inland road that runs parallel to Gloucester Avenue. Essentially a fast-traffic route straight through MoBay, Queen's Drive is popularly known simply as the "top road" (Gloucester Avenue being the bottom road). Pavements are sporadic along the top road and walking can be risky, though the views over the bay are fantastic.

East of the roundabout, Queens Drive skirts the airport and the low-income community of Flankers. After a mile or so, there's a left-hand fork following the perimeter of the airport to the fishing community of **WHITEHOUSE**, a quiet residential zone – bar the noise from the airport – seldom visited by tourists and refreshingly hassle-free. Roadside vendors sell excellent fried fish and festival, and there are a couple of great seafood restaurants (see p.264).

The beaches

The Strip, of course, wouldn't exist were it not for Montego Bay's prize asset: a dazzling bay with miles of protected coral reef (see box on previous page) and some beautiful beaches. Much of the coastline has been snapped up by the hotels and carved into private chunks, but there are three main managed **public beaches**, all with showers, changing rooms, snack outlets and watersports concessions and a minimal entrance fee.

At the time of writing, **Cornwall Beach** was closed for renovation; check at the adjacent tourist board office for an update on entry fees and facilities. Separated from Doctor's Cave Beach by breeze-block walls, Cornwall Beach is a compact but gorgeous swathe of white sand, with a bar built around a giant almond tree in the middle, and gently shelving waters with good snorkelling possibilities.

Closest to downtown and opposite Fort Street Craft Market, **Walter Fletcher Beach/Aquasol Theme Park** (daily 10am–10pm; J$200; ⓦ www.aquasoljamaica.com) has the most comprehensive sports facilities on the Strip. It offers all watersports (half-hour rates: jet ski US$75; glass-bottom boat rides US$12; snorkelling US$12), tennis (J$200 per hour) and basketball courts and a go-kart track (J$200 per ride). An attractive decked bar (which stays open until late every night), a decent seafood restaurant and the wide expanse of gently curving sand have made the beach popular with young tourists and the attendant hangers-on as well as Jamaican families. Changing rooms and showers are scrupulously clean. You might want to avoid swimming here after heavy rain, when downtown gullies discharge pollutants into the water.

Half a mile further north lies the famous **Doctor's Cave Beach** (daily 8am–sunset; J$200; ⓦ www.doctorscavebathingclub.com), Montego Bay's premium portion of gleaming white sand and warm see-through water. The beach was put on the map in the late nineteenth century when local doctor and sea-bathing advocate Alexander McCatty founded the *Sanatorium Caribbee*, an exclusive private bathing club that's still in existence today. In the 1920s visiting English chiropractor Sir Herbert Baker was so impressed by the curative potential of the waters that he published an article in the English press extolling their efficacy. The beau monde flocked and MoBay's tourist industry was born. The rapidly deepening waters really are the best in town and facilities are excellent, though there is little shade and it gets very crowded at the weekend. You'll pay a steep J$250 for daily rental of an umbrella or inflatable mattress, and J$200 for a chair; snorkelling equipment is J$400, but there's little to see under the water here. The swanky **clubhouse** to the left of the entrance, with pool tables, a games room, a gym, sauna and steam room, is members-only; it's J$4025 for

Montego Bay is justifiably famed for its deep turquoise waters and abundant reef systems, some close enough to swim to from the main beaches. Discarded rum bottles and tyres can be disconcerting, but the deeper reefs are alive with fish, rays, urchins and the occasional turtle and nurse shark. There are hosts of similarly priced **watersports operators** on each beach and within the larger hotels; naturally, we list the most reputable below. Pamphlets and information are always available from the Montego Bay Marine Park office.

Diving and snorkelling

The following offer guided dives (around US$40), certification courses (from US$350) and equipment rental (from US$15). Like every other watersports operator in Montego Bay, they also rent **snorkel gear** for around US$10 a day – most also offer guided snorkelling tours of the best reefs.

Captain's Watersports and Dive Centre, *Round Hill Hotel*, Hopewell ☎956 7050, ext 378.

Fun Divers, *Wyndham Rose Hall Hotel,* Rose Hall ☎953 3268.

Jamaica Scuba Divers, *Half Moon Hotel*, Ironshore ☎953 9266.

Resort Divers, *Holiday Inn Hotel* ☎953 9699.

Boat trips

Boat trips, with an open bar and sometimes lunch, are always popular and usually fun. Most depart from the Pier One complex downtown and sail around the bay to the airport reefs, with a stop for snorkelling. MoBay Undersea Tours (☎940 4465 or 952 4285) run trips aboard *Calico*, the only wooden sailing ship in town (3hr daytime cruise US$35; 2hr evening cruise US$25). Sailing from *Sandals Montego Bay*, two well-equipped and beautifully maintained catamarans, *Tropical Dreamer* and *Day Dreamer,* cruise along the coast to *Margaritaville*, where passengers can get out and have a go on the water slide; there's a snorkelling stop on the way (☎979 0102; 3hr cruises US$48). More sedate family cruises aboard the catamarans are also available.

Other watersports

There's a comprehensive watersports service at Aquasol Theme Park on Walter Fletcher Beach. From *Margaritaville*, MoBay Undersea offer **parasailing** (from US$60 for 15min). They also have several **semi-submersible** vessels that take you ten feet underwater (Mon–Sat 11am & 1.30pm; US$34, US$40 including transfers from local hotels). Go in the morning for the best light or try a night tour to catch the nocturnal marine life. From Doctor's Cave Beach, Chukka Blue (☎979 6599, ⊛www.chukkablue. com) offer "Seatrek" **undersea walks** (25min; US$67); you don a special air-filled helmet and walk along the seabed at a depth of 14ft to view coral and fish. A more conventional option, **glass-bottom boats** operate from all the main beaches and sail out to the airport reefs (30 min; US$12–15); particularly recommended is *Birthday.* Jet skis are available all over the place for US$75 for half an hour. Alternatively, a fully equipped **sport-fishing boat** costs around US$700 per day; try the *Irie Lady* (☎953 3268), *No Problem* (☎936 6702), or call *Cariblue Hotel* (☎953 2250). Captain's Watersports at *Round Hill Hotel* has several boats and also rents out *Stoshus*, a 36ft yacht costs US$120 per hour or US$600 per day).

annual membership. However, the regular changing rooms are clean and well equipped. There are several restaurants along the back of the beach, from the inexpensive *L'Oven Best* patty and sandwich shop to the *Groovy Grouper,* with a more extensive menu (see p.264). There are also a couple of craft shops adjacent to the restaurants, one offering overpriced Internet access.

If the big three are too crowded for your tastes, head past the Strip and out of town toward Ironshore. Well signposted from the main road, **Caribbean Beach Park** (Tues–Thurs 9am–6pm, Fri–Sun 9am–8pm; J$100) is a much quieter, privately operated white-sand stretch with changing facilities and a bar selling snacks and drinks. The huge grassy area is often used for stageshows. Alternatively, backing onto the airport perimeter wall on Kent Avenue (the northern continuation of Gloucester Ave), and consequently dogged by the racket of landings and takeoffs, **Buccaneer Beach** (or Dead End/Sunset Beach) is a thin but attractive strip of public sand, popular with Jamaicans. The water is shallow and there are no facilities, but snorkelling is good and the view over the bay is fabulous, providing the best free sunset seat in town.

Downtown

After the flamboyance of the Strip, **downtown** MoBay announces itself with its very own stretch of undeveloped shoreline right opposite the dividing roundabout. With its gentle curve of white sand, **Dump-Up Beach**, as it's known, looks pretty enough, particularly from a distance. But this is one of the dirtiest parts of the bay; untreated waste and garbage from downtown squatter settlements drain directly into the sea via the many rainwater gullies here. It's not a place to swim or spend much time, although it's the popular venue of local soccer matches and packed gospel meetings with Jamaicans in their Sunday finery overflowing the marquees erected for such occasions.

Shooting off from the roundabout, the main route into the centre of town is **Fort Street**, a clamorous thoroughfare with dancehall flooding out from store-fronts and all manner of pushcarts and vehicles jostling for space with the thick human traffic. A short way along, there's a little garden area housing the useful **parish library** (Mon–Fri 9.30am–5.30pm, Sat 9am–4pm; ☎ 952 4185), which carries a fair stock of Caribbean books. It would be a tranquil spot were it not for the cigarette and newspaper vendors who noisily tout their wares from the garden wall. Past here, over the bridge across North Gully, you enter town proper. The covered market to the left is popularly known as **The Gully** (the correct name, William Street Market, is seldom used). It's a lively fruit and vegetable market where hard-dough bread and calalloo are sold out of super-market trolleys and bartering is common at the stalls; a Jamaican companion will ensure reasonable prices. This is a prime area for pickpockets – don't take out wads of cash when paying for small items, use ATM machines in daylight only, and keep cameras in a closed bag.

Running parallel to Fort Street to the east, **Orange Street** is lined by shabby shops and dingy bars that back onto the Canterbury squatters' community. The zinc-roofed clapboard dwellings cover the entire valley behind Orange Street, petering out at the red-earthed playing fields of MoBay's main high school, Cornwall College. To the west, Bay West shopping mall is squeezed into the space between Fort Street and Howard Cooke Boulevard; pop in to sample the ice cream sold at the Devon House outlet within.

Sam Sharpe Square and the craft market

St James Street comes to an abrupt end at **Sam Sharpe Square**, the heart of downtown. Characterized by its central fountain and seemingly permanent stream of honking, gridlocked traffic, this cobbled pavement area was until recently dominated by illegal vendors, every pavement obscured with displays of leather sandals, cheap watches, toys and bootleg designer imports. As part of the islandwide government initiative to place vendors in malls, local police have been successful in clearing the streets here – much to the disgust of the vendors, who feel they've lost their livelihoods.

The square is bordered by a jumble of old and new architecture, including **The Cage**, built in 1806 as a lock-up for disorderly seamen and runaway slaves; their shenanigans so damaged the original wooden walls that they were replaced with the red-brick and stone that stands today. In 1811, the rooftop belfry was installed. It was originally used to ring out a 2pm curfew warning; after the second ring at 3pm, any slaves still on the streets were locked up. Just outside, National Hero Sam Sharpe (see p.90) is commemorated in a **bronze statue** by Jamaican sculptor Kay Sullivan, which depicts him in full evangelical flow before a crowd of converts.

To the left of the cage is MoBay's brand new town hall, **Montego Bay Civic Centre**. Opened in 2001, the Georgian-style structure was built to replace the old one, which was destroyed by fire. Inside, there's an unmemorable museum and a theatre space. Shooting both east and west of the square next to the centre, Market Street holds the hulking, unattractive **Burchell Memorial**

Sam Sharpe and the Christmas Rebellion

During the course of just over a week, slavery in Jamaica received the blow that would kill it forever. The **Christmas**, or **Baptist, Rebellion** began on December 27, 1831; by its end on January 5, 1832, twenty thousand slaves had razed nearly 160 sugar estates, causing damage to the value of £1 million – a massive drain on the British exchequer. It was the largest slave uprising in Jamaican history, and it set in motion the process that led to the abolition of the slave trade in 1834 and full emancipation in 1838.

The rebellion was led by **Sam Sharpe**, a house slave working for a MoBay solicitor. Though this nascent martyr took on the surname of his master in accordance with tradition, his sideline as deacon of the town's Burchell Baptist Church made him anything but servile. At the time, the Baptists were Jamaica's most radical and outspoken critics of slavery and were rightly seen as a threat by the British establishment, particularly as religious congregations were the only gatherings legally allowed to slaves. The church taught Sharpe to read, and through international newspapers he learned of English anti-slavery sentiments and became convinced that emancipation in Jamaica was imminent, a reality that planters were trying to suppress. A powerful orator, Sharpe formed a secret society dedicated to banishing slavery and planned a nonviolent withdrawal of labour over the Christmas period. Talk of the insurrection spread fast through St James estates, and even the planters became uneasy as December 1831 drew to a close. By the night of the 27th, passions were running high. The peaceful protest soon degenerated into anarchy; tipped off by the estate owners, the militia were out in force, and the more militant slaves responded by lighting bonfires at the highest point of the Kensington estate to signify the start of a full-scale rebellion. Others followed suit and within days western Jamaica was burning as the cane fields and great houses were destroyed one by one. The response of the British militia was brutal. Though damage was predominantly restricted to property and only fourteen whites died, soldiers gunned down one thousand slaves, and Montego Bay magistrates handed down a further three hundred execution orders during the emotionally charged six-week trial that ensued. Sharpe himself was hanged in the MoBay square that today bears his name and buried in the harbour sand, though his remains were later exhumed and interred in the vault of Burchell Memorial Church.

△ Cooking fish stew for Accompong Maroon Festival

Church, where Sam Sharpe lies buried, to the east. The western section of the street, towards the sea and the town's main **craft market**, has been pedestrianized. The market is a surprisingly hassle-free place to shop if you don't treat the inventive sales pitches as bamboozling. The 200-odd stalls sell every type of Jamaican craft (see p.267), and there are a couple of good, cheap restaurants, patronized mostly by the vendors.

Church Street

The four streets that feed off Sam Sharpe Square are MoBay's busiest, packed with stores and offices. Of these, **Church Street**, branching off from the square's southern corner, is the most architecturally interesting. Dominating the street is **St James Parish Church** (if locked, ask at the rector's office opposite or call ☎952 2775), built from creamy cut stone in the shape of a cross. It was considered the showpiece of the parish when the original structure was completed in 1782. In 1957, an earthquake destroyed the foundations and the building underwent major repairs. Inside the church, the virtues of Rosa, first wife of John Palmer of Rose Hall (see p.270), are commemorated in a John Bacon verse and sculpture set to the left of the altar, while lovely stained-glass windows depict the crucifixion. Outside, the rather neglected graveyard contains the ornate but weathered graves of deceased planters, many standing at erratic angles since the earthquake.

Facing the church is the elegant facade of the **Town House**, its weathered stone walls and stately grace rendering the surrounding concrete even more ill-favoured. Constructed in 1765 by local merchant David Morgan, the building served as a private home, church manse, Masonic lodge, warehouse, synagogue and hotel (Queen Victoria spent the night) before becoming the smart restaurant, favoured by lunching ladies, it is today (see "Eating", p.264).

Dome Street and Jarrett Park

At its very top Church Street becomes **Dome Street**, which loops down to Water Lane, Creek Street and the South Montego Gully. The principal feature of an otherwise quiet street is **Dome House**, built as a wealthy planter's residence in the late eighteenth century and now restored to its former glory after a long period of disuse. Though it's currently in commercial use, it's still a princely building, with the classic proportions of plantation architecture, large sash windows, cool cut stone and an interior rich with original mahogany floors and fittings. Aqueous street names hint at the centrality of water to the history of this part of town. The now-disused well in front of Dome House was originally linked to the **Dome** on Creek Street below. A solid stone circle topped with a peeling wooden roof, the Dome was originally built in 1837 to protect the point at which a stream bubbled up from underground. (The stream, which provided Creek Street with a name, is still flowing along concreted banks.) The Dome looks rather incongruous these days in the midst of what has long been the building site for a new drainage system and racing traffic. Its thick walls mask two floors; the upper portion was originally occupied by the "Keeper of the Creek", who supervised collection from what was Montego Bay's main and only source of fresh water until a piped supply was made available in 1894.

Moving west from the Dome along Creek Street, you reach the junction with the second half of **St James Street**, downtown's liveliest shopping strip. Tatty hole-in-the-wall emporia vie for space with neon store-fronts and sidewalk vendors, all fighting to be noticed against a background symphony of nonstop reggae and shouts of "sky juice" and "peanuts and Wrigley's". East of here, Creek Street rises sharply uphill, changing names and eventually reaching **Jarrett Park** (☎940 3710), MoBay's cricket ground and the original site of Reggae Sunsplash (Bob Marley and the Wailers made their only festival appearance here in 1979). Even if you're not a cricket fan, attending a match is highly entertaining, as much for the crowd-pleasing dancehall that booms out during every break in play as for the aficionados' impassioned running commentaries. Tickets (US$4–8) are sold at the gate, but you should get to the high-profile test and one-day matches early to ensure a seat; alternatively, you could follow the local example and catch the match for free from one of the surrounding hills.

Barnett Street and Charles William Gordon Market

The least tourist-friendly part of downtown, **Barnett Street** – reached by following St James Street south from Sam Sharpe Square – is a raucous belt of supermarkets and mini-malls choking in a constant fug of traffic fumes. After St James Street, this is where you'll find the best shopping in town, though not of the duty-free T-shirt and packaged rum variety. Barnett Street is also the site of the town's notorious main **police station** and lock-up, so run-down that the inmates sleep ten to a cell on concrete floors and the officers make regular appeals for donations. Turn down Railway Lane for the main fruit and vegetable outlet, **Charles William Gordon Market** (also known as Fustic Market). Straddling the disused railway tracks and the impoverished houses that make up MoBay's most notorious "ghetto" (though it's luxury by Kingston standards), the market is a visceral whirl of tarpaulin-covered stalls selling enormous mounds of earth-covered yams, sweet potatoes and cassava alongside deep-orange pumpkins, bunches of scallion and thyme, fat fingers of green bananas or plantain and a kaleidoscope of fruits. Goat belly and cheap chicken back are bartered in the pungent indoor meat section, where higglers make up temporary beds beside their pitches at the end of a day's trade. Main days are Wednesday and Saturday, but goods are always on sale and you get better deals here than at Gully Market. You can refresh yourself with a jelly coconut or Day-Glo sky juice from one of the ever-present vendors.

At the end of Barnett Street, the traffic opens up and passes over Montego River. Here, the roadside takes on an incongruously lush aspect; giant bulrushes and emerald reeds flourish in the greyish semi-sewage, and egrets roost in the few remaining poinciana and palm. Beyond the river is Westgate shopping centre, where a fairly good road branches off towards Adelphi and ultimately Cockpit Country.

West of town

Barnett Street shoots off from the dividing roundabout to become the A1 and takes you through MoBay at its least inspiring, a grim industrial estate perfumed by the slaughterhouse. The flotsam-filled yards and warehouses don't let up until well past the painted zinc fence circumventing **Catherine Hall Entertainment Centre**, stageshow venue and home of Reggae Sumfest (see p.50). The road ends at a T-junction, the right prong leading to **Freeport Peninsula**, a depressingly empty thoroughfare suspended in a limbo of factory fronts and marshland backing onto the Bogue Lagoon. Fuel silos block out the view of the bay and hundreds of cars sit marooned on the wharves until their owners can afford to get them through customs. The sole sign of life is at the **cruise-ship piers**, an incongruously flashy mass of expensive shops and restaurants that springs into action on docking days. Otherwise, you might wander up here for an early evening drink on the roof of the *Houseboat Grill* restaurant, which overlooks Bogue Lagoon, or a game of pool and a tasty lunch at the posh **Yacht Club**, ostensibly for members only but covertly accessible to tourists; shared taxis ply the route.

The left fork at the top of Howard Cooke Boulevard, Alice Eldemire Drive leads past new shopping malls and the Palace Multiplex to another T-junction. Turning left takes you toward Barnett Street, past the Gallery of West Indian Art (see p.267), while turning right takes you to Reading and, ultimately, Negril (see chapter 5). The initial stretch shoots past the town's new sewage treatment plant and what's left of the cane fields of the Barnett Estate.

Eating

Montego Bay's resort status ensures a fair share of swanky **restaurants** alongside the more usual Jamaican eateries, though many offer bland "international" fare or watered-down Jamaican dishes at inflated prices. Pricier tourist restaurants almost always offer free pick-ups; look out for flyers around town with various seasonal deals and special offers. Aside from notable exceptions such as *The Native*, Jamaican food is at its best in small-scale cook shops and restaurants; for local-style **fish**, head for Whitehouse. There are plenty of US-style **fast-food** outlets around town, including the Caribbean's largest *KFC* and an adjacent *Pizza Hut* opposite downtown's Dump-Up Beach; *McDonald's,* at the Baywest Shopping Centre on Harbour Street, Westgate Plaza and the Blue Diamond Shopping Centre in Ironshore; and *Burger King* branches on Gloucester Avenue and St James Street. There's a *Domino's Pizza* on Miranda Ridge; call ☎971 5887 for delivery. The concrete balustrades of Dead End Beach are a popular spot for take-away consumption. If you're after Sunday **brunch**, head to the *Wexford* hotel on Gloucester Avenue, where an all-inclusive Jamaican feast (US$10) is served on the terrace overlooking the bay.

We've given a phone number only for those places where you might need to reserve a table or you'd like to take advantage of a free pick-up.

Queen's Drive, downtown and around

Brandon Hill Village 11 Coke Ave, Brandon Hill ☎952 7665. Laid-back, very Jamaican hotel restaurant that does a good lunch trade with MoBay workers. Tables are set on a breezy porch affording downtown views, and the inexpensive menu ranges from baked chicken to curry mutton or fried fish. On Saturdays, there's free food for bar patrons.
Crafts Cafeteria Harbour St Craft Market. Excellent open-air bar and restaurant serving very reasonably priced Jamaican food, cooked to order. Popular with both stall-holders and tourists; the atmosphere is friendly and surprisingly hassle-free.

Georgian House Corner of Orange and Union streets. Attractive eighteenth-century building with a garden, serving well-made, inexpensive Jamaican take-aways.
Houseboat Grill Freeport Road ☎979 8845. Fantastic, unique setting in a beautifully converted houseboat moored on Bogue Lagoon. You board by way of a rope-pulled launch, and a window in the floor allows perusal of the marine life gliding underneath. The menu is superlative and sophisticated, mixing Jamaican cooking with international dishes; the pepper shrimp with scotch bonnet beurre blanc is unmissable, and the desserts are pure indulgence. Best choice in town, though not cheap.

For **patties**, calalloo loaf, coco bread and pastries, head to *Butterflake* on Union Street, *Tastee* on Barnett Street or *Juci Beef* on St James Street; Juicy Beef patties are available from Weekenders store, on Gloucester Avenue adjacent to Doctor's Cave Beach, and, on the beach itself, from the *L'Oven Best* snack outlet, which also does burgers. The Montego Bay (LOJ) shopping centre on Howard Cooke Boulevard has an excellent **food court** with a great view over the bay; Centerpoint Mall on Harbour Street has a branch of *Island Grill*, serving Jamaican fast food, and a *Pizza Hut*. Cheap and tasty jerk and filling soups are sold at the *Pork Pit* on Gloucester Avenue, while delicious box lunches (meat with rice and peas) come from *Wayne's* cook shop in the Fantasy Craft Market opposite Cornwall Beach. In the row of shops outside the market, *Tony's Pizza* (☎952 6365) is very popular with the locals, selling pizza and sub sandwiches late; free local deliveries are available. Downtown, *24-7*, on the corner of St. James Street and the Gully Market, serves **all-night** macaroni cheese or calalloo and saltfish with dumplings, but be prepared to jostle with crowds of hungry Jamaicans fresh from the clubs. Sweet teeth can be satisfied at the **frozen yoghurt** outlet underneath the *Pork Pit,* while *24-7* is the best **ice cream** outlet downtown.

I'N'I Paradise, Queen's Drive. Rastafarian vegetarian restaurant just beyond the airport entrance serving inexpensive, authentic Ital food in red-gold-and-green bamboo shacks. Excellent natural juices including roots wine and cane juice.

Smokey Joe's 19 St James St. Cheap and tasty local, serving no-nonsense Jamaican lunches and dinners in a comfortable atmosphere.

Tigers 23 St James St. Inexpensive, buffet-style Jamaican café frequented almost exclusively by locals. All the usual dishes, with some vegetarian food available. Enormous Jamaican breakfast served from 7am.

The Town House 16 Church St ☎952 2660. Genteel basement restaurant in a beautiful eighteenth-century building, reeking of old-world gentility. The dinner menu (New York steak, red snapper papillot, shrimp and lobster creole) is expensive, but the daily lunch special, taken at one of the pews in the lounge area, is great value.

Gloucester Avenue and around

Adwa City Centre Mall, Fort St. Fabulous air-conditioned vegetarian diner on the mall's top floor, offering breakfast (ackee, porridge); wholewheat ackee, veg or soya patties; salads; and lunches/dinners of ackee and tofu stew, curried tofu, veggie "chicken" and "lamb" dishes and all manner of pulse and vegetable combinations. Smoothies, natural juices and power drinks also available.

Akbar Gloucester Ave ☎979 0113. The sister of the renowned Kingston purveyor of fine Indian cooking serves excellent, justifiably expensive, curries in an air-conditioned dining room with tasteful Indian decor.

Baba Joe's Whitehouse. Roadside fish joint just past *Sandals*, with typically basic Jamaican-style decor and simple but gorgeous seafood: steamed, fried or escovitched fish, sea puss (octopus) and a tasty conch soup.

The Brewery Miranda Ridge, Gloucester Ave. Late-opening spot above the Strip. Extremely varied menu with daily specials, a big burger selection, lots of salads and some Mexican fare. Good value and pretty views.

Bullseye Gloucester Ave. Air-conditioned US-style steakhouse, serving prime imported cuts and some seafood, too. A reliable, if uninspiring, mid-range choice.

Evelyn's Kent Ave, Whitehouse ☎952 3280. Locals' seafood joint right on the water, serving all things piscatorial with rice, bammy or roti. Great cooking, inexpensive prices and a casual, laid-back vibe.

Groovy Grouper Doctor's Cave Beach ☀www.groovygrouper.com. On a raised deck overlooking the sand, this moderately priced seafood restaurant comes into its own at night, when lights twinkle in the greenery and the bay views are fabulous. But it's good for a local-style meal anytime, serving pepper shrimp, crab cakes and jerk calamari as well as fish, lobster and chicken. Best value is the all-you-can eat Friday night seafood buffet (US$19.95).

Guangzhou Miranda Ridge, Gloucester Ave. The only Chinese restaurant on the Strip, and very good it is, too. The indoor dining room is a bit gloomy in the daytime, but a 15-percent weekday lunch discount pulls in the punters. Prices are generally moderate.

Ma Lou's *Coral Cliff* 165 Gloucester Ave ☎952 4130, ⊚www.coralcliffjamaica.com. Upscale, indoor air-conditioned restaurant serving an intermittently successful range of moderate to expensive Caribbean-wide specialities; stick to the Jamaica specials and you can't go far wrong. The *Rum Jungle* in the gaming lounge has lighter fare.

Margaritaville Gloucester Ave. The loudest place on the Strip. Mid-priced international menu with a Mexican flavour, and American-style service with the emphasis on fun. Hidden behind an aquatic wall mural, *Marguerites* (☎952 4777) next door has elegant decor, upscale atmosphere and a more expensive continental menu specializing in seafood; there's a flambé grill for table-side cooking as well. Outdoor terrace dining over the bay makes it very popular with honeymoon couples.

The Native 29 Gloucester Ave ☎979 2769. The best place on the Strip for a sit-down Jamaican meal – but not cheap, so take advantage of reduced-rate buffets and lunch specials. Try the "Boonoonoo's Platter" of ackee, curry goat, jerk chicken and escovitched fish, rice and peas and plantain.

The Pelican Gloucester Ave ☎952 3171. Long-established, mid-priced restaurant popular with locals and tourists. Highlights include cornmeal porridge or American/Jamaican breakfast, the daily lunch specials (from fricassee chicken to cow foot) and desserts (rum pudding and coconut- or banana-cream pie).

Pork Pit Gloucester Ave. Stop by for a inexpensive, delicious jerk and substantial soups.

Raine's St James Place, Gloucester Ave. Popular kiosk café situated between Doctor's Cave and Cornwall beaches. Local and American breakfasts, burgers and home-made cakes are served all day.

Scotchies Ironshore, near the *Holiday Inn Hotel*. A bit out of the way, but worth the effort if you're after some excellent jerk cooking; pork, chicken, fish and seafood are served with festival, breadfruit, yam or sweet potato. You eat at palm-thatch-shaded tables set back from the road.

Sunset Restaurant and Bar Gloucester Ave. Tiny, easily missed place that's the only really authentic Jamaican bar and restaurant along the Strip, as suggested by the clientele – taxi drivers and Jamaican couples. Recommended, especially for the home-made ginger beer. Inexpensive.

Tapas Corniche Rd ☎952 2988. Innovative and delicious Mediterranean food in a place that's upscale but affordable, and blessedly detached from the Strip (take the small road to the left of *Coral Cliff* hotel). Try such delights as shrimp- and crab-stuffed butterfish, chicken pesto crepes or pork with pimento.

Voyage Walter Fletcher Beach. Good, moderately priced Jamaican cooking in a lovely seaside setting. Your choices include pepperpot, conch or pumpkin soups, burgers and fries, salads and mains such as spicy shrimp, fish fingers with lemon-pepper mayonnaise, Red Stripe snapper, curried mutton and chicken or oxtail and beans.

Drinking, nightlife and entertainment

Surprisingly, Montego Bay is not particularly lively at **night**; the Strip takes on a ghostly hush as the cruise ships glide out of the harbour and visitors hole up in their all-inclusives. Walter Fletcher (Aquasol) and Doctor's Cave beaches are great for a drink by the sea, and there's usually something going on at *Dead End Bar*, at the end of Kent Avenue – the bar's music competes with the in-car sound systems of locals parked up by the sea wall. For a more sedate evening, *Coyaba* hotel in Ironshore has jazz and free finger food on Fridays during its half-price cocktail hour (from 6.30pm). For the most part though, MoBay's nightlife is conveniently centred around **Margaritaville** and **Coral Cliff** on Gloucester Avenue, both of which are full most nights. If you're feeling lucky, the *Coral Cliff* **gaming lounge** has over a hundred slot machines, free drinks for punters and a US$50,000 jackpot. *The Brewery* and *Pier One* are popular enough at weekends, while several enjoyably seedy downtown joints attract a crowd of die-hards; all get going by 11pm and keep the pace until the small hours. Cover charges vary, but you're unlikely to pay more than US$10 unless it's an all-inclusive night, when the entrance fee might run about US$15.

Bars and clubs

Bayside Jerk Centre Bogue Crossing. A low-key outdoor bar attached to a guesthouse, it's a nice place to sink a few beers alongside the locals. There's a good oldies session on Friday nights, and jerk food to soak up the beer.

Blast Bar Gloucester Ave, next to *Caribic House* hotel. This is a small, locally run bar with pool tables and a couple of slot machines; good for a late-night drink.

Bottle Inn 11 Union St. Late-opening club with ultraviolet light and a certain louche charm. Wednesday is dancehall night, Thursday is old hits. Recommended for a taste of real Jamaican clubbing. Open nightly.

The Brewery Miranda Ridge, Gloucester Ave. Friendly bar-cum-nightclub, permanently packed at the weekends with an up-marketish crowd of mostly young Jamaicans who spill out onto the attractive decked bar. Tuesday and Friday are highly entertaining karaoke nights, popular with both game locals and partying tourists, and there's usually a big-name DJ at the weekends.

Coral Cliff 165 Gloucester Ave ☎952 4130, ✆www.coralcliffjamaica.com. All is glitz and glamour inside the *Rum Jungle* bar here. There's free live music nightly from the very professional in-house band, a non-dancehall music policy and occasional comedy or theme nights. Attracts a mixed crowd of tourists, the more well-to-do locals and flashily dressed gigolos. Busy when all else is quiet, and open 24 hours.

Dead End Bar (renamed *Po'k Knockers*) Kent Ave. Open around the clock, this is a laid-back spot perfect for sunset- and plane-watching or a game of pool. Thursday night is given over to a sound-system beach party, with a comprehensive mix of reggae, soca and hip hop. Sunday is oldies night, with classic reggae and rocksteady churned out until the last punter leaves, and there's karaoke on offer at other times.

Flamingo Sugarmill Rd, Ironshore. The usual X-rated go-go dancing and all-round lasciviousness occasionally make way for phenomenally popular jams by the best of the Kingston-based sound systems. Open nightly.

Goldfingers Market St. Dingy dancehall club downtown favoured by kissing couples and expert Jamaican dancers – make sure you know your butterfly from your Diwali. Open nightly.

Groovy Grouper Doctor's Cave Beach. Pretty setting for a seaside cocktail or beer, with sports events on big-screen TVs.

Hi-Lites Café 19 Queen's Drive. Very sleepy bar, but a great escape from the Strip and worth visiting for the wonderful view across the bay.

Keg 2 Barnett St, on the corner of Harbour St. Friendly local hangout with a popular oldies session every Wednesday. Open nightly. Cover charge US$3.

Margaritaville Gloucester Ave ☎952 4777, ✆margaritavillecaribbean.com. Hugely popular bar-cum-club with sports events on big-screen TVs, 52 different flavours of margarita and 32-ounce "bongs of beer" to help keep the atmosphere buzzing. Themed parties, which usually culminate in a packed dance floor, include Wednesday night pyjama parties (US$15 all-inclusive, half-price if you come suitably attired), and Thursday Latin nights. There's a "World Party" on Fridays; Saturdays see well-known guest DJs and drinks promotions; and there's karaoke on Sundays. If you're looking for guaranteed action this is the place, and if you don't mind gigolos galore and sunburnt tourists, it's great fun. Open nightly; dance floor opens at 10pm. Cover charge US$5 Sun–Tues.

Nick's Reading. Right on the main road near the turnoff for Anchovy, this seaside spot with a smoking jerk centre is a great place for a drink, with pool tables and games (draughts, ludo, dominoes, darts and backgammon) on offer. There's an oldies jam session from 9pm on Fridays. Open nightly.

Pier One Howard Cook Blvd ✆www.pieronejamaica .com. MoBay old-timer that's as popular as ever. Oldies on the boardwalk during the week and a pumping club at the weekends. Small cover charge.

Randles Hart St. Brilliant oldies club (ska, R&B, soul) in a large open-air building downtown. Popular with an eclectic mix of Jamaicans, and though you won't feel unwelcome, this is strictly non-tourist territory so go with a local. Thurs & Sun only. Small cover charge.

Richmond Hill Inn Union St ☎952 3859. A brilliant spot for a sunset drink by the pool. The setting – on its very own hill at the top of Union St – is spectacular and intensely romantic; the view covers the whole bay.

Voyage Bar Walter Fletcher Beach. Right by the sea, the open-air bar is a lovely spot for a quiet drink (try the excellent margaritas). The cavernous all-wood function area upstairs is opened up for regular nightly events; currently, there's DJs on Tuesdays, and a teen party on Saturdays. Cover charge of around J$300 for some events.

Live music, theatre and cinema

Unless you're content with a diet of tired in-hotel floor shows, you'll often be climbing the walls for **live entertainment** in MoBay. **Music** is the town's strongest suit, with regular live reggae at various Strip venues and at the beaches, where you'll occasionally find stageshows and open-air sound-system nights, generally more pleasant than the hot and smoky indoor venues. Walter Fletcher Beach/Aquasol is a popular venue for sporadic visits from Jamaica's top **DJs**, as are *Pier One* and *The Brewery.* **Live stageshows** (including Reggae Sumfest in August and Air Jamaica Jazz and Blues in January or February) are held at the Catherine Hall Entertainment Centre on Howard Cooke Boulevard, Caribbean Beach Park in Ironshore or *Club Inferno* in Rose Hall; they're advertised on Irie FM and by way of banners and posters all around town.

There are two **cinemas** in town: the brand new Palace Multiplex off Alice Eldemire Drive (℡979 8359) is the more luxurious, while over in Ironshore, there's the Diamond Cinema at the Blue Diamond Shopping Centre (℡953 9540). **Roots plays** are staged at the Montego Bay Civic Centre and occasionally at the Chatwick Gardens Centre, 10 Queen's Drive (℡9522147). For serious theatre, catch one of the excellent Montego Bay Little Theatre Movement productions at Fairfield Theatre (℡952 0182).

Shopping

As a major cruise-ship port, much of MoBay's consumer activity centres around **in-bond shopping**, with countless flashy malls given over to identical jewellery, perfume and leather goods outlets. They're all much of a muchness, but City Centre Mall on Fort Street is the least ostentatious. The Montego Bay Shopping Centre – usually referred to as the LOJ (Life of Jamaica) Mall – on Howard Cooke Boulevard is better for general purchases and has a couple of decent clothes shops, as well as a branch of the excellent Fontana Pharmacy, which is great for gimmicky souvenir mugs, pens, stationery and knick-knacks. The Baywest Mall on Harbour Street is also recommended for clothes; a particularly good shop here is Sahara, featuring linen shirts and shorts.

You can't move for **crafts** in MoBay. The best market is the huge Harbour Street complex (daily 7am–7pm) packed with straw and wicker work, belts, clothes, jewellery, T-shirts and woodcarvings; more unusual woodcarving can be found at Unit 4, while Betty at Unit 81 will sew the design of your choice onto a range of baskets. The Fort and Fantasy craft markets along the Strip (daily 8am–7pm) are worth a look but tend to be a little more expensive with less variety. Elsewhere, check out Irie Creations, upstairs in the City Centre Mall. The **Bob Marley Experience** at Half Moon Shopping Village has the largest collection of Bob Marley T-shirts in the world, as well as all kinds of other Marley memorabilia.

Head downtown for the best **art** shopping. The **Gallery of West Indian Art**, 11 Fairfield Rd, Catherine Hall (Ⓦwww.galleryofwestindianart.com), has a huge range of works and is renowned for its hand-carved and painted wooden animals. The tiny Heaven's Art Gallery, 1 Church Lane, houses, among the tombstones (carved and engraved here), the wonderful paintings of the late Hector Heavens, Montego Bay's most talented naive artist. For Jamaican and Cuban prints and originals, at upscale prices, try Ambiente Gallery at 10 Fort

St. On the Strip, below the Cultural Arts Centre at 31 Gloucester Ave, Elgo's exhibits and sells the Cubist paintings of the eponymous artist.

Downtown **record stores** offer the Jamaican speciality of custom-made reggae tapes (around US$3) as well as CDs and vinyl. Worth a visit, for the enthusiasm of owner Ainsworth Palmer coupled with his large collection of classic sounds, is Federal Records, 14 Strand St. Other shops include El Paso, at 3 South Lane overlooking Sam Sharpe Square, and Top Rank in Westgate Plaza. For sound-system session tapes and bootleg recordings of recent stageshows (US$5) check Clapper's Mobile Music Box in the Church Lane car park; the quality is surprisingly good, but ask for a test play before you buy.

For miscellaneous odds and ends, browse around the untouristy stores downtown. St James Street holds a branch of the dependable Sangster's **bookstore** chain and Dominion Stationery, with an excellent selection of 1970s postcards and a small but good-quality selection of yellowing books, while Barnett Street is best for useless souvenirs. If you want to take home some **rum**, the cheapest option is to club together and buy it wholesale from C&J Liquors on Harbour Street, though the Jamaica Farewell pre-packed boxes from in-bond shops are easier to carry and only a little more expensive.

Listings

Airlines Air Jamaica ☏1-888-359 2475 (toll-free) or 952 4100; Air Jamaica Express ☏952 5401; American Airlines ☏1-800-744 0006 (toll-free); and British Airways ☏952 3771. All are based at the airport.

Airport enquiries Sangster International Airport's ticket, flight and baggage information line is ☏952 3124, or visit ✆www.sangster-airport.com.jm.

American Express Grace Kennedy Travel Ltd, right by the craft market at 2 Market St (☏979 5912), can replace lost or stolen Amex travellers' cheques.

Banks and money Several banks congregate around Sam Sharpe Square; most efficient are Bank of Nova Scotia (also at Westgate Shopping Centre) and NCB (with other branches on Gloucester Ave opposite Cornwall Beach and at the airport); all have ATMs. Citizens Bank is at Montego Bay (LOJ) Shopping Centre, also with an ATM. With good rates and a convenient location, FX Trader (Mon–Sat 9am–5pm), above the Pelican restaurant, is the best place for currency exchange and also handles Western Union wire transfers. There are several other cambios along the Strip; others are Alvin Wallace, Unit 144, Harbour Street Craft Market, and Cambioman, 8 Market St.

Car and bike rental Car rental companies have offices at the airport or on Queens Drive/Sunset Boulevard. International companies: Bargain ☏952 0762; Budget ☏952 3838; and Hertz ☏979 0438. Local operators are usually cheaper; most reliable are: Alex's ☏940 6260; Beaumont's ☏971 8476;

Horizon ☏952 0185; Island, Sangster Airport ☏952 5771; Prospective, 28 Union St ☏952 011; Sunbird ☏952 4975; Sunshine ☏952 4218; United ☏952 307.

Consulates Only the Canadian Consulate (☏952 6198) and US Consulate (☏952 0160) have offices in Montego Bay; both are on Gloucester Ave. UK citizens should call the British Honorary Consul John Terry (☏953 3301 or mobile 999 9693). Embassies and other consulates are all based in Kingston.

Dentists Dr Marlene Foote, 14c Market St ☏952 3016; Dr Vernon Gardiner, 90 Barnett St ☏952 5742.

Doctors Most hotels have a doctor or nurse on duty or on call. A recommended practitioner is Dr Anthony Vendryes, whose surgery is at the *Royal Court* hotel on Sewell Ave (☏979 3333); or call Dr Ramanujam Prathap (☏979 0053) or Dr Sonia Nixon (☏952 0256).

Hospitals Cornwall Regional Hospital, Mount Salem (☏952 5100 or 6683), is the best public hospital outside Kingston. The best private institutions are Doctor's Hospital in Fairfield (☏952 1616) and the MoBay Hope Medical Clinic at Half Moon Shopping Village, Rose Hall (☏953 3649 or 9310). In an emergency dial ☏119 for an ambulance.

Immigration Immigration Office, Floor 3, Overton Plaza, Union St ☏952 5381; Mon–Thurs 8.30am–4pm, Fri 8.30am–4pm. For visa extensions, go early to avoid the queues.

Internet The best place to check email, at around

J$50 for 15min, is Cyberhaus, upstairs adjacent to *Sunset Restaurant*, 37 Gloucester Ave (Mon–Sat 9am–midnight, Sun 9am–10pm). The St James Parish Library has a small computer lab that allows half an hour of free Internet access.

Laundry Most hotels have a laundry service, but there are some fairly good coin-operated laundries. Try Bay Fabricare Centre at 4 Corner Lane (☎952 6987), Westgate Fabricare in Westgate Plaza (☎940 1143) or Ironshore Fabricare in Blue Diamond Shopping Centre, Ironshore (☎953 8918).

Pharmacies There are plenty of pharmacies downtown. Best equipped are Clinicare on Sam Sharpe Square (Mon–Sat 9am–8pm, Sun 10am–6pm); Fontana, Montego Bay (LOJ) Shopping Centre (Mon–Sat 8am–7pm); and Hilton's Pharmacy, 27 St James St (Mon–Sat 9am–8pm). There are no pharmacies on the Strip; the Sunset Supermarket sells basic toiletries.

Photography You can buy or develop film at Photo Express, Fort St (☎952 3120); Salmon's, 32 St James St (☎952 4527); and Ventura, 22 Market St (☎952 2937).

Police Montego Bay has four police stations. The largest and newest is inconveniently located in Catherine Hall (☎952 4997) and the nearest downtown station is at 14 Barnett St (☎952 1557). Visitors are usually told to take complaints or crime reports directly to the Tourism Liaison Unit at Summit station on Sunset Blvd (☎952 1540). If your car is impounded, you should go to the station at 27 Church St (☎952 5310). In an emergency, dial ☎119; the Woman Inc rape crisis line is ☎952 9533.

Post offices The two main post offices are Number 1, on the corner of Fort St opposite the library, and Number 2, at 120 Barnett St. There is a postal agency (Whitesands PO) on Gloucester Ave next to Doctor's Cave Beach; you can pick up post-restante mail at all three, but Whitesands is the least frenetic.

Supermarkets There are large supermarkets in Westgate Plaza on Barnett St, Overton Plaza on Union St, and Blue Diamond Shopping Centre in Ironshore. Mini-marts on Gloucester Ave are pricey but convenient; try Sunset Supermarket and Deli opposite *Casa Blanca* hotel or New Eagle Supermarket in the *MoBay Club* building, which stays open until 10pm daily.

Taxis Reliable taxi ranks on the Strip are operated from both *The Gloustershire* and the *Coral Cliff*; best of the lot, though, is the Doctor's Cave stand (☎952 0521), opposite the *Doctor's Cave Beach Hotel*. Downtown, locals take taxis from the Market St stand. Recommended drivers for longer distances and custom-made tours are Dale Porter, aka Rasta Shaka (☎806 8147 or 375 7918); Keith Tomlinson (☎971 5420 or 990 5637); and Danny Paterson (mobile ☎707 4767 or 979 4103).

Telephones The Strip is fairly well served by public phones, and there's a large bank of them opposite the Cable and Wireless building on Church St. Overseas calls can be made cheaply at Teleworld on Miranda Ridge, Gloucester Ave, though it's easier to buy a World Talk card and dial from your hotel.

Travel agents Friendly Travel Service, 18 Strand St ☎979 5797; International Travel Service, 14b Market St ☎952 2485; Vaughans, 3 Corner Lane ☎952 5140.

Around Montego Bay

Away from the shops and the beaches, there's plenty to see around Montego Bay, and though many of the attractions – like **Rose Hall**, with its ghoulish reputation and theme-park ambience – are so hyped-up that you couldn't miss them if you tried, others, such as the **Rocklands Bird Sanctuary** or the **Belvedere Estate**, have a quiet charm and natural beauty that are effortlessly seductive.

Other than for **raft trips** down the Great River from Lethe, few people head into the **St James interior.** That's a shame because the rolling hinterland pastures are spectacular in places. St James was prime plantation territory under the British and a few of the old estates have kept their land and opened it up to the public. Polished boiling pots and repointed stone mills illustrate the mechanics of the sugar industry, and lavishly restored great house interiors froth over the planters' lifestyles. However, there's little to commemorate one of the most significant phases in Jamaican history: the **Christmas Rebellion** of 1831, which began in St James and set the wheels in motion for the abolition of slavery.

East along the coast

With its endless reefs and postcard beaches, the eastern stretch of coast beyond Montego Bay has long been the preserve of the more expensive all-inclusive hotels. As a consequence, the A1 coast road is a pleasure to drive. Straight and smooth, it zips through the plush residential belt of **IRONSHORE**, home to three of the island's best **golf courses:** the independent Ironshore Golf and Country Club (℡953 2800), the Ritz Carlton hotel's White Witch course (℡518 0100) and the Half Moon Golf Club (℡953 2211). The area was once part of a vast sugar plantation; from Sugarmill Road you can see the remains of crumbling chimneys and an aqueduct.

Some of the island's best **horseback riding** is found at the Half Moon Equestrian Centre (℡953 2286; daily 9am–5pm), an immaculate facility within the *Half Moon* hotel that's home to some of the best-kept mounts in Jamaica, most of them ex-racehorses. Beginners are welcome on the Jungle Jaunt, a forty-five-minute trek that starts with a short lesson (US$30); more experienced riders can take the Tryall Trail, a longer ride along bridle paths into the Jamaican countryside (1hr 45min; US$60). By far the best option, though, is the Sand Shuttle (1hr 45min; US$60), a ride through the hotel gardens and onto the beach (passing the resort's new dolphin enclosure, closed to non-guests), where you strip off to your swimsuit and ride out into the waves. Unlike other Jamaican beach rides, where the horses simply trot through deep water, this allows you to actually swim your horse back to shore – far less strain on the legs and immeasurably more fun. Dressage, showjumping and polo lessons are also on offer, as are pony rides for kids (US$10).

Rose Hall

Romanticized plantation history comes into its own at **ROSE HALL**, six miles east from MoBay and site of the infamous **Rose Hall Great House** (daily 9am–6pm; US$15). The house is the inspiration for Jamaica's best-loved piece of folklore, the tale of a voodoo practitioner who ruthlessly disposed of her husbands and is still said to haunt the corridors. Built between 1770 and 1780 by its first owner, planter and parish custos (the old English term for a mayor) John Palmer, the dazzling white stone structure, set back from the A1 and surrounded by gardens, woods and a swan-filled pond, is difficult to miss. Rose Hall makes much of the vastly embellished legend of Annie Palmer, the "White Witch of Rose Hall", and the rather mechanical guided tours that run every fifteen minutes milk it shamelessly. You gasp at blurred photos that supposedly show the face of an unknown woman in the mirror, and you gawp at Annie's bedroom, symbolically redecorated in shades of red, and the terrace from which she allegedly pushed a maid to her death. As the house was unoccupied and widely looted during the nineteenth century, almost all of its current contents have been transported from other great houses or from overseas. The silk wallpaper, magnificent mahogany staircase and furnishings are attractive

Jamaica's most famous horror story centres on **Annie Palmer**, the "White Witch of Rose Hall". A beautiful young woman of Anglo-Irish descent, Annie Mary Patterson's early years are cloaked in mystery. Born in either England or Ireland, she was the only child of small-time property owners John and Juliana Patterson, who brought her to live in Haiti as a little girl, where she learned the voodoo art. The date of her arrival in Jamaica is unknown, but it's said that she came to Kingston as a fresh-faced seventeen-year-old in search of a husband. Being young and white, she was granted access to high society functions and her brooding good looks soon captured the attention of John Palmer, incumbent of Rose Hall and grand-nephew of its architect, also named John Palmer. They married in March 1820, but the union was not a happy one; seven years on and bored with her insipid husband, Annie took a young slave lover. Palmer found out and whipped her severely; Annie took her revenge by placing poison in his wine, smothering the dying man with a pillow. She went on to stab and strangle two more husbands and seduce and murder a succession of white book-keepers and black slaves. She was a cruel and sadistic mistress – even to those slaves she wasn't sleeping with – meting out excessive punishments for minor misdemeanours.

However, Annie's cruelty proved to be her undoing, and she was murdered in her bed in 1831. No one knows for sure whose hands encircled her neck, but some accounts point to an old and powerful balmist whose pretty granddaughter had been in competition with Annie for the attentions of a young English book-keeper until the older woman set an "ol' hige" vampire upon her rival, killing her within a week.

Gripping as it is, there's barely a shred of truth in the story (though it is retold in bodice-ripping style in Herbert DeLisser's novelized version; see *Contexts*). Annie Palmer did exist (she's buried in a concrete grave to the left of the house), but by all accounts she was a peaceful woman with no discernible tendencies to sadism or lechery. She may have become confused over the years with Rosa Palmer, the original mistress of Rose Hall, who did have four husbands, but she was said to be unwaveringly virtuous. Nonetheless, most Jamaicans choose to believe in something more sinister, and visiting mediums swear to strange visions and the discovery of buried effigies in the grounds.

(if not from the right period), but the fake food and on-site Olde English pub – legacies of a gaudy refurbishment in the mid-1960s – rather spoil the romance.

Nevertheless, the grounds are lovely, although these too have a violent past, this one authentic. On Good Friday in 1963 the district was the site of the **"Coral Gardens Massacre"**, a bloody altercation between police and Rastafarians – then commonly viewed as vicious, anti-white, drug-crazed maniacs – whose right of way through the Rose Hall grounds to their vegetable plots was being threatened by property speculators developing the house into the tourist attraction it is today. After months of contention, a policeman sent to arrest the dissidents was attacked with a spear, and a petrol station was set on fire. The army was called in, and during the ensuing bloodbath eight Rastas died. The police then declared an unofficial "war on Rastas" islandwide, and hundreds were thrown into jail, their locks forcibly sheared off. Obviously, nothing marks the spot, though local Rastafarians commemorate the killings at Sam Sharpe Square each Easter.

The Rose Hall empire extends a few miles east along the coast to the non-descript roadside community of **LILLIPUT**, where **Rose Hall Beach Club** (daily 9am–6pm; US$6 including beach lounger; ⓦwww.jamaicawatersports .com) is a prettily landscaped beach with full tourist amenities. It's advertised as the safest beach in Montego Bay – presumably because the entry fee precludes entry to most local people. It's a lovely place to swim, though, with plenty of shade, beach volleyball, a restaurant and bar and comprehensive watersports facilities.

The towering *Wyndham Rose Hall* resort (see below) dominates the rest of the Rose Hall district. Its expansive (and expensive) **golf course** contains a beautiful waterfall seen in the Jamaican James Bond classic *Live and Let Die*. It's an excellent spot for a walk even if you don't play golf – though you should check at the hotel before entering. The hotel is also home to the **Sugar Mills Falls**, a water complex billed as the Caribbean's most spectacular, with cascading waterfalls, a 280ft thrill slide, three terraced pools, and bridges from which to watch all the fun. Unfortunately, the falls are only open to guests at the *Wyndham* hotel, though the friendly management may make an exception for visitors keen to test the waters.

Practicalities

The *Wyndham Rose Hall* hotel (ⓣ953 2560; ⓦwww.wyndham.com; ⓦ) is an ugly high-rise with an incongruously plush lobby, a pristine private beach and five bars and restaurants. A simpler **place to stay** is *Dunn's Villa Resort,* two miles inland (ⓣ953 7459, ⓦwww.dunnsvillaresort.com; ⓦ), a small family-run resort with a pool, jacuzzi, restaurant and mountain bikes for rent. Rooms are pleasantly decorated but somewhat overpriced, so haggle; rates include breakfast.

The fanciest place to **eat** in the area is the *Ambrosia Restaurant* at *Wyndham Rose Hall* (ⓣ953 2560 ext 459)*,* serving top-notch, top-whack Mediterranean dishes with an accent on seafood.

Greenwood

Five miles east from Rose Hall, the A1 passes through scrubby mangrove swamps and opens up with a magnificent sea view at diminutive **GREEN-WOOD**. Perched on a hill overlooking the sea, the dull white stone of **Greenwood Great House** (daily 9am–6pm; US$12) provides a classy deviation from the concrete new-builds below. Surrounded by luscious flowering gardens, the house itself has none of the flashy allure of Rose Hall, but is of far more interest, having managed to retain most of its original contents as well as a wonderfully listless, frozen-in-time eighteenth-century ambience. Built in 1790 by relatives of the Barrett family of Wimpole Street fame (see p.234), the house was used primarily for recreation and entertaining. It contains the owners' original library and a wonderfully eclectic collection of objects including ancient (and still functioning) musical instruments, a court jester's chair and custom-made Wedgwood china. The Barretts clearly had an eye for scenery, as the seventy-foot veranda commands a panoramic view of the sea unbroken by land, and, doubtful as it may seem, you really can see the curvature of the earth. The tour, which ends in the bar set up in the original kitchen area, is much more enjoyable than the breakneck run round Rose Hall. There's little on the property's slave history, however. The Barretts owned 84,000 acres hereabouts, worked by some 2000 Africans, but the tour includes just a cursory reference to a man trap used to catch runaways and a leg iron displayed on the wall like an ornament. Meanwhile, with an apparent lack of irony, the female guides are dolled up as eighteenth-century servants.

Nearby (but closed to the public), **Cinnamon Hill Great House** was also built by the Barretts, but is now the private home of country-and-western star Johnny Cash. He's a local hero both as a singer (country music is incredibly popular in Jamaica) and for his regular contributions to children's charities and schools.

Just outside Greenwood, fluttering flags and red, gold and green huts mark the first buildings of the **Bob Marley School for the Arts** (T 954 5252), an ambitious project that is slated to spread out over two hundred acres of land here. The school, which aims to be the island's premier musical training centre, is the brainchild of reggae expert Astor Black; check out his website for further details (W www.bobartsinstitute.edu). Until it's up and functioning, Black presides over a beach bar and regular Rasta drumming sessions.

Practicalities

Though this is a bit of a desolate stretch (shared taxis back to MoBay are J$40), there are a couple of accommodation options in and around Greenwood. *Sea Castles* (T 953 9117, W www.seacastlesjamaica.com; 4) is a sprawling complex of self-contained apartments right on the coast between the *Wyndham* hotel and Greenwood, with a pool, private but tiny beach, watersports and two restaurants. On the same stretch of road, but with a prettier seaside setting, is the *All Seasons Resort* (T 953 1448, F 1449, W ww.colorgraphix.net /allseasons; 5), an intimate grouping of white-painted apartments around a driftwood-decorated bar. Finally, *Royal Reef* (T 953 1700, W www.royalreefjamaica .com; 6), just up the road from *All Seasons*, is a rather incongruously glitzy newish place offering tropical chintz and all mod cons in its luxurious rooms, as well as a pool, a murky beach and a restaurant.

For **eating and drinking**, the *Far Out Fish Hut*, eastwards along the A1 just half a mile beyond Greenwood, has renowned fish and bammy and a laid-back seaside setting. More Jamaican food is available at *Turtles Inn*, half a mile further down the road and worth a visit for the home-made conch soup alone; fish and chicken are also available. Slightly more tourist-oriented, *Last Chance,* just up the A1, also offers delicious fish and friendly staff.

The St James interior

Shooting off from Reading on Montego Bay's western flank, the well-signposted B8 inland road plunges straight into tropical St James. The initial steep incline, known as Long Hill, parallels the Great River valley and affords occasional glimpses of the lush palms and ferns of the chasm below. Most visitors venture here to raft the river and hike at **Lethe**, although there are more worthy attractions further on, including the superlative **Rocklands Bird Sanctuary** and the unique German settlement of **Seaford Town**. The B8 is the quickest route to Savannah-la-Mar and the south coast, so traffic is pretty heavy. Striking west out of downtown Montego Bay, Fairfield Road (locally known as Trucker Road due to the constant presence of juggernauts en route to quarries hereabouts) takes you into a strikingly beautiful landscape. Country roads overhung with dripping foliage pass over swift streams and hug the edges of the Cockpit foothills, and the tarmac barely grips the edges of steep valleys lined by tiny hamlets such as **Kensington**, the key flashpoint of the Christmas Rebellion.

If you don't have a car, you'll often find **transport** a problem in the interior. Buses are practically nonexistent towards Kensington, so your best bet, if you're heading somewhere fairly near the B8, is to hop on a Sav-la-Mar bus, get off as near to your destination as possible and complete the journey on foot. It's much easier to join an organized tour or hire a private driver (see p.248).

Lethe and around

Less than ten miles south from MoBay and well signposted from the B8, **LETHE** is a pretty village set amid cool and vividly green hills, with a graceful stone bridge, built by slaves in 1820, straddling the gushing Great River. The village's focal point, on your left as you enter, is **Lethe Estate** (☎956 4920, lethe@cwjamaica.com). From here you can go **rafting** along the Great River; the 45-minute trip (US$34 for two people, US$44 including pick-up from MoBay) takes you past banks dripping with vines and overhung by trees. It rains a lot up here, so the water often takes on a muddy aspect, but it's still safe for swimming. There are a few rather turbulent spots where the shallows tumble and bubble over rocks; the bamboo rafts scrape the bottom a little, but the punt-handlers are far too experienced to sink.

On the road up to Lethe you'll notice signs for the **Nature Village Farm** (Mon–Fri 10am–6pm, Sat & Sun 11am–7pm; free; mobile ☎912 0172), several miles along an appallingly potholed road at the appropriately named Eden. It's a very scenic spot on the Great River with manicured lawns, bamboo groves, an open-air restaurant on a deck overlooking the water, a go-kart track and a sweeping collection of basketball, volleyball and netball courts and soccer pitches. The cooked-to-order Jamaican food, from curried shrimp to sandwiches, salads, omelettes and fries, is excellent and inexpensive. You can swim in the river from several places and kick back with a game of pool afterwards. This is a marvellous spot to get away from it all.

Just two miles beyond Lethe at Copse, the road curves; look out for a dirt road to the left by a lightpost, which will takes you down to **Animal Farm** (Mon–Fri tours by arrangement, Sat & Sun 10am–5pm; J$200; ☎815 4104, ⓦfly.to/animalfarm). A delightful, environmentally conscious and well-tended smallholding, run completely on solar energy, it makes a worthwhile stop, especially if you're travelling with small children. It has a huge array of exotic birds, a petting zoo and a herb garden, all with good labelling. Below the main part of the property there's a swimmable river.

Rocklands Bird Sanctuary and Feeding Station

Back on the B8, the first community after the Lethe turnoff is **ANCHOVY**, little more than a school, post office and a couple of snack bars as well as the popular *Bojangles* dancehall; partygoers travel from miles around to take in some of Jamaica's top DJs here. Just before the town proper, a battered JTB sign indicates the hugely potholed turn-off for the fabulous **Rocklands Bird Sanctuary and Feeding Station** (daily 2–5pm; US$8; ☎952 2009). The flowered former home and gardens of the late Lisa Salmon, a celebrated ornithologist, this is the only place on the island where hummingbirds are confident enough to drink sugar water while perched on your outstretched finger. Feeding peaks at around 4pm, when the air thrums with tiny wings. More than a hundred varieties of bird have visited here, including orange quits, vervain and the streamer-tailed doctor, Jamaica's national bird. A nature walk through the gardens is included in the entry fee, but serious ornithologists should call ahead to arrange more specific bird-watching hikes. The extremely knowledgeable Fritz can take you on bird-watching trails through the property and beyond (US$10). At the time of writing, two guest rooms were under construction here; call for an update.

Montpelier

About three miles further along the B8 from Anchovy is **MONTPELIER**, 2000ft above sea level and surrounded by citrus groves, arable land and cattle meadows. The crumbling stone buildings in front of the hilltop Anglican **church** (declared a national monument in 1999), reached along a muddy track off the main road, are all that's left of one of the largest sugar estates in western Jamaica, burned to the ground during the Christmas Rebellion (see box, p.259). A rusting plaque marks the spot of the ensuing skirmish between British forces and the "black regiment". If you're in Montpelier visiting the church, it's worth knocking on the door of the adjacent rectory; the Rev Antony Otty is a highly entertaining character and welcomes visitors. Pat, his wife, is an authority on the history of the village and its environs.

A further fifteen minutes' drive along the track, the eight-hundred-acre **Montpelier Blue Hole Nature Park** (daily 8am–5pm; US$4; mobiles T 423 8241 or 389 8643) claims to be a botanical garden but is more like a pastoral retreat, visited mostly by schools and church groups on outings. The views across the hills are awesome, and there is a huge swimming pool, an aqueduct dating back to 1747 and a series of breathtaking swimmable and climbable waterfalls along the Blue Hole River, a tributary of the Great River. You can **camp** in the park for US$6 per person; simple **food** is sometimes available from the thatched bar if you call ahead, or you can bring your own picnic and cook on the barbecue.

Just beyond Montpelier, the B8 forks; a right turn takes you over the interior mountains to Shettlewood and on to Savannah-la-Mar in Jamaica's far west. It's an incredibly pretty route, made even more pleasant in season by the accompanying smell of orange blossoms from the surrounding citrus plantations. The communities along the road are diminutive; only **Ramble** boasts a petrol station and a police station. Just before Ramble, and signposted off the road at Haughton Grove, you can **stay** and absorb the pastoral calm at *Countryside Villa* (mobiles T 601 3583 or 817 9120; ❷), a surprisingly modern little complex with a fishing pond, large pool, tennis courts, a small gym and a restaurant. Rooms are pleasant and simple, with cable TV and fan or a/c. There are lots of hiking possibilities around here, as well as plenty of breezily positioned hammocks in which to recover.

Seaford Town

Back on the B8, taking the left fork at Montpelier leads you through some marvellous countryside to **SEAFORD TOWN**. At first glance, this is just another rural community, but you'll soon notice that a lot of the older residents are white. In 1834, the British administration, fearing that forthcoming emancipation would result in widespread chaos and a mass exodus from the sugar plantations, began a pre-emptive programme of European settlement throughout the island's interior. To establish a "civilizing" white presence throughout Jamaica, and, more importantly, snap up the best land and labour before the slaves could (thus keeping Africans at work on the lowland plantations), it drafted in more than a thousand Germans over the next two years, promising them land and prosperity after a set period of indentured toil. Between 1834 and 1836, 251 Germans settled in Seaford Town, a five-hundred-acre plot of land donated by Lord Seaford of nearby Montpelier. The rest of the immigrants scattered throughout Jamaica's interior and blended into existing communities; Seaford Town remains the only Jamaican town to be deliberately established by the government.

The new arrivals, many unused to farm labour, found life in rural Jamaica difficult, and when the rations they'd been allocated for the first year ran out, became as impoverished as their black neighbours. Intense hardship and tropical diseases depleted their numbers, and within just a couple of years many of the survivors emigrated to the US. Enough remained, however, for their legacy to be obvious today. Despite some racial intermixing over the years, a tradition of intermarriage has ensured that quite a few of the town's residents still have blonde hair, blue eyes and (almost) white skin.

The diminutive **Seaford Town Historical Museum** (daily 9am–5pm; US$2), on a grassy knoll below the Catholic Church of the Sacred Heart, was closed for renovation at the time of writing. Once reopened, it'll tell the story of Seaford's German heritage, with photographs of the original settlers and a plaque listing their names and occupations (one man was a comedian). Beyond the museum, however, little German culture has been retained around town. Traces are seen in the pointy roofs and gingerbread fretwork of some of the older houses, but German speakers are restricted to the very old, and local residents are more likely to have rice and peas than sauerkraut for their dinner.

If you want to **stay** here, the Seaford Town HEART/NTA training school operates the *Training Villa* guesthouse (☎995 2067; ❷), staffed by students. It's a lovely old wooden building, and rooms have fan and TV; breakfast is included. Otherwise, pillar of the local community Jeanette Lynch offers B&B in her modern and comfortable home, *Tree Tops* (☎640 6134; ❷), overlooking a verdant valley (which encompasses the boundaries of St James, Westmoreland and St Elizabeth) in the nearby community of Bridgewater. Rates include breakfast.

The Cockpit fringes and Kensington

From Seaford Town, you can drive east through the pretty hilltop village of **ST LEONARDS**, site of the Hilton High Day Tour (see p.249). Just north of here, the ragged road takes you through tiny **MARCHMONT** – look out for the local bush doctor's home, painted red, gold and green, just off the road. Just a short way beyond Marchmont, you pass signs for **Croydon Estate**, 132 acres of pineapple plantation occupying the last stretches of accessible land before the Cockpit hillocks make large-scale farming a commercial impossibility. A mile north down the same road is **CATADUPA**, once the main tourist stop of the now-derelict train line that ran from Montego Bay to Kingston. Today, cows and goats pick at the grassed-over sleepers, though the gingerbread-style station house, with its peeling paint and panelled walls, exudes a faded romance.

From Catadupa, the road lurches crazily along the western fringes of Cockpit Country, passing lazy-looking communities like **MOCHO**, where untethered goats stare wild-eyed at the sun and housewives hang their washing out to dry on hedges. City folk disparage the residents of this backwoods village as unsophisticated country bumpkins. There are several villages called Mocho in Jamaica, all located in remote rural areas. A common colloquial insult is to tell someone they're from "up a Mocho sides", and the *Dictionary of Jamaican English* interprets the name as "a place of symbolic remoteness – a rough, uncivilized place".

Three miles on, at diminutive **FLAMSTEAD**, the road splits; right heads for

MAROON TOWN, which despite its name has no contemporary Maroon connections, while left takes you the four miles north to **KENSINGTON**. Despite huge historical significance as the place where the first fires of the Christmas Rebellion were lit (see p.259), the only hint of the past is a roadside plaque. Past Kensington, the views over gaping valleys are marvellous; John Crow vultures whirl high on the thermals and you get the occasional glimpse of the sea behind the trees. You're only thirteen-odd miles from Montego Bay, but the contrast couldn't be more striking. If you want to **stay**, head for *Orange River Ranch* (☎979 6523 or 919 1017, ⓦwww.whittergroup.com/orangeriver; ③), set in 998 acres of land complete with a swimmable river, a 110-year-old great house and countless groves of raggedy banana trees. Rooms are simple and functional, each with a balcony, and there's a restaurant, bar and pool as well as some of the nicest hotel staff you'll encounter. Horseback riding and hiking are both available from the hotel.

Cockpit Country

The most bizarre landscape in Jamaica, **COCKPIT COUNTRY** (ⓦwww.cockpitcounty.com) is an uncanny series of improbable lumps and bumps covering roughly five hundred square miles of Trelawny parish, just south of Montego Bay. Thousands of years' worth of rain and river water flowing over the porous limestone surface has created a rugged **karst topography** of impenetrable conical hillocks dissolved on each side by a drainage system of sinkholes and caves. The region is one of the most intriguing parts of the island, not least because of the place names peppered throughout it: Me No Sen You No Come, Wait-a-Bit (where the police station sign is subject to many a photographer's lens), Quick Step and Rest and Be Thankful District, though the last appears on aged maps only. Cockpit Country is also known as the "**District of Look Behind**", in reference to the justifiable paranoia of English soldiers who made hot, comfortless and usually ill-fated missions through the area tracking **Maroons**, whose superior local knowledge and guerrilla strategies brought most of the sorties to a bloody end. To this day, the Cockpits are thought by some to be the stamping ground for all manner of spirits and duppies and are avoided by more superstitious Jamaicans.

Save for a few pockets on the outskirts and along the central ten-mile trail from Windsor to Troy, Cockpit Country is uninhabited. Hunters make regular forays into the interior in search of feral pigs, but otherwise the few locals congregate at **Windsor**, **Albert Town** and **Accompong**, their economy based on small-scale farming, coffee production and – cloaked by the region's thick foliage – ganja growing. The legendary Coptic, one of Jamaica's wealthiest ganja exporters, allegedly grew his stock here when he was in business in the 1970s and 1980s.

Only a fraction of this land is accessible, and you can't get far independently, so what follows is not a geographical tour but a few of the highlights. Wherever you go, the scarcity of tourists and the lack of environmental damage make Cockpit Country unforgettable. It's a sanctuary of incredible untouched beauty, particularly in the early mornings when low-lying mists and a silence broken

Despite popular disbelief, **hiking trails** do exist in Cockpit Country, usually maintained by local residents, though the further you get into the interior the rougher they become. Windsor and Albert Town are the most accessible starting points for hiking, where you should hire a local guide, essential not only to stop you getting lost but in case of any accident – if you fall down a hole here, there will be nobody around to get you out. The main ten-mile trail through Cockpit Country starts at Windsor and runs straight through the middle to Troy on the southern outskirts, though it gets very overgrown towards the middle. The first few miles are relatively easy and foliage-free, but in the heat of the day it's an arduous eight-to-ten hour trek that few would want to undertake. You're in the midst of foliage most of the time, so there are few open vistas and little to interest you after the first couple of hours. But you'll certainly feel a sense of achievement if you complete it. Of course, you don't have to go the whole way; the first couple of hours from Windsor give you a pretty good idea of what's to come. If you set out from Troy, the trail is mostly downhill and a lot easier-going – the best plan is to base yourself at Windsor, hire a guide there and drive to Troy early enough to make the hike back to Windsor before nightfall.

A number of informed and well-organized **guided tours** pointing out rare plants and birds seen along the pig-hunting trails that network the Cockpit interior are available from Sun Venture in Kingston (☎960 6685, ☻www.sunventuretours.com). Similar tours are offered by a local community group, Cockpit Country Adventure Tours (☎610 0818, ☻stea@cwjamaica.com), a division of environmental NGO South Trelawny Environmental Agency (STEA), which also organizes nature walks, trips to caves such as Rock Spring (be prepared for lots of bending double and wading through water), campfire picnics in the bush and walks along Barbecue Bottom Road in search of medicinal plants; trips range from US$20 to $50 per person. As the going is rugged you'll need a stout pair of shoes or boots with good grip, a waterproof jacket or rain slicker, something warm (winter evenings are pretty cold), a torch and a water bottle. Don't forget heavy-duty mosquito repellent: Cockpit Country's limestone pools are an ideal breeding ground. Allow double your usual walking time, as an ostensibly simple trek can take hours longer if you have to chop at foliage to clear your path.

Cavers would find Cockpit Country irresistible were it not for the lack of infrastructure. Though 250-odd caves network the area, only Windsor is easily accessible; the rest are little explored and there is no specialized group to guide you. However, both Sun Venture and Cockpit Country Adventure Tours run trips into local caves; recommended is the cathedral-sized **Quashie River Sink Cave**, though it's a tough scramble down steep slopes to reach it and is not for the unfit or fainthearted. Alan Fincham's essential book *Jamaica Underground* lists and measures all the island's caves; you can also visit his website (☻www.fincham.co.uk). The excellent "Caving in Jamaica" website (☻users.skynet.be/sky33676/index1.html) is another good source of information.

only by bird calls give it an almost primeval feel. Plans to turn the whole of this region into a national park funded in part by the World Bank will ensure, with careful management, that the area remains protected and unique.

Getting there and around

If you're **driving** in from Montego Bay, you can take either of the roads that lead off the A1 near Westgate Plaza, though as these are narrow, potholed country lanes, a quicker route is to drive along the coast to Falmouth (see p.235) and head inland at Rock along the B11. As with most of the Jamaican interior, Cockpit Country is poorly served by **buses**. A limited daily service runs from Falmouth to Clarks Town and Sherwood Content, the best places from which to catch a lift to Windsor; buses for Albert Town depart from Falmouth. If all that sounds like hassle, you might want to consider joining an **organized tour** from MoBay (see p.248). Maroon Attraction Tours (℡952 8753; from US$50 pp) are the only carriers authorized to visit Accompong, but big companies like Caribic offer trips to Windsor on demand.

Once you're there, by far the best mode of transport is a **car**. Most makes of regular car will suffice, but a four-wheel-drive is preferable. Otherwise local people are extremely amenable with **lifts**, usually for free but sometimes for a small charge; just flag down anything that passes.

Windsor

Smack in the middle of Cockpit Country's accessible northern edge and reached via a dirt track from the tiny village of Sherwood Content, **WINDSOR** is the most visited settlement in the region, as tour buses occasionally pull in to its main attraction, **Windsor Cave**. Documented to stretch as far as three miles underground, the cave is an eerie maze of dripping water and huge twisting columns of fused stalagmites and stalactites. Its innocuously small mouth exhales a constant, clammy wind, except at dusk, when hundreds of bats – the cave is home to eleven species – sweep majestically out on feeding forays. Experienced cavers or the foolhardy can explore on their own, following the slippery path for about two and a half hours before emerging deep in the mountains and walking back to Windsor overground. As it's completely undeveloped and pitch black inside, the best way to see the cave is with a guide. Franklyn Taylor, owner of the village's convivial red-gold-and-green-painted bar, leads tours for US$10–20 dependent upon group size; the duration of the tour depends on the requirements of the group but averages at around ninety minutes.

Franklyn's also your man for **hiking**, a big activity here as Windsor is the starting point for the only trail that crosses Cockpit Country. If you're of a botanical bent, resident Windsor biologist Susan Koenig leads informative half-hour walks for US$35; for the best experience, go at night. There's not much else to Windsor save for a few fields of coffee and a couple of nice swimming spots along the Martha Brae River, which rises by the cave. The stately **Windsor Great House** (℡997 3832, ⓦwww.cockpitcountry.com; ❷), recently renovated and privately owned, has a huge open veranda and a couple of basic **rooms** (though only those with a committed interest in Cockpit Country are really made welcome); meals are available at extra cost. Every Wednesday, the house's owner, Mike Schwartz, hosts a "meet the biologists" meal (four courses US$25 per head plus alcohol), part of an ongoing project to develop Windsor into a research station for scientists and other related parties. This meal is perhaps the best way to experience the natural allure of the Cockpits; dusk sees a procession of bats leaving their roosts under the great house's roof, while the interminable insects that can drive you to distraction here finally cease their attentions, and the shrieking, whistling sounds of the forest take over. Alternatively, Franklyn Taylor or Mike Schwartz can organize simple accommodation in a nearby house owned by Texan Patrick Childres (❷); camping is also possible here.

Flora and fauna

Soil forms only a thin cover over the Cockpit limestone, and as the limestone soaks away most of the rainfall, the area's **plant life** has had to adapt itself in order to survive. As a result, visitors to this region will see a proliferation of species that make the most of their rather limited means. Bromeliads collect dew and rainwater in the tanks between their leaves, while the thick, waxy leaves of other plants, such as the tiny orchids that colonize dead wood, take advantage of the high humidity. The Cockpits also support a huge range of **bird life**, including 27 of Jamaica's 28 endemic species of bird; this is one of the few places where you'll see – and hear – profusions of shrieking green parrots. The feral **pigs** that root through the undergrowth are descended from those reared by the Maroons, and with hundreds of caves, **bats** are common – 21 varieties are found in the region. The limestone also provides a perfect cover for the **Jamaican boa**, or **yellow snake**. For more on the area's unusual environment, visit ⊛www.cockpitcountry.com.

Albert Town

The best way to see the southern Cockpits is from **ALBERT TOWN**, an isolated but friendly hillside community at the southeastern edge of the area (though expect plenty of staring from the school kids). It's fairly small, with thirty-odd buildings dotted around a central square and residential areas extending down into the valley below. It's also the best starting point for any trips, hiking or otherwise, into the area; the excellent **South Trelawny Environmental Agency** (STEA) and its tour company, Cockpit Country Adventure Tours (☏610 0818, ✉stea@cwjamaica.com), are based here and offer a wealth of advice, useful information and official guides.

Some 67,000 farmers produce yams in Trelawny, a fact celebrated in Albert Town's annual **Trelawny Yam Festival**, a hugely popular celebration of the area's most typical food, held on and around Easter Monday. Thousands of people, locals and tourists, jam the streets to witness culinary displays, best-dressed goat and donkey competitions, yam head-balancing races and ultimately the crowning of the Yam King and Queen. Associated events include a 10km road race, DJ and singing competitions and gospel concerts.

Practicalities

The easiest driving route into Albert Town is via the B11 from the north coast at Rock. At Clarks Town, you join the B10, a poor excuse for a road that offers fantastic views and some of the best white-knuckle driving in Jamaica. The road takes you past the **Barbecue Bottom** district, notable for the scarily steep cliffs that sheer off from the roadside and provide superlative views of the Cockpits and cane fields below. STEA can also do pick-ups from Falmouth or the airport, and shared taxis and buses run up from Falmouth for J$120–150.

There's no formal **accommodation** in Albert Town, but a number of local families offer bed and breakfast, most with private bathrooms and meals at extra cost (contact STEA for reservations; ❷–❸). Basic but tasty Jamaican **food**, including vegetarian and Ital options on request, is served up at *Donna's* cook shop, just off the square (take the road to the left of the STEA offices); there are a couple of other basic restaurants on the square, including a good soup vendor. Jerk chicken and pork are cooked at weekends on the main square. Of Albert Town's five bars, G. *Reid's* on the square is the best place for a **drink**, with typical rum-shop ambience and some gravity-defying murals on the walls. Finally, there's **Internet** access at the Western Union office (Mon–Fri 9am–5pm; J$150 per hour).

Accompong

Sitting on one of the steep hillocks that make up outer Cockpit Country, **ACCOMPONG,** the last remaining Maroon settlement in western Jamaica, boasts breathtaking views. Named after the brother of Maroon hero Cudjoe, Accompong came into being in 1739, when, as part of the peace treaty that ended the first **Maroon War**, the British granted the Maroon people 15,000 acres of land upon which to create a semi-sovereign community. (However, a missing zero meant that only 1500 acres were made available, a matter of continuing contention.) Several such communities, including Trelawny Town in St James, were also given land, and the Maroons set about a peaceful life in the hills, raising animals and farming. In 1795, however, a Trelawny Town Maroon caught stealing a pig in downtown Montego Bay was publicly flogged, ironically by one of the runaway slaves the Maroons had captured and returned to the plantations in accordance with the peace treaty. His kinsmen rebelled once again and the second Maroon War flared up. Though the Trelawny Town Maroons could muster only 300 fighters, the British took no risks and sent in 1500 soldiers and hunting dogs to track them down and wreck their villages. Accompong, the only Maroon village in western Jamaica that chose to remain neutral, was allowed to stand.

Accompong is still ruled by a **colonel**, elected every five years – the current incarnate is the charming Sidney Peddie (it's considered proper protocol to call on him when you arrive in town). Accompong colonels still hold real power; they must ensure citizens abide by the town's written constitution, and mete

Accompong Maroon Festival

Every **January 6**, Maroons from all over the island come home to celebrate the most important day in their calendar – the anniversary of the 1739 peace treaty. Like everything else in Jamaica, the Accompong festivities start late. Under a towering mango tree on the outskirts of the town (known as the Kindah Tree), a suckling pig (always male according to Maroon tradition) is roasted on a spit and eaten communally – it's supposed to bring luck to all that partake. Then comes the real highlight of the day (at around 10am), when Maroon leaders, adorned by the vines used as camouflage by their ancestors, make their way up from the **Peace Cave,** where they have drummed, danced and chanted since dawn. Goombay drums beat complicated rhythms in anticipation, and the town's aged hornblower sends the haunting tones of an **abeng** horn (a cow horn once used as a musical instrument and means of communication) echoing across the hills, signalling the approach of the elders. The drumming reaches a climax as the parade arrives and the assembled mass joins in with call-and-response Akan war songs. At around 2pm, the procession moves through the village, paying respects at the homes of former colonels and those too old to participate, finishing at the **Bickle Village** parade ground for speeches and performances from traditional Maroon dance groups, who whirl around and are sprinkled with a traditional dash of white rum. Eventually, the drums make way for towers of speaker boxes, and the party continues in an all-night sound-system jam and live reggae performances at Bickle Village. Note that there's a J$300 entry fee to the village on the festival day, and that the timings given above can vary.

out justice in instances of petty crime. Though most Maroons value their level of autonomy from the state (they pay no taxes or rates), this independence has also ensured years of state neglect. However, things are looking up: the village now boasts a spanking-new access road, and the advent of mobile phones means that it's now easy to keep in touch.

Though modern Accompong is making a determined effort to retain its heritage and traditions, there's a sense that it's a losing battle. Though older residents claim direct descendancy from fearsome Maroon leaders Nanny and Cudjoe, there are relatively few "real" Maroons left in the town. During the last thirty years over two-thirds of the population have left to pursue jobs in urban areas or abroad. The secret "Coromantee" language has vanished from daily use, resurfacing only in traditional songs and ceremonies, and the survival of Maroon culture has become less important to a younger generation more interested in dancehall than Goombay drums or Akan chants. The best and most interesting time to visit is for the annual **Accompong Maroon Festival**, held on January 6 to celebrate the signing of the peace treaty, when traditional culture is honoured and celebrated and the streets are lined with vendors selling all manner of Maroon (and non-Maroon) artefacts.

The village

Accompong is ranged along a precipitous main street; as you drive in to town, you'll most likely be met by one of the excellent **tour guides** who conduct visitors around the village (US$15 per person), relating the town's history and introducing you to local characters along the way. First stop is usually the **community centre**, with some lovely murals on the walls and a plaque detailing local history. In a side room, a small museum contains exhibits on the wider history of black Jamaicans as well as that of the Maroons, with items ranging from the ubiquitous calabash gourds to an Ashanti stool and a Taino axe on display, as well as a detailed panel on the making of goat-skin goombay drums. Next door is a skills training centre for local residents, equipped with a shiny bank of computers and a small library (book donations are appreciated). From the museum, you'll be led up the hill to **Bickle Village**, the scene of the main action during the annual festival and boasting thatch-roofed huts built in traditional Maroon style. Next stop is the sacred **Kindah Tree**, a giant specimen of the common mango, adjacent to which there's a battered sculpture of a Maroon in battle by Leonard Perkins. Then it's on to the **Herbal Garden,** where the local women who tend the plants will give an overview of their medicinal uses. The **Peace Cave**, where the treaty with the British was signed, is in the valley below the garden. You should be able to persuade your guide to take you there, but it's so small and insignificant-looking that it's hard to imagine that history was on the site; it's a couple of miles' walk through pretty, undulating hinterland that's more of an attraction than the destination. Other sights consist of a **church** on a hillock overlooking the main town, and, on the lower half of the main road, a **memorial to Cudjoe**, co-signatory of the 1739 treaty.

Practicalities

There are several ways to get to Accompong, the easiest by heading north from Maggotty in St Elizabeth (see p.352) to Vauxhall, and following the signs there. It's a fabulous drive, affording spectacular vistas over the rolling Cockpits, though the sheer drops can be a bit disquieting, especially when you meet another vehicle. You can also drive up from Albert Town, skirting the southern edge of Cockpit Country along the B10/B6, or travel via Elderslie and Jointwood. There are a couple of places to **stay** in town, and you can **camp** by arrangement (call Mark Wright, mobiles ☎855 9116 or 812 4797), but the best choice by far is *Mystic Pass Villas* (mobiles ☎770 3680 or 792 6166; ❹), two gorgeous thatch-roof round building perched on the hillside and affording wonderful views over the Cockpits; waking up here is an unforgettable experience. The wood-floored villas are surprisingly modern inside, with mossi-netted double beds upstairs, as well as an immaculate bathroom, an outdoor hot-water shower with a view, and a fridge (full kitchens are planned). *Peyton Place Pub* on the main street is the place to have a **drink** after your tour. There are no formal restaurants, but several shops sell the usual Jamaican **snacks** and meals can be arranged if you give advance notice; ask your tour guide.

The countryside around town is absolutely stunning and makes for some great walking (albeit with plenty of ups and down over the hillocks). If you're interested in **hiking**, call tour guide Mark Wright (see above); rates depend on the length of the walk and the size of the party.

Travel details

Buses

Buses from the main bus station in Montego Bay can take you throughout the island, but you'll have to change midway for longer journeys. The terminal is pretty well organized by Jamaican standards and even has signs directing you to each route, but there are no timetables. Your best bet is to turn up the day before and ask, particularly if your destination is off the beaten track. Below are the main routes covering places listed in this chapter. Services run from around 6am until 6pm. There is a reduced service on Sundays, with little or nothing after 5pm.

Montego Bay to: Anchovy (10 daily; 40min); Catadupa (4 daily; 1hr 30min); Falmouth (every 20min; 30min); Reading (every 30min; 10min); Rose Hall (every 30min; 15min); Savannah-la-Mar, where you change for Negril (every 40min; 40min).

Flights

Montego Bay to: Tinson Pen, Kingston (Mon–Fri 8 daily, Sat–Sun 5 daily; 35 min); Negril (3 daily; 20min); Ocho Rios (3 daily; 30min); Port Antonio (1 daily; 45 min).

Negril and the west

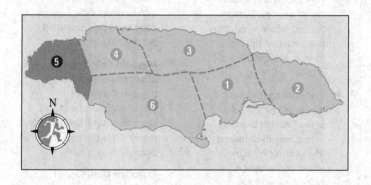

CHAPTER 5 # Highlights

* **Cousin's Cove** A low-key but lively coastal village with inexpensive accommodation and interesting, engaging residents. See p.295

* **Half Moon Bay beach** No jet skis, no hustlers and no hotels – just this peaceful and pristine stretch of sand. See p.295

* **Snorkelling and scuba diving** Negril's coral reef is the finest in Jamaica, with a wealth of marine life, year-round warm water and excellent visibility. See p.305

* **Sunset-watching** An institution in Negril, where everyone heads to the cliffs of the West End for happy hour drinks and the most spectacular sunsets in Jamaica. See p.310

* **Royal Palm Reserve** Tranquil and lovely nature reserve with wooden walkways snaking through the groves of majestic royal palm trees and abundant bird life. See p.307

* **Mayfield Falls** A series of waterfalls and river pools in the hills of Westmoreland whose extreme natural beauty remains, for the present, unspoilt. See p.289

* **Culloden Café** One of the finest restaurants on the island, it offers delicious nouvelle Jamaican cooking and a relaxed, attractive setting in a seafront garden. See p.325

△ Negril beach

Negril and the west

Though Jamaica's **western tip** is often associated only with the seven miles of sand at **Negril**, there's a lot more than beach life to the parishes of Hanover and Westmoreland. At only 174 square miles, **Hanover** is the island's smallest parish, and despite the deceptively steep-looking coastal rise to the 1789ft peak of the central Dolphin Head range, it's also the flattest, ensuring the **lowest rainfall** in Jamaica and invariably sultry weather in the extreme west. Sleepy capital **Lucea**, with its Georgian buildings and decaying grandeur, is slated for heritage development, but for now remains a languid and charming shrine to the past. Other than the ever-hopeful roadside refreshment stops and craft shacks, there's little tourism development along its stretch of coast. The smooth cattle pastures and deserted white-sand coves beg for exploration, while the odd abandoned windmill and crumbling walls of long-deserted estates remain untouched.

Split in two by Hanover and Westmoreland, sybaritic **Negril** has a front-row sunset seat, the longest continuous stretch of white sand in Jamaica and a geographical remoteness that provides this ultimate chill-out town with a uniquely insouciant ambience. "Discovered" by wealthy hippies in the 1970s, Negril is still immensely popular with those who favour fast living and corporeal indulgence, and it's easily the best place outside Kingston for **live reggae** and **nightclubs**, though its reputation as "sin city" means an over-quota of ganja and cocaine hustlers and an inevitable edginess. However, even though the main menu items are sun, sea, smoke and sex, there are plenty of natural attractions around Negril, including the **Great Morass**, the **Royal Palm Reserve** and some marvellous **reefs**. Beyond Negril, the landscape stretches out into the flat south coast plains and tourism gives way to agriculture. Irrigated by the meandering Cabarita River, **Westmoreland** was once Jamaica's foremost **sugar-growing** parish, and though rice is now an equally popular crop, cane plantations still surround the main commercial town and parish capital **Savanna-la-Mar**. Exports have significantly declined in recent years, leaving districts without tourism receipts struggling to find new industries and lending an air of pastoral neglect to the quiescent coastal villages. Although the ground has been broken for a huge all-inclusive hotel near Whitehouse, which is due to be completed in 2004, the **southwesterly point** remains deliciously quiet, with beaches dedicated to fishing rather than aloe massages and sun loungers. **Bluefields** and neighbouring **Belmont**, birthplace of the late reggae revolutionary **Peter Tosh**, are small but lively once you scratch beneath the surface, and have the best undeveloped beaches in Westmoreland. Fishing also dominates **Whitehouse**, a main port of call for north coast hotel food buyers; both towns are ideal if you want peace, quiet and few other foreign faces.

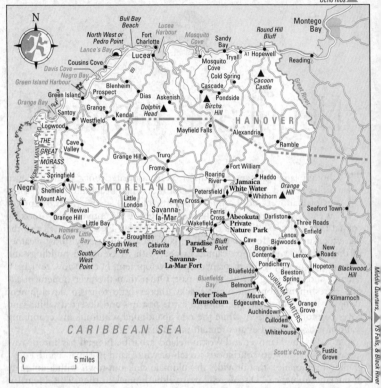

West towards Negril

The west tip of Jamaica begins where Montego Bay ends. Past the bridge over the mouth of Great River, the new super highway to Negril follows the old coast road as it twists and turns past **Hopewell**, home of *Round Hill,* one of the finest hotels on the island, and then takes a straighter route, bypassing some of the pretty coastal scenery on this stretch of the island, though unmarked turn-offs still lead down to the sea. There's little to occupy you in the interior here other than the swimming at **Mayfield Falls** or the mini-museum at Alexander Bustamante's **Blenheim** birthplace, and as most people choose to remain within sight of the Caribbean Sea, much of the land remains uncompromisingly indifferent to tourism; even the many hiking possibilities of the central **Dolphin Head** range are unexploited. Market town **Lucea** breathes a little life into the area, and further west the build-up to Negril begins, with a closer concentration of roadside bars and rest stops around **Green Island** and **Orange Bay**. Riding and diving at bounteously situated **Rhodes Hall Plantation** and swimming at the marvellously secluded **Half Moon Bay beach** are the last vestiges of calm before the onslaught of Negril.

Hopewell

The first sizeable town west of Montego Bay, dormitory town **HOPEWELL** is quite content to let MoBay deal with the tourists, to the extent that some residents positively seem to resent a foreign face. Other than browsing through the general stores that surround the bedraggled and unjustifiably pricey **vegetable market** (main day Saturday), there's little in this one-street town to keep you busy. The hills around are scattered with multiple zinc-and-plaster fundamentalist **churches** – *The Watchtower* is the unofficial village newspaper – and an evangelical mood dominates, broken only on Friday evenings, when a local sound system strings up on the main road and blocks traffic way into the night. The **coastline** around town is not ideal for swimming, but there are occasional sandy spots; most popular is **Steamer Beach,** just past the murky fishermen's beach, marked by the rusting iron shell of a wrecked boat. The slim white stretch gets packed in the early evening and on weekends, when kids descend for an after-school bathe and dominoes slap down on the verandah tables of the *Old Steamer Tavern.* Before moving on from Hopewell, take time to visit the small **gallery** of local potter Sylvester Stephens – it's just past the Shell petrol station on your left as you drive west. His garden, in front of the gallery, is a bizarre collection of giant pots and clay figures nailed to wooden posts.

There is just one **hotel** in Hopewell – *Round Hill*, PO Box 64 (℡ 956 7050, Ⓕ 7505, Ⓦ www.roundhilljamaica.com; ❻) draped across an entire hillside just east of town – but it is one of the classiest in Jamaica. Designed in part by Ralph Lauren, with an elegant 36-room hotel building and 29 eclectically furnished villas, the 98-acre property exudes taste and opulence. JFK and Jackie, Audrey Hepburn, Clark Gable and Queen Elizabeth II gave the hotel a reputation for glamour that today attracts an autograph book of famous names. Ordinary Joes may use its facilities – the main pool, tennis courts, gym, art gallery, restaurant and all watersports – for a US$50 daily fee. On Mondays, *Round Hill* hosts a wonderful candlelit beach party with tables and chairs shifted onto the sand, barbecued food and live music (US$55 per head). Otherwise in Hopewell, there are plenty of possibilities for **private rentals** if you ask around, and as the town is nicely detached from MoBay but close enough to enjoy its benefits, it's worth having a go.

You won't go hungry in Hopewell. There's an excellent bakery renowned for its hard-dough bread, and a couple of good **restaurants.** *Love Bird,* on Bamboo Hill, churns out ackee and saltfish, chicken and curry goat for its local regulars. Further up the hill is *Quatro Negocios*, which serves basic Jamaican fare on a breezy terrace and hosts a calypso and oldies night every Thursday. Just west of town, seafood dominates at a couple of simple restaurants directly in front of the fishing beach; they get packed at weekends with locals tucking into conch soup and steamed or fried fish and competing in noisy dominoes games. Shared taxis run between Hopewell and MoBay; fares are around J$50. Cars leave every 10min from the main street and terminate on St James Street

Tryall and Mayfield Falls

Three miles west of Hopewell, a towering **water wheel** at the roadside marks the old **Tryall Estate**, a once huge sugar plantation destroyed in the Christmas Rebellion (see p.259) that's now Jamaica's most prestigious **golfing hotel**. Until 1996, *The Tryall Club*, PO Box 1206, Montego Bay (℡ 956 5660,

ⓕ5658, ⓦwww.tryallclub.com; ⑧), hosted the annual Johnnie Walker golf tournament, now held at various Asian courses. The smoothly undulating eighteen-hole course is the best-kept, and reputedly most challenging, on the island, though you'll need deep pockets to examine it; non-*Tryall Club* guests pay US$150 per round plus mandatory caddie service. The hotel, in the plantation's refurbished great house, is unstintingly luxurious; rooms come with every conceivable trapping and most of the self-contained villas have private pools. The 800yd beach is fully equipped for watersports, and there are tennis courts and a waterfall pool on site.

The road that turns inland here overlooks the foothills of the **Dolphin Head Mountains**, a languid series of low-lying hills said to resemble a dolphin (though no one seems to know *where* you get this perspective). Most of the hillocks are partially cultivated by small-scale farmers, and there's none of the cool air or remoteness of full-scale ranges like the Blue Mountains (see Chapter Two). A right fork at **Cold Spring** leads to the appealing surrounds of **Pondside** and **Cascade**, where there are plenty of undeveloped waterfalls. You'll need local help to find the falls and to do any walking in the area, as this is prime ganja-growing territory. The best way to get a flavour of the Dolphin Head area is to visit the 22 mini-cascades and numerous swimming spots at **Mayfield Falls**. Two private tour operators, Original Mayfield Falls (☎971 6580, ⓦwww.mayfieldfalls.com) and Riverwalk at Mayfield Falls (☎957 5555, ⓔseemenomore@hotmail.com), have sites a hundred yards apart on the same stretch of river and charge the same basic entry fee (US$10). Both offer the identical experience of a tranquil walk through bamboo-shaded cool water with swimming holes every twenty yards – a fabulous, sensuous treat compared to the contrivances of the more famous Dunn's River Falls (see p.196). Mayfields Falls, however, is not the easiest of places to find: signs dot the route from Tryall via Pondside, but you'll probably have to ask for directions about a dozen times. To avoid getting lost, go with a local or join round-trip tours offered by both the above companies, with transport from Montego Bay or Negril and lunch included (US$65 per person). Upon arrival at Mayfields Falls, the procedure for starting your tour is similar with both operators: you'll be allocated a guide (leave a tip) who helps to carry your belongings, points out the easiest route and the best naturally formed swimming pools, and will tell you the local names of the trees, flowers and vines along the banks. Wear a swimming costume and bring flip-flops as the stones are tough on bare, wet feet – mosquitoes can also be a problem. Once at the end, you walk back through richly fruited, hilly pastures dotted with yam banks and fluffy clusters of bamboo. Hiking guides are available for walks in the surrounding mountains, and on Mondays and Fridays, the Original Mayfield Falls puts on a show of African song and dance (1.30pm; no extra charge) in front of the bar.

Sandy Bay and Mosquito Cove

Three miles west of Tryall, sleepy, suburban **SANDY BAY** was founded by Baptist missionaries as a free village for newly liberated slaves. (See Contexts, p.401, for more on free villages.) Today it's just a strip of shops, cafés, bakeries and bars, with great views back along the coast to distant Montego Bay, and the incongruous *Lollypop on the Beach*, a seaside entertainment centre that has seen better days but still gets busy on Friday nights and is the occasional venue for sound-system nights and stageshows. As you leave town you'll pass the more cheerful *Rita and Steve's Café,* a local bar strewn with fairy lights and serving up tasty and cheap fried fish.

Just west of Sandy Bay is the starting point for popular **Chukka Blue Adventure Tours** (☎979 6599, ⓦwww.chukkablue.com). The well-organized tour company offers several kinds of trip into Jamaica's western interior – if you're short of time or without transport, these are an easy and convenient way to explore little-known areas of the island. Tours include a Horseback Ride 'n' Swim (2.5hr, US$60 per person), which takes riders through lush mountain scenery to the sea; river tubing down the Great River (2.5hr, US$50 per person); and a Jeep safari over the hills above Montego Bay (4 hr, US$60 per person, lunch included). All tours must be booked in advance.

Further west, a turn-off from the new highway at *Eddie's Highway Pub* leads to pretty **MOSQUITO COVE**, named for the perfect breeding ground of the Maggoty River shallows; several tributaries meet here, spanned by a tiny stone bridge. The pesky mites didn't deter the Amerinidians – remains of **Taino settlements** have been found around here, though there's not a hint of the settlement remains today. Instead there's a small **beach** of pebble-strewn yellow sand lined by wind-bent palms – assorted flotsam and jetsam hint at the strong undertow that makes swimming risky, so stick to paddling. There are a couple of bar-cum-jerk spots and craft stalls at the edges of the bay.

Inland of Mosquito Cove, horses graze in clipped pastures dotted with the odd run-down windmill, relics of the plantation days when the land was part of the Kenilworth estate. A superb example of old industrial architecture, Kenilworth's **great house** now serves as the HEART (Human Employment and Resource Training) Academy, a further education college, signposted off an inland track just past the cove (daily 9am–5pm; free). There are no guided tours, but you can go in and have a look around the surrounding mills, boiling houses and distillery, all now under the protection of the Jamaica National Heritage Trust.

Lucea

Built around a crescent-shaped natural harbour, where Henry Morgan (see p.112) moored ships during his respectable period as lieutenant-governor of Jamaica, **LUCEA** (pronounced Lucy) was a flourishing port town during the plantation era, its wharves thronged with ships exporting locally produced sugar. These days, only the occasional shipment of molasses leaves the docks, but the town has another card up its sleeve: the exceptionally tasty **Lucea yam**. A floury-textured tuber with excellent storing properties, it was exported in vast quantities to the thousands of Jamaicans who migrated in the late nineteenth century to work on Central American sugar plantations or as labourers on the Panama canal, and is still crucial to Lucea's economy.

The Town

Despite being the capital of Hanover, Lucea is no showpiece; peeling paint pervades, and even the best buildings display the odd broken window or sagging wall. The faded allure of the Georgian town hall and gingerbread fretwork of the older houses have long prompted calls for Lucea's development as a heritage resort, though in true Jamaican "soon come" style, nothing much has yet happened – except that the town hall has been renovated and was officially rededicated on May 17, 2000 – and Lucea remains a sleepy sort of place. It's a beguiling town, a perversely aesthetic jumble of austere stone architecture and salt-and-sun-bleached clapboard houses, gaudy store-fronts, and snack and rum bars, all clustered around a seething central bus park that hums with the raucous shouts of minibus touts and peanut vendors and the tinny strains of reggae tape stalls. The main road twists straight through the centre of Lucea, past the bus park and the covered entrance of **Cleveland Stanhope Market**, which spills out onto the streets on Saturdays and draws villagers from miles around.

Just beyond the bus park is the imposing exterior of the once-majestic **town hall** and old **courthouse**, recently restored after years of neglect to its original Georgian grandeur. The roof of the courthouse is topped by an incongruously large **clock tower**. Still keeping perfect time after more than 170 years, the size of the clock betrays its misplacement – it was originally destined for St Lucia (Lucea's Spanish name was Santa Lucea) but was mistakenly sent to Lucea. Locals became so attached to it that they refused to exchange it for the more modest timepiece originally ordered, raising the difference through public collections. The tower was built with funds donated by a local planter of German origin on the condition that he had a hand in its design, hence the distinctive nippled dome of a German army helmet that forms its roof. The town hall overlooks the official town square, which serves as a traffic roundabout. Formally dedicated as **Alexander Bustamante Square** by England's Queen Elizabeth in 1966, the square was used as a period set for parts of the movie *Cool Runnings*.

Lucea's western portion contains most of the older buildings; particularly noticeable from the road is the towering cut-stone steeple of **Hanover Parish Church**, which dates back to 1725. The church boasts some fine monuments, one by the British sculptor John Flaxman. The cemetery's walled area is a **Jewish burial ground**, presented in 1833 to the large Jewish community who settled here during Lucea's commercial heyday. Toward the sea behind the church, **Rusea's School** (Mon–Sat 8am–4pm; free) was established in 1777 by a benefaction from French religious refugee Martin Rusea, who was so grateful for the help he received when he was washed ashore at Lucea that he bequeathed his accumulated estates to the parish; his disgruntled relatives were not quite so benevolent and contested the will for ten years after his death in 1764, without success. Originally located at the current Wesleyan mission house, the school was moved to the present site, an old army barracks, in 1900. Just past the school, through a small truck-repair yard, is near-derelict **Fort Charlotte**, restored in 1761, though no one is sure when the foundations were first laid. Three of the original cannons remain, and the fort gives a fabulous sweeping view across the harbour.

The beach and the Hanover Museum

As you leave town heading towards Negril, scrubby playing fields mark the way to Lucea's main bathing spot, windblown **Watson Taylor Beach**. This is not one of Jamaica's best beaches; it's generally the preserve of locals, who pick up the rubbish and maintain the rudimentary facilities. The miniature cove is sheltered by rocks, and there's a little sea grass, but the swimming is good and the water clean. Overlooking the beach is the excellent **Hanover Museum** (Mon–Sat 10.30am–4.30pm; J$150; ☎956 2584). A former British barracks, the red-brick building has also seen service as a prison, police station and firing range – you can see the original stocks and lock-up rooms complete with newly concreted stone "beds". Blackened timbers attest to the fire that almost destroyed the structure in 1985; it suffered a further battering from Hurricane Gilbert in 1988, the year it was awarded the prestigious Heritage Architecture Award. In honour of the settlements discovered at nearby Mosquito Cove (see p.401), re-creations of Taino dwellings and canoes stand in the backyard, flanked by a traditional canoe hollowed from a silk cotton tree. Other artefacts have been made by present-day Amerindians living in South America and the Caribbean. The main museum offers a surprisingly comprehensive glimpse into local history, with several aerial photos of Hanover, and old English weights and measures displayed alongside records of the West African ancestors of various Lucea citizens, maps, jackass rope tobacco (a long coil of dried tobacco leaves, resembling the rope used to tether a donkey and smoked by poor Jamaicans in the nineteenth century), a chunk of Lucea yam, and a copy of a harbour map hand-drawn by Captain William Bligh, who lived in Lucea for four years. The Ian Robinson Research Centre upstairs has a small collection of West Indian history books, and there's a good gift shop selling locally made crafts. The museum is also the base for the Hanover Historical Society (ⓦwww. jamaicahistory.org), the best source of in-depth local information.

The Lucea **Infirmary** is adjacent to the museum, just off the main road leading to Negril and adjoining Watson Taylor Park (☎956 2911). A visit to this infirmary in 1995 inspired American gerontologist Paul Scott Rhodes to set up JAFI (Jamaican and American Friends of the Infirmary), a charity that brings practical aid, such as wheelchairs, sheets and toiletries, to cash-starved Jamaican homes for the elderly and also encourages visits to the residents, who welcome company. If you wish to help or take part in JAFI's annual working vacations, contact JAFI in the US (☎310/249 7112, ⓔPSRMD@aol.com) or ring the infirmary directly.

Around Lucea

From the Lucea town centre, a twenty-minute drive inland along the B9 will take you to **BLENHEIM**, birthplace of National Hero Alexander Bustamante (see box overleaf). The shack in which Jamaica's first prime minister grew up has been converted into a small but interesting **museum** (daily 9am–5pm; J$130) celebrating Bustamante's life and achievements. The grounds surrounding the museum make a great picnic spot, with a large mango tree for shade and staggering views over the hills.

The other inland road parallels the Lucea East River and circumvents the **Dolphin Head Mountains**, an undeveloped wilderness area known for its abundant bird life and 23 endemic plants, including species of orchid and bromeliad. At present there are no **organized tours** into the area; you may be able to arrange an ad hoc guide at the tiny village of **Askenish**, the nearest settlement to the highest peak, or at Mayfield Falls (see p.290).

Practicalities

You can see Lucea's sights on foot in a day, but it's an engaging kind of place and if you do choose to **stay,** a good choice is *Global Villa* (☎956 2916, 0121 554 1410 in the UK, ⓦwww.caribbeanet.com/globalvilla; ❸), a small, clean guesthouse and restaurant situated slightly west of town at Esher. Delicious jerk chicken is served up daily, the bar is frequented by entertaining locals, and there's a popular karaoke session every Saturday night. The friendly owners also organize informal local tours for guests. *Global Villa* is a far better option than the overpriced, anonymous *West Palm Hotel*, near the Hanover parish church on western end of Lucea (☎956 2321; ❷). Also a possibility are *Leila Cousin's*

Chief Busta

Wild-haired and brutishly handsome, Sir William Alexander Bustamante's physical stature, charismatic appeal and legendary appetite for women earned him a fond notoriety in the ribald world of Jamaican politics. Born Alexander Clarke on February 24, 1884, into an impoverished family working on the Blenheim estate, Bustamante was architect of his own destiny, rising to political prominence through a mixture of insight, cunning and cynical manipulation of the illiterate populace who came to worship him as "Busta" or simply "Chief".

He left Jamaica at nineteen in search of better prospects, and his years away are veiled in mystery. Though he's said to have begun cutting cane and labouring alongside other migrants, he returned nearly thirty years later with an assumed surname and enough wealth to become a small-time money lender, a shrewd move that gave him clandestine influence before he entered the political arena.

The Jamaica that Bustamante returned to was still firmly under Britain's imperial grip and languishing as a result. Pay and working conditions for those lucky enough to have a job were abysmal, and the polarities between the ruling browns and whites and the black majority were as sharp as ever. Settling in Kingston, Bustamante allied himself with the workers and became their unofficial spokesman; his outspoken condemnation of these inequalities began to win support. By 1938 his "fire and brimstone" warnings of racial violence and black revolution (designed to scare the colonial authorities into action) were almost realized; fanned by Bustamante's inflammatory rhetoric, a violent confrontation between police and workers broke out at the West Indies Sugar Company in Frome, Westmoreland, sparking a wave of rebellions and strikes that brought the whole island to a near standstill for months. Eclipsing the tentative support for black nationalist labour leader William Grant, Bustamante formed the **Bustamante Industrial Trade Union** – still the island's main union – and became the leader of the labour movement among the rank and file.

In 1940, distressed at the volatility of his speeches, the government seized on Bustamante's union involvement and imprisoned him as the ringleader of the 1938 unrest – he spent seventeen months in jail plotting his future. On his release in 1942, he formed the **Jamaica Labour Party** and swept to victory in the island's first election in 1944, trouncing his first cousin Norman Manley's People's National Party so decisively that Manley lost even in his own constituency. Though the PNP enjoyed a few years of power between 1955 and 1961, it was the JLP that ruled when Jamaica was granted independence in 1962, and Sir Bustamante (he was knighted by Queen Elizabeth II in 1954) who danced with Princess Margaret during the ensuing celebrations. He remained active in politics until 1967 and died a National Hero on August 6, 1977, at age 93.

homely rooms at Malcolm Heights, PO Box 4742 Lucea (contact the Hanover Museum, ℡956 2584; ❸ with breakfast included).

For **eating**, there's the Rasta-striped shack *Vital Ital*, on your right as you enter Lucea from Montego Bay, serving delicious bowls of soup and vegetable stew. For spaghetti and burgers try the *D&S Restaurant and Grill* in town, and if it's Jamaican food you're after, *Sarducces*, in the uptown shopping centre, is a popular local choice. For delicious box lunches of chicken, rice and peas, try any of the number of cook shops in the large market.

Practically all of the **buses** and **minibuses** that connect MoBay and Negril terminate at Lucea's central bus park; you simply change services to complete the journey. To avoid long waits, ignore the touts and choose a bus that's almost full. The fare from Lucea to Negril is around J$70.

Cousin's Cove, Orange Bay and Rhodes Hall

West of Lucea, the coastal scenery is immensely attractive; foliage drips down over the road from the inland side and deserted coves swing temptingly into sight around each precarious corner. **Bull Bay Beach**, five minutes west of Lucea at Esher, is a pretty strip of whitish sand with calm water. It's a popular local spot for a swim, though during the week it's usually deserted. At **Lance's Bay**, three miles west of Lucea, **Ron's Arawak Cave** (daily 9am–5pm; 2hr tour; US$10) is signposted from the road. The impressive cave is a mile long, with plenty of intricate stalactite and stalagmite formations, a mineral pool and faint markings on the wall made by bat guano miners, long since gone, to help them navigate the various chambers and tunnels. Ron himself is an engaging tour guide, pointing out anthropomorphic shapes in the cave walls and playing the stalagmites like a musical instrument. You can stay in the area at *Sweet Breezes* (❷ with breakfast), an attractive collection of simple rooms set in a grassy clearing with space for camping (US$15 per couple per night). *Sweet Breezes* is situated in a small residential neighbourhood in the hills just above the cave – follow the signs from the road.

Lances Bay stretches seamlessly into **COUSIN'S COVE**, a lively coastal community that is widely but controversially acknowledged to be the inspiration behind *One People*, Guy Kennaway's hilarious novel about Jamaican village life (see p.432). Now cut off from the main highway to Negril – take the turn-off marked "Jamzen" to follow the much more scenic route through the village – Cousin's Cove is extremely laid-back, with a lovely enclosed bay and several great places to **stay**. Just before the turn-off is *Sunset Village* (☎956 6197; ❶), a simple local bar offering lodging in a couple of wooden huts in its well-maintained garden and plenty of space for camping (US$5 per person per night). *Jamzen*, just after the turn-off (☎956 6216, ⓦwww.jamzen.com; ❸), is more funky, with four rooms in its extensive cliffside grounds, great snorkelling from an offshore fringing reef and a bar that hosts oldies nights every Friday, Saturday and Sunday. *Cove House* is in the heart of the community, next door to *Byron's Bar*. An attractive four-bedroom house owned by Guy Kennaway, it rents for US$500-1000 a week; for reservations contact Sue Morris in Wales, UK (☎01987 861904, ⓔto-the-worlds-end@supanet.com). From *Byron's Bar* you can persuade Byron or one of the other local youths to take you out fishing or for a boat ride (rates negotiable). For further information and details of other properties available for rent, check the community website: ⓦwww.cousinscove.org.

While Cousin's Cove has a lot of rootsy appeal, there are very few good reasons to stop in **GREEN ISLAND**, a scruffy harbour town six miles west of Lucea, which is also home to the only secondary school for miles around – consequently most of Negril's burgeoning youth population commutes to it daily. Just out of town, small, clean, fan-cooled **rooms** are available at *JJ's Guesthouse* (☎956 9159; ❷), on a breezy hill off the main road.

Three or four miles down the coast, **ORANGE BAY** boasts the unspoilt **Half Moon Bay beach** (☎957 6467; daily 8am till late), full of the paradisical charm that originally brought tourists to Negril. The wide curve of white sand has no braiding booths, jet skis or hassle, just a little sea grass and some small islets; nude bathing is perfectly acceptable, snorkelling equipment is cheap, and the **restaurant** (daily 8am–10pm) serves excellent chicken, fish and sandwiches. The overgrown flat track behind the restaurant was once an illegal airstrip used for ganja smuggling; today it hosts occasional dirt-bike races. Set back from the sand, there are three wooden cabins (②) for overnight stays. **Camping** is also possible (US$10 per tent); security is provided. The *Hurricane Bar*, in the small strip of bars past the beach, is the perfect place for a seafront beer.

Just past Orange Bay, **Rhodes Hall Plantation** (☎ 957 6883, ⓦ www.rhodes resort.com) is a 550-acre coconut, banana, plantain, pear and coconut farm with two private **beaches** – one a shallow sea-grassy reef beach with a fresh-water mineral spring bubbling under the brine, the other a more convention-al sugar-sanded curve. Volleyball and football pitches and a restaurant /bar back onto the beaches, as do two luxurious two-bedroom **cottages** (⑤). **Horseback riding** is also an option; the well-kept mounts trot into the hills and along the beach (US$50/60, depending on length of ride). The property also covers an area of pristine **mangrove swamp**, home to a few wild Jamaican **crocodiles** – if you can't see any in the open section, you'll usually find some sunning themselves in a fenced-off enclosure.

Negril

Jamaica's shrine to permissive indulgence, **NEGRIL** has metamorphosed from deserted fishing beach to full-blown resort town – easily the most popular on the island now – in little over two decades. Though it's hard to imagine once you've seen today's overdeveloped strip, in the late 1960s the population was well under a hundred and the only visitors were day-tripping Jamaicans. By the 1970s, hippies had discovered a virgin paradise of palms and pristine sand, and the picture of beach camping, ganja smoking and chemically enhanced sunsets set the tone for today's free-spirited attitude. Thanks to deliberately risqué resorts like the infamous **Hedonism II**, Negril is widely perceived as a place where inhibitions are lost and pleasures of the flesh rule. The traditional menu of ganja and reggae (Negril has a deserved reputation for its **live music**) draws a young crowd, but the north coast resort ethic has muscled in, too, All-inclu-sives pepper the coast and, even though undeveloped beachfront land is now extremely limited, are still being built, while hustling has increased to an irri-tating degree.

Nonetheless, Negril shrugs off these minor irritations and remains supreme-ly chilled-out – every conversation starts and ends with "Irie" or "no problem" – and addicts come back year after year for the best sunsets in Jamaica and a resort that offers pretty much everything anyone could ask for on holiday. Pristine miles of sand with comprehensive watersports facilities, open-air danc-ing to rated Jamaican musicians, a wide range of eating and drinking joints and gregarious company are all on offer here. Many visitors have stayed on perma-nently, and the consequent blurring of the distinctions between tourists and locals make for a relaxed, natural interaction that's a refreshing change from other resorts. For a humorous and entertaining introduction to Negril, read resident and hotelier Mark Conklin's novel, *Banana Shout* (see p.432), based on

"Rent-a-dread"

Jamaica is a carnal kind of country, and while there's no sex tourism industry as such, monetary-based holiday liaisons are a well-established convention. Fuelled by tropical abandon and the island's pervasive sexuality, the lure of the "big bamboo" prompts some unusual partnerships. Middle-aged women strolling hand in hand with handsome young studs have become such a frequent sight that pejorative epi-thets – **"Rent-a-dread"** or **"Rastitute"** – for the young men who make a career out of these cynical liaisons have entered the lexicon.

The butt of many jokes, the stereotypical Rastitute is a muscle-bound model of the latest mini-trunks and expensive sneakers, with a head topped off with dreadlocks – or hair extensions if he can't manage the real thing. However, not all gigolos come in the same package; a Rastitute is equally likely to appear in the form of an Ital-style Rasta who woos with talk of natural living and preaches sex with white tourists as an expression of racial unity.

In a country of scant possibilities and high unemployment, becoming a gigolo is a practical career move for many young Jamaicans. Negril is a centre for this kind of trade-off, and many women regularly return specifically to partake of an injection of "Jamaican steel", some forming relationships that span several years of holiday time. This makes life rather difficult for women whose holiday plans do not include sex with local men; single women are almost universally assumed to be out for one thing only. Prepare yourself for a barrage of propositions.

Male tourists are less involved in the holiday romance scenario, but **female pros-titutes** are common and men should expect to be frequently propositioned; in Negril the prostitution scene is firmly ingrained. If you do choose to indulge, make sure that you practise safe sex; one in five prostitutes are HIV-positive and STDs – including syphilis – are rife in Jamaica (see *Basics*, p.23).

the outlandish real-life events that shaped the beginnings of Negril as a tourist resort.

Some history

Negril's isolation – until very recently it was completely cut off from the main-land by the Great Morass, Long Bay and the smaller Bloody Bay – has been central to its history. Even its Spanish name, *Punto de Negrilla* or "dark point", referred to the west tip's remoteness as much as to the black eels that once thrived in its rivers. During British rule, Negril's seclusion was used both to protect British ships sailing home under the cover of armed men-of-war and to attack Spanish vessels straying off course to Cuba. It also provided an ideal hideout for **pirates** in the eighteenth century (see box p.229), and for the export of **ganja** in more recent years. In 1996, over-zealous coast guards opened fire on a seaplane owned by Island Outpost boss Chris Blackwell, assuming that the cargo was drugs rather than, as was the case, various mem-bers of the band U2 and country and western singer Jimmy Buffet; fortunately the volleys missed and pop fans were spared a tragedy, though the shamefaced coast guards were cornered into a public apology. The town has also played a part in war: in 1814, fifty English warships and some 6000 men, including 1000 Jamaicans from the West Indian Regiment, sailed from Negril to Louisiana to fight the Battle of New Orleans.

In 1959, a coast road was laid from Green Island, and Negril was for the first time connected to the rest of Jamaica. Its beauty was soon discovered by for-eign hippy travellers, who brought Negril's charms to wider attention and spawned a **tourist industry**. Developers were quick to step in, and by the early 1980s the once-empty curve of beach was smothered with all the trappings of a full-blown resort. International attention was captured by tales of debauchery at the notorious *Hedonism II* resort, and Negril's reputation as Jamaica's devil-may-care holiday hotspot was assured.

In recent years the town has worked hard to solve its infrastructural problems: Negril now has an efficent central sewage system and a new main supply of water, and is also now linked to Montego Bay (and the airport) by a brand new highway – which has almost halved the journey time between the two towns. The flip side of all these improvements is that the resort continues to grow. Even Bloody Bay – the last piece of virgin beach remaining in Negril – is no longer unspoilt, with one large all-inclusive on its sands and another being built. Nevertheless, it is still possible to find the laid-back charm and gorgeous scenery that first brought tourists to Negril.

Arrival and information

Arriving in Negril is straightforward; **buses** from Montego Bay and Lucea drop off passengers just before the central roundabout – if you're staying on Norman Manley Boulevard, bus drivers will drop you off outside your hotel. Buses from Savanna-la-Mar terminate at the top end of Sheffield Road, from where you can charter a **taxi** to the West End or beach (see p.304) for US$3–5. Private taxis charge around US$70 for the MoBay to Negril ride; alternatively, try hitching a lift with a hotel transfer bus for approx US$20 per person each way. Domestic **flights** land at Negril Aerodrome at Bloody Bay; taxis are waiting but fares can be ridiculous – a reasonable price would be US$10.

The **Jamaica Tourist Board office** is on the first floor of Coral Seas Plaza, opposite the roundabout (Mon-Fri 9am-5pm, Sat 9am-1pm; ☎957 4597); it stocks various local freesheets, all of which carry local maps, listings and news. Pretty pink JTB **information booths** are located at the main craft market by the roundabout and on West End Road opposite *Tensing Pen* hotel.

Alternatively, the Yacht Club (☎957 9224, ⓦwww.yachtclub.com) on West End Road has set itself up as a one-stop shop, offering not only accommodation, watersports, bike rental and taxi services but also informal advice; the staff are friendly and trustworthy.

Orientation and getting around

Negril doesn't really have a "town centre", just a roundabout right on the coast that feeds its three streets: **Norman Manley Boulevard**, which runs parallel to the Long Bay and Bloody Bay beaches and the Great Morass wetlands; the quieter **West End/Lighthouse Road,** which winds along the cliffs to Jamaica's west tip; and **Sheffield Road**, the route to Savanna-la-Mar.

You don't need a **car** if you're going to stay in town. **Shared taxis** run the length of the beach and West End Road all day every day, and charge between J$30 and J$50 from the roundabout to the lighthouse or Bloody Bay – you can flag them down anywhere en route. **Chartering a taxi** can be expensive, particularly at the far reaches of the cliffs, but competition is high, so you should be able to haggle – US$5 from the roundabout to Bloody Bay is reasonable.

Negril's drug culture

As any aficionado can tell you, Jamaica's best **ganja** (marijuana) – well-flavoured and incredibly potent – grows in the fertile Westmoreland earth. The trade to eager tourists plays a significant, if covert, part in the local economy. Many devotees make annual pilgrimages to find a place to chill out and partake of the local weed. Herb is a part of daily life in Negril, so don't be surprised if your first potential supplier is your hotel porter, and you lose count of the men who hiss "sensi" as you pass them in the street. Don't feel that you can light up wherever you choose, though – marijuana is as illegal here as it is anywhere else on the island, and there are plenty of undercover police around town who can and do arrest tourists and locals alike for possession.

Though Negril has been an unofficial ganja centre since its hippy heyday, there's also a great deal of **cocaine** and **crack** use around town. It's not especially noticeable and crackheads won't accost you on the street, but a certain furtiveness around the late-night beach bars lets you know that it's there for the taking. Negril is also one of the few places on the island where you're likely to be offered locally abundant **magic mushrooms**, considerably larger and stronger than those in cooler countries. Some restaurants include them in cakes, omelettes or pizzas. *Miss Brown's,* on the beach, and *Jenny's Favorite Cakes* (also serving up potent ganja cake), on the West End Road, are the spots for foul-tasting mushroom tea, while *Tedd's,* on Sheffield Road, mixes up mushroom-flavoured daiquiries.

There is no local bus service to the roundabout from the beach or cliffs. Other than **walking**, the most popular ways of getting around are moped, motorbike or bicycle. **Dirt bikes** rent for around US$40 per day, mopeds from US$30, and bicycles from US$10. Alternatively, if you're staying on the cliffs, you could try flagging down a glass-bottom boat on its way to the beach – *Famous Vincent Elvira* is a good choice, though at US$7–10 one way, not the cheapest way to travel.

Organized tours

As Negril tends to attract those who want to stay put and relax, the roster of available tours in Negril is pretty paltry in comparison to the options in Ocho Rios or Montego Bay. Most tour operators offer the same roster listed in the Montego Bay chapter (p.248), along with a few tours in southern Jamaica. Standard trips include a Black River safari (approx US$60 per person), with a visit to the YS Falls, a typical Jamaican lunch and a crocodile search along the Black River; a nature tour to Mayfield Falls (US$65 per person); and a beach party (US$35 per person) with folklore show, creole picnic and rum punch on the beach. Local operator Divine Tours Limited (☎957 3838, ⓦwww .divinetoursjamaica.com) is an experienced outfit and offers all of the above tours, as does Sammy's Jamaican Tours (☎381 8129, ⓦwww.sammysjamaicantours .com). Conch Tours (☎869 0900, ⓦwww.conchtours.com), run by friendly American LeeAnne Criscenti, is a smaller operation with a more individualized service.

Bicycle tours are an excellent way to explore the countryside; Rusty's X-cellent Adventures, situated past the lighthouse on West End Road (☎957 0155, ⓦwww.webstudios/rusty.com), has a series of trails through the ganja landing strips and deserted beaches of greater Negril; the top-of-the-range mountain bikes and the pace demand good riding ability. Rusty's is also the headquarters of the Jamaica Mountain Bike Association, which organizes an

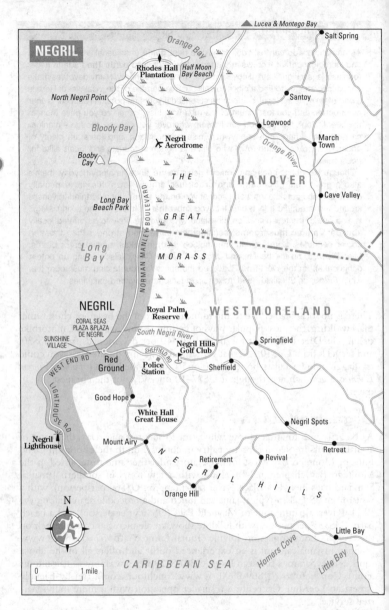

annual Fat Tyre Festival in Negril (during the second week in February) with championship mountain-bike races and bicycle bashments.

Alternatively, hire a **local driver** and set off on your own. Tony Vassell at Tykes Bikes (☎957 0388), opposite *Tensing Pen* hotel; Kenny Tours taxis, which operate from *Rockhouse;* and Floyd Wilson of Pink Floyd Tours (☎771 0962) are all recommended. Otherwise call the Negril branch of JUTA (☎957 9197).

Spring Break

Every year, between the end of February and the Easter weekend, upwards of twenty thousand American college students arrive in Jamaica for **Spring Break** – and well over half go straight to Negril. Heavily promoted by the Jamaican Tourist Board in their widening quest for niche markets, Spring Break– a nonstop carnival of fun if you're nineteen, and a rude shattering of the (relative) peace if you're not – is the one time of the year in Jamaica when hotels can still guarantee one-hundred-percent occupancy, with many given over entirely to Spring Breakers. If wet T-shirt competitions, drinking challenges and dancing in pina-colada flavoured foam are your thing, then this is the time to head for Negril – otherwise be warned. *Margueritaville* is the self-appointed headquarters for Spring Break, in both MoBay (also popular with Spring Breakers) and Negril; *Legends, Risky Business* and the *Yacht Club* all put on **special events**, and the season is sponsored by both Red Stripe beer and Appleton's Rum. This is also a good time to see **live music**, with some of Jamaica's best DJs and bands making the most of a large, enthusiastic audience. Travel agents that specialize in Spring Break packages include *Apple Vacations* (℡1-800/727 3400 in US), *Student Travel Services* (℡1-800/648 4849 in US) and *Sunsplash Tours* (℡1-800/426 7710 in US, ⓦwww.sunsplashtours.com). For further information check website ⓦwww.springbreakinjamaica.com.

Accommodation

Negril has several thousand **beds**, far more than any other resort in Jamaica and with a much wider variety – from five-star all-inclusives to backpacker shacks, and gorgeous boutique hotels to undistinguished accommodation blocks. The lodging options are split between the beach and the cliffs. Easily the more popular location, the **beach** reeks of commercial vitality and is the place to stay if you want to be right at the centre of Negril's party culture. Most hotels have commandeered semi-private areas of beach with sun loungers and security guards, while smaller hotels and those on the inland side of the road simply use whatever piece of sand is closest. Inland properties are often cheaper, but as they back straight onto the Great Morass, bugs can be a problem. The quieter **West End** has a degree of privacy lacking at the beach and several of the loveliest hotels in Jamaica, as well as some attractive budget options, though its steep open-access cliffs make it a bad choice if travelling with children.

With so many hotels to choose from, there are fewer self-contained **villas** and **apartments** to rent in Negril than on the busy north coast. But some of those available are particularly lovely and can be rented on a nightly basis. On the beach, *Moon Dance Villas* (℡1-800/621-1120 in US, ⓦwww.moondancevillas .com; US$1500 per night for 5 bedrooms) are the most luxurious choice, a collection of beautifully designed and furnished houses with huge rooms, full staff and all mod-cons. *Crystal Water Villas* (℡957 4287, ⓕ4889, ⓦwww .crystalwaters.net; from US$110 per night) are cheaper units, with sea-view patios and an informal family atmosphere. On the cliffs, two of the more attractive villas to rent are *Llantrissant* (US$3200-4000 per week; ℡957 4259, ⓔnegril @beachcliff.com) and *Seagrape* (from US$135 per night for two bedroom units; ⓕ419/793 6647 in US, ⓦwww.seagrapevillas.com). One of the original holiday properties in Negril, *Llantrissant* has dark wooden floors and two private beaches, while *Seagrape* comprises three octagon-shaped houses and is set in lovely flowered gardens. The all-inclusives congregate around **Bloody Bay**, well away from the polluted South Negril River, on some of the prettiest stretches of Negril's beach. Notable among these is *Hedonism II* (T957 5200, W www.superclubs.com; ●), the original "risqué resort", with its nude beach, swingers' month and night-time fun in the hot tub and elsewhere. *Grand Lido Negril* (T957 5010, W www.superclubs.com; ●) is particularly luxurious, while *Couples Swept Away* (T957 4061, W www.couples.com; ●) boasts a fully comprehensive sports complex – the best on the island.

As Negril's planning regulations prevent building anything higher than a palm tree, a lot of accommodation is in traditional circular palm-thatched **cottages**. Though much cooler than concrete, many of these are ludicrously easy to break into. Also popular in Negril is the **pillar cabin**, a round cottage set on top of a stone column, with a shower below and the advantage of catching the best breezes. Locals cite the lonely reaches of West End Road as problematic in terms of **security**; wherever you stay, always make sure that doors and windows are secure and check ID before you let anyone in. Twenty-four-hour security is sensible if you plan to **camp**, though if you're willing to rough it and risk it, there are plenty of cabins and campsites with few facilities and negligible security on the morass side of Norman Manley Boulevard.

The beach

Beachcomber Club PO Box 98, Norman Manley Blvd; T957 4170, F4097, W www.beachcomberclub.com. Garishly painted accommodation blocks amidst gardens. The spacious rooms have four-poster beds, and there's a pool, games room and Italian restaurant. Under 12s stay free and baby-sitting is available. ●

Charela Inn PO Box 33, Norman Manley Blvd T957 4277, F4414, W www.charela.com. French-Jamaican–owned place with gardens, pool, carpeted rooms with four-poster beds, and an air of cultured elegance. Rates include a weekly cruise, watersports and folklore shows. Three night minimum stay. ●

Chippewa Village Hotel Norman Manley Blvd T & F957 4676, W www.chippewavillage.com. Friendly and laid-back resort with attractive self-contained apartments and wooden cabins. Overlooks the Great Morass and Negril hills. Swimming pool, jacuzzi, sun deck and communal dining area are other pluses. ●

Country Country Negril P.O, Norman Manley Blvd T957 4273, F4342, W www.countrynegril.com. Brightly painted cottages set in pretty garden with small strip of beach. The rooms are spacious and each has a fridge, a/c and ceiling fans. There are two restaurants on site, including the only Chinese restaurant in Negril.

Golden Sunset PO Box 21, Norman Manley Blvd; T957 4241, F4761, W www.thegoldensunset.com. Long-established and reliable, though across the road from the beach, it offers clean rooms or cabins with fans, kitchenettes and private or shared bath. ●

Idle Awhile Norman Manley Blvd T957 3302, F9567, W www.idleawhile.com. Sophisticated small hotel with beautifully designed and furnished rooms, all with a/c, cable TV and phones. Rates include free pass to *Swept Away*'s sports facilities. ●

Kuyaba Norman Manley Blvd T & F957 4318, W www.negril.com. One of the beach's classiest hotels, with imaginative and stylish Mexican tiling, calico fabrics and large bathrooms. Good restaurant on site. ●

Mom's Place Norman Manley Blvd T957 3349. Run by a friendly Jamaican couple, this is a simple and homely set of rooms on the beach. All have bright decor, fans and private bathrooms. Café and bar on the premises. ●

Negril Cabins PO Box 118, Norman Manley Blvd T957 5350, F5381, W www.negril-cabins.com. Well-equipped cabins in a garden backing onto the Great Morass. Excellent food and a full range of facilities, including a "private" section of Bloody Bay. Good for kids: under-12s stay free and there's a playground on the beach. ●

Negril Tree House PO Box 29, Norman Manley Blvd T957 4287, F4368, W www.negril-treehouse.com. A clean, comfortable and appealing complex of rooms and villas. Two bars, one built around a tree, along with a restaurant, pool and watersports. ●

Negril Yoga Centre PO Box 48, Norman Manley Blvd T957 4397, W www.negrilyoga.com. Yoga centre and guesthouse overlooking the Great Morass. Attractive cottages of varying degrees of comfort, surrounded by heaps of greenery. Wholefood cooking and yoga classes available. ●

Nirvana on the Beach Norman Manley Blvd T957 4314, F9196, W www.nirvananegril.com. Semi-luxurious wooden cottages in an unusually beautiful sand garden shaded by tall trees and dotted with sculptures and hammocks. Friendly atmosphere, kooky decorative touches and free pass to *Swept Away*'s sports facilities nearby. ⑤

Perseverance PO Box 17, Norman Manley Blvd ☎957 4333. Budget accommodation across the road from the beach; clean and comfortable rooms with fans and shared or private bath. ②

Roots Bamboo Norman Manley Blvd ☎957 4479, ☎9191, ☻rootsbamboo.com. Friendly, efficient place that's one of Negril's most popular budget lodging options and live-music venue. Cottages are small but cosy; some have private showers, and there's also a communal row. Also on site: a cheap Jamaican restaurant and a campsite with 24-hr security and showers. Often noisy due to thrice-weekly gigs. ②

Sunny Cottages Norman Manley Blvd ☎957 4741. Friendly guesthouse on the beach. Basic rooms, with hot water and fans. Breakfast café and shop on site. ②

Swept Away PO Box 77, Norman Manley Blvd ☎957 4061, ☎4060, ☻www.COUPLES.com. Extensive landscaped gardens and copious sports facilities make this one of Negril's finest all-inclusives. There are tennis, squash, basketball and racquetball courts, a gym, regular and Olympic-size pools with lap lanes, jacuzzis, saunas, steam rooms, an aerobics room, a fitness circuit, spa facilities and watersports. Rooms are elegantly furnished, the beach grill and veggie bar serve up healthy snacks, and the main restaurant is award-winning. Three night minimum stay. ⑧

Westport Cottages PO Box 2626 ☎957 4736. Budget travellers' haven at the roundabout end of the beach. The basic cabins are starkly furnished but comfortable, with fan, mosquito nets, outdoor bathroom and communal cooking area. ①

Whistling Bird Norman Manley Blvd ☎957 4403, ☎3252, ☻www.negril.com. Beach cottages set in a lovely garden with cook-to-order restaurant. Very private. ⑤

West End

Addis Kokeb PO Box 78, Summerset Rd ☎640 2313, ☻addiskokeb@yahoo.com. Private rooms in the main building or handsome hardwood cabins in fruited and flowered gardens. Cooking facilities are shared, and you can use the pool at *Summerset Village* next door. ②

Banana Shout PO Box 4, Lighthouse Rd ☎ & ☎957 0384, ☻www.negril.com/bananashout. Simple but attractive cottages in gardens or right on the cliffs. Each unit features a kitchenette, ceiling fan, hammocks on the verandah and Haitian art. The cliff portion has a diving platform, sun

deck, its own cave and exceptional sunset views. ③

Blue Cave Castle PO Box 66, West End Rd ☎957 4845, ☻www.bluecavecastle.com. Pastel-painted castle on the rocks, a curious mix of high kitsch and elegant luxury. Individually decorated rooms are built over a cave that extends underneath the road. Excellent swimming in the sea in front of the hotel; there are ladders into the water from the hotel's garden. ③

Citronella PO Box 2662, West End Rd ☎957 0379/0550. A private and tranquil resort next to the *LTU Pub*, with five self-catering cottages and a restaurant set in sprawling cliffside gardens. ⑤

The Caves PO Box 3113, Lighthouse Rd ☎957 0270, ☎4939, ☻www.islandoutpost.com. Gorgeous small hotel set behind Fort Knox-inspired gates and patronized by celebrities who are heli-coptered in. Cottage-style rooms are funkily designed and come equipped with batik bathrobes and CD players. On-site facilities include a spa, jacuzzi and sauna. ⑧

Home Sweet Home PO Box 2, West End Rd ☎957 4478, ☻www.homesweethomeresort.net. Small, cheerful resort, popular with Canadians, boasts a swimming pool, jacuzzi, restaurant, and cliffside sun deck. All rooms have ocean views. ⑤

Jackie's on the Reef Negril PO, Lighthouse Rd; ☎957 4997, ☻www.jackiesonthereef.com. Breezy alternative-style place with all sorts of holistic therapies on offer – massage, yoga, t'ai chi, you name it. Private cottages or expansive units in the main house, all simply but carefully decorated. Swim in the saltwater pool if the sea gets too rough. Four-night minimum stay. ⑥

Lighthouse Park PO Box 3, Lighthouse Rd ☎957 4490. Basic but serviceable A-frame cabanas, villas and camping on a sprawling, densely vegetated section of cliff top. There's a communal kitchen and a gazebo with hammocks. Gay-friendly. ②

LTU Villas PO Box 2875, West End Rd ☎957 0382, ☻www.negril.com/ltuvillas. Spacious rooms in quiet gardens opposite one of Negril's best bars, the *LTU Pub*. A great-value option, offering rooms with living room, fridge and balcony. ③

Mariners Inn PO Box 16, West End Rd ☎957 4474, ☎0391, ☻www.marinersinn. Medium-size retreat with attractive wood-panelled rooms. Facilities include a dive centre, swimming pool and games room used by local pool wizards. Great sea swimming and a boat-shaped bar. ④

Moonlight Villa West End Rd; ☎957 4838, ☻www.moonlightvilla.com. Spacious rooms in an attractive oceanfront villa, all with large beds and fridge. Private sun deck and outside grill for barbecues. ④

New Moon Cottage West End Rd ℡957 4305. Clean and quiet rooms in a Jamaican family home, with communal cooking facilities. Camping available. **②**

Primrose Inn c/o Gus Hylton, Negril PO ℡771 0069 or 640 2029, ⊛www.negril.com. Basic "home from home", set back from the road in a yard dominated by a large ackee tree. Rooms are off an open corridor laced with hammocks; each has a fan and double bed, and most have a cold-water bathroom. Bad dogs take care of security. **①**

Rockhouse PO Box 3024, West End Rd ℡957 4373, ⅌0557, ⊛www.rockhousehotel.com. Enviable location, Mediterranean styling, magnificent thatched bar/restaurant and saltwater pool on a rock peninsula create a unique, stylish and comfortable retreat. Thatched studios or villas, each with glass-doored patio overlooking the ocean, outdoor shower, fan and bamboo four-poster bed draped with muslin nets. Innovative and deservedly expensive restaurant. **⑤**

Summerset Village PO Box 80, Summerset Rd ℡957 4409, ⅌4078, ⅇsummersetvillage @cwjamaica.com. Set in seven acres dotted with fruit trees, this property, popular with Brits, offers a large pool, restaurant, bar and games room. Eclectic accommodation options range from regu-

lar room blocks to a five-bed wood-panelled thatch house. **③**

Sundown Lighthouse Rd ℡640 2174 or 817 1770. Gorgeous and comfortable little cottage with kitchenette, cable TV and sun deck in a cliffside garden. **④**

Tensing Pen PO Box 13, Lighthouse Rd ℡957 0387, ⅌0161, ⊛www.tensingpen.com. Stylish and exclusive retreat in pretty clifftop gardens. Imaginatively decorated bamboo and wood cottages are graced with individual touches; there's a well-equipped communal kitchen/lounge and on-site yoga room. Some of the cliffs are linked by a tiny suspension bridge. **⑦**

Villas Sur Mer Negril PO, Lighthouse Rd ℡957 0377, ⅌957 0177. Thoughtfully designed and decorated luxury villas right on the cliffs, with marble bathrooms, breezy living rooms, full staff and a wooden boardwalk complete with pool and jacuzzi. **⑤**

Xtabi, PO Box 19, West End Rd ℡957 4336, ⅌0827, ⊛www.xtabi-negril.com. Well-organized West End veteran with flowering gardens and a network of caves. Oceanside rooms are in wooden cabins with private sun deck and sea access, or two-storey concrete cottages with kitchens. Also features a pool, open-air restaurant and bar, and countless swimming platforms. **④**

The Town

Negril doesn't really have a centre – just a roundabout feeding its three main roads – and most people leave the beach or cliffs only to change money, buy petrol or find a ride out of the area. However, **Sheffield Road** is the least tourist-oriented part of town and the closest approximation of a real heart. The police station, market stalls, petrol station, restaurants and constant crowds dodging beeping mopeds create an animation that's absent in the boulevard's beach life and the West End's studied tranquillity. To the right of the roundabout are two rather tatty **shopping plazas** – Coral Seas Plaza and Plaza de Negril, the latter used by locals more than tourists; the car park in front is known as **Negril Square**, a base for taxi drivers, low-key hustlers and would-be guides. Nestled behind is **Red Ground**, a seldom-visited residential area that houses most of Negril's permanent population.

The beach

Negril beach is a near-perfect Caribbean seashore. The whiter-than-white sand is lined by palms and sea grapes, the water is translucent and still, and the busy reefs ornately encrusted. It's also packed with tourists, locals and holidaying Kingstonians, and while it's great for lively socializing – the banter runs as freely as the rum cocktails, and everyone and everything is on show – the high concentration of human traffic inevitably draws a hard core of vendors and hustlers. The hassle is constant and high-octane, and as well as the usual crafts, hair braiding and aloe massage (the last must have been invented in Negril), you'll be offered sex and drugs with alarming frequency.

Though hotels guard "their" portion of beach with security men and strings of floating buoys, the law keeps beaches public up to the shoreline and you can walk the entire seven miles in an hour or so, though it's a hot and thirsty business in the sun. The beach is roughly divided by the bank of all-inclusives at the outcrop splitting Long Bay and Bloody Bay. Stretching north from the roundabout, **Long Bay** is the most heavily developed section of beach, by day a rash of bronzing bodies and flashing jet skis; by night a chain of disco bars dedicated to reggae, rum punch and skinny dipping. At the northern end, the hotels give way to the grassy stretch of **Long Day Beach Park**, with picnic tables, changing rooms, a snack bar and considerably fewer people. **Cosmo's**, a long-established restaurant further north towards Bloody Bay, is one of the best places to hang out if you're not staying at a beach hotel, with a pretty strip of sand strung with hammocks (J$100 entrance).

The final stretch of Negril's seven miles of beach is crescent-shaped **Bloody Bay**. Named for the crimson innards of whales once butchered on the beach, this was until very recently the least-developed stretch of beach in Negril, much favoured for nude bathing and general chilling-out, and almost deserted

Watersports

Two large reefs running parallel to the West End cliffs and four along the beach make **snorkelling** and **scuba** major Negril highlights. Despite environmental damage, the reefs are sumptuous, crowded with soft and hard coral, brilliantly coloured sponges and fish, octopuses, sea stars and even the odd turtle or nurse shark. There are several **sunken wrecks** that have become artificial reefs, including a ganja-smuggling plane that misjudged its landing at Negril airstrip, and another that was sunk deliberately. Snorkel equipment is available at most hotels and from all watersports operators at around US$10 per day. For snorkels, scuba gear, guided dives and certification courses, try Marine Life Divers (☎957 9783, ⓦwww.mldiversnegril.com) at the *Samsara Hotel*, Negril Scuba Centre (☎957 4425/9641/0392, ⓦwww.jamaica-irie .com) at both *Mariners' Inn* and *Mariner's Negril Beach Club,* and Sun Divers (☎957 4503 or 9943, ⓦwww.divenegriljamaica.com) at *Point Village* and on the beach. Both **water-skiing** (US$25 per lesson) and **jet ski** rentals (US$40 per half hr) are available on the beach. **Parasailing** is also possible; try Aqua Nova Sports at *Mariner's Beach Club* (☎957 4323, US$25 for 20min).

Glass-bottom boats are well represented along the beach and cost roughly US$15 for a ninety-minute trip; touts also sail along the cliffs, as do **canoe owners**, offering impromptu pleasure or fishing trips. Rates vary greatly depending upon the mood of the owner but average at about US$40 per half day; you can also ask at the fishermen's beach behind the craft market. If you're really serious you can hire a **sport-fishing boat** from most of the cruise operators listed below – try also The Spread Eagle Fishing Co (☎957 5170) or Stanley's (☎957 6341/0667) – and go after deep-water blue marlin, sailfish, wahoo and tuna. Bait, tackle, ice and beverages are usually included in half-day rates of around US$400. **Cruises** are an excellent way to see the local coastline, particularly at sunset (US$30 per person), although daytime cruises include Rhodes Hall Plantation or Half Moon Beach (US$40–55); most operators throw in snorkelling and snacks and all have an open bar. Try Cool Runnings (☎957 4323), Red Stripe (☎640 0873) or Wild Thing (☎957 5392).

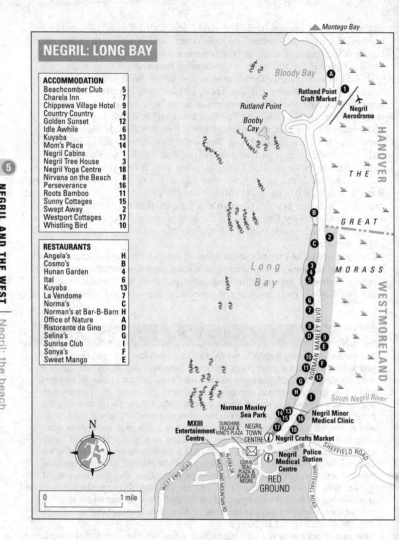

NEGRIL: LONG BAY

▲ Montego Bay

Bloody Bay

Rutland Point Craft Market

Rutland Point

Negril Aerodrome

Booby Cay

HANOVER

THE

GREAT

Long Bay

MORASS

WESTMORELAND

NORMAN MANLEY BLVD

South Negril River

Norman Manley Sea Park

Negril Minor Medical Clinic

MXIII Entertainment Centre

SUNSHINE VILLAGE & KING'S PLAZA

NEGRIL TOWN CENTRE

Negril Crafts Market

Police Station

WEST END ROAD

ALSICA DR

WESTLAND MOUNTAIN RD

CORAL SEAS PLAZA & PLAZA DE NEGRIL

Negril Medical Centre

RED GROUND

SHEFFIELD ROAD

WHITEHALL ROAD

N

0   1 mile

ACCOMMODATION

Beachcomber Club	5
Charela Inn	7
Chippewa Village Hotel	9
Country Country	4
Golden Sunset	12
Idle Awhile	6
Kuyaba	13
Mom's Place	14
Negril Cabins	1
Negril Tree House	3
Negril Yoga Centre	18
Nirvana on the Beach	8
Perseverance	16
Roots Bamboo	11
Sunny Cottages	15
Swept Away	2
Westport Cottages	17
Whistling Bird	10

RESTAURANTS

Angela's	H
Cosmo's	B
Hunan Garden	4
Ital	6
Kuyaba	13
La Vendome	7
Norma's	C
Norman's at Bar-B-Barn	H
Office of Nature	A
Ristorante da Gino	D
Selina's	G
Sunrise Club	I
Sonya's	F
Sweet Mango	E

during the week. Unfortunately it is now home to one particularly unattractive all-inclusive resort, the *Hotel Rui Tropical Bay,* and another is currently being built by the same company at the far end of the beach. Between the two lies the last remaining piece of the bay free of construction. This is where you'll find the *Office of Nature,* an open-air barbecue run by friendly Rastafarians, and lots of local activity – cricket matches, picnics – on public holidays and Sundays. The beach is backed by dense scrub and woodland, and on quieter weekdays it's best to keep a eye on your belongings.

Ironically, the track from the main coast road down to this stretch of Bloody Bay is opposite the local office of the Urban Development Corporation, the body theoretically responsible for protecting land in Jamaica, and patently failing to in the case of this particular stretch of beach. (Bloody Bay was

One of Negril's proudest moments came when the reign of **Calico Jack Rackham**, the most famous and notorious buccaneer to terrorize Jamaican waters, was brought to an end here in November 1720. Rackham – called "Calico" in reference to his preferred underwear – and his crew had moored their captured sloop in Bloody Bay to celebrate recent plunders along the north coast, unaware that their every move was bring shadowed by one Captain Barnet of the British Navy. Made inattentive by rum punch, the pirates were quickly overwhelmed. Some surrendered instantly, but two, in particular, put up a mighty struggle – even turning their weapons on their more malleable crew members. Eventually, these last two were subdued – at which point naval officers were astonished to find that they were **women** in disguise. Famously bloodthirsty in battle, **Anne Bonney**, Rackham's former mistress, and **Mary Read** formed a ruthless double act and were instrumental in earning Rackham his infamy as a freebooter. At their trial, victim Dorothy Thomas noted that "they wore men's jackets and long trousers… each of them had a machete and a pistol in their hands, and cursed and swore".

Rackham was executed, his body displayed in an iron frame at the Kingston cay that now bears his name. Bonney and Read were also sentenced to death, but were spared when they declared themselves pregnant and were eventually reprieved. Anne Bonney disappeared from recorded history, while Mary Read died of yellow fever and is buried in St Catherine.

considered officially protected public land until several years ago, and the building of the new all-inclusives is still a contentious issue among locals.)

The small forested islet in the centre of Bloody Bay, **Booby Cay**, appears in the epic movie *20,000 Leagues Under the Sea*, based on the Jules Verne novel. The isle is named after the **booby bird,** or sooty tern, an ocean dweller that takes a brief respite to lay eggs on offshore cays, though centuries of egg collection and hunting mean you're unlikely to clap eyes on one these days. The all-inclusives hold barbecues here, though you can usually get a local fisherman to transport you for about US$15 – ask at the fishermen's beach behind the main craft market.

Beyond Bloody Bay, past the Orange River bridge, there are several deserted white-sand coves fringed by mangroves, creepers and trailing vines, favoured by Jamaicans for weekend beach parties. To get to them, take any of the dirt tracks that lead into the trees. Past reports of robberies and assaults make going in a group sensible.

The Great Morass and Royal Palm Reserve

Jamaica's second-largest **wetland**, the **Great Morass** comprises six thousand acres of rivers, peat bogs and grasses running directly parallel to the beach. Fed by rivers flowing down from the Orange and Fish River hills, the morass lies at the bottom of Negril's watershed recharge area and is crucial to the area's supply of fresh water. Acting as a giant natural filter, the wetlands also protect the reefs from being smothered by silt and earth runoffs, and are a sanctuary for insects, shrimp, rare plants and birds – commonly seen species include Jamaican euphonias, parakeets and woodpeckers. Land crabs enjoy one of the

△ Glass-bottom boat

Environment matters

Rapid growth and unplanned development have had a devastating effect upon Negril's delicately balanced ecosystems. Norman Manley Boulevard cuts straight through what was originally swampland, while jet skis and anchors have played havoc with the reefs, and mangrove-felling has allowed the sea to slim down the precious beach and smother portions of reef with earth and sand that the trees once filtered. The population explosion has meant that until recently houses built on captured land lacked water supplies, garbage removal services and sanitation facilities. However, the long-term picture is far from hopeless: Negril now has a US$15-million water treatment plant and reservoir at nearby Logwood, which ought to minimize the amount of untreated sewage flowing into the sea, although link-up is proving beyond some people's means. With healthy support from Negril citizens, the **Negril Coral Reef Preservation Society** (NCRPS) has placed 45 mooring buoys at key points on the reefs and successfully lobbied for marine park status like that afforded the Montego Bay waters (see p.255); it was granted in March 1998. The **Negril Environmental Protection Trust** (NEPT) has a wider brief, declaring eighty square miles from Green Island to Salmon Point as the **Negril Watershed Environmental Protection Area**. To find out more about both groups, visit their offices at the back of the main craft market (℡957 9607).

few remaining perfect habitats in Jamaica and are a common sight during the summer breeding months – often, unfortunately, squashed at the roadside.

This rare habitat has long been threatened by pesticide and sewage pollution and proposals to remove peat fuel, but public outrage at the obvious destruction put a stop to the cut-and-drain activities of the government-owned Petroleum Company of Jamaica (PCJ). In addition, the 200-acre **Royal Palm Reserve** (daily 9am–6pm; US$10; ℡957 3736, ⓦwww .royalpalmreserve.com) was created in the 1980s towards the south side of the morass as a means of protecting this crucial wetland and the plants and animals within. The royal palm cluster here is one of the largest single collections of the tree in the world, and it is magnificent. Tall and graceful but devoid of coconuts, the palms have a stately presence that lends the reserve a patently tropical air. Wreathed in creepers and vines springing up from the nutrient-rich bog below, the trees are thick enough in places to block out views of the hills behind. Peat channels are now fish ponds, and there's a rickety bird-watching tower; a system of boardwalks allows you to go deep into the morass without getting wet.

The reserve land is still owned by the PCJ, which, after years of mismanagement and apathy, finally leased it in 2001 to the Negril Environmental Protection Trust (NEPT; see box). There's now an on-site café and a small museum with rather desultory exhibits and explanations of wetland ecosystems and bird varieties. However, the guide who takes visitors on the standard 45-minute tour is wonderfully informative and enthusiastic, and there are now useful labels posted on trees and other plants in the reserve. Dawn or dusk bird-watching is available with advance booking, and there are plans to introduce horseback riding and jitney tours. The area remains difficult to get to, though – finding it can be tricky, but most locals know the way from the Negril Hills Golf Club. At present, there are no organized boat trips into the morass, but you may be able to hire one of the fishing or glass-bottom boats moored at the mouth of the South Negril River (by the town roundabout) for a glimpse of its perimeter.

The West End

Beyond the overpriced cocktails and hallucinogenic sunset-watching at the infamous *Rick's Café*, the **West End** cliffs are the last vestige of truly laid-back Negril. The ostensible serenity, however, masks the depression of an extended period of economic decline. Disruptive sewage works between 1995 and 1997, combined with the more obvious appeal of the beach, have almost eclipsed the West End's formerly massive popularity, though the remoteness, immaculate reefs and the thrill of diving from a cliff straight into fifteen feet of the crystal-clear Caribbean remain unbeatable, and the quietude often means that you've got some of the best places entirely to yourself. The sleepiness of the West End might change in the future, however. The winding road that twists and turns for five miles along the clifftops has been dramatically resurfaced, and several popular evening joints are bringing life slowly back to the area.

The West End begins at the roundabout in the centre of town and meanders along the cliffs for some three miles, becoming Lighthouse Road at Negril lighthouse and winding inland to Orange Hill and ultimately Sheffield Road. The first stretch is the liveliest, with jerk shacks, bars, juice stalls and craft shops – including the official A Fi Wi or Vendor's Plaza **craft market** – lining the inland side, and restaurants hanging over the sea's edge. There are a couple of ramshackle **beaches** where fishermen moor their canoes, but the murky water makes swimming inadvisable. The road opens up a little once you get to the fancy King's Plaza and Sunshine Village shopping malls, but the true West End begins over the next blind bend; the road narrows, the water clears and the hotels that carve up the rest of the cliffs begin in earnest.

As this is Jamaica's extreme westerly point, the **sunset view** from the West End is the best you'll see. Most evenings the sky blazes with absurdly rich oranges, pinks and blues that intensify as the sun dips behind the horizon, eventually merging into the deepest of blues, with a moon reflected way out to sea. Sunset-watching is an institution here; most bars and restaurants offer sunset happy hours (see p.310) and the half-hour or so before dusk is the closest the West End gets to hectic. Coach parties descend in droves upon Negril's biggest tired cliché: undeservedly popular **Rick's Café**. The place has the trade sewn up – you pay for your drinks with plastic tokens, cameras click and local lads play the jester by diving off the cliffs for dollars.

Rick's marks the last of the major development; from here on the road becomes a country lane and the hotels are interspersed with near-wild coastline. A main point of interest is **Negril Point Lighthouse**, standing 100 feet above sea level at Jamaica's westernmost tip. Built in 1894, the 66-foot tower flashes a solar-powered beam 10 miles out to sea. The lighthouse still contains the carefully preserved acetylene gas canisters that first provided the power, the original hand-wound pendulum that once regulated the beam, and plenty of brass fittings. Port authority workers who live on site are usually willing to take you up all 103 leg-quivering steps to the top. Look out for the quaint crumbling outhouses, preserved as listed buildings, and the far-reaching roots of a huge silk cotton tree.

Negril Hills

Beyond the lighthouse the coast swings out of sight, but there's plenty of undeveloped land perfect for exploration by **bicycle** (see p.299 for outlets and cycling guides). As the cliffs and calm water diminish into a windblown ruggedness, there are fewer people, practically no hassle and a markedly rural

NEGRIL: WEST END

Savanna-la-Mar

Orange Hill and Retirement

Little Bay

0   500 yds

South Negril River

SHEFFIELD ROAD

Gas Station

AFIWI PLAZA

Negril Medical Centre

Police Station

CORAL SEAS PLAZA & PLAZA DE NEGRIL

SUNSHINE VILLAGE & KING'S PLAZA

WHITEHALL ROAD

White Hall Great House

RED GROUND

GOOD HOPE

ALASKA DRIVE

WEST END ROAD

WESTLAND MOUNTAIN ROAD

Joseph's Cave

SUMMERSET ROAD

Central Park Entertainment Centre

LIGHTHOUSE ROAD

Negril Lighthouse

HYLTON AVENUE

NEGRIL HILLS

CARIBBEAN SEA

N

ACCOMMODATION

Addis Kokeb	8
Banana Shout	14
Blue Cave Castle	1
The Caves	17
Citronella	16
Home Sweet Home	2
Jackie's on the Reef	19
Lighthouse Park	18
LTU Villas	15
Mariners Inn	10
Moonlight Villa	3
New Moon Cottage	4
Primrose Inn	6
Rockhouse	7
Summerset Village	9
Sundown	12
Tensing Pen	11
Villas Sur Mer	13
Xtabi	5

RESTAURANTS

The Carrot	J
Chicken Lavish	D
Choices	F
Erica's	K
Hallzers International	N
Hungry Lion	L
Jackie's on the Reef	19
Just Natural	H
LTU Pub	15
Peppa Pot	B
Pirate's Cave Bar and Grill	I
Ragga-Muffins	C
Rockhouse	7
Silver Star Café	E
Sips and Bites	M
Sweet Spice	A
Three Dives	G

Many **hotels** will let you swim from their piece of cliff for the price of a drink, and though they all look pretty similar, some stand out. *Drumville Cove* has a friendly attitude towards non-guests and a spectacular portion of cliff, while *Rockhouse* boasts a stylishly surreal saltwater swimming pool, a bar, excellent sea access and complete seclusion. The limestone cliffs are riddled with **caverns**, with a popular network below *Xtabi* hotel, though the rather chic *Pirate's Cave* restaurant and bar is in prime position for the exploration of **Joseph's Cave**, one of the largest along the West End, made famous in the movies *Dr No*, *Papillon* and *20,000 Leagues Under the Sea*; there's a staircase carved into the rock which leads from the bar down into the cave. The cliffs are at their highest around *Rick's Café*, the venue of sunset **cliff-diving** demonstrations; a less prominent place to have a go yourself is the *LTU Pub* next door or at *Pirate's Cave*. Below the lighthouse is a beautiful **cove** unconnected to any hotel, reached via a precarious wooden ladder, with rocks smooth enough to lie on and a small cave. Past the lighthouse, the cliffs peter out, coastal winds whip the sea into a frenzy and swimming becomes a little risky, but there is a sheltered spot just past the point where Lighthouse Road turns inland – turn straight onto the piece of undeveloped land and climb down the rocks.

atmosphere. Inland, the terrain rises into the dry limestone peaks of the **NEGRIL HILLS**, habitat of the nonvenomous **yellow boa snakes** occasionally seen slithering across the road. The coast road becomes a dirt track here, and the tarmac swings into the interior through quiet **ORANGE HILL**, with flowered duck ponds on its outskirts and a host of quietly convivial **bars** along its single street. Orange Hill merges into residential **RETIREMENT**, home to the distinctive **Jurassic Park Restaurant and Lounge**. Marked by giant cast-iron painted flamingos at the gates, this is the creative outlet of a local ironworker, whose enormous metal pterodactyls, hibiscus flowers and a five-foot-long centipede overlook the basketball court, bar, restaurant and a shady gazebo set up for domino tournaments.

Past Retirement the route either continues to weave round to Little Bay (see opposite) or loops back to Sheffield Road, giving wonderful views of the cane fields in the basin below and passing **Whitehall Great House**, a crumbling piece of colonial architecture that enjoyed a brief stint as a disco in the early 1980s, but has lain uninhabited since being gutted by fire in 1985. Only the stone shell and black-and-white floor tiles remain, but you can climb the foundations for a magnificent sweep over West End, the beach and the Great Morass. A peaceful spot for **horse rides**, the 187 acres of grounds contain an enormous silk cotton tree with grotesquely twisting limbs and quite possibly the widest girth of any on the island. The estate is also home to the grave of Robert Parkinson, a plantation owner, who had the dubious honour of giving his name to Parkinson's disease. There's a **bar** adjacent to the house, staffed by men who will offer to guide you round the house and grounds for a small tip.

Homer's Cove and Little Bay

If you're heading for the coast immediately southeast of Negril, you can either continue on from Retirement or go directly from Negril along the shore (although you won't be able to drive all the way; a bicycle is a much better bet for traversing the dirt track) until you arrive at the pleasant but rather dishevelled inlet of **HOMER'S COVE** (also known as **Brighton Beach** to locals).

The once-pristine beach has been mostly eroded by sand mining, but it's still a nice place for a swim, and there are a few vendors selling drinks and snacks.

Past Homer's Cove lies **LITTLE BAY**, the last piece of unspoilt coastline in the Negril hinterland and for now an extremely attractive, tranquil place. It may not remain so for much longer, however; increasingly, escapees from the noise and mania of Negril are choosing to visit and even stay in Little Bay. The *Humble Boy Club* is the closest Little Bay gets to a **hotel**, with a restaurant, bar and rooms (℡ 426 6205; ❸) set on the loveliest stretch of the beach. Next door is *Seaspray Villas* (℡ 392 6890, ⓦ www.seasprayvillas.com), a lovely oceanfront house that sleeps four to six people and rents for US$1500 per week; the rate includes all food and the services of a cook. You can rent kayaks from *Seaspray* (US$60-100 for half a day), which is also the base for excellent guided kayaking tours (ⓦ www.seasprayadventures.com). Another accommodation option is *Romie's Bar,* which has several simple cabins (℡ 707 0864; ❷) as well as bikes for hire. *Coconuts* (℡ 1-800/962 5548 in US, ⓦ www.jamaica-cottages.com) is a collection of attractive stone and cedar cottages right on the ocean's edge. Rates, which include three meals a day, start from US$645 per person per week.

For eating, *Uncle Sam's* has delicious conch soup and fresh fish served in the grooviest bar around; follow the signposted right fork opposite the school in the middle of the village. *Uncle Sam's* is also the venue for one-off sound-system dances and an annual unmissable **Donkey Derby** (held on the first Sunday in February). You can also **camp** here at US$10 per pitch.

Although it's currently locked up behind high gates as a result of ownership disputes, you might be able to find a local who can take you round **Bob Marley's Place**, an attractive wooden house built by Bob Marley in 1972. Marley and then-girlfriend Esther Anderson lived in the house for several years, and it was also the setting for Marley's *Talking Blues.* The grounds have a small mineral spring pool, large enough to swim just a couple of strokes.

Eating

Negril caters to a cosmopolitan crowd and offers some of the finest cuisine in Jamaica as well as an eclectic range of dining experiences. Negril's hippy associations are manifest in the high proportion of **vegetarian** options alongside the usual chicken and fish. You'll also find a lot of **pasta** and **pizza**, with many restaurants run by ex-pat Italians – these places are popular with the huge number of young Italians who visit en masse in the early summer. Italian eateries are generally moderately priced, while places that serve Jamaican fare have lower prices and the hotel restaurants tend to be expensive. Vendors based at the first stretch of West End Road sell roast or fried fish, jerk chicken and soup; as many of these are no more than a shack, names come and go and phones are infrequent, but generally the less flashy the place, the cheaper the product. There are dozens of jerk vendors in Negril, all wheeling out their oil-drum barbecues as dusk falls, but particularly recommended for jerk chicken are *The Best in the West* on Norman Manley Boulevard, *Simple and Fuzzy* in Negril Square and *Chicken King* on West End Road. Many of the smarter restaurants offer free pick-up; call in advance. The beach bars catering to American students, *Risky Business*, *Legends* and *Margueritaville,* all serve various forms of hamburgers and chips, and there is now a small *Burger King* opposite ScotiaBank.

Sheffield Road

Sweet Spice Sheffield Rd. The best place on Sheffield Road for delicious Jamaican food – though it's no longer as cheap as it used to be – to take away or eat in.

Peppa Pot Sheffield Rd. Excellent, inexpensive jerk centre with tasty chicken, pork and fish served with side orders of breadfruit, sweet potato or yam. Mellow atmosphere, with oldies hits on the sound system and tables painted with checkers and chess boards.

The beach

Angela's *Bar-B-Barn Hotel*, Norman Manley Blvd ℡957 3345. Excellent, mid-priced Italian restaurant on breezy and attractive upstairs terrace. Delicious thin-crust pizza, pasta dishes and other Italian specialities.

Cosmo's Norman Manley Blvd ℡957 4330. One of the best, busiest spots on the beach, equally popular with Jamaicans and tourists. Excellent seafood – conch soup is a speciality – and the usual selection of chicken variations. Prices are moderate.

Ristorante da Gino *Mariposa* resort, Norman Manley Blvd ℡957 4918. Excellent, expensive Italian restaurant set on pretty outdoor terrace. The usual range of pasta and seafood dishes; *scallopine al burro* (scallops in butter) is particularly good, as is lobster linguine.

Hunan Garden *Country Country* hotel, Norman Manley Blvd ℡957 4359. Excellent Chinese restaurant in attractive dining room with a vast, somewhat expensive, menu. Eat in or take out.

Ital *Idle Awhile*, Norman Manley Blvd. Tasty, moderately priced vegetable stews are cooked up by a funky Rasta chef in chic hotel gardens on the beach.

Kuyaba *Kuyaba* hotel ℡957 4318. Thatch-roofed, open-sided and expensive restaurant with innovative decor, consistently good food and regular crowds. The frequently changed blackboard menu might include lobster in white wine and garlic, imported Italian pasta, steaks, snapper stuffed with crab in an orange sauce and vegetarian dishes.

Norma's *SeaSplash* hotel, Norman Manley Blvd ℡957 4041. This expensive spot is award-winning chef Norma Shirley's latest project. The menu features nouvelle Jamaican cuisine, with creative salads, pasta and jazzed-up jerk chicken and grilled fish.

Norman's at Bar-B-Barn Norman Manley Blvd. Lively beach restaurant with up-market, moderately priced menu, including blackened mahimahi and rack of lamb.

Office of Nature Bloody Bay. Funky barbecue joint under canvas on the beach. Lobster, fish and chicken are moderately priced and cooked to order.

Selina's Norman Manley Blvd. Excellent breakfast joint with friendly service, moderate prices and extensive menu – eggs, filled bagels, delicious banana pancakes. Blue Mountain coffee roasted on site is sold, and there's a good book and magazine exchange.

Sunrise Club Norman Manley Blvd. This small Italian-run resort on the Great Morass side of the beach road has three restaurants – Jamaican, lobster and Italian – with moderate prices. The latter offers unusual but tasty pink gnocchi, among other treats. Great cocktails and proper espresso, too.

Sonya's Norman Manley Blvd. Delicious, inexpensive Jamaican food cooked over a wood fire. This spot also serves the classiest patties in Negril – try the Italian with tomato and mozzarella.

Sweet Mango *Rondel Village,* Norman Manley Blvd. Inexpensive health-food shop with salad bar, vegetarian lunch buffet and good fruit drinks and smoothies.

La Vendome *Charela Inn* ℡957 4648. Celebrated, sophisticated, expensive French/Jamaican cuisine – duck à l'orange, veal with veloutée sauce, snapper in coconut. Some vegetarian dishes as well. Also home-made ice cream, excellent bread and a good wine list.

West End

The Carrot West End Rd. Inexpensive natural juice bar and vegetarian café with on-site herbal consultant. Seafood dishes include excellent conch soup.

Chicken Lavish West End Rd ℡957 4410. Choice spot for domino players. It serves chicken and fish, Jamaican- and Chinese-style, steaks and pork chops, all inexpensive.

Choices West End Rd. Brightly painted outdoor café with low prices and all the Jamaican staples. Popular with both locals and tourists, particularly at breakfast.

Erica's Opposite the *Rockcliff Hotel*, West End Rd. Small shack featuring home cooking by Erica herself. Seafood is a speciality, with excellent, and reasonably priced, lobster.

Hallzer's International West End Rd. Extremely welcoming bar and restaurant run by sociable and kind-hearted Scots. Serves large breakfasts, including full English ones, and moderately priced home cooked dishes such as steak pie with mashed potatoes, fish and chips and home-made sausages. Boasts the best-stocked bar in Negril, with wide range of malt whiskies and other more obscure liquors.

Snacks

For snacks and patties, try *Tan-Tan* at the back of the Plaza de Negril – its callaloo and cheese loaf and vegetable and beef patties are the best and cheapest in town. *3C's Pastry,* at the start of the West End Rd, is open around the clock, serving chicken, fish and curry goat alongside the pastries. *Mr Slice's Pizza* (☎957 0584), opposite the Yacht Club on the West End and at the beach, sells real thin-crust pizza and will deliver. Ice-cream and fruit vendors make regular rounds of the beach if you can't be bothered to move; otherwise look out for *La Bella Italia,* delicious Italian-style ice cream made in Negril and sold at various outlets in town, including a small booth in Times Square and the *Blue Water Ice-cream Parlour* on the West End Road.

Hungry Lion West End Rd; ☎957 4486. The best vegetarian food in town, with seafood too. A walled courtyard affords privacy, and the food, though expensive, is always good. The menu offers meatless shepherd's pie with green lentils, lobster in lemon butter, black bean chilli, pasta primavera, and other specialties. The coconut cream pie is unmissable. Expensive.

Jackie's on the Reef Lighthouse Rd ☎957 4997. Meals must be ordered in advance, but the menu is innovative and health-food oriented, and the setting romantic and unusual. Moderately priced dishes include grilled tuna with sesame noodles, sun-dried tomato pasta and chicken marinated in rosemary.

Just Natural West End Rd. Inexpensive, fresh Jamaican food, callaloo omelettes, pasta, burritos and vegetarian options, in a beautiful shady garden.

LTU Pub West End Rd ☎957 0382. Laid-back venue with cliffside dining, relaxed atmosphere and a moderately priced, mixed menu: seafood, stuffed jalapeno chillis, callaloo filled with callaloo and cheese, and some German dishes, too.

Pirate's Cave Bar and Grill West End Rd. Newly – and beautifully – renovated restaurant in prime

spot over Joseph's Cave, with chic decor, moderate prices, excellent grilled chicken and ribs and a long cocktail list. Entertainment includes cliff diving and a darts board.

Ragga-Muffins West End Rd. Pretty Canadian-run café with great breakfasts, home-made banana bread and well-priced lunch and dinner menus.

Rockhouse West End Rd; ☎957 4373. One of Negril's finest restaurants, romantically set on a boardwalk right over the sea. Expensive, but with excellent service and an imaginative menu that includes vegetable tempura, seafood linguine with garlic, and conch fritters.

Silver Star Café West End Rd. Long-established, moderately priced café with excellent hippy breakfasts – yoghurt, muesli, banana pancakes – some vegan meals and peaceful verandah set back from the road.

Sips and Bites West End Rd. Large open yard, popular with taxi drivers, serving unadulterated Jamaican cuisine at very reasonable prices.

Three Dives West End Rd. Popular, inexpensive jerk centre in a cliffside garden, with particularly good lobster and a nightly bonfire.

Drinking and entertainment

Most **bars** want you to spend the **sunset** with them and provide drinks promotions or happy hours as an incentive. As the cliffs give the best view, bars along the West End tend to be livelier at dusk, with the action moving to the beach after dark. The larger places are distinctly tourist-oriented, with neon, imported drinks, satellite TV and an air of enforced indulgence. If you want some local flavour, try the darkened interiors of the **rum bars** and **beer shacks** along Sheffield Road or West End Road near the roundabout.

As there is only one proper **club** in town, *The Jungle* (see p.317), most of the weeknight dancing is offered by **beach bars** using their portion of sand as a dance floor. These have agreed to a nightly rotation system to share the business around a little. DJs play dancehall or Euro-disco, and the **live music** usually consists of a no-name reggae band singing Bob Marley covers – though the *Hurricane Band,* who play every Wednesday at *Roots Bamboo,* are a distinct cut above the rest. Otherwise, Tuesdays, Fridays and Sundays at *Alfred's* and Saturdays at *Bourbon Beach* (formerly *De Buss*) are particularly lively dance nights. Jazz fans should note that the John Wheatley Quartet play on Mondays at the *Charela Inn Hotel,* and *Roots Bamboo* has live **jazz** every Sunday afternoon. *Home Sweet Home* on the West End hosts a talented local group of **nyabingi drummers** on Fridays between 7 and 9pm. Nights vary and new venues pop up with alarming regularity, but most locals keep abreast of the current hot spots. As the beach venues are free you can walk from one to another in any case.

Large **stageshows** featuring well-known reggae artists are advertised on roadside billboards and through a car-with-megaphone system. They're supposed to start at 9.30pm and finish at 1.30am, but rarely begin before 11pm and often go on until 3 or 4am. Well-known artists and DJs perform regularly during the winter season; if a major artist is scheduled to play, it's always worth checking that they are actually there before you pay your money, as some have a reputation for unreliability. Main **venues** for large shows are *Roots Bamboo* on the beach, which frequently hosts big-name bands, and less regularly *MXIII* in the West End; cover charge is usually in the region of US$10. *The Samsara Hotel* and *Central Park* (both on the West End Road) have occasional live events and open up properly, several nights a week, during the Spring Break period in March; the *Bella Donna* restaurant on Summerset Road has live reggae music on Wednesdays and sporadic big-name gigs.

Sound-system jams take place every weekend in Red Ground, Orange Hill and the surrounding communities. There's often a jam at the large lawn in front of the *One Love Rastawant,* off West End Road behind Coral Seas Plaza. Though the Negril Reggae Festival is a thing of the past, there's usually a huge **reggae extravaganza** around Spring Break time. Two set fixtures in the local calendar are **Negril Carnival** and the **Bob Marley Birthday Bash. Negril Carnival,** held annually in late April, features costume parades and all-night dancing in the streets – contact the JTB for further information. The other main event, the annual Bob Marley birthday celebration (see p.47), takes place at *MXIII* each February 6 and usually attracts top reggae performers.

Bars

Alfred's Ocean Palace Norman Manley Blvd. Busiest bar on the beach, with thrice-weekly live reggae and crowds of happy holidaymakers dancing on the sand. This is where all the action is and it's great fun, but watch out for the hustlers, particularly on gig nights.

Boat Bar Norman Manley Blvd. Long-standing bar on the beach with swing seats, genial low-key atmosphere and tasty Jamaican food.

Bourbon Beach Bar Norman Manley Blvd. The trademark London bus (now looking very tatty) used in *Live and Let Die* stands outside. There's piped or live music every night in a large covered area and section of the beach. The jerk chicken is famously good.

Errol's Norman Manley Blvd. Small 24hr beach bar with reggae videos, an overdose of fairy lights and hard-core drinking by guests who rent basic but adequate rooms in the yard behind the bar.

LTU Pub West End Rd. Very cool bar, and vastly superior to next-door *Rick's*; it offers cliffside drinking, diving, snorkelling and food to boot. Ask the barman to make you a Bob Marley – and then try and drink it.

Margueritaville Norman Manley Blvd. Large beach bar with nightly bonfire, beach volleyball, two-for-one drink offers and big TV screens for sports fans. Themed nights include karaoke and weekly Friday all-inclusive parties. Hugely popular with American students.

Mi Yard West End Rd. High-rise bar that's tourist-friendly but positively Jamaican. Open 24hr for music, dominoes, drinking and jerk; always packed once the beach bars start to slow down after 2am.

Natural I Lighthouse Rd. Groovy 24hr bar run and frequented by Rastas. It's a long way from downtown Negril, which makes it chilled-out and quietly sociable.

Naturelle Juice Bar On the beach, about midway. Delicious fresh fruit juices are the speciality at this funky little place run by Rastas. Drinks made with coconut, squeezed by hand, are superb.

Rick's Café West End Rd. Overpriced tourist trap with appallingly tuneless band playing reggae cover versions alongside the traditional spectacle of local boys diving from the high cliffs. The West End's main sunset event.

Sexy Rexy's West End Rd. Just beyond *LTU*, this small shack has as good a clifftop view as anywhere in the West End. Rexy is an entertaining local character and will cook up tasty fried fish if you're hungry.

Yacht Club West End Rd. Large thatched bar, with a long and colourful history, overlooking the sea. Cheap Red Stripe all day until 7pm, live music at weekends and wonderfully shady clientele. Come for a heavy drinking session with the hippies who "discovered" Negril, and other local characters; the staff are helpful and friendly. It's surprisingly safe and often great fun.

Clubs

Close Encounters Kings Plaza, West End Rd. Every town has one, and this is Negril's premier go-go club, where scantily clad women gyrate for the drinkers. Don't go before midnight. Open nightly; weekends are especially popular. Cover US$5.

The Jungle Norman Manley Blvd. Large glitzy purpose-built nightclub across from the beach, with gaming lounge, sports bar and jerk food. Thursday, "Ladies' Night", is most popular (free for women until midnight). Open Wednesday through to Sundays until 5am. Cover US$9 for men, US$6 for women.

Shopping

Crafts are available practically everywhere you go in Negril. Dedicated craft shops pepper the West End, and though the resort police and Chamber of Commerce have cracked down on mobile vendors by building dedicated plazas and patrolling the streets, plenty still roam the beach. The best place to buy is the main craft market at the roundabout end of Norman Manley Boulevard, with around a hundred stalls and a full spread of merchandise. Also good is A Fi Wi Plaza, on West End Road between the roundabout and Sunshine Village. The Rutland Point market opposite Bloody Bay deals mostly with guests of the all-inclusives, so it can be more expensive, but it's often quiet enough to make bartering worth the vendors' while, as is the ramshackle collection of huts opposite the *Rockhouse Hotel*.

For unusual items try the shop at *Kuyaba* restaurant on the beach, which prides itself on stock that you can't find anywhere else in town, like painted tin "country buses" and primary-coloured enamelled tropical fish. Well-known Negril-based artist Geraldine Robins sells excellent **batik** and hand-painted T-shirts and fabrics from her shop at *Margueritaville*, and Gallery Hoffstead in A Fi Wi Plaza has prints, originals and sculpture by owner Lloyd Hoffstead. The *Rockhouse* gift shop has the town's prettiest array of **beach wraps**, among other attractive items; Sarongs to Go on the West End Road also has a good selection. Roots Man Corner, on the main Negril roundabout, is the place to get natural remedies, while *Pamela's* craft stall on the West End sells attractive stripey bags and other hand-made items. Ja-Ja Originals promotes and sell paintings by local Jamaican artists as well as elegant gold and silver **jewellery** and will create custom-made items; you'll find the shop at the *Coco La Palm* hotel on Norman Manley Boulevard. Times Square is a fancy shopping mall that specializes in thousand-dollar watches, though several shops sell decent beach clothes, bags and jewellery. Other **in-bond shops** are situated in hotels and in Sunshine Village, which is also the best choice for kitsch holiday souvenirs and swimwear.

Basic **food** needs are met by the well-stocked Hi-Lo in Sunshine Village, or the smaller Valuemaster in Plaza de Negril. The stalls at the top end of Sheffield

Road have cheaper and fresher fruit and vegetables. If you don't want to stray too far from your hotel, *Café Taino* on Norman Manley Boulevard has a small selection of deli items and wine; *Wise Choice,* opposite *Tensing Pen*, is a comprehensive grocery store that's incredibly convenient if you're loathe to leave the West End. Daley's liquor store, near the post office on West End Road, offers discounts on bulk buys of **beer** or **spirits,** a good idea if you have a fridge in your room.

Listings

Airlines Air Jamaica ☎952 4300 or 4100; Air Jamaica Express ☎957 5251; American Airlines ☎952 5950; British Airways ☎952 3771; Continental ☎952 4495 or 1-800/230-0856 in US; Timair ☎957 5374. Only Air Jamaica Express and Timnair have offices in Negril.

Airport The information line for Negril Aerodrome is ☎957 3016.

American Express Bank of Novia Scotia, Plaza de Negril (Mon–Thurs 9am–2pm, Fri 9am–4pm).

Banks and money The Bank of Nova Scotia, Plaza de Negril, has a 24hr ATM machine, as does the National Commercial Bank in Sunshine Village (hours for both banks: Mon–Thurs 9am–2pm, Friday 9am–4pm); there's also an ATM at the Petcom petrol station by the Negril Aerodrome. Both banks offer currency exchange and cash advances on credit cards; rates are substantially better than in hotels but around the same as the town's best official cambio, Gold Nugget, on Norman Manley Blvd (Mon–Sat 9am–5pm). Black market touts hang around Negril Square; if you choose to risk using them, try and get a Jamaican to accompany you. Moneygram wire transfers can be collected at the National Commercial Bank and the cambio at the Time Trend Financial Co on Norman Manley Blvd (Mon–Fri 9am–5pm, Sat 10am–3pm; ☎957 3242); Western Union (Mon–Thurs 9am–5.30pm, Fri & Sat 9am–6pm) has an outlet at Hi-Lo supermarket in Sunshine Village.

Car and bike rental Choices ☎957 3490; Jus Jeep, West End Rd ☎957 0094/5; Vernon's, Plaza de Negril and Norman Manley Blvd ☎957 4522 or 4354. Bikes can be rented from Dependable (☎957 4764), Elvis (☎957 4732) and Jah B's (☎957 4235), all on Norman Manley Blvd, and from Banmark (☎957 0197), Kool Bike Rental, (☎957 9224) and Tykes Bikes (☎957 0388) on West End Rd.

Doctors and clinics There are plenty of doctors and private clinics; try Negril Minor Emergency Clinic on Norman Manley Blvd (☎957 4888; open

24hrs) or Dr Dale Foster (☎957 9307). There is an optician in Kings Plaza, West End Rd.

Golf Negril Hills Golf Club (☎957 4638) is an extremely hilly and attractive 18-hole, 6,600-yard, par-72 course in the hills above town. The topography makes for a challenging game, and there's a clubhouse and restaurant on site.

Hospitals The nearest hospitals are at Savanna-la-Mar (☎955 2533 or 2133) and Lucea (☎956 2233). In an emergency, dial ☎119 for an ambulance.

Internet You can pick up and send emails (from US$4 per hr) from *Café Taino* on Norman Manley Blvd or the *Irie Vibes* bar on the beach. On the West End, try the *Yacht Club* (🖳www.yachtclub.com), the *Easy Rock Internet Café* or *Mi Yard* (open 24hrs).

Laundry Most hotels will wash clothes, but it's cheaper to hire a local lady. Ask around – a load should cost US$5–7. West End Cleaners, off Hylton Ave at the top of Lighthouse Rd (☎957 0160), is rather inaccessible but will pick up and deliver between 8am and 10pm daily. Washing costs J$50 per pound, including soap. The Village Laundry (☎957 0165), on the back road behind Coral Seas Plaza, is more expensive but conveniently located.

Massage Massage is a Negril institution. Try Nadine Loeb at *Catcha Falling Star* hotel (☎957 0390); *Jackie's on the Reef* (☎957 4997); Catherine McLean (c/o *Tensing Pen*, ☎957 0387); or Beverly Haslam at the *House of Dread* bar on West End Rd (☎957 4833). Dr Peggy Daugherty (☎957 9924 or 818 0682) is a naturopathic doctor specializing in deep tissue and cranio-sacral massage.

Petrol Negril has two petrol stations: on Sheffield Rd at the junction of the right fork to Whitehall and Retirement (daily 6.30am–11pm), and Petcom by Negril Aerodrome (daily 6.30am–11pm).

Pharmacies Key West Pharmacy is at 11 Sunshine Village (Mon–Sat 9am–8pm, Sun 10am–6pm); Negril Pharmacy is at 14 Coral Seas Plaza (Mon–Sat 9am–7pm, Sun 10am–2pm).

Photography Colour Negril, at Plaza de Negril, and Photo Prints, on West End Rd, both offer free pick-up and delivery and one-hour processing.

Post office Negril post office is on West End Rd next to A Fi Wi Plaza; open Monday to Friday 9am to 5pm.

Taxis Candycabs ☎957 9224 or 972 0190, ⊛www.candycabs.com; Negril Transportation Services ☎815 6782; JUTA Negril ☎957 9197.

Telephones and communications There is a bank of phone boxes opposite the main craft mar-ket and another in Plaza de Negril; phonecards are available from pharmacies or the post office. Other than Sunshine Village, the West End is poorly served; there are two phone booths by *Catcha Falling Star* and one by the *House of Dread* bar. The Negril Calling Centre (9am–11pm) in Plaza de Negril offers relatively cheap local and overseas calls and fax service; you can also send faxes and make photocopies from the Negril Chamber of Commerce office at A Fi Wi Plaza (Mon–Fri 9am–5pm).

East of Negril

After Negril's glittering hedonism, the rest of the southwest can come as quite a surprise. Restaurants remain wholeheartedly Jamaican, with mannish water and eye-rollingly insouciant service replacing waffles and exhortations to "have a nice day". Locals tend to be more genuinely friendly, if a little surprised that you've torn yourself away from a resort, and unfettered by high-rises and serviceable roads, the countryside is magnificent. Westmoreland's longest river, the multi-tributaried **Cabarita**, meanders down central hills through the vast cane fields around **Frome Sugar Factory** and the alluvial plains surrounding the concrete capital of **Savanna-la-Mar**, where brisk trade and honking horns fight against the soupy humidity. A few miles to the east, **Roaring River** marks its entrance above ground with a spectacular blue swimming hole, having carved out an inky cave on its way. Water is central to Westmoreland, irrigating the sugarcane and reducing turf to swamps, or noticeable by its absence as you near the parched fields and dry riverbeds towards St Elizabeth. Since Indian workers first entered the scene in the mid-nineteenth century, the region's extensive wetlands have been mostly employed for the cultivation of rice. The potential for bird-watching and boat safaris has not been capitalized as it has further down the south coast, nor have the miles of beach at **Bluefields** or the unhurried charm of fishing villages **Belmont** and **Whitehouse**.

Little London and Frome

Once out of Negril proper, Sheffield Road opens up into the pockmarked, fast-moving and truck-dominated route to Savanna-la-Mar, sweeping past cane fields neatly bordered by the stunning Fish River hills. After about nine miles, a cluster of buildings around a gas station signifies the start of **LITTLE LONDON**. Though the years have blurred racial origins, the local population was at one time dominated by Indians who came to Jamaica in the nineteenth century as indentured workers to labour in the cane fields and sugar factories. Most people pass through Little London with hardly a sideways glance, as there's little of obvious interest. If you're hungry, stop at the *Kingfish Kitchen* for

Sugar wars

The centre of some of Jamaica's most violent labour disputes, **Frome sugar factory** was built in 1938 by British company Tate and Lyle's subsidiary West Indies Sugar Company as the most modern facility in the West Indies. It is now government-run under the Sugar Company of Jamaica.

The factory has long been beset by industrial disputes. Constructed during a period of high unemployment, it drew job seekers in their thousands. Most were unlucky, and even those who were given jobs received a pittance far lower than the salary they'd been promised. Under the fiery leadership of **Alexander Bustamante**, the workers banded together in protest. The dispute swiftly turned ugly; cane fields were set on fire and a full-scale riot broke out on May 3, 1938. The unrest left four dead from police bullets and one hundred demonstrators, including Bustamante, in jail.

Frome's volatile reputation endures, and it has been the centre of more recent difficulties, triggered by the decline of the Jamaican sugar industry. Machinery has never been updated, leaving the factory unable to compete with more efficient producers and operating at a loss. Re-mechanization is, arguably, the only solution, but the inevitable loss of hundreds of manual jobs has understandably generated animosity. Frome remains the largest single employer in Westmoreland and its success is crucial to the overall prosperity of the area.

traditional Jamaican cooking; the large lawn out back serves as an occasional venue for sound-system dances, and the proprietors and regulars usually have a small party on a Sunday. There's no **accommodation** in Little London proper, but turning right at the central crossroads in town will take you down a relatively smooth track to **BROUGHTON** and the *Lost Beach Resort* (T 640 1111, 1-734/761-7444 in US, F 640 1008, W www.lostbeach.com; ●), which has spacious rooms on Hope Wharf fishing beach, a swimming pool, a restaurant and a bar. Horseback riding, watersports and an adventure package are also available, and the place itself is an idyllic getaway spot with friendly and welcoming staff.

Flat savannah lands, ideal for the cultivation of cane, have long meant strong local ties to the **sugar industry**. The largest cane-processing factory in the area is **FROME**, about five miles northeast of Little London, which handles most of the cane from neighbouring plantations (see box above). Though the factory is not officially open to the public, you should be able to arrange a tour by calling ahead (T 955 6080).

Savanna-la-Mar

Capital of Westmoreland it may be, but there's little to keep you in the rather soulless confines of commercial **SAVANNA-LA-MAR**. It's the area's main shopping centre, but as the profusion of low-lying concrete keeps the air still and makes it a hot and uncomfortable place to wander about, most people depart as quickly as possible and there are no developed tourist attractions. The elements have given the town a battering – successive hurricanes flattened it in 1748, 1780, 1912, 1948 and 1988; in 1748 the wind drove the sea far enough up central Great George Street that boats were left dry-docked in the middle of the road.

Other than a couple of attractive gingerbread dwellings on the outskirts, you're stuck with the negligible appeal of **Great George Street**, the needle-straight main thoroughfare. The **courthouse** and parish administrative offices stand next to a cast-iron **fountain**. The rest of the street is taken up with pharmacies and general stores, most selling the usual assortment of imported designer bootlegs, though if you want some true Yard-style ragga string vests, Jamaican flag bandannas or barely there dancehall attire, this is the place to go. Great George Street ends abruptly at the seashore; here you'll find the main fruit and vegetable **market** (main day Saturday), and the ruins of **Savanna-la-Mar Fort**. The latter was declared "the worst fort in Jamaica" by a visiting admiral in 1755, who discovered that though vast sums had been devoted to defending the town, the fort was unfinished and one third of what there was had collapsed into the sea. Opposite is the West Indies Sugar Factory **pier**, from which sugar from the Frome factory is loaded for export. There's little to see other than crumbling walls and moored fishing boats.

Practicalities

Savanna-la-Mar is a main junction of the Montego Bay/Negril route; all **buses** stop at the main bus station at the top of Great George Street, and you can connect with services to the south coast and beyond. If you're driving, there's an incredibly complicated one-way system round town – follow the signs. With so many pleasant options nearby, few choose to **stay** in Savanna-la-Mar, but you could join Jamaican regulars and rent a basic but air-conditioned room at *Orchard Great House* (℡955 2737; ❷); there's a restaurant, bar and a pool on site. Simpler but much more attractive is the *Lochiel Guest House*, east of town on Sheffield Road (℡955 9344; ❶), an atmospheric old house in lovely grounds. For **food**, try *Susie V's* on Great George Street or, for the best vegetable patties for miles around, *Lucky Tree Pastry*, on the road leading out of town eastwards to Bluefields.

Around town: Roaring River Park and Abeokuta Nature Park

An easy escape about five miles north of Savanna-la-Mar is gorgeous **ROARING RIVER PARK** (daily except Saturdays 9am–5pm; US$10) near the small community of **Petersfield**, approached on a rutted road that you'll probably need directions to find, though there are signposts from town. Set in a former plantation and still surrounded by cane fields, a dazzling blue **mineral pool** and extensive **caves** have been developed with tourists in mind, though not on the scale of Dunn's River (see p.196). The site's reputation for unpleasant hassling has largely been dealt with by its current managers, the Tourist Product Development Company (TPDCO): a guide meets you as you arrive, leads you helpfully to the ticket office and then takes you on a trip round the caves and surrounding gardens. On Saturdays the caves are accessible, but the landscaped park and gardens are closed, and there are no official guides. (You may be met by locals on motorbikes keen to "guide" you – shake them off firmly.) It's all very pretty – watercress grows wild along banks planted with palms and crotons, and the forested hillside rises up unbroken. Steps up to the mouth, concrete walkways, and lighting let you appreciate the full magnitude of the caverns, which range from broom cupboard to auditorium in size. Bats flit about, and there are two mineral pools for a disquieting swim in pitch-blackness – the water is said to rejuvenate. The caves are marred only by graffiti carved into the rock and jagged edges where the quartz has been levered off and sold.

The village is located further on, past the main swimming spot at **Blue Hole Garden** (daily 8am–6pm; US$4). Overhung with trees and flowers, this thirty-foot-wide natural spring of refreshing chilly azure water is said to be bottomless – the true depth has never been charted. The surrounding gardens are well kept but not over-landscaped, packed with unusual trees, anthuriums, narcotic white trumpet flowers, and every variety of heliconia; there are several spots to immerse yourself amid gushing mini-waterfalls.

If you want to **stay** in Roaring River, there are two cool thatched cabins (❶) in the Blue Hole Garden. Facilities are simple (outdoor shower, mosquito screen and pit toilet), but the setting is incredible. You can also **camp** at perfectly appointed tent sites for US$10. **Food** and **drink** are available from the *Lover's Café* in Blue Hole Garden; for a relatively remote spot, the menu is excellent and includes vegetable patties, garlic bread, spicy dumplings and fish.

Close to Petersfield, on the Cabarita River, is a new adventure-sports outfit, Jamaica Whitewater (℡ 387 9342, Ⓦ www.jamaicawhitewater.com), which runs kayaking and rafting trips over the river's rapids. Trips consist of 3.5 hours on the water and an initial hour of comprehensive instruction and cost US$80 per person. You'll need to book in advance by phone; organizers will then arrange to meet you in Petersfield or Savannnah-la-Mar and take you on to the site.

Also north of Savannah-la-Mar, in Deans Valley, is the **ABEOKUTA PRIVATE NATURE PARK** (daily 9am–5pm; US$10, US$15 with guided tour; ℡957 7719). Owned by a friendly Jamaican family, the "park" is a large private garden with lovely views, a ruined great house and a huge natural pool fed by the Sweet River, which runs through an aqueduct built by slaves over 300 years ago. There are plans to create a café and accommodation on the premises; meanwhile, it's possible to **camp** (US$30 per tent with breakfast). The park is a wonderfully tranquil place, perfect if you're looking for some peace and quiet. To reach Abeokuta, take the road from Savannah-la-Mar to Bluefields and turn left at the Ferris Cross junction to Deans Valley. The park is situated opposite the Deans Valley Housing Scheme on the old ice factory road.

Bluefields and Belmont

East of Savanna-la-Mar, the coast road becomes the A2 and after the crossroads at Ferris Cross sticks close to the sea on its way to Bluefields and Whitehouse. Just before Ferris Cross, **Paradise Park** (Mon–Sat 8.30am–4.30pm; US$5), marked by a drive of royal palms, is an extensive cane plantation offering swimming in the Sweet River, hiking in beautifully varied terrain (guides are available), and two-hour horse rides (between 9am and 3pm; US$30). It's a worthwhile diversion before you reach **Bluefields** and **Belmont**, contiguous, laid-back communities of picturesque fishing beaches and reef-fringed shallows.

Henry Morgan (see p.112) sailed from **BLUEFIELDS** in 1670 to attack Panama, and the calm seas and sheltered bay have attracted every generation of Jamaican settlers. It was one of the first Spanish settlements, and the local community association (see p.324) is attempting to reopen the old Spanish road to Martha Brae in Trelawny as a hiking route – though the distance and thick plant cover make this a rather distant possibility. The most interesting building in modern Bluefield is privately owned **Bluefields House,** next to the police station. It was once a temporary home to Philip Gosse, "father of Jamaican ornithology" and inventor of the modern aquarium, who researched *Illustrations of the Birds of Jamaica* and *A Naturalist's Sojourn in Jamaica* during an eighteen-month residence in 1844–45. In the gardens stand a **breadfruit tree** said to be the first in Jamaica, planted by Captain Bligh when he brought seedlings from Tahiti. The house is virtually derelict now, but it is possible to stay in very basic but wonderfully atmospheric accommodation (**①**).

Bluefields merges imperceptibly into **BELMONT**, birthplace of the late **Peter Tosh** (see box below). His body lies in a small red-gold-and-green **mausoleum** (daily 9am–5pm; donation) just off the road, decorated with stained glass, photos and press cuttings. It's much less of an affair than the Marley mausoleum in St Ann (see p.228) and usually deserted. Recent upgrading by Peter Tosh's family – his mother lives in a modest house at the back of the property – means there's a car park now, along with CDs on sale and hand-painted signs that exhort you to light up a spliff on your way in.

Peter Tosh

Consciously controversial, **Peter Tosh** (born McIntosh) was Jamaica's best-known lyrical agitator. Born an only child in Belmont on October 19, 1944, he was raised by an aunt in the West Kingston tenement yards dominated, at the time, by the explosion of hopeful harmony groups that transformed post-independence Kingston into a hotbed of aspirations. Every newly arrived country "bhuttu" (or bumpkin) wanted to be a singer and Tosh followed suit, embarking on a mission to reveal home truths from a ghetto perspective. He saved to buy his first guitar and in 1964 formed vocal trio The Wailers with teenage allies Bunny Livingstone and Bob Marley. In 1972 the Wailers signed to Chris Blackwell's Island label, and recorded *Catch a Fire* and *Burnin'* together while Tosh put out tracks on his own Intel Diplo HIM label (Intelligent Diplomat for His Imperial Majesty), all the time becoming increasingly bitter over pay and personal disputes with the man he referred to as "Whiteworst". By 1974, he and Bunny Livingstone had gone their separate ways.

Having already earned a reputation as the Wailers' social conscience and an uncompromising egotist, Tosh took on the mantle of chief critic of what he called Jamaica's "Babylon shitstem" (system), publicly berating politicians for double standards and hypocrisy and lighting spliffs on stage with a cool disregard for the law. His bellicose militancy did him no favours with the island's police; in 1975 he was busted on a trumped-up ganja charge and beaten to within an inch of his life. As soon as his wounds had healed, he answered back with *Whatcha Gonna Do*, a cocky release chiding the futility of police brutality, smokers' anthem *Legalize It*, and the defensive *Can't Blame the Youth* – inevitable airplay bans ensured record sales and Tosh cemented his position as the roots reggae revolutionary.

Tosh stayed in Jamaica, but his ever-increasing status and fortune – collaboration with the Rolling Stones in 1978 and a deal with EMI attracted global recognition – drew awkward parallels with the sufferers' lot he expostulated. In a country where money and fame draw a barrage of demands from old friends, needy causes and shady characters, the intensely spiritual and suspicious Tosh began to display signs of paranoia, believing himself both a victim of an establishment assassination conspiracy and haunted by duppies. His prophecies of destruction were fulfilled on September 11, 1987, when gunmen opened fire in Tosh's living room, killing him and two friends, and wounding five others. Rumours of the motive spread swiftly, some arguing that head assassin and renowned "bad man" Dennis "Leppo" Lubban was demanding financial retribution for a recent prison stint he saw as Tosh's rap, others muttering of a government-backed gagging.

Remembered by Jamaicans as a formidable ladies' man with a razor-sharp wit, Tosh himself provided his best biography; the "Red X" tapes, shot on scratchy film in a darkened room, show him philosophizing on his personal mantra, reggae and Rastafari and form part of the essential Tosh documentary *Stepping Razor Red X*.

Practicalities

The two villages are served by regular **buses** and route taxis from Savanna-la-Mar. If you want to **stay** around **Bluefields**, try *Casa Mariner*, in Cave, to the west of town (℡995 9897; ❷). It has nine budget rooms with fans and air conditioning, a restaurant, a popular bar, pool tables and slot machines, and an upstairs "conference room" that serves as a weekend disco. Also in Cave is a one-bedroom cottage to rent (❶) right on the waterfront, behind the *Sandpiper Jerk Centre and Bar,* which hosts regular **sound–system parties**. Another inexpensive and unusual option, *Shafston Great House*, c/o Frank Lohmann, Bluefields PO (call ahead for free pick-up; ℡955 8081 or 997 5076, Ⓦwww.shafston.com; ❸) sits above the bay, with fabulous views, and offers large attractive rooms with en-suite or shared bathroom. There's a pool, bar and cheap restaurant, pool table, hammocks and extensive grounds; **camping** costs US$10. Frank is a useful source of local knowledge and often takes guests out sightseeing. If you're looking for a luxurious option, scattered through the bay are five beautifully designed and furnished villas that comprise the casually elegant *Bluefields Villas* complex (℡202/232 4010 in US, Ⓕ703 549 6516, Ⓦwww.bluefieldsvillas.com; ❻).

In **Belmont**, both *Sunset Cottage* (℡955 8007) and the *Belmont Cabins* (℡955 8728) offer basic but clean accommodation at low prices (❷); both are well signed and located on the one road that runs through the village. By far the most exciting place to stay in the area, though, is the fabulous *Moun Tambrin Retreat* (℡918 4486, Ⓕ4487, Ⓦwww.jamaicaescapes.com; ❽) at **Darliston** in the hills above the bay. It's the private work in progress of American artist Russ Gruhlke, with one of the loveliest gardens in Jamaica, a stupendous view and an on-site collection of bizarre but beautiful follies, sculptures and woodcarvings. All meals are included in the rates and there's a three night minimum stay.

A few **bars** and **restaurants** are grouped around the police station and post office in the "centre" of Bluefields. Just past the police station is *Cool Runnings*, an oceanfront bar that also offers boat tours. Further south, *KD's Keg Lawn and Restaurant* (aka *Sands* to the locals) and the cavernous *Ocean Edge Pub and Restaurant* are both fine, but for really good local food cooked alfresco, try *Robert's* at the far end of Belmont. Also good is the *Fresh Touch* fish restaurant in the Bluefields Beach Park; the park is a rather characterless collection of landscaped units selling snacks and drinks and is part of a highway project which now bypasses the beach. In Belmont, the highlight of the annual **Peter Tosh birthday celebration** in mid-October is a live concert held in one of the village's bars and featuring "roots and culture" performers.

Just beyond Belmont is the **Oasis Spa** (℡ & Ⓕ955 8075, Ⓦwww.oasisspajamaica.com), set in a cool and elegant house with gardens down to the sea. Treatments include facials, body scrubs and massage using natural local products like papaya, coffee and sugarcane.

For all local **information**, contact the Bluefields People's Community Association (℡373 6435, Ⓦwww.bluefieldsjamaica.org.jm), whose ongoing programme of community tourism operates from its headquarters next door to the *Ocean Edge Pub*.

Whitehouse and Scott's Cove

As you continue along the A2 – through land known as **Surinam Quarters** in honour of the English who resettled here when the British colony was captured by the Dutch in 1667 – the scenery becomes drier but more agricultural, with swathes of pasture and plenty of cattle and goats. The road swings away from the coast, but there are still some nice places to swim; ask locals to direct you to the best spots.

One of the main fishing ports on the south coast, **WHITEHOUSE**, five miles down the road, offers little beach life but plenty of commercial bustle. Turn off the main strip of shops at the fruit and vegetable **market** (Wednesday & Saturday); the track will take you past some dusty cows and resigned-looking higglers before it deposits you in the midst of the clapboard shacks and run-down bars at the **fishing beach**. If you get there early enough, you can watch the chicken wire traps being baited up with cow skin, balanced on canoes and sailed out to the shallows, where the meat attracts lobster and fish. Later in the day, huge hessian bags of flapping specimens are weighed and bartered over, while women scale furiously and cats prowl for scraps. Fish caught at Whitehouse is transported islandwide, and this tiny place hums with action (and odour) as the boats return from trips that can last as long as a week. A new octagonal-shaped fish market is the result of a project for development of small-scale fisheries in Jamaica and was completed in 1999 with a grant from the government of Japan as a token of friendship and cooperation between the two countries. After years of apathy and stalling, the fish vendors have moved into their new space, though you'll need to arrive early in the morning to get the best of the day's catch.

Past Whitehouse, the coast road marks the Westmoreland/St Elizabeth border with a cache of purpose-built fish and bammy stalls at **SCOTT'S COVE**, manned by a friendly team of vendors who crowd around anything that stops. The fish is usually excellent, but ensure that your bammy has been soaked and fried – it's become commonplace to offer tourists the uncooked supermarket version.

Practicalities

There are quite a few places to **stay** in Whitehouse, most of them – like the large, airy *South Sea View Guesthouse* (☎963 5172, ℱ5763; ❸) – deserted. A much better option for both accommodation and food is the wonderful *Culloden Café* (☎963 5344, ℗www.cullodencafe.com; ❹ including breakfast) where you can stay in one of several bohemian cottages in the grounds. Other pluses include a small beach and waterfront or garden dining. A superb restaurant serves modern Jamaican cuisine at ridiculously reasonable prices, and the café has a gorgeous indoor bar with a decent wine selection, should you just want a drink.

Travel details

Buses

Tour company buses make daily runs from Sangster Airport in Montego Bay to Negril (US$30), but public buses are as haphazard as everywhere else in Jamaica.

Lucea to: Montego Bay (16 daily; 1hr); Negril (20 daily; 40min).

Negril to: Lucea (20 daily; 40min); Savanna-la-Mar (20 daily; 40min).

Savanna-la-Mar to: Bluefields (9 daily; 40min); Montego Bay (20 daily; 1hr); Negril (20 daily; 40min); Whitehouse (16 daily; 50min).

Flights

Negril to: Kingston (2 daily; 1hr 15min); Montego Bay (3 daily; 20 min); Port Antonio (1 daily; 1hr 15min).

The South

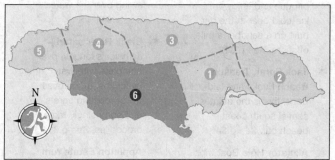

CHAPTER 6

Highlights

- ✳ **Pepper shrimp, Middle Quarters** Spicy, delicious and extremely moreish, the salty, peppered river shrimp sold at the roadside here are legendary. See p.351

- ✳ **Pelican Bar boat trip** Thwack through the waves in a fishing pirogue and enjoy an ice-cold beer at the bar, built on a sandbar a mile offshore. See p.342

- ✳ **Jack Sprat, Treasure Beach** Funky and laid-back, this is the quintessential south coast beach bar. See p.346

- ✳ **Alligator Hole** Boat trips up this lazy, crystal-clear backwater are the ideal way to appreciate the area's quiet beauty – and get a glance at the elusive manatee. See p.347

- ✳ **Milk River Spa** This wonderfully ramshackle colonial-era spa hotel offers the chance to soak away aches and pains in the second-most radioactive water in the world. See p.348

- ✳ **YS Falls** Surrounded by spectacular rainforest-edged farmland, the falls here come equipped with a Tarzan-style rope swing over the water. See p.351

- ✳ **Black River safari** Jamaica's longest river, complete with water hyacinths, mangroves full of roosting egrets and surprisingly tame crocodiles. See p.334

- ✳ **Appleton Estate rum distillery tour** Hemmed in by the egg-box cockpits in the gorgeous Nassau Valley, the scenery here is as spectacular as the effect of tasting seventeen luscious varieties of rum and liqueur. See p.352

△ Jack Sprat Bar, Treasure Beach

6

The south

Mass tourism has yet to reach Jamaica's **southern** parishes. None of the all-conquering all-inclusives have opened here yet, and the beaches aren't packed with sun-ripened bodies, but there are some fantastic places to stay and great off-the-beaten-track places to visit. It takes a bit of extra effort to get here – and you'll need a car or a tour to see one or two of the "hidden" highlights – but it's definitely worth it. If you're after watersports and heavy-duty nightlife, stick to the coastal resorts, but if you want to catch a glimpse of Jamaica as it was before the boom, head south.

The parishes that make up south-central Jamaica are immensely varied, with the landscape ranging from mountain to scrubby cactus-strewn desert, and from typically lush vegetation to rolling fields more redolent of the English countryside. To the west, in the beautiful parish of St Elizabeth, **Black River** is the main town – an important nineteenth-century port that today offers popular **river safaris** and a handful of attractive colonial-era buildings. If you're after somewhere to stay and swim, **Treasure Beach** is a better target – it's an extremely laid-back place with lovely black-sand beaches and some unique accommodation options that's fast becoming the south's major destination. As for touring around, you can make for the **Appleton Estate rum distillery** on the cockpit fringes, the fabulous **YS waterfalls**, or drive around the tiny villages of the attractive and untouristed **Santa Cruz Mountains**.

Further east, the parishes of Manchester and Clarendon are less diverse and a little less appealing. Manchester, with its cool evenings and misty mornings, has the major town of **Mandeville** – a very English inland touring base that makes a pleasant, if unspectacular, change from the coast – and the much smaller market town of **Christiana**, an unspoilt retreat with a single, delightful old hotel. Along the coast, there's marvellous river and sea swimming, and some great fish restaurants at **Alligator Pond**, while the combination of mineral spring and black-sand beach at **Guts River** provides one of the most picturesque spots on the entire island. The parish of Clarendon is total farming country, with large citrus groves in the north and sugarcane fields everywhere else, but it offers a handful of unusual places to visit, including the mineral spa at **Milk River** and the seventeenth-century **Halse Hall**, just south of the market town of **May Pen**.

Bauxite is the crucial economic commodity in the area, mined at seams in the central highlands (particularly around Mandeville) and processed at refineries scattered over the parishes. **Agriculture** is also key: despite the dry climate (particularly west of the Santa Cruz Mountains), St Elizabeth produces much of the country's agricultural surplus and is known as Jamaica's "breadbasket". Recently, **tourism** has begun to make an impact, though it is unlikely ever to

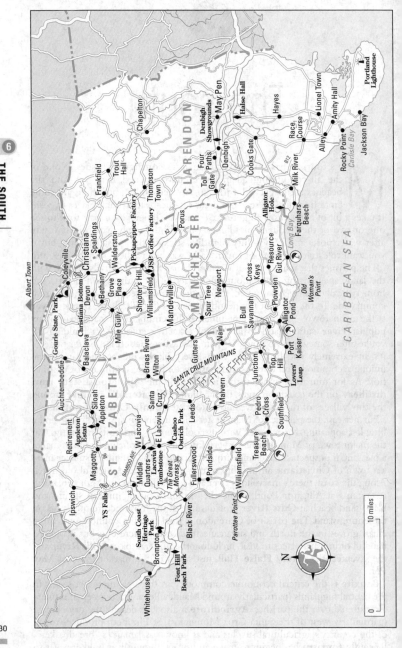

approach north coast levels – the emphasis is on small-scale "community tourism", avoiding the disruption to traditional lifestyles that the industry has caused elsewhere on the island.

Getting around

Regular **buses** and **minibuses** ply the main routes between Kingston and Negril, giving easy access to the main towns of May Pen, Mandeville, Santa Cruz and Black River. From these centres, a network of buses fans out to smaller towns like Christiana, Treasure Beach and Malvern, though these services are much less frequent. Be warned, also, that many of the main attractions in the interior, like the YS Falls, Apple Valley and Appleton, are somewhat off the beaten track and can be hard to reach by public transport. **Driving** is the best way to see the hidden parts of the south; the roads are mostly good, but watch out for gullies on the smaller, coastal roads – they'll take the bottom out of your car if you hit them too fast.

The south coast

Though without the turquoise seas and white-sand beaches of the north, Jamaica's **southern coastline** is among the most spectacular on the island, and a series of tiny but relatively pothole-free minor roads make it possible to drive along large stretches of it, particularly between Black River and Milk River, without losing sight of the sea. The scenery is wild and unspoilt down here, with giant cacti standing sentry at the roadside and thickets of makka thorn bushes, wetland morass and twisted mangroves giving way to glimpses of undeveloped coves, the volcanic sand twinkling in the sunlight. You'll need a car to see most of it, though, as buses and minibuses tend to stick to the main, inland roads, making side trips down to coastal villages as required.

Of the area's towns, **Black River**, the largest in St Elizabeth, merits a visit for its crumbling architectural gems and **river safari** into the Great Morass. Further round the coast, close-knit, laid-back **Treasure Beach** is probably the best place on the island to just stop, chill out and de-stress for a couple of days. It offers a brand of community tourism that's entirely different to anywhere else in Jamaica – a fact that the island's visitors are fast catching on to. Further east still, there's a great coastal drive from the seafood restaurants and quiet beaches of **Alligator Pond** to the tiny nature reserve at **Alligator Hole**, and you can stop off for a splash in the vividly blue **Gut River**. Finally, and usually the quietest place of all, the mineral spa at dry and dusty **Milk River Bath** is the perfect place to soothe away any aches and pains.

If you spend any time in this part of Jamaica, you'll appreciate the importance of the local **fishing industry**. Tiny fishing villages are scattered along the coast, with boats pulled up on stretches of the beach; even in tourist areas like Treasure Beach, fishing remains vital to the local economy. Many of the fishermen head for the **Pedro Banks**, a series of sandy cays in rich – but treacherous – fishing waters some eighty miles south. Over the years, full-scale communities have become established on these tiny blips in the ocean, and the abandoned behaviour of the fishermen and the few women who live on them semi-permanently are the stuff of local legend. However, things on the cays are more organized these days, with a police post ensuring some semblance of order, and two-way radios, provided at cost price by the Treasure Beach community organization BREDS (see p.343), giving fishermen a vital link with the mainland. The cays are the preserve of Jamaica's hardiest fishermen, so not a destination for a day-trip, but if you want to try your hand at fishing JA-style, ask around at any of the fishing villages.

Black River and around

Although it's St Elizabeth's largest town, **BLACK RIVER** is a quiet spot, and most travellers only nip in briefly to take a boat trip on the river in search of crocodiles, or stay a couple of nights whilst exploring the delights of western St Elizabeth. It wasn't always this way, though: in the mid-nineteenth century the town derived substantial wealth from the trade in **logwood**, used to produce black and dark-blue dyes for the textiles industry and exported in great quantities from Black River's port. For a brief period the trade helped to make the town one of the most influential in Jamaica, with electricity, the telephone and the car all first introduced to the island here, and a big racecourse west of town. However, with the introduction of synthetic dyes, the trade in logwood began to dry up, and today, the only signs of those illustrious days are some wonderful but decrepit old gingerbread houses. If you have time to spare, Black River's somnolent charms are worth a couple of days' gentle exploration.

Arrival and information

Buses and **minibuses** stop in the typically chaotic bus park behind the market, just off the High Street. Five minutes' walk away, the **Jamaica Tourist Board** (Mon–Fri 9.30am–4.30pm; ☎965 2074) has a small office on the upper floor of the Hendricks building, 2 High St, but don't expect much in the way of useful information. Globe Communications, on High Street next to *Waterloo Guest House* (Mon–Sat 8am–7pm), offers cheap international phone calls and **Internet access** for J$75 per half-hour. There are several places offering **currency exchange** on High Street, including branches of Scotiabank and NCB banks, and a cambio at the Naps supermarket (Mon–Sat 9am–5pm).

Accommodation

Given that few tourists stop over in Black River, there's a surprisingly good selection of **places to stay**. Most of the cheaper options are just east of town on Crane Road, across the iron bridge and running parallel to the rather scrappy beach, but there are several good choices in the town centre. As things are so quiet hereabouts, it's well worth doing a spot of bargaining, particularly if you plan on spending more than a couple of nights.

Ashton Great House ☎965 2036, ⊛www
.ashtongreathouse.com. In a completely stunning
hilltop setting, with eye-popping views over the St
Elizabeth/Westmoreland plaines and the Santa
Cruz Mountains, the 200-year-old great house
here is bursting with period charm, all creaking
waxed wood floors and antique furniture. Rooms in
the main house are the most characterful, but
there are also appealing newer ones; all have a/c
or fan, cable TV and phone. A restaurant, pool and
bar are on site. Extremely friendly and one of the
best choices in the area. ❹

Bridge House Inn 14 Crane Rd ☎965 2361,
☎2081. Friendly, industrious sort of place on the
east side of town. Rooms are clean but nothing
special; the cheapest are fan-only, but others have
a/c, fan and cable TV, and can sleep four. Rates are
excellent for all. ❶–❷

Invercauld Hotel High St; ☎965 2750,
⊛www.invercauldgreathouse.com. Lovely property
centred around a beautifully restored great house
with gabled roofs, bay windows, intricate fretwork
on the projecting verandahs and original wood
floors. Rooms in the great house are really atmospheric, with antique furnishings and balconies,
while rooms and suites in the new block have all
the trappings of a resort hotel. There's a huge
pool, and a bar and restaurant on site. ❹–❺

Parottee Beach Parottee ☎383 3980 or 990
6385 (mobiles), ⊛www.parottee.com. A ten-
minute drive from town (take the signposted right
at the roundabout at the end of Crane Rd, and it's
straight on), this is the most resort-like place in

the area, on a clean stretch of black-sand beach.
Ideal if you want self-contained seclusion, the two-
bedroom townhouse-like units have full kitchens,
living rooms with cable TV, and lovely decor, and
there's a pool and bar on the premises. Breakfast
is included if you book online. ❺

Port of Call Hotel 136 Crane Rd ☎965 2410,
☎965 2360. Newish beachside place with a less
soporific atmosphere than its neighbours. The spacious en-suite rooms are excellent value, with
queen beds, tiled floors, a/c, cable TV and phone;
cheaper ones have smaller beds. There's a pool
and a bar/restaurant right on the sand. ❷–❸

South Shore Guesthouse 33 Crane Rd ☎965
2172. Small, tidy guesthouse with very well-
stocked bar, in a breezy beachside spot east of
town. Rooms are en suite, with double beds and
cable TV; those facing the sea are more expensive,
with a/c. ❷

Sunset Beach Club 29 Crane Rd ☎965 2462 or
634 3938 (mobile). Quite possibly the most eccentric hotel in Jamaica: three buses converted into
very basic rooms, some with fan and private bathroom, set on the beach and adjoining a friendly
local bar. Owner Cliff Senior is highly entertaining.
Not for the faint-hearted. ❶

Waterloo Guesthouse 44 High St ☎965 2278,
☎waterloo@cwjamaica.com. The first hotel in
Black River, with atmospheric, spacious, fan-only
en-suite rooms in the ancient main house, and
smarter units, with a/c, cable TV, phone and fridge,
in a new block. A pool and a good restaurant, too.
❷

The Town

The nicest thing to do in Black River itself is to take a stroll along the **waterfront**, particularly attractive towards sunset, and check out the old wooden
buildings, many with gorgeous colonnaded verandahs and gingerbread trim
and most in a perilous state of near-collapse. The **Waterloo Guesthouse**, built
in 1819, is reputed to have been the first place in Jamaica to get electricity –
installed to provide air conditioning for racehorses kept in the old stables – and
to have boasted the island's first telephone. Nearby, the gleaming white
Invercauld Hotel, built in 1889, reflects the confidence of the town during
its heyday. As you head back towards the town centre, you'll see goats roaming
the grounds of **St John's**, the tidy parish church; it dates from 1837 and has
marble monuments to Robert Munro and Caleb Dickenson, benefactors of
two of the schools at nearby Malvern.

Though the busy High Street is mostly taken up with new concrete buildings housing the usual array of supermarkets, pharmacies and fried-chicken
outlets, it does hold some more attractive old buildings, particularly the brightly
coloured **Hendricks building** beside the bridge, built in 1813 and now housing the Jamaica Tourist Board on its first floor. From here you can wander
down to the shore, where you'll see men and boys fishing and maybe the odd

crocodile feeding or hanging out by the ocean. Scant traces of the once fashionable town can be found a couple of miles west of here along the main road: **Abundant Spring** is an old spa, once attracting people from all around the area with its restorative waters but now a run–down and forlorn spot by the sea, while nothing at all remains of the nineteenth-century **racetrack** that stood across the road.

The Great Morass and the Black River safari

The main reason most people come to the town is for a **boat safari** on the **Black River** itself, which, at 44 miles, is Jamaica's longest. The river – so named because the peat moss lining the river bottom makes the crystal-clear water appear an inky black – is fed by various tributaries as it makes its way down from Balaclava, on the Manchester/St Elizabeth border. It's the main source for the **GREAT MORASS** – a 125-square-mile area of wetland that spreads north and west of Black River and provides a swampy home for most of Jamaica's surviving crocodiles as well as some diverse and spectacular bird life. It's the best place to spot the **crocodiles**, a rapidly dwindling bunch now protected by law, who once lived in great numbers around the coast of Jamaica until hunting and the deterioration of the swamplands began to take their toll.

The boat tour is a very pretty trip into the Great Morass, although the term "safari" promises rather more excitement than it delivers. You do have a virtually guaranteed sighting of crocodiles (albeit fairly tame ones, most of which answer to their names), and there are some marvellous **mangrove swamps** where you can normally spot flocks of roosting egrets as well as whistling ducks, herons and jacanas, and you may run into the occasional shrimp- or crab-fisherman in his dug-out canoe. The boats run about eight miles upriver to Salt Spring Bridge, where you can get some refreshment and take a swim – most people decline the opportunity, though crocodiles are rarely spotted this far north – before heading back down. To go on the ninety-minute tour (US$15 per person), turn up at the dock or contact St Elizabeth River Safari (☎965 2374) or Black River Safari Boat Tours (☎965 2513). Theoretically, tours leave at 9am, 11am, 12.30pm, 2pm and 3.30pm, but if you turn up at other times you should be able to go straight away. Otherwise try the fisherman's bar, *Boney's*, at the back of the marketplace and ask for Teddy; he advertises a mini-cruise that goes beyond the bridge and up to Cheese Rock. If you're interested in further exploration of the river, contact Irie Safaris (☎965 2211). It's run by wetland ecologist Lloyd Linton, who not only puts a more scientific spin on the standard safari tour but also runs **specialized ecology trips** (by prior arrangement only; rates negotiable) with bird-watching experts, fishing trips and occasional forays into virgin stretches of the morass. You can also include the Black River Safari on a boat trip from Treasure Beach (see p.342), which tends to be a less touristic way to see the river and its inhabitants.

Font Hill Beach Park

Still little-visited by tourists, but a popular spot amongst locals for a day out by the sea, the **Font Hill Beach Park** (Tues–Sun 9am–5pm; J$120, or $150 if you come with a picnic), which runs alongside the main road a couple of miles west of Black River, is all that's currently open to the general public of the Font Hill Wildlife Sanctuary. It's a lovely, if compact, stretch of clean white sand with sparkling water and good snorkelling at several offshore reefs, and a restaurant and bar on site. Lockers are available to rent, and there are lots of picnic tables dotted around in shady spots.

The sanctuary, a three-thousand-acre reserve originally established to provide some unspoiled land for swimming and nature walks, continues to serve as a refuge for the endangered **American crocodile**. About two hundred of the crocodiles live in the swamps at the eastern edge, and many bird species – doves, pelicans, egrets and herons – also inhabit the sanctuary. The Petroleum Corporation of Jamaica, who own the land, apparently have plans to re-open the place, and if you have a special interest in wildlife or ecology you may well be able to enter the park anyway (phone in advance, ☎929 5380 or 818 6088). **Buses** between Black River and Sav regularly pass the entrance on the main road and will drop you off outside if you ask.

South Coast Heritage Park

A couple of miles before you get to Font Hill, on the road west from Black River, a minor road swings inland toward Luana. A mile or so along, at the nondescript community of Brompton, signs at the roadside announce the **South Coast Heritage Park** (no set hours; free), a hillside reclaimed from the bush and boasting sweeping lawns, lots of flowers and fabulous views down to the coast. Essentially a venue for the family fun days that Jamaicans are so fond of, it serves as a suitably windy venue for an Easter Monday kite-flying contest and is a pretty place to stop at any time of the year. At the top of the hill, a newly built wooden building houses a couple of guest rooms (under construction at the time of writing); it's a lovely spot if you fancy getting away from it all for a couple of days.

Eating and nightlife

Black River is a quiet town and, though there are a couple of good **places to eat**, the evening **entertainment** options are strictly limited. On Fridays, there are convivial after-work jams in the bar of the *Waterloo Guesthouse* and at the *Riverside* bar by the St Elizabeth River Safari office; both are also easy-going places for a drink on other nights. East of town along Crane Road, the *Sunset Beach Club* has a similarly earthy feel, with locals playing dominoes and drinking rum. *Cloggy's,* also on Crane Road, is perhaps the liveliest spot, open till late every night for drinks, accompanied by quality reggae on the sound system; it has karaoke on Fridays from around 8.30pm, and occasional sound-system jams.

For **snacks** during the day, High Street has a Juicy Beef patty shop, a branch of Chester Fried Chicken and a couple of good bakeries; jerk chicken vendors sell at weekends. Look out also for the soup man, who plies his delicious vegonly pumpkin soup from a pushcart.

Abundant Spring West of town. Open-air and inexpensive restaurant alongside the old mineral spa, serving roast fish and Jamaican staples. Only open sporadically for lunch but worth checking out; the food is home-cooked and really delicious.

Bayside 19 High St. Reasonable café serving breakfasts, the usual chicken and fish lunches and dinners and a good selection of cakes and ice cream.

Bridge House Inn 14 Crane Rd. Cavernous indoor dining room that's lacking in atmosphere, this is an official lunch venue for coach tours doing the safari. The Jamaican food – curry goat, stew beef, ackee etc – is consistently good and moderately priced.

Cloggy's on the Beach Crane Rd. Lovely setting by the sea, with tables under thatched gazebos, on the sand or inside by the bar. This is the best place in town for a cup of conch soup, curry conch or lobster, or a plate of fish (steamed with okra and pimento is lovely), served with rice, bammy and festival.

Idler's Rest Parrotee Rd. Beach bar off Crane Rd, a ten-minute drive from the centre of town, that's a pleasant spot for a quiet drink or dominoes session. Sound-system dances are held occasionally.

King Lion Reggae Centre Black River bus park. Tasty Ital food in a Rasta-decorated hut – with fierce biblical quotations on the walls – that doubles up as a record shop. Nineteen different natural juices are served.

Turns High St. Popular ice cream parlour also serving snacks and standard Jamaican fare. Its central locality and large windows make this a good spot for watching the town go about its business.

Treasure Beach and around

South of the main A2 road between Black River and Mandeville, snoozy **TREASURE BEACH** is the bright spark of south coast tourism. A string of laid-back fishing villages tucked under the Santa Cruz Mountains amidst some of Jamaica's most beautiful countryside, the area is the ultimate antidote to the island's more commercialized resorts. Tourism is very much a community concern here: many of the accommodation and eating places are owned by local families, and as there are no fenced-off all-inclusives to create a barrier between the locals and the visitors, everyone mixes easily together. One of the safest areas in Jamaica, this tight-knit, proud community has both a solid tourist infrastructure and a strong sense of its own traditional values. It's a tiny spot, with no neon beach bars or jet skis and sun loungers on the beaches, and attracts a mix of hip, bohemian jetsetters and young, backpackerish travellers who simply want to unwind and absorb Jamaica's gentler, more pastoral side. There's a good and ever-expanding range of **accommodation** options, including a delightfully eclectic collection of villas and beach cottages to rent, some great places to **eat** and a couple of diverting attractions, while the bays that make up the area boast some spectacular undeveloped black-sand **beaches**.

The **Santa Cruz Mountains** (see p.354) rise up from the sea just east of Treasure Beach and run northwest, providing a scenic backdrop for the village and protecting the area from rain clouds coming from the north. As a result, Treasure Beach has one of the **driest** climates in the country, and the scrubby, desert-like landscape – red-earth savannahs strewn with cactuses and acacia trees – is often reminiscent of the African plains. Despite the dry weather, though, this is very much farming country, and you'll see rolling plantations of carrots, scallions, thyme, onions and watermelons scattered around the area. You may also notice that many of the residents have a very distinctive appearance – red or blonde hair; blue, green or yellow eyes; light skin and freckles – that is said to be the result of intermarriage between locals and a crew of Scottish sailors who were shipwrecked here in the nineteenth century. Whatever the reason, Treasure Beach's "red" men and women, as they're known, are famed islandwide for their unusual beauty.

Treasure Beach itself is made up of a string of loosely connected fishing settlements; the community is the closest point in Jamaica to the **Pedro Banks**. Many locals make month-long trips to the cays, braving dangerous seas and the elements in order to bring home what are often very rich pickings. The chances are that you'll stay on the long sandy sweep of **Frenchman's Bay**, where tourism has largely displaced fishing as the main industry, or smaller **Calabash Bay**, where you can still see brightly coloured fishing boats pulled up on the beach below the newly constructed hotels and guesthouses. To the east, **Great Bay** remains a basic fishing village with a sprinkling of guesthouses

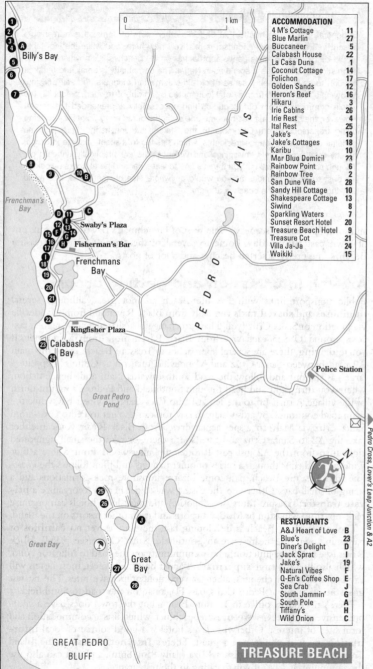

0 _____ 1 km

ACCOMMODATION

4 M's Cottage	11
Blue Marlin	27
Buccaneer	5
Calabash House	22
La Casa Duna	1
Coconut Cottage	14
Folichon	17
Golden Sands	12
Heron's Reef	16
Hikaru	3
Irie Cabins	26
Irie Rest	4
Ital Rest	25
Jake's	19
Jake's Cottages	18
Karibu	10
Mar Blue Domicil	23
Rainbow Point	6
Rainbow Tree	2
San Dune Villa	28
Sandy Hill Cottage	10
Shakespeare Cottage	13
Siwind	8
Sparkling Waters	7
Sunset Resort Hotel	20
Treasure Beach Hotel	9
Treasure Cot	21
Villa Ja-Ja	24
Waikiki	15

RESTAURANTS

A&J Heart of Love	B
Blue's	23
Diner's Delight	D
Jack Sprat	I
Jake's	19
Natural Vibes	F
Q-En's Coffee Shop	E
Sea Crab	J
South Jammin'	G
South Pole	A
Tiffany's	H
Wild Onion	C

Billy's Bay

Frenchman's Bay

P E D R O   P L A I N S

Swaby's Plaza

Fisherman's Bar

Frenchmans Bay

Kingfisher Plaza

Calabash Bay

Great Pedro Pond

Police Station

✉

Great Bay

Great Bay

GREAT PEDRO BLUFF

TREASURE BEACH

337

In general, the tourist **hustle** that bedevils other parts of Jamaica is refreshingly absent in Treasure Beach. Tourism is relatively new here, and while the inevitable would-be gigolos do make gentle approaches on the beaches, it's nowhere near as sophisticated and jaded a scene as in Negril. The community is small and tightknit enough to have retained a sense of old-time Jamaican manners and self-policing; following a recent theft from a hotel (committed by an out-of-towner), practically the whole community went out in pursuit and successfully apprehended the culprit. However, the south coast has become one of the favoured entry points for **cocaine** being transhipped from Colombia to the States, and inevitably, there is some cocaine use among younger residents, which has led to a slight upsurge in **crime**, mostly theft from hotels (muggings and violent crime are practically unheard of). Though some locals will tell you that it's fine to leave car and hotel doors unlocked, it's best to be as cautious as you would anywhere else on the island, and avoid walking alone along the beaches at night.

and some spectacular scenery, while west of Frenchman's Bay the road runs out of town past **Billy's Bay**, home to several of the classiest villas in Treasure Beach, some pretty deserted beaches and a lot of goats.

Arrival, information and getting around

Public transport links with Treasure Beach are not great, although several **minibuses** and **shared taxis** run daily from Black River and from Mandeville via Junction or Santa Cruz (you'll have to change bus/shared taxi). A regular taxi costs around US$25 each way from Black River, more from Mandeville. If you're **driving**, there are several approaches to Treasure Beach. From the main A2 road between Santa Cruz and Mandeville, turn off at Gutters (opposite a large gas station) and follow the road south towards Nain and then Junction, where you turn right and head through Southfield and Pedro Cross, just north of the village. A turn-off to the left at Pedro Cross leads to Great Bay, while the main road continues towards Calabash Bay. You can also get to Pedro Cross from Santa Cruz via Malvern, a spectacular drive. From Black River, you can either take the A2 to Santa Cruz and turn south there, or take the small signposted right turn from the A2 just past Parottee at Fullerswood, from where a tiny, winding road runs though a series of quiet hamlets and then follows the coastline into Treasure Beach, past some bizarre ironshore rock formations and a string of small bays. Otherwise, the easiest way to get here is to organize a **private transfer**: Treasure Tours (see opposite) and most local hotels can organize pick-ups from Kingston or MoBay airports and from other resorts on the island.

Though Treasure Beach is developing fast, there are as yet no **cambios** or banks in town; the nearest are in Southfield, Santa Cruz (see p.354), Black River (see p.332) or Junction, a busy community on the road to Alligator Pond, which also boasts a large **supermarket** and a **bank**. However, most hotels will exchange cash and cheques, albeit at very noncompetitive rates. The nearest **gas station** is out at Pedro Cross, pass Flagaman on the road to Southfield.

There's no tourist office in Treasure Beach, but the town does have a comprehensive **website**, ⊛ www.treasurebeach.net, which lists accommodation and local sites of interest. Otherwise, *Jake's* hotel is a good source of local **information**, even if you're not a guest. There's **Internet access** at the Island Treasures gift shop in Kingfisher Plaza (daily 8am–8pm), and you can also use the computer at *Jake's* if you're eating in the restaurant.

As signs dotted along the roadsides announce, Treasure Beach is "bike country", and given the often awful state of the roads, periodically reduced to gullies following the severe flooding that has hit the area in recent years, a bicycle is an excellent way to **get around**. Numerous guesthouses and restaurants rent mountain bikes for around US$10 per day; a central outlet is *Q-En's Coffee Shop* in Swaby's Plaza on the main road in Frenchman's Bay.

If you're interested in seeing the YS Falls, Guts River, Alligator Pond or other parts of the south from a base here, Treasure Tours (℡965 0126, ⓦtreasuretours .info), run by friendly, efficient and very knowledgeablc American émigré Rebecca Wiersma, offers an excellent and reasonably priced **tour service** (from US$35 per person), and offers pickups from MoBay and Kingston airports and from other resorts.

Accommodation

There is a wide variety of **accommodation** in Treasure Beach, from full-blown resorts and chic boutique hotels to numerous guesthouses, the latter charging lower rates ($35 per double is average) than in more developed parts of the island. More places are springing up all the time and, in addition, seemingly every other house is a rentable **villa**; these vary from simple beach cottages to luxurious and elegant homes with all mod-cons. The villas listed below are a recommended selection of the dozens available, and it's worth bearing in mind that while some of these options are simply much cheaper and more private than a hotel, several of the more expensive villas are very beautiful indeed, with spectacular oceanfront settings and rates to match. Unless otherwise stated, prices quoted (all in US dollars) are for the whole house in low season (many offer reductions for just two people), and include staff (most have a housekeeper and/or cook and a groundsman/security man) but not food (you buy provisions and can ask the staff to cook it for you), or alcohol. We've specified those properties that will rent a room as well as the whole house.

Camping – available at *Four M Cottages* and *Ital Rest/Irie Cabins* for US$10–15 per tent – is more feasible here than in most parts of Jamaica; the community is still small enough for crime to be very rare.

Many of the properties below have pages on ⓦwww.treasurebeach.net; we haven't noted each one that does, but it's always worth taking a look at the site if you're pre-booking accommodation, as new places are appearing all the time.

Hotels and guest houses

Calabash House Calabash Bay ℡965 0126. Right on the sea, this is a cute, clean little place with simple decor and excellent rates. You can have the whole place for US$125 per night, or rent a room only. ❷

4 M's Cottage Frenchman's Bay ℡965 0131, ⓔfourmscottage@hotmail.com. Six small, simply furnished and appealing fan-only en-suite rooms, presided over by the dynamic Miss Effie, in a friendly house opposite the *Treasure Beach Hotel*. Beds are swathed with mosquito nets and windows are screened. There's a kitchen that guests can use (though meals are available) and a bar in the front garden. ❸

Golden Sands Frenchman's Bay ℡965 0167, ⓔgoldensandsguesthouse@yahoo.com. Long-

standing and deservedly popular budget option in a prime position right on Frenchman's beach. The basic, tile-floor rooms have fan, screened windows and a bathroom, and share a communal kitchen. One self-contained a/c cottage is also available (❹), and there's a bar and restaurant on site. ❷

Irie Cabins Great Bay ℡964 3111 or 3231. Adjacent to *Ital Rest* (see below) and with the same laid-back vibe, these thatch-porched wooden cottages are great value, with double beds and use of a shared kitchen. ❷

Irie Rest Billy's Bay ℡965 0034, ⓦwww.geocities .com/irierestguesthouse. Extremely friendly place set back from, but within walking distance of, the beach. Rooms are simple and inviting, with a/c, screened windows and en-suite bathrooms; some have huge screened verandahs. There's a bar-cum-restaurant and a cool communal area with a stereo and satellite TV. Brilliant value. **②**

Ital Rest Great Bay ☎965 3231 or 412 8909 (mobile). Two cottages only at this gentle, friendly and beautifully landscaped place within walking distance of a lovely swimming cove; each has separate rooms upstairs and down (ask for upstairs for the views and the breeze) and a kitchen. A small bar with ping-pong table, a restaurant (which can do vegan food as well as regular dishes) and a herbal steam room are on site. Turn right just before the *Sea Crab* restaurant and then take the first right. **②**

Jake's Calabash Bay ☎965 3000, ⊛www .islandoutpost.com/jakes. With its easy-going but cultured atmosphere, this delightful venue in beautifully landscaped gardens at the seashore is the most appealing, and liveliest, hotel in the area. Run by the dynamic Jason Henzell, perhaps the main player in the local tourism scene, *Jake's* is a unique spot, bursting with imagination and personality, and the inspiration for an ever-growing number of imitators islandwide. Each of the gorgeous, quirky rooms has its own hand-done decor, with funky, earthy colours and intricate attention to detail; common touches include verandahs slat-roofed with local yam poles, and outdoor showers mosaiced with shells and coloured glass. No rooms have TV or phone (seen as distractions from the elemental joys of the sun and the sea), but do feature mosquito nets, CD players and coffee makers. There's a fabulous saltwater pool, a good restaurant, and the bar draws a genial local crowd. **⑥**

Karibu Frenchman's Bay ☎965 0149, 617/354 1719 in US, ⊛www.karibucottage.com. Two-storey building with a verandah overlooking the sea and access to the roof for sunning and night-time chilling out. Two of the clean, simple bedrooms have fans, hot water and kitchen facilities; the other has a fan and more rudimentary cooking equipment, and is significantly cheaper. **②–④**

Mar Blue Domicil Old Wharf, Calabash Bay ☎965 3408, ⊛www.marblue.com. Spanking-new German-run place right on the beach, with fabulous attention to detail. Thoughtful extras include use of a cellphone for all guests, and rooms equipped with bathrobes, hairdryers and irons with boards. Spotless and fresh, rooms have a/c, balconies overlooking the sea, and CD and DVD players, too. There's a bar and an excellent restaurant, and breakfast is included in the rates. **⑥**

Sandy Hill Cottage Frenchman's Bay ☎965 0149 or 837 7231 (mobile). Adjacent to *Karibu* on a breezy hilltop above the beach, this is a slightly chaotic place run by the amiable Prof, offering very basic rooms with fan and cold-water bathrooms,

and use of kitchen facilities. Great for those on a budget. **①**

Shakespeare's Cottage Frenchman's Bay ☎965 0120. Excellent budget option, with four basic but clean rooms with fans and shared bathrooms, and a kitchen for guests' use. **①**

Siwind Billy's Bay ☎965 0582, ⊛www.siwind.com. Tranquil and very friendly hotel with amazing views and steps down to a secluded little beach. Rooms are simple, classy and clean, with screened windows and ceiling fans. You can prepare your own meals in the kitchen. **⑤**

Sunset Resort Hotel Calabash Bay ☎965 0143, ⊛www.sunsetresort.com. Incongruously and fabulously kitsch resort in a lovely seaside setting, with Astroturf round the central pool and wonderfully gaudy Hawaiian-esque decor in the rooms. All are spacious, with a/c, fans, satellite TV and coffee maker; self-catering cottages are also available. There's a restaurant on site. The staff are extremely friendly. A bit of a departure from the usual bohemian TB vibe, but great if you value home-comforts and efficiency. **⑤–⑥**

Treasure Beach Hotel Frenchman's Bay ☎965 0110, ⊛www.treasurebeachjamaica.com. Huge, rather incongruous full-blown resort on one of the best stretches of beach, with two pools, extensive gardens and a restaurant and bar. Modern suites with oceanfront views all have a/c, ceiling fan and satellite TV. **⑤**

Waikiki Calabash Bay ☎965 0448. Rangy place set back from the road and overlooking the beach, with basic, clean rooms with fans and shared or private bathrooms. Brilliant if you're on a budget. **②**

Villas and cottages

Blue Marlin Great Bay ☎965 0459, ⊛bluemarlinvillas.freeservers.com. Located on the site of a Taino settlement and set right on (but enclosed from) a protected beach amid sweeping lawns, with a gazebo where hammocks swing in the sea breezes, these two beautiful three-bedroom former family homes ooze understated class, both strewn with Taino artefacts and colonial-era heirlooms collected by the owner. It's the perfect place to sink into an antique four-poster. Weekly rates for both are US$1400 for four people, US$1700 for six and US$2000 for eight.

Buccaneer Billy's Bay ☎703/765 7566 in US, ⊛www.jamaicaescapes.com. Spectacular four-bedroom villa designed in funky Santa Fe-meets-Morocco style by Sally Henzell, the woman behind *Jake's*. Facilities include a pool, satellite TV, a gorgeous outdoor shower and a well-equipped kitchen.

The setting, on a bluff overlooking the bay, is marvellous. Weekly rates range from US$2050 for one to two people to US$3050 for seven to nine guests.

La Casa Duna ☎965 0429, 215/297 0592 in US, ⊛www.jamaicaescapes.com/casaduna. Secluded three bedroom, two-bathroom house on a bluff above the beach, with gardens out back and spreading down to the sea, and a huge ocean-facing verandah complete with hammocks. Full kitchen and living room, and brilliant staff. US$1500 per week.

Coconut Cottage Frenchman's Bay ☎807/473-7606 in Canada. Sweet and homely cottage opposite Frenchman's Bay in downtown Treasure Beach. It includes two en-suite, mossi-netted bedrooms with fans and screened windows, a fully equipped kitchen, a garden and a roof terrace. The whole thing rents for US$50 per night – a real bargain. More rooms were under construction on the roof at the time of writing.

Folichon Frenchman's Bay ☎904 5454/965 0012, or mobiles ☎816 5809, ☎877 7335, ⓔasutton @cwjamaica.com. Close to *Jake's* and surrounded by gardens, this is one of the area's oldest rental villas, built in 1937 in Art-Deco style by a Russian count. There's a pleasantly antique feel, with mahogany furniture and a seahorse theme running throughout. Four bedrooms (though only one with a double bed), two bathrooms, kitchen, living room, verandah and screened windows. Very secluded. US$150 per day.

Heron's Reef Frenchman's Bay (contacts as per *Folichon,* above). Adjacent to *Folichon,* and with the same owners and a similarly genteel, shabby-chic feel. One bedroom (and a sofabed, so sleeps four), mossi nets, living room and kitchen. US$75 per day.

Hikaru Billy's Bay ☎860/247-0759 or 800/526-2453 in US, ⓔdononoel@cs.com. Homely house with a bedroom on each side of the verandah (one with a queen bed, the other with two singles). The big garden, spreading down to a slightly rocky stretch of beach, contains tennis courts, a pool and a croquet lawn. US$1325 per week.

Jake's Cottages Calabash Bay ☎965 3000, ⊛www.islandoutpost.com/jakes. Under the umbrella of Jason Henzell's ever-expanding Treasure Beach empire and boasting the same distinctive and funky style, these refurbished former private homes are close to the action, right at the sea's edge to the east of *Jake's*. Smart *Sweet Lips* has a sea-facing verandah, two bedrooms (unusually, these have a/c) and one bathroom; *Mussels* features three bedrooms, two bathrooms, a lovely verandah and a rooftop patio for stargazing sessions. Occupying a mini-peninsula and surrounded by the sea, *Jack Sprat* is pleasantly private, with two bedrooms, one bathroom and two verandahs. *Tiki Tiki II* consists of a two-bedroom, one bathroom unit attached to the one-bedroom *Tiki Tiki I,* and is a good bet for two couples travelling with kids. With the exception of *Tiki Tiki I,* which rents for US$75, per-night prices are US$125 for one to two people, US$150 for three to four.

Rainbow Tree Billy's Bay ☎703/948-0651 in US, ⊛www.rainbowtreevilla.com. Set back from the road in 5.5 acres of gardens with a pool and a path down to the beach, this is a stylish and luxurious place bedecked with lovely photos of local characters. There are two en-suite, a/c master bedrooms and two smaller ones with ceiling fans and a shared bathroom, a spacious lounge, a kitchen with all creature comforts and a verandah encircling the whole property. US$1850 per week for four people, plus ten percent for each additional person. Just east of here, the same owners have *Rainbow Point,* a three-bedroom villa that rents for US$1550 per week for four, plus ten percent per extra guest.

San Dune Villa Great Bay ☎965 0367, mobile 377 7724. Two beautifully refurbished 100-year old wooden houses with original floorboards and heaps of quirky character. Bedrooms (one has four, the other two) have queen beds and fans, and there are fully equipped kitchens, living rooms and a washing machine. One house has a breezy verandah, and there's a pool and a bar on site. Really unusual, and in a secluded spot with fabulous

Relaxation therapies

Treasure Beach's relaxed vibe lends itself well to a bit of pampering, and two local operators offer massage. Based in Great Bay, local herbalist **Shirley Genus** (☎965 3231 or 3111) offers a great herbal steam bath, prepared with organic herbs and a fantastically soothing experience. This can be combined with a 15-minute pore-cleansing massage (US$40) or a 50-minute full massage with essential oils (US$60); an hour's massage is US$60. Pick-ups from local hotels are available.

Practising from the therapy room at *Jake's,* **Joshua Lee Stein** (☎965 0583, mobile 389 3698; 1hr US$60, 1hr 30min US$80) blends massage with movement and healing energy work and is great for deep-tissue massages.

views back over the undeveloped hills. US$100 per night for two people, US$150 for three or four.

Sparkling Waters Billy's Bay ⓣ965 0486, ⓦwww.sparklingwatersvilla.com. Two two-bedroom villas with contemporary decor in earthy primary colours. One has a fabulous verandah right over the water, the other an attractive sun deck and porch. Each has a fully equipped kitchen, satellite TV and a/c in the rooms, and there's a jacuzzi and huge pool on site. Rates include breakfast. US$1500/1800 per week, or US$3000 for both.

Treasure Cot Calabash Bay ⓣ965 0635, ⓦwww.islandoutpost.com/jakes. Part of *Jake's Cottages* but entirely different in style and feel, this is a gorgeous, atmospheric and intensely private little house, with two a/c en-suite bedrooms, where Alex Haley stayed whilst writing portions of *Roots*. Elegantly battered antique fittings combine beautifully with the photographs of local life on the walls, and there's a sweet little sea-facing verandah enclosed by greenery on each side. US$1050 per week for four people.

Villa Ja-Ja Old Wharf, Calabash Bay ⓣ965 3536, ⓔvillajaja@yahoo.com. Unusually designed two-bedroom place in a quiet spot east of *Jake's*. The octagonal, sunken master bedroom, flooded with light by huge windows, opens straight onto the verandah, and the bathrooms, done out in mosaic tiles, are lovely. Very romantic. The second bedroom is smaller, so no more than three people can stay. US$175 per day or $1200 per week for two; US$225 per day or US$1500 per week for three.

The town and the beaches

Spread on either side of the main coast road, Treasure Beach has no town centre as such, though things are busiest between *Jake's* in Calabash Bay and the *Treasure Beach Hotel* at the western corner of Frenchman's Bay, where restaurants and hotels line the road. Most people, though, divide their time between their hotel and the beautiful undeveloped **beaches**, most of which have fine black sand, body-surfable waves and crystal clear water once you get out past the breakers; however, you'll need to watch the **undertow**, which can get strong at times – ask locally about present conditions. The best swimming is along the wide sweep of **Frenchman's Bay**, where there are few underwater rocks and several beach bars for snacks and drinks. The sweep of sand here is wide enough for late-afternoon football games amongst local lads, and it's a great spot to watch the sun go down. If you're not staying along Frenchman's and thus don't have direct access to the sand, you can get onto the beach via numerous footpaths; there's also a rocky little side-road onto the beach from the main road to the right of *Golden Sands* resort. Although rocky headlands create occasional obstacles, you can stroll along the shore in either direction from Frenchman's (head west if you want to cover some distance).

Frenchman's is also the departure point for **boat trips** along the coast, a brilliant way to see the area. You'll probably be approached by various operators on the beach (some of whom have questionable safety standards); best plan is to ask at your hotel or get in touch with Dennis Abrahams (ⓣ965 3084, mobile 359 7213), an excellent and experienced boatman whose fishing pirogue is the fastest in Treasure Beach and a regular winner of the Hook 'n' Line festival races (see p.344). An excellent and unusual excursion is to **Pelican Bar**, a sandpit offshore of Parrottee Point, where enterprising local man Floyd has constructed a bar on stilts in the middle of the sea (4hr; $60). Other boating excursions offered by Dennis include a trip to the bigger **Sunny Island** Cay for sunbathing and snorkelling, followed by lunch at *Little Ochi* (6hr; $90); a ride up the coast and along Black River to see the crocodiles (6hr; $90); and line fishing ($35 per hour). He'll also take you east to Guts River and Milk River for a negotiable rate. All prices are for two people, and there are good reductions for larger groups.

West of Frenchman's, the road swings away from the coast for a while and then heads back to the sea around **Billy's Bay**. There are several undeveloped stretches of sand where you could easily spend a day by the sea without seeing a soul, and the arid, cactus-strewn countryside is spectacular.

BREDS

A non-profit association established in 1988 to promote local awareness of black Jamaican cultural heritage and the environment, and to provide educational opportunities and healthcare for the residents of Treasure Beach, **BREDS** (☎965 3000, ⊛breds.org), short for "bredrin", Jamaican slang for friend, has had a tangible positive impact on quality of life in Treasure Beach. The brainchild of, among others, Jason Henzell of *Jake's* fame, BREDS embodies the strength of this close-knit community, very much a place where people look out for one another. By way of grants and endowments, as well as the profits from annual events such as the triathlon and fishing tournament (see overleaf) and sale of T-shirts and postcards, BREDS has constructed some thirty homes for less well-off locals, provided computers and office equipment for the local school, added a marine light to Frenchman's Beach to ensure safe navigation through the reef and conducted regular beach and town clean-ups. In late 2002, BREDS established the **Treasure Beach Response Unit**, training 27 local volunteers in various basic medical techniques to become "first responders" in the event of emergencies. There are now at least four volunteers on call 24 hours a day to respond to emergencies – an essential service in a town with no hospital (the nearest is in Black River) and where the majority of residents (and visitors) don't have access to a car.

The organization is always on the lookout for visitors who can contribute to the cause, whether materially or in terms of skills sharing, and BREDS merchandise is on sale at *Jake's*. For more on upcoming projects, visit the website above.

Great Bay and out to Lovers' Leap

On the outskirts of Treasure Beach, just beyond Pedro Cross police station, a turn-off to the right leads to **Great Bay**, the least geared for tourism of Treasure Beach's mini-communities, but perhaps the most physically beautiful, with a fabulous beach and a sprinkling of low-key guesthouses. This is primarily a fishing community, as demonstrated by the large Fishermen's Co-op building on the beach where the paved road ends, and many of the locals are regulars at the Pedro Banks. Aside from exploring the beach (there are several paths over rocky outcrops that lead to secluded coves), the only other thing to do in Great Bay is to head for **Back Seaside**, a magnificent portion of undeveloped coastline in the shadow of Lovers' Leap that's home to numerous types of cacti and supports several species of sea bird. On the other side of the Great Pedro Bluff, and reachable via a fifteen-minute walk through strangely English-looking pastureland (only the palm trees give the game away), it's a great spot for a coastal walk or a spot of shell collecting. The land here is private, though, so to visit you'll need to arrange a trip with Great Bay resident Damian "Reds" Parchment (☎965 0225 or 3101, mobile 864 9020), who conducts walking or mountain-biking trips to Back Seaside that include snorkelling (around $30 per person); he can also organize night-time cookouts here.

Out to Lovers' Leap

At some point, most Treasure Beach visitors take a trip out of town up to the sheer cliffs of **LOVERS' LEAP** (daily 10am–6pm; J$120), where the Santa Cruz Mountains drop nearly two thousand feet to the sea. According to legend, two young lovers – slaves at a nearby plantation – came here while running away from their owners. They were followed to the edge of the cliffs and, preferring to die rather than be separated again, threw themselves into the sea. It's hardly gripping stuff, but there's a restaurant and bar on site, and it's a good spot for a breezy lunch or an evening drink while watching the sun go down.

Annual events

Though Treasure Beach is usually pretty quiet, three annual events bring an injection of life to the area and, this being a small community, tend to overwhelm the whole place; if you plan on visiting during any of these events, you'll need to book accommodation ahead. In early May, the **Jake's Off-Road Triathlon** (☏965 3000, ⓦbreds.org) is one of the biggest events, drawing a large and loud crowd to cheer on the 200 local and foreign participants, some seasoned professionals, others triathlon first-timers. The race itself consists of a 500m ocean swim, a 25km mountain bike ride and a 7km country run. There's also a new under-14s Aquathon, in which kids (mostly locals) swim 50m and then run down the beach for another 250m. Lots of parties and special events are held simultaneously.

Later in May, held over the US Memorial Day Weekend and drawing some 600 people each day, the **Calabash Literary Festival** (☏965 3000, ⓦwww.calabash festival.org), also centred around *Jake's*, is a brilliant free festival featuring readings and seminars given by novelists, poets and cultural commentators from the Caribbean (with emphasis on Jamaica) and the rest of the world. Past participants have included Nobel Prize winner Derek Walcott, musicians Ibo Cooper, Ernie Smith and Lady Saw, and novelists Colin Channer and Rachel Manley. There are several organized events each day, and an open mic session each evening.

The next big event, over Heroes Weekend (the third in October), the **Hook 'n' Line Fishing Tournament** (☏965 3000, ⓦbreds.org) is a mix of serious competition and serious fun. Treasure Beach's best fishermen take to the sea armed only with, unsurprisingly, a hook and line, and compete to bring in the biggest specimens, usually kingfish weighing 35 pounds or more. There's usually a sound system on the beach, and associated events include a bikini competition, tug-of-war, dominoes tournament and, most excitingly, a race between the fastest of the local fishing pirogues.

It's also worth heading to Treasure Beach for the annual community Christmas celebration, on **Christmas Eve**, and for **New Year's Eve**, when Jake's traditionally put on a fireworks display and a high-calibre concert on the beach; past performers include the marvellous Toots and the Maytals.

The view from the restaurant verandah over the cliffs and out to sea is pretty spectacular. If you're feeling reckless you can scramble down the cliff path to the beach, a hot and strenuous 1.5 hours each way – you can, of course, just go part of the way down for an even better look at the drop. There's also a small **museum** displaying, among other things, cassava graters, yabba pots and, rather chillingly, a dried cow cod (penis) used to beat slaves.

Lovers' Leap is signposted off the main road at Southfield seven miles east of Treasure Beach. On the way back to the coast, you can stop and admire the view over the farmlands and out to the coast at *Treasure View Restaurant*, an expansive white-painted building by the side of the road in Southfield, where there's solid Jamaican fare on offer – curry goat, fried chicken and soups – and tables on the verandah. There are a couple of lovely **rooms** upstairs for rent (☏965 6238; ❷–❸).

Eating and drinking

Evenings are pretty low-key in Treasure Beach, but there are plenty of excellent options for **food**, most offering, unsurprisingly, excellent locally caught seafood. Most of the places are small-scale affairs, but a few – *Jake's*, *Tiffany's*, *Blue* – accept credit cards.

If you're cooking for yourself, you'll find several small **groceries** in Treasure Beach – both *South Jammin'* and *Q-En's* restaurants have a limited selection of goods – but for a big shop, you'll need to go to Black River or Junction. A van selling **fruit and veg** passes through Treasure Beach a couple of times a week; ask locally.

Cafés and restaurants

A&J Heart of Love Frenchman's Bay. Formerly the renowned *Trans-Love Café*, and maintaining the excellent reputation of its predecessor, this laid-back thatched patio run by two friendly women is the essential stop for breakfast or brunch, with fresh bread, cakes and fruit salads, muesli, French toast, home-made fruit jam, marvellous Spanish omelettes, baguette pizzas, sandwiches and salads. Open till 5pm.

Blue's *Mar Blue* hotel, Old Wharf, Calabash Bay ☎965 3408. Stylish in-hotel restaurant right by the sea, serving sophisticated, imaginatively presented, moderate to expensively priced dishes concocted by the German owner/chef. The menu changes daily, but staples include soups (crab or tomato with gin), cheese plates, curry chicken and shrimp and lobster with aioli.

Diner's Delight Frenchman's Bay, opposite Swaby's Plaza. Simple local place, serving Jamaican food only at excellent prices: callaloo with saltfish, liver, steamed fish with okra, etc.

Jack Sprat Calabash Bay. Part of the *Jake's* empire, this fabulous beachside café, in a gingerbread-fretworked former home, demonstrates what eating out in Jamaica should be like. With tables under the sea-grape trees, a sandy path down to the beach and a verandah dining area decked out in antique Appleton rum signs and boasting an old-time juke box (a traditional feature of the Jamaican rum shop), this is the perfect place for a relaxed meal. Baguette sandwiches and seafood – fish cooked any style and served with bammy, as well as shrimp, curry conch, and conch soup – are available alongside excellent pizzas (bases are handmade on the spot, and toppings include jerk chicken and proper peperoni). Pastries, cakes and Devon House ice cream satisfy the sweet tooth, and prices are very reasonable.

Jake's Calabash Bay. Open-air restaurant within the hotel, this is usually one of the busiest places in town, serving moderately priced Jamaican fare with a sophisticated twist. The breakfast, lunch and dinner blackboard menus change daily; highlights include breakfast banana porridge, pumpkin soup, curried shrimp and lobster cooked in various ingenious ways. Tables are under shade trees, and there's a good, if small, wine list.

Natural Vibes Frenchman's Bay. Small concrete building by the roadside, with some tables outside, serving basic, inexpensive and tasty home-cooking. Open late.

Q-En's Coffee Shop Swaby's Plaza, Frenchman's Day. Open from 7.30am daily for great breakfast omelettes or ackee and saltfish (the latter cooked without oil and utterly delicious), and good Jamaican lunches. Pastries and coffee are available all day. This is a good spot to catch up with the local gossip.

Sea Crab Great Bay. Friendly local restaurant near *Ital-Rest*, with good and inexpensive Jamaican staples like escovitched fish and curry goat.

South Jammin' Frenchman's Bay. Unpretentious and popular open-sided bar offering a comprehensive mix of burgers, pizza and seafood; local and international breakfast fare is served, too. Other highlights include a pool table, a cute pocket-size garden and sports events on satellite TV.

South Pole Billy's Bay. Cavernous indoor dining room serving up some serious – and inexpensive – Jamaican food: ackee or eggs for breakfast and oxtail, stew beef, fish and seafood for lunch and dinner.

Tiffany's Frenchman's Bay. Rather incongruously smart place, with candle-lit tables inside or on the terrace, good service and a range of moderately priced (from around J$300) lobster, octopus and fish dishes.

Wild Onion Frenchman's Bay. Newish spot in pretty landscaped gardens set back from the road, and deservedly popular for the excellent cooking of its owner, an irreverent Scotsman who migrated to Jamaica decades ago. All meals come with a soup starter and are served on a sizzling skillet at the table with rice and potato wedges; portions are mammoth. The escovitched kingfish is particularly delicious. There's an all-inclusive barbecue on Friday evenings, with a live band (J$280), and a good Sunday Brunch from 10am featuring all the Jamaican specialities (J$300).

Nightlife and entertainment

Treasure Beach isn't a **nightlife** hotspot, and during the week, evenings out will generally consist of after-dinner drinks at any of the restaurants listed above (*Tiffany's* occasionally put on karaoke nights) or at the area's few **bars**, which often keep quite late hours if the punters are drinking. In addition to the places listed below, there are numerous rum shops in and around town for a spot of white rum drinking and ol' talk. Things get busier at the weekends, when Treasure Beach's one club gets fairly busy; for a dancehall fix in a dedicated nightclub, head to the thoroughly Jamaican *Gally's Entertainment Lounge* in Junction (Fri & Sat). Ask around to see if anyone's staging one of the hugely entertaining **in-car sound-system clashes** occasionally put on hereabouts; several local men have installed ridiculously powerful sets in their cars, and the clash usually consists of two rivals attempting to outdo each other in terms of sound quality and selection, as decided by crowd response.

Bars and clubs

Dougie's Bar *Jake's*. Relaxed in-hotel bar that's usually filled with a friendly crowd of sophisticates and locals. A great spot for a sunset cocktail or a glass of wine.

Fishermen's Bar Frenchman's Bay. Up the lane beside *Tiffany's*, with a small indoor disco and pool table out back, this thatched bar is an easy-going local hangout that's open after everywhere else has closed. Very popular at the weekends with both locals and tourists.

Jack Sprat Calabash Bay A good place for a drink or a lesson in the art of dominoes, with a great selection of music – from rocksteady to roots reggae – courtesy of the genial manager, Fabulous. The Sunday Fish Fry, from 6pm, features a domino or bingo competition, and a bonfire on the beach after sunset.

Sparrow's Bar Frenchman's Beach. The friendliest of the beachside drinking spots, and an excellent place to watch the sun set.

Alligator Pond to Alligator Hole

At first glance, the ramshackle fishing village of **ALLIGATOR POND** – ten miles east of Treasure Beach, and reachable from the A2 via a direct road from Gutters – is not one of the most attractive spots on the south coast. But if you're passing, it's worth stopping to get the feel of a part of Jamaica pretty much unsullied by tourism, and to eat some superb **seafood**. Where the main road into Alligator Pond opens up into an unofficial town square, a dirt road to the right leads to several small shacks selling lobster and fish fresh from the boats. By far the most popular of these is *Little Ochi*, with a lovely setting right on the fishing beach and a collection of tables housed in reconditioned, brightly painted fishing boats on stilts. There's always a steady trade here, but it's particularly busy on weekends, with hungry folk pouring in from Mandeville and even as far as Kingston, and reggae blaring from columns of speaker boxes. The fresh fish, shrimp, lobster and conch – cooked in every way possible and served with bammy and festival – certainly taste great eaten in the sea air, but the wait can be horrendous: an hour or more at busy times. If you consider serious seafood more important than a sea view, head back down the main road and take the left turn just before the Cayman church. In an orange-painted thatch-roofed shack, with tables in the garden out back, *Bunch of Grapes* is a family-run affair that beats *Little Ochi* hands down in terms of taste. Fish, conch and lobster are sold by the pound (you select what you want from the fridge) and either brown-stewed, steamed, fried or curried and served with rice or bammy. Further north towards Gutters, on the right just before the left-hand turn-off to the Kaiser bauxite-loading plant, *Different Taste* is an open-air seafood place that's notable for its sublime conch soup, made daily in season.

There's little reason to **stay** in Alligator Pond itself, though the *Venue Sunset Lounge* (☎ 965 4508; ●) in Wards Bay, a five-minute drive east of *Little Ochi,* is a small, friendly guesthouse run by an English Jamaican. Rooms are basic and rather dingy, but cheap, and it's a lovely spot for a drink in the sea breeze or a plate of fish. In the other direction from *Little Ochi* (take either of the Kasier turn-offs, and follow the road past the Sports Ground), the *Sea-Riv Hotel* (℡962 7265; ❶–❷) is a far better option, right on a nice stretch of black-sand beach, with a swimmable river running into the waves. Rooms are surprisingly appealing, with ceiling or standing fans, tile floors and plain white linens.

There's no tourism scene here as such, but there's a bar at the water's edge, and local families arrive at the weekends for a day on the beach. It's also a great spot for watching the sunset – or the moon rise over the hills to the east, which slip down to the sea in the unmistakeable shape of an alligator's head. A couple of local Rastas run snorkelling trips to Sunny Island (rates are negotiable), and there are some battered paddle boats that kids can rent to splash around in the river, but otherwise it's just you and the beach. Incidentally, the usual peace of this very secluded area is interrupted once a year when Tony Rebel's **Rebel Salute** stageshow is held at the Kaiser Sports Ground; if you're attending the show, try and get a room at the *Sea-Riv*, as traffic jams on the minor roads leading to the A2 are horrendous.

Alligator Hole

From the square in Alligator Pond, a road leads east for eighteen miles to Alligator Hole and Milk River. What Jamaicans call a "lonely road" (with a shiver of misgiving), it's a lovely drive through an isolated area known as **Canoe Valley,** or the Long Bay Morass, much of it along the coast, with goats and sea birds usually your only company. The area is barely touched by development and remains a naturalist's paradise, with the dry, cactus-strewn slopes in the west giving way to mangrove swamps as you head further east – brilliant for bird-watching. In several places, you can access the beautiful, completely deserted stretch of brown-sand **beach** along Long Bay (look out for a clearing on the right, where a small bar sells drinks by the sea). It's not really a place to swim – the water is usually rough and currents strong – but it's a marvellous spot for a walk, with plenty of driftwood and shells to collect. Halfway along this stretch, the road passes **Guts River**, one of the most picturesque places on the south coast. The river runs under the road towards the sea, emerging in a

Manatees

The **manatee** – an aquatic mammal that looks rather like a large, fat seal with a bigger snout and a smile – is found in the warm waters of the Atlantic Ocean and in the Caribbean Sea. Known locally as the sea cow, it's a very secretive creature; little is known about its reproductive habits, for example, and scientists have found it tricky to monitor its numbers. The nature park at Alligator Hole is the only place in Jamaica, and one of few places in the world, where you've an excellent chance of seeing them in the wild.

Fully grown, manatees can reach up to fourteen feet in length, although the great size is no cause for concern as they are strictly vegetarian – eating as much as four hundred kilos of sea grass per day – and known for doting on each other and their young. Columbus probably spotted them when he first came to Jamaica in 1494 (although he claimed that he had seen mermaids), and there were certainly plenty around back then. Sadly, their slow and gentle lifestyle meant that they were (and are) easy prey for fishermen; accordingly, even though they are now protected, fewer than three thousand are believed to survive in the Caribbean and only a hundred in Jamaica.

clear blue stream edged by coconut palms and huge aloe plants, where you can swim, snorkel and jump off the rocks. Frigate birds and egrets flap lazily around, and even the best efforts of local developers, who have put up an intermittently operating **café** and **bar** and fenced-off the area, can't spoil the beauty. At the time of writing, no one was in charge of the facility, but the unofficial caretaker sometimes charges a small fee for visitors to enter the fenced-off area. Vendors cook up chicken dishes at the weekends.

Continuing east towards Milk River, you'll pass the tiny nature park of **Alligator Hole** (daily 9am–4pm; free), the part-time home of a small number of **manatees**. It's a peaceful place to stop, with a small visitor centre housing displays on manatees and Caribbean ecosystems. If you're lucky, you'll see the manatees come in for their daily feed, usually in the late afternoon, supplied by the caretaker-managers who hang out by the park, drinking, playing dominoes and selling cold beer and soft drinks. A boat trip downriver to look for the manatees is highly recommended (J$300 per person); ask to go all the way to the end, where the river flows into the sea and there's a tiny deserted beach. It's a truly paradisiacal spot. **Crocodiles** (known locally as alligators) also inhabit the area, although they are seen less often, and lots of people swim in the cool, clear waters here.

About 200m up the road towards Milk River, and reachable via a path on the left (inland) side of the road, **God's Well** is a deep sinkhole, surrounded by greenery and with a deep-blue pool just visible at the bottom. Said to be inhabited by the ghosts of a Taino maiden and a scuba diver who drowned here whilst trying to establish the sinkhole's depth, it's a rather eerie spot. Throw a stone over the edge and it seems to take an age to reach the water, the sinkhole's sheer sides providing a satisfyingly loud and deep thump as it hits. The guys at Alligator Hole will usually be able to take you here if you ask.

Milk River Spa

The **hot mineral springs** near **MILK RIVER**, only a couple of miles inland from Alligator Hole, were first discovered in the early eighteenth century. Mineral spas were subsequently built in the area – first opened to the public in 1794 – and are today housed in the basement of the *Milk River Hotel* (☎902 4657, ⓕ4974; ❸). The hotel is a lovely old wooden building, with comfortable, if rather sparse, mostly en-suite rooms and inexpensive meals on offer, and, though there's nothing spectacular about the area, the dry climate and the laid-back atmosphere make it a very pleasant place to spend a night.

Many of the guests at the hotel and spa are return visitors who swear by the curative powers of the water for a range of ailments from rheumatism to gout, nerve diseases and sciatica. Other visitors find their curiosity tinged with concern about the high radioactivity levels of the baths – more than fifty times that of the waters at Vichy in France – although the staff will assure you that this is quite harmless so long as you don't stay in for more than fifteen minutes at a time. The nine sunken tiled baths are big enough to have a good splash around, although you'll probably just want to float and relax. You get free use of the spas if you're staying at the hotel; if you're visiting, they cost J$100 for fifteen minutes.

Other than the spa, there's little to the village of Milk River other than the usual crowd of schoolchildren and smattering of churches, although there are rumoured plans to build a large all-inclusive hotel close to the spa. The river itself is named for its colour in the early morning, when it is shrouded in mist; swimming is not a great idea, given that the river is the home of a number of

△ YS Falls

crocodiles. Opposite the hotel, a vendor sells drinks and will point out the specimens that are usually found lurking in the shallows. You could try the **Milk River Mineral Pool** – an open-air swimming pool 150 yards from the hotel – though it's only filled these days on special occasions. Two miles beyond the spa, past rows of giant cactuses, is the tiny fishing village of **FARQUHARS** which has, at its western end, a passable black-sand beach where you can swim in the ocean. Expect lots of good-natured attention from the locals, as tourists very rarely venture this far.

East of Milk River

From Milk River, you can either head north to the main road for Mandeville and May Pen or continue east towards Lionel Town. After six miles, the latter B12 road passes through the quiet village of **ALLEY**, where **St Peter's Church** is one of the oldest and most attractive churches on the island. Although the church was founded in 1671, the present building mostly dates from the early eighteenth century. Inside, check out the tablets on the upper west wall, engraved with the Lord's Prayer and the Ten Commandments, and the 1847 organ. Outside there are a mass of crumbling tombs, many of the inscriptions ravaged by time. If the church is locked, try asking for the key at Amity Hall library (see below).

Beyond Alley you'll pass a unique octagonal building at tiny **AMITY HALL**. Originally a sugar mill, probably built around 1800, the building now houses the **parish library** (Mon–Fri 11am–5pm), with the rooms above occupied by a local family (though you can ask to look around). Constructed from imported brick rather than Jamaican limestone, this was an unusual building even in its own time. Ruins of the old sugar works, which closed in 1926, are dotted around nearby, and there is a present-day refinery at **Monymusk**, a mile away. Unlikely as it now seems, Amity Hall was the site of an important battle during the French invasion of 1694. The French landed at Yallahs in the east of Jamaica (see p.148) and crossed the island, destroying sugar estates as they went. At Amity Hall, though, they lost over a hundred men in one short engagement with the British (probably on the site of the sugar mill) and fled, never to return, burning the coastal village of **Carlisle Bay** in spite as they left.

East of Amity Hall, the B12 road turns north for the bustling market town of **LIONEL TOWN**, crowded with traders, fruit and vegetable stalls and school-children. If you continue past the turn-off and head south instead, you'll reach some of the most isolated places in Jamaica. **JACKSON BAY**, roughly five miles from Lionel Town, is a scruffy fishing village with a not particularly attractive beach. A much better option for a swim is the gorgeous strip of sand 500 yards to the west; take the right fork on your way down to Jackson Bay. Very few tourists ever come to this part of the island, and your presence will awaken considerable local interest. If you have a four-wheel-drive vehicle, you can head east before you reach the bay, and a rough track will carry you out along the deserted and scrubby **Portland Ridge,** past mangrove swamps and muddy plains dotted with stunted acacia trees. Inhabited only by a few fishermen and the occasional abandoned car, the peninsula is an eerily atmospheric place. The track continues on through the private grounds of the PWD Hunting and Sporting Club, which are closed to the public, and comes to a halt at Portland Lighthouse. For the adventurous, a canoe ride through the mangrove swamps and inland swamp lakes may be arranged with some of the local fishermen at Portland Cottage, starting at the beach, or, in local parlance, at "Bar Mout".

Inland to Mandeville

The A2 highway speeds inland from Black River, passing through some attractive countryside before making the long climb up Spur Tree Hill to **Mandeville**. The main road passes through **Bamboo Avenue**, with its walls of tall bamboo, and there are several interesting detours worth taking, particularly in the interior of St Elizabeth. There are gorgeous **waterfalls** at YS, **hiking** possibilities in the **Black River Gorge**, and the quiet and completely untouristed villages of the **Santa Cruz Mountains**. You can also visit a **rum factory**, beautifully placed among fields of sugarcane at Appleton, on the southern edge of Cockpit Country (see Chapter Four).

Accommodation options in the area are limited, though there are a couple of decent places at Santa Cruz and Maggotty, and you may want to consider visiting on day-trips from a base on the south coast or in Mandeville. **Getting around** is a breeze if you've got a car; public transport links into the interior are not brilliant, though minibuses and route taxis do run to most parts – for a couple of places, including YS, you'll need to charter a taxi for a short part of the trip.

Middle Quarters and YS Falls

As you drive northeast from Black River, you'll reach an intersection directing you north for Montego Bay or east towards Santa Cruz and Mandeville. Head east and you'll soon pass **Middle Quarters**, a small crossroads where groups of women sell spicy, salty **pepper shrimp** collected from the Black River. Feel free to sample from the proffered bags before you buy; reckon on around J$150 for a small bag. Buy some to add to your picnic if you're heading to the YS Falls or take a few minutes out to crunch them on the roadside and have a chat with the women. Incidentally, don't be intimidated by the fiercely competitive approach of the sellers – they are often all members of the same family and if one is lagging in sales for the day, she will usually be thrust forward to clinch the deal. However, to enjoy some shrimp in a more relaxed setting, head past the ladies to *Auntie's One-Stop,* a wooden shack to the left of the road, with a shady grove behind in which to eat. Trade is busy here, and the shrimp always fresh and delicious (they also tend to be bigger than those sold on the road); fabulous janga (shrimp) soup is also available.

Shortly after Middle Quarters, a left turn takes you two and a half miles north to **YS** (pronounced "why-ess"), an area dominated by the **YS farm**, home of the magnificent YS Falls. The name is thought to derive from the farm's original owners in 1684, John Yates and Richard Scott, whose initials were stamped on their cattle and the hogsheads of sugar that they exported. Today the farm covers around 2300 acres and raises pedigree **red poll cattle** – a Jamaican breed that you'll see all over the country – and grows papaya for export.

The **YS Falls,** a series of ten greater and lesser waterfalls, are great fun (Tues–Sun 9.50am–3.30pm; US$12). A jitney pulls you through the farm's land and alongside the YS River to a grassy area at the base of the falls, where there are changing rooms and toilets. You can climb up the lower falls or take the wooden stairway, which leads to a platform beside the uppermost and most spectacular waterfall. There are lianas and ropes for aspiring Tarzans, and pools for gentle bathing at the foot of each fall; you can swim under the main falls and climb up into a cave behind them. Early morning is a good time to go, before the afternoon clouds draw in; take a picnic and a book and you can comfortably spend a few hours loafing around on the grass and in the water. Cold beers, soft drinks and food are sold in the gazebo at the base of the falls.

A **car** is extremely handy if you're heading for the falls, as they're a little off the beaten track, but if you're relying on public transport, **buses** run along the main A2 highway south of YS between Black River and Santa Cruz. Ask the driver to drop you at the junction, and you can usually find taxis waiting to run passengers up to the YS farm. There's nowhere to **stay** at YS – the nearest options are Maggotty (see below) or Black River (see p.332).

Maggotty

East of YS and seven miles from the main A2 highway, **MAGGOTTY** resembles a small Wild West frontier town. It's a dry, dusty place, most of whose inhabitants work at the **Appleton Estate** rum distillery nearby (see below). Though there's little to see in town, there is some beautiful scenery nearby – including the YS Falls – and a couple of accommodation options.

Just south of town, atop a hill in the middle of the teeming rainforest, the red-roofed *Apple Valley Guesthouse* (☎963 9508, ✉pennesev@hotmail.com; ❷) has five very basic rooms. It's a handy base for some good walking, and the owners can provide guides. The best **hike** is across the local farmland and down into the **Black River Gorge**, a deep and attractive ravine carved by the island's principal river. Around twenty minutes' walk from the guesthouse you reach the first of a series of 28 **waterfalls**, and you can either wallow around there or trek for an hour or so down to the bottom. It's a straightforward walk to get down into the gorge, although the climb back up can be a bit strenuous.

The guesthouse's industrious owners also run the **Apple Valley Park** back in town. It's a small nature park with ducks and geese, paddle-boats and go-karts for kids, explanations of the medicinal value of Jamaica's herbs, and a little farm. Unfortunately a decline in custom means that the park is only open by appointment these days; you might be lucky and arrive at the same time as a school group (J$250 if you're not booked with a party). If you want to stay in town, there are simple, clean rooms at *Poinciana Guesthouse* (☎963 9676; ❷), up a slight hill opposite the police station; ask for Miss Williams at the *Happy Times* restaurant down in town if no one's around. *Happy Times* is also good for basic Jamaican meals and snacks.

Infrequent **minibuses** run to Maggotty from Black River and Santa Cruz. If you're **driving**, the road north from the A2 highway is in far better condition than the road running east/west between Maggotty and YS.

The Appleton Estate Rum Tour

Three miles east of Maggotty, the **Wray and Nephew rum distillery** at **APPLETON** (Mon–Sat 9am–4pm; US$12; ☎ 923 6141 9 ❽www.appletonrum .com) has a great setting in the Nassau valley among thousands of acres of sugarcane fields. At 250 years old, this is the oldest rum producer in the English-speaking Caribbean and the best known of Jamaica's several brands. All of the rum produced here is sent for barrelling in Kingston (though some barrels are sent back here to age), and blending and bottling are also carried out there.

Rum and raison d'être

Rum – once known as rumbullion or kill-devil – is Jamaica's national drink, and you couldn't choose a better place to acquire a taste for the stuff. Jamaica was the first country to make rum commercially and it still produces some of the world's finest. **Over-proof** is the drink of choice for the less well-off – it's cheap, lethally strong (64 percent alcohol) and, supposedly, cures all ills. If you can't handle the overproof, the standard **white rums** are the basis for most cocktails, while more refined palates go for the **darker rums**. During the ageing process these rums acquire colour from the oak barrels in which they are stored and, as they get older, they slip down increasingly smoothly with no need for a mixer.

Distilling of sugarcane juice started in Jamaica during the years of Spanish occupation, stepping up a few gears when the British took over in 1655 and rum became famous as the drink of the island's semi-legitimate **pirates** and **buccaneers**. The production process hasn't changed much over the centuries, although it has become fully mechanized, putting a number of donkeys out of work in the process. The sugarcane is squeezed to extract every drop of its juice, which is then boiled and put through a centrifuge, producing molasses. In turn, the molasses is diluted with water, and yeast is added to get the stuff fermenting away. After fermentation, the liquid "dead wash" is sent to the distillery, where it is heated, and the evaporating alcohol caught in tanks. It sounds simple enough – and it is. But when you discover that it takes ten to twelve tonnes of sugarcane to produce half a bottle of alcohol, which is then blended with water and a mixture of secret ingredients (molasses is almost certainly among them) to make the finished product, you begin to appreciate all those fields of swaying cane a little more.

You'll need a car to get here, or you can take a taxi from Maggotty. Though you're free to drop in, it's a good idea to call ahead to arrange a guided visit, if only to avoid your visit coinciding with a big tour party. The hour-long **tour** starts with a complimentary drink and video session, followed by a visit to the factory (heavy with the sweet scent of molasses) and cobwebby ageing house, and then outside to an old sugar press, where donkeys used to walk in circles to turn a grinder that crushed juice out of the sugarcane. Today it's all mechanized, though a donkey has been put back into service to demonstrate old techniques. All sorts of pots, boilers and barrels used for the production process are placed artistically around the site. The tour concludes in a "tavern", where you get to sample all seventeen kinds of rum and various rum-based liquors.

Bamboo Avenue and Lacovia

Back on the main A2 highway, **Bamboo Avenue**, halfway between Middle Quarters and Lacovia, enlivens the drive to Mandeville. For several miles, *bambusa vulgaris*, Jamaica's largest species of bamboo, has grown up on either side to create a pretty arch over the road. The place was once almost completely shaded by the bamboo, but the sun now streams in through gaps created by Hurricane Gilbert and, some say, by official neglect. There are several rest stops along the road where you can get a jelly coconut or a cold beer.

Just east of Bamboo Avenue, the village of **LACOVIA**, one-time capital of St Elizabeth, was once an important inland port for shipping sugar and logwood down to Black River for export. Today it is most notable for its **twin tombs**, just outside the Texaco petrol station, believed to contain the bodies of two

353

young men killed in a local duel in 1723. One of the deceased is identified as Thomas Jordan Spencer and the coat of arms on his tombstone suggests a connection with the family of Winston Churchill and Diana Spencer. Lacovia is also home to the **Cashoo Ostrich Park** (Sat & Sun 10am–5.30pm; J$250; ☎966 2222); take a right turn over the old Lacovia bridge and follow the signs towards Slipe. The park – named after its former crop, cashew nuts – is a family-orientated place that features a pool with a children's area, a bumper-car track ($100 per ride), a petting zoo and a play area as well as the ostriches themselves. Jamaicans haven't yet warmed to the appeal of eating ostrich, and they're being bred here for export. A guided tour of the grounds concentrates on ostrich facts but also takes in the park's comprehensive and rather pretty herb garden. You can go down to the river, which runs through the property, for a swim. Plans are afoot to create a **butterfly farm** here, too; the owners hope to start a breeding programme for Jamaica's giant swallowtail butterflies (see p.395).

Santa Cruz, Malvern and Spur Tree Hill

If you're in this part of the country, sooner or later you're likely to pass through **SANTA CRUZ**, the main settlement along the A2 and reckoned to be the hottest place in Jamaica. This rapidly expanding market town, once famous as a livestock trading centre, is noisy and frenetic at the best of times, and there's no particular reason to stop off here, although you can fill up on fresh patties and delicious juices at *Paradise Patties* on Main Street. If you need to spend a night, the friendly *Danbar Guest House* (☎966 9382; ❷), at Trevmar Park just south of the main road towards the west side of town, has seven very cheap rooms and the owners will cook to order.

The road south from Santa Cruz to Treasure Beach and the coast (see p.336) is a beautiful (if slow) drive over the Santa Cruz Mountains. The drive takes you through a series of tiny villages and the quiet town of **MALVERN**. Like Christiana further north (see p.362), this is one of Jamaica's **coolest** towns, at around 2500ft above sea level. In the early twentieth century, it was an important summer retreat for foreigners and wealthy Jamaicans, though it's now almost bereft of tourists. Today, apart from a handful of top-notch schools and colleges established here in the 1850s, there's not much to the town, although the presence of returning residents who've made their money abroad is injecting an air of affluence – with grand houses springing up on the hilltops – and it's a pretty place to cruise around for a little while. Jason Henzell of *Jake's* in Treasure Beach (see p.340) is currently building some luxurious holiday homes up here that may be available to **rent**, and *Mikarabee* (☎966 5537, Ⓦwww.mikarabee.com; ❸–❹), a lovely family home just outside town, offers rooms in the main house as well as a separate cabin; there's a pool on site. Otherwise, the nearby *Chariots Hotel* (☎966 3860; ❷–❸) in **LEEDS**, midway between Santa Cruz and Malvern, is a surprisingly large place, with a small pool and decent en-suite rooms with screened windows, phone, a/c, ceiling fan and cable TV; there's a restaurant on site. *Dolly's* restaurant and ice cream parlour, next to the petrol station in Malvern, has standard Jamaican **food** if you're after some lunch.

Heading east from Santa Cruz, the A2 continues to **Gutters**, on the Manchester/St Elizabeth border, where it begins the long and rather tortuous climb up **Spur Tree Hill** to Mandeville. Once known as "man bump", the switchbacking hill provides dramatic views over the southern plains, the Santa

Cruz Mountains, and down to the sea, and there are a couple of good **bars** and **restaurants** to stop off at and enjoy the view: *All Seasons* has a variety of local dishes and a verandah, while, 400 yards further up, a handful of small bars specialize in curry goat and mannish water – *Alex's Curry Goat Spot* is known islandwide.

Mandeville and around

You can almost feel the wealth in **MANDEVILLE**, Jamaica's fifth-largest town. Big money started to arrive here in the 1950s as a result of the very visible **bauxite industry** (see p.358) that grew up around the town. More recently, returning expatriate Jamaicans, attracted by the cooler climate and the relatively low crime rate, have begun to invest their accumulated savings in large homes and small businesses around town, and Mandeville has grown at an unprecedented rate. Tourism has been rather an unimportant sector in recent years, although from the early days of the *Mandeville Hotel* in the 1890s, the town was popular with British soldiers who came to escape the heat of the coastal areas and to recuperate from their fevers and diseases.

Nowadays, Mandeville is still a quiet town and by no means an essential stop on your tour of the island. However, it is a pleasant place to get away from the hustle and bustle of Jamaica's more touristed areas – you'll probably notice the lack of hassle – and makes a reasonable base for exploring the south and centre of the island. The hilly setting also means a pleasantly cool climate; winter evenings can get quite cold, and you'll need a sweater. If you're here for any time, check out the old great house at **Marshall's Pen** and the more contemporary mansion at **Huntingdon Summit**, or while away an hour with a visit to a local **factory**.

Community tourism

The creation of big tourist "ghettos" on Jamaica's north coast has completely disrupted traditional lifestyles there and means that, often, the only contact overseas visitors have with Jamaicans is when they are serving drinks or driving tour buses. In the face of its own gradually developing tourist scene, Jamaica's south coast, where the absence of large-scale beach resorts offers visitors more of a feel of the "real" Jamaica, is keen to escape such insensitive development. Planners and hoteliers are showing increasing interest in the concept of "**community tourism**", which aims to contain and control tourism by fostering closer connections between the tourist and the community – through visits to schools, farms and craft centres – and persuading developers not to despoil the area. It's a positive, optimistic approach, but it remains to be seen whether the organizers' noble intentions will rein in some of the short-termist developers, who are beginning to sniff big possibilities on the south coast. For more information on the scheme, contact the inimitable Diana McIntyre-Pyke at Mandeville's *Astra Inn* (☎962 3725 or 7758, ℮countrystyle@ mail.infochan.com), where you'll also find the community tourism operator Countrystyle Ltd.

Arrival, information and getting around

Buses into Mandeville arrive at the south end of Mandeville Square, a small village green in the town centre surrounded by banks, supermarkets and, usually, a crowd of people. Buses and minibuses for Kingston, Christiana, Santa Cruz and Black River (less often for the west and north coasts) leave from the same place at regular intervals, and the town's main **taxi rank** is alongside. If you're **driving** there are three separate entrances to town signposted from the highway – it's simplest to take the middle one, at the major roundabout, and follow New Green Road all the way into town. For sightseeing, a car is definitely a major asset; although you can see everything in the town centre on foot, getting out to Marshall's Pen or Huntingdon Summit will require wheels. If you don't want to navigate the town alone, Countrystyle (see p.355) offer a daylong "Marvellous Mandeville" tour (US$40) that includes a visit to a local home, Mrs Stephenson's garden, a school and the SWA Craft centre; the highlight, though, is the trip out of town to the lovely rural community of Resource, just outside town, where you visit a private home for a delicious home-cooked lunch and to see traditional methods of bammy preparation.

There is no longer a **tourist board office** in Mandeville, so you'll have to rely on your hotel staff and the usual flyers around town for news of what's going on. Diana McIntyre-Pike at the *Astra Inn* is especially helpful and a great source of information on the local area. The *Astra Country Inn* and the *Mandeville Hotel* both organize tours of the local sights, as does the *Kariba Kariba Guesthouse*, whose genial owner Derrick O'Connor has a lovely retreat, **Little Rippon Farm** in Mile Gully, to which he takes guided visits through the fruit orchards, carefully planted flowering shrubs and woodland trails; horseback riding is also available.

Accommodation

Mandeville's **hotels** largely cater for business travellers as tourists are relatively few here, although there are a couple of decent budget places. Countrystyle Tourism (c/o the *Astra Country Inn*, see below) can organize bed and breakfast accommodation in some of Mandeville's loveliest homes.

Astra Country Inn 62 Ward Ave ☎962 3725, ⊕1461, ⊛www.access-ja.com/countrystyle. A little out of the town centre, and a bit short on character; the place used to be a nursing home and still feels a little sterile, though renovations are underway. The rooms range in size, price and facilities (the budget ones are a great deal), and all have cable TV. There's a small pool, the food is good and the hotel is the base for the area's community tourism scheme (see box p.355). ❸

Fleur Flats Resorts 10 Coke Drive ☎962 1053. Tidy self-catering apartments with cable TV in a small complex a five-minute drive from town – follow the Manchester Road south from the central square, keeping right at the petrol station, and take the first left. ❸

Glen Rock 3a Greenvale Rd ☎961 3278, ⊕3279, ⊕glenrock@cwjamaica.com. Excellent new guest-house conveniently located on the main road into the town centre. The eleven en-suite rooms, with fan, cable TV and phone, vary in size, and there are some reasonably priced singles. Breakfast is available and guests can use the kitchen. Brilliant staff and good rates, too. ❷ –❸

Golf View Hotel 51/2 Caledonia Rd ☎962 4471, ⊛www.thegolfviewhotel.com. Modern, well-equipped hotel designed around a central court-yard with a pool. The en-suite rooms, either a/c or fan-only, have attractive wood furnishings, phone, cable TV and balcony, and there's a restaurant and bar on site. ❹

Hilltop Hotel Northern Caribbean University, Manchester Rd ☎625 2296, ⊕taicentre @wicollege.edu. Clean, spacious and comfortable en-suite rooms with phone and cable TV, and a communal kitchen for preparing snacks and hot

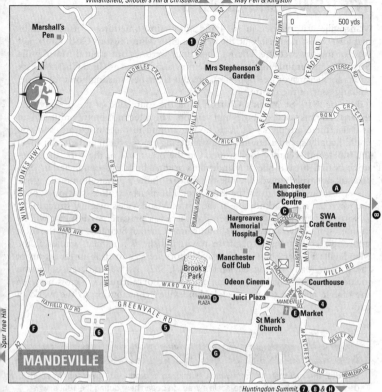

Huntingdon Summit, **7**, **8** & **H** ▼

ACCOMMODATION			
Astra Country Inn	**2**	Kariba Kariba	
Fleur Flats Resorts	**7**	Guesthouse	**1**
Glen Rock	**5**	Mandeview Flats	**6**
Golf View Hotel	**3**	Mandeville Hotel	**4**
Hilltop Hotel	**8**		

RESTAURANTS			
Astra Inn	**2**	International Chinese	
Bamboo Village	**D**	Restaurant	**H**
Bloomfield Great House	**G**	Jerky's	**F**
Centenary Rastarant	**E**	The Link	**B**
The Den	**A**	Mandeville Hotel	**4**
Gee's Café	**C**		

drinks. Most guests are visitors to the university, so there's not much of a holiday feel, but the staff are friendly and helpful. Rates include breakfast. ④

Kariba Kariba Guesthouse Winston Jones Highway (A2), New Green Rd roundabout ☎962 8006, ⊛www.karibaholidays.com. Friendly little guesthouse on the edge of Mandeville. Lovely parquet floors throughout, and large rooms with appealing, understated decor, balconies, cable TV and fan. Rates are negotiable if you stay more than a couple of nights, and include breakfast. ③

Mandeview Flats 7 Hillview Drive, Balvanie Heights ☎961 8439, ⊛www.mandeviewhotel.com. Built on a hillside affording great views over town, this small guesthouse is in a quiet setting along a

pretty residential street. It features spacious and comfortable rooms, some with kitchenette and all with cable TV, phone and fan, and a very friendly owner. Meals are available, and breakfast is included in the rates. ④

Mandeville Hotel 4 Hotel St ☎962 2460, ⊛www.mandevillehotel.com. One of the oldest hotels in Jamaica and, though almost totally reconstructed and refurbished, still a pleasant and easy-going place to stay right in the heart of town. A little on the expensive side for the standard of accommodation, however. Facilities include a restaurant, bar and large pool, and the rooms and studios have phone and cable TV. Check out the enormous sandbox trees near the entrance. ⑤

The Town and around

Mandeville was founded in 1814 and still retains something of its early colonial air – most noticeably at the very English **Manchester Golf Club**, just west of the town centre. The first buildings were set out around **Mandeville Square**, a rather unkempt grassy space now also known as Cecil Charlton Park after a former mayor (see opposite), and this is the best starting point for a brief walking tour of the centre.

Built in 1819, **St Mark's Church** is on the south side of the park, behind the massed ranks of taxis, buses and vendors. The interior is pretty ordinary, but, as usual, there are plenty of goats nosing around in the churchyard, and you could happily spend a few minutes wandering among them and checking out the nineteenth-century tombstones. On the other side of the park, the limestone **courthouse** is one of Mandeville's original buildings, completed in 1820 and still normally crowded, while the **rectory** (now a private home) alongside the courthouse dates from the same year. The nearby **police station** – once the town jail and workhouse – is the last of Mandeville's original structures.

North of here, at 25 New Green Rd, there is a **private garden** that will be of interest if you've a passion for anthuriums. Carmen Stephenson has the most impressive collections of plants in town, and she is a regular winner at the Mandeville Flower Show every May. Visitors are free to drop in for a tour of the garden (daily during daylight hours; US$2); its well-ordered collection includes the rare white anthurium, orchids and **ortaniques** – a cross between the orange and the tangerine and Mandeville's contribution to the world of fruit.

Jamaica's bauxite

Bauxite, the raw material from which aluminium is produced, is present in abundance in Jamaica's earth. Large-scale extraction began here during the 1950s, when three North American companies started local operations, and the mining and processing operations remain very visible as you travel around the country's interior. Much of the mining is open-cast, resulting in gruesome-looking red mud lakes like the one just outside Mandeville, while the ugly refineries spoil the landscape at various places around the country.

It may not be pretty, but the "**red gold**" is vital to Jamaica's economy. After tourism, it's the second most important contributor, employing around five thousand people and, more importantly, contributing about a quarter of the government's income and a half of the nation's export earnings. A third of the raw bauxite is shipped abroad for processing; the rest is processed at the island's four alumina refineries, and the resulting alumina is then sent abroad for conversion to aluminium. This last stage – the most profitable part of the process – cannot economically be carried out in Jamaica because of the lack of a cheap energy source.

The industry took a big hit during the 1970s, when Michael Manley's PNP administration imposed higher taxes on the multinational companies involved in extraction. The bauxite companies scaled down their operations dramatically, and in the face of increasing world competition and a declining price, it was a decade before the local industry recovered to a perceptible degree. Today, the industry remains under pressure, with world prices relatively low and new production centres in Australia and South America challenging Jamaica's market position. With little else to fall back on, the island has to hope that the industry it has relied on so heavily for nearly five decades can survive its modern challenges.

Marshall's Pen and Huntingdon Summit

Mandeville's more interesting sights are both a bit of a drive out of town. **Marshall's Pen** (tours daily by appointment, ☎904 5454; US$10) is a lovely old great house, built around 1795 and originally used in the preparation of coffee beans for export. The driveway you enter through was the "barbecue", where the beans were laid out to dry in the sun, and the ground floor of the house, with its massive cedar floorboards, was where they were polished prior to their shipment to the US and UK for roasting and grinding. Nowadays this area has been converted to living quarters and also serves, together with a couple of rooms upstairs, as an interesting **museum**. Ann Sutton, owner of the house, has been a relentless collector over the years, and the museum features fabulous collections of shells and stamps, from both Jamaica and abroad; Japanese and Chinese artefacts; and a tiny array of Taino relics.

The grounds are great for **birdwatching**, and serious ornithologists can arrange to stay at the house for around US$30 per person per night. Even if you are just passing through, you are likely to see a doctor bird or two flitting around the gardens.

A more modern mansion is **Huntingdon Summit** (daily by appointment ☎962 2274; free), a Jamaican version of Elvis Presley's Graceland that's the home of the town's former mayor and self-made millionaire Cecil Charlton – you'll see his **off-course betting shops**, from which he made his fortune, all over town. The octagonal extravagance features a giant living room replete with antique furniture, seven bedrooms colour coded by their carpets and often esoteric furnishings, and a library stuffed with trophies and photographs of the great man meeting Jamaican and foreign dignitaries. The extensive grounds of the house have their own bamboo avenue as well as great views over the neighbouring countryside. There's even a swimming pool with swim-up bar that you enter via a tunnel inside the house. The whole place is gloriously kitsch and offers an interesting perspective on Jamaica's nouveaux riches. If Mr Charlton is at home, try and persuade him to show you round – he's predictably a larger-than-life character.

To get there, follow the Manchester Road south out of Mandeville, keeping right at the Texaco station. At the T-junction where the road ends, turn right onto Newport Road, then first left onto May Day Road for just under a mile, turning left down George's Valley Road until you reach the big green gates on your left.

Coffee and Pickapeppa sauce

If you have some time to kill while you're in Mandeville you can visit a nearby factory. The **coffee factory** of Jamaica Standard Products (Mon–Fri by appointment; free; ☎963 4211) is a couple of miles north of the town centre in Williamsfield. JSP makes a number of different foodstuffs – including tea, sauces and spices – but coffee, which they've been producing since the 1950s, is their mainstay; the factory roasts, grinds and packages beans for the superior Blue Mountain coffee as well as JSP's own "High Mountain" and Baronhall brands, grown at lower elevations. Since seventy percent of coffee drunk in Jamaica is instant, most of the coffee packaged here is exported – largely to Japan. The tour of the coffee plant, conducted by staff members and with an entirely uncommercial air, is brief but informative, taking you through all stages of processing from grading the beans to roasting – and the entire place smells wonderful. Afterwards you have a chance to buy the products at excellent prices.

Just beyond Williamsfield at the bottom of Shooter's Hill, the **Pickapeppa factory** (Mon–Fri 8.30am–noon & 1.30–3.30pm; 45min tour J$200; ☎603 3441) makes a great detour, especially if you've developed a taste for its extremely addictive main product. In operation since 1921 and equipped with masses of ancient-looking, Heath Robinson-esque machinery, the factory is best known for its delicious Pickapeppa seasoning sauce, a piquant blend of tomatoes, onions, mangoes, raisins, tamarinds, hot peppers and a secret concoction of fourteen spices; once made, the sauce is aged for at least a year in oak barrels. The end product, sold mostly overseas but nonetheless a firm favourite on Jamaican restaurant tables, is utterly delicious and not as fiery as the Scotch bonnet sauce that's also made here. The **tour** starts in the lab, where ingredients are subjected to stringent quality-control checks, and moves on to the factory floor, where you see the ageing barrels, vats of simmering ingredients and, finally, the bottling process. It's all a very hands-on affair, and many of the staff have been working here for decades. You should be able to get a tour if you turn up, but it's best to call ahead.

Eating, drinking and nightlife

As you'd expect from such a peaceful town, Mandeville **nightlife** is pretty tame, though there is a newly opened cinema, the *Odeon*, on Caledonia Avenue (☎962 7646). But there are some good **restaurants** and a lot of fast-food options, including *KFC* and *McDonald's*, and snack outlets at the ubiquitous malls (particularly at the Manchester Shopping Centre); *Juici Patties* is at the corner of Ward and Caledonia avenues. The central bus park at twilight is your best bet for jerk chicken and delicious roast yam. You'll also find a handful of decent **bars** and a rather run-of-the mill **nightclub**.

Restaurants and snack bars

Astra Inn 62 Ward Ave. Good and moderately priced hotel restaurant, though not worth the trip out if you're staying in town.

Bamboo Village Ward Plaza, 35 Ward Ave ☎962 4515. Pretty good Chinese restaurant, halfway between the town's main square and the *Astra Inn*.

Bloomfield Great House Bloomfield ☎962 3116. Wonderfully restored great house, with grand steps leading up to a verandah dining area that affords lovely views over Mandeville. The menu is varied, fairly sophisticated and expensive, with mains ranging from filet mignon, chicken parmigiana and lamb chops to coconut curry shrimp or lobster and chickpea veg stew. But the cooking can be a bit hit-and-miss, with heavy-handed seasoning. Nonetheless, it's well worth eating here at least once, and the wine list is short but good. If you're not dining come anyway for an early evening drink.

Centenary Rastarant Marketplace. Tiny café with freshly squeezed orange juice and home-cooked Jamaican food. A great spot for watching the hustle and bustle of the market.

The Den 35 Caledonia Rd. One of Mandeville's busier restaurants, set in an ancient colonial-era house. The moderately priced menu is quite wide-ranging, from curry chicken and other Jamaican dishes to fish and chips, kebabs, pork chops, pizzas and sandwiches. The Friday night jam here plays host to live music in the garden, often jazz.

Gee's Café Manchester Shopping Centre. Best of a number of good eateries, juice bars and pastry shops at the back of this shopping plaza, with excellent Jamaican breakfasts and good cheap food throughout the day.

International Chinese Restaurant 117 Manchester Rd. Chinese food from an extensive menu, a short drive from town.

Jerky's Winston Jones Highway. Lively, newish spot for good and inexpensive Jamaican food, with tables in the open air on a thatched gazebo, and in the bar area. Jerk (chicken, pork, lobster and fish) is the mainstay, but barbecue chicken, hot wings and roast fish also are available, as is a worthy conch soup.

The Link 80 Caledonia Ave. Along the far reaches of Caledonia Avenue (look out for it on a little hillock on the right as you drive out of town), this is a genial place for an inexpensive dinner. Jerk chicken and pork, fish and pizza are served.

Mandeville Hotel 4 Hotel St ☎962 2460. Consistently good, central hotel restaurant, though often low on atmosphere, with a varied mid-priced menu of steaks, fish and curry goat. Excellent breakfasts are served on a poolside terrace.

Bars and clubs

Dicky's Sports Bar Ward Ave. Friendly, thoroughly Jamaican basement hangout, excellent for a white rum or a game of pool; occasional sound-system dances held outside.

Eclipse 33 Ward Ave, next to the Ward Plaza. Small, indoor nightclub, with a mainly dancehall playlist and youngish clientele. It gets seriously crowded at weekends. Open Fri–Sun.

Jerky's Winston Jones Highway. One of Mandeville's busiest places in the evenings, with a nice, semi-open-air bar and pool tables. Open late.

The Link 80 Caledonia Ave. Cosy, friendly little bar with a games night (Wed), very raucous karaoke on Thursdays and Saturdays, a Friday happy hour (6–8pm), and an oldies session on Sundays. Sports events are shown on the big-screen TV, and there's the occasional bingo night, too. Usually busy, with a mixed crowd –young and old, local and foreign.

Manchester Arms *Mandeville Hotel*. Pleasant quiet bar, fashioned after an English pub. Opens late most nights.

Manchester Club Corner of Caledonia Rd and Ward Ave. Definitely a colonial feel at this golf club, but a decent place for an early evening drink if you're cruising around.

Mystic Sports Bar Juici Plaza, Caledonia Ave. Popular upstairs pool club that's good for a few games.

Shopping

Shopping malls are everywhere in Mandeville. Probably the most extensive is the Manchester Shopping Centre, opposite the junction of Caledonia Road and New Green Road, where you'll find banks, an excellent Hi-Lo supermarket, craft stores, and a number of fast-food restaurants. Bookland at the shopping centre has **books** on Jamaica and recent UK and US **newspapers** and **magazines**. There are two more **supermarkets** – Moo-Penns and Super Plus – beside Mandeville Square on East Park Crescent. The vibrant and colourful local **marke**t, at the southeast corner of Mandeville Square, is a great place to shop for fruit and vegetables.

If you're nearby, drop in at the **SWA Craft Centre**, 7 North Racecourse, behind the Manchester Shopping Centre, which evolved as a way of dealing with the problem of youth unemployment for girls. They are trained in various craft skills, such as embroidery, dressmaking and cooking, and many of the products are sold in the centre. If you're not interested in the crafts, there's normally some cooking going on and patties or plantain tarts worth trying.

Listings

Banks and exchange Among the numerous banks around town are NCB at the Mandeville Centre, which is situated at the top end of Manchester Rd just off the main square, and Bank of Nova Scotia, at Caledonia Rd and also the Manchester Shopping Centre. If you're changing money, there's an FX Trader (Mon–Sat 9am–5pm) in the plaza on the corner of Ward and Caledonia avenues, opposite the gas station, and Brumalia Cambio (Mon–Fri 8.30am–4pm, Sat 8.30am–1pm) at 1 Ward Ave, just past *Juici Patties*.

Car rental Hemisphere, 51 Manchester Rd ☎962 1921; Maxdan, 183 Ward Ave ☎962 5341. Rates are from US$60 a day.

Dentist Manchester Dental Associates, 11 Manchester Rd ☎962 1560.

Golf The nine-hole Manchester Golf Club, at the corner of Caledonia Rd and Ward Ave (☎962 2403), is the oldest club in the Caribbean. A round costs US$17, plus caddy.

Hospitals The public Mandeville Hospital is at 32 Hargreaves Ave (☎962 2067); newly refurbished, it's referred to by most as the "hotel hospital". The private Hargreaves Memorial Hospital shares the same address (☎962 2040). In an emergency call ☎961 4221 for a private ambulance.

Internet You can get online at the Mandeville Business Centre, in Manchester Shopping Centre (Mon–Sat 8.30am–5.30pm).

Library The Manchester Parish Library (Mon–Fri 9.30am–5.30pm, Sat 9am–1pm) is on Hargreaves Ave, just above the hospital.

Pharmacies Haughtons, 18 West Park Crescent (Mon–Sat 8am–10pm, Sun 9am–9pm); Fontana, Manchester Shopping Centre (Mon–Sat 8am–7pm).

Police The main station is on the north side of Mandeville Square (☎962 2250). In an emergency call ☎119.

Post office South Racecourse.

Taxis The main rank is on the south side of Mandeville Square, near the parish church, or call Garth Taxi Service (☎625 5681).

Christiana and May Pen

The south's two other main towns sit in splendid isolation, with the emptiness of the interior between them. North of Mandeville, the hills around the small market town of **Christiana** offer a view of a very different, more rural, Jamaica, while unattractive **May Pen**, to the east, is only worth a visit for its annual agricultural show.

Christiana and around

The steep Shooter's Hill heads north from Mandeville, climbing up above the ugly Alcan bauxite plant, with its lake of red mud. Just over halfway up the hill, you'll come to **WALDERSTON**, a small village at the crossroads; turn left and left again up a dreadful track to reach the sweet little **Magic Toy factory** (daily 9am–5pm; ☎603 1495). The small workshop makes the very colourful wooden fish, jigsaw puzzles and similar playthings that you'll see in hotel gift shops all over Jamaica – and you can buy them here at a considerable discount. It's housed in a lovely old house with attractive gardens and fabulous views over the surrounding area.

Continue ten miles north for **CHRISTIANA**, a small market town for the surrounding agricultural community, where potatoes, yams, ginger, coffee and cocoa are grown. Lofty and cool, three thousand feet up in the hills, the town was a popular resort for "old-style" tourism in the 1940s and 1950s, when beaches and tanning were less fashionable than they are today. It's a simple one-street town with just a single hotel and not a huge amount to see – though you can organize a hike or two and a spot of caving – but if you're looking for a peaceful escape from the heat of the coast, it's an excellent choice. If you have a car, Christiana also makes a decent base for visiting Appleton and Maggotty to the west (see p.352) or Bob Marley's mausoleum to the northeast in Alexandria (see p.228).

A hike to the lush gorge at **Christiana Bottom** is the big thing to do here. Take a right turn by the post office in town and then follow the left fork at the crossroads to a standpipe where you can park if you're driving, though it's perfectly walkable from the centre of Christiana. Continue down an often muddy track through prolific ferns and bamboo to a **waterfall** and a cold but refreshing **pool**. (It's not easy to find the way, so if you get lost ask for the "blue hole".) North of town, beyond the village of **Coleyville**, the **Gourie State Park** (daily during daylight hours; free) has a number of lovely hiking trails through its pine woods; the cool air up here makes for especially pleasant hiking. To get to the park from Christiana, turn left off the main road towards Albert Town at the signposted potato-processing factory; follow the road, bearing left, and keep going until you reach a thatched gazebo in a clearing. (The road is pretty rough, but is usually driveable.) To the right of the gazebo, trails lead into the forest (look out for wild strawberries at the side of the path), while to the left are **Gourie Caves** and **Oxford Caves**, which offer some challenging caving. With a good flashlight you can explore on your own, but the underground routes are tricky and a guide is strongly recommended; contact STEA in Albert Town, or get in touch with Trevor Anderson, a Christiana resident who's great for hikes hereabouts and trips to Christiana Bottom (from $15 per person; ☎964 5088, Ⓔfoxtoo@hotmail.com).

If you have a car, it's also worth taking a brief trip west of Christiana to **BETHANY**. Head back downhill towards Walderston, take a right turn beside the petrol station and bear left down a winding road that leads through the cute village of **Devon** and some very English scenery. Nineteenth-century Moravian missionaries – the first Christian missionaries to come to Jamaica – built a number of **churches** in the local area, and Bethany's, modelled on one in Hernhut, Germany, and perched on the mountainside, is the most impressive. The large, red-roofed church was founded in 1835, and the views over the Dom Figuereoa Mountains and up to Cockpit Country are staggering. There isn't much to the church interior, but if it's locked, you can get a key at the adjacent rectory, prettily gabled with gingerbread trim. The countryside around here is green, rolling and quite un-Jamaican with hedgerows and dry-stone walls. But don't come out this way if you're short of time – it's easy to get lost driving around as there are no road signs and minor roads spin off all over the place.

Practicalities

Hotel Villa Bella (☎964 2243, Ⓦwww.jamaica-southcoast.com/villabella; ●), three miles from the town centre and the only **hotel** in Christiana, is one of the most delightful small hotels in Jamaica. There's no pool or unnecessary fripperies, but the place retains a colonial-era feel and is dotted with interesting curiosities – plenty of art deco furniture, nineteenth-century china, old prints and the hotel's original guest book from 1941. The *Villa Bella* also organizes a variety of **tours** of the local area, including mountain biking, caving and hiking, for between US$10 and US$35 per person.

The **restaurant** at *Villa Bella* has standard international and Jamaican fare at moderate to expensive prices and a nice indoor dining area (you'll find it's too cold to eat outside in the winter months). But for really good food, head to the tiny *Aketeh* (mobile ☎796 2782), a vegetarian restaurant on the lower floor of a small bar/supermarket complex on the south side of town (look out for the huge sign). Cooked up by the Rasta chef/owner, the food here – ackee and callaloo breakfasts, and lunches and dinners of steamed fish with brown rice and vegetables, or soya chunks and stewed tofu – is absolutely delicious and very inexpensive. The natural juices are great, too. Otherwise, options in town include *Christiana*, located opposite the Syldian Court shopping centre and serving cheap, local fare. The main road has a smattering of inexpensive snack bars and patty shops; in the evenings, look out for Norman and his pushcart, selling boiled corn and vegetable soup from Thursday to Saturday. **Nightlife** is pretty much nonexistent (the main street is all but deserted after about 8pm), though the *Lamplight Club* in town opens most weekend, with a dancehall playlist.

Regular **minibuses** run up Shooter's Hill from Mandeville and head straight into town – ask them to drop you off if you're heading for *Hotel Villa Bella*. If you're driving, the hotel is signposted on your right just before you enter town; bear left and keep straight on for the town itself.

May Pen and around

Heading east from Mandeville, the A2 road runs out of the parish of Manchester through **Porus** – a lengthy village easily identified by its displays of citrus fruit strung up by the roadside (though the planned Kingston–Montego Bay highway bypasses this colourful place) and into **Clarendon**, one of Jamaica's least enthralling parishes. A right turn at Toll Gate takes you down to Milk River Bath on the south coast (see p.348), while continuing straight ahead brings you to the parish capital of **MAY PEN**, a light industrial centre and an important market town with a population of over forty thousand. The highway actually bypasses the town, which is handy as there is no reason at all to stop there unless your bus is breaking its journey. However, if you're here during the **Denbigh Agricultural Show**, a three-day fair held in the Denbigh showgrounds just west of town – normally over the last weekend in July or the first weekend in August – then it's certainly worth stopping off. The event features displays of agricultural produce from each of the country's parishes, exhibits of prize livestock and a showjumping event. There's also plenty of live entertainment, including singers, dancers and reggae bands, and the usual array of food vendors and craft stalls. If you're planning to stay over, try to arrange a room well in advance.

The best place to **stay** in town is the *Hotel Versalles*, just off the highway at 42 Longbridge Ave (℡986 6384, ⓦwww.hotelversallesjamaica.com; ❸–❹). If you're driving, take the right-hand exit towards May Pen at the main roundabout; there's a small signpost for the hotel about 400 yards down on your left.

The **restaurant** at *Versalles* serves reasonable food, but there's an excellent café and ice cream parlour, *La Maria*, in the Crown Eagle Centre on Brooks Avenue. The café is also the centre for the Clarendon Countrystyle Tourism Association and offers all kind of local information. You'll find a number of **patty shops** around the clock tower in the market square (where most of the buses originate and terminate).

Halse Hall

The great house at **Halse Hall**, due south of May Pen, is certainly worth a visit. However, the house is no longer officially open to the public, and tours have to be arranged through its present owners, bauxite company Jamalco (℡986 2561). The basic structure was built in the late seventeenth century by Thomas Halse, an English soldier who was active in the war against the Spanish, although the present building mostly dates from the 1740s. The wealth of the erstwhile owners is evident from the interior design; the sturdy mahogany doors and window frames in the airy living room are particularly impressive. The front of the house (you drive up at the back) has commanding views over miles of plantations and, to the south, over the less attractive alumina works of Jamalco. Don't miss the tiny **cemetery** behind the house, which holds the tombs of Halse and some of his descendants.

Halse Hall is just off the A2 highway from May Pen. Take the exit south from the main roundabout towards the Jamalco alumina plant; the house is one mile down on your right. Several **buses** a day run past the house en route from May Pen to Lionel Town (see p.350).

Travel details

Buses and minibuses

It is impossible to predict accurately the frequency of buses and minibuses running the following routes – services are often chaotic and delays and cancellations frequent – so the figures given below are only rough estimates. However, on the most popular routes you should be able to count on getting a ride within an hour if you travel in the morning; things normally quieten down later in the day. On less popular routes, you're best off asking for probable departure times the day before you travel.

Black River to: Kingston (3 daily; 5hr); Mandeville (5 daily; 2hr 15min); May Pen (3 daily; 3hr 30min); Montego Bay (4 daily; 2hr 15min); Negril (2 daily; 2hr 20min); Santa Cruz (8 daily; 1hr); Treasure Beach (3 daily; 1hr 15min).
Christiana to: Kingston (3 daily; 3hr); Mandeville (8 daily; 30min).
Mandeville to: Christiana (8 daily; 30min); Kingston (6 daily; 2hr 45min); May Pen (6 daily; 1hr 15min).
May Pen to: Kingston (6 daily; 1hr 30min); Milk River (3 daily; 1hr); Spanish Town (8 daily; 1hr).

Contexts

Contexts

The historical framework

The first human inhabitants of Jamaica were the Tainos, an Amerindian people speaking the Arawak language, who arrived in Jamaica around 900 AD, making their way from present-day Venezuela and Guyana aboard dug-out canoes. They were a peaceful people with a primitive Stone Age culture – fishing and foraging for subsistence – and they lived in scattered settlements all over the island, settling around sites with a good water source. Estimates of Taino numbers at the time of Columbus's arrival in Jamaica are hugely varied, but it is possible that there were as many as a million. Although Tainos living in the small islands of the eastern Caribbean were under attack by the more war-like Caribs by the fifteenth century, there is no evidence of any Carib attacks on Jamaica.

The arrival of the Spanish

Christopher Columbus made his first expedition from Spain in search of a western sea route to Asia in 1492. During his second "voyage of discovery", he landed at Rio Bueno on Jamaica's north coast, on May 6, 1494. The Tainos had learned of the violence of Columbus's men from their neighbours in Hispaniola (today's Haiti and Dominican Republic) and there was a brief skirmish, easily won by the Spanish with their armour, dogs and superior weaponry. Columbus had little interest in the island (which he named Santiago) but claimed it for Spain and moved on in search of China. During his fourth and last voyage in 1503, Columbus made an unfortunate return to Jamaica, his ships running aground on the coral reefs at St Ann's Bay. The explorers were marooned on the island for a year before a rescue ship could be summoned from Hispaniola. It carried them back to Spain, where Columbus died two years later.

Spanish settlement of Jamaica began in 1510, when a group of settlers from Hispaniola, headed by Governor Juan de Esquivel, set up a base at Sevilla Nueva on the north coast. The initial plan was to look for gold, but other than the few trinkets the Tainos had collected in trade with other islands, there was none to be found. Nor was Sevilla Nueva a good site; surrounded by swampy land, the tiny Spanish population soon found its numbers threatened by fever. In 1534, King Charles I permitted a transfer of the capital, and the Spanish decamped to a better location near the south coast; Villa de la Vega, known today as **Spanish Town**, was to remain the island's capital until 1874.

Despite the successful settlement of Spanish Town, and the agricultural bounty that the country offered, Jamaica remained a backward colony until well into the seventeenth century. Early colonists established farms across the country – introducing cattle, horses and various food crops such as bananas and sugar cane – but mostly the island served as a stopping-off point between the mother country and the richer colonies of the Spanish Main. Ships stopped for cleaning and repairs, and supplies of maize, cassava, pork and beef were taken on. Despite the low level of activity on the island, though, the Spanish soon managed to obliterate any traces of the native population. The Tainos fell victim to European diseases in their thousands and suffered severely, too, from the legendary cruelty of the Spanish, who subjected them to the *encomienda* system of slavery. By the time of the British conquest of Jamaica in 1655, the entire Taino population had been wiped out.

Because of the inability of the Tainos to provide the Spanish with the labour force they required, the importing of **slaves** from Africa began within a decade of the Spanish settlement of Jamaica. This was not a novel practice – slavery from Africa had been going on for centuries – but the new gold and silver mines of South America required a mass labour force, and the trickle of slaves slowly became a flood. Again, most of the traffic bypassed Jamaica, but there was a steady growth of slavery on the island and there is evidence from this period of the first runaway slaves, who gradually developed settlements of their own and were to prove a constant thorn in the side of the British after 1655 (see box on p.374–375).

The British conquest

Spanish Jamaica was not a well-protected colony. In 1596, Sir Anthony Shirley, an English adventurer, landed with five hundred men at Passage Fort near present-day Kingston and completely **sacked** Spanish Town. In 1643, the same thing was done by a small force led by a Captain William Jackson. Spain provided little or no assistance in defending the place, and gave scant impression of caring for its colonists.

In 1654, Britain's "Lord Protector" Oliver Cromwell, distrustful of sections of his armed forces whom he suspected of plotting the restoration of the monarchy, decided to send them against Spain's American possessions, far away from home. The British were well aware of the immense Spanish wealth in the area; for over a century, British pirates and buccaneers like Francis Drake had been making a good living from looting Spanish ships and cities. Cromwell sent fifteen ships under the command of General Robert **Venables** and Admiral William **Penn**, the father of the founder of Pennsylvania. The ships were fitted out in British Barbados before launching an assault on the city of Santo Domingo, capital of Hispaniola.

The assault on Hispaniola was a catastrophe for Penn and Venables. The Spanish resistance was well thought-out and the British troops were incompetently managed, retreating to their ships having lost around a thousand men yet without having properly engaged the enemy. There was little will for fighting on, but the leaders knew that to return to Britain without anything to show for their trip would be fatal. Jamaica was known to be a modestly prosperous and poorly defended place, so they set sail for the island, landing at **Passage Fort** in May 1655.

After the previous sackings, there were few Spanish left to fight for Jamaica: Spanish Town was quickly overrun, but the Spanish settlers were able to withdraw to the north coast, where they held the British at bay for another five years. The Spanish king hadn't given up entirely: in 1657, an invasion force from nearby Cuba engaged the British, but were defeated in a battle at Los Chorreros, present-day Ocho Rios. In 1660, British governor Edward D'Oyley led a force that defeated the Spanish at the battle of **Rio Nuevo**, near Ocho Rios, and the last of the Spanish finally left for Cuba. In the process of leaving, the Spaniards freed and armed their slaves to continue the fight; these freed slaves proved an important boost for the growing band of **Maroons**.

Having anticipated further incursions, the Spanish had removed their valuable goods to the mountains before 1655, so there was little booty to show for the capture of the island. Penn and Venables returned to Britain and, despite the conquest, were promptly imprisoned in the Tower of London. Nevertheless, despite his disappointment over Santo Domingo, Cromwell soon came to appreciate the strategic importance of Jamaica and issued a proclamation encouraging emigrants, from Britain and from other colonies like Nevis, and offering land to settlers.

Port Royal and the buccaneers

Immediately after the British conquest, large tracts of Jamaica were divided up between the officers who had served with Penn and Venables, their legacy still very apparent today. Officer Thomas **Hope** was given a huge estate near present-day Kingston, while Thomas **Halse** and John **Colbeck** established properties at or near modern-day Halse Hall and Colbeck Castle. The first priority of these new British settlers, though, was defence, to ensure that they could keep their newly won colony. Recognizing the strategic position of what is now Kingston harbour, they began immediately to build **fortifications** on either side of it, particularly on **Port Royal**. Five separate forts were built on the uninhabited island, including the still-standing Fort Cromwell, renamed Fort Charles in 1660 when King Charles II was restored to the British throne.

In 1661, Edward D'Oyley became Jamaica's first non-military governor and, in 1664, the first **local assembly** was summoned. Sir Thomas Modyford became governor and encouraged local **buccaneers** to make Port Royal their base for attacks on Spanish dominions. These buccaneers had started out as a ragged collection of outlaws from their European homes, living on the island of Tortuga near present-day Haiti. By the mid-seventeenth century, they had evolved into a disparate but skilled collection of pirates, attacking ships around the region. The British saw a way of using these buccaneers to their advantage. By giving them official sanction as **privateers** and letting them use Port Royal as a base, they would provide some defence for the young colony; equally important, they would harass the Spanish enemy, attacking their treasure ships, and would be obliged to deliver ten percent of their haul to the British authorities in Jamaica.

Port Royal became a boom town. The security provided by the forts and the wealth provided by the privateers encouraged traders to set up, exporting sugar and spices and importing slaves and supplies for the growing population. Although Spanish Town remained the capital city, government figures set up home on the island alongside the merchants, and Port Royal became one of the wealthiest places in the world, with rents rivalling London's classiest districts. However, its ascendancy was to be short-lived; a devastating **earthquake** in 1692 plunged most of Port Royal into the sea, and sent its residents fleeing for a new home across the harbour in modern-day Kingston.

By the 1670 **Treaty of Madrid**, the Spanish recognized British rule in Jamaica, and the brief era of the privateers was over, though there was to be one last fling. Henry Morgan, most famous of the privateers, launched an attack on the Spanish colony of Panama, sailing from Bluefields Bay on Jamaica's southwest coast. Though he claimed that he was unaware of the peace treaty, Morgan and Governor Modyford were recalled to Britain. Modyford was sacked to appease the Spanish, while Morgan, having insinuated his way into royal favour, was made lieutenant-governor in Modyford's stead, returning to Jamaica with a new brief – to stamp out piracy by persuading his former colleagues to turn to a life of peace.

Naturally enough, many of the privateers, now officially termed "**pirates**" to mark their loss of favour, refused to give up their thrilling and financially rewarding lifestyles and continued to torment shipping in the Caribbean throughout the eighteenth century. But their heyday was past, and a succession of high-profile successes by the authorities – particularly the capture in 1720 of Calico Jack Rackham, with his female aides Anne Bonney and Mary Read – inexorably turned the screw on the remaining bandits.

Sugar and development of the Jamaican economy

After the British had taken possession of Jamaica, and particularly after peace was made with the Spanish in 1670, settlers were encouraged to come out from the mother country with the offer of land grants and other financial incentives. Slowly, the island began to embark on the massive transformation from tiny colony towards its present shape, and the key factor in that change was **sugar**. Though first imported and grown by the Spanish, cultivation of sugarcane was to become a major phenomenon only under British rule, turning its West Indian colonies into much-prized possessions.

At first, there was little enthusiasm for sugar. **Tobacco** was the crop of choice, but the Jamaican harvest was unable to compete with the produce of Virginia. However, the settlers quickly realized the potential of sugar, which flourished in Jamaica's tropical conditions, and as the taste for the stuff boomed in Europe, the cultivation of sugarcane grew in leaps and bounds. The number of sugar estates in Jamaica expanded eight-fold between 1673 and 1740, and during the course of the eighteenth century, the island became the **biggest producer** of sugar in the world.

As Jamaica developed, more and more settlers were tempted out from the mother country, although most of the estate-owners, known as **planters**, were absentee landowners who spent most of their time in Britain and delegated control of their estates to overseers. The planters amassed extraordinary fortunes from their Jamaican possessions and, as their wealth increased, it brought with it significant political power and influence in London. In turn, this new-found influence was used to nourish and protect the sugar trade, with huge duties levied on sugar imported from elsewhere and the price of Jamaican sugar kept artificially high. Given the lavish lifestyle led by the planters in Britain, practically none of the profits of sugar were ploughed back into the colony, although every plantation had its **great house** – the elegant mansions that often survive today (despite the fact that they were normally the first target during any slave revolt).

Slavery

The success of the sugar industry, and the wealth of the planters, was, of course, predicated upon the appalling inhumanity of **slavery**. Like sugar, slaves had been in Jamaica during the Spanish rule, but on a tiny scale. Under the British, the development of the sugar estates called for a mammoth workforce and, with no indigenous labour available, the planters embarked upon the importation of slaves from Africa in earnest.

The **slave trade** was dominated by British merchants. Their ships sailed first to the west coast of Africa – from where most of the slaves were taken – carrying trinkets and other goods to barter for the human cargo. From Africa, the ships were loaded with slaves, and sailed direct to Kingston, the most important transshipment point in the region, where the "chattel" (slaves were not considered worth referring to as human beings) strong enough to have survived the **Middle Passage** were unloaded into warehouses and sold at auction. From there, the ships would return to Britain, now laden with the Jamaican products of sugar, rum and spices. It's estimated that between **twelve and fifteen million** people were transported from Africa as slaves, and this triangular traffic brought great wealth to the traders, reflected among other things in the development of the major port cities of Bristol and Liverpool. Little attention was paid, though, to the plight of the West Africans, drawn principally from the tribes of the Coromantee, the Fula, the Ashante, the Ibo and the Mandingo. In the early days of slavery, many of these Africans were already prisoners before they were shipped, bought from local **chieftains** who had captured them in war.

As the needs of the colonies expanded, **raiding parties** were sent into the African interior to hunt for more victims, who were then marched across the continent to stockades on the coast. From there, the journey to Jamaica could take between six and twelve weeks, with the slaves kept in chains in the hold of the ship, packed into galleries one above the other, and jammed into spaces so small that they couldn't stand or lie at full length. With no sanitation facilities and barely any food, huge numbers died of disease or malnutrition; many others committed suicide if the chance arose, sometimes leaping from the ship rather than continue in captivity.

Despite the high rate of loss, it continued to be profitable for the slavers to ply their trade, and every year, several thousand slaves survived to become labourers on the estates or, on a smaller scale, domestic workers in the home. Unsurprisingly, many of the transported slaves – uprooted from home and family and prohibited from using their own language – found the prospect of life on the plantations impossible, and there was continual **conflict** between slaves and slave owners. Discipline, accordingly, was brutal, with severe punishment for any wrongdoer – torture, followed by a slow, painful death, was commonly imposed as a deterrent to others.

Though the **living conditions** of the slaves varied a little from estate to estate, it's clear that they were all utterly squalid, with little living space or privacy. Slaves were at the whim of cruel overseers, few of whom would ever be taken to task, however badly they treated those in their charge. As time went by, however, conditions slowly improved, albeit very marginally. **Religion** played a part in this – once converted, slaves were usually given Sundays off to attend church, and church leaders encouraged slave owners to treat slaves as human beings for the first time. When food supplies to the island were disrupted in the 1770s during the American War of Independence, for example, slaves were often given the opportunity to cultivate and market their own foodstuffs. Yet this was hardly an altruistic gesture – malnourished slaves did less work, so it was in every planter's interest to keep his lifeblood alive at the least possible cost to himself. For every slave owner who made some small effort to ensure the physical well-being of his slaves, there were ten more who cared little or nothing for their well-being – if a few slaves died, it was easier and cheaper to simply buy some more.

Hence life on the plantations remained unimaginably horrible for all but the slave owner and his family.

Rebellion

Given the grim living conditions on the estates, it's hardly surprising that **slave revolts** were a feature of Jamaican life from the time of the British conquest right up until emancipation in 1838, always dreaded by the authorities and invariably crushed with appalling brutality. Insurrection was commonly punished by the dissenter being slung up from the waist in the sun for four days, before being taken down to have the soles of the feet and the armpits seared, the heart and entrails removed and burned in front of the still-living victim, and then to be quartered, with the body parts displayed as a warning to others considering rebellion. Despite such grisly punishments, slave rebellions in Jamaica – occurring, on average, every five years during the eighteenth century – were both more numerous and on a

The Maroons

The Spanish armed and freed most of their slaves when they finally quit the island in 1660; these Africans joined comrades who had escaped from Spanish owners previously, and formed a band known as the *cimarrones*, a Spanish word meaning "wild" or "untamed" that the British corrupted to **Maroons**. The Maroons lived in small communities in inaccessible parts of Jamaica's mountains and forests – particularly in the Blue and John Crow mountains in the east and Cockpit Country in the west – and, after the British arrival, found their numbers gradually swollen by new runaway slaves, particularly after slave rebellions such as the Clarendon revolt of 1690.

Most of the original Maroons were of **Coromantee** descent, from the region of modern-day Ghana, and, despite the upheaval of slavery, their shared language and traditions helped them to organize strong communities in their new environment. As their numbers grew, they periodically plundered British settlements for arms, animals and supplies, and they proved an effective deterrent to colonists who were considering settling in inhospitable areas like Portland.

Although British soldiers made regular forays against them, the Maroons had become such a serious threat by the 1720s that it was decided to take conclusive action against them. Forts and barracks were built at the edges of their territories, and the British military might was turned towards wiping out this troublesome fifth column. Special troops were brought in, including a large party of Mosquito Indian trackers from Nicaragua, but, in extremely difficult and confusing terrain, they were often outmanoeuvred by the skilled **guerrilla tactics** of the Maroons. In places that now carry evocative names like "The District of Look Behind", whole parties of British soldiers were slaughtered, though one was normally left alive to carry the message of comprehensive defeat back to the authorities.

By 1739, though, the superior firepower of the British had gained the upper hand, although it was apparent to them that winning a war against this "invisible enemy" would be costly and drawn-out. Accordingly, the First Maroon War was ended by a **peace treaty**, signed in the Maroon stronghold of Accompong by British commanding officer Colonel Guthrie and **Cudjoe**, the Maroon chief. The terms were that the Trelawny Maroons should stop attacking British settlements, return all future runaway slaves and provide assistance in the event of internal rebellion or foreign inva-

larger scale than in the United States or elsewhere in the British West Indies.

There were a number of reasons for this. First, there was an unusually **high ratio of slaves to whites** and, particularly during the seventeenth and eighteenth centuries, a relatively high ratio of African slaves to creole slaves (those born on the island and generally considered less rebellious). The island's mountainous geography encouraged rebels by providing places to which they could escape and hide, and the high level of absentee slave owners probably also encouraged revolts either through the cruelty of those left in charge or, conversely, because of a lack of attention to the risks of rebellion. In addition, though not exclusive to Jamaica, **social and religious ideas** fomented disorder, particularly at the turn of the nineteenth century, as abolitionists argued the case against slavery and missionaries challenged the religious orthodoxy about keeping black people in their "place". Finally, Toussaint L'Ouverture's revolution in **Haiti** in 1799, which threw out the French colonialists and created the first independent black republic in the world, provided slaves with a concrete example of a successful revolt.

The first major slave rebellion faced by the British came in 1673, when

sion. In return, they were granted freedom, fifteen hundred acres of land in Cockpit Country (around present-day Accompong), and a remarkable degree of autonomy, including the administration of justice in all cases except for those involving the death penalty. One year later, the Windward Maroons – those encamped in the Blue Mountains – signed a similar deal with the British.

For two generations the peace held, and the Maroons lived as a semi-sovereign state within Jamaica. Both sides kept to the agreement, most notably in 1760 when a major **slave rebellion** broke out in St Mary, led by a runaway slave named **Tacky** (see p.376). Tacky and his followers took to the mountains, anticipating support from the Maroons, only to find that the poacher had turned gamekeeper, helping the British to suppress the uprising. However, in 1795, the public flogging of two Maroons in Montego Bay outraged the Maroon community in Trelawny, and with temperatures raised and neither side prepared to compromise, hostilities quickly flared again. Plantations were burned and planters killed, and the British army rushed to quell this internal conflict. For a while, the **Second Maroon War** followed the path of the First, with soldiers ambushed as they ventured into unfamiliar territory, and the Maroons inflicting heavy losses.

However, the British were better organized this time and had at their disposal both enormous hunting dogs – imported from Cuba and quite terrifying to the Maroons – and warriors and trackers from Jamaica's other Maroon settlements. A generous peace offer was made by British General Walpole and the Maroons surrendered their arms, although not until several days after the terms of the peace offer had lapsed. Using this pretext, the British revoked the promise that the Maroons should be allowed to stay on their land, and five hundred of the Trelawny Maroons were **deported** to the freezing cold of Nova Scotia, although not before General Walpole had resigned in disgust at the authorities' duplicity. The deported Maroons stayed in Nova Scotia for just a year, setting sail for Sierra Leone from where, generations earlier, many of their ancestors had been brought to Jamaica as slaves.

Most of the Maroon communities in Portland and at Accompong in Cockpit Country remained relatively undisturbed by the ructions of the Second Maroon War and, protected by the 1739 peace treaty, continued to maintain a semi-independent status within the island that persists to this day.

around three hundred Coromantee slaves from present-day Ghana, working at a large plantation in St Ann, murdered their owner and fled inland, massively swelling the ranks of the Maroons. Their success encouraged further revolts, and in 1690, five hundred slaves from the same part of Africa instigated a rebellion in Clarendon, though most were either killed or captured.

Tacky's rebellion in 1760 (see p.375), again with Coromantee slaves at its heart, was the major slave revolt of the eighteenth century, occurring during Britain's Seven Years War against France and Spain and lasting for five months. For the first time, a rebellion spread islandwide; sixty whites were killed, more than a thousand slaves were either killed or transported from the island, and there was colossal damage to property across Jamaica. After the rebellion was crushed, the British authorities continued to fortify the island, bolstering the armed forces and encouraging firmer dealings with the slaves.

For a while, perhaps in reaction to the savageness of the British response to the Tacky rebellion, the level of revolts died down, but in 1831, the **Christmas rebellion** was to prove the most serious slave uprising in the island's history. Though it lasted for just ten days, as many as 20,000 slaves were involved. By now, Jamaica's slaves were aware of moves towards abolition in Britain and of the fierce hostility to such a move felt by the island's planters. There were strong rumours that slavery had actually been abolished, and that no one in Jamaica was going to tell the slaves.

Sam Sharpe, the rebellion's leader, was a slave in Montego Bay, reasonably educated and a leader in the Native Baptist church. Through the church, he organized a campaign of passive resistance, designed to coerce the slave owners into declaring the end of slavery, but this had little chance of success and quickly erupted into a full-blown revolt throughout the island's western parishes. Though Sharpe and another five hundred slaves were either killed or executed, the seriousness of the rebellion and the brutality with which it was crushed intensified the abolition debate, both in Jamaica and in Britain, and accelerated the emancipation that Sharpe had been seeking.

Foreign affairs 1670–1800

The threat of slave rebellions, and the two wars with the Maroons, were not the only problems faced by the Jamaican authorities during the eighteenth century. Although Spain had recognized British control of the island in 1670, the risk of **foreign invasion** was far from removed. In 1694, Ducasse, the French governor of nearby San Domingo (present-day Haiti), launched an invasion of Jamaica; troops landed in St Thomas in the southeast and did tremendous damage to sugar estates across the country before they were repulsed at the battle of Amity Hall. Regular skirmishes with the French followed, with British Admiral Benbow killed during another defeat of Ducasse in 1702.

The frenzy of **fort building** with which the British began their occupation of Jamaica was continued, with military establishments being put up around the coast, as well as in parts of the interior where regiments were being maintained to contain the threat of the Maroons. All of Britain's great naval commanders served time on the island, normally based at Port Royal, and the presence of such force undoubtedly contributed to the fact that there was not to be another foreign invasion.

In 1775, the **American War of Independence** had a profound effect on Jamaica. The Jamaican assembly sympathized with the thirteen colonies when they made their declaration of independence, but the British refused to concede and blockaded the eastern coast of North America, depriving the island of its ability to trade with the Americans. The resulting food shortage was dramatic – around fifteen thousand slaves are believed to have died of starvation – and prompted significant change on the island. Estate owners began to encourage slaves to grow food on small allotments, while the introduction of the **breadfruit** from Tahiti in 1793 helped the island take a big step towards self-sufficiency in terms of food production.

The French were not slow to take advantage of Britain's war with its former colony in North America, and a series of invasions of her West Indian possessions left Britain holding just Jamaica, Barbados and Antigua. In Jamaica itself, invasion seemed inevitable, but a crucial sea battle off the Windward Islands in 1782 – the Battle of **Les Saintes** – saw the destruction of the French Navy by British forces under Admiral Rodney, and removed the threat of attack from the island for several generations.

Jamaican politics 1700–1834

From the early days of British occupation of Jamaica, the chief authority on the island was the **governor**, appointed from Britain. An assembly of estate owners was convened in 1661 to advise the governor on local matters, but control of key issues was kept in the hands of the British Crown. However, it wasn't long before conflicts arose between the interests of the early settlers and those of the mother country, coming to a head towards the end of the century in discussions over the abolition of slavery. As creole society developed, and a new generation grew up who had actually been born in Jamaica, there were increasing demands for political power to be kept entirely on the island. Accordingly, in 1729 the British Crown recognized the **local assembly** as the source of all legislation on Jamaican matters.

Throughout the eighteenth century, power remained in the hands of the white planter class, with the right to vote given only to property owners. Gradually, given the sexual proclivities of the planters, a "mulatto" or **mixed race class** emerged who looked to their white fathers for an education and opportunities that were denied to people of pure African origin. Although this mulatto class were not officially granted equal rights until 1832, many of its members exercised considerable political influence and were to prove far more sympathetic to the black cause that anyone from the planter class had previously been.

By the end of the eighteenth century, the present-day **racial composition** of Jamaica was already pretty much in place, with the black population outnumbering the whites by more than ten to one. Though political power rested with the whites, forces inside and outside Jamaica were soon to bring about a sea change in the fortunes of the different racial groups.

The abolition of slavery

In 1807 the British parliament prohibited its colonies from trading in slaves, but the **abolition of slavery** itself – heavily opposed by the West Indian lobby, who feared the collapse of the local economy – was not finally passed until 1834. Despite the islandwide jubilation, though, the slaves were not yet given unconditional freedom; they were expected to continue working for their former masters, unpaid, for a six-year "apprenticeship". In 1838 the apprenticeship system was abandoned and the former slaves were, at last, free to demand wages or work elsewhere.

Many former slaves left the hated estates at the first opportunity, renting or squatting on a little landholding and establishing small farms. Across the country, missionaries set up "**free villages**", buying land, subdividing it and either selling or donating it to former slaves, who would also normally help with building the local church and school that the villages were based around.

The drain of workers from the estates, and the reluctance of many estate owners to pay proper wages, forced them to turn to alternative sources of cheap labour. Already, during the 1830s, 1200 Germans had been brought to Jamaica, with the promise of land grants once they had worked on the estates for five years. Other workers were brought from China, the Middle East and other parts of Europe, but it was India that was to provide the great majority of the new **indentured labour**.

Under a scheme approved by the Jamaican assembly in 1845, 35,000 **Indians** were brought to the island before the Indian government banned further traffic in 1917. The estate owners promised that, once the workers had paid off the cost of their passage from India, they would be able to earn decent money to send home, before returning themselves at the end of their contracts. In practice, the Indians became the new slaves – working for scant pay under appalling conditions – and the majority never had the chance to return home.

Jamaica's sugar industry took another major blow in 1846, when a **free-trade** minded British government passed the Sugar Duties Act, forcing Jamaica's producers to compete on equal terms with sugar producers worldwide. At the same time, the development of **beet sugar** in Europe also hurt the industry, contributing to the drop in the price of sugar and reducing demand for the West Indian product.

Although the sugar industry was far from dead, this series of setbacks forced the island to diversify and move beyond its reliance on a single crop. A Royal Commission report recommended the encouragement of peasant proprietors and the substitution of other tropical products – such as coffee, coconuts and citrus fruits – for sugarcane. **Banana** cultivation was introduced in the 1860s and, for a while, became the boom crop as demand for the new fruit soared in Europe and America. By the end of the nineteenth century, the older economic pattern of the Jamaican community had faded completely and a new organization was emerging. Only the scattered ruins of the plantation great houses and sugar mills – still found in even the remotest districts – now speak of the once great days of sugar.

Post-emancipation problems

Jamaica's estate-owners were given a total of £**20 million compensation** for the loss of their slaves (most of which went to repay debts owed to merchants in Britain). There was no such compensation for the newly freed slaves. Life for them was far from easy and, in the mid-nineteenth century, there were two issues which caused black Jamaicans particular concern.

The first problem was **land**. Unless they could get somewhere to farm, black

Jamaicans had little choice but to return to the plantations and work as poorly paid wage labourers; getting their own plot of land guaranteed a degree of independence and gave them a bargaining tool for higher wages. Unfortunately for black Jamaicans, the planters were equally aware of this issue and made it as hard as possible for the ex-slaves to get land, imposing high rents and taking action against squatters who tried to take possession of unused land. The second, related, issue was the one-sided **administration of justice**; the landowners generally dominated the magistrates' courts and imposed heavy-handed penalties for squatting and other minor wrongs.

The downturn in the country's economy that followed the abolition of slavery and the introduction of free trade in sugar also took its toll on the freed slaves. Wages were kept pitifully low, taxes were imposed and unemployment rose as plantations were downsized or abandoned altogether. There were numerous **riots** and conspiracies, particularly in the early years of emancipation as rumours of re-enslavement were given strong currency, and there was even talk – fuelled by dissatisfied planters – of the island being annexed to the United States as a slave state. The last straw came during the American Civil War of 1861–65, when naval blockades cut off crucial supplies to Jamaica, causing food shortages and intensifying the economic problems of the poor.

The grievances of Jamaica's black population came to a head in 1865, when a major **rebellion** broke out in **Morant Bay** in St Thomas. Problems here were particularly acute and were compounded by the authorities, who removed a magistrate seen as too impartial and also removed from the parish council **George William Gordon**, a mixed-race businessman openly sympathetic to the cause of the poor black Jamaicans. On October 11, a band of rebels marched on the town, looting weapons from the police station, releasing prisoners from jail and attacking the courthouse, killing eighteen soldiers and council members.

The attack on the courthouse was swiftly followed up by minor rebellions on outlying plantations in the area, and, fearing that the rebellion would spread throughout the island, Governor Eyre ordered a show of strength from the armed forces. Little mercy was shown as 437 people were killed and executed, including the rebellion leader, **Paul Bogle**. The government also took advantage of the situation to execute leading political dissidents such as Gordon. Thousands more people were flogged and terrorized, and the brutal suppression caused horror throughout Jamaica and Britain. For more on Paul Bogle and the rebellion, see p.150.

After Morant Bay

Although the Morant Bay rebellion did not spread outside St Thomas, and there was no evidence of an islandwide conspiracy, it provoked considerable change in the colony. After the rebellion, Governor Eyre was ordered back to Britain and dismissed for his part in the atrocities. His assembly abolished itself, and in 1866, Jamaica became a **Crown Colony**, with direct rule from Britain. This meant that, rather than having elected representatives, the governor appointed members of a legislative council who were responsible for policy on the island. Although this set back the cause of responsible government on the island for almost a century, it enabled certain reforms to be passed that would never have got past the planters and their representatives in the assembly.

Governor Grant, who replaced Eyre, brought in important measures that helped to give Jamaican society a more modern shape. New courts were established, a new police force created and the Church of England was disestablished on the island. Roads and irrigation systems were improved, more money was spent on education, and in 1872, the capital city was transferred from Spanish Town to **Kingston**. This move was long overdue; most of Jamaica's trade – from slaves to rum – had been processed through Kingston's harbour for two centuries, bringing colossal wealth in its wake, and by any criteria the city was the right place for the seat of government.

There were downsides to the changes, of course. Taxes were raised to finance the reforms, and the unrepresentative political system frustrated the island's fledgling democratic movement for nearly eighty years. There was scathing criticism of the government by landowners for financial extravagance and inefficiency, while black leaders bemoaned the lack of any radical change and the continuities with the old system of government. On the whole, though, the new system kept the peace while preserving the status quo; the whites retained all political and social authority, while the blacks were sufficiently mollified that there was little threat of upheaval for the rest of the century.

Away from politics, meanwhile, innovation in Britain's prized colony continued as the mother country continued to reap the rewards of its industrial revolution. In 1845 Spanish Town and Kingston had been joined by **railway** – the first outside Europe and North America – while, in 1891, the **Jamaica Exhibition** was held in Kingston and Spanish Town and drew a crowd of around 300,000 people. Also during the 1890s, early **tourists** were brought to Jamaica, many sailing from North America on the banana boats that plied between the US east coast and Port Antonio in Portland. Trends were being started that would prove of crucial significance in the coming century.

Jamaica in the twentieth century

The early twentieth century saw considerable **economic prosperity** in Jamaica, with particular booms in the banana and tourism industries. And the new wealth was no longer confined to the whites – **George Stiebel**, Jamaica's first black millionaire, used his fortune to design some fine buildings, particularly Devon House in Kingston, and his example proved an inspiration to others. Inevitably, though, most of the new wealth bypassed the black masses, and serious **poverty** remained throughout the island. People were increasingly drawn to the new capital city to look for work, but many were left stranded in slums on the city's western edge with little prospect of income or employment. **Natural disasters** also took their toll. In 1907, Kingston was partially flattened by a devastating earthquake, and there were major hurricanes throughout the 1910s.

By the 1930s, as the **Great Depression** took hold worldwide, the positive effects of the economic boom had pretty much evaporated. The banana crop had been decimated by disease, never to regain the exporting heights of the early century, while sugar exports fell precipitately as overseas demand dried up. In the face of the Depression, US immigration laws tightened up, and the blocking of this perennial pressure valve resulted in further problems, sending unemployment figures spiralling. Riots in Kingston and around the island were commonplace, and **strikes** erupted too, with a major clash in 1938 between police and workers at the West Indies Sugar Company factory in Frome leaving several people dead. Protests and looting followed islandwide.

In fact, 1938 was to prove a key year in the development of modern Jamaica. Partly as a result of the battle in Frome, strike leader **Alexander Bustamante** founded the first **trade union** in the Caribbean – the Bustamante Industrial Trade Union (BITU). An associated **political party** was born too, with the foundation of the People's National Party (PNP) by the lawyer **Norman Manley**. Both events gave a boost to Jamaican nationalism, already stirred by the campaigning of black consciousness leader **Marcus Garvey** during the 1920s and early 1930s, and increased the pressure for political reform and improvement in the condition of the workers.

World War II and after

As it did worldwide, **World War II** fuelled the pressure for change in Jamaica, dramatically weakening European countries and loosening their grip on their colonies. It was also a major catalyst for development in economic terms – Jamaica was an important Allied base during the war and Britain was obliged to increase financial aid to the island. Jamaica was also called on to provide increased supplies of food to the mother country, and as sugar and other food industries expanded again, the disruption of shipping supplies led to the creation of local servicing industries and small manufacturing businesses. This all continued after the war and was boosted by major tourism and bauxite, whose commercial export began in 1952. Islanders also contributed to the war effort more directly, with thousands of Jamaican men volunteering to fight for Britain.

On the political front, a **new constitution** in 1944 introduced universal adult suffrage and the same year saw the first elections for a government to work in conjunction with the British-appointed governor. In 1943, Bustamante had split from Manley's PNP to form the Jamaica Labour Party (JLP) and it was the JLP that won the elections, succeeding on a populist appeal for "Bread and Butter", rather than the PNP's more intellectual call for independence. The two parties gradually drifted in different ideological directions, with the JLP adopting a basic liberal capitalist philosophy, and Manley's PNP leaning more towards democratic socialism. The JLP won again in 1949, not ceding power to the PNP until the election of 1955.

Taking office in 1955, one of Norman Manley's first priorities was the issue of independence. Both he and the British government considered that it was impractical for the Caribbean islands to "go it alone", and the idea of a West Indian federation was floated. However, right from the start such a federation faced awesome challenges. First, **economic development** in Jamaica and in Trinidad and Tobago during the 1950s – fuelled by the exploitation of bauxite and oil respectively – convinced many in both countries that they were strong enough economically to stand on their own feet. Second, **public opinion** in the large islands was largely anti-federation, with traditional rivalries between islands coming to the fore and many Jamaicans suspicious that they would have to subsidise the others. Third, the progress of self-rule, albeit somewhat limited, in Jamaica created a class of local **politicians** who felt they could manage the island's affairs themselves and were reluctant to share power with others in the Caribbean.

Accordingly, though the **West Indies Federation** was launched in January 1958, with its capital in Port of Spain, Trinidad, it never really stood a chance. Jamaica refused to accept the principle of federalism, arguing that it must be allowed to protect its own economic interests, even where these clashed with the other islands. Following the threat of sanctions from the federal government, Bustamante declared his opposition to the union in 1960, and in a **referendum** called by Manley in September 1961, the Jamaicans voted categorically to leave, prompting the rapid disintegration of the federation. Disheartened though they were, the British had little choice but to accept the decision of the electorate. Within a year they had granted Jamaica its **independence**.

Independence

On August 6, 1962, Jamaica became an independent state within the British Commonwealth, with Bustamante as its first prime minister. The early years of independence were marked by rising prosperity, as foreign investment increased, particularly in the bauxite industry. **Hugh Shearer** succeeded Bustamante after his retirement in 1967 and the JLP continued in power until the key elections of 1972. By then, the difference between the two main parties had become marked, with the JLP espousing a US-friendly liberal economic programme and the PNP – now led by Norman Manley's charismatic son **Michael** – an avowedly **democratic socialist** party.

Michael Manley's victory in 1972 led to eight years of PNP rule, a period regarded by almost all Jamaicans as instrumental in fashioning the country of the late twentieth century. Until 1972, economic and political power had rested predominantly with white and mixed-race Jamaicans. Manley's slogans, such as "Power for the people", set out his desire to improve the conditions of the black majority; to accomplish this, however, he had to challenge the status quo.

The major reforms introduced by the PNP included a minimum wage, a literacy campaign, the distribution of land to small farmers, more public housing, and an improvement in funding for the island's education and healthcare sectors. To finance these "**people's projects**", Manley turned to businesses that had been largely protected from taxation, in particular the internationally owned bauxite industry. Increased levies on the industry proved counterproductive, though, as bauxite companies promptly scaled down their Jamaican operations, reducing the country's foreign exchange earnings. This blow was quickly followed by the effects of the 1973–74 oil crisis, which led to a tripling in the cost of the island's imported oil and further increased pressure on government spending. In the light of this, Manley sought to promote a greater degree of **self-sufficiency**, encouraging the use of Jamaican, rather than imported, products.

In **foreign affairs**, too, Manley followed a different line to his predecessors. Rejecting close ties with the United States, the prime minister turned to the nonaligned movement, calling for increased aid and better terms of trade for developing countries, and forged particularly close ties with Fidel Castro's Cuba. Needless to say, the American reaction was furious; economic sanctions were applied and it became increasingly difficult for the island to attract foreign investment. Manley's problems were compounded by the **exodus** of wealthy white Jamaicans, withdrawing their capital and skills from the island at the time that they were most needed. Most left because they feared higher taxation and even the introduction of communism, but the rhetoric of Manley and his supporters didn't help – they gave broad hints to anyone dissatisfied with his regime that there were plenty of flights leaving the island every day, and if they didn't like it, they should get on one.

During the Manley years, politics in Jamaica became as polarized as they had been since self-rule was reintroduced in 1944. The opposition JLP, led now by **Edward Seaga**, launched blistering attacks on the "communist" administration, and the 1976 election – won by the PNP again – saw a disturbing increase in **political violence**. This was particularly true in the ghetto constituencies of Kingston, which the political parties had turned into "garrisons" – distributing guns to their supporters and encouraging them to recruit voters and drive opponents away through intimidation. Despite criticism from human rights groups, Manley's response to the violence was to impose a **state of emergency**. The government established a non-jury "Gun Court" and passed severe anti-crime legislation providing, for example, a life sentence for anyone convicted of unlawful possession of a firearm.

During the PNP's **second term**, the lack of capital to finance his projects sounded the death knell for Manley's brand of democratic socialism. Foreign investment had fallen precipitately, local capital had been withdrawn from the island, and despite the empty shelves in the supermarkets, the cost of imports continued to outstrip exports. The government was forced to turn to the International Monetary Fund for assistance, and the resulting curtailment of public spending and the drastic cuts in social programmes alienated many erstwhile supporters. Violence flared again during the 1980 election campaign, with hundreds of people killed in shoot-outs and open gang warfare. Amid the carnage, the Jamaican people turned to the JLP for a new vision for their country.

The JLP in power

Immediately after Ronald Reagan won the 1980 US presidential election, Jamaica's new prime minister Edward Seaga was the first foreign leader to visit him in Washington, and the **realignment** of the two neighbouring countries was perhaps the most important change in policy that Seaga brought about. The US took steps to open its markets to foreign imports and to encourage outward investment, most notably with the enactment of the Caribbean Basin Initiative (economic aid in return for free elections and cooperative governments), and foreign capital began to find its way back to Jamaica. However, Seaga was obliged to continue the cutback of government services, begun under the PNP, and his honeymoon with the Jamaican people proved short-lived.

In 1983 Jamaican troops assisted the US **invasion of Grenada**, launched to depose the Marxist leaders who had overthrown and executed prime minister Maurice Bishop. Taking advantage of a brief surge in popularity (and the absence of opponent Manley from the island), the JLP called a snap election. In protest at government tactics, the PNP boycotted the election, leaving the JLP in sole control of Jamaica's parliament, and re-elected prime minister Seaga gave himself various portfolios in the resulting government, including minister for finance, defence and culture. However, although his skills as minister of finance were widely praised, Seaga was unable to give the island's economy the boost it required, and in the face of rising poverty and unemployment, his lack of charisma and the concentration of power in his hands led to a fall in support. In 1989, Michael Manley and the PNP were returned to office.

Despite widespread fears of a return to the politics of the 1970s, the new-look Manley administration proved very different. The emphasis now was on continuity of policy, and although foreign relations with Cuba were restored, there was no more anti-American and anti-white rhetoric. The demands of the

World Bank and the IMF continued to be met and a generally liberal economic policy followed. In 1992 Manley resigned the premiership on the grounds of ill-health, leaving his successor, **P.J. Patterson**, to continue the policy of continuity. In 1993 Patterson – the first black man to become Jamaica's prime minister – defeated Seaga and the JLP in the general election, and since then Seaga hasn't been able to recover his previous levels of support.

Jamaica today

The backbone of the modern Jamaican economy is provided by tourism, bauxite and agriculture. A colossal amount of money is spent on encouraging **tourism** and counteracting the negative images of the island that have been seen abroad in recent years, although arrival figures have been pretty stable for several years, at around a million and a half people per year. **Bauxite** production has recovered from the blow the industry took in the 1970s, although falls in prices worldwide have meant overall lower earnings.

Agriculture – particularly sugar and bananas – accounts for around twenty percent of export earnings. The potential of the sector remains vast, with great products and superb farming conditions, but the imagination required to expand and diversify output has been sorely lacking. A daunting problem that Jamaica faces, along with other West Indian islands, is the removal by the WTO of their privileged access to European markets, leaving small-scale and often inefficient Jamaican farms unable to compete with the giant US-owned and funded plantations in Latin America. Also on the agricultural side, **ganja** farming and export – illegal but very widespread – makes a major, if unofficial, contribution to the island's economy, despite the efforts of the US "War on Drugs".

Unfortunately, Jamaica's export earnings from these industries are quite unable to keep pace with the nation's spending habits. Jamaica carries a massive burden of **debt** to foreign banks – some J$617 billion at the time of writing – and much of the foreign currency earned is required to repay interest and capital on that debt; a staggering 65 percent of the total expenditure in the 2003 budget was allocated to service debt repayments. As a result there is little money available for urgently needed domestic programmes, such as education and health. Retrenchment, built on interest rates that average around fifty percent, has hit hard – officially, unemployment stands at around seventeen percent (though the real figure is probably significantly higher), and the glamour of the tourist resorts belies a lot of poverty in Kingston and rural areas.

The imbalance between earnings and spending has been compounded in the last decade by a staggering increase in foreign **imports**. The streets and shopping malls of the cities and towns are chock-full with flash cars and other foreign accessories, though there is no sign of any corresponding increase in export production to pay for it all. **Remittances** from Jamaicans working overseas help to reduce the earnings gap, but even this is creating problems – it is widely felt that "easy money" from relatives abroad is creating a class of idle youngsters, who refuse to countenance the prospect of hard work. To add further insult to injury, the Jamaican farming industry, which has struggled to remain viable in the harsh economic climate, now has to compete with produce imported from the US; go to any market in Jamaica, and you'll see American potatoes, cabbages and carrots on sale for significantly less than their locally grown equivalents – hardly an incentive for the hard-pushed consumer to buy Jamaican.

On the **political** scene, major ideological differences remain a thing of the past. In 1995, JLP veteran Bruce Golding left the party to set up a third political force, the **National Democratic Movement**, but there's little to indicate that the party has any new ideas on dealing with the country's problems. Golding defected back to the JLP just before the 2002 election, and other recently established parties have attracted so few voters that they're not seen as serious competition for the JLP and PNP. The political scene, then, continues to limp along. Having been re-elected in the 1997 poll, P.J. Patterson's PNP won a fourth consecutive victory in the 2002 elections, albeit with a reduced majority. Patterson cuts a rather insipid figure and draws little popular support from an electorate clearly disillusioned with the political process; less than fifty percent of the population turned out to vote in 2002.

Many of the important political issues in Jamaica today are familiar ones throughout the Caribbean, although given the size of the island relative to its smaller neighbours, they are often felt more extremely here than elsewhere. Given the island's unwelcome distinction of having one of the highest per-capita murder rates in the world – around 1000 per year – **crime** is the key issue in Jamaica today. The "garrison communities", first established by politicians in Kingston during the 1970s, have become safe havens for gangsters and drug barons no longer in need of political support. Convicted Jamaican criminals have been deported to their home country from North America and Britain, but as they have committed no local crime, they are free as soon as they arrive home. With their overseas contacts, these **deportees** (numbering around 1500 a year) have reinforced the gangs, turned the drug business into a billion-dollar industry and brought criminality to ever more sophisticated and brutal levels.

Facing an ever-increasing barrage of violent, organized crime, the Jamaican government has responded by creating a series of high-profile specialist divisions within the police force, from the Eradication Squad of the 1980s to the ACID initiative of the 1990s, each with a mission to target gangs, area "dons", extortion rackets and the importation of guns. The most recent division, the Crime Management Unit (**CMU**), headed by controversial Senior Superintendent **Reneto Adams**, was disbanded in June 2003 in the wake of several incidents in which Adams and his officers appear to have taken the law into their own hands. To the chagrin of human rights organizations, the CMU is charged with meting out "**vigilante justice**" to alleged offenders (for more on which, visit ®www.jamaicansforjustice.org or ®www.amnesty.org). The 2001 police killing of the "Braeton Seven" in St Catherine, and the May 2003 deaths of four people, including two women, at Kraal in Clarendon, have attracted wide condemnation and high-profile investigations and are just two of the incidences of so-called police executions that have taken place over recent years. Some 600 people have been killed by officers since 1999, many in disputed circumstances, but not one policeman or woman has been convicted of an extrajudicial killing since that year. Some argue that with crime at an all-time high, the actions of officers such as Adams are to be applauded. It's this atmosphere of fear that led P.J. Patterson, in June 2003, to ratify the establishment of a new **Caribbean Court of Justice** to replace Britain's Privy Council as the final court of appeal for prisoners on Jamaica's death row–and thus allow Jamaica to resume hangings, widely seen as the only real deterrent to criminality.

Despite the establishment, in early 2003, of a Corruption Prevention Commission to scrutinize ministers' conduct, **political corruption** remains another much-lamented problem, with the party in power seen to dispense favours to its supporters and believed to use every available ploy to get itself re-elected. In the face of this cynicism, and a general feeling that successive governments have done little to alleviate poor economic conditions, disillusionment with politics is growing and a selfish materialism and a dangerous fatalism have both taken over large sectors of society.

Despite these problems, there remains much to be positive about in Jamaica. Democracy is still firmly rooted and there is a vigorous **culture of debate**, most noticeable in the numerous talk shows that compete with reggae for radio airtime. Leading entrepreneurs – most notably **Chris Blackwell**, former head of Island Records, and **Gordon "Butch" Stewart**, owner of Air Jamaica and the Sandals hotel chain – have elected to stay in Jamaica and invest their considerable fortunes in the island's development; Stewart's purchase and overhaul of the once-decrepit Air Jamaica has been particularly inspiring. With cruise-ship arrivals in the winter 2002 season higher than ever before, and a new, leaner Jamaica Tourist Board going great guns in promoting the island's culture as well as its beaches, **tourism** is also on the upsurge. The government has also managed to improve Jamaica's notoriously poor roads via the construction of coastal highways – which were in various stages of completion at the time of writing – and has upgraded public transport in the capital and in Montego Bay with the introduction of government-run bus services. Nonetheless, those not in a position to experience the prosperity enjoyed in some sectors of the tourism industry and business community continue to find life in Jamaica extremely hard, and small-scale street protests are a regular feature of island life.

Away from politics, Jamaican culture remains vibrant, and the island continues to produce leading figures in **music** and **sport**, from Buju Banton to Sean Paul, a rising star in both the US and Jamaica, as well as the Reggae Boyz and cricketer Courtney Walsh, who remains the leading wicket-taker in the world since reaching the 500 mark before his retirement in early 2000. Whatever the challenges, it is hard to quench the island's spirit, and while many islanders predict that "things will get worse before they get better", Jamaica's future, on balance, seems bright.

The environment

Jamaica's four thousand-plus square miles make it the third-largest island in the Caribbean archipelago, after Cuba and Hispaniola. Unlike many of its neighbours, however, more than half of it stands over 1500ft above sea level, providing mist-shrouded peaks as well as brilliant white-sand beaches.

From parched savannah plains and dry limestone forest to low-lying rainforest and wetland swamps, with richly vegetated, undulating hills and lush pastures in between, Jamaica's landscape and topography vary immensely. Other than the metamorphic, sedimentary and igneous volcanic rocks of the Blue Mountains – Jamaica's oldest geological feature – most of the island's surface area is covered with soft, sedimentary **limestone**, at its thickest in central and western areas such as Cockpit Country (see pp.277–283), where rivers have carved out a labyrinthine network of conical hillocks surrounded by deep sinkholes and caves. Also abundantly present in Jamaica's earth is **bauxite** (see p.358), though the island's largest export mineral comes at a price: caustic red mud deposits, which are still inadequately disposed of in unlined pits and seep into the watersheds and poison rivers and lakes.

There are about 120 **rivers** in Jamaica, the longest being the 44-mile Black River in St Elizabeth. **Mineral springs** bubble up from the earth throughout the island, many within caves and a few hot, such as at Bath in St Thomas (see p.153).

Over half of the land area is given over to **agriculture**, with vast plantations cultivating coconuts, bananas, sugarcane, cocoa, coffee, citrus, rice and tobacco.

Natural disasters

Jamaica's geographical location and geological origins make the island highly susceptible to the elements, particularly during the rainy seasons, which run roughly from May to June and September to mid-October, when pre-hurricane tropical storms can cause islandwide flooding, landslides and road closures. After a few days of relentless sun and calm seas, these intense tropical storms can be exciting, but it's wise to avoid swimming or golfing during a violent electric storm.

Though the Caribbean is ranked third in the worldwide scale of annual **hurricane** occurrence, full-scale tempests are relatively rare in Jamaica. Twenty hurricanes hit between 1886 and 1991, the worst being Allen in 1980 and Gilbert in 1988 (see p.154). News bulletins carry regular updates on the position and force of storms in the region; the Office of Disaster Preparedness, 12 Camp Rd, Kingston 5 (℡972 9941 or 4101), issues guidelines for coping with a strike; and most hotels are well prepared during the season, which runs from June through November.

Jamaica is also prone to **earthquakes**; the most violent occurred in 1692, destroying Port Royal (see p.111), and in 1907, when much of Kingston was levelled. Most of the major faults are found in the east of the island – there have been over twenty earthquakes per century in Kingston and St Andrew, but only five in the western region. The last earthquake occurred in Kingston on January 13, 1993, a scale two quake that caused extensive damage.

The most pressing recent concern has been **flooding.** Torrential rains in late 2001 and 2002 caused extensive damage islandwide and put a huge strain on the island's finances; new bridges were built to replace those washed away in 2001, only to be obliterated again in 2002, while hundreds of families whose homes have been destroyed bemoan the lack of adequate government compensation.

However, farming has had a negative effect upon the island's environment; unstable mountain slopes are cleared for cultivation, resulting in landslides and soil erosion, while use – and misuse – of pesticides and fertilizers has led to loss of productivity. Slash-and-burn farming methods destroy acres of forest and animal habitats annually. The Jamaican gardener's adage – "whatever you throw, it grow" – is borne out in the island's abundance of trees and plants; of the **3003** varieties of flowering plant, some 28 percent are endemic, and many have been introduced by successive colonists. Jamaica has always been an island, so all of its fauna and flora have evolved from ancestors that crossed a marine barrier. There may be relatively few indigenous species, but as Jamaica boasts many variations found only on the island, it's an important centre of **endemism**.

Aside from its creepy crawlies and bats, Jamaica's animal life is pretty poor in comparison to its flora, and there are few large mammals. **Camels** made a brief and embarrassing appearance in the eighteenth century, transported by planters to carry sugar and rum on the estates, but their preference for smooth ground and sand dunes made them unsuited to Jamaica's uneven and precipitous terrain. They spooked other livestock and had more or less died out by the late nineteenth century, when historian Edward Long described them as "the most useless animals on the island".

Trees and shrubs

Though only five percent of Jamaica's natural woodlands remain, the island's tropical fertility ensures a richly variegated landscape. Trees are often planted for their shade-giving properties; the **guango**, with its symmetrical spreading branches, is popular, but the most arresting and majestic is the towering **silk cotton**, which often reaches more than 130ft in height, its buttressed roots spreading elegantly to meet the ground. Regarded as sacred in Ashante folklore, the silk cotton is surrounded by superstition; the silver roots are said to hide duppies, and the trees are associated with Myalist ceremonies. Naturally buoyant and easily carved, silk cotton trees were hollowed out into dug-out canoes by Tainos, and the fruits contain the cotton-like kapok. **Logwood** is extremely common and was once grown commercially for the dark-blue dye extracted from the trunk and roots. In 1893 it surpassed cane and coffee as the island's main export, but synthetic alternatives subsequently ended the trade. Bees flock to the perfumed yellow blossoms, and logwood honey is said to be the best available. The **annotto** was also exploited for the intense orange-red dye extracted from seed pods growing in clusters around its attractive pink flowers. Tainos used it as their principal body paint and it was a prime commodity during Spanish occupation, though it's extremely rare today.

You'll encounter the marbled, blue-tinted wood of the **mahoe**, the national tree, in countless craft items. Fast-growing and indigenous, the mahoe has a short straight trunk that grows up to 65ft, broad leaves and distinctive hibiscus-like flowers that change from yellow to orange and deep crimson as they mature. The rich red wood of Jamaican **mahogany** is regarded as the best in the world and has been so heavily exported that few trees are left – the custom of stripping the bark from young trees to extract a dye also helped to decimate populations. Those remaining grow in remote areas such as Cockpit Country and the Blue and John Crow mountains and can attain a height of

130ft. Another prized tropical hardwood, true **ebony** is found only in Jamaica and Cuba, though trees called "ebony" grow in other places. It's now rare in primary forest, but the orange and crimson flowers make it a popular garden shrub if trained.

Characteristically Caribbean, there are several varieties of ornamental **palm** in Jamaica. Often used to mark out driveways, the graceful **royal palm**, at around 100ft, is shaped like the perfect postcard palm, while close relative the **cabbage palm** manages a whopping 130ft and has thicker, messier-looking fronds. There are several pseudo-palms in Jamaica – the unusual **screw pine** is easily distinguishable by its yucca-like leaves and spidery "silt-roots" that branch off from the bottom of the central trunk. Commonly planted in hotel gardens, the most attractive pretender is the magnificent **travellers' palm**, a member of the banana family – the name refers to mini-ponds at the base of the leaves that provide a convenient water source. Fronds fan out from the base in an enormous peacock's tail shape that can measure 30ft.

Flowering trees and shrubs

If you fly over Jamaica's interior or look closely at any rural panorama, the greenery will doubtless be broken by occasional patches of deep red, courtesy of the **African tulip** or "flame of the forest". Flowering sporadically through-out the year, the clusters of blooms often cover entire outer branches; each bud contains a pouch of water which children squirt out to make a natural water pistol. Commonly planted in towns and hotel gardens for its distinctive and gorgeous crown of deep-scarlet blossoms, the **poinciana** or "flamboyant tree" produces long brown seed pods, often polished and used as shaker instruments. Equally popular and familiar as a Christmas pot plant, the **poinsettia** displays a huge spread of bright green leaves that turn deep red in the cooler winter months; however the leaves are highly poisonous if eaten. Twenty-nine varieties of **cassia** are found in Jamaica; most common are the pink and yellow flowering types, widely planted in urban parks. The showy blossoms cascade downward in tight clusters and develop into brown seed pods up to 2ft long. The smaller shrub *Cassia occidentalis* is equally pretty but known as "piss-a-bed" and "stinking weed" due to its nauseating odour.

The tree of life, **Lignum vitae** – so called because of its many medicinal uses – blooms with Jamaica's **national flower**, a subtle light blue shower that cov-ers branch tips and makes a splendid show from afar. Trees are fairly small, with twisting branches, heart-shaped fruits and a dense cover of dark and waxy leaves. Highly resinous, the wood is heavy enough to sink in water and was extensively used in shipbuilding and as a suitably painful material for trun-cheons. The gum has long been used as a purgative and a treatment for syphilis and gout, while the detergent action of the leaves still usurps soap powder in remote areas. An urban staple known as "poor man's orchid", the **bauhinia** is a prolific purple-flowered shrub also known as "bull hoof" in reference to the cloven-shaped leaves.

Fruit trees

Bearing Jamaica's national fruit, the 30ft **ackee** tree is one of the most common in Jamaica, with glossy ovoid leaves and crimson seed pods, the latter bursting open when ripe to reveal the yellow arils (see p.38 for more). Almost as preva-lent are the spreading branches of the **breadfruit**, decorated by serrated, hand-like leaves and pockmarked, matt-green fruits; less widespread is its cousin the

breadnut tree, similar in appearance but producing a two-inch edible nut.

Cashew trees are common and produce both fruits and nuts. Similar in appearance to red ackee pods, cashew apples produce the cashew nut but can also be cooked and eaten. The oily liquid in the shell is poisonous, while the sap produces an indelible ink. The **calabash** is a 30ft spreading tree bearing large globular fruits that are hollowed and dried for use as dishes and containers, or filled with pebbles to make musical instruments like the "shakka" or maraca. It's an odd-looking tree, with leaves clustered in condensed spirals along long, thin branches. **Cocoa** trees are easily identifiable, with shiny dark-green or red leaves and ten-inch oval pods that grow in clusters from branches or sometimes the trunk, turning from light-green to brown when ripe; the sweet pulp around the beans inside can be eaten when raw.

Versatile **coconut palms** are everywhere, with every part of their fruit used – be it for food or floor mats. The Jamaica Tall coconut palm has been largely eradicated by lethal yellowing disease and is widely replaced by the hardier hybrid **mayapan**, a squat ten-footer with straggly yellowed leaves and orange-tinted nuts. Diminutive **guava** trees grow wild throughout the island and are also cultivated commercially for their green-skinned, pink-fleshed fruits. Fairly common in the interior, **jackfruit** trees grow up to 65ft and produce a globular, strong-smelling sweet fruit with pronounced pimples that can weigh as much as 40lb. With a satisfyingly rounded crown of leathery leaves over a short trunk, **mangoes** are one of the most beautiful trees in Jamaica, also boasting admirable shade cover and delectable fruits. Stumpy and rather nondescript, **naseberry** trees grow to around 50ft, with hairy brown fruits better known as sapodillas. Suited to wet areas, **nutmegs** attain a height of 60ft; they have plain but oily dark-green leaves and inconspicuous flowers, which spawn a creamy yellow fruit that contains the nutmeg kernel. When ripe, the fruit splits to reveal the red aril (mace) and the nutmeg, soft enough to be chewed at this stage.

Coastal trees

Mangrove swamps grow along the Jamaican coast and are central to the health of coastal ecosystems, affording protection from hurricane surges, filtering earth sediments and nutrients and providing a protected nursery for fish and crustaceans. Yet they often fall victim to shortsighted development, bulldozed to make way for housing and to facilitate sand mining or used as fuel for charcoal kilns. Though not naturally a coast-dweller, the **Indian almond** can withstand drought and flourishes along the length of Jamaica's shores. Branches grow symmetrically, and though they don't taste much like conventional almonds, the nuts can be eaten once the outer pods turn brown. A staple of all Jamaican beaches, the **sea grape** varies considerably in shape according to its environment; on exposed shores it lies low and twisted, but with less buffeting it can attain a height of 50ft. The flat, round leaves are distinctively veined and turn a deep red as they mature. Once they've turned purple, the grapes are edible, if a little sour. Fortunately very rare and definitely one to avoid is the **manchineel**, which grows to about 40ft, with a wide-spreading canopy dotted with indistinct green fruits and flowers, all of which are extremely poisonous – even standing below a manchineel during rain incurs blistering. Luckily, you're only likely to chance upon a manchineel in the most remote areas, and cases of run-ins are unheard of.

Plants

Borders and fences island-wide are enlivened by the multicoloured **croton** shrub; the yellow, red, orange and green leaves are extremely hardy and are also used in bush medicine. More than 550 species of **fern** thrive in Jamaica's hot, moist climate; silver and gold ferns are common, coated with a waxy substance on the underside which makes a natural tattoo. **Cactuses** are best suited to the dry scrub of the Hellshire Hills and south coast plains, where some, such as the two **dildo** varieties, grow as tall as 20ft stretching skywards between clumps of viciously thorned **makko** bushes. The inner stems of **torchwood** cactuses are dried and lit as homemade torches in rural areas and bear a yellow fruit, while the **dildo pear** (*Stenocereus hystrix*) has a red fruit; both are edible. **Prickly pear** and the "smooth pear" or **cochineal cactus** are also common, the latter known as "roast pork" for its taste when cooked. Of climbing cactuses, most spectacular is the **queen of the night**, which boasts a huge and powerfully scented flower that only blooms at night. The endemic **god okra**, with edible stems and crimson fruits, is often vested with supernatural powers as its aerial roots spread so far over rocks and trees from their triangular main stem that they appear to have no earth to support them. The epiphytic **spaghetti cactus** has 6ft skinny green stems that hang down from dead or living trees and bears miniature white flowers and berries. The flat-lobed prickly **tuna** cactus is widely used in bush medicine, said to cure dandruff, reduce swelling and relieve chronic pain.

Of Jamaica's **vines**, the rampant forest **cacoon** has a huge circular bean pod the colour of a burnished conker, while the rare, triffid-type **duppy fly trap** bears the largest flower in Jamaica – an eight-inch purple heart-shaped centre from which 23-inch fly-catching spurs extend. A rotting-meat odour attracts flies to the inside of the flowers, where they are covered in pollen and released

Ganja cultivation

Though there are two annual growing seasons, Jamaica's most infamous crop is mainly reaped between August and October, when the buds have received the full benefit of the summer sun. The 7ft bushes are usually grown amongst other tall crops at very remote and usually small plantations. After the plants are harvested, the outer leaves are discarded and the potent buds hung up and cured. Marijuana, or **ganja**, is not particularly easy to raise – many cultivators liken the task to bringing up a sickly child. Seeds must first be carefully germinated, then planted in open ground and stringently guarded against pests and birds. As buds attain maturity, the farmer must spend increasing amounts of time at the plot, feeding, watering and tending his crop as well as defending the valuable stems against thieves. Many farmers use pesticides and expensive conventional fertilizers, though this is frowned upon and seen to produce a tainted version of the real thing; organic fertilizers such as bat guano are preferred to ensure top potency. Growers also face losing it all to the hands of the Jamaica Defence Force, who conduct regular eradication programmes as the fields reach maturity. Helicopters scour the hills for likely plantations, while a ground crew sweeps through the countryside burning or spraying the plants with powerful insecticide. Unscrupulous soldiers are frequently known to accept a bribe in return for burning only a portion of the fields or not arresting the farmer, though as many policemen sell or smoke cannabis themselves, undocumented and highly profitable confiscations are reputedly common. For more on ganja in Jamaica, visit ⊛www.cannabisnews.com.

to pollinate other plants – contrary to popular belief, the insects are not consumed. Strings of shiny red and black seeds from the **John Crow bead vine** turn up on craft stalls island-wide; dangerously so, as this is one of Jamaica's most toxic plants. Growing prolifically throughout the island, the mimosa family's fascinating **shame'o'lady**, resembling a miniature bracken, closes its leaves to expose thorns on its stem at the slightest touch as protection against foraging animals. Equally intriguing is the epiphytic **wild pine bromeliad**, its 3ft pineapple-like leaves flourishing wherever there's a tree to host it. The rainwater collected between the leaves supports a variety of insects and even frogs, and the most protected specimens boast a pale crimson flower.

Flowers

Jamaica's perennial summer keeps flowers constantly in bloom, and the rich soil supports a huge variety of **flowers**, from the lavish exotics of the lowlands, exported worldwide, to the delicate iris, begonia and azaleas of cool mountain climates. One of the most familiar sights is the brush-like deep pink **red gingers**. The bracts hide the small white true flower that grows from each tip once fully open, and the shiny, banana-like leaves are teamed with the blooms as a staple of flower arrangements. A close relative is the **torch ginger**, which boasts one of the showiest heads in the world, a deep-crimson cluster of thick waxy petals nestled among leaf blades that grow to 15ft. Also ubiquitous are the forty vividly coloured varieties of the **heliconia** genus. Most popular are the various red shades of aptly named **lobster claw** and the red, gold and green cascade of the **hanging** heliconia, which looks like a series of fish hanging from a rod. Equally prevalent is the artificial-looking **anthurium**, a heart-shaped and shiny red, pink or white bract with a long penile stem protruding from the centre, and the spectacular **bird of paradise**, a mauve, bent stem which resembles a bird's head graced by a deep orange crest.

Jamaica boasts 237 species of **orchid**, approximately 25 percent of which are endemic. Most are epiphytic and grow on living or dead plant or tree matter, and many are so small that you'll need a magnifying glass to appreciate them. There are far too many varieties to mention, but some of the most notable are pea-sized miniature orchids like **Lady Nugent's purse**, commonly seen in the pristine Blue Mountain and Cockpit Country forests.

Hedges and fences are beautified by several varieties of **flowering shrub**; the ubiquitous **bougainvillea** ranges from red to deep magenta, white, orange and pink, the colour provided not by the comparatively insignificant flowers but by the surrounding papery bracts. **Hibiscus** take on an abundance of hues and shapes but are distinguishable through the generic pollen-tipped stamen that grows from the centre. The lacy **coral hibiscus** has a cluster of tiny curling red petals and an unusually long stamen topped by another red frill, and there are hundreds of hybrid varieties. **Mexican creeper** is a clambering shower of delicate pink or white flowers used to beautify fences and walls. The unusual **angel's trumpet** boasts large white horn-shaped flowers that are mildly hallucinogenic, so don't get too close when inhaling the musky scent. **Bladderwort** is a carnivorous plant found mostly in the Black River morass, bearing trailing yellow flowers that float on water and feeding on insects lured by sweet nectar.

Fauna

Jamaica's geological isolation precludes a rich variety of animals, and human habitation has decimated indigenous mammal species; an estimated 37 species have become extinct since the first settlements. Much damage was done by the introduction of the **mongoose** in 1872, which wiped out the Jamaican cane and rice rat population in little more than three years. Together with rats and mice first introduced via the galleys of Spanish ships, burgeoning populations of mongoose pose a significant threat to other Jamaican creatures, including the Jamaican hutia or **coney**, a nocturnal rabbit-sized rodent that lives in hollowed trees or rock crevices. Other than **feral pigs,** first introduced by the Spanish and still living wild in the interior 200 years later, Jamaica has no large land mammals, although semi-feral cats, dogs and, particularly, goats roam every corner of the island and are especially prevalent in urban areas. The only other indigenous mammal is the **bat**, of which there are 21 varieties; Jamaicans call them all "rat-bats" (the country's huge moths are called rat-bats, too). Some bats are solitary tree dwellers, but huge colonies inhabit Jamaica's caves, from which their droppings, or guano, have been harvested as a fertilizer, particularly prized for its effect on ganja plants.

Birds

Approximately 250 species of bird frequent Jamaica's skies, though many are migratory or come to the island only to breed. There are 25 indigenous species and 21 varieties found nowhere else in the world, which represents a greater level of endemism than in any other Caribbean island. Quick-moving, brightly coloured **hummingbirds** epitomize Jamaican bird life at its most spectacular; the red- or black-billed streamertail, or **doctor bird,** is the national bird, though only males have the characteristic trailing double tail feathers (reminiscent of an old-fashioned doctor's coat) and iridescent green breast. At under two inches, the **vervain**, or bee hummingbird, is the second-smallest bird in the world. Its darting aerial techniques, surprisingly loud squeaky call and bee-like buzzing are far more notable than its grey-brown plumage. The endemic two-tone black and purple **mango hummingbird** is seldom seen in the urban flower gardens frequented by its braver cousins, preferring peace and quiet and defending its rural nesting sites with dive-bombing assaults and a sharp curved beak. Another nectar addict, the black and yellow **banana quit** punctures flowers with its curved bill and often hangs upside down from a twig to ensure a favourable feeding position. Equally eye-catching is the bright green back and red crest of the Jamaican **tody**, which digs a nest two feet underground during its breeding season. Squawking green **parakeets** and rare red- and black-billed parrots are found in quiet forested areas like Cockpit Country. Glossy black, sharp-beaked **greater Antillean grackles** are to Jamaica what pigeons are to England. Their staring yellow eyes have resulted in the common name "shine eye", though they are also known as "cling clings" or "tinglings". Noisy and social, they live in groups and their harsh clacking call, broken by a gentler whistle, forms a constant background music wherever there are food scraps to be found. Commonly seen around cattle, the **white egret** often roosts on a ruminating rump in a mutually rewarding relationship that provides the egret with a constant supply of insects and the cow some relief from bloodsuckers.

Few sights are more evocatively Jamaican than the sight of a distant **John Crow vulture** swooping high over the hills. Though ugly and awkward on the ground, this scavenging carrion bird comes into its own in the air as it scans the land for the scent or sight of dead meat. Typically scrawny, its messy black plumage and bald red neck and head make it a convenient euphemism for people considered dirty, lazy or ugly. Easily recognizable by its harsh rasping cry is the 2ft **red-tailed chicken hawk**, dark-brown and black with a white breast and russet tail feathers, which feeds on rats, mice and occasionally chickens. Jamaica has two types of night-hunting **owls**, both surrounded by superstition. The unworldly call of the "**screech owl**", or white owl, is said to bring bad luck, despite its useful function as a vermin exterminator. Owls are generically referred to as **patoos** (their Ghanaian name), and the **Jamaican brown owl** is rarely known as anything else. Seldom seen away from country areas, the patoo feeds on moths and lizards and has a deep, hoarse cry that's said to be a harbinger of death and destruction – it's certainly disquieting on a dark night. The charismatic sea-dwelling **brown pelican,** or "old Joe", frequents fishing harbours, where it feeds on discarded scraps, though out at sea it dives – spectacularly – for fish. Despite its dull brown coat, the pelican has an expressive face, though its squat body, thin neck and long hooked bill with a food pouch on the underside give the bird a faintly ridiculous aspect.

Reptiles and amphibians

There are 24 species of **lizard** in Jamaica including the **iguana**; the Jamaican version, *Cyclura collei*, native of the Hellshire Hills near Kingston, is found nowhere else in the world. A dinosaur-like beast, it attains a body length of 5ft. However, most of the lizards you'll see are one of the seven varieties of *Anolis* lizard – all are despised by many Jamaicans, who refuse to enter the same room as a lizard and squash them like vermin. *Anolis lineatopus* has a mixed pattern of brown markings, while *Anolis grahami* and *garmani* are bright green and can darken their skin if threatened. A variety of gecko, **croaking lizards** provide a throaty night-time call and are extremely common. The 2ft-long, dark-brown **galliwasp** has a particularly unfortunate reputation that has led to a massive decline in numbers; African superstition falsely argues that the bite is fatal and that if bitten, you must run to the nearest water source – if you get there before the galliwasp, you'll live. Though decimated by the mongoose, there are still six varieties of **snake** in Jamaica, none of which are poisonous. Most snakes inhabit remote forests but are found in small numbers throughout the island. The largest is the Jamaican **yellow boa,** or nanka, which grows to around 7ft and is bright yellow/orange when young, maturing into a beautiful yellow and black; during the day it rests in trees and sinkholes and is rarely seen. Popularly called the trophy dophy, the 0.5m **thundersnake**, cream-coloured with rows of brown squares along a russet stripe, is said to be able to soothe sprains; chunks of its body are marinated in white rum, which is rubbed into the skin – its willingness to be handled makes it easy to catch. Jamaica's two species of **grass snake** (*Arrhyton funereum* and *dromicus*) are also known as black snakes, both attain a size of 0.5m and are uniformly brown with a white underside; they're found under logs or leaf litter. The **two-headed snake** or worm snake is so named because of its tiny head and larger tail, which comes equipped with a small "thorn" used to burrow into the earth. Fairly common throughout Cockpit Country, you'll usually find one through lifting stones or digging.

A south-coast swamp inhabitant, the American **crocodile** has been so extensively hunted that it is now classed as endangered and has been protected by law since 1971. The Black River Morass is one of the last places it lives wild, growing up to 12ft, though smaller specimens are more common. Generally nonaggressive unless threatened, Jamaican crocodiles live mostly on small fish. There are 22 varieties of **frog** in Jamaica. Since their introduction in 1890 by the then-governor's wife Lady Blake, who apparently found their sound soothing, whistling frogs provide a regular night-time chorus throughout the island. There is one variety of **toad**, commonly called "bull frog", introduced from Barbados in 1844 as an insect killer, but most often seen squashed flat on country roads.

Insects

By far the most noticeable Jamaican insects are the 120 varieties of **butterfly** and **moth** ("rat bats" to Jamaicans), which appear in all shapes, sizes and colours. Most striking but extremely rare is the six-inch **giant swallowtail** butterfly, seen only in the lower slopes of the eastern John Crow Mountains, matched in size by the multiple species of giant moths. One variety of solitary **wasp** (*Auplopus bellus*) prefers meat to pollen and stores its food in a self-built larder of loosely connected mud cells, incarcerating spiders by chewing their legs off, while cave-dwelling flies capture prey with silken home-spun fishing lines dangled from the ceiling. **Spider** species are comparatively few, and though there are none of the huge and hairy tarantula types, there are some pretty big ones; the orange, red and black **silk spider** measures around six inches. Its many-layered webs are an arachnaphobe's nightmare; at 3ft wide with attachment lines extending as far 6ft, they have been known to trap small birds. Encountered only by the foolishly inquisitive, **brown** and **black widows** live under rocks and leaves, and though dangerous do not carry a fatal bite. Heavily armoured, dull brown and apparently without a sense of direction, **news bugs** are easily recognizable by their habit of bumping into walls and people; if one lands on you, it's said that important news is to come. Diamond-shaped, lime-green and with an equally poor sense of direction, "stinkie bugs" are named after their offensive smell. Often referred to as "white ants", Jamaica's seventeen species of **termites** construct huge nests along tree trunks and wooden buildings.

Marine life

Much diverse marine life is found around Jamaica's reefs. The sixty or so coral varieties include rotund **brain** coral, patterned with furrowed trenches; branching umber **elkhorn** and **staghorn;** stalagmite-like **pillar** coral; and cool-green **star** coral. Extremely striking are the **gorgonian** group of intricate soft coral **sea plumes**, **sea whips** and purple **sea fans**. Around the reefs, brilliant yellow **anemones** and red, brown, purple and green **sponges** provide a splash of colour, some growing up to three feet in diameter. **Crabs**, **Caribbean spiny lobsters** and spotted **moray eels** inhabit the crevices between corals. Harmless unless provoked, when they can inflict serious bites, morays open and close their mouths in a constant snarl as they draw oxygenated water over the gills. The patches of sandy sea bed and sea-grass fields between reefs provide a habitat for many animals. Spiny black sea **urchins** are an obvious hazard – their needle-sharp barbed and venomous spines splinter off into the skin if stepped on (see Basics, p.22). Often picked up for a closer inspection by scuba guides, round white urchins have spines that are too short to puncture skin. **Sea cucumbers** are long, thin and off-white, sifting through the sea floor to feed on deposited nutrients, while five-armed orange and green **starfish** and queen **conch snails** move slowly along, encircling grass blades with their stomachs to ingest encrusted organisms. One of the most stunning inhabitants of the sea floor is the flat manta or **stingray**, often partially buried in sand. Though nonaggressive, it has a serrated tail spine that is venomous but can only be used if the ray is partially immobilized by a bite or a badly placed foot. The camouflaged **scorpion fish** rests motionless on coral or sand looking exactly like a barnacle-encrusted rock – the spines of its dorsal fin carry a virulent poison.

Despite the effects of over-fishing (see "Threats to the environment", below), there are still over seven hundred varieties of **fish** in Jamaican waters. The commonest include multicoloured **parrot** fish, electric-blue creole **wrass**, red and yellow **snappers**, ornate **damselfish**, striped **grunts**, glassy **sweepers**, spiny **puffers** and rarer **tarpon** and **trigger fish**. The slender yellow and blue **trumpetfish** suspends itself vertically in the water awaiting smaller victims to drift by and into its mouth. Larger fish include **groupers**, **jackfish**, **dolphin**, **kingfish**, **tuna**, **marlin**, **bonita** and **wahoo**. The scourge of spear fishermen, silvery-sleek predatory **barracudas** impart a nasty bite if provoked, though the common **nurse shark** is benign unless attacked or cornered. In deeper water, **dolphins** are a common companion to boats, and pleasure cruisers often carry a conch shell to blow in answer to their squeaks.

Though increasingly rare, hawksbill and loggerhead **turtles** still lay their eggs on Jamaican shores, despite the continuing threat of capture. Though it is illegal to kill, capture or possess any part of a turtle, living or dead, the trade in their meat and shells is lucrative. The Caribbean **monk seals** that once inhabited offshore cays are now believed to be extinct, and Jamaica's cutest sea mammal, the **manatee**, or sea cow, is extremely endangered; there are only about a hundred left in Jamaican waters, mostly along the less developed inlets of the south coast.

Threats to the environment

As a developing country, the Jamaican environment has long suffered the effects of unplanned development and a lack of environmental awareness. While many of its **reefs** are still the beautiful underwater gardens of hotel brochures, they are under serious threat. Studies have reported that the island has damaged 95 percent of its reefs in the last fifteen years as a result of over-fishing (and destructive fishing practice), sand mining, coral collection, industrial pollution and mass tourism. Dynamiting and chemical bleaching, which stun fish up to the surface for an easy catch, have had disastrous effects upon reefs, which depend upon clean, clear water for their survival. A symptom of unusually high sea temperatures, coral bleaching has been reported on eighty percent of reefs around Jamaica's shores – killing the algae within the polyps and leaving the still-living coral to starve.

On land, **deforestation** and its associated problems are a major concern. Stripped slopes are overly susceptible to soil erosion and landslides, threatening hundreds of already rare animal and insect species and wreaking havoc with the island's ecosystems. Deforestation has been particularly severe in the Blue Mountains, which represent the watershed for the entirety of eastern Jamaica, causing annual droughts. For an island with such a high rainfall, Jamaica is in the perverse situation of facing a permanent drought entirely of human making. In the Yallahs Valley, a century of misuse – slopes cleared for coffee cultivation or slash-and-burn farming techniques – has left the area vulnerable to the torrential rainy season deluges, which have flooded the valley and dumped huge amounts of earth onto former farmlands, leaving the slopes above bald and impossible to cultivate. The situation became so desperate that the government intervened as early as 1961, creating the Yallahs Valley Land Authority to rehabilitate the area through planting Caribbean pine, mahoe and eucalyptus to restabilize the slopes, although a lack of funding has resulted in poor maintenance.

Elsewhere, though eighty percent of household waste is collected by the government, the remaining twenty percent is simply dumped in open areas and gullies, resulting in poor hygiene, increasing levels of vermin and polluted water.

However, all is not lost. Thanks to the efforts of nongovernmental conservation organizations, there has been a marked increase in public awareness of environmental issues over the last few years. Jamaica has established three **national parks** (Montego Bay Marine Park, Negril Marine Park, and the Blue and John Crow Mountains National Park) as the first phase of the 1995 Protected Areas Resource Conservation (PARC) Project, and the area offshore of Negril has also been designated a marine park. A further six sites are proposed for protected status, including Cockpit Country, the Dolphin Head Mountains in Hanover, Black River, the Hellshire Hills and the coastline around Port Antonio.

Environmental and conservation associations

Environmental matters in Jamaica are the responsibility of the **National Environmental Planning Agency**, John McIntosh Building, 10 Caledonia Ave, Kingston 5 (℡754 7546, ⊛www.nepa.gov.jm), a government agency established in 2001 and encompassing the former Natural Resources Conservation Authority. Its mission is to ensure sustainable development and to devise and enforce environmental legislation. The **Jamaica Conservation and Development Trust**, 95 Dumbarton Ave, Kingston 10 (℡960 2848, ⊛www.greenjamaica.org), have responsibility for Jamaica's national parks, among other things.

More directly active are the voluntary conservation agencies, also useful for obtaining information on specific environmental concerns. The **National Environment Societies Trust** (**NEST**; ℡969 6502, ⊛www.jsdnp.org.jm/nestjamaica) act as an umbrella organization for environmental nongovernmental agencies listed below.

Bluefields People's Community Association, Bluefields PO, Westmoreland ℡955 8792.

Environmental Foundation of Jamaica, 1b Norwood Ave, Kingston 5 ℡960 6477.

Friends of the Sea, 6 James Ave, Ocho Rios ℡974 9832, ⊛www.friendsofthesea.org.

Jamaica Environment Trust, 58 Half Way Tree Rd, Kingston 10 ℡960 3693.

Negril Coral Reef Protection Society and **Negril Environment Protection Trust**, PO Box 27, Negril ℡957 3735.

Portland Environmental Protection Association, 6 Allen St, Port Antonio ℡993 9632.

South Coast Conservation Foundation, 91a Old Hope Rd, Kingston 6 ℡978 4050.

Southern Trelawny Environmental Agency, Albert Town PO, Trelawny ℡610 0818, ⊜stea@cwjamaica.com.

St Ann Environmental Protection Agency, PO Box 21, Runaway Bay ℡973 4305.

St Elizabeth Environment Association, 2 High St, Black River ℡965 2074.

Trelawny Environment Protection Agency, c/o Trelawny Chamber of Commerce, Shop 6, Albert George Shopping Centre, Falmouth ℡954 4087.

△ Lee "Scratch" Perry at Black Arc Studios

Religion

With over 250 denominations and the highest number of churches per capita in the world, religion is a Jamaican vocation. Most Jamaicans are devoutly religious, and in this fundamentally non-secular society, faith features in every aspect of daily life. Over eighty percent of the population describe themselves as Christian, but there are also Jews, Quakers, Moslems and Hindus practising on the island. Popular ideology is governed by Biblical dogma, and most Jamaicans have an astonishing ability (and propensity) for quoting lengthy passages of scripture. Sunday piousness is fervently observed, reggae stars read from the Bible on stage and devote entire performances to unadorned preaching, graffiti artists decorate Kingston walls with apocalyptic Biblical verse rather than obscenities, and the most popular newspaper agony columnist is addressed "Dear Pastor". Churches are at the heart of all Jamaican communities, providing subsidized housing, education, healthcare and a strong social focus – and this centrality is fundamental to Jamaican religion, in all its myriad forms.

The development of Jamaican religion

The antecedent of most contemporary Jamaican cults and Christian sects is a wider **African** religious tradition that arrived with the first wave of slaves. Considered living machines with no human rights, slaves were denied formal religious instruction until the late eighteenth century. This privation, together with the constant influx of new slaves, allowed for a continuing reinforcement of African tradition – although the planters attempted to quash it by banning drumming and persistently breaking up ceremonies.

Missionaries began arriving on the island in the late-eighteenth century. Fighting against the indifference of the planters, they slowly began proselytizing increasing numbers of slaves, while also attempting to convince the planters that slavery in itself was inherently un-Christian. Owners were faced with a choice between having their slaves attend church on a Sunday or flaunt their heathen proclivities on a daily basis; they grudgingly bowed to the former, and a mass church culture was born.

Sunday mass became the only sanctioned gathering for slaves, and, ironically, contributed to emancipation, as firebrand black-activist preachers used their sermons to whip congregations into political action.

After emancipation, the British took a belated interest in the spiritual lives of black Jamaicans and tried to "civilize" them into orthodox Christianity. But decades of religious neglect had permitted African belief systems to survive and flourish, and former slaves preferred to openly practise aspects of their folk culture or combine their traditions with western Christianity. The time was ripe for a uniquely African-Jamaican phenomenon.

Some twenty years after the abolition of slavery, a new religious fervour swept Jamaica, initially carried along by the momentum of the newly popular Native Baptists and other Christian denominations but essentially resting upon the Revival, Pukkumina, Zion and Myal Afro-Jamaican cults that have remained active in Jamaica ever since. The **Great Revival** of 1860–61 was one of several

Though the number of Jamaican Jews has never risen much higher than 1000, **Judaism** has been practised on the island since the sixteenth century, when small numbers of Sephardic Jews fled to Jamaica from Spain and Portugal during the Spanish Inquisition. Though they still had to worship in secret in a Spanish colony, the "Portugals" or "Marranos" could at least live without the threat of being tortured to death. Eager to avoid continued persecution, Jamaican Jews assisted the English in their capture of Jamaica by piloting ships and acting as negotiators in the Spanish surrender. Under English rule, Jews were not only able to worship openly but were granted both English citizenship and the right to vote; they went on to play a prominent role in contemporary civic and commercial life despite making up less than one percent of the population. The island's Jewish population was only minutely increased by the **"Syrian"** Jews who emigrated to Jamaica from the Middle East in the late nineteenth century. Though Jamaican Jews have only one recognized synagogue – the United Congregation of Israelites in Kingston, where the majority of believers are based – their commercial success has attracted anti-Semitic sniping, though the community's prime economic position in Jamaican society means that Jews suffer little direct persecution. For more on Jamaica's Jewish population, visit ⊛www.sephardim.org.

religious revivals (others took place in 1831, 1840, 1865 and 1883) that signified a resurgence both of religious practices banned under slavery and of a desire among blacks to rediscover and celebrate their African origins. It marked the beginning of a Jamaican religious tradition that threatened carefully constructed colonial hierarchies, and white Jamaicans were horrified at this "grossly perverted religious fervour" and "scenes of debauchery and hideous caterwauling".

By the end of the nineteenth century, the Jamaican elite was panic-stricken by the phenomenal popularity of the church led by self-declared messiah (and eventual lunatic) **Alexander Bedward**. His August Town branch of the Native Baptist Church adapted conventional theology, proffering a combination of black power and faith healing – Bedward blessed the waters of Hope River and thousands flocked to Kingston for baptism or a miracle cure. He also prophesied that he would sprout wings and fly to Zion on December 31, 1921, and Bedwardites from all over Jamaica and the Caribbean descended upon Kingston to witness his departure; Bedward stayed put, but used the mass gathering as an opportunity to spread the message. Inevitably, Bedward's black nationalist tendencies led to several clashes with the state; in 1895 he was tried for sedition but acquitted on the grounds of insanity, and eventually he was arrested as a vagrant and committed to Kingston's Bellevue asylum, where he died in 1930.

Christianity

Christianity arrived in Jamaica with the Spanish, who built the island's first **Roman Catholic** church at Sevilla Nueva in St Ann (see p.217) in 1524. The British promptly outlawed Catholicism in 1655, and it was not freely practised again until 1792; only between five and eight percent of Jamaicans are Catholic today.

The British replaced Catholicism with the Church of England and divided the island into the ecclesiastical **parishes**, each of which had a church as its spiritual centre. The church later became known as the **Anglican Church of**

Jamaica and is far and away the island's dominant faith, though the Moravian, Baptist and Methodist missionaries who arrived on the island from 1754 established denominations that still thrive in force today.

The **Baptist** church is the second-largest Christian denomination, first brought to Jamaica by African-American ex-slaves **George Lyle** and **Moses Baker** in 1783. The Native Baptist movement, as it was then known, incorporated numerous African rituals into more orthodox forms of worship and was widely supported at its peak, with impressively large and still-functioning churches springing up all over the Jamaican interior throughout the nineteenth century. Following emancipation, the Baptists were the first to set up **free villages** for liberated slaves and became a main instigator and provider of free education for black Jamaicans.

Approximately ten percent of Jamaicans are **Methodists**, a faith strongly influenced by the African religious tradition and often connected to Revivalism (see below). Many black Jamaicans were converted to Methodism by missionaries from the Wesleyan Missionary Society, who arrived in Jamaica in 1789 to set up the Coke Church in Kingston, assuring potential converts that their own religious traditions would survive within the blanket of the Methodist Church.

In recent years, the fundamentalist tenets of US Bible Belt churches have proven immensely popular, with many Jamaicans becoming Seventh Day Adventists and Jehovah's Witnesses, while the Pentecostal church and the Church of God also have significant followings.

Revivalism and Kumina

Essentially spiritualistic, the **Revival** movement, which came into being during the Great Revival, combines African and European religious traditions into a uniquely Jamaican form. It centres on the African acceptance of a synthesis between the spiritual and temporal worlds, an "animist" philosophy of a supernatural power that organizes and animates the material universe. Spirits are seen

African death rituals

Believed to be a prime time for the release of wicked duppies, **death** in Jamaica is still surrounded by rituals designed to smooth the passage from one world to another, though these days many are remembered only by the elderly and restricted to rural areas. Within hours of expiration, the body is washed by two family members who begin at the head and feet and meet in the middle; the water is saved and poured into the grave. Mirrors are turned against walls to prevent reflections that may portend further deaths, and the house is ritually swept out with new palm brooms. If death occurred in bed, the body is placed so that the head rests at the foot of the bed to confuse any lurking duppies, and the mattress may be turned over. Once the corpse leaves for the funeral home, the bed is left outdoors for three days to air out any negative spiritual residue. **Nine Night**, or "death watch", ceremonies traditionally take place over the nine days and nights following a death, with friends and relatives "setting up" to remember and celebrate the deceased and ensure that their duppy doesn't return to haunt the living; food is cooked and consumed, stories told, rum imbibed and traditional dances performed. Today observance is usually restricted to the ninth night only, and sound-system speakers often take the place of drums and anecdotes.

to have a distinct influence upon the living and, accordingly, must be respected, pacified, praised and worshipped through ritual dances, offerings and prayer. There are two branches within Revivalism: **Zionism** and **Pukkumina**. More overtly Christian, Zionism deals only with the heavenly spirits and angels of the Bible, while the more African Pukkumina worships earthbound "ground spirits" such as deceased ancestors. Known as **bands** (the collective plural is always used), Revivalist congregations have a female (**mother**) or male (**shepherd** or **captain**) leader who acts as general adviser and governs meetings. Ceremonies are held in consecrated **mission/seal grounds** or **poco yards,** which are specifically designated by spirits and marked by a tall central pole flying coloured flags to attract passing spirits and identify the site. The **tabernacle** – decorated with symbolic candles, fruits, herbs, flowers and holy pictures, and containing an earthenware jug of water used in the rituals – is either in the open air, a temporary bamboo structure or, increasingly, a concrete building. Liturgies include the singing of "Sankeys" (hymns penned by the American evangelist Ira David Sankey), dancing, drumming, clapping, and multiple-spirit possession (sometimes called **trumping**) induced by the hypnotic rhythms, controlled circular wheeling and dancing movements, and the technique of **over-breathing**, a self-induced hyperventilation that results in a trancelike state of possession. Once inside a physical host, the spirit becomes an adviser to the whole flock and is controlled by the shepherd, who interprets messages received in "tongues" or through the movements of the possessed. The drumming, chanting and dances are all of African origin, as are the traditional goatskin burru or kette drums (see "Music", p.410). Revivalism is concentrated in the eastern end of the island, and flocks are typically comprised of the working-class, with a higher proportion of women than men. Followers wear flowing white or coloured robes and cover their heads in a turban-style wrap.

Usually described as the most African of Jamaican cults, **Kumina** (also concentrated in the east) is less formally organized than Revival, and though still centred on connections between spiritual and temporal worlds and the evocation and worship of dead ancestors, it focuses on **music** to a far greater extent. Indeed, Kumina is regarded as an art as much as a religion; the intricate and precise patterns of its **drumming** have had far-reaching influence upon latter-day forms such as reggae, and Jamaica's national dance company, NDTC, incorporates numerous Kumina **movements** into performances. Call-and-response chants backed by complicated drumming rhythms provide the music for the worshippers, who dance around the drummers in a ring; women often take an aggressive, sometimes sexual stance, dancing their male partners into the ground in a proud show of female power.

Obeah

Obeah (from the Ashante term *obayi*, meaning a malicious spirit) is the belief in a form of spiritual power or witchcraft that can influence events – from curing disease to providing good fortune or wreaking revenge – and that also manifests itself in individual ghosts or **duppies** (see box opposite). Though dismissed by many as primitive nonsense – and theoretically outlawed, though prosecutions are rare – obeah, or "duppy business", is taken seriously, and it's not uncommon for Jamaicans, particularly in rural areas, to call upon the serv-

Duppies

The Jamaican name for ghosts, **duppies** can be good but are almost always seen as malevolent. The idea of the duppy originates from the African belief that each person has two souls; after death, one goes up to heaven while the other may linger in the temporal world and can be easily persuaded by an obeah-man to do good or evil to the living. Believers consult obeah-men if they feel they've been "fixed" or cursed, and there are countless rituals, charms and substances used to ward off or invoke the spirits. A traditional superstition warns that when walking on lonely roads at night, you should carry handfuls of stones or matches and drop them as you go to ensnare any inquisitive ghoul – unable to count beyond three, the duppy is forced to remain on the spot in a perpetual inventory.

Alongside the ghosts of regular people, there are also specific fiends that haunt children's bedtime stories and have become intermeshed with Jamaica's folklore and culture. The **Ol' Hige** is a bloodsucking hag who leaves her skin at night to seek out succulent babies and feast on their blood. A crossed knife and fork and Bible are kept near a child's crib to ward off her attentions, but she can only be stopped by finding her skin and dousing it with salt and pepper. The **Rolling Calf** is a staple night phantom that appears as an enormous red-eyed bull draped with clanking chains and walking with a sickly rolling gait; to see it is dangerous and to be attacked means certain death. Missing a foreleg, the **Three-Foot Horse** is sometimes ridden by the **Whistling Cowboy** and its breath is said to be deadly. The only duppy to appear during the day, the **River Mumma** combines the African belief in a river spirit with the Western mermaid legend. Appearing as a ravishing young woman, she sits near deep pools on river banks and exposed rocks, bewitching passing males with her beauty; once beguiled, the love-struck victims are pulled down to the river bed and drowned. The River Mumma is also one of the most commonly invoked spirits in Revivalism, particularly when ceremonies are held near running water.

ices of an obeah practitioner in special circumstances. **Obeah-men** are paid to invoke or dispel a curse and usually dole out brown bags of special powders – the "powder of compliance", for instance, is comprised of roots and herbs, ashes, earth, blood, feathers – to sprinkle on the subject and bring on the desired effect, which is reversible only by a more powerful obeah-man. "Good" obeah-men are sometimes called **myalmen**; they use specific ceremonies to counteract evil or mischievous obeah and rid those possessed by duppies in a "shadow catching" ceremony, commonly held around the roots of a silk cotton tree, where duppies are said to hide. Myalmen are usually respected members of rural communities who prescribe herbal medicines for physical and spiritual complaints (see Basics, p.23) and minister at ceremonies to mark births, illness, and death – dangerous times when spirits are particularly active.

Rastafari

From the reds, golds and greens that colour everything from shop hoardings to belts and buses, and the beaming dreads that adorn commercials and tourist brochures, the outer trappings of Jamaica's newest and most visible religious movement are inescapable. **Rastafari** has influenced all aspects of society from art and craft to politics, academia, language and particularly music, but the movement was not always looked upon so favourably. The last thirty years have

Inherently patriarchal, the traditional Rastafarian attitude towards **women** takes direction from Biblical concepts of woman as an evil, impure and a potentially corrupting influence upon man. Initially, women ("daughters" or "sistren") could only be recognized within the movement and be shown their own innate sin through the guidance of a "king-man", the physical and spiritual ruler of the Rasta queen who takes responsibility for balancing her thoughts and for her spiritual development – without a man, women cannot know the faith. Women are expected to be receptive to spiritual instruction at all times, and – unlike males – they are required to cover their hair when praying. They must never be seen in public without a hat or headscarf and must dress modestly, avoiding revealing clothes (particularly trousers) and make-up. They are considered unclean during menstruation, when they are not permitted to prepare food for others or attend communal prayer sessions, and in camps are often completely isolated and excused from chores. Traditionally, women are also greatly excluded from worship, prohibited from leading rituals and sharing the chalice and sometimes excluded from the most significant nyabinghis. However, since the 1970s, and the rise of the more egalitarian Twelve Tribes group, women have begun to assert themselves within the Rastafarian movement, taking respected positions in the hierarchy and participating in all celebrations, often with the active support of progressive, usually young, male Rastas.

seen a complete societal volte-face from widespread revulsion and persecution (a favourite police pastime in the 1960s was to arrest Rastas on ganja charges and shear off their locks – as sacrilegious as the cutting of hair is to Sikhs) to the tentative acceptance of today. Nevertheless older Jamaicans still retain a deep-seated prejudice against the "Blackheart Man", and despite a few notable exceptions, dreadlock-wearing Rastafarians are poorly represented within the professions. Some more well-to-do supporters prefer to defend the faith without displaying the frowned-upon outer trappings – wearing locks is not deemed essential to "knowing" Rastafari, as followers assert that they do not merely "believe" in Rastafari, but know and feel their faith.

Beliefs and rituals

The Rastafari faith has its roots in the teachings of black activist and National Hero **Marcus Garvey** (see p.218). He advocated an anti-imperialistic, pro-black philosophy and prophetically urged Jamaican followers to "Look to Africa, where a Black King shall be crowned". When **Ras Tafari Makonnen** was crowned Negus of Ethiopia in 1930, taking the title Emperor Haile Selassie, King of Kings, Lord of Lords, Conquering Lion of the Tribe of Judah, Jamaicans looked to their Bibles and interpreted his title as proof of divinity. Garvey was christened the **Black Moses** and Selassie became a messiah sent to redeem black people from their suffering at the hands of white oppressors.

Rastafari places Africans as the direct descendants of the original Hebrew Israelites, and Africa as the promised land, offering a restructuring of black identity and an emphasis on black culture lost and maligned by centuries of "slave mentality". As a colonized country, Jamaica is part of the white, Western system of corruption and "downpression" – **Babylon** – which will ultimately destroy itself through its own innate wickedness in an appropriately apocalyptic manner.

The first tenet of Rastafari is the acceptance of Haile Selassie as the second coming of God, or **Jah**. **Kebre Negast**, the Ethiopian version of the Christian

Bible, places him in a legendary line of Ethiopian kings stretching directly back to King Solomon and Queen Sheba; it states that the Ark of the Covenant (and therefore the God of Israel) rests in Ethiopia rather than Jerusalem, and that Selassie is the 225th incarnation of the divinity – a latter-day Christ. Though the Rastafarian elders granted a private audience with Selassie during his 1966 visit to Jamaica reported that he said "Holy priests, warriors and traitors, be still and know that I am He", Selassie never publicly acknowledged himself as a god and was said to be frightened rather than gratified by the adulation he received. Selassie died in 1975, but to Rastafarians, he became even more powerful – it is believed that only the evil truly die, and as the Rastaman lives his life in the appropriate spiritual manner, his soul is immortal.

A second central doctrine of Rastafari is African **repatriation.** This became a real possibility through Haile Selassie's gift of land at Shashamene in Ethiopia for black people to return "home" to. Though the few who made the journey found life in Shashamene just as harsh as it was in Jamaica, the belief in Africa – particularly Ethiopia or **Zion** – as a spiritual home persists amongst older Rastas. Younger followers, though, point to Selassie's 1966 public comments, in which he advised Rastafarians to "liberate themselves in Jamaica" before removing to Africa. The new cry of "liberation before repatriation" emerged, alongside a new politicization. Traditionally, Rastas do not vote and refuse to enter the corrupt world of "politricks" – but following Selassie's words, the movement became intensely political, with popular adherents such as Peter Tosh publicly decrying the manifestations of the bloodsucking Babylon "shit-stem" (system). This politicization has been taken further in the new millennium, with several Rastas standing for office in the 2002 elections. Meanwhile, Rasta groups have applied to the British Queen Elizabeth for reparations in compensation for slavery; the request was denied on the grounds that the UK "can't be held responsible for something that happened 150 years ago".

Most Rastafarians abide by basic principles based on interpretations of the Bible. Proverb 15:17 – "Better is a dinner of herbs where love is, than a stalled ox and hatred therewith" – is the source of the strict **Ital** (natural and unprocessed) **diet**: no salt in cooking, no meat (pork, lobster and shellfish are particularly avoided, though many Rastas eat small fish – anything larger than 12in is probably predatory and representative of cannibalistic Babylon), and few dairy products. Some even abstain from rice and bread, eating only home-grown vegetables and pulses. Animal by-products such as lard are also prohibited, as are alcohol, cigarettes and chemical stimulants. However, **ganja** – or "herb", as Rastas prefer to call it – is seen as a religious sacrament, as referred to in Psalm 104:14 "He causeth the grass to grow for the cattle, and the herb for the service of man". Though many followers smoke pretty much continually to aid their meditations, or "reasonings", ganja is primarily used at prayer meetings, when the communal pipe (chalice, cutchie or chillum) is stoked with the finest herb available, blessed with a prayer and passed round the group to the left. Alleged to have first grown around King Solomon's grave, the "holy herb" is said to enable deep penetration of thought as well as permitting a higher level of spirituality that transcends the petty distractions of the Babylonian world. **Reasoning** is central to the Rastafari faith, designed to reveal truth and elucidate the wickedness of the world and the Rasta position within it. Alongside these ad hoc sessions, Rastafarians hold more organized gatherings, usually outdoors, known as **grounations** or **nyabinghis**, which go on for as long as three days.

Dreadlocks are also believed to be a biblical directive; Leviticus 21:5 commands that "They shall not make baldness upon their head, neither shall they shave off the corner of their beard, nor make cuttings in the flesh". Orthodox Rastafarians cover their hair in a wrap or a knitted hat called a **tam**, believing it indiscreet and immodest to show it off. The reference to cutting the flesh informs Rasta opposition to surgery; most prefer to trust in herbal **bush medicine** and supplement their diet with a variety of stamina-building fruit drinks and herbal tonics such as the "roots wine" concoction consumed by Rastas and nonbelievers islandwide.

Finally, the Rastafarian **colours** of red, black, gold and green have a deep significance. Red symbolizes the blood spilled in Jamaican history, black is the African skin of 97 percent of the population, gold is the hope for the victory over oppression and green represents the fertile land of Jamaica – and Ethiopia.

The development of the faith

Kick-started in 1930s Kingston by Marcus Garvey, the **Rastafarian** movement centred on the capital and quickly attracted some vociferous advocates, provoking widespread antagonism in the broader society. One of the most provocative early sympathizers was **Claudius Henry**, head of the self-made Kingston-based African Reform Church and something of a charlatan. Aligning himself with Rastas through public speeches on white corruption and the necessity of repatriation, in 1959 he enraged the poorest sections of Jamaican society through the sale of thousands of cards purporting to be tickets back to Africa. Hundreds of eager exiles sold all their furniture and descended upon Kingston on October 5, only to be disappointed as Henry reneged on his promises. The movement was further maligned when Henry's church was raided and a quantity of detonators, guns, swords and conch shells packed with ganja were seized. Henry was imprisoned, but reports that his son was training a crack team of armed Rastas in preparation for an overthrow of the government led to a national manhunt and an islandwide state of emergency – a public-relations disaster for a movement that prides itself on pacifism and tolerance.

Among early Rasta elders of a more sincere nature, **Leonard Howell** stands out as one of the most influential father figures. He established a Rasta commune at **Pinnacle**, an abandoned great house near Sligoville in St Catherine, where converts lived a self-sufficient lifestyle praising Jah, growing food crops and cultivating ganja. Despite countless police raids, the community flourished for more than thirteen years until Howell's 1953 arrest and permanent committal to the Bellevue asylum. Those Pinnacle members who were not incarcerated drifted back to the slums of West Kingston, establishing the Back'o'Wall and the Dungle strongholds described in Orlando Patterson's seminal novel *The Children of Sisyphus* (see "Books", p.433) and setting up Jamaica's oldest Rastafarian camp at Bull Bay, east of Kingston. By the late 1950s, Rastafari was a serious faction in the volatile sphere of Jamaican religion, with at least fifteen different sects practising in Kingston alone. Yet the wider view, fuelled by hysterical press reports, was of a drug-crazed, violent underclass plotting the mass murder of white Jamaicans. Police harassment ensued throughout the 1960s, with Rastafarian communities bulldozed without notice and countless followers beaten and thrown into jail.

However, by the 1970s, things began to look more favourable for Rastafarians. Poor Jamaicans in their thousands began to identify with the movement's militant analysis of a wicked state and its apparent disdain for the lot of the black sufferer. The socialist Michael Manley was the first politician to use the Rasta faith to his advantage. During a visit to Ethiopia in 1970, Manley was presented with an ornamental staff by Haile Selassie; a sacred relic that he

Rastafari websites

®**www.rastafari.org** Good-looking site with a chat room, music-based features and links.

®**www.rastafari.de** "Home" site of a Rastafari webring.

®**web.syr.edu/~affellem/raslinx.html** Lots of info and links.

®**www.onedropbooks.com** Rasta literature.

®**www.jrdcommunity.org/JRDC.html** Website of the Rastafarian community in Shashamene, Ethiopia; ®www.shashamane.org a US-based support foundation.

®**houseofbobo.com** Bobo dread site, with a chatroom, links, and plenty of discussion of the Rasta faith al la Prince Emmanuel.

dubbed the "**Rod of Correction**" and transported to every election meeting in every small village during the 1972 election campaign. Always up for a little showmanship, Jamaicans greeted the appearance of the sacred rod with evangelical fervour, and Manley reinvented himself as the Rastas' ally, employing their lexicon in speeches and calling himself the "people's Joshua", able to lead Jamaicans into deliverance. He swept to victory on election day with the tacit support of the Rastafarian community and its many sympathizers. Governmental recognition of Rastafari was lent untold weight by the worldwide influence of **Bob Marley and the Wailers**, who brought international attention to Jamaica and forced an acknowledgement of the movement's legitimacy at home, and suddenly – almost overnight – the tide of public antipathy turned. Dreadlocks became chic, and reggae Jamaica's number-one export, but these halcyon days were short-lived. With popularity came a certain commercialization of the faith, with many Rastas turning to the financial gains of the international ganja trade rather than to Jah. Conspiracy theories about infiltration by the CIA were supported to a degree even by Manley, who believed that his programme of "economic socialism" was deliberately destabilized by the US government. Twinned with the death of chief ambassador Marley in 1981, this general degeneration meant a loss of international prominence and local momentum, but Rastafari continues to develop its political and ideological strategies on home ground, remaining one of the most unique, challenging and fascinating of twentieth-century religions.

Though true figures are probably far greater, it is estimated that there are around 100,000 Rastafarians in modern Jamaica, many of whom have a more egalitarian view of the faith than older adherents, allowing women a more prominent role (see box on previous page) and even questioning the divinity of Selassie and criticizing his questionable human rights record. It's worth bearing in mind though, that not all contemporary Rastafarians are orthodox followers. Many embrace the faith superficially, wearing locks as a hairstyle rather than an expression of faith, becoming "Rent-a-dreads" (see p.297), smoking the sacred herb and pontificating about Jah, Ethiopia and their personal friendship with brother Bob but lacing their ganja with cocaine and washing down their jerk pork with white rum.

Sects

Though there have been many attempts to coordinate the Rastafarian movement, there are hundreds of divergent belief strands, sects and methods of worship. The **Rastafarian Centralization Organization** represents the newest attempt to unify the disparate chapters of Rastafari, holding yearly conferences and speaking for the wider movement on common issues. In recent years, the development of new sects with differing interpretations of the faith have caused some level of internal division. Some (including several of the Marley family) have moved towards the more Christian-oriented **Ethiopian Orthodox Church**, while others have opted to join the **Twelve Tribes of Israel** sect (as Marley himself did). Well-organized and well-connected, Twelve Tribes is now one of the more prosperous branches of Rastafari, with chapters in the UK and America, as well as one of the more progressive, with women taking a far more equal role. Members must read a chapter of the Bible every day and are assigned a name and a colour based on twelve "houses" related to birth months (see box) and corresponding to the twelve tribes. Music plays a strong part in ceremonies. Controversially, members of the Twelve Tribes sect believe that redemption will be limited to only their 144,000 chosen few, and use the names Haile Selassie and Jesus Christ interchangeably when referring to God.

At the other end of the spectrum, members of the reclusive and strictly orthodox **Bobo Shanti** sect are the high priests of Rasta, following the teaching of the late Prince Emmanuel Charles Edwards in choosing to reject wider society and live self-sufficiently in semi-rural communes called **camps**, wearing their locks wrapped tightly in a cloth turban rather than the conventional knitted tam. Prayer meetings are continuous, and members leave only to sell the palm brooms and leather sandals made on site or to purchase foodstuffs that the commune is unable to produce.

Houses and colours of the Twelve Tribes of Israel

The Twelve Tribes of Israel assigns followers **houses** and **colours** that correspond to their birth months. The year begins in April, according to the ancient Egyptian calendar used by the Hebrews or "Children of Israel". The houses and colours are: April: Reuben, silver; May: Simeon, gold; June: Levi, purple; July: Judah, brown; August: Issachar, yellow; September: Zebulun, pink; October: Dan, blue; November: Gad, red; December: Asher, grey; January: Naphtali, green; February: Joseph, white; March: Benjamin, black.

Music

Close your eyes practically anywhere in Jamaica and you'll hear music. Radios blare on the street, buses pump out nonstop dancehall and every Saturday night the vibrations of a thousand sound systems waft through the evening air. Music is a serious business here, generating an average of a hundred record releases per week and influencing every aspect of Jamaican culture from dress to speech to attitude. Reggae, and specifically DJ-based dancehall, dominates, but Jamaicans are catholic in their musical tastes: soul, hip-hop, jazz, rock'n'roll, gospel and the ubiquitous country and western are popular.

The evolution of Jamaican music

Jamaica has long been a musical island. The simple rhythms of the Amerindian Tainos were adopted by the Maroons; the drumming, Coromantee chants and songs of their **Myal** religious ceremonies and related **Kumina** dance movements (see "Religion", p.402) became the island's first established musical form. Principal instruments included the bamboo and Coromantee nose flutes, abengs (cow horns), conch shells and strum-strums – home-made banjos fashioned from a hollowed calabash strung with horsehair. These provided the melody, but by far the most important instruments were the gumbe and ebo **drums**, supplemented by **percussion** from shakers, scrapers and graters. But while the Maroons were sounding their drums and abeng horns through the hills, plantation slaves were expressing themselves in a considerably more restricted environment. Recognizing the drum as a principal instrument of African warfare, the British tried to smother the provocative music of their minions, going so far as to prohibit "the beating of drums, barrels, gourds, boards or other such-like instruments of noise".

Yet African musical traditions survived on the plantations, most notably in the annual **Jonkonnu** masquerade parade, contemptuously dubbed "Pickaninny Christmas" by the whites. Jonkonnu was originally a religious ceremony using music and dance to evoke spirits – and named for its principal rhythmic component, the jawbone of a cow or horse played by scraping a stick across the teeth – and appropriated on the plantations to become a secular travelling pantomime. It incorporated British fife and drum marching rhythms and featured the fixed characters of a cow- or horse-headed leader followed by a king, queen and policeman, with companies of **Set Girls**, grouped by coloured sashes and skin tone. Jonkonnu is resurrected today as a tourist attraction. Other celebrations, such as those marking the end of the plantation year, were more European in flavour, with English maypole and morris dancing, and French quadrilles.

Another significant development was the rise of the **folk song**, created by workers in the cane and banana fields as a way to alleviate the arduous hard labour – an oral tradition that survives today. In the enormous canon of Jamaican folk music, there are traces of African, British, Irish and Spanish musical and vocal traditions, and heavy doses of Nonconformist hymns, arrangements

Traditional Jamaican dance forms

The syncretism of African and European culture in the plantations and beyond is particularly visible in traditional **dance**. Much of it emanates from the moves performed at Myal or Revival religious ceremonies, and most dances are purely African, often revolving around "dip and kotch" up-and-down movements or shuffling, hip-swinging styles that parallel the counterclockwise movements of ritual dance. One of the most interesting dances is **etu**, danced at Nine Night ceremonies (see "Religion", p.401), but otherwise performed only in Hanover by descendants of the original community of Nigerian slaves. It revolves around a process called "shawling", where the Revival Queen throws a scarf around the neck of a fellow dancer who is ceremoniously dipped back, giving each individual a chance to demonstrate some solo footwork from the standard pose of a slight but flat-footed bent-kneed crouch. Still actively practised in Portland, **brukin' party** is danced to celebrate the emancipation of Africans from slavery; groups of red and blue sets perform in a mock contest before the king and queen of each colour.

Many of Jamaica's most well-known dance forms are incorporated into performances by the island's professional dance companies, and you can see practically every style ever danced at the annual Heritage Festival held each October all around the island.

and singing styles. Each of these influences is blended with characteristic Jamaican wit, irreverence and creativity. There are songs for courting, marrying, digging, drinking, playing ring games, burying – and just for singing, too. One of the all-time classics is "*Hill and Gully Rider*", a timeless ode to transport on an island strong on hills and weak on roads.

The roots of reggae: burru to mento

After emancipation, the influx of free African workers rekindled support for the less European aspects of Jamaican music and society. The Great Revival of 1860–61 (see p.399) saw a massive resurrection of support for Myal, Kumina and Afro-Pentecostal Revival religious forms within which drumming, chanting and singing form an integral part of worship. The new prominence of the master **burru** drummer and his topical, wickedly humorous social commentary signified the return of the **drum** to the heart of Jamaican music. A version of the African griot (a travelling one-man information agency who brought gossip and news to rural communities), the burru man originally accompanied fertility rites and played in plantation cane fields to keep machetes swinging to a steady pace, but later became a sort of smutty strolling minstrel. Burru songs were commonly associated with sinful and indecent practices and dealt with situations seen as taboo in everyday speech. Musically influenced by Pukkumina and Revivalist drumming, the burru man would accompany himself on a three-part set of drums known today as **akete**, with complicated rhythms that would eventually work their way into Rastafarian music and develop into ska, rocksteady and finally reggae.

Over time, the burro man added a booming rhumba box (a wooden box with a hole on one side covered by metal strips that are plucked for an elementary bass sound) and home-made bamboo fifes, piccolos and fiddles to his repertoire.

By the turn of the twentieth century, groups of burro men were banding together to perform at jump-ups and parties, singing souped-up and sophisticated versions of traditional folk songs – burru had become **mento** and Jamaican popular music was born. With a syncopated rhythm that got hips gyrating and bodies dipping forward or back in Kumina-esque abandon (a style of movement revived in the "bogle" dance of the early 1990s), pelvis-centred mento was closely related to calypso – the music of nearby Trinidad and Tobago – through both a predilection for rhythmic and lyrical sexual bawdiness and its humorous social commentary. Mento dominated the Jamaican music scene for the first decades of this century. You'll still see mento trios – often referred to as calypso bands – performing welcome songs at north-coast hotels or forming the "authentic Jamaican culture" portion of an all-inclusive floor show.

Big bands to ballads

By the early 1940s, mento was waning in popularity as thousands left the island to fight for Britain in World War II or find work in Cuba, Latin America and the US. They returned with a taste for new rhythms and musical styles – rhumba, salsa and merengue – as well as new musical technology – phonograph records and cheap radio sets, widely available and affordable for the first time. Taking their influence from Count Basie and Duke Ellington, **big bands**, such as the Eric Deans Orchestra, found moderate success playing international standards and cleaned-up versions of mento hits at hotel floor shows. The best of these were put on vinyl by West Indies Recording Limited (WIRL), a record label owned by then-entrepreneur and later prime minister Edward Seaga. However, despite the quality of these tightly orchestrated performances, the big bands were bypassed by the majority of Jamaicans in favour of the radio stations beaming black American R&B from transmitters in Florida.

By the early 1950s, Jamaica's music scene was concentrated largely in a few pockets of southwest Kingston that were later to spawn the island's best-known musical luminaries. The desperately poor communities of Trench Town, Jones Town, Denham Town and Greenwich Farm offered plenty of dancehalls and street corners where quick-thinking impresarios like **Duke Reid**, **Prince Buster** and **Clement "Coxsone" Dodd** played for the people on huge mobile disco sets, taking the latest R&B or blues to areas where few could afford to see a big band play live. Reid and Dodd were the first to exploit the full commercial potential of the **sound system** (see box on p.415), vying with each other to see who could spin the best selection, often acquired on record-buying sorties to the US, and employing the braggadocio that characterizes today's dancehall posturing. An ex-policeman who always carried a firearm, Reid was prone to arrive at a dance dressed to the nines in sequins and leather, his guns cocked and ready to discipline any contenders to his throne.

By the mid-1950s, R&B's star had faded and the fickle Jamaican consumer was tiring of American imports. Quick to catch on to a new opportunity, men like Reid, Dodd and Leslie Kong began recording music themselves – primarily soft and soulful ballads – using established vocalists and players who had cut their teeth on the big band circuit. The Gaylads, Jackie Edwards, Owen Grey, Jackie Opal, Laurel Aitken and Bunny and Skully were backed by some of the best session musicians Jamaica has ever produced – Roland Alphonso, Tommy McCook and "Deadly" Headley Bennett on saxophone, Don Drummond and Rico Rodriguez on trombone, Jerome "Jah Jerry" Haines and Ernest Ranglin on guitar,

Lester Sterling on trumpet and keyboard virtuoso Jackie Mittoo. Initially, the producers used the WIRL (now Dynamic) and Federal (now Tuff Gong) studios to record, but as soon as finances allowed, Reid and Dodd (among others) built their own rudimentary studios, naming them after their most popular labels, **Treasure Isle** and **Studio One** respectively. Around this time as well, in 1959, Chris Blackwell founded Island Records, which would go on to become arguably the most famous label in Jamaican music. It was a halcyon age for Jamaican music, a time of cooperation and innovation. Ken Boothe, who began his career with Coxsone in the late 1950s, described the era in this way: "Music was nice in them times; you could just go and sing on a corner, go look for some other singers and everybody used to talk and smoke and sing together."

Ska licks

By the late 1950s, musicians and singers began flirting with the philosophies of **Rastafari**. Some went down to the Dungle in Kingston or Adastra Road in the Rasta-dominated Wareika foothills and jammed with master drummers like **Count Ossie** (Oswald Williams) and his **Mystic Revelation of Rastafari** band, collaborations that produced the first-ever recording for the Jamaica Broadcasting Corporation (JBC). Reworked in 1993 to massive commercial success by Jamaican DJ Shaggy, their *Oh Carolina* was one of the most influential tracks recorded, a perfect example of the fusion of Kumina drumming, harmonic singing and unique rhythm that was later to develop in to ska, rocksteady and finally reggae. The Rasta drummers became well known on the Kingston entertainment scene via the popular Vere Johns Opportunity Knocks variety show (held every week at the Ambassador Theatre in Jones Town). Star Marguerita Mahfood refused to appear in the show unless she was backed by Ossie and Mystic Revelation. Unwillingly, Johns complied; to his surprise the drummers were a huge hit and went on to perform regularly at Kingston venues.

For Jamaican musicians, the late 1950s and early 1960s were a time of intense creativity, a period of exploring new rhythms and pushing the boundaries of jazz, R&B and Rasta drumming – an explosive combination that sometimes saw drummers and instrumentalists pitched against sound-system wattage. Meanwhile, session musicians were conducting their own experiments, using the exaggerated shuffle rhythm of R&B and syncopated mento sounds. Somewhere along the way, the staccato, guitar-and-trumpet-led sound of **ska** emerged and captured the Jamaican musical imagination with effortless ease.

Following independence from British colonial rule in 1962, the future seemed full of possibilities. You can hear the euphoria in the music of the time – joyous, up-tempo ska tunes that seem now not to express a care in the world. And the small independent record labels in West Kingston were at the cutting edge. Ska lyrics provided a window into the evolution of Jamaica and its music, and with its home-grown roots and dancefloor beat, ska expressed the mood of the ghetto dweller. Tommy McCook grouped together the cream of the session musicians to form the now-legendary **Skatalites**, who released a host of massively popular instrumental tracks, like *Guns of Navarone*, and backed most of the era's popular singers – including Millie Small, who shot to international fame with *My Boy Lollipop*, produced by Chris Blackwell for Fontana. Other prominent ska tracks included Justin Hinds and the Dominoes' *Carry Go Bring Come*, the Ethiopians' *Train to Skaville* and a host of others on Beverley's, Federal, Treasure Isle and Coxsone's Studio One and Coxsone labels.

Rude boys to rocksteady

As the post-independence glow began to fade, the ghetto youth became increasingly dissatisfied with their meagre slice of the pie, and the **rude boy** era of violence, police brutality and ghetto dissent began. Rude boys were cinematically celebrated by Jimmy Cliff's portrayal of urban rebel Ivan in *The Harder They Come*, and musically documented in early Wailers cuts like *Rule Them Rudie* and *Let Him Go (Rudie Get Bail)*. Their fractious stance also generated the Wailers's 1964 *Simmer Down*, an appeal for calm among the youth.

While the musical critique of free Jamaica continued in releases like the Skatalites' 1966 *Independent Anniversary Ska*, subtle changes occurred in the music itself as Jamaicans began to demand something more leisurely. Producers accorded and began to slow down the tempo, guiding their artists toward a more benign lyrical output. Though the rude boy lament continued in cuts like *007 (Shanty Town)* from Desmond Dekker and the Aces, by 1966 Hopeton Lewis had produced *Take It Easy*, and Stranger and Patsy were singing emollient **rocksteady** tracks about love and relationships in *When I Call Your Name*. *Happy Go Lucky Girl* and *Only A Smile* by John Holt and the Paragons, *Queen Majesty* and *You Don't Care* by the Techniques with Slim Smith and Pat Kelly and *You Don't Need Me* and *I Caught You* by Brent Dowe's Melodians also did something to temper the pressure in West Kingston. Characterized by the addition of the "one drop" drumming style and a more melodic tone, rocksteady carried the swing and swiftly eclipsed the ska sound. The king of the era was Alton Ellis, who put a name to the movement with his *Get Ready Rock Steady* track. It was a prolific time for Jamaican music, with labels like Studio One and,

The art of the rhythm track

Through what's known in Jamaica as the **rhythm track**, the bass lines and chord sequences laid down during the rocksteady and reggae eras have become the foundation for practically all Jamaican music recorded thereafter. Realizing that there are only so many chords to play, or pressed for time when studios charge by the hour, musicians and producers like Bunny Lee (one of the first to release multiple versions of the same rhythm) have capitalized on the best chord and bass-line combinations, manipulating and reinterpreting them so often that most of the classic rhythm tracks have established names, usually gleaned from the song title with which they first appeared. Working as full-time studio session musicians throughout the rocksteady and early reggae eras, the likes of singer, bassist and arranger Leroy Sibbles and the "rhythm twins", **Sly Dunbar** and **Robbie Shakespeare**, created many of the rhythms that backed hundreds of 1970s' reggae cuts and are still reworked into today's dancehall. Hence the famous bass line that underpinned Eric Donaldson's *Cherry Oh Baby* was reworked by UB40 in the 1980s with their cover version of the tune, and by Tony Rebel in the 1990s with *Sweet Jamaica*. Many of the older rhythm tracks (and some new ones) have been digitally reworked to become hugely popular backing tracks, and surface on as many as six hundred versions. Within contemporary dancehall, certain rhythms – such as "punany", "pepper-seed", "liquid" and "diwali", to name just a few – become hugely popular, with all the big-name artists voicing versions and dances created to fit the beat. The upshot is that listening to Jamaican music can feel like an exercise in déjà vu; you may or may not have heard a particular song before, but once you've listened to a fair portion of rocksteady and early reggae, you'll certainly be familiar with most of the classic rhythm tracks. And once you've listened to the radio for a couple of hours, you'll know the currently popular dancehall rhythms.

primarily, Treasure Isle literally pumping out the tunes, many set to rhythm tracks that still continue to be heard to this day (see box on previous page). However, rocksteady was a short-lived movement, and by 1968 it had been superseded by the tighter guitars, heavier bass and sinuous rhythm of reggae.

Reggae to roots rock

So many artists contributed to the development of **reggae** that it's impossible to say who originated the genre – it's most likely that this ubiquitous Jamaican sound developed organically as a natural progression from rocksteady, but Toots and The Maytals' 1968 single *Do The Reggay* (sic) certainly cemented a name that Rastafarians will tell you derives from *rex*, meaning king. Hence reggae is the "king's music" – an apt allegory, as the appearance of reggae coincided with an explosion in the popularity of the Rastafarian movement.

From 1970 onwards, Jamaican music took an increasingly religious stance, with its main lyrical themes drawing reference from the tenets of Rastafari: repatriation, black history, black pride and self-determination. "**Roots and culture**" were the lick, and reggae became a fully fledged protest music. It was anathema to the establishment, who saw a menacing, subversive message from a dirty and violent source and banned it wherever possible, though the rum bar jukeboxes played whatever the radio stations wouldn't. It wasn't until after Bob Marley and the Wailers signed with Island Records in 1972, to international acclaim (see p.228), that reggae was given islandwide approval for the first time.

A time of intense musical productivity, the 1970s stand out as the classic period of Jamaica's best roots reggae. But while **Burning Spear** was singing *Marcus Garvey* and *Slavery Days* and Joseph Hill's **Culture** provided apocalyptic warnings of the time when *Two Sevens Clash*, the era also offered a sweeter side; the angelic crooning of more mainstream artists like **Dennis Brown** and **Gregory Isaccs** found an eager audience, their style becoming known as **lovers' rock**. Though their lyrics rested mostly on love and affection, lovers' artists also had some bite; tracks like Junior Byles' *Curly Locks* (a song about the controversial move of falling in love with a Rastaman) highlight the uneasy relationship that Rasta and reggae still had with wider Jamaican society.

Dub to DJ business

As the 1970s wore on, studio technology became increasingly sophisticated. Producers began manipulating their equipment, using reverb or echo machines, overdubbing techniques and snatches of dog barks or gunshots to produce some of the most arresting and penetrating music ever to emerge from Jamaica – **dub**. Employing a remarkable level of inventiveness with often limited means, Jamaican engineers such as dub pioneers **King Tubby**, **Prince Jammy** and **Scientist** predated the advent of the digital sampler by ten years and brought reggae back to basics, stripping down songs so that only bass, drums and inflections of tone remained. Snippets of the original vocals were then mixed in alongside sound effects and two-line DJ sound bites. Like ska, dub remained a primarily instrumental music for a short time. Before long, scores of DJs clamoured to produce a dub voice-over, and producers plundered

The cult of the sound system

Since the mid 1950s, when Duke Reid and Coxsone Dodd discharged the first shots in a battle of heavy wattage, mobile discos known as **sound systems** have been intrinsic to the Jamaican music scene. Laying the foundations of each stage in reggae's development, sound systems provide an opportunity to test crowd response to new lyrics or rhythms and inspire Jamaicans to follow their sound of choice with vehement loyalty. A simple arrangement of high-powered amplifiers and momentous columns of speakers customized to give a heavy, belly-rolling bass, the sound system began as a way of bringing the music to those who couldn't afford nightclub or stageshow cover charges. And so it remains; the sound system is now the major form of entertainment for young Jamaicans. Some come to hear their favourite **selector**, the man who employs an almost clairvoyant intuition to play just what the crowd wants, while others come for the prospect of hearing DJs chatting live lyrics over a rhythm track – a tradition that began with a couple of introductory one-liners as the music played and expanded to full-blown commentaries. Overall though it's the unique "dancehall vibe" that most people come to savour. Whether it's a country dance or a high-fashion session in downtown Kingston, the scene is the same: sweaty patrons bubbling alone or intertwining loins in a sensuous exchange of body heat, rum and ganja fumes mingling with the steam and smoke from pots of mannish water soup or jerk barbecues, and shouts of "Wheel and come again!" ("play that one again") as the music reaches its peak.

Since the early days when Dodd would set up on an opposite Kingston corner to Reid and try to poach his crowd with a mightier bass and a craftier playlist, **rivalry** has been central to sound-system culture. The battle to be known as the best is fought out at "**clashes**", where two sounds play on one night, and crowd appreciation is the mark of the winner. Buying a larger amp or a new set of speakers is one way of achieving dominance, but the most popular method is still to spin an exclusive record, a one-off "dub-plate" acetate voiced over by the latest DJ or singer.

The main players in the Jamaican sound-system scene are **Stone Love**, whose raw reputation and killer selectors Rory, Billy Slaughter and Wee Pow prompt followers to travel for miles to hear them play. Other sets to watch out for are the Twelve Tribes sound, Jah Love, as well as Killamanjaro, Metro Media, Fire Links, Coppershot, Adonai and Renaissance, the latter popular amongst more well-heeled Jamaicans. Even with this glory, though, the position of the sound system in its land of origin is increasingly fragile. Following noise pollution legislation and the closure of Kingston clubs such as *House of Leo* and *Skateland* in the late 1990s, the days when a sound system could simply set up in the street and play until the early hours are drawing to a close.

their archives and released dub versions of old cuts, while DJs provided the voice-over and even vocal tracks had a dub flip side.

The cult of the DJ had begun in the sound systems, with resident DJs improvising a couple of lines of introductory patter at the beginning of a record. The ecstatic crowd responses encouraged them to spin it out, and soon they were delivering full-length monologues over the music, discussing topical events as well as the state of play on the dance floor. The craft was mastered by **U-Roy** – inspired by the earlier efforts of Count Machouki and Sir Lord Comic – who released talk-based singles to great success throughout the 1970s with roots sound systems like the venerable King Tubby's Hi-Fi, Tippertone, Sir George and Killamanjaro providing the backing for their live appearances. Meanwhile, the DJs' trade was expanded when Big Youth started talking over records in his cultural style, followed by the likes of King Stitt, Dennis Alcapone, I-Roy, Jah Stitch, Tappa Zukie, Prince Jazzbo and Dillinger, whose *Cocaine Running*

The Producers

From the late 1950s to the late 1960s, Duke Reid and Coxsone Dodd dominated Jamaica's music scene, commanding heavyweight respect among the music fraternity and churning out the majority of the island's hits. This pair of musical titans are widely credited with controlling Jamaican recording as the industry shifted focus from ska to rocksteady. Their "big fish in a small pond" infamy has shaped the way that the industry works at a basic level: A producer raises enough funds to buy a studio. He then hires a team of musicians or a master keyboard programmer to lay down the rhythm tracks, and scouts for a talented arranger to look after the daily running of recording sessions and auditions of hopeful vocalists. The producer then selects the right combination from his pool of vocalists, songs and rhythm tracks, puts it all together, presses vinyl copies and releases the record, sometimes taking no chances on its success by handing out favours to ensure the tunes are played on the radio and at dances.

Though the reign of Dodd and Reid remained watertight until the late 1960s, the prevailing mood had changed by the early 1970s. Artists got sick of being paid a single fee while the producers reaped the royalties, and in-house arrangers balked at doing all the work while the producers sat back and enjoyed the rewards. As starting a label was merely a matter of raising the funds for studio time and record pressing, a new breed of **independent producer** emerged. Many lasted no longer than a couple of releases, but the likes of Jack Ruby, Harry "J" Johnson, Bunny "Striker" Lee, Henry "Junjo" Lawes, Sonia Pottinger and Clancy Eccles were more longstanding, and produced some of the finest reggae of the era. The most infamous and instrumental independent producer, though, was the eminent "Upsetter", **Lee "Scratch" Perry**, who started out as a bouncer for Prince Buster and graduated to running Coxsone's Studio One, where he worked with Marley and the Wailers on the definitive singles (*Small Axe*, *Sun Is Shining*, *Duppy Conqueror*, *Satisfy My Soul*) that were later reworked on albums for Island Records. In the late 1960s, Perry built his **Black Ark** studio and established the famous Upsetter label, releasing classic tracks such as Junior Murvin's *Police and Thieves*, Max Romeo's *Sipple Out Deh* (*War Inna Babylon*) and the definitive roots reggae LP *Heart of the Congos*. Perry remained at reggae's cutting edge until the late 1970s, becoming one of the chief innovators of dub as a patron of the late King Tubby. But his legendary – and often consciously cultivated – mental instability (planting records in his garden, burning down his studio in a fit of pique) and refusal to compromise his increasingly eccentric musical vision led to a decline in sales.

In the digital age dominated by electronically generated dancehall rhythm tracks, producers were able to release material with even fewer resources behind them. Producers such as Prince Jammy have taken centre stage alongside fellow luminaries Bobby Digital, Gussie Clarke, Mikey Bennett, Donovan Germaine, Dave Kelly, Philip "Fatis" Burell, Steely and Cleevie, and Jeremy Harding.

Around My Brain scored a hit in the UK. As the violent elections of 1976 and 1980 saw the pressure in Kingston building up, the sound systems multiplied and the DJs "chatted" on the mike about the times, analyzing the position of the ghetto youth in Jamaica from a dread perspective and offering cultural distractions by setting the psalms to song. Newcomers U-Brown, Ranking Joe, Josey Wales, Charlie Chaplin and Trinity continued in the same vein, touring Jamaica and the Caribbean with sound systems, and paving the way for the dancehall explosion of the 1980s.

In 1981, the Jamaican reggae industry was left in shock as Bob Marley succumbed to cancer and the music fraternity realized the enormity of their loss. Jamaica came to a standstill for two days as mourners viewed his coffin and lined the roads to watch the entourage on the final procession to Nine Miles. Though not the greatest singer to emerge from Jamaica, Marley's influence and song-writing talent were immeasurable, and following his demise, reggae struggled to regain its direction and purpose. Groups like **Black Uhuru** recorded a succes-sion of roots albums for Island, but the musical tide had already turned towards the DJ, and Marley's legacy of cultural consciousness began to seem less appro-priate to the world of cocaine-running and political warfare in the ghettos. The scene also took a blow in 1999 with the death of the "Crown Prince of Reggae", Dennis Brown, one of Jamaica's most prolific – and sweetest – singers.

Slackness in the dancehall

These days, you're far more likely to be assailed by a clamorous barrage of raw drum and bass and shouty patois lyrics than hear Bob Marley or Burning Spear booming out from Jamaican speaker boxes. Known as **dancehall** (because that's where it originated and where it is best enjoyed), or **ragga** (from "ragamuffin", meaning a rough-and-ready ghetto dweller), this is the most popular musical form in contemporary Jamaica. The genre first surfaced around 1979 and was cemented in 1981 when a flamboyant albino DJ named **Yellowman** exploded onto the scene with his massive hits *Married in the Morning*, *Mr Chin* and *Nobody Move*. Yellowman's lyrical bawdiness and huge popularity signified the departure

Dancehall queens

Weekends in Jamaica mean sound-system dances islandwide, and fashion goes hand-in-hand with the music. In a society where women are often the sole breadwin-ners of single-parent families, parties are a time to let loose and forget the domestic drudgery in favour of some of the rudest dancing and most glittery glamour on the planet – as demonstrated in the 1997 Jamaican movie *Dancehall Queen* (see p.430).

Whether it's a latticework leatherette g-string and bra ensemble or a concoction of carefully arranged silver plastic straps, topped-off with a neon wig, thigh-high boots or killer heels, dancehall wear is loud, proud and deliberately ostentatious. The cos-tumes are for one purpose: the sheer hype and self-promotion of "modelling" for the crowds who'll step aside to watch the wearers "skin out" and "shock out", per-forming the suggestive gymnastics of the latest dances to the most overtly sexual tracks. Dancehall queens, as the wearers are called, are the icons of sound-system culture, a league of ghetto princesses ruled for years by a light-skinned uptown Kingstonian named Carlene, whose killer dress sense, athletic dancing style and pneumatic body have earned her the local status of a Hollywood film star. New faces are constantly arriving on the scene, but in 2002, Japanese dancer Junko "Bashment" Kudo stunned Jamaicans by out-dancing her local rivals in the annual Dancehall Queen competition staged in Montego Bay – itself an excellent opportu-nity to get a flavour of this quintessentially Jamaican phenomenon.

Each new rhythm that appears on the dancehall scene spawns not only a hundred DJ or singer versions but – if it becomes really popular – a **dance** of its own, usual-ly based around sensual gyrating of the hips and lower body and always best dis-played by dancehall queens. The "winding", "skanking" or "water pumping" of the early 1980s were a fairly innocuous way of slow-dancing, but in recent years, some of the dances have become ever more explicit. Some of the best to look out for – or have a Jamaican companion demonstrate – are the classic bogle and butterfly or the more current "Pon the River, Pon the Bank", "Row the Boat" or "Diwali."

from roots reggae and cultural toasting (the original term used to describe the Jamaican talking-over-music that inspired US rappers) to the sexually explicit and often violent DJ-ism that took hold in the 1980s. Though none were rawer than Yellow, who added energetic stage performances and self-deprecating humour to the expletives, other DJs – fuelled by a positive response from their Jamaican audience – emulated his lewd approach, and sexually explicit lyrics – or "**slackness**" – began to proliferate.

In 1985, Wayne Smith's hit *Under Me Sleng Teng* – voiced for a King Jammy-created rhythm of the same name – heralded the start of the computer age in the dancehall. Studios switched from analogue to digital recording formats, and producers seized upon computerized rhythms as a quicker and cheaper way of putting out a record. The mixing board had become an instrument unto itself, with a new breed of producers like Bobby Digital, Donovan Germaine, Mikey Bennett, Dave Kelly, Jeremy Harding and Patrick Roberts becoming the Reids and Dodds of the 1990s and DJs becoming the island's biggest stars. Vocalists also clamoured to ride the digital rhythms – singers like Frankie Paul, Michael Palmer, Little John, Beres Hammond, Barrington Levy, Pinchers, Wayne Wonder and Sanchez got the sweetness out of the rhythms and continue to record today.

Dancehall is massive in contemporary Jamaica, though it's not to everyone's liking. Many charge the genre with wider moral decline as the DJs become the gangsta rappers of reggae with gold chains, flash cars, and in some cases, a seemingly limitless enthusiasm for automatic firearms and violent sex. However, though some songs do seem intent on a glorification of violence, most simply reflect the lives of a thousand ghetto dwellers for whom violence and guns are a

Reggae websites

Below are some of the best reggae-related websites. As new pages pop up with increasing frequency (and we've only the space to list a few), it's well worth conducting your own search, too.

@**www.bobmarley.com** Official Bob page, with essays on the man and his life, music clips, and information on the continuing activities of the Marley clan.

@**www.dancehallminded.com** One of the best dancehall sites, with reviews, pictures, features, music downloads and links to the cream of like-minded sites.

@**www.dancehallreggae.com** Reviews of sound-system dances and stageshows, as well as artist interviews and a rather macabre list of Jamaican artists who've passed away.

@**www.downsoundrecords.com** Downloads of the best and most current sound clashes and stageshows, direct from Kingston.

@**www.jahworks.org** Intelligent site with a cultural reggae bent that has some of the best reggae articles you'll find online.

@**www.niceup.com** Essential all-round site better known as the "Jammin Reggae Archives", with excellent background material and up-to-date information on every aspect of reggae and dancehall, plus lots of links.

@**www.reggaeambassadors.org** Culture-oriented, with heaps of links, music downloads, and features, but rather unappetizing to look at.

@**www.reggaesource.com** US reggae charts, the newest rhythm tracks and an online reggae CD shop.

@**www.reggaetimes.com** Website of this excellent magazine, with excerpts from articles and archived issues.

@**www.reggaetrain.com** Reggae portal with reviews, charts – and the weather in Kingston.

daily reality. Essentially, dancehall is a raw, rude, hard-core music designed to titillate and tease its Jamaican audience on home ground and beyond. Whether you like the lyrics or hate them, it's unlikely you'll be able to resist dancehall's compelling rhythm and infectious hype, and while you're in Jamaica, it's futile to try.

Reggae in the twenty-first century

Undoubtedly, dancehall dominates contemporary Jamaican music. Yet those worried about moral depravity can take heart: dancehall culture is going through another transitional phase, as the battle between cultural and slackness artists intensifies. In 1993, the conscious lyrics and staunch Rastafarian stance of singer **Garnet Silk** managed to conquer the dancehalls at the time when "gun bizness" and sexual slackness were the sole signifiers, and his immense popularity started the momentum for today's resurgence of cultural reggae. In 1994, Silk was killed in an explosion, but the likes of the massively popular Morgan Heritage and **Luciano** have carried on where he left off, using musicians rather than keyboards and writing their own material.

It seems that the righteous are triumphing over the slack. In the late 1990s, even the original "gold teeth, gold chain don gorgon" **Ninjaman**, a long-term crack addict and firearms advocate, resurrected himself as Brother Desmond, a gospel-singing born-again Christian (though he's since reverted to his old antics, making the news after handing over an illegal gun to top cop Reneto Adams at a New Year's Eve 2002 stageshow and being accused of sexual assault by a female relative), while megastar **Buju Banton** – who famously encouraged the murder of homosexuals, to mercifully widespread condemnation – has renounced his early lyrical vitriol, converted to Rastafari and now sings of Jah to the sufferers. Meanwhile, "veteran" artists John Holt, Leroy Sibbles, Ken Boothe and the Mighty Diamonds do the stageshow rounds to satisfy the demand for "**oldies**" hits. So-called "sing-jays" such as Sizzla, Capleton, Anthony B, Warrior King and Spragga Benz (who made a conscious decision to sing positive lyrics after his conversion to Rastafari) keep up the cultural pressure in the dancehall with a mix of conscious lyrics and singing, and singers Sanchez, Abijah, Beres Hammond and Wayne Wonder provide sweet love songs for the romantically inclined, while Lady Saw, Tanya Stephens, Cecile, Nadine Sutherland and Lady G provide the woman's touch. Reggae has even made moves into the pop arena: Grammy-award-winner Shaggy scored worldwide hits with *Boombastic* and *It Wasn't Me*, and reggae's current leading light, platinum-selling uptown boy **Sean Paul**, has scored several No.1s on the US *Billboard* chart.

The ongoing DJ feud between **Beenie Man** and the poor-man's champion **Bounty Killer** continues to rumble on, despite regularly declared truces, while other luminaries such as **Sean Paul**, **Elephant Man** and **Vybes Cartel** continue to release hit after hit. You'd be hard-pressed to find anywhere with a music scene as influential, vibrant and liberated as Jamaica's, and with thousands of young Jamaicans dreaming of being the next Marley or Lady Saw, it looks as though reggae's future prosperity is secure.

The selection below doesn't represent the definitive list of Jamaican releases, but suggests a few collection essentials and some favourites of the authors.

Compilations

Various *Tougher than Tough: The Story of Jamaican Music* (Island, UK; 4-CD set). This is quite an investment, but it would be hard to imagine a better compilation of Jamaican music. The discs cover just about every phase of the Jamaican musical story, from 1958 to 1993, beginning with a superb selection of pre-ska R&B, then moving through the ska and rocksteady hits of the 1950s and '60s to an overview of reggae's manifold styles and sub-genres. The songs are gathered from a wide variety of labels – not just from the Island catalogue – and there are superb, virtually book-sized sleeve notes from Steve Barrow.

Various *This is Reggae Music Volumes 1–5* (Mango, UK). More crucial anthologies, if you prefer to pick your reggae years.

Roots and Mento

Count Ossie and his Mystic Revealers of Rastafari *Grounation* (various labels). Traditional Rasta drumming accompanied by bebop and cool jazz horn lines, apocalyptic poems, and much chanting.

The Jolly Boys *Pop'n'Mento* (Cooking Vinyl, UK/First Warning, US) and *Sunshine'n'Water* (Rykodisc, US). Sunny and lewd, this is classic good-time mento from a band who have been playing it for decades. Strongly recommended.

Luciano *Where There Is Life* (Island Jamaica, UK). An exceptionally well-crafted set that's a landmark in modern roots music.

Various *Drums of Defiance* (Smithsonian Folkways, US) and *The Roots of Reggae* (Lyrichord, US). Two excellent, well-annotated anthologies of the deepest roots music of Jamaica from the Maroon communities.

Various *From Kongo to Zion and Churchical Chants of the Nyabinghi* (Heartbeat, US). Traditional Rasta music from nyabinghi ceremonies.

Various *Jamaican Roots: Bongo, Baccra and Coolie, Volumes 1 & 2* (Folkways, US). The first volume includes more or less the only Kumina music on record, plus Indian Hindu (baccra) music; the second has Revival Zion plus carnival music.

Ska and Rocksteady

Alton Ellis *Cry Tough* (Heartbeat, US). Alton invented the sound of rocksteady – and the name – with his song "*Get Ready to Rock Steady*".

Ethiopians *The World Goes Ska* (Jetstar, UK). Classic 1960s ska, with songs full of ghetto life in Kingston.

Skatalites *Music is My Occupation* (Trojan, UK) and *Hog in a Cocoa* (Esoldun, France). Led by trombonist Don Drummond, the Skatalites had an all-star musical cast and produced simply the greatest ska sounds. The first disc here is a showcase for Drummond, Tommy McCook and Baba Brooks; the second has them backing the best singers of the 1960s at Duke Reid's studio.

The Techniques *Run Come Celebrate* (Heartbeat, US). Classic rocksteady from one of the great vocal trios.

Various *Duke Reid's Treasure Chest* (Heartbeat, US). Rocksteady gems from the producer who ruled the sound.

Reggae

Abyssinians *Satta Massagana* (Heartbeat, US). A legendary dread album.

Big Youth *Hit the Road Jack* (Trojan, UK). One of the great toaster records of the 1970s.

Dennis Brown *The Dennis Brown Collection* (Jetstar, UK). A fine, wide-ranging hits compilation from 1993.

Burning Spear *Marcus Garvey* and *Garvey's Ghost* (Mango, UK). Spear's 1976 Marcus Garvey tribute was full of exquisite vocals and horns, and given a sublime dub treatment on *Garvey's Ghost*, packaged with it on this bumper CD. Spear's 1990 album, *Mek We Dweet* (Mango, UK), marked a return to form, updating his sound with heavy guitar hooks.

Jimmy Cliff *The Harder they Come* (Mango, UK). No reggae collection is complete without this 1972 movie soundtrack, combining early reggae standards with Cliff songs like the title track and *Many Rivers to Cross*.

Culture *Two Sevens Clash* (Blue Moon, UK/Shanachie, US). The band never equalled this debut, with its gorgeous vocals.

Eek-a-Mouse *Wa Do Dem* (Greensleeves, UK/Shanachie, US). One of the wittiest, most imitated 1980s toasting discs.

Marcia Griffiths *Naturally* (Sky Note, Jamaica). Greatest hits compilation from Jamaica's top woman singer, and former leader of the I-Threes, Bob Marley's backing trio.

Beres Hammond *Music Is Life* (VP, US). One of the best-ever albums from one of reggae's most brilliant and consistent performers.

Ijahman *Haile I Hymn* (Mango, UK). Ijahman Levi's unique, soulful, meditative brand of reggae at its (1978) best.

Gregory Isaacs *Night Nurse* (Mango, UK). Isaacs has been releasing Jamaica's best love songs for the past thirty years. This set, from 1983, is the finest of the lot to date.

King Tubby and Yabby You *Time to Remember* (Yabby You, Jamaica). Ethereal and heavy dub – just as it should be.

Bob Marley and the Wailers highlights include:

Songs of Freedom: The Complete Bob Marley Collection (Tuff Gong/Island, UK). The definitive Bob anthology: four CDs and 78 songs, dating from 1962 to his death in 1980, including virtually all the classics, plus lots of rare treasures.

Legend (Island, UK). If you want just a single disc, this is a near-faultless "best of" selection.

Burnin' (Island, UK). The sound of the original Wailers in 1973, with Marley and Tosh at their songwriting best on "*Get Up, Stand Up*" and "*I Shot the Sheriff*".

The Lee Perry Sessions (Charly, UK). Many consider these the greatest of all Bob's recordings: songs include "*Lively up Yourself*", "*Sun is Shining*" and "*Kaya*".

Mighty Diamonds *Mighty Diamonds* (Mango, UK). Fine selection from one of reggae's best vocal harmony groups.

Morgan Heritage *Don't Haffi Dread* (VP, US). The best release yet for this family-based band, featuring the smash hit title track as well as the uplifting *Reggae Bring Back Love* and *Send Us Your Love*.

Junior Murvin *Police and Thieves* (Mango, UK). The title song, inspired by election violence in Jamaica, was a massive hit on the island and in Britain in 1977. Lee Perry produced and shared writing credits.

Augustus Pablo *King Tubby Meets Rockers Uptown* (Jetstar, UK). Augustus Pablo and producer King Tubby (the Upsetters' keyboard player, Glen Adams) invented dub in the early 1970s and perfected things on this wonderful and innovative album.

Frankie Paul *20 Massive Hits* (Sonic Sounds, UK). One of the best – of innumerable – Frankie Paul compilations.

Lee "Scratch" Perry and the Upsetters *Reggae Greats* (Mango, UK). Jamaica's greatest and craziest arranger is responsible for too many classic reggae albums to mention. This compilation has generous doses of his 1970s *"Super Ape"* outings, with wild dub. For true devotees, Greensleeves have released three triple-CD sets that pull in most of Perry's greatest moments, with the Upsetters and as arranger. These are titled *The Upsetter Compact Set*, *Open the Gate* and *Build the Ark*.

Sly and Robbie *Reggae Greats* (Mango, UK). This drums and bass duo are even more prodigious producers than Lee Perry. This is their own stuff – dub at its most sophisticated.

Mikey Smith *Mi C-yaan Believe It* (Island, UK). An album of powerful dub poetry from a radical exponent, Mikey Smith, murdered by JLP gunmen shortly after its release.

Third World *Reggae Greats* (Island, UK). Third World were often too slick for their own good, but their late 1970s songs like *96 Degrees in the Shade* and *Now That We Found Love* are pop reggae at its sweetest.

Toots and the Maytals *Reggae Got Soul* (Mango, UK). The title says it all – Toots Hibbert is the man who put soul together with reggae.

Peter Tosh *Legalise It* and *Equal Rights* (Virgin Frontline, UK). These two records were recorded after Tosh split from the Wailers, with most of the band along. They're militant songs with razor-sharp backing.

Twinkle Brothers *Twinkle Inna Poland Style* (Twinkle, UK). And if Toots put soul into reggae, the Twinkles' Norman Grant was the man who put Polish folk into the genre, on this, the latest of a series of recordings with the Trebunia family. Strangely enough, it works brilliantly.

Yellowman *Reggae on the Move* (Ras, US). Yellowman was the biggest toaster of the 1980s, and his slack lyrics, full of crudity and anti-feminist and anti-gay raps, were a precursor of the more offensive contemporary ragga habits. This is one of his better outings.

Various *Chatty Chatty Mouth Versions* (Greensleeves, UK). Twelve cuts of this hugely popular rhythm.

Various *If deejay was your trade: the Dreads at King Tubby's 1974–77* (Blood & Fire, UK). Sixteen dynamite tracks from Kingston's premier DJs of the 1970s – U Roy, Dr Alimantado, Dillinger, Tapper Zukie and others – produced by Bunny Lee.

Various *Solid Gold, Coxsone Style* (Heartbeat, US). The likes of John Holt, the Abyssinians and Dennis Brown singing their hearts out for Studio One.

Dancehall, ragga and cultural ragga

Abijah *Abijah* (VP, US). The debut album from Jamaica's newest cultural singer, including the haunting *Why*.

Buju Banton *Voice of Jamaica* (Polygram, UK), *'Til Shiloh* (Loose Cannon, UK), *Inna Heights* (VP, US), *Friends For Life* (VP, US). The first album has bad-boy Buju at his baddest, the second sees him in more reflective cultural mood, and the third and fourth build on the Rasta theme, though with the odd lascivious track.

CONTEXTS | Music

Beenie Man *Many Moods of Moses* (VP, US), *The Doctor* (VP, US). Two seminal albums from Jamaica's hottest and most versatile DJ, including most of the hits over the last few years.

Bounty Killer *My Xperience* (VP, US), *The Mystery* (VP, US). Both albums from the ultimate hard-core ragga DJ include his major dancehall hits alongside some scintillating fresh material.

Capleton *One Mission* (J&D, US), *Prophecy* (DefJam, US), *More Fire* (VP, US), *Still Blazing* (VP, US). Capleton's own brand of fiery cultural ragga, complete with nyabinghi drumming to boot.

Cocoa Tea *Kingston Hot* (Ras, US). A silky-smooth dancehall voice, produced by Henry "Junjo" Lawes.

Chaka Demus and Pliers *Tease Me* (Mango, UK). Mid-1990s ragga, mixing in Curtis Mayfield soul and hip-hop rhythms, and produced by the ever-inventive Sly and Robbie.

Junior Gong *Halfway Tree* (Motown, US). Debut album from by far the most musically promising of Bob Marley's offspring, featuring the haunting hit *It Was Written*.

Luciano *Where There Is Love*, *Serve Jah* (VP, US). Cultural reggae's great hope does his finest.

Sugar Minott *Slice of the Cake* (Heartbeat, US). Sweet sounds from "Sugar Sugar", including the great *No Vacancy.*

Sanchez *Stays on My Mind* (VP, US). The latest from this longstanding king of dancehall crooning, featuring most of his recent hits.

Sean Paul *Dutty Rock* (VP, US). The platinum-selling uptown boy's excellent first album.

Shabba Ranks *As Raw as Ever* (CBS, US). Hip-hop meets reggae in this pioneering ragga album from 1991.

Garnet Silk *It's Growing* (Vine Yard, UK; VP, US). The album that established the late Garnet Silk as one of the prime vocalists of the 1990s – a celebration of physical and spiritual love.

Sizzla *Praise Ye Jah* (Xterminator/Jet Star, UK), *Black Woman and Child* (Greensleeves, UK), *Da Real Thing* (VP, US). The deeply serious Bobo dread Sizzla chatting over the pick of the rhythms from Philip "Fattis" Burrell and Bobby Digital.

Various *Reggae Hits – Volumes 1–25* (Jetstar, UK). Essential dancehall and lovers' rock compilations from 1984 on.

Various *Strictly the Best* (VP, US). New breed of compilations with the best in dancehall and sing-jays.

Mr Vegas *Heads High* (Greensleeves, UK). Mr Vegas' best-received album, including the smash title track.

Warrior King *Virtuous Woman* (VP, US). The first album from this promising cultural sing-jay, featuring the smash- hit title track.

Wayne Wonder *No Letting Go* (VP, US). Making waves in the US, this R&B-flavoured album sees Wonder at his best.

Jamaican art

Though the island has a centuries-old artistic tradition, interesting Jamaican art is very much a modern phenomenon. Before the 1920s, Jamaicans were, on the whole, simply too busy making ends meet to turn to art. Today, however, the island is considered one of the artistic centres of the Caribbean.

The earliest Jamaican art was the work of the Amerindian Tainos, who lived on the island prior to the arrival of Columbus in 1494. A few relics of their art remain – **cave paintings**, for example, at Mountain River Cave, near Spanish Town – and suggest that they were rather primitive woodcarvers and painters. The Spanish, who controlled the island from 1513 to 1655, imported artisans from Spain to produce **limestone carvings**, notably for the now-destroyed governor's castle at Sevilla Nueva on the north coast, and these carvings incorporated Jamaican subject matter such as the figures of Taino women. In contrast, the dominant features of art in Jamaica during the period of British rule were **commemorative sculpture** – produced in Britain by British sculptors – and **portrait and landscape paintings** by British artists who paid occasional visits to the island.

Some of Britain's finest sculptors had their work commissioned for the Jamaican market. **John Bacon** (1740–99) produced the Spanish Town memorial to Admiral Rodney and the smaller but more impressive monument to John Wolmer in the Kingston Parish Church. **John Flaxman** (1755–82), probably the finest English sculptor before Henry Moore, carved the monument to planter Simon Clarke that sits in the church at Lucea. More interesting is the "documentation" of eighteenth- and nineteenth-century Jamaica in the landscape paintings of **George Robertson** and **Joseph Bartholomew Kidd**, who paid visits to Jamaica during the 1770s and the 1830s respectively, and the nineteenth-century photographic records of **Adolphe Duperly** and **V.P. Parkhurst**. A more voluminous artistic legacy of the period is a series of portraits of governors and wealthy planters and their families painted, again, by itinerant British artists like **Philip Wickstead,** who was in Jamaica in the 1770s.

A new art movement

Even after the abolition of slavery, it inevitably took three or four generations before a true Jamaican art began to flourish. Ironically, the prime mover in the new phase was an English sculptor – **Edna Manley** (1900–87) – who had married prime minister-to-be Norman Manley and moved to Jamaica in 1921. Several of her sculptures may be seen as turning points in Jamaican art. *Beadseller*, from 1922, is the small bronze figure of a Jamaican street vendor, carved in a way that echoes European Cubist and Art Deco movements of the period; her 1935 *Negro Aroused* – a black body uncoiling out of bondage – depicts early enthusiasm for national independence in art form.

In 1939, around forty artists in Manley's circle stormed into the annual meeting at the island's main (and rather sedate) art museum, the Institute of Jamaica. They demanded an end to the domination of Anglophile attitudes to art and the replacement of the colonial portraits that hung in the art galleries with works by local artists. The event was more symbolic than revolutionary, marking a new departure point for Jamaican painters and sculptors. Classes began at the institute in 1940; organized initially by Manley, they helped to give direction to a new wave of Jamaican artists.

For several decades the primary aim of these pioneers of the island's new art movement – painters like **Albert Huie** (born 1920), **Carl Abrahams** (born 1913) and **Gloria Escoffery** (born 1923) – was to represent Jamaican people and their surroundings. Whereas earlier painters had focused on the simple beauty of nature, ignoring local people, artists now showed the landscape as a place where Jamaicans lived and worked. Paintings like *Crop Time* by Albert Huie, for example, showed the sugar plantations in action, with workers cutting, bundling and loading the cane, while in Huie's *Constant Spring Road*, his citizens go about their daily business on the streets of Kingston – chatting, selling and reading newspapers.

There were two distinct artistic styles in the work of this new wave of painters and sculptors. The predominant style was **European-influenced**, following twentieth-century trends in European art. Plenty of Jamaicans studied in Britain on British Council scholarships during the 1940s and 1950s, and an exposure to foreign art trends is reflected in much of their work. Most followed a classical approach, with artists like Huie and **Barrington Watson** (born 1931) using natural forms and landscapes as reference points, though Watson's later paintings, like *The Banana Loaders*, show the influence of Post-Impressionism. Of the early European-influenced painters, Escoffery shows the greatest interest in abstract art, stretching her figures along wide, panoramic canvases that depict a range of subjects, from quiet pastoral scenes to the traditional Saturday market.

More distinctive, the **Afro-Caribbean approach** was characterized by the paintings of the self-taught, known as "intuitive", artists. One of the first, and most unusual, of these intuitives was the prodigious **John Dunkley** (1891–1947). Dunkley was a barber in Kingston, famous for covering every square inch of his shop with pictures of trees, vines and flowers; his later paintings continued his obsession with dark, brooding scenes from nature. Though scorned by the critics during his lifetime, Dunkley's work has become far more appreciated and sought after in recent years and is excellently represented at the National Gallery in Kingston.

As you would expect on an island where religion plays such a large role, many of Jamaica's other successful intuitive artists have focused their art around **religious imagery**. **Mallica Reynolds** (1911–89) – the shepherd (head) of a Revivalist group in Kingston, better known as **Kapo** – is the best known of these artists. During the 1950s he became the first self-taught Jamaican painter to be fully accepted by local and foreign viewers, and is still seen as the island's foremost intuitive sculptor and painter. Other intuitives such as **Albert Artwell** (born 1942) and **Everald Brown** (1917–2002) – a priest in the Ethiopian Coptic Church – concentrate on Rasta beliefs, their paintings rich in religious symbolism and Rasta colours, showing kings and queens living an idyllic existence in heaven (Zion).

Jamaican artists grew in confidence during the 1960s and 1970s, many of them spurred by the promises and hopes of nationalism and independence. **Black iconography** was prominent in the work of artists like **Osmond Watson** (born 1934), who painted miniature portraits of a black Christ and black madonnas, as well as large, spiritual African archetypes. At the same time Jamaican art became more experimental, most noticeably in a specifically Jamaican surrealism represented by the work of **David Boxer** (born 1946) and

Australian-born **Colin Garland** (born 1935). Garland's paintings, inspired by the works of Haitian intuitives, seem to tell a story but instead dissolve into bizarre fantasy. His triptych *In the Beautiful Caribbean*, for example, appears to be a familiar summary of the island, with its jumble of birds, fish and religious figures -- until you spot the incongruous parachutist and the soldier with a seashell on his head.

Today, Jamaica's art scene continues its diversity. At the bottom end, it is dominated by the huge carving and painting industry that has grown up around mass tourism and, although much of it is relentlessly mediocre, there is some reasonable-quality art at the craft markets in Kingston and across the north coast, and in Kingston's clutch of galleries. The establishment of the National Gallery in Kingston in 1974 has given the island's art an important institutional infrastructure, and its regular exhibitions of the best of Jamaican art continue to encourage the development of young painters and sculptors, as witnessed by the proliferation of studios and galleries islandwide.

A short history of Jamaican film-making

How does an island with a relatively small population and a lack of technical infrastructure compete in the global marketplace against multinational media empires? Independence in 1962 gave Jamaicans the right to political self-determination, but it didn't provide an opportunity to see themselves or their cultural traditions represented in film. In the same year Jamaica became the primary location for *Dr No*, the first in the series of James Bond films. *Dr No* set the pattern for the first type of "Jamaican" film-making: the island is exploited as a tropical backdrop against which tales of international adventure and romance, aimed at the North American and European marketplaces, are set. Films like *Club Paradise* and *The Mighty Quinn* continue the tradition of Hollywood's many remixes of the "Jamaican experience" on celluloid, but the competing, alternative strand of Jamaican film-making, which came into being with *The Harder They Come* in 1972, continues to gain ground and respect both at home and abroad.

The Harder They Come

In 1972, for the first time in the nation's history, a film set out to document island life and placed its distinct regional history and culture at the centre of its narrative. **The Harder They Come**, directed by Perry Henzell, is both the story of Ivan (played by Jimmy Cliff) as he comes to try to make a better life for himself in Kingston, and an indictment of Jamaican society that implicates the church, music industry and police in Ivan's eventual estrangement from authority, new career as a criminal, and violent death. The film has become the standard by which authentically Jamaican films are judged. Its radical synthesis of social realism, political consciousness and popular culture introduced a new regional voice to world cinema that built on the artistic traditions established within the Caribbean through carnival celebration and religious worship. The film sets out to document contemporary social injustice but places these elements of realism in a critical flux with imported conventions from American crime and "spaghetti western" genres. In the same way that ska and reggae throughout the 1950s and 1960s transformed imported American rhythm and blues songs to generate a totally Jamaican style of popular song, *The Harder They Come* appropriated an eclectic range of influences, drawn from America and Europe, to produce a unique cinematic vernacular that spoke directly to the majority of Jamaican citizens.

Finance for *The Harder They Come* was raised from a small network of Jamaican investors, and the film took three years to make, with two long breaks in the shooting schedule. During these interludes Perry Henzell, the film's producer, co-writer and director, edited material and hunted down more funds to complete the project. At home the film was a success, winning the first of many box office clashes between indigenous and imported titles, while abroad the film gained almost universal critical acclaim but suffered from limited distribution.

Directed by Jamaican playwright and co-writer of *The Harder They Come*, Trevor Rhone, the hilarious **Smile Orange** (1974) features Ringo, a head waiter in a resort hotel, played by Carl Bradshaw, who uses all his guile and wit on tourists to overcome the harsh economic realities of contemporary Jamaica. "If you're a black man and you can't play a part, you'll starve to death", he advises a novice waiter under his training. The film's drama tests Ringo's ability to manage other people's perceptions of him, as he alternately seduces and cheats American tourists out of their dollars while avoiding being caught in the act by his wife and the hotel manager. Finally, his acting skills pay off when the hotel manager mistakenly believes that Ringo made a concerted effort to save a guest who drowned in the hotel pool and rewards him financially. Like Henzell's earlier film, *Smile Orange* also deals with the economic dominance of America and the class and race divisions within Jamaica. Unlike Ivan, Ringo chooses to make a truce with the repressive forces of the wider society if only the better to fool them into granting him a chance for a more profitable survival. Social injustice and discrimination are an occasion for farce and satirical commentary in this film rather than anger, violence and revolt.

The 1980 film **Children of Babylon**, written, directed, edited and produced by Lennie Little-White, focuses on Jamaican society through a set of character archetypes: a beautiful Marxist graduate student, a bourgeois painter, a Rastafarian farmer, a white plantation owner and a mute servant girl. The story follows these characters through a series of romantic affairs set on a plantation that reveals the class and ethnic divisions in Jamaican society. The film featured the seminal reggae songwriter Bob Andy, as Luke the Rastafarian farmer. Bob Andy had given up on music at that time in favour of acting with the theatrical workshop at the University of the West Indies. The film's cinematographer, Franklyn St Juste, maintained that the film's poor critical reception in America was due to the fact that it confounded long-held expectations about the low-budget visual style of Third World cinema.

"Dread at the Control"

The continuing worldwide popularity of **Jamaican music** has set the commercial pattern for most Jamaican film production. **Rockers** (1978) by Greek film-maker Theodoros Balfaloukos featured a cast of contemporary Jamaican musicians playing both themselves and fictional roles. Balfaloukos lived in Jamaica for two years before shooting the film, making personal contact with the musicians who came to feature in it. The story is a modern-day fable in which the Rastafarian musician, played by Leroy "Horsemouth" Wallace as himself, takes revenge on the Trench Town gangsters that have stolen his bike. The film points to many of the cultural tensions within Jamaican society. Such tensions are exemplified in scenes like Leroy and Dirty Harry's hijacking of the turntables at a disco to play reggae to the well-off Jamaicans who patronize the club. "Dread at the control!" shouts Leroy as he replaces the imported sounds from America with Rastafarian rhythms. Throughout the 1970s and early 1980s it was the music of Jacob Miller, Gregory Isaacs, Burning Spear, Robbie Shakespeare, Big Youth, Dillinger and Theophilos Beckford, all cast members in *Rockers*, and the counterculture of Rastafari that came to be Jamaica's best-known cultural export and therefore a vital component of an emerging film industry.

Chris Blackwell has long been able to see the potential export value of Jamaican music and has devoted himself to establishing profitable links with

Europe and North America. After acting as location scout on *Dr No* in 1962, Blackwell came to London and as co-founder of Island Records promoted and recorded Jamaican music in Britain, eventually releasing the classic film sound-track album from *The Harder They Come* on his Island label. In the early 1980s, following the enormous international success of Bob Marley, Blackwell sought to extend Island Record's portfolio into film production. He envisaged that advances in technology, especially the advent of home video recorders, would eventually circumvent the traditional chain of cinema distribution, and he established Island Pictures in 1982 with the production of **Countryman**, directed by Dickie Jobson. The film exchanges the urban realism of *The Harder They Come* or *Rockers* for a bucolic mysticism inspired by its eponymous hero's deep faith in Rastafarian theology. The plot revolves around a scheme operated by corrupt governmental officials to discredit the political opposition through the framing of two innocent Americans as CIA gunrunners to the island during a forthcoming election. Through Countryman's religious beliefs, kung-fu fighting skills and certain supernatural helpers, the young Americans are rescued from the corrupt politicians and allowed home. The film's endorsement of the Rastafarian rejection of the modern world and its materialism contrasts strongly with Ivan's quest in *The Harder They Come* to better his conditions of living by all means at his disposal. *Countryman* was made during a time of almost open civil war between Jamaica's two main parties, the JLP and PNP, but whereas *The Harder They Come* had attempted to expose the economic motivations behind this new breed of political gangsters, *Countryman* wanted to avoid the political implications of its own timely plot in favour of a more supernatural contest between a rural spiritual faith and the urban forces of corrupted and westernized "progress".

During the 1980s Blackwell concentrated on the non-Jamaican side of his film company, achieving international success with productions such as *Kiss of the Spider Woman* and *She's Got To Have It*. Eventually he sold his film and record companies, while continuing to manage them, to European entertainment giant Polydor. For small independent producers based in Jamaica at this time, the costs involved in feature production seemed prohibitive. In Britain, television in the form of Channel 4 acted as a crucial catalyst for feature film production, but in Jamaica film and video producers were forced to actually buy air time on JBC themselves before broadcast was possible.

In 1991 Blackwell returned to Jamaican subject matter with **The Lunatic,** directed by American songwriter and music video director Lol Creme. Like *Smile Orange*, the film makes broad comedy out of the Jamaican tourist industry and featured Aloysius, played by Paul Campbell, who has an affair with Inge, played by British actress Julie T. Wallace. The pair become embroiled in a plot to rob the local white landowner, with hilarious consequences. Adapted by Jamaican author Anthony Winkler from his own novel, the film is an engaging, achingly funny mixture of burlesque humour, folklore and satirical comment on the sexual tourism prevalent in Jamaica.

Digital Futures

In the 1990s the cost of feature film productions was greatly reduced by the arrival of new digital video technology. Chris Blackwell's hope at the start of the 1980s that technological progress would eventually lead to greater opportunities for smaller producers operating outside Hollywood now seemed much closer to reality. Blackwell eventually left Polydor and went on to form Palm Pictures. Both **Dancehall Queen** (1997) and **Third World Cop** (1999) were financed by Blackwell and made on a limited budget using small digital cameras for release onto the video market, although they were eventually given a theatrical release by the transference of the digital format to film. *Dancehall Queen*, directed by British music-video veteran Don Letts and Rick Elgood, adapts elements of the musical and crime genres to a Jamaican context. The film follows the fortunes of its heroine, Marcia (played by Audrey Reid), as she struggles to break free from her existence as a street vendor and to distance her daughter from the sexual advances of "Uncle" Larry. Her escape route is to become queen of the dancehall and receive the cash prize that goes with it. The film generated controversy in Jamaica upon its release, as it was seen to raise difficult questions over the representation and exploitation of women within society, and in the island's cinemas its popularity ensured it competed successfully with *Men in Black*. *Third World Cop*, directed by Christopher Brown, continues the ongoing creolization of American cinema conventions by Jamaican producers. It takes the stock characters, action sequences and narrative cliché associated with the modern Hollywood action thriller and fleshes them out with distinctively Jamaican motivations and language.

The Jamaican film industry has also made a brilliant entry into documentary making via the feature-length **Life and Debt**, produced and directed by local woman Stephanie Black and with a voice-over adapted from Jamaica Kincaid's celebrated novel *A Small Place*. An investigation into the ways in which Jamaica's debt burden – and the agendas of agencies such as the World Bank, Inter-American Development Bank and the IMF – have affected everyday life for the island's residents, it makes essential viewing, with cameos from Buju Banton and Yami Bolo as the icing on the cake. Juxtaposing carefree tourist frolics at a resort hotel with footage of the 1999 gas riots and a look at the farming and dairy industries, as well as the "free zones" in Montego Bay and Kingston where Jamaicans work for mostly US-based companies for often pitiful wages, it's not easy viewing, but certainly puts the lot of the average Jamaican into context.

Almost thirty years after the release of *The Harder They Come*, there are still only limited film production opportunities on the island, and producers are often forced to seek an audience outside Jamaica to gather a return on their investment. American studios, on the other hand, continue to take advantage of local tax concessions and dollar exchange rates. Don Letts, director of *Dancehall Queen*, warns that digital technology can bring down only the cost of what takes place behind the camera, not in front of it. For the time being at least, it seems those wishing to make films about the reality of Jamaican society will continue to occupy a disadvantaged place within the world's media, while the processes of globalization continue to support the dominance of European and North American culture. Although the number of authentic Jamaican films produced over the years has been small, within this handful of films is the beginning of a cinematic tradition, one that turns its own economic disadvantages into positive aesthetic values and absorbs foreign cultural influence to transform it into the unique historical synthesis that is Jamaican cinema.

John Fortnum

Books

T he selection of books below represents the best available books written about Jamaica, alongside some of the authors' personal favourites. All are available via websites such as ⓦwww.amazon.co.uk and ⓦww.amazon.com, or from specialist Caribbean publishers such as Sangsters (ⓦwww.sangsterbooks.com), UWI Press (ⓦwww.uwipress.com), Peepal Tree (ⓦwww.peepaltreepress.com) and LMH (ⓦwww.lmhpublishingjamaica.com). Titles marked with a star are particularly recommended.

Travel and diaries

Patrick Leigh Fermor *The Traveller's Tree.* The classic Caribbean travelogue describing Leigh Fermor's visit in the late 1940s, before tourism had really started in the region, though only the last chapter covers his time in Jamaica, with specific reference to the developing Rastafari movement in West Kingston.

★ **Linda Gambrill** (ed) *A Tapestry of Jamaica.* A collection of the best articles from thirty years of Air Jamaica's brilliant in-flight magazine. Covering sport, music, travel, fashion, people, art, history and folk tales, as well as a whole section on the inimitable Miss Lou, this is an essential collection, made all the more poignant by the sheer love of the island that comes through in the final "memories" section.

Margaret Hodges (ed) *Blue Mountain Guide.* Useful pocket guide to the peak trail, with a sketch map of the stages up and accounts of the surrounding environment, geology, fauna and flora, and human impact.

Brian J. Hudson *The Waterfalls of Jamaica.* A wide-ranging ode to Jamaica's gorgeous cascades (though not a guidebook in the practical sense), it looks at the main waterfalls and their exploitation as tourist attractions, with illustrations ranging from eighteenth-century prints to contemporary photographs. Food for thought as you idle away an afternoon at YS.

Mattthew Lewis *Journal of a West Indian Planter.* Fascinating diaries of Lewis, an early nineteenth-century English novelist, describing his brief visits to his Jamaican estates and cataloguing the lifestyle and living conditions of the island's slaves.

Margaret Morris *Tour Jamaica.* A Jamaican's view of Jamaica, recommending seventeen different driving tours around the island. Lots of history and folklore titbits, and plenty of detail, but short on practicalities.

Lady Maria Nugent *Journal of Residence in Jamaica 1801–5.* Lady Nugent was the wife of one of Jamaica's governors, and her diary, though often naive and patronizing, paints an interesting picture of how the "ruling class" lived.

★ **Chris Salewicz** *Rude Boy – Once Upon a Time in Jamaica.* Part history of Jamaica, part travelogue written by a true Jamaicaphile, it evokes some of the innate paradoxes of Jamaica with humour and delicacy.

★ **Frank Fonda Taylor** *To Hell with Paradise.* Exhaustive history of the beginnings of the Jamaican tourist industry, with great black-and-white photos and early adverts. Offers some marvellous insight into the prejudices and condescensions of the first visitors.

Anthony Winkler *Going Home to Teach*. Engaging story of novelist Winkler's own experiences as a white Jamaican returning to live on his native island during the "anti-white" climate of the late 1970s. Very

good on the politics and atmosphere of the period.

Paul Zach (ed) *Jamaica: Insight Guides*. Glossy guide, short on practical information but long on colour photographs, and a decent souvenir book.

Fiction

★ **Louise Bennett** *Anancy and Miss Lou*. Jamaica's oral tradition of storytelling may be fading, but these are the classic folk tales – from the greatest of modern Jamaican storytellers – told in patois and including the story of the crafty spider Anancy.

★ **Margaret Cezair-Thompson** *The True History of Paradise*. Poignant and beautifully written history of Jamaica as told by various generations of a Jamaican family, from the Scottish wife of a planter to an African ex-slave to a modern-day uptown girl in Kingston. Evocative and brilliant.

Colin Channer *Waiting In Vain*. This tale of a modern-day romance between a Jamaican man and an American woman perfectly evokes the Jamaican communities of England, New York and Jamaica itself. Great holiday reading.

Mark Conklin *Banana Shout*. Engaging and occasionally hilarious account of an American draft dodger's adventures as he sets up home in Negril during the 1970s, and an essential oral history of the development of the resort.

Kwame Dawes *A Place to Hide*. Short stories set in Jamaica, often with a rather pessimistic slant, which reveal all the intricacies of island society.

Herbert de Lisser *The White Witch of Rose Hall*. A blend of Gothic horror and purple prose, this richly embellished account of the island's best-known ghost story tells the tale of Annie Palmer, mistress of Rose Hall Great House, whose three husbands all died in suspicious circumstances.

Victor Headley *Yardie*. Easy-reading, thought-provoking (if not that well-written) tale of a drug-running "mule" who rises to the top of a UK-based drugs racket, shedding light on the whole sordid business along the way.

★ **Perry Henzell** *Power Game*. Long, entertaining story of power seekers at different levels in Jamaican society – politics, the army, the banks, the drug trade. Henzell catches local language and atmosphere with the same skill he used in his movie *The Harder They Come*.

Evan Jones *Stone Haven*. Long-winded but readable historical novel that picks its way through modern issues, from 1920s attitudes to colour to the problems of post-independence.

★ **Guy Kennaway** *One People*. Entertaining and brilliantly funny take on life in a tiny coastal town in Westmoreland. It perfectly evokes rural Jamaican life, from the patois chat to the clandestine shenanigans of the locals. Essential.

★ **Roger Mais** *The Hills Were Joyful Together, Brother Man* and *Black Lightning*. *Hills* is a bleak, compelling picture of life in a Kingston ghetto in the 1950s, with a harsh look at law and order Jamaica-style, by one of the country's earliest novelists. *Brother Man* details the emergence of Rastafari in Kingston via the gentle "Brother Man" himself, while *Black Lightning* is an intense and atmospheric account of the life of a brooding sculptor living in the Jamaican bush.

Terry McMillan *How Stella Got Her Groove Back*. In McMillan's lightweight but enjoyable tone, this semi-autobiographical tale tells the story of a holiday romance that turns serious, written as a result of the author's experiences during holidays in Negril.

Brian Meeks *Paint the Town Red*. Moving portrayal of an uptown Kingstonian's first day of freedom after serving a prison term for his involvement in a politically motivated shooting in the run-up to the 1980 election. The descriptions of life in the ghetto are particularly gripping – and brutal.

Colin Moon *Obeah*. Fascinating and sinister fictional introduction to the world of Jamaican witchcraft.

★ **Orlando Patterson** *The Children of Sisyphus*. Famous, uncompromising picture of the poorest of Kingston's poor, fighting for survival on the margins of society, and of Dinah, a prostitute who tries to leave them behind and move up in the world. One of the first novels to try to present a fair picture of the Rasta community.

★ **Geoffrey Philp** *Benjamin, My Son*. A Jamaican living in Miami returns to the island for the funeral of his father, a politician loosely modelled on several recognizable Jamaican leaders, and becomes embroiled in the shady world of

Jamaica's political scene: gunmen, obeahmen and all.

V.S. Reid *The Jamaicans*. Juan de Bolas was a slave liberated by the Spanish when the English captured the island in 1655; Reid's fictionalized account tells of his life in hiding and struggle against the English.

★ **Jean Rhys** *Wide Sargasso Sea*. Poignant, beautifully written view of post-emancipation Jamaica, with Antoinette, a young creole girl, and Rochester, her English boyfriend, trapped by declining financial circumstances and his inability to understand the realities of local life. Written as a prequel to Bronte's *Jane Eyre*.

Kim Robinson & Leeta Hearn (eds) *Twenty-two Jamaican Short Stories*. Excellent short-story collection that covers some of the more chilling psychological aspects of Jamaican life. Venerable authors include Olive Senior, Dennis Scott, Hazel Campbell and Trevor Fearon.

Tony Sewell *Jamaica Inc*. Gripping and intelligent fictional history of a strangely familiar political family dynasty.

Vanessa Spence *The Roads Are Down*. Excellent and amusing first novel of a cross-cultural love affair, set in modern-day Kingston and the Blue Mountains.

Michael Thewell *The Harder They Come*. Novel inspired by Perry Henzell's brilliant movie, telling the story of Rhygin – country boy turned rude boy – who comes to Kingston and gets caught up in gangs and ganja.

★ **Anthony Winkler** *The Great Yacht Race, The Painted Canoe* and *The Lunatic*. Set just before independence, *The Great Yacht Race* is a hilarious look at the lifestyle of Montego Bay's erstwhile "ruling class" as the lawyers, journalists and hotel owners go through scandal after scandal in preparation for their annual boat race. *The Painted Canoe* is a powerful, evocative tale of a Jamaican fisherman and his relationship with the sea, while *The Lunatic* is a poignant but amusing tale of a Jamaican madman, who wanders the island talking with the trees and bushes, and his encounter with Inge, a sexually voracious German tourist (see also p.429).

History and politics

Warren Alleyne *Caribbean Pirates*. Alleyne debunks the myths about the region's leading pirates – from Blackbeard to Henry Morgan – in a series of brief portraits.

★ **Clinton Black** *Port Royal* and *Tales of Old Jamaica*. *Port Royal* is a solid history of the city once known as the "wickedest place on earth"; *Tales* has brief accounts of some of the key events in the island's past, recalling the capture of Jamaica by the British, the story of "Three Fingered" Jack Mansong, and the women pirates Anne Bonney and Mary Read.

Mavis Campbell *The Maroons of Jamaica 1655–1796*. Scholarly work that traces the origins of the Maroons during the English invasion of Jamaica in 1655 and follows their development as a community up to the Trelawny war of the late-eighteenth century.

James Ferguson *A Traveller's History of the Caribbean*. Concise and well-written overview that provides a good introduction to the region's history.

John Gilmore *Faces of the Caribbean*. Excellent and essential sociohistory of the Caribbean, covering everything from slavery to reggae, cricket and the environment.

Michelle Harrison *King Sugar – Jamaica, the Caribbean and the World Sugar Economy*. Solid history of the Jamaican sugar industry – and the fortunes it made for British planters.

★ **Gad Heuman** *The Killing Time: The Morant Bay Rebellion*. Detailed and articulate study of the 1865 rebellion, its causes and the aftermath, and a review of the tradition of protest in Jamaica.

Darrell E. Levy *Michael Manley: The Making of a Leader*. Detailed biography of the controversial leader, though it never really captures Manley's sparkle, and Levy lets him off rather lightly on some of his acknowledged errors.

Rupert Lewis & Patrick Bryan (eds) *Garvey: His Work and Impact*. Twenty-one articles on the historical background to Garveyism, his influence on Jamaica and his worldwide legacy.

Michael Manley *The Politics of Change – A Jamaican Testament*. Interesting overview of the proposed transformation of the island under Manley's PNP government, written as it got underway in the early 1970s.

★ **J.P. Parry, Philip Sherlock & Anthony Maingot** *A Short History of the West Indies*. The best concise history of the region, taking the story up to the mid-1980s, and good on general issues such as regional cooperation and debt crisis.

★ **Carey Robinson** *The Fighting Maroons of Jamaica*. Accessible, general history of the Maroons up to 1800, fairly easy to get in Jamaican bookshops.

Olive Senior *The A-Z of Jamaican Heritage.* Concise but useful dictionary, with brief entries on everything from Garvey to Manley, Rastas to Pocomania.

Tony Sewell *Garvey's Children: The Legacy of Marcus Garvey.* Readable account of Garvey's black power movement and the inspiration it has provided for black nationalists in Jamaica and abroad.

Verene Shepherd *The Experience of Indians in Jamaica, 1845–1950.* Short, scholarly look at Indian indentured labour and its social and economic consequences.

John Stewart (ed) *In Old St James.* Small collection of stories of the early English settlers, focusing particularly on the ancestors of Elizabeth Barrett Browning.

Religion, culture and society

Mervyn Alleyne *Roots of Jamaican Culture.* Academic but fascinating exploration of African-Jamaican culture and society covering history, language, music and religion.

Leonard Barrett *The Rastafarians and The Sun and the Drum.* The former is one of the most comprehensive accounts of the movement, explaining its origins and politics and looking at related religious movements like the Twelve Tribes of Israel sect. The latter is an in-depth look at the influence of African traditions in Jamaican culture, including language, witchcraft and folk medicine.

Marcel Bayer *In Focus Jamaica: A Guide to the People, Politics and Culture.* Excellent little handbook, with lucid and relevant sections on history, politics, the economy, society and culture.

Derek Bishton *Black Heart Man – A Journey into Rasta.* Succinct, well-researched foray into the origins and development of the Rastafarian movement in Jamaica, with discussion of Garvey and a host of less well-known black theorists.

Adrian Boot & Michael Thomas *Babylon on a Thin Wire.* Evocative photographic portraits of 1970s Kingston from one of the most renowned photographers of Jamaican culture, backed up by cynical and informed text.

Lloyd Bradley *Bass Culture – When Reggae Was King.* Very readable history of reggae, written, for once, by a man of Jamaican origin rather than a US academic. Entertaining and pretty comprehensive, though a bit short on contemporary detail.

Edward Kamau Braithwaite *Folk Culture of the Slaves in Jamaica.* Fact-packed mini-book with an excellent introduction to black culture under slavery as seen through the eyes of a contemporary black Jamaican university professor. Detailed descriptions of the customs among slave societies, including death rituals, religion, music and dance, dress, entertainment tastes, language and even household decor.

Horace Campbell *Rasta and Resistance from Marcus Garvey to Walter Rodney.* Academic but militant discussion of the development and influence of the Rasta religion and philosophy.

Laurie Gunst *Born Fe Dead* (US Henry Holt/UK Payback Press). Gripping account of the dark side of political and drug-related violence in Jamaica, recently reissued with updates and a new postscript.

Ably researched with the help of Jamaicans in Kingston and New York, this traces the development of Jamaican posses from political lackeys to drug-trafficking gangsters.

★ **Polly Pattullo** *Last Resorts – The Cost of Tourism in the Caribbean*. Important, well-researched critique of the tourist industry and its impact on the islands.

Edward Seaga *Revival Cults in Jamaica*. Anthropological descriptions of the beliefs, rituals and practices within Pocomania, Kumina and Zion religions by former prime minister Seaga.

M.G. Smith, Roy Augier & Rex Nettleford *Report on the Rastafari Movement*. Published in 1960, the first academic study of Jamaica's home-grown religion. Dated but accurate description of the contemporary make-up, history, beliefs and rituals of Rastafari.

Music, art and sport

★ **Steve Barrow & Peter Dalton** *The Rough Guide to Reggae*. Comprehensive, definitive handbook on reggae music, with sections on the UK, US and African scenes as well as a comprehensive rundown on things in Jamaica.

Cedella Booker *Bob Marley*. Very personal account of Marley's life and death written by his mother, light on the music but heavy on family anecdotes, plus the occasional (and most entertaining) catty swipe.

★ **Adrian Boot & Chris Salewicz** *Bob Marley – Songs of Freedom*. Boot's fabulous photos and Salewicz's spot-on text make this one of the better Marley bios, with lots of input from the family and first-hand interviews.

★ **David Boxer & Veerle Poupeye** *Modern Jamaican Art*. Lavish tome with text from Jamaica's premier art historians, and high-quality plates of the best and most familiar works.

Stephen Davis *Bob Marley – Conquering Lion of Reggae*. Businesslike and exhaustive examination of Marley's life and work, with lots of gossip thrown in.

Dermott Hussey & Malika Lee

Whitney *Bob Marley*. Coffee-table heavyweight, with lots of illustrations, interviews with all the principal characters and text by Jamaicans who were part of the unfolding scene.

★ **Lee Jaffe** *One Love – Life with Bob Marley and the Wailers*. An American photographer who hung out with Bob et al in the 1970s, Jaffe tells his story via interviews with Roger Steffens. The text is interspersed with Jaffe's wonderful photographs (some previously unpublished), which perfectly document the era.

Brian Jahn & Tom Weber *Reggae Island*. The story of reggae told mainly through interviews with key players, from the young Garnet Silk to Buju Banton, Bunny Wailer, Ken Booth and Mykal Rose, but lacking in contemporary insight.

David Katz *Solid Foundation* and *People Funny Boy*. *Solid Foundation* is a history of the first thirty years of Jamaican music, from mento to the dawn of dancehall, as told by the musicians themselves. The 200-plus interviews include producers (Coxsone Dodd, Prince Buster, Junjo Lawes), musicians (Sly and Robbie) and all the essential artists, from members of the Skatalites and Toots and the Maytals to Burning Spear, U-Roy and Frankie Paul. Katz's *People Funny Boy* is the definitive biography of the eccentric genius Lee "Scratch" Perry.

★ **Beth Lesser** *King Jammy's*. Brilliant bio of the Waterhouse dancehall maestro, which provides the definitive lowdown on the man himself as well as a host of artists from the 1980s onwards, from Wayne Smith to Bounty Killer.

Michael Manley *A History of West Indies Cricket*. The late prime minister's superb history of the Caribbean contribution to the world's greatest game.

Dennis Morris *Bob Marley – A Rebel Life*. Brand-new coffee-table tome detailing Marley's 1970s stint in London, as seen through the lens of a then-young British-Jamaican photographer. Some lovely never-before-seen shots paint an intimate portrait.

★ **Chris Morrow** *Stir It Up*. LP-sized tribute to Jamaican record-cover artwork, with all the best efforts in full colour.

Norman C. Stolzoff *Wake The Town and Tell The People*. Though rather academic in tone, and written firmly from the somewhat anthropological perspective of a non-Jamaican, this nonetheless provides some solid background to the sound system scene, from the genre's early days to a blow-by-blow account of a Killamanjaro dance.

★ **Petrine Archer Straw & Kim Robinson** *Jamaican Art*. Comprehensive account of the development of modern Jamaican art, well illustrated with the work of all of the major painters and sculptors, from Edna Marley to Kapo.

Don Taylor *Marley and Me*. Taylor was Bob Marley's one-time manager, and his chatty if rather badly written account – focusing on girlfriends, politics and controversy – is more sensationalist than White's (below).

★ **Timothy White** *Catch a Fire*. Exhaustive and loving biography of Bob Marley (including a detailed discography), with an in-depth look at the early Jamaican music scene and plenty of obeah and superstition.

Language and humour

L. Emile Adams *Understanding Jamaican Patois*. User-friendly and intelligent description of patois grammar and language usage, with a small dictionary.

Viv Burnett *Mi Granny Seh Fi Tell Yu Seh*. Entertaining collection of some of Jamaican proverbs, including: "Ard 'ears pickney nyam rockstone" (children that don't listen learn the hard way) ; "dem like batty an' bench" (they're as thick as thieves); "dem like clothes pin: squeeze dem head, foot open" (a description of a promiscuous per-

son); and "Ah nuh every kin teen a laugh" (not every smile is genuine).

S. Knight & T. Lowrie *Hustling Jamaican Style*. Light-hearted and sarcastically incisive trip through the familiar tourist town hustlers.

★ **Kim Robinson, Harclyde Walcott & Trevor Fearon** *The How To Be Jamaican Handbook*. Humorous lessons on appropriate behaviour in the resorts and beyond, with painfully accurate - if very 1980s – caricatures of archetypal Jamaican and tourist types.

Flora and fauna

★ **C. Dennis Adams** *Flowering Plants of Jamaica*. Useful introductory guide to Jamaican flora.

James Bond *Field Guide to Birds of the West Indies*. The classic bird book, from which Ian Fleming took the name of his fictional hero, though generally considered to have been supplanted by the Downer/Sutton book.

★ **Audrey Downer & Robert Sutton** *Birds of Jamaica: A Photographic Field Guide*. The definitive field guide on the island's birds, with handy sections on the island's principal habitats and birding "hot spots".

Susan Iremonger *Guide to the Plants in the Blue Mountains of Jamaica*. Useful field guide if you've a serious interest in the area's plant-life, with line drawings and lots of colour plates.

Eugene Kaplan *A Field Guide to the Coral Reefs of the Caribbean and Florida*. Attractive guide to the region's reefs.

★ **G.W. Lennox & S.A. Seddon** *Flowers of the Caribbean; Trees of the Caribbean; Fruits and Vegetables of the Caribbean*. Handy pocket-size books, with glossy, sharp, coloured pictures, and a good general introduction to the region's flora.

Diane Robertson *Jamaican Herbs*. Thorough description of the medicinal properties of commonly used herbs, roots, fruits and vegetables, with advice on preparation.

Food and drink

Norma Benghiat *Traditional Jamaican Cookery*. Handy and engagingly written guide to the island's traditional dishes, from ackee and saltfish to curry goat and rice and peas, with all of the classic recipes and a lot more. *The Food of Jamaica*, by Benghiat and John Demers, is another reliable option.

Mike Henry *Caribbean Cocktails and Mixed Drinks*. All of the classic recipes based mostly on rums and fresh juices.

Laura Osbourne *The Rasta Cookbook*. The low-down on classic Ital cooking with main courses, puddings and (of course) blended health drinks.

Caroline Sullivan *Classic Jamaican Cooking*. The Jamaican version of Mrs Beeton, little changed since its first publication in 1896. Excellent recipes, anecdotes and the essential "Herbal Remedies and Household Hints".

Helen Willinsky *Jerk – Barbecue from Jamaica*. Do-it-yourself jerk manual.

Language

Language

Language

Jamaicans enjoy nothing better than a good debate – you can join in at any rum shop or simply switch on the radio. They take great delight in outwitting each other in verbal battles that Anancy, the sharp-brained spider who's a favourite Jamaican folk hero (see box p.442), would be proud of. Although Jamaica's official language is English, patois is the working mode of expression for most Jamaicans. Its validity as a legitimate language or corrupted slang continues to provoke much debate on the island.

Jamaican patois is an incredibly creative and constantly evolving idiom; new words are coined almost daily to suit every development and fall into common use with astonishing speed, while older phrases – yesterday's "buzzwords" – disappear without a trace. Sex and related topics are generously covered in the patois lexicon; there are no less than four names for the penis in its various stages from boyhood ("pem pem") to teenage years ("tutu"), and countless names for the female genitalia. Patois also forms the basis for Jamaica's myriad **proverbs**, spouted by grannies and rude boys alike, such as "what sweet nanny goat ago run him belly" ("what you like may not necessarily be good for you"); "every hoe have him stick a bush" ("there's an ideal partner for everyone") or "tree nah grow in yuh face" ("you're not ugly").

An explanation of some of the more obvious idiosyncrasies will go some way to unravelling the labyrinth of patois. If you want to delve deeper, consult the books listed on p.437, and keep your ears wide open.

- Women are commonly referred to as "him": "Wha! Shelley pregnant! Him never tell me!"
- "H" is often not voiced, but makes up for the discrepancy by adding itself to plenty of other words. Hence "So yu is 'Enry from Hin-glan, don't?" ("don't" is used to mean "aren't you", or "isn't it?").
- There are plenty more inexplicable additions and absences: "shrimp" is often "swimp", "spliff" is "scliff", "vex" is "bex", "little" is "likkle", "ask" is "aks".
- Plurals are either ignored or conveyed by adding "dem"; hence "two feet" becomes "two foot", and "the girls are cooking for me" is "de gyal dem a cook fe de I".
- If somebody calls you "fatty", "whitey" or "big batty gyal", they are simply being direct rather than attempting to insult. Follow Jamaicans in their directness and convey your meaning as simply as possible. Don't waste time with endless unnecessary pleasantries – please and thank you will suffice.

Rasta linguistics

The Rasta challenge to all things Babylonian includes an assault upon all that "downpresses" the black man in the English language. As a means of resistance, Rastas have embarked on a new classification of words that attempt to correct what is seen as bias against their experiences, perceptions, personal choices and world view as black people. While this may sometimes seem pedantic (greeting

Anancy

The Twi word for spider, **Anancy** is a Jamaican hero and the principal character of most of the island's traditional folk stories; even tales without him are often referred to as "Nansi stories". Living by intellect rather than substance, the half-man, half-spider Brer Anancy always outwits his adversaries in a triumph of cunning over force – an allegory of the historical and contemporary struggles of black Jamaicans.

Anancy's Machiavellian use of deception and cunning in his triumphs mean each story has to end with the words "Jack Mandora, me no choose none" – Mandora is the keeper of heaven's gates, and the narrator has to disassociate him- or herself from Anancy's wicked ways. Anancy stories are best told in Louise Bennett's *Anancy and Miss Lou* (see "Books", p.432).

a Rasta with "hello" might illicit the cool response "We're not in hell and I'm not low"), language does have a strong effect upon the formation of hierarchies and prejudices, and Rasta linguistics is one of the most creative elements of Jamaican patois. Rastas generally counteract negatives with positives and vice versa, breaking down each word and analysing its syllabic connotations, often reading significance into every nuance; hence understand becomes **overstand** (because if you comprehend something, you're above it rather than beneath it), oppress (up-press) becomes **downpress.** The most recognizable aspect of Rasta linguistics is the use of "I" to emphasize unity (Inity) and positivity as well as to protest against the coercive control of language. Hence create becomes **I-rate**, continually becomes **I-tinually**, creation is **I-ration**. Selassie I is interpreted as proof of Haile Selassie's omnipresence: **Sela***see eye*. It isn't difficult to see why there are so many cryptic messages embedded in 1970s roots reggae lyrics.

Rasta linguistics are not restricted to the Rastafarian community; the Rasta greetings "hail", "yes Rasta" or the acknowledgement of understanding in "seen Iyah" have become normal phrases for Jamaican (particularly male) youth. Rasta words that have slipped into daily usage are listed below. For a full description of the Rasta lexicon read Velma Pollard's *Dread Talk*.

Patois glossary

The common words and phrases below have been written semi–phonetically, a sometimes clumsy medium but the only way in which to convey their sound in the available space.

Ago Verb meaning will or going to do something: "Me ago check yuh tomorrow".

Agony Rough sex (or just sex).

Almshouse Militant or negative behaviour, a favourite attitude during sound-system clashes.

Babylon Government or the established and oppressive social system; also an insulting title for police.

Baby mother/father A person with children.

Badmind Jealous, covetous, bad intentions.

Baggy Female underwear.

Bakra White man, traditionally a slave owner, probably derived from the Ibo "mbaraka".

Baldhead Non-Rasta, or person of unsound views.

Bandulu Trickery or a swindle.

Bangarang Noise or disruptive commotion, often used by rival sound systems: "Pack up you old time bangarang" ("Pack away your pathetic array of tinny equipment").

Bare Only; as in "she ave bare plantain fi sell".

Bashment A huge party or dance, or anything or anybody current, appealing and worth making a fuss over; also shortened, as in "me ave one bashy dress fe wear to de dance".

Battery dolly A woman who makes a habit of having sex with more than one man simultaneously.

Batty Backside/bottom.

Battyman/boy Homosexual male.

Batty riders Tight lycra hot pants worn by dancehall queens for maximum buttock exposure.

Bawl Cry out or call, particularly to register anguish: "Him a bawl out over the taxi fare".

Beenie Small or diminutive: "Me buy a likkle beenie amplifier".

Bhuttu Unsophisticated, simple country bumpkin; used as an insult.

Big Up Boost yourself up (verb): "Big up yu chest" or "Big up yu status/yuself".

Bimma BMW: "Who got the keys to my bimma?".

Blood Principally a swear word used with claat and hole. Can also be used as a respectful greeting signifying unity; as in "Wh'appen, blood?".

Blouse and skirt An exclamation of surprise.

Bly An opportunity, chance or escape from an unwanted chore: "De rain gimme a bly – me nah haffe go a wuk".

Bombo Offensive expletive meaning backside, usually in conjunction with claat or hole: "Move yu bombo-claat face from me".

Boops Rather 1980s term for a man who financially supports his (usually much younger) girlfriend.

Boots Condoms: "Me wear me boots everytime, zeen!".

Bow Verb meaning to indulge in oral sex; "bow cat" is a participant.

Brawta A little extra to make a better bargain, usually employed when bartering in a market: "Gimme me brawta, nuh?"

Breddah Friend, usually male: "Yes mi breddah!". **Bredren** is the plural form, used both as a noun and as an adjective; **breds** is the shortened version.

Browning Light-skinned woman.

Bruk Broken.

Brukout To let loose, usually at a party.

Buck To meet somebody: "Me will buck up wid yu later".

Buddy Penis.

Buff Bay Relating to the vagina; if a woman is "buff", she has large and appealing vaginal lips.

Bumper Backside/bottom.

Bun or **burn** Literally, burn. Used in terms of smoking: "Me bun de ganja long time"; as a condemnation: "Bun out de politician dem" (also see "fire"); and to connote infidelity: "She bun im with a nex man".

Cargo Bling-bling gold jewellery, as favoured by dancehall DJs.

Cat Vagina.

Chalice Pipe for smoking ganja, usually communally.

Charged Intoxicated, stoned: "Me get charged las' night".

Check Pay a visit: "Me ago check yu tomorrow". Also a term of platonic or sexual appreciation, as in "Me check fe di man's argument", and as a term for sexual advances: "De young bway try an' check big woman".

Chi-chi man Pejorative term for a homosexual man, popularized in dancehall music.

Cho Expression of surprise or distaste: "Cho! Me nah wan no man inna me life".

Claat/clot Literally, cloth, used with ras, pussy, bumba as an expletive: "Tek yuh blood-claat hands off me!"

Clean de rifle Perform fellatio.

Cook an' curry Everything's been taken care of, as in "Me clean de whole house; everyting cook an' curry now".

Copasetic Cool, good: "Everyting copasetic".

Cork Full, as in "the dance cork tonight".

Cotch Rest up, chill out: "Sit dung and cotch with me". Also a verb to mean where a person sleeps: "Me a cotch by Evelyn's". Also used to denote bracing something: "Cotch de wheel wid' a rock".

Craven Greedy, desperate.

Criss Attractive, beautiful: "Maxine a criss, criss gyal".

Criss-biscuit Anything of excellence but seldom used these days.

Crub Dance with a partner slowly and suggestively.

Cuss-cuss Argument.

Cut-eye A malevolent look: "Pure cut-eye me get from him".

Dads Don, a well-respected man: "Zekes a de dads fe Matthews Lane" ("Zekes runs Matthews Lane").

Dally To go: "Me mus dally now".

Dawta Young woman, interchangeable with sistah.

Dead-stock Quiet, a non-event: "Dem promote pure dead-stock dance".

Dege-dege Small, measly: "She gimme one dege-dege piece of yam".

Deh-deh Be somewhere: "Me deh-deh" ("I am here").

Deh-pan Doing it, in control of matters: "Me deh-pan the repairs, man".

Deportee Humorous term used for the huge number of Japanese estate cars imported in recent years, so-called because, like wayward Jamaicans deported from "foreign", the unwanted cars have been sent here because no one else wants them.

Dis Disrespect: "Him a dis de programme" ("He's rudely disrupting our plans").

Don Literally an area leader, but also used to describe any respected male: "Him a de don". Also used in conjunction with gorgon or dada to mean the best or the toughest: "Me a di don gorgon/don dada" ("I'm the man!").

Draw card To trick or deceive; pull something sneaky.

Dread A person with locks (not necessarily of Rastafarian faith), or an adjective used to describe a bad situation: "De times dread".

Duns/Dunsa Money.

Dutch pot Heavy cooking pot.

Dweet Do it: "Me dweet sweet, sis".

Eat under a two-foot table A man performing oral sex on a woman.

Ends A place: "Mi deh pon a ends, still" ("I'm off to go somewhere").

Facety Impertinent, rude: "De touris' facety to rass".

Fassy Literally vagina, combined with "hole",

as in "Yow, fassyhole, who you talk to so?". Also, generally nasty, dirty and foolish.

Feel no way Don't worry about it.

Fenky-fenky Weak, pathetic behaviour or demeanour.

Fire Popularized by Rastafarian dancehall DJ Capleton, whose militant catchphrase is "more fire"; used to castigate the unrighteous by means of the cleansing power of fire: "Fire pon all de politician dem!". Often combined with "bun".

Fish Homosexual man.

Flex A person's way of behaving: "Ah so me flex, my yout" ("That's how I operate, young man").

Flop Losing face, usually in public and often associated with the performance of an artist or sound system.

Fowl pill Poultry steroid taken by women to increase the size of their breasts and backsides.

Friend Apart from the usual meaning, can be used (rather confusingly) to refer to one's sexual partner.

Fuckery Irritating, bothersome, out of order: "Dis man is pure fuckery" ("This man is badly behaved").

Ganja Marijuana.

Ganzey String vest or light-knit T-shirt.

Gates Home: "Check me at me gates".

Ginnal Con man or trickster.

Glamity Female genitals.

Gravalicious Greedy or avaricious.

Grind To have sex. A grindsman is a man particularly skilled between the sheets.

Guidance An inspirational goodbye meaning "Let God be with you".

Gwan Go on or carry on (verb). Also used to mean "go away" or "going to".

Gweh Go away. Can also be used as an affectionate retort to foolish actions or speech.

Gyal Girl or woman.

Heartical Conscious esteemed person: "He's my heartical bredren".

Herb Ganja, herbal marijuana.

Higgler Female market trader, or a woman who brings goods to Jamaica from abroad to sell, often also called an ICI (Informal Commercial Importer).

High grade Premium-quality ganja.

Hol' it down Be cool and restrained, to be on a low profile or stay quiet.

Hood Penis, also called a **wood**.

Hottie-hottie An attractive female: "She one hottie-hottie gyal".

Hush Used as an expression of sympathy.

I an' I Rasta-speak meaning me, I, we, mine, myself. **I-man** equally applies.

Idren Used by Rastas to mean friends or bredren.

Irie Adjective meaning fine or good: "You lookin' Irie tonight". Also used as a greeting.

Iron bird/fish Airplane or boat; used mostly by Rastas.

Ishence Ganja.

Ital Anything natural (an Ital car wash is a river) or pure (a spliff without tobacco). Also describes Rastafarian meatless food cooked without salt.

Iyah Greeting to a friend: "What a gwan Iyah".

Jacket Child raised by a man who isn't his father (the father usually doesn't know).

Jagabat Nasty, unclean, sluttish woman.

Jamdown Jamaica. **JA** is also frequently used.

Joe White man.

Joe Grind Term for a man sleeping with someone else's partner.

Jook Stab or pierce: "De rass fish hook jook me". Also a common term for the act of penetrative sex.

Juggling Sound-system tactic of playing several tracks on the same rhythm, mixing them smoothly via two decks. Also just playing records in a dance.

Kiss me neck! An expression of surprise: "Kiss me neck! Price of cornmeal gone down!".

Labrish Gossip, small talk. **Labba-labba** is to talk too much.

Let off Give something: "She nah let off she tings" ("She won't have sex with me").

Lick To strike a blow: "(H)im a lick down the pear tree". Also to smoke: "Me a lick de chalice Iyah". Also an adjective meaning hot: "Beenie Man a de lick!" ("Beenie Man is the best").

Lick shot Literally or figuratively firing a gun to demonstrate appreciation in the dancehall.

Likkle more See you later.

Live blanket Human body: "Darlin', you need a live blanket?" ("Would you like to have sex with me?")

Lock off Cease, desist; also hold a low profile.

Maaga Thin, scrawny: "You sorry fe a maaga dog, maaga dog turn an bite you".

Maama man Effeminate, probably gay man.

Mampy Fat woman, not necessarily derogatory.

Massive Crowd of friends or people: "Strictly for de dancehall massive".

Matey Girlfriend, often used to denote one of an attached man's multiple sexual partners.

Men Used in the plural form to denote a homosexual male.

Merino Men's tank top or string vest.

Modeller Fashionable, attractive woman, not necessarily a model; also used as an adjective, as in "me moddelin' in me criss Versace".

More time Another way of saying "See you soon".

Mule Woman without children, usually incapable of conceiving. Also a person that smuggles cocaine internally.

Natty Used as an adjective or adverb to describe dreadlocks, also a greeting to a Rasta: "Wh'appen, Natty?".

Nature Libido, also penis.

Navel string Placenta; it's traditional for a new baby's navel string to be planted under a young tree.

Nuff Abundant or copious: "Me have nuff gyal". Often twinned with respect as a courteous greeting: "Nuff respect me breddah".

Nyam To eat, from the Hausa word "nyamnyam".

Obeah Jamaican witchcraft.

One love Greeting or farewell salutation. "**Love**" is used in the same way: "Love Iyah".

Ongle Only.

Oonu You, them: "Oonu wan' eat tonight?" ("Do you want any dinner?")

Pappy show Something utterly ridiculous and foolish.

Phat Adjective applies to a fit, attractive woman, so-called because she has all the right things in all the right places "Pussy, Hips, Ass and Tits".

Piece A gun, a girl, or sex: "Me get a nice piece las' night" ("I had sex with an attractive woman last night").

Pikney Child.

Pirogue Fishing canoe.

Pon On or upon.

Prentice Apprentice or protégé, usually young man; also shortened to prenta.

Profile Status; someone who's intent on showing off their designer clothes is profiling.

Pum pum Vagina.

Punany Vagina – again.

Pussy or punny printers Shorts even tighter than the batty rider.

Queen Respectful title for a woman, usually a Rastaman's partner.

Raas Loosely translated as backside ("mi fall dung pon me raas"), and an expletive when used with claat or hole: "That man is one nasty raashole". Can also express surprise or emphasize a point: "Wha de raas claat man a deal wid?"

Raggamuffin Respected and wily ghetto sufferer, often used in a musical context. Also used to refer to "street" style.

Rahtid Mild expletive or an expression of surprise.

Ramp Usually used in the phrase "ramp wid", meaning to interfere with or irritate.

Rastitute See "Rent-a-Dread", below. Not to be confused with Ras, the abbreviation for Rasta, often used as a respectful greeting: "Wha'ppen Ras?"

Rat-bat Large moth – or regular bat.

Reason Discuss and debate a subject: "Me a reason wid mi bredren"; Nyabinghi Rastas gather for formal "reasonings" sessions.

Red Used to refer to a light-skinned person: "See de red man deh". Red also describes someone who has been smoking ganja.

Red-eye Greedy, envious.

Renk Extreme insolence or rudeness: "De man talk to me so renk it is a shame". Also

foul-smelling, nasty.

Rent-a-Dread A man with locks who makes a living out of sexual relationships with tourists.

Respect Perhaps the most commonly used greeting or farewell in Jamaica.

Risto From "aristocrat"; someone from (or who thinks they're from) high society.

Roughneck Ragamuffin rascal.

Rude bway Bad boy.

Runnings Happenings, things that are going on: "Bway, runnings hard dis year" ("Things are tough this year").

Rush Assail: "Watch dem rush de gates" ("Look at them forcing their way in").

Salt Used as a verb to describe something unlucky or gone wrong; ie "Windies gwine lose the series – we salt fe true".

Schoolers Schoolchildren.

Science Obeah.

Screw Be annoyed, and look like you are. A "screw face" is a miserable character.

Seen Understand or comprehend what someone is saying. Usually used as a reply to a statement, as in "Uh-huh". **Zeen** has the same meaning.

Sensimillia High-grade herbs; also shortened to sensi.

Session Sound-system jam: "Stone Love session gwine be wicked!"

Shock-out Looking good: "Me ago shock-out tonight ina mi criss new suit".

Shotta Rude boy, with all the appropriate notoriety that such status demands.

Sipple Slippery, precarious, as used in Max Romeo's hit song *Sipple Out Deh*.

Skank Rip off, con: "Me get skank at the mechanic today". Also an old-time dance.

Sketel Promiscuous, provocatively dressed woman.

Skin-teet Smile.

Slackness Improper, lowdown, dirty, base behaviour; also used to describe rude dancehall lyrics.

Slam The sexual act.

Spar Friend.

Spliff Marijuana joint.

Star Used as a salutation or qualifier in greetings: "Wh'appen, star".

Stoosh Snooty, condescending from a position of assumed superiority. Also means something of quality.

Structure The body: "Min' you structure" ("Get out of the way").

Sufferah Poor but righteous ghetto dweller.

Sweetboy Man who is financially supported by his lover.

Talawah Small but strong, applied to Jamaica itself in the motto: "She little but she talawah".

Talking to Can also be used to mean sleeping with someone, as in "She been talkin' to de man for de longest time".

Tall Long, usually referring to hair: "Yuh hair get tall!".

Tan Stay or stand: "Tan so back" ("Hold back").

Ting Object or woman: "A my ting dat" ("That's my girlfriend"). "Tings" can be male and female genitalia. Also the Jamaican pronunciation of "things": "Tings a gwan rough sah".

Trace To curse somebody.

Version A cut of a popular rhythm track.

Vex(ed) Irritated or annoyed.

What a gwan "What's going on?"

Wind/Wine Dance closely and suggestively.

Wuk Regular work or sex.

Wutless Combination of worthless and witless: "Pure wutless bway me meet at the show" ("I met some awful men at the show").

X-amount Huge, incalculable amount: "Me have x-amount of loving".

Yahso Here: "Park yuh car yahso".

Yard Home, also used as an alternative name for Jamaica: "No where no better dan Yard".

Yush A greeting.

Index
and small print

Index

Map entries are in colour

A Rough Guide to Rough Guides

In the summer of 1981, Mark Ellingham, a recent graduate from Bristol University, was travelling round Greece and couldn't find a guidebook that really met his needs. On the one hand there were the student guides, insistent on saving every last cent, and on the other the heavyweight cultural tomes whose authors seemed to have spent more time in a research library than lounging away the afternoon at a taverna or on the beach.

In a bid to avoid getting a job, Mark and a small group of writers set about creating their own guidebook. It was a guide to Greece that aimed to combine a journalistic approach to description with a thoroughly practical approach to travellers' needs – a guide that would incorporate culture, history and contemporary insights with a critical edge, together with up-to-date, value-for-money listings. Back in London, Mark and the team finished their Rough Guide, as they called it, and talked Routledge into publishing the book.

That first *Rough Guide to Greece*, published in 1982, was a student scheme that became a publishing phenomenon. The immediate success of the book – with numerous reprints and a Thomas Cook prize shortlisting – spawned a series that rapidly covered dozens of destinations. Rough Guides had a ready market among low-budget backpackers, but soon also acquired a much broader and older readership that relished Rough Guides' wit and inquisitiveness as much as their enthusiastic, critical approach. Everyone wants value for money, but not at any price.

Rough Guides soon began supplementing the "rougher" information about hostels and low-budget listings with the kind of detail on restaurants and quality hotels that independent-minded visitors on any budget might expect, whether on business in New York or trekking in Thailand.

These days the guides – distributed worldwide by the Penguin Group – offer recommendations from shoestring to luxury and cover more than 200 destinations around the globe, including almost every country in the Americas and Europe, more than half of Africa and most of Asia and Australasia. Our ever-growing team of authors and photographers is spread all over the world, particularly in Europe, the USA and Australia.

In 1994, we published the *Rough Guide to World Music* and *Rough Guide to Classical Music*; and a year later the *Rough Guide to the Internet*. All three books have become benchmark titles in their fields – which encouraged us to expand into other areas of publishing, mainly around popular culture. Rough Guides now publish:

- Travel guides to more than 200 worldwide destinations
- Dictionary phrasebooks to 22 major languages
- History guides ranging from Ireland to Islam
- Maps printed on rip-proof and waterproof Polyart™ paper
- Music guides running the gamut from Opera to Elvis
- Restaurant guides to London, New York and San Francisco
- Reference books on topics as diverse as the Weather and Shakespeare
- Sports guides from Formula 1 to Man Utd
- Pop culture books from Lord of the Rings to Cult TV
- World Music CDs in association with World Music Network.

Visit www.roughguides.com to see our latest publications.

Rough Guide Credits

Text editor: Mary Callahan
Managing Director: Kevin Fitzgerald
Series editor: Mark Ellingham
Editorial: Martin Dunford, Kate Berens, Ann-Marie Shaw, Helena Smith, Ruth Blackmore, Geoff Howard, Claire Saunders, Gavin Thomas, Alexander Mark Rogers, Polly Thomas, Joe Staines, Richard Lim, Duncan Clark, Peter Buckley, Lucy Ratcliffe, Clifton Wilkinson, Alison Murchie, Matthew Teller, Fran Sandham, Sally Schafer, Matthew Milton, Karoline Densley, Andy Turner (UK); Andrew Rosenberg, Yuki Takagaki, Richard Koss, Hunter Slaton, Chris Barsanti, Thomas Kohnstamm (US)
Design & Layout: Helen Prior, Julia Bovis, Dan May, John McKay, Sophie Hewat (UK); Madhulita Mohapatra, Umesh Aggarwal, Sunil Sharma (India)

Cartography: Maxine Repath, Ed Wright, Katie Lloyd-Jones (UK); Manish Chandra, Rajesh Chhibber, Jai Prakash Mishra (India)
Cover art direction: Louise Boulton
Picture research: Sharon Martins, Mark Thomas
Online: Kelly Martinez, Anja Mutic-Blessing, Jennifer Gold, Audra Epstein, Suzanne Welles, Cree Lawson (US); Manik Chauhan, Amarjyoti Dutta, Narender Kumar (India)
Finance: Gary Singh
Marketing & Publicity: Richard Trillo, Niki Smith, David Wearn, Chloë Roberts, Demelza Dallow, Claire Southern (UK); Geoff Colquitt, David Wechsler, Megan Kennedy (US)
Administration: Julie Sanderson
RG India: Punita Singh

Publishing Information

This third edition published November 2003 by **Rough Guides Ltd**,
80 Strand, London WC2R 0RL.
345 Hudson St, 4th Floor,
New York, NY 10014, USA.
Distributed by the Penguin Group
Penguin Books Ltd,
80 Strand, London WC2R 0RL
Penguin Putnam, Inc.
375 Hudson Street, NY 10014, USA
Penguin Books Australia Ltd,
487 Maroondah Highway, PO Box 257,
Ringwood, Victoria 3134, Australia
Penguin Books Canada Ltd,
10 Alcorn Avenue, Toronto, Ontario,
Canada M4V 1E4
Penguin Books (NZ) Ltd,
182–190 Wairau Road, Auckland 10,
New Zealand
Typeset in Bembo and Helvetica to an original design by Henry Iles.
Printed in Italy by LegoPrint S.p.A

480pp includes index
A catalogue record for this book is available from the British Library.

ISBN 1-84353-111-9

The publishers and authors have done their best to ensure the accuracy and currency of all the information in **The Rough Guide to Jamaica**, however, they can accept no responsibility for any loss, injury, or inconvenience sustained by any traveller as a result of information or advice contained in the guide.

Help us update

We've gone to a lot of effort to ensure that the third edition of **The Rough Guide to Jamaica** is accurate and up-to-date. However, things change – places get "discovered", opening hours are notoriously fickle, restaurants and rooms raise prices or lower standards. If you feel we've got it wrong or left something out, we'd like to know, and if you can remember the address, the price, the time, the phone number, so much the better.

We'll credit all contributions, and send a copy of the next edition (or any other Rough Guide if you prefer) for the best letters. Everyone who writes to us and isn't already a subscriber will receive a copy of our full-colour thrice-yearly newsletter. Please mark letters: **"Rough Guide Jamaica Update"** and send to: Rough Guides, 80 Strand, London WC2R 0RL, or Rough Guides, 4th Floor, 345 Hudson St, New York, NY 10014. Or send an email to **mail@roughguides.com**

Have your questions answered and tell others about your trip at
www.roughguides.atinfopop.com

Acknowledgements

The authors would like to thank the staff of the Jamaica Tourist Board for their help and support, as well as Sarah Patten and Fay Osborn at Biss Lancaster and Alexia Evans and Louise Moore at BGB. Thanks also to Andrew Rosenberg for his guidance and generosity, Mary Callahan for cool editing and enduring patience with missed deadlines, Sharon Martins for spot-on photos, Michelle Bhatia and Helen Prior for smooth typesetting, Katie Lloyd-Jones for excellent maps, John Fortnum for the lowdown on movies, and Steve Barrow and Greg Salter for their original contributions to the music piece.

Polly Thomas: Huge and heartfelt thanks go to all those in Jamaica who offered their help and expertise so freely, and who make the island so special everytime – much respect. Extra special thanks go to the inimitable ladies: Marjorie Morris, Andrea Lewis, Simone Eschmeier and Elaine Gower. Thanks also to Pam and Lorna Morris, Petroline Lewis and family, Andre McGann of *Doctor's Cave Beach Hotel*, Patricia Maher of Digicel, Colin McDonald of Our Story Tours, Jason Henzell and the *Jake's* crew, Laura Gambrill, Roy Watkin at *Cariblue*, David Cook of Autobookers, Hugh Dixon, Donovan Haughton and Donna McLean of STEA, Mrs Buckle and Fuzzy in Albert Town, Damian "Reds" Parchment and Carlene, Terry James, Ossy Osman, Robert Kerr, Delroy "Callo" Collins, Donahue Jarrett, and Roydell "Congo Ashante Roy" Johnson, Daniel Jacobs, Daniel "Bozra" Barrett, Micheal Barnett of Heineken Startime, Diana McIntyre-Pike and all at Countrystyle, Cookie Kinkead, and Ainsley Henriques; also to Polly RB for working so hard, for sharing a deep love for all things Yard and for the lifesaving car contra. Lastly, the biggest thank-you to the west London crew who supported and encouraged me all the way: Adrian Edwards (and Mrs Edwards for delicious Sunday dinners), Imogen and Isabella Spencer, Emma Sturgess-Leif, Amanda Rolandini Jensen and of course to my mum Celia and dad Matt.

Polly Rodger Brown: Special thanks and much love to Polly Thomas for her massive support, encouragement and infectious enthusiasm. Many thanks also to the following for their generous advice, hospitality and friendship, which helped to make my job possible and my stay in Jamaica so much fun (again!): Jon Baker, Antonia Beamish, Neason Brown, Scott Crawford, Easy Rock Sue, Graham Duffus, Michael Fox, Mike Gleeson, Maria Carla Gulotta, all the staff at Hallzers, Donna Hussey, Paul Hussey, Casey McGlue, Greg Naldrett, Tony Moncreiff, Sista P, Lesley Tae-Tan-Que at Bargain Car Rental, Vanessa Taylor, Helmut Steiner, Oliver Weir, Woody and Cherry. Above all, huge amounts of gratitude and love - I miss you! - to wonderful gorgeous Nancy Beckham, Paul Salmon and Lisa Schnepf.

Readers' letters

Thanks to all the readers who took the trouble to write in with their comments and suggestions (and apologies to anyone whose name we've misspelt or omitted):

Shaen Cathewood, Tawnya Fay, Jonathan H, Heather Hamer, P.E. Howes, Karine and Ricky, Bill Malaynch, Sarah Salih, Philippe Savoie, Glenn Woodley and Peter Paul Zahl.

Photo Credits

Music Reference Guides

Classical *music*

Country
THE ROUGH GUIDE

Jazz
THE ROUGH GUIDE

World music
THE ROUGH GUIDE

Opera

Rock
THE ROUGH GUIDE

Reggae *music*

Soul
THE ROUGH GUIDE

World Music
Africa, Europe and the Middle East

World Music
Latin and North America, Caribbean, India, Asia and Pacific

Music USA
THE ROUGH GUIDE

Country
THE ROUGH GUIDE

Jazz
THE ROUGH GUIDE

Blues
THE ROUGH GUIDE

CD Guides

classical music
THE ROUGH GUIDE

Opera
THE ROUGH GUIDE

Latin
THE ROUGH GUIDE

Reggae
THE ROUGH GUIDE

Rock
THE ROUGH GUIDE

Mini Guides

House
THE ROUGH GUIDE

Hip-hop

Irish Music

Techno
THE ROUGH GUIDE

Cuban Music

"The Rough Guides are near-perfect
reference works"
Philadelphia Inquirer

www.roughguides.com

Rough Guide Music Guides

key: 🌏 map   ⊞ phrasebook   ⊙ cd

Rough Guides publishes new books every month

Rough Guides music & reference

Music Reference Guides

Classical music

Country THE ROUGH GUIDE

Jazz THE ROUGH GUIDE

Opera

Rock THE ROUGH GUIDE

Reggae music

World Music
Africa, Europe and the Middle East

World Music
Latin and North America, Caribbean, India, Asia and Pacific

Music USA

CD Guides

Classical music

Opera

Latin

Reggae

Rock

Mini Guides

House THE ROUGH GUIDE

Hip-hop

Irish Music

Techno THE ROUGH GUIDE

Cuban Music

"The Rough Guides are near-perfect
reference works"
Philadelphia Inquirer

www.roughguides.com

Rough Guide Music Guides

NOTES

The ideas expressed in this code were developed by and for independent travellers.

Learn About The Country You're Visiting

Start enjoying your travels before you leave by tapping into as many sources of information as you can.

The Cost Of Your Holiday

Think about where your money goes - be fair and realistic about how cheaply you travel. Try and put money into local peoples' hands; drink local beer or fruit juice rather than imported brands and stay in locally owned accommodation. Haggle with humour and not aggressively. Pay what something is worth to you and remember how wealthy you are compared to local people.

Embrace The Local Culture

Open your mind to new cultures and traditions - it will transform your experience. Think carefully about what's appropriate in terms of your clothes and the way you behave. You'll earn respect and be more readily welcomed by local people. Respect local laws and attitudes towards drugs and alcohol that vary in different countries and communities. Think about the impact you could have on them.

xploring The World – The Travellers' Code

ing sensitive to these ideas means getting more out of your travels -
d giving more back to the people you meet and the places you visit.

Minimise Your Environmental Impact

Think about what happens to your rubbish - take biodegradable products and a water filter bottle. Be sensitive to limited resources like water, fuel and electricity. Help preserve local wildlife and habitats by respecting local rules and regulations, such as sticking to footpaths and not standing on coral.

Don't Rely On Guidebooks

Use your guidebook as a starting point, not the only source of information. Talk to local people, then discover your own adventure!

Be Discreet With Photography

Don't treat people as part of the landscape, they may not want their picture taken. Ask first and respect their wishes.

We work with people the world over to promote tourism that benefits their communities, but we can only carry on our work with the support of people like you. For membership details or to find out how to make your travels work for local people and the environment, visit our website.

www.tourismconcern.org.uk

TourismConcern
Campaigning for Ethical and Fairly Traded Tourism